4/03

Theatre in Europe: a documentary history

This is the only volume available to bring together a wide selection of primary source materials from the theatrical history of the Middle Ages. The focus is on western Europe between the fall of the Roman Empire and the emergence of markedly Renaissance forms in Italy. Early sections of the volume are devoted to the survival of classical tradition and the development of the liturgical drama of the Roman Catholic Church, but the main concentration is on the genesis and growth of popular religious drama in the vernacular which had its artistic culmination in the ambitious mountings of Bible plays presented in a wide variety of contexts in the later Middle Ages. Each of the major medieval regions is featured, while a final section covers the pastimes and customs of the people, a record of whose traditional activities often only survives in the margins of official recognition. The volume has been compiled by a team of leading scholars in the field and over 700 documents are presented in modern English translation.

The book contains numerous illustrations, the source location for each document and a substantial bibliography. It will be of interest to scholars and students of theatre history, medieval studies, European language and culture, and sociology.

Theatre in Europe: a documentary history

General editors

Glynne Wickham
John Northam
W. D. Howarth

This series presents a comprehensive collection of primary source materials for teachers and students and serves as a major reference work for studies in theatrical and dramatic literature. The volumes focus individually on specific periods and geographical areas, encompassing English and European theatrical history. Each volume presents primary source documents in English, or in English translation, relating to actors and acting, dramatic theory and criticism, theatre architecture, stage censorship, settings, costumes and audiences. These sources include such documents as statutes, proclamations, inscriptions, contracts and playbills. Additional documentation from contemporary sources is provided through correspondence, reports and eye-witness accounts. The volumes also provide not only the exact source and location of the original documents, but also complementary lists of similar documents. Each volume contains an introduction, narrative linking passages, notes on the documents, a substantial bibliography and an index offering detailed access to the primary material.

Published

Restoration and Georgian England, 1669–1788, compiled and introduced by David Thomas and Arnold Hare, edited by David Thomas

National Theatre in Northern and Eastern Europe, 1746–1900, edited by Laurence Senelick

German and Dutch Theatre, 1600–1848, compiled by George W. Brandt and Wiebe Hogendoorn, edited by George W. Brandt

Naturalism and Symbolism in European Theatre, 1850–1918, edited by Claude Schumacher

French Theatre in the Neo-classical Era, 1550–1789, edited by William D. Howarth

English Professional Theatre, 1530–1660, edited by Glynne Wickham, Herbert Berry and William Ingram

Theatre in Europe: a documentary history

The Medieval European Stage, 500–1550

Edited by

WILLIAM TYDEMAN
University of Wales Bangor

Associate editors

MICHAEL J. ANDERSON
University of Kent at Canterbury

NICK DAVIS
University of Liverpool

LOUISE M. HAYWOOD
University of Cambridge

PETER MEREDITH
University of Leeds

LYNETTE R. MUIR
University of Leeds

THOMAS PETTITT and LEIF SØNDERGAARD
University of Odense

ELSA STRIETMAN
University of Cambridge

JOHN E. TAILBY
University of Leeds

CAMBRIDGE
UNIVERSITY PRESS

PUBLISHED BY THE PRESS SYNDICATE OF THE UNIVERSITY OF CAMBRIDGE
The Pitt Building, Trumpington Street, Cambridge, United Kingdom

CAMBRIDGE UNIVERSITY PRESS
The Edinburgh Building, Cambridge CB2 2RU, UK
40 West 20th Street, New York, NY 10011–4211, USA
10 Stamford Road, Oakleigh, VIC 3166, Australia
Ruiz de Alarcón 13, 28014 Madrid, Spain
Dock House, The Waterfront, Cape Town 8001, South Africa

http://www.cambridge.org

First published 2001

Printed in the United Kingdom at the University Press, Cambridge

Typeface Monotype Photina 10/12.5 pt   *System* QuarkXPress™   [SE]

A catalogue record for this book is available from the British Library

Library of Congress Cataloguing in Publication data

The medieval European stage / edited by William Tydeman.
        p.   cm. (Theatre in Europe)
Includes bibliographical references and index.
ISBN 0 521 24609 1 (hardback)
    1. Theatre – Europe – History – Sources.   2. Liturgical drama – History and criticism.
I. Tydeman, William.   II. Series.
PN2570.M39   2001
792'.094'0902 – dc21   00-067610

ISBN 0 521 24609 1 hardback

Contents

List of documents

Asterisks before titles indicate illustrated documents

V   The Church's view of theatrical activity

III   Biblical plays from Byzantium and the Orthodox East

IV   The Feast of Corpus Christi and the plays

II Reactions and responses

III Secular theatre

I The theatre of the mystères

IV Drama in the bilingual cities: Metz

SECTION F: THE GERMAN-SPEAKING AREA

I Religious drama

Preliminaries

IV Plays for political and religious occasions

SECTION J: TRADITIONS OF THE PEOPLE: CUSTOMS AND FOLK
DRAMA

I Pre-Christian origins?

II Seasonal customs

Seasonal observances in churches and churchyards

Christmas and New Year

General editors' preface

In appointing appropriately qualified editors for all the volumes in this documentary history it has been our aim to provide a comprehensive collection of primary source materials for teachers and students on which their own critical appraisal of theatrical history and dramatic literature may safely be grounded.

Each volume presents primary source documents in English, or in English translation, relating to actors and acting, dramatic theory and criticism, theatre architecture, stage censorship, settings, costumes and audiences. Editors have, in general, confined their selection to documentary material in the strict sense (statutes, proclamations, inscriptions, contracts, working drawings, playbills, prints, account books, etc.), but exceptions have been made in instances where prologues, epilogues, excerpts from play-texts and private correspondence provide additional contemporary documentation based on an author's authority or that of eye-witnesses to particular peformances and significant theatrical events.

Unfamiliar documents have been preferred to familiar ones, short ones to long ones; and among long ones recourse has been taken to excerpting for inclusion all passages which either oblige quotation by right of their own intrinsic importance or lead directly to a clearer understanding of other documents. In every instance, however, we have aimed to provide readers not only with the exact source and location of the original document, but with complementary lists of similar documents and of secondary sources offering previously printed transcripts.

Each volume is equipped with an introductory essay, and in some cases introductory sections to each chapter, designed to provide readers with the appropriate social background – religious, political, economic and aesthetic – as context for the documents selected; it also contains briefer linking commentaries on particular groups of documents and concludes with an extensive bibliography.

Within this general presentational framework, individual volumes will vary considerably in their format – greater emphasis having to be placed, for example, on documents of control in one volume than in another, or with dramatic theory and criticism figuring less prominently in some volumes than in others – if each volume is to be an accurate reflection of the widely divergent interests and concerns of different European countries at different stages of their historical development, and the equally sharp differences in the nature and quality of the surviving documents volume by volume.

Glynne Wickham (Chairman)
Bristol University, 1997

Editor's preface

However prescriptively or liberally one may choose to define the term 'medieval theatre', both chronologically and geographically the scope of this collection of documents must be far more formidable than that of others in the *Theatre in Europe* sequence. (The contrast would have been even more pronounced had an associate editor with the necessary specialised knowledge of the eastern European stage been recruited to contribute on that subject.) The challenge of adequately encompassing the theatrical history of the medieval centuries was originally envisaged as requiring two volumes each as large as this, but as the project developed, publishing exigencies and financial constraints involved distilling the proverbial quart into what is, if not exactly a pint-pot, a vessel of considerably reduced dimensions from those first contemplated. The consequent effort to compress without distorting, to render a scaled-down selection truly representative, along with several modifications of plan and personnel partly arising from the multiple changes in the character of British academic life over the past decade, has undoubtedly extended the period during which this work has been in gestation. I should therefore like to acknowledge here the faith shown by the general editors and the Cambridge University Press in the final outcome of the labours of an editorial team whose determination to complete their task has only been achieved in the teeth of numerous frustrations and setbacks.

My warmest thanks are due to my nine stalwart fellow contributors who, along with Professor Barry Baldwin formerly of Calgary University, have produced what we believe to be as coherent an account of theatrical activity in the Middle Ages as is consistent with our present state of knowledge. I am particularly grateful to Professor Baldwin for putting at our disposal his versions of Byzantine material, and to the three contributors from Leeds who twice arranged for colleagues to meet there in a beneficially relaxed environment. It is also a pleasure to thank Professor Glynne Wickham, Chairman of *Theatre in Europe* Editorial Board, for inviting me to undertake this rewarding but demanding assignment, and for his benevolent guidance and advice as it gradually progressed. I must pay tribute too to Sarah Stanton and Vicki Cooper at the Cambridge University Press, not only for their willingness to negotiate and liaise, but for their friendship and encouragement when my own confidence faltered. Linda Jones, Research

Administrator in the Department of English, University of Wales Bangor, has given the volume editor invaluable support by maintaining contact between us all, and in ultimately assembling our several contributions. Hilary Hammond has once again proved a most conscientious and vigilant copy-editor, handling a type-script which bristled with problems, not least that of ensuring corporate consis-tency. Collectively we thank her for painstakingly saving us from our several fallibilities.

Acknowledgements

While the editors have depended on each other for much mutual support and advice, they alone are responsible for what appears under their individual names. They would also wish to thank partners, friends, colleagues and fellow scholars who have generously given them the necessary sustenance and expertise to bring this volume to a successful conclusion. We are grateful to all the individual editors and theatre historians cited in these pages, and in particular to Alessandra Anderson, Bernard Bentley, Rolf Bergmann, David Bevington, Richard Byrn, John Cartwright, Robert A. Clark, Stephen D. Corrsin, Clifford Davidson, Alan D. Deyermond, Alan J. Fletcher, Peter Foote, Will Fowler, Carmen García de los Rios, Sarah Graves, Leslie Hewitt, Sydney Higgins, Wim Hüsken, Kurt Villads Jensen, Alexandra F. Johnston, John Ellis Jones, Pamela M. King, Alan E. Knight, Anthony Lappin, Peter Llewellyn, Ann Mackenzie, Brian O. Murdoch, Nerida Newbigin, Alan Paterson, John Pitcher, Richard Rastall, Nancy Regelado, Tomos Roberts, Graham A. Runnalls, Steven Ryle, Reinhold Schröder, Max Siller, Eckehard Simon, Eric Turner, Angela Williams, Elizabeth Williams, Robert Wilson, Diana Wyatt and the late John E. Varey.

We must express our indebtedness to Peter Baxter and Helen Taylor for their specially drawn sketch maps featured in sections H and I.

We should also like to thank the following for their willingness to grant us permission either to reproduce in the body of this work pictorial material in their possession, or to make use of versions of documents in which they hold the copyright.

Illustrations: Bibliothèque Nationale, Paris; Bodleian Library, Oxford; British Museum, London; Musée Condé, Chantilly; Conway Library, Courtauld Institute of Art; Folger Shakespeare Library, Washington; Münster Unserer Lieben Frau, Konstanz; Orvieto Cathedral; Princeton University Art Museum; Rijks Universiteit, Leiden; National Library of Wales, Aberystwyth; the President and Fellows of St John's College, Oxford; the Trustees of Sir John Soane's Museum, London; Victoria and Albert Museum.

Copyright materials: Boydell and Brewer; Cambridge University Press; Catholic Press of America; Center for Medieval and Early Renaissance Studies, State University of New York, Binghamton; Columbia University Press; Edizione Il

Polifilo, Milan; Edizioni dell'Orso; the Folklore Society; the Hakluyt Society; Liverpool University Press; Dr John McKinnell; Modern Language Association of America; Oxford University Press; Taylor and Francis Ltd (Routledge); Thomas Nelson & Sons; the editor and publishers of *Past and Present*; University of Toronto Press; Yale University Press.

We also gratefully acknowledge our indebtedness to the staff of the following institutional libraries, on whose facilities and resources we have drawn: Biblioteca Nacional, Madrid; Bibliotèca Nazionale, Florence; Bibliothèque Nationale, Paris; British Library, London; Libraries of the Universities of Cambridge, Kent at Canterbury, Leeds, Liverpool, Odense, St Andrews, and the University of Wales Bangor.

Dr Louise M. Haywood is indebted for research funding to the Russell Trust, School of Modern Languages, University of St Andrews.

In order not to obscure its presence among the welter of publications cited in the text and bibliographies, attention should be drawn to a work to which every contributor to this volume owes a particular debt, direct or indirect. The existence of *The Staging of Religious Drama in Europe in the Later Middle Ages: Texts and Documents in English Translation*, edited by Peter Meredith and John E. Tailby (Early Drama, Art and Music Monographs Series 4, Western Michigan University, Medieval Institute Publications, Kalamazoo, 1983) – referred to in the text hereafter as *Staging* – has considerably eased our labour as well as providing us with a high standard to which to aspire. Items reproduced from the book are reprinted by kind permission of the Board of the Medieval Institute of Western Michigan University, for which we are most grateful to Professor Clifford Davidson.

Historical table

Many of the events listed below are primarily of theatrical significance, although references to salient historical events have occasionally been introduced as 'signposts'. A large number of the dates which appear are merely approximations, particularly where evidence for dramatic performance or composition is concerned.

AD	
395	Roman Empire divided between sons of Theodosius the Great
c. 397–8	St Augustine completes *The Confessions*
c. 425	Augustine's *De civitate Dei* [The City of God]
429	Vandals invade Roman Africa
c. 470–542	Caesarius of Arles
476	Odoacer deposes Romulus Augustulus and ends western Empire
527–65	Justinian Emperor of the East
540	Rule of St Benedict drawn up
c. 580	Death of Cassiodorus
590–604	Papacy of Gregory I ('the Great')
602	Augustine establishes see of Canterbury
632	Death of Mohammed
c. 633	Isidore of Seville completes his *Etymologiae*
672–735	The Venerable Bede
c. 675–c. 749	John Damascene
711	Islamic conquest of Iberian Peninsula begins
725–54	St Boniface converts Germany to Christianity
c. 731	Bede's *Historia ecclesiastica gentis Anglorum* [The History of the English Church and People]
732	Arabs defeated by Charles Martel near Poitiers
755–96	Reign of King Offa of Mercia
768–814	Reign of Charlemagne; Carolingian reforms to liturgy
800	Charlemagne crowned Holy Roman Emperor, Rome
c. 800	Epitaph for the mime artist Vitalis composed

804	Death of Alcuin
c. 818–30	*The Book of Cerne* (Anglo-Saxon miscellany) copied
821–35	Amalarius of Metz, *Liber officialis*
826	Council of Rome condemns dance-songs
859	Norsemen begin invasion of Mediterranean
878	Arabs conquer Sicily
899	Death of Alfred, king of the West Saxons
910	Foundation of the Abbey of Cluny
c. 920–50	Composition of earliest *Quem queritis* tropes as part of Latin liturgy
c. 935–c. 1002	Hrotswitha of Gandersheim
c. 935	Constantine VII Porphyrogenitus *De caeremoniis*
c. 965–75	Compilation of the *Regularis concordia* for English use
c. 1000–c. 1100	Composition of the earliest Latin liturgical dramas
1020–53	Norman conquest of southern Italy
1054	Schism between Catholic and Orthodox churches
1066	William of Normandy gains English crown
1073–85	Strife between Emperor Henry IV and Pope Gregory VII (formerly St Hildebrand)
1077	Emperor Henry IV does penance at Canossa
1079–1142	Peter Abelard
1095–99	The First Crusade
1096–1141	Hugh of St Victor
1098	The Order of Cistercians founded
c. 1100	*Gemma animae* (Honorius of Autun); *Paschon Christos* (?); the *Sponsus* (Limoges); the Ripoll Troper
c. 1110	Geoffrey of Gorham stages play of St Katherine, Dunstable
c. 1115–80	John of Salisbury
c. 1120	Benediktbeuern Passion Play
c. 1140	Hilarius composes *Historia de Daniel*
1142	Canon Benedict of St Peter's *Liber politicus*
1146–74	The Anglo-Norman *Adam*
1147–9	The Second Crusade
c. 1150	Montecassino Passion Play
c. 1150–c. 1185	Neo-Roman comedies include *Geta, Aurularia, Pamphilus, Babio*
1154–89	Henry of Anjou king of England
c. 1155	*Ordo Virtutum* (Hildegard of Bingen); *Auto de los Reyes Magos* (Play of the Magi Kings)
c. 1159	John of Salisbury's *Polycraticus*
c. 1160	Tergensee *Ludus de Antichristo*
1162	Gerhoh von Reichersberg, *De investigatione Antichristi*
1170	Murder of Archbishop Thomas à Becket

c. 1175	Anglo-Norman *La Seinte Resurreccion*; William Fitzstephen commends London's pious 'representations'
c. 1180	Beauvais *Ludus Danielis*
1187	Passion plays at Hagenau
c. 1188	Giraldus Cambrensis, *Itinerarium Cambriae*
1189–92	The Third Crusade
1193	La Confrérie du Puy founded, Amiens
1194	Regensburg *Ordo Creacionis*
1198–1216	Papacy of Innocent III
c. 1200	Siena Passion Play; Saxo Grammaticus, *Gesta Danorum*
c. 1200–*c.* 1250 (?)	The *Cyprus Passion*
1204	*Ludus Prophetarum* staged in Riga
c. 1205	*Le Jeu de St Nicolas* by Jean Bodel of Arras
1207	Pope Innocent III condemns clerical excesses in Poland
1209–10	Order of Franciscans established
1210–29	Albigensian Crusades against Cathar heretics
1215	Fourth Lateran Council pronounces doctrine of Transubstantiation an essential belief
1216	Dominican Order receives papal approval
c. 1220	Thomas de Chabham (or Chobham) condemns aspects of performance in his *Summa confessorum*
c. 1220	Alleged miracle at a Beverley Resurrection play
1223	St Francis of Assisi's *presepe* at Greccio
c. 1225–74	St Thomas Aquinas
c. 1225	*Courtois d'Arras*
1226–70	Louis IX (St Louis) king of France
1234	Pope Gregory IX quotes Innocent III on religious plays in his *Decretals*; 'gloss' added 1263
1244	Padua Passion and Resurrection Play
1250–1300	Kloster Muri Passion Play
1252–84	Reign of Alfonso X ('the Wise') of Castile (*Primera Partida*, *c.* 1260)
1264	Feast of Corpus Christi established by Pope Urban IV's *Transiturus de hoc mundo*
1265–1321	Dante Alighieri
1265–74	St Thomas Aquinas' *Summa theologiae*
1267	Annunciation play, Feast of St Mark, Venice
1269	Royal reception for Alfonso of Castile, Valencia
1272–1307	Edward I king of England
1273	Celebratory *festa* in Siena
c. 1276	*Le Jeu de la Feuillée* (Adam de la Halle)
c. 1280	*Le Miracle de Théophile* (Rutebeuf); *Le Garçon et l'Aveugle* (Flemish farce)

c. 1283 (?)	*Le Jeu de Robin et Marion* (Adam de la Halle)
c. 1284	Origny-Saint-Benoîte *Ludus Paschalis*
1285	Death features at the wedding of Alexander III of Scotland; Scottish priapic dance at Easter
c. 1285–9	Death of Adam de la Halle, possibly in Naples
1286	Coronation of Alfonso III of Aragon, Saragossa
1290	Citizens of Cahors perform in cemetery of St Martial
1291	First Bruges *ommegang* of the Holy Blood mentioned
	Trade guilds parade in London to mark English victory at Falkirk; Cividale Pentecost cycle (also in 1304)
1299	An Arthurian entertainment for Edward I's wedding (?)
c. 1300	*De clerico et puella*; *La Passion du Palatinus*; *La Passion d'Autun*; Vienna Passion Play
c. 1300–1350	St Gall Passion Play
1301	Prioress of Clerkenwell complains to Edward I of damage caused by Londoners' sports and pastimes
c. 1303	Robert Mannyng's *Handlyng Synne* freely translated from William of Wadington's *Manuel des Pechiez*
1304	Spectacle on the Arno; bridge collapses
1309–77	Papacy located at Avignon
1313	Pageants for Edward II's visit to Paris
1314	Scots defeat English at Battle of Bannockburn
1317	Observation of the Feast of Corpus Christi promulgated
1327–77	Edward III king of England
1328	Coronation of Alfonso IV of Aragon, Saragossa
1328–84	John Wycliffe
c. 1330	*Le Jour de Jugement* (Besançon)
1333	Bishop de Grandisson censures clerics of Exeter Cathedral; Christmas play in Toulon
1336	The visit of the Magi staged, Milan
1337	Beginning of the Hundred Years' War between France and England
1339	Guild of St Dominic, Perugia, draws up inventory of stage costumes
c. 1339–82	*Les Miracle de Nostre Dame* written and staged
1346	English defeat French at Battle of Crécy
1347–50	First phase of the Black Death
1348–53	Giovanni Boccaccio's *Il Decamerone*
1350–1400	The Frankfurter *Dirigierrolle* drawn up
1352	Bishop de Grandisson forbids proposed play against Exeter shoemakers
1355	Passion play presented, Pollença, Majorca
c. 1360	John Bromyard, *Summa praedicantium*

1363–76	Barking Abbey's *Visitation* devised under Katherine of Sutton
1370	Earliest reference to the Elche Assumption
1371	First known *confrérie* set up at Nantes
1372	Philippe de Mezières' *Presentation of the Virgin Mary in the Temple*, Avignon
1374	Death of Francesco Petrarcha at Arquà
c. 1375	The Cornish *Ordinalia* created; the Maastricht *Passion* (?)
1376	Resurrection play, Cambrai Cathedral; first mention of a York 'pagine'
1377	Citizens' mumming, Kennington; coronation celebrations for Richard II; Beverley 'pagine' first mentioned
1378–1417	The 'Great Schism' in the western Church
1379	Pentecost spectacle presented, Vicenza
c. 1380	St Genevieve manuscript compiled; *Estoire de Griselidis*
1381	The Peasants' Revolt in England
c. 1382	Dramas possibly incorporated into Lille procession
post 1383	Ypres *Thundach* established
1388–9	Confraternity founded to organise York Paternoster Play
1389	Turks defeat Serbs at Kossovo
1390–1409	Clerks perform scriptural plays, Skinners Well, London
1391	Innsbruck Easter Play
1392	First mention of Coventry 'pagent'; *Robin et Marion* played, Angers
1399	Coronation celebrations of Martin I of Aragon, Saragossa
1400	Passion play performed, Avignon; earliest reference to the 'ludo de ly haliblude' (Corpus Christi play), Aberdeen; death of Geoffrey Chaucer
c. 1400	*A Treatise of Miraclis Pleyinge*
c. 1400–*c.* 1425	*The Pride of Life*; *The Castle of Perseverance*; *La Passion d'Arras* (Mercadé)
1402	La Confrérie de la Passion et Resurrection receives its charter from Charles VI of France
1409–80	René of Anjou
c. 1410	Van Hulthem manuscript includes four *Abele Spelen*; *Dives and Pauper* written
1413	Passion play staged in Amiens; Bautzen St Dorothy Play performed
1414	Coronation of Fernando of Antequera, Saragossa; Lisbon *momos* recorded, Zurara's *Crónica da Tomada de Ceuta*
1415	First extant list of Barcelona Corpus Christi pageants; York's *Ordo paginarum ludi Corporis Christi* drawn up; spectacles greet Henry V's return from Agincourt

1416	Execution of John Hus at Constance
1417	Christmas play performed at Council of Constance
1418	Earliest reference to Toledo Corpus Christi procession; disguised perambulations forbidden in London
1420	Henry V enters Paris with Charles VI; Prades Assumption, Tarragona
c. 1420	Swabian Boy-Bishop's Play
1422	Deaths of Henry V of England and Charles VI of France
c. 1425–30	John Lydgate's 'momeries' written and performed at English court
1429	Play of St George staged, Turin
1430	Duke of Savoy bans pre-Christmas *quêtes*
1431	Joan of Arc burnt at Rouen
1435	Council of Basel condemns Feast of Fools
1437	Metz stages Passion and *Vengeance* plays
1439	Archbishop Abramo of Souzdal witnesses Florentine Annunciation and Ascension spectacles
1440	Valencia Assumption; Platonic Academy at Florence
c. 1440–1513	Hans Folz, author of German *Fastnachtspiele*
1443	Norwich procession of Christmas and Lent
1444	Turks defeat Christian alliance at Battle of Varna
1448	Plays of Seven Joys of Mary follow Brussels *ommegang*; dramatic presentations accompany Good Friday sermon at Perugia
c. 1449	Reginald Pecock, *The Repressor of Over Much Blaming of the Clergy*
c. 1450	John Capgrave's *Ye Solace of Pilgrimes*
c. 1450–70	Greban's *Le Mystère de la Passion* composed
1451	Wedding celebrations for Leonor of Portugal and Emperor Frederick III, Lisbon
1452	Sibyl play, León Cathedral
1452–78	*Les Actes des Apôtres* composed
1453	Fall of Constantinople to Turks ends Byzantine Empire
1454	Notable Florentine *festa* for the Feast of John the Baptist includes plays on floats
1455–85	The Wars of the Roses in England
1456	Angers stages Resurrection play
1457	Margaret of Anjou visits Coventry to see cycle plays
c. 1460	Jean Fouquet's St Apollonia miniature of the Heures of Etienne de Chevalier; St Alexius fragment
c. 1460–1539	Annual Good Friday Passion play performed in the Colloseum, Rome
1461–2	Disguisings at court of Constable of Jaén

1462	First mention of the Chester plays
1464	Redentin Easter play performed
1465	*Passion* performed at Saumur
c. 1465–70	*Mankynde* composed
1467	Princess Isabel appears in disguising by Gómez Manrique
1468	Metz stages play of St Catherine of Siena
1469	Ferdinand of Aragon marries Isabella of Castile
1473	John Paston II alludes to Robin Hood interludes
1474	*Le Mystère de l'Incarnation et de la Nativité de Jésus-Christ* played at Rouen
c. 1475	Manuscript of N-Town Plays compiled
1479	Crowns of Aragon and Castile united under 'the Catholic Monarchs'
c. 1479–1522	The *Künzelsauer Fronleichnamsspiel* performed
c. 1480	Jean Michel's *Passion* composed
c. 1480–1520	*Mary Magdalene* and *The Conversion of St Paul* (Digby manuscript) composed
1481	First extant reference to Passion cycle, Cervera
1484	Plautus' *Aulularia* performed in Rome
1485	Lorenzo de Medici's play on St John and St Paul staged by the *Vangelista*, Florence; Battle of Bosworth Field brings Henry Tudor to the English throne
1486	Vitruvius' *De architectura* published; Angers performs Jean Michel's *Passion*
1487	Presentation of a Nativity play before the Catholic Monarchs, Saragossa
1487–92	Completion of the Reconquista in Spain
1488	Life of John the Baptist performed, Casteldurante
1490–2	Three-day Revello Passion Play staged
1492	Conquest of Granada celebrated, Gerona; Jews expelled from Spanish kingdoms; Columbus discovers America
1493	Badius Ascensius' edition of Terence published, Lyon
1494	Emperor Maximilian enters Antwerp; troupe of interlude players established at English royal court
c. 1495	*Den Spieghel der Salicheit van Elckerlijc* (*Everyman*) composed
1496	*Le Mystère de St Martin* staged at Seurre; Amboise presents the Nativity (?)
c. 1497	*Fulgens and Lucres* (Henry Medwall) staged at Lambeth Palace
1498	Dublin list of Corpus Christi pageants
1499	Classical comedies presented, Ferrara
c. 1499–1503	Anrique de Mota's *A Lamentaçao da Mula*
c. 1500	*Gracisla* written; Toledo shepherds' dance

1501	Passion play staged at Mons; Alsfeld Passion Play staged; wedding celebrations for Prince Arthur, London
1502	Plautus' *Menaechmi* presented before Pope Alexander VI
1504	Manuscript of *Beunans Meriasek* (Cornish); Queen Anne of Brittany enters Paris
1507	Zerbst Corpus Christi play and procession
1509	*Le Mystère des Trois Doms* performed, Romans; Ariosto's *I Suppositi* staged, Ferrara; Henry VIII ascends English throne
c. 1509–*c.* 1538	Cornelis Everaet of Bruges active
1510	Châteaudun and Vienne present Passion plays
1513	First production of *La Calandria*, Urbino
1514	Bozen (Bolzano) Passion plays performed (Death of Benedikt Debs, 1515)
1516	80,000-seat theatre built at Autun
1517	Bozen Ascension Day Play presented; Martin Luther's 95 theses against papal indulgences
1517–18	Gil Vicente's *Auto da Barca*
1518	Pierre Gringore (Mere Sotte) joins Duke of Lorraine's court at Nancy
1520	Masked perambulations forbidden, Denmark
1522	Pageants greet Charles V in London
1530	Charles V installed as Holy Roman Emperor
1534	Issoudun presents Passion play
1535	Thomas More executed
1536	*Les Actes des Apôtres* staged at Bourges
1539	La Confrérie de la Passion transfers to Hôtel de Flandres, Paris; *Le Sacrifice d'Abraham* played before François II; great play contest staged at Ghent
1540	Contract between Gonzalo Guerra and Seville Tanners; Linlithgow performance of Sir David Lindsay's *Ane Satyre of the Thrie Estaitis*
1541	La Confrérie de la Passion stages *Les Actes des Apôtres*; Boy-Bishop perambulations banned in England (along with plough-trailing, 1548)
1542	Procurator-general reports adversely on La Confrérie de la Passion
1543	Lope de Rueda's Assumption Play, Seville
1545	Jacob Rueff's Protestant Passion Play, Zurich
1547	Valenciennes Passion play staged
1548	La Confrérie de la Passion acquires part of Hôtel de Bourgogne; Paris Parlement forbids performances of religious plays

1549	Trade guilds present Corpus Christi plays, Béthune; Hugh Latimer condemns Robin Hood 'gatherings'
1550–60	Hans Sachs writes his major *Fastnachtspiele*
c. 1552	*Thrie Estaitis* performed, Cupar, Fifeshire (Edinburgh presentation, *c.* 1554); earliest manuscript of Welsh interludes; death of Vigil Raber (Sterzing)
1553	Thomas Kirchmayer [Naogeorgus] *Regnum papisticum* (trans. as *The Popish Kingdome* by Barnaby Googe, 1570)
1555	Olaus Magnus, *Historia de gentibus septentrionalibus*; Philip II enters Antwerp
1556	Thomas Cranmer burnt; death of Ignatius Loyola
1558	Elizabeth I succeeds to English throne
1560	New Romney Whitsun plays performed for last time
1561	Splendid *landjuweel* held in Antwerp
1565	Lope de Rueda dies in Córdoba
1569	Valencia *Assumption* begins; final performance of York Cycle
1572	Ecclesiastical Commissioners suppress Yule ceremony, York
1575	Final performance of Chester Cycle; Coventry Hocktide show presented at Kenilworth
1583	Renwart Cysat's first presentation of the Lucerne Passion Play (does so again in 1597); Philip Stubbes, *The Anatomie of Abuses*
1595–1600	Llabrés manuscript (the Palma codex) compiled
1604	Corpus Christi play, Freiburg im Breisgau
c. 1609	Archdeacon Robert Rogers' *Breviary* on Chester antiquities written up

Glossary of technical and specialised terms

The following conventions have been used in the glossary below: Cast.: Castilian; Cat.: Catalan; Dut.: Dutch; Fr.: French; Ger.: German; It.: Italian; Lat.: Latin; Port.: Portuguese; Sp.: Spanish. Words in **bold** indicate entries in the glossary and can be used as cross-references.

abele spelen (Dut.) ['ingenious plays'] Four fourteenth-century plays on secular subjects, three having romantic themes, preserved in the Van Hulthem MS of *c.* 1400.

acolyte Attendant on the priest and **deacons** in celebrating **Mass**.

admonitor (Lat.) Monk who ensured that the monastic rule was maintained.

Advent The 'coming' of Christ; liturgical season immediately preceding Christmas. Advent Sunday (the first Sunday of the season) was the beginning of the Christian year.

alb Garment reaching to the feet, normally of white linen, with tight sleeves and girded round the waist, worn by clerks and choirboys assisting at the **altar** as well as by the priest and other ministers. In rich churches, albs made of white silk were often worn on festivals. (See fig. 3; see also **apparel**.)

almuce Hood and cape of fur with pendants. (See figs. 1–2, 4.)

alne (Sp.); *aune* (Fr.) A unit of linear measurement (approx. 1.182 metres), see **ell**.

altar Within a church, a structure of stone and wood containing relics of saints at which **Mass** was celebrated. When side altars were introduced, the main altar was often referred to as the 'high altar'.

amice Linen hood tied round the neck and thrown back in manner of a collar; to its upper or front edge was sewn an **apparel** which formed a collar. (See fig. 3.)

antiphon Sentence, often scriptural, recited or sung at the beginning and end of a psalm or canticle in the **Office** or **Mass**. (See also following entry.)

antiphonal chant Originally, simply a piece sung by two alternating choirs, one singing the psalm and the other repeating the refrain (**antiphon**) between each verse.

antremeses: (Port.); *entremés* (Cast.); *entremesos* (Cat.) Disguising or court entertainment, possibly using pageant wagons; the wagon itself (cf. **pageant**).

apparel (a) of the **amice**, an oblong strip of rich material sewn to one edge and

1

forming a collar about the neck; (b) of the **alb**, oblong pieces of rich material or embroidery, sewn on the front and back of the skirt and on the cuffs of its sleeves. (See fig. 3; see also **dalmatic**.)

araceli (Sp.)   Piece of aerial machinery which descended from and ascended to the dome or roof of a church, operated by a system of winches, and was strong enough to carry a number of actors.

aune (Fr.)   See **alne**.

auto (Sp.)   Short play, usually religious; *autos sacramentales* were plays often associated with the Feast of Corpus Christi.

Ave Maria (Lat.)   'Hail Mary'; act of devotion based on the angel Gabriel's salutation to Mary.

benefice (Fr.)   Profit from the entrance money shared between the performers.

breviary   Portable, abridged, combined **Office** book, first used in the thirteenth century.

bulto (Cast.)   Bust, statuary; usually of a religious nature.

cadafal (Sp.); *cadahalso, cadalso, cadefal, catafal* (Cat.)   Wooden structure on which plays were performed (cf. **scaffold**).

camerspel (Dut.)   Chamber play, i.e. one performed indoors.

canon of the Mass   Central sequence of prayers in the **Mass**, including the prayer of consecration of the bread and wine (eucharistic prayer).

cantor (Lat.)   One who led the singing in church.

cantrix (Lat.)   Nun who led the singing in church.

capellán mayor (Cast.)   Senior chaplain.

carées (Fr.)   Literally 'cartings'; performances on horse-drawn wagons.

carro, carrete (Sp.)   Wheeled float or wagon used for indoor and outdoor performances.

castillo (Sp.)   Stage castle; occasionally just a mobile float.

cavaliers salvatges (Cat.)   Literally 'wild knights'; performers who fought in duels and occasionally performed battles (cf. **salvajens**).

censer   Also called a thurible; metal vessel to hold charcoal in which incense was burned.

Chambers of Rhetoric; *Rederijkerskamers* (Dut.)   In the Low Countries, confraternities of rhetoricians (poets and actors).

chasuble   Outer and principal vestment of a priest or bishop at **Mass**. It was often ornamented with **orphreys** front and back in the form of a Y, but later with a vertical strip in front and a cross behind. (See figs. 3–4.)

choir-cope   Cope worn by monks during services in the quire. Often very rich and elaborate for festivals. (See fig. 1.)

ciborium   canopy or canopied shrine; receptacle for the **Host** with a canopied lid or cover. (See also **pyx**.)

comedia (Lat.)   Dramatic work, play, not necessarily comic.

Compline   Last of the eight daily Hours. (see **Office**.)

Confiteor (Lat.)   'I confess'; the opening of the usual form of confession in the western Church.

consueta (Sp.)   Customary; book providing details of liturgical ceremonies; term sometimes used for a play.

cope   Semicircular cloak with ornamental **orphreys** on edges . The original hood later became a stiff, rounded flap of rich embroidery hanging behind the neck. (See fig. 2.)

dalmatic   Outer vestment of the **deacon** in the form of a long tunic with tight sleeves, slit part way up the sides, and fringed along the edges. Its **apparels** were often narrow bands of rich material over each shoulder reaching to the bottom fringe. (See fig. 4.)

deacon   Middle rank of minister, between the priest and the **subdeacon**; assisted the priest at **Mass** but could not consecrate the bread and wine.

devisa (Sp.)   See ***envenções***.

disciplinati (It.)   Flagellants; groups of laymen who met to do penance for the sins of the world; the movement arose in the late thirteenth century and was especially widespread in Italy. (See ***laude***.)

disguising   In Britain, aristocratic pastime involving dressing-up, singing and dancing.

echaffaut (Fr.)   See **scaffold**.

ell   See ***alne/aune***.

entremés (Cast.); *entremesos* (Cat.)   See ***antremeses***.

envenções (Port.); *invención, invençiõn* (Sp.)   Occasional piece usually comprising a *devisa* (a visual component, generally a device on a helm) and a *letra* (a verse composition ranging from one short line to several octosyllabic stanzas).

episcopellus (Lat.); *obispillo* (Sp.)   Boy-bishop.

esbat[t]ement (Fr., Dut.)   General word for an amusement or entertainment.

estado (Sp.)   Unit of measurement ('the height of a man').

estrio (Sp.), *histrio* (Lat.)   Performer or actor.

factie (Dut.)   Originally a text written by a ***factor***; later the term used to indicate a short play performed as street theatre.

factor (Dut.)   Official of a Chamber of Rhetoric, responsible for teaching members how to write in the correct forms, for composing and directing plays and general administrative duties.

farseur (Fr.)   Farcer, player of farces.

Fastnachtspiel (Ger.)   Urban Shrovetide entertainment, often though not necessarily a secular play.

feinte (Fr.)   Stage device employed to produce some striking effect, or the effect itself.

feretory   Portable shrine containing a saint's relics.

feria (Lat.)   Used in liturgical books for the days of the week. Monday is *feria* II since Sunday, though a feast day and referred to as *festum* and not *feria*, counts as *feria* I.

fiesta (Sp.)   General term for feast days.

genuflection   Formal bending of the right knee as a sign of reverence.

Hail Mary   See ***Ave Maria***.

histrio   See *estrio*.

Holy Week   Week leading up to Easter Sunday; beginning with Palm Sunday and ending with Maundy Thursday, Good Friday and Holy Saturday.

Host   Wafer ('the bread') representing the Body of Christ, consecrated during the **Mass**.

hourd, *hourdement* (Walloon dialect of Fr.)   Large wooden structure for performance. The term is also used to refer to the whole enclosed 'theatre' (cf. *echaffaut*, **scaffold**).

humeral [veil]   Silk scarf worn by the priest over his shoulders and covering his hands when carrying the consecrated **Host**.

incipit (Lat.)   'It begins';   the opening words of a liturgical or other composition, or of an individual dramatic speech, where the remainder may be omitted.

infernum (Lat.)   'The lower place'; term often used to designate the location of Hell on the medieval stage.

interlude   Generic term applied in England and Scotland to a wide variety of small-scale dramatic entertainments, sometimes only 'games' but also involving dialogue.

Introit   Liturgical piece sung during the entry into the church. Its opening words were used to identify a particular Sunday (for an example, see **Sunday *Esto mihi***).

invención   See *envençõentes*.

jeu de personnages (Fr.)   Play with live actors.

jeu de retorique (Fr.)   Play by rhetoricians.

joc (Sp.); *jochs* (Cat.); *jogos* (Port.); *juegos* (Cast.)   Sport, game or play including stage plays (cf. *ludus*).

jogrol (Port.); *juglar* (Cast.)   Minstrel.

joueur d'appertige (Fr.)   Acrobat, rope-dancer or similar performer (from *appertisses* 'acts of skill').

landjuweel (Dut.)   Play contest held in Brabant.

laude (It.)   Literally 'praises'; vernacular sung pieces, some in dialogue form, developed by Umbrian ***disciplinati*** in the latter part of the thirteenth century. They evolved first into sung and then into spoken drama.

Lauds   Second of the daily Hours. (See **Office**.)

lectio (Lat.)   'Reading'; the portions of the Bible, saints' lives, etc. read during **Mass** or the **Office**.

letra   See *envençõentes*.

liturgy   Term used for the prescribed form of a corporate act of worship officially organised by the Church, but especially for the **Mass**.

ludus (Lat.)   Sport, game or play (cf. *jeu*, ***joc***, *spiel*).

Mass   Principal service of the church in which the consecration of the bread and wine as the Body and Blood of Christ commemorates Christ's actions at the Last Supper on Maundy Thursday.

Matins   First of the daily Hours (see **Office**), celebrated during the very early morning.

Mere Sotte; *Mere Folle* (Fr.)   Leader and principal female role (played by a man) in a group of **sots**.

missal   Volume combining the three books needed for celebrating **Mass**: Sacramentary (containing the prayers); Lectionary (containing the scriptural readings); and Cantatorium (containing the sung items).

misterios (Cat.); *mystère* (Fr.)   Play or tableau on a serious subject.

monstra (Sp.)   Spectacle or performance.

monstrance/*ostensorium* (Lat.)   Richly decorated vessel of precious metal with window to display the consecrated Host safely. Often used in processions, notably those of Corpus Christi.

monstre (Fr.)   Parade; often mounted to publicise a forthcoming performance.

mote (Sp.)   Device.

mumming   In Britain, mimed entertainment, or one with a mimed element as a major component, often with presenting or receiving gifts as its focus.

mystère   Chiefly applied to the large-scale religious plays of France, but see **misterios**.

mystères par signes (Fr.)   Tableaux or mimes.

Neidhartspiele (Ger.)   Group of secular plays in which the knight Neidhart avenges himself on the peasants who have caused his disgrace.

neophytes   Those newly converted, usually still under instruction.

Nones   Sixth of the daily Hours (see **Office**).

obispillo (Sp.)   See **episcopellus**.

octave   Week following a major feast or the last (eighth) day of such a week.

Office/*Officium* (Lat.)   The Church's prescribed series of short daily services (Hours, namely: Matins, Lauds, Prime, Terce, Sext, Nones, Vespers and Compline), found, with the psalter, in the **breviary**. The term could also be applied to a drama subsumed in the **liturgy** (cf. **ordo**).

ommegang (Dut.)   Procession, often highly elaborate in style.

ordo (Lat.)   'Arrangement'; agreed form of religious observance, also applied to a play included as part of the **liturgy** (cf. **officium**).

original   In Britain, master copy of a play-text from which individual scripts derived.

orphreys   Strips of rich embroidery used to ornament vestments. (See fig. 2.)

Our Father   See **Pater Noster**.

pageant   In Britain, wheeled or portable vehicle on which dramatised scriptural episodes were presented; the tableau or play mounted on it.

parc (Fr.)   Enclosed area containing playing space and audience accommodation.

Pater Noster (Lat.)   'Our Father'; the Lord's Prayer.

place; *place* (Fr.); *platea* (Lat.)   Principal area of performance; usually an unspecified locality fringed by **scaffolds**.

plen an gwary (Cornish)   Literally 'level place'; in Cornwall, amphitheatre constructed to accommodate various pastimes including stage-plays.

pontificals   Vestments and insignia of a bishop.

Prime   Third of the daily Hours (see **Office**)

prose   Liturgical sung item.

pulpitum (Lat.)   Stone screen with doorways, separating the **quire** and the nave of a major church and usually providing a raised platform that could be used for liturgical ceremonies.

puy (Fr.)   In France, literary society; in the French-speaking Low Countries also used for a group of rhetoricians.

pyx   Lidded vessel to hold the **Host**.

Quinquagesima (Lat.)   Sunday before Lent, i.e. at the height of the Shrovetide/ Carnival season (see also **Sunday *Esto mihi***).

quire   Part of the church containing the seats of the clergy or singing monks, also often spelt 'choir'.

Rederijkerskamers (Dut.)   See **Chambers of Rhetoric**.

refitolero (Sp.)   'Rationer'; the monk or brother in charge of the refectory and its provisioning.

remembranza (Sp.)   Term used for a play.

remonstrances par seignes (Fr.)   Dumbshow.

representació (Cat.); *representación* (Cast.); *representações* (Port.); *representatio* (Lat.) Play or performance.

responsory   Liturgical item consisting of a versicle (V) and a response (R), short texts which were recited or sung alternately.

rocas (Cat.)   Literally 'rocks'; floats, on wheels or carried, often used in processional drama, such as Corpus Christi processions.

rochet   A modification of the **surplice,** having no sleeves, worn by the clerk when serving the priest at **Mass**. Sleeved rochets, like short **albs**, were also worn.

rubric   Ritual or ceremonial direction in a service book; usually written in red.

sacrarium (Lat.)   Sacristy, room in church for keeping sacred vessels, and for priests (and others involved in the service) to robe.

sacre rappresentazione (It.)   A mainly Florentine form that adopted the narrative *ottava rima* of poets and street performers for dramatic purposes. Staged indoors and outside, often very elaborately, by religious confraternities.

salvajens (Sp.)   'Wild men'; knights with animal masks and hair in royal processions.

scaffold   In Britain, platform serving different theatrical purposes, deployed about a playing area/**place** (sometimes on the circumference of a circular arena) and capable of being curtained off or used as spectator accommodation (cf. ***cadafal, echaffaut***).

sequence   a **trope** (see below) originally designed to embellish the final syllable of the chanted Alleluia, from which independent hymns were evolved.

sinnekens (Dut.)   **Vice figures** in Dutch drama especially the ***spel van sinne***.

sot (Fr.)   Actor dressed as traditional fool.

sottie (Fr.)   Satirical play performed by ***sots***.

spel van sinne (Dut.)   Morality play written on a theme (*questie*) for a contest and including **sinnekens**.

stage   In Britain, basic scenic component or accommodation for audience; virtually synonymous with **scaffold**.

station   (a) in a church, a stopping place for a procession; (b) in Britain, one of several designated locations where a mobile play (or a section of one) stopped to perform.

stole   Long and narrow strip of material fringed at the ends and worn round the neck as a scarf. By bishops it was worn straight; by priests crossed over the breast; and by **deacons** over the right shoulder and fastened under the left arm. Its colour was the same as the **chasuble**. (See figs. 3–4.)

subdeacon   Member of the lowest order of clergy; one of the ministers at High **Mass**, with the priest and **deacon**.

sudary/*sudarium* (Lat.)   Napkin or cloth used to wipe sweat or tears from the face (especially that used by Veronica to wipe Christ's face); cloth used to wrap the head at burial (especially Christ's); a shroud.

Sunday *Esto mihi*   **Quinquagesima**; identified by the first words of the **Introit**.

surplice   Loose garment of white linen with wide sleeves, in its amplest form reaching to the feet. (See figs. 1–2.)

tafelspel (Dut.)   Literally 'table play'; one usually performed at dinner.

Te Deum (Lat.)   'We praise thee, O God'; canticle sung during Matins, and also often used at the end of special festivals or plays.

Tenebrae (Lat.)   Ceremony involving the gradual extinguishing of the candles in church, included in **Matins** and **Lauds** of the last three days of **Holy Week**.

Terce   Fourth of the daily Hours (see **Office**).

thurifer   One who carries a censer or thurible; an incense-bearer.

toise (Fr.)   Six *pieds* (feet) or 1.949 metres.

trope   Short series of sung words used to amplify or embellish a text in the **Mass** or the **Office**.

tunicle   Outer vestment of the **subdeacon** and the **acolyte**; worn also by taperers, cross-bearers, censer-bearers in some churches. It resembled the deacon's dalmatic, but was less ornamented. Later the two were made more alike and were called 'a pair of tunicles'. (See fig. 4.)

unguentarius (Lat.)   'Ointment-dealer'; the traditional figure of the merchant (*mercator*) from whom the three Maries buy ointments on their way to Christ's sepulchre.

ustensiles (Fr.)   Stage properties.

versicle   See **responsory**.

Vespers   Seventh of the daily Hours (see **Office**).

Vice figures   Dramatic characters embodying evil and acting as its agents, integral to the Dutch ***spel van sinne*** and the English/Scots morality play.

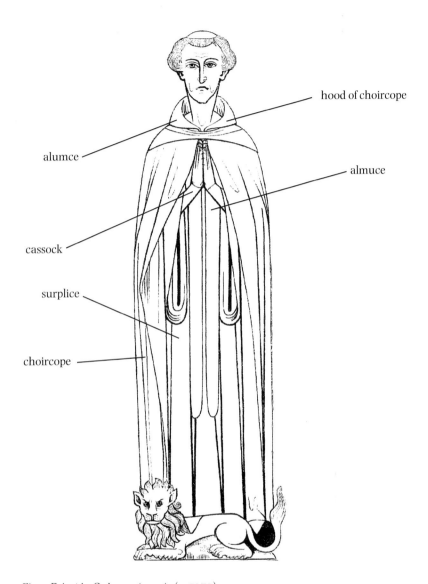

hood of choircope

almuce

alumce

cassock

surplice

choircope

Fig. 1 Priest in Quire vestments (c. 1370).

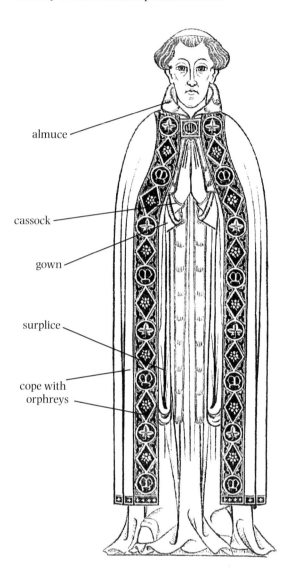

almuce

cassock

gown

surplice

cope with
orphreys

Fig. 2 Priest in Processional vestments (1432).

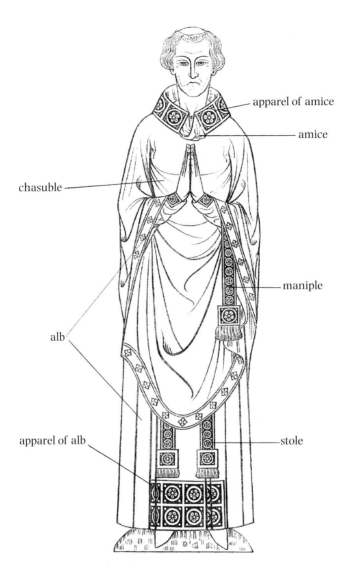

apparel of amice

amice

chasuble

maniple

alb

apparel of alb

stole

Fig. 3 Priest in Mass vestments (1375).

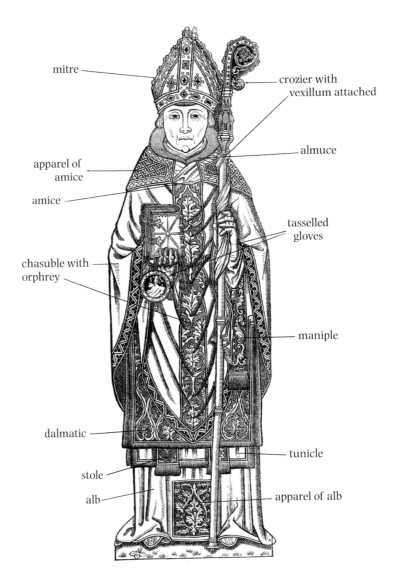

Fig. 4 Bishop in Mass vestments (1554).

Note on the treatment of texts

Where translations have been taken with permission from published editions, the source is specified in the attributions for individual entries; in other cases, unless otherwise indicated, the versions which appear are those of the editors. Occasionally where it seems helpful or of interest the original terminology has been supplied enclosed inside square brackets, which are also employed throughout to signal editorial emendations, adjustments or explications within the document.

MONEY

For language abbreviations, see glossary above. Money values and rates of exchange varied enormously during the medieval period. They can, however, be divided into two main kinds: money of account and actual coins minted. (Detailed information about medieval money and relative values can be found in Peter Spufford's *Handbook of Medieval Exchange*, London: Royal Historical Society, 1986. The same author's *Money and its use in Medieval Europe* (Cambridge, 1988) has a list of the coins most commonly in use in the Middle Ages as Appendix I.)

Money of account
For much of western Europe this was some form of £ s d: *libra, solidarius* and *denarius*. The *libra* (Lat.); *livre* (Fr.), used only as a money of account and abbreviated as either £ or lb, was originally a pound weight of silver. It was usually divided into 240 silver *denarii* (Lat.); *deniers* (Fr.); *dineros* (Sp.) and sometimes into 20 *solidarii* (Lat.); *sous* (Fr.); *sueldos* (Sp.).

France and the Low Countries mostly used the *livre tournois* (£T), worth 20 *sous*, but sometimes the *livre parisis* (£P) worth 24 *sous*. Where no indication is given, the *livre tournois* was probably meant.

Elsewhere, £ s d was expressed as the *pfund* (Ger.); pound (of sterlings) (Eng.); *esterlin* (Fr.); *Engelske punt* (Dut.). They were divided into 20 *schillings* (Ger.); shillings (Eng.; Dut.); each of 12 pence (Eng.); *pfennigs* (Ger.).

In South Tyrol the £ s d units were: h. kr. d. (See Bernd Neumann, *Geistliches Schauspiel im Zeugnis der Zeit*, 2 vols., Munich and Zurich, 1987, pp. 102–3.)

Spain used *maravedis* (abbreviated as *mrs*). A coin first minted in Almovarid

Spain (1093–1148) and later used as the currency of accounting.

A number of other terms were used mainly or solely as accounting terms; for example, the 'mark': in England worth 13s 4d and in Germany worth 12s/16s.

Currency and coinage

All the monies of account except the *libra* and its equivalents were also, at some time or other, used as coins. The following coins are also mentioned in the documents. Relative values, where given, are to the basic monies of account of the period.

carolus (Fr.)   Gold coin with head of King Charles VIII (1470–98) on it.

cruat (Cat.)   Coin minted in Barcelona worth 12d (cf. ***grooten d.***, etc.; ***gros***, etc.).

ducado (Sp.)   'Ducat'; gold coin of variable value.

ecu (Fr.)   Gold coin worth about a *livre*.

florin   Originally a coin from Florence but used widely in different countries; gold coin equivalent to 16s.

franc (Fr.)   Gold coin worth a *livre*, first minted in the thirteenth century.

great/thick penny   Silver coin first minted in thirteenth century (see ***grooten d.***, etc.; ***gros***, etc.).

groat   English coin worth 4d.

grooten d.; d.groot, (Dut.)   **'Great penny'**; worth about 12d. (For the change from 'penny' to 'great/thick penny' and its complex consequences, see Spufford, *Handbook*, p. xxiii.)

gros (Provincial Ger.), *groschen* (Ger.); *grossi* (Ital.)   Variations on the **'great penny'**.

heller (Ger.)   Small coin worth half a *pfennig*.

kreutzer Ger.   Silver coin of varying value.

mouton royal (Fr.)   Gold coin with a sheep on it.

real (Sp.)   Coin valued at 34 *maravedis*.

stuiver (Dut.)   Silver coin minted in Burgundian Netherlands, worth about a shilling.

taler (Ger.)   Large silver coin first minted in the sixteenth century. (The name derives from Joachimsthal in Bohemia, and is the origin of the American word *dollar*.)

General introduction

The urge to perform – and to watch others perform – may not be as fundamental a human instinct as are eating, sleeping and making love. Yet documentary evidence harvested from the field of western European sources between *c. AD* 500 and *c.* 1550 would certainly be of considerable assistance in sustaining the thesis that histrionic aspiration is universal among humanity. The mere existence of theatre in the Middle Ages denotes a recurrent pattern of victories over adversity. For all but the latter part of the period performance conditions were rarely other than rudimentary; ignorance and misunderstanding obscured the dramatic achievements of 'insolent Greece, or haughty Rome'; a religious faith pre-eminent in every sphere of life looked askance at forms of artistic expression unconducive to the furtherance of pious devotion. Yet by the end of the first Christian millennium not only had the theatrical impulse survived in its more basic, even illicit, manifestations, but was becoming assimilated albeit unconsciously into the sanctified routines of organised worship. Five centuries later, supported through the spiritual zeal of the laity, fuelled by late Gothic or Renaissance virtuosity, it would have proceeded to register some of its most remarkable triumphs.

Art rarely thrives in tranquillity. The factors inimical to the medieval stage's outbursts of creative vitality were not those cataclysmic population shifts, recurrent conflicts (as much ideological as political), periods of socioeconomic instability, territorial disputes between secular powers, doctrinal rivalries within and between religions, manifestly characteristic of the epoch. What is perhaps surprising is that, despite a lowering background of anti-theatrical prejudice and highly articulate opposition, dramatic ventures were not only tolerated but often actively encouraged by the establishment. Generally speaking, the material chronicling stage activity during the Middle Ages offers ample testimony to the apparent indestructibility of humanity's desire to perform and to witness performances.

But indestructibility does not imply immutability. The initial reaction of terrestrial institutions, whether lay or religious, is to mistrust theatre, unless its allegedly unruly energies and disruptive tendencies can be harnessed to advance ends not of its own creation. Around the crossroads where East confronts West, and the late classical era retreats before the advancing Middle Ages, hovers the elusive figure of the Byzantine Empress Theodora (*c.* 503–*c.* 548) who epitomises the incorporation of the wayward perversity of her twin professions into the fabric of official acceptability. Graduating from child prostitute to the erotic entertainer whose lurid routines Procopius details in his *Secret History* of *c.* 550, Theodora first became mistress to Justinian, nephew and adopted son to the senile Emperor Justin I, and then his wife. In 527 she succeeded with him to the joint rule of the Eastern Empire, a role she ruthlessly fulfilled by exercising metaphorically the same naked effrontery as she had exhibited literally in the arena.

Though Theodora's is undoubtedly an extreme case, her career highlights the perennial battle for supremacy waged throughout history between stern guardians of the spiritual, political, social and moral order, and those free spirits whose temperaments and actions lead them to subvert it unless firmly suppressed or taken into partnership. Too potent a phenomenon to be ignored, too suspect to be given its head, the histrionic appetite has often been disciplined or subdued by being tailored to suit the requirements of self-proclaimed good government or diverted into self-delineated paths of righteousness. The intermittent pulse of statutes, edicts, injunctions, and decrees emanating from bishops and burghers alike which punctuates the following pages bears witness to nervous efforts to control theatre's irreverent excesses, or to deflect its lawless dynamism into channels of which Church and State could approve.

Yet it would be unfair to suggest that medieval officialdom's suspicion of the stage was universal. Enlightened minds (which included those of Hugh of St Victor, Pope Innocent III and St Thomas Aquinas) welcomed responsible performances as a source of harmless recreational pleasure and as a vehicle of effective religious instruction, provided that they were set forth in the proper place at the proper time and in the proper manner. Sovereigns and royal personages could prove generous patrons of the players or take performers into their personal entourages; they might even condescend to tread the boards themselves provided that the company was sufficiently select. Drama presented itself not only as an accessible popular amusement for distracting the community, but as an appropriate means of upholding political, religious, ethnic and social values and continuities. Rational authority and regularised anarchy could often achieve a state of mutually supportive rapport: perhaps the best way of regarding the history of the medieval theatre is to view it as a sequence of constant readjustments between contending forces which time and again succeeded in creating conditions favourable to the emergence of great theatrical art.

It is impossible to say to what extent the tribal migrants who swarmed westwards across Europe from the fourth century onwards nurtured the stage or appreciated its appeal. Since in many occupied territories they would certainly have confronted survivors from the Roman entertainment industry, discovery of these thespian refugees – whether *mimi, histriones, scurrae, joculatores* – may well have been a revelatory experience whatever talents those labels conceal. Procopius may imply as much when describing the Vandals' spectatorial tastes after gaining possession of Libya in 429:

[they] passed their time [. . .] in theatres and hippodromes and in other pleasurable pursuits [. . .] they had dancers and mimes and all other things to hear and see which are of a musical nature or otherwise merit attention among men [. . .][1]

It may have been their novelty value which enabled post-Roman entertainers to reach an accommodation with Vandals, Goths, Celts and other intruders, even if they found their natural exuberance checked, as Apollinaris Sidonius (*c.* 430–*c.* 480) indicates when speaking of restraints placed on even musical performers at the court of Theodoric II, Visigoth ruler of Gaul from 462 to 466:

the badinage of farcical jesters is certainly introduced during dinner, though seldom and only on condition that no guest is assailed by the bitterness of a biting tongue [. . .] no lyre-player or flautist, no leader of dances, no girl tambourinist or cithara-player, performs there, the king being charmed only by stringed music whose virtue delights the soul no less than its melody soothes the ear [. . .][2]

By what means theatre was kept alive through the so-called Dark Ages it is hard to say. Soon after Sidonius' death the mirror of history becomes too misted over to enable us to chart the survival of dramatic entertainments with any precision. But that the stage remained popular in the West during the early medieval centuries is undoubted, if only from the agonised injunctions which emanated from both temporal and ecclesiastical officials castigating the wanton behaviour into which performances could entice the weaker-willed clergy. The medium, whether realised in actuality or deplored as one further suspect feature of pagan antiquity, exercised the troubled consciences and occupied the legislative energies of medieval rulers and church leaders. They could argue that there had been no less distinguished a witness to the stage's harmful allure than the redoubtable St Augustine himself (354–430), whose Carthaginian wild oats were partly sown from theatrical seed. Several centuries later Hrotswitha of Gandersheim (*c.* 935–*c.* 1002) unquestionably found herself sufficiently engrossed by the classical comedies of Terence to feel compelled to transform their unabashedly secular Latinity into picquant celebrations of Christian virtue, even if performance was perhaps not her goal.[3] To churchmen and women the stage was dangerous even as an ally: under its influence the sinful pleasures of a transient existence could too easily blur humanity's vision of the life to come.

Obviously not every hostile diatribe or stern directive which Church or State launched against the allegedly damaging effects of stage performance or its presenters' presumed turpitude was based on first-hand testimony. The early medieval church in particular inherited an endemic hostility to the theatre by way of patristic prejudice stemming from at least as far back as the *De Spectaculis* of Tertullian (*c.* 155–*c.* 222), and there were few opportunities for allowing objective observation to overthrow venerable convention. We must therefore be wary of drawing any dogmatic or inferential conclusions from a range of documents inevitably coloured by doctrinaire bias.

Not that the Church set itself up as the implacable scourge of every indication of the dramatic tendency. As passages of apparent dialogue and acts of quasi- or partial representation became drawn into the developing pattern of Christian worship, the clerisy began to acknowledge the theatre's potential for reinforcing spirituality and increasing devotion, both among initiates and aspirants. This is not to argue that participants in religious ceremonies saw themselves in any sense as performers or regarded what they presented as plays. The fluctuating line dividing religious observance from theatrical performance largely depends on contextual circumstances, though it is clear that some churchmen – Amalarius of Metz (c. 780–c. 850) and Honorius of Autun ('Augustodunensis'; c. 1075–c. 1156) among them – interpreted the Mass service as a drama with the celebrant 'playing the part' of Christ as he repeated His words during the consecration of the bread and wine. Such a conviction, while not universally adopted, may nonetheless have contributed to the constructive environment theatre required in playing its future role as an integrated element in Christian worship.

The impulses animating the conception and growth of the Church's Latin liturgical music-dramas remain obscure and controversial,[4] but it seems at least arguable that by the year 1000 a specialised form of Christian theatre had won ecclesiastical acceptance in several parts of Europe, constituting a major new development which would eventually spread across the entire continent. With a minimum of disguise achieved through judicious use of standard church vestments and only limited attempts at impersonation, clerics had begun to present within monastic or cathedral churches elementary scenarios or 'routines' constructed from chanted texts and mimed actions adapted from their service books. These presentations were closely associated with the annual pattern of ceremonials which followed the sequence of events commemorated in the Christian year, the highlights not surprisingly being the week leading up to Easter, Easter itself, then Christmas and the twelve days which succeeded it.

The point of origin is usually acknowledged as being the Easter ceremony known as the Visit to the Sepulchre (Visitatio sepulchri), of which the 'script' is provided by the so-called Quem queritis trope. This is one of many similar tenth-century textual and musical embellishments to standard Gregorian plainchant, and takes the form of a set of alternating (antiphonal) exchanges imagined as being delivered on the first Easter morning between the three Maries seeking Christ's sepulchre and the angel seated at its entrance. Fittingly enough, it was sung as a prelude to the first Mass of Easter Day, though its place within the programme of Easter services could vary from region to region.

The Visitatio with this dialogue at its heart proved capable of extension to incorporate other portions of the Easter narrative: the revelation of Christ's Resurrection to the apostles Peter and John and their race to view the empty sepulchre; the lament or planctus of Mary the Virgin; Mary Magdalene's encounter with Christ in His unrecognised guise as a gardener – the so-called Hortulanus; the three Maries' purchase of spices from the merchant (the unguentarius), the first non-scriptural character to appear in medieval religious drama. Showing only relatively minor variations one from another, numerous instances of the core version of the *Quem queritis* and its satellite episodes have come to light from across the whole of Europe.

There will always be debate as to whether the status of true drama can be claimed for the *Visitatio sepulchri*, or how far it represented a true partnership between the requirements of worship and the histrionic tendency. It was not a routine separable from its liturgical or service book context; formalised materials alone supplied its sung dialogue; 'costumes', 'props' and 'setting' were confined to the normal accessories of Christian devotion. Nor was it presented for the benefit of an audience in any real sense of that term; its participants were not called on to portray figures who required 'bringing to life' and so prove convincing human characters.

Yet the earliest version of the *Visitatio* to survive (in the *Regularis concordia* of c. 970[5]) has persuaded many that, as described, something more significant than another church ceremonial is afoot: a 'performance dimension' has appeared. For example, in this instance the *Visitatio* does not act as an introduction to the Easter Mass, but has been given its own position after the third lesson or *lectio* of the Easter Matins service. The clerics standing for the Maries may not be required to impersonate them, but they are specifically instructed to come forward 'tentatively' and wander about 'as if looking for something', suggesting that an element of mimesis, though not characterisation, is felt desirable. As for the ostensible lack of an audience, one might argue that the instruction that the Maries should display the burial cloth 'before the clergy' is a tacit admission that at this juncture non-participants briefly fulfil the function of spectators. Overall many scholars accept that, however carefully we qualify the statement, with the *Visitatio* and its subsequent liturgical extensions theatre becomes firmly identified with the furtherance of religious belief, its principal keynote throughout the Middle Ages. The Church had acknowledged and turned to its own advantage an innate human disposition to perform while others bear witness.

Liturgical music-drama enjoyed its creative heyday in the eleventh and twelfth centuries, and continued to be composed and presented until the middle of the sixteenth century, but remained essentially a preserve of the Church. Although its representation was gradually liberated from strict attachment to the appropriate season of the Christian year, places of worship remained its customary venue and Gregorian plainchant its esoteric medium. Even when in the twelfth century its executants were permitted to stage the plays outside sacred edifices, and to intersperse with the Latin texts lines couched in such European vernaculars as the *langue d'oc* of the Provençal troubadours, the laity's desire to receive divine truths through its native idiom remained frustrated. An account of a Latin play staged at Riga in 1204 illustrates both the proselytising incentive for popular religious performances – 'that those of the heathen persuasion might learn the rudiments of the Christian faith through the evidence of their own eyes' – and the potential crowd control problems inherent in couching them in an unfamiliar tongue:

The content of this play [. . .] was carefully explained through an expositor to the neophytes and the pagans who were present. However, when Gideon's force fought against the Philistines, the pagans, frightened that they themselves were about to be slaughtered, began to run away, but they were brought back again, although very wary.[6]

The duplication of Latin as a vehicle of dramatic expression parallels the evolution and spread of vernacular communication in worship. It is compatible too with the Church's thirteenth-century evangelistic mission to reach out to the non-Latin-speaking community, and to privilege the revised doctrinal thrust which placed at the heart of the faith Christ as a human figure living and suffering on earth for humanity's redemption. Such an approach was powerfully reinforced by the emphasis which Francis of Assisi (c. 1181–1226) and Dominic de Guzmán (1170–1221) – founders of dynamic orders of friars in the early years of the century – placed on the urgent necessity of employing the demotic tongues to preach salvation through Christ to the common people. Franciscan influence played a notable role in securing for popular Christian theatre a positive reception, not only within Italy but across the whole of western Europe.[7]

Certainly by 1350 drama was flourishing in the major western European languages, though mounted under a broad range of auspices, in a wide variety of circumstances, and in forms independent of liturgical occasion and inspiration. For most scholars these newer, freer vernacular plays represent a departure from, rather than a mere extension of, their liturgical counterparts, a view memorably expressed by V. A. Kolve in arguing that while a church play was 'simple, dignified, ritualistic, limited in its means',

When the drama moved into the streets and the market place, into a milieu already the home of men's playing and games, it was redefined *as* game and allowed to exploit fully its nonearnest, gratuitous nature at the same time as its range of subject and its cast of sacred personae grew.[8]

Clearly, in order to appeal to a broader, more variegated audience the non-Latin plays drew on a less restricted range of source materials, incorporating into their action aspects of common, often comic, everyday life largely alien to the more restricted, hieratic ambience of the liturgical stage. Probably the Church encouraged a more liberal treatment of scriptural and spiritual matters in the vernacular plays partly because it saw the necessity of appealing through them to those who might resist unembellished religious instruction. Similarly, ecclesiastics may have deliberately engineered the improved opportunities for lay participation which non-Latin drama offered the community, building perhaps on the increasing popularity of widespread public declarations of faith and of corporate expressions of urban solidarity.

One prime example is the post-mid-thirteenth-century vogue which engulfed the Abruzzi, Umbrian and Tuscan regions of Italy, where ardent assemblies foregathered to chant *laude* or hymns of praise in honour of Christ or the Virgin. Such hymns could sometimes adopt semi-dramatic form, and in these, as the fourteenth century wore on, spoken words replaced sung melody, and striking staging effects came to assume a more prominent role. Ingenious and ambitious spectacles were certainly a feature of the notable successors to the *laude*, the *sacre rappresentazioni*, a genre which reached a peak of artistic and technological elaboration in the churches and streets of fifteenth-century Florence. Here the popular desire for expression through drama became powerfully interwoven with celebrating the splendours of the de' Medici family regime, Lorenzo himself composing at least one piece for public consumption.[9] Perhaps with the *sacra rappresentazione* the citizenry of Florence allowed an assertion of secular power and political supremacy to usurp the place formerly occupied by an act of divine worship, although the distinction is unlikely to have been preoccupied many.

Elsewhere in western Europe, Church and laity frequently blended forces to ensure that the dramatic urge could be overtly indulged at the same time as the claims of religious observance and civic pride were sincerely honoured. Such an alliance helped to create much that is artistically distinguished in late medieval culture, and it almost certainly accounts for the swift escalation of the annual summer procession associated with the celebration of the Feast of Corpus Christi from about 1320 onwards.[10] This festival, instituted as part of the Church's calendar by Pope Urban IV's bull *Transiturus de hoc mundo* of 1264 but not observed universally before 1317, though no longer viewed as the 'only begetter' of the high summer of medieval theatre, did offer secular officials and lay organisations the perfect chance to engage in creative collaboration with the clergy. As one of its obligations a Corpus Christi guild or fraternity might occasionally sponsor a dramatic performance, but for many companies it was enough to dress up and march alongside community leaders and ecclesiastics in the yearly eucharistic parade with the Holy Sacrament as its central focus. Thereby medieval laymen used a diluted form of theatrical activity not only to identify themselves with the upholders of the Christian religion and its hallowed ceremonies, but to affirm their place in the civic hierarchy. The spirit inspiring such an integration of motives would eventually lead members of town councils, neighbourhood groups, or trade and craft guilds (notably at British, French, German and Flemish venues) to sponsor, mount and take responsibility for communal presentations of scriptural plays, though progress from merely parading to mounting full-length performances was by no means inevitable or universal.

The semi-dramatic procession was at all events an integral part of the medieval theatrical scene, supplying a cogent outlet for the prevalent spirit of festivity and celebration. The occasion might be secular, marking a coronation, a royal visit, the signing of a treaty, or a popular victory in war, while the Church's extensive calendar of festivals also offered ample opportunity for parades through the streets, Corpus Christi being only one such opportunity for communal rejoicing. The Feast of the Assumption of the Virgin Mary, for example, was observed throughout western Europe with sumptuous perambulations, many of which became associated with theatrical performance; the citizens of Lincoln celebrated the Feast of

St Anne by the same means, as did those of Florence in commemorating their patronal saint John the Baptist. Medieval street pageantry deployed a wide variety of devices to create the ambience deemed proper to the occasion: public monuments including bridges, conduits and fountains were decorated; triumphal arches erected; static or mobile floats bearing *tableaux vivants* displayed; banners, torches, candles, and simple devices such as wheeled ships or costumed figures paraded through city or town thoroughfares. But the scope of such activities never embraced full-scale drama except at a relative handful of locations.

Only here and there did the ambience of the festive occasion allow the theatrical imperative to develop a more prominent role. From the welter of processional activities feasible by the end of the fourteenth century, a less haphazard pattern of procedures seems to emerge. The likeliest conjecture is that as the processing vehicles, the static tableaux, the walking characters' costumes became more elaborate, so the dramatic dimension became more pronounced. No standard method of evolution predominated, and practices clearly differed from place to place. At some centres live performers in costume presented short scenes at ground level or on stages along the processional route; elsewhere participants in static or mobile tableaux who might have initially mimed the building of the Ark or the Visit of the Magi began to deliver passages of dialogue from the moving floats. In one city wagons might stop at designated 'stations' to allow the crowd to watch and listen; at another, street-level performances took place while the procession was actually in slow motion, as appears to have been the practice by 1558 at Draguingnan in southern Provence:

[. . .] the Corpus Christi play [. . .] shall be played along with the procession as heretofore and also as many shorter plays [episodes ?] as possible. The latter shall be performed as the procession moves on, without anybody who is acting stopping, in order to prevent things becoming too long drawn out and to prevent confusion both in the procession and in the performances [. . .][11]

At many centres religious processions never generated a literal drama of any kind; even when they did, there was no uniformity of presentation. At Bologna, for example, the only Italian Corpus Christi text to survive was set forth in the streets on wagons, but was also accompanied by tableaux and walking figures. In Bruges the processing floats supported tableaux alone, while dramatic performances were presented by players on foot; at Zerbst in 1507 actors displaying texts appear to have mimed a sequence of episodes alongside portable tableaux. In Brussels players probably gave mimed performances along the route taken by the *ommegang* in the morning, presenting the plays proper that afternoon in the Nedermarkt. In some countries the plays would be staged in church before being taken on to the streets; at certain centres the performances were even executed on a different day from the sacramental procession.

Despite popular belief, not every play set forth was part of a 'cycle' of integrated biblical episodes. France and German-speaking areas tended to focus on the life and death of Christ; of the thirty-three plays performed processionally in Toledo between 1493 and 1510 none formed part of a cyclic sequence. In 1549 craft guilds in Béthune, the ancient seat of the Counts of Flanders, near the present Franco-Belgian border, mounted a processional presentation consisting of twenty-eight episodes stretching from the Annunciation to Doomsday, but it was not a recurrent event. Only at certain centres in England were nurtured the growth and the regular production of that idiosyncratic succession of connected scriptural plays which encompass the Christian vision of human history from Creation to Doomsday, and of which the cycles of York, Chester and Wakefield (and in a limited sense the N-Town Plays) furnish the best extant examples. Two at least of these were shaped into literary texts late in their existence; all are best regarded as relics of an amorphous, fluid, fluctuating repertory. Only at York, Coventry and Chester were plays now extant indubitably mounted processionally, and even in this limited context their relationship with and their relevance to the Feast of Corpus Christi has been much debated, as has their mode of presentation.

Yet such spiritual festivities occasioned that characteristic fusion of local and ecclesiastical resources which is the hallmark of so many medieval play performances. Inseparably intertwined with genuine religious devotion, a strong sense of corporate identity and communal pride gave a vital impetus to the mounting of productions, and is particularly characteristic of some of the ambitious French civic *mystères*. Typical is the justification given for performing the *mystère* of St Martin at Seurre in 1496:

[. . .] so that on witnessing it acted the common people would easily be able to see and understand how the noble patron of the said Seurre lived a holy and devout life. [12]

One of the numerous strengths of medieval performance is that its roots plunge deep into the soil of its immediate surroundings, and are fed from indigenous resources. These plays represent community drama in the best sense of the term.

Nevertheless we should not assume that willing assistance was spontaneously made available or that the entire populace could be relied on to give a production its unquestioning support. The existence of a whole reef of contracts and regulations, sureties and recognisances which legally bound participants, both performers and labour force, to honour their pledges shipwrecks these sanguine beliefs. When setting up a presentation, authority could obviously not rely on the histrionic impulse alone to promote cooperative cohesion; organisers could never afford to leave recalcitrant human nature out of the reckoning.

By way of counterbalance, however, given that presentations were expected to constitute a justifiable cause for local pride and satisfaction, they could act as a very effective form of social cement. The desire to perform creditably must be accompanied by a parallel desire to watch creditable performances, or theatre perishes. So the irksome labours undertaken and the copious sums laid out to ensure that dramatic offerings did not forfeit the approval of spectators or incur the derision of rivals represent not only the desire to fulfil what may be a basic human need, but also a determination to create an experience which would cast reflected glory on those under whose auspices it had been conceived and executed. Undoubtedly in certain instances the profit motive also inspired town and city traders in particular to see that performances worthy of patronage attracted audiences with money to spend.

The immense organisational demands made on urban dwellers, let alone the residents of villages and hamlets, cannot be overemphasised. Even when the incentive or invitation to perform came from church officials, regional magnate or the local council, from the entire community or from individuals within it, this was only a preliminary to setting up an appropriate command structure, selecting adequate supervisors, raising the requisite funding, securing the needful permissions or accepting the stipulated conditions from the secular or religious authorities, and persuading sufficient personnel to contribute to the proceedings in whatever capacity they could and would. As the Church's grip loosened on the logistics of staging drama outside its own buildings, so teams of lay persons assumed at least joint responsibility for the multiple facets of public performance, and at many venues even took complete control. The existence of religious, trade or craft associations such as the town and city guilds in England considerably facilitated the organisation of performances; where no such ready-made cooperatives could supply the requisite degree of cohesion and dedication, analogous structures and systems had to be put in place. Groups like the *puys* of France and French-speaking areas of the Low Countries, the Parisian *Confrérie de la Passion*, and Rome's *Gonfaloniere di Santa Lucia* banded together with the presentation of plays as one of their principal aims. Of all such play writing and producing organisations which came into being, the amateur literary guilds of the Low Countries – the Chambers of Rhetoric or *Rederijkerskamers*, with their highly organised competitions – are perhaps the most remarkable. But in many other places secular authorities mounted drama as one of their public responsibilities.

The general pattern emerging from the plethora of records which survive is that while the ruling power in a region was usually the ultimate source of permission and appeal, bishop or city council, cathedral chapter or local nobleman, would almost invariably delegate the detailed aspects of presentation to reliable deputies acting as either administrators or executives. Their number might include local government officials, prominent members of town or city councils, and individuals chosen for specific experience or expertise. Occasionally, as at Valenciennes in 1547, the players themselves elected some of their number to exercise absolute jurisdiction over proceedings, with powers to fine their fellows for any misdemeanours. Elsewhere one or more directors would be appointed to supervise the entire project, not excluding the off-stage arrangements: it was not for nothing that Lucerne selected their meticulous town clerk, Renward Cysat, to take charge of their Whitsun Passion play in 1583. Payments to organisers were not unusual: Alonso del Campo who supervised the arrangements for the Toledo Corpus Christi performances in 1493 received an annual salary of 1,000 maravedis, but like many of his ilk, had to agree to store and maintain materials, properties and other stage impedimenta. Along with the right to exercise their own discretion, continental directors seem to have enjoyed an invaluable measure of autonomy, supported by generally proficient staffs who worked under them.

Since expenses were often high, particularly if local prestige was at stake (and in many places performers were rewarded for their services), the allocation of financial responsibility was of serious concern. Players might be asked (as at Mons in 1501) to supply their own stage costumes, construct their own set as at Diest in Brabant or New Romney in Kent or at least, as at Seurre in 1496, decorate it, but generally these matters were executed by others. However, it was certainly not unknown for participants to be required to pay for the privilege of performing: at Lucerne actors agreed to invest a gold écu in the production as a contribution to expenses, returnable if the show broke even or made a profit. But the bulk of a production's funding came from outside sources.

Church authorities are seldom found contributing more than a proportion of the total expenditure, though in the Toledo accounts for 1493 the Corpus Christi expenses were met half by the cathedral treasury, half by its fabric office, and the cost of erecting the magnificent timber amphitheatre at Autun in 1516 was shared between town and surplice. Occasionally, too, we hear of the wealthier classes offering or being invited to subsidise a production. But in the main it was local communities who paid for plays to be put on, either directly from public funds or as a levy on citizens in their private capacity or as conscientious members of some type of guild. At Romans, a compromise was reached before the 1509 presentation of the *Mystère des Trois Doms* whereby the cathedral chapter and members of the Chapel of St Maurice shared half the costs, leaving the town with only the other half to find. Craft guilds participating in Lille were paid expenses from the city's coffers. Elsewhere citizens were less fortunate: at Bourges many investors claimed to be almost ruined after the 1536 *Actes des Apôtres*, the result of overestimating the attendances intended to reimburse them for their outlay. Resistance to the notion of contributing financially to dramatic presentations is thus not surprisingly a marked feature of some sets of records.

But many others appear to have paid without question the contribution required of them as local residents or members of their guild or religious confraternity, Rome's *Gonfaloniere di Santa Lucia* allowing their directors twenty ducats out of their funds to stage a Passion play in the Colosseum. In England, in particular, legislation was enacted to ensure that all craftsmen or traders, whether guildsmen or not, contributed the 'pageant pence' due from them in order that some of their number might perform. Even smaller communities whose populations had no binding obligation to subsidise performances usually seem to have given what was required. At the same time expenditure might be recovered from takings, since not all productions guaranteed free admission. In France, particularly for the large-scale civic *mystères*, a graduated scale of prices backed by stringent arrangements to ensure that payment was received could even secure the organisers a profit. At York the authorities levied a percentage fee from those citizens who set up scaffolds at stations along the processional route; later this privilege was put out to competitive tender. In other places it was more common to take up a collection during performance or to 'gather' contributions in advance.

The lack of custom-built playhouses created many of the problems encountered by management groups, although it no doubt made them more inventive in their efforts to press into service a wide range of disparate buildings, or to present their offerings at a variety of outdoor sites, some carefully constructed or adapted, others left in their natural state. The most common indoor venue, sanctioned through time-honoured use as the home of liturgical performances, was of course the local church or diocesan cathedral. Church buildings were often a *sine qua non* when elaborate machinery was required to sustain the dramatic effect of ascents or descents like those in Florence which impressed Bishop Abramo of Souzdal in 1439 and which still feature in the Elche *Assumption* today. Here the Italian *laudesi* found their ultimate home; plays from the Palma Codex, including the vernacular music-drama of Esther and King Ahasuerus, were almost certainly staged in Palma Cathedral; in less spacious circumstances a Palm Sunday play occupied the church at Bozen (Bolzano) in 1514. Failing such edifices, several communities built their own structures, some of the most celebrated being the wooden amphitheatres constructed at Autun 'on the field of St Lazarus' in 1516, at Doué-la-Fontaine near Saumur in 1539, and at Issoudun near Bourges in 1545.

Far more common were performances mounted out of doors, using varying configurations of platforms set up either within well-defined areas of public assembly, or on specially prepared sites in open spaces. By variously combining the use of level ground (the 'place' or *platea*) with that of raised platforms ('scaffolds'), medieval players developed a sophisticated repertory of staging techniques which met most dramatic exigencies. Such natural places of resort as city squares and marketplaces were ideally suited to this style of presentation; Rouen's Place du Neuf Marchié was the site of a Nativity piece in 1474, the stages being set up on four sides of the central square. At Mons for the famous Passion play of 1501 a single central platform was thrust out into the Grand Markiet, some of the surrounding houses being commandeered as part of the setting. Lucerne's Weinmarkt, the city's most important public square similarly employed in 1583, featured scenic components distributed across its wide expanse. But a whole range of enclosed spaces including cemeteries and monastic or castle courtyards were annexed as the occasion demanded it.

Not unnaturally performances at locations where more expenditure of time and effort was required to mount presentations effectively are less commonly encountered. But Cornwall's *Ordinalia*, originally staged around the middle of the fourteenth century, and East Anglia's *The Castle of Perseverance*, first presented early in the fifteenth, while adopting the 'place and scaffold' principle, appear to have been set forth at open-air sites away from busy communities. These plays seem to have taken place in either natural or specially prepared circular arenas where audience and scenic units shared the circumference of the 'round'. Such a configuration has clear affinities with the type of theatre depicted in the celebrated Fouquet miniature of *The Martyrdom of St Apollonia*, whose factual reliability has been the subject of much recent speculation.

As often observed, drama had the status of a medieval mass medium, and even allowing for a measure of exaggeration, we cannot dismiss as fanciful claims that 2,800 spectators attended each of the two daily stagings of the Valenciennes *Passion* of 1547; that 9,000 could be accommodated for the performance of the *Mystère de Trois Doms* at Romans in 1509; or even that a prodigious 80,000 watched the play of St Lazarus over four days at Autun seven years later. From 1460 to 1520 the Colosseum at Rome (said to have held 40–50,000) was the venue for an annual Good Friday performance of the Passion; the same number are alleged to have attended a Florentine performance in 1451 involving the decollation of St John the Baptist.[13]

It would be unfortunate, however, if we allowed such statistics to govern our impression of the staging of popular religious drama in the Middle Ages. Attention tends to focus on the more massive, spectacular and ambitious ventures such as the French *mystères*, the English cycles, or the Florentine *sacre rappresentazioni*, whose presentation still catches the imagination after over 500 years. But undoubtedly there were more intimate productions which relied less on grandiose effects and mass responses – the plays of the Dutch Rhetoricians, the French *Miracles de Nostre Dame par personnages*, the modest morality-style pieces played out in a variety of courtyards, halls and refectories for the benefit of more select audiences. These slender threads too have their place in the tapestry.

Perhaps because of the universality of medieval religious expression, far fewer remnants of purely secular stage activity remain to reward investigators, though the distinction may sometimes be more a modern than a medieval one.[14] The comparative scarcity of surviving documents reflects governmental and ecclesiastical priorities in furthering the twin purposes of Christian propaganda and political allegiances, looking to the stage to make its contribution to those approved goals. In the majority of cases theatre with other ends in view, unless designed by the aristocracy or dedicated to their pleasure, was liable to suffer either proscription or neglect. From the relatively sparse evidence for popular theatre one might never register that non-Christian, non-official entertainments, both professional and indigenous, also maintained a flourishing and colourful existence throughout the period and were enjoyed across a wide social spectrum. Regrettably, what has been left behind conveys only a dim impression of the satisfaction and delight which observing these customs and engaging in these pastimes must once have brought to so many drab, harsh and wearisome lives. As already indicated, many of these expressions of the medieval imagination met with official disapprobation for a variety of reasons genuine and spurious. Thankfully, enough records of such 'coarser pleasures' as the *Fastnachtspiel* and the Neidhart play exist to invoke the lost revelry celebrating earthy happiness and 'glad animal movements'.

However, while many imprints of 'people's theatre' have disappeared, ample records survive of lavish court ceremonies and dramatic festivities, and of the elaborate street pageantry which periodically lightened the medieval citizen's daily burden. Kings, princes and governors made plentiful use of professional performers and organisers in demonstrating their own importance within the scheme of things, as well as enthusiastically participating in theatricals themselves. Glowing accounts of these activities provide us with access to one aspect of medieval profane dramatics, albeit an almost exclusively patrician one. Though purists might wish to enforce a distinction between public spectacles and staged plays, it seems somewhat pedantic to avert our eyes from the presence of elements common to, say, chivalric tournaments, entertainments at court, parades through the city streets, and communal presentations of scriptural drama. To say the least, their executants had in common similar problems – technical, aesthetic, logistical – to confront and overcome. Moreover, the relish with which chroniclers describe the minute details of such spectacular celebrations confirms the theatrical orientation and impact of all these variant forms of conspicuous display which so signally reinforced contemporary concepts of power, order and degree. Even without a full understanding of the several social, political and economic contexts in which such performances were embedded, one becomes aware that secular theatre served as an integral part of the life of its time.

Certainly in the realm of knightly accomplishment, many aspects of both the individual joust and the general *tournois* – confrontational encounter, reversal of expectation, the ultimate resolution of conflict – undoubtedly paralleled the fundamental strategies of drama, as did such more obvious parallels as role-playing and dressing-up in emblematic disguises. Nor did aristocratic influence on theatre stop with the tournament. The countless forms of banquet entertainment encountered in court and castle – the lavish royal *entremés* mounted on the Iberian Peninsula perhaps the most notable of them – fostered the development of such esoteric forms as mummings, disguisings or interludes which prefaced those dramas of wider appeal that ushered in the early modern period.

While only a well-born élite might savour the arcana of the tournament and the banquet, commoners could at least share and enjoy vicariously the overspill from upper-class activities in the extensive (and expensive) provisions often made in major towns and cities for celebrating important events. Formal 'entries' and triumphs painstakingly arranged to welcome a monarch or illustrious visitor offered the municipal or civic hierarchy an opportunity to deploy ornate ritualistic pageantry within the public domain, not only to demonstrate their own dynastic loyalties and enhance local prestige, but to foster a sense of common values and a communal identity on which they might rely for reciprocal expressions of solidarity at times of crisis. Here, by capitalising once again on the theatrical instinct, those in authority ensured that it played an important part in underpinning a complex structure of political, economic and social relationships.

A work which 'covers' the theatre of the Middle Ages must be assigned an appropriate termination point, yet the decision is problematic in that most commentators view the period as coming to a close at different times in different geographical areas. As one historian writes: 'However revolutionary humanist and Renaissance ideas were to become, their origins are firmly rooted in medieval culture, to the extent that it is difficult to pin-point the beginning of the movement.'[15] Certainly, if we focus exclusively on techniques of theatrical presentation, in many parts of Europe much of what we think of as the drama of the Middle Ages is in fact sixteenth-century in provenance.

When, then, does 'the medieval theatre' cease to be medieval? Even if we grant (as many historians do not) that some kind of transformation of western European hearts and minds had occurred by the time the Platonic Academy was established in Florence in 1440, or Greek scholars were driven west following the Turkish conquest of Constantinople in 1453, we may still wish to accept that it took many decades for the new spirit to become a living cultural presence in countries outside Italy. Even when it did emerge, particularly in northern Europe, it would chiefly serve to season the late Gothic artistry of such men as the elder Cranach, Albrecht Dürer, and the younger Holbein, rather than to transmogrify the native artefact at a single stroke. It therefore makes little sense to allow some kind of chronological guillotine to slice off the rich material dating from after 1500 which typifies the heritage of the late Middle Ages. Intellectually and aesthetically medieval presuppositions and preoccupations permeate most areas of sixteenth-century creativity, as an admittedly archaised work like Spenser's *The Faerie Queene* (1590–6) demonstrates so magnificently.

Undoubtedly, in the theatrical sphere, innovations arising from Italian technological initiatives far outstrip anything achieved or even contemplated contemporaneously elsewhere on the European continent or in Britain. Designers and engineers employed in the great city states of northern Italy pioneered and fine-tuned marvels of scenic illusion largely evolved from exploring the stage possibilities of the principles of perspective. Ambitious experiments in theatre-building flourished following the stimulus provided by the first printing of Vitruvius' *De architectura* in 1486. But in many other territories organisers and directors remained true to improvised structures and non-illusionistic modes of staging deployed in traditional ways. As with other art forms, in theatrical terms medieval and neoclassical conventions coexisted into the seventeenth century, as the versatility of Lope de Vega and Ben Jonson as dramatic authors testifies.

There are thus many obvious reasons why the later sections of this work contain material dating from the mid to late sixteenth century (and in several instances from after 1600). Many documents from this period provide us with our only evidence for certain facets of medieval stage practices; others represent the most graphic or reliable information which survives. In several areas much of the documentation pre-dating 1500 is so scanty that we are forced to trust such later sources as, for example, Archdeacon Rogers' 'Breviary' with its uncorroborated account of the Chester Whitsun performances. The most striking demonstration of the vital importance of late evidence arises in the case of the Lucerne Passion Play, staged in the city's Weinmarkt at regular intervals from *c.* 1450 until its final presentation in 1616. It would clearly be foolhardy to rule out extracts from the marvellously detailed records kept by Renward Cysat for the Lucerne presentation of 1583 on the grounds that by then, pedantically speaking, the Middle Ages are over. As F. M. Salter wrote in *Medieval Drama in Chester* (Toronto, 1955), 'it is the type of drama, rather than the period, that is in question'. Elucidation, not exactitude, has been our goal.

As a result, editorial guidelines as to what constitute 'medieval' items eligible for inclusion and 'Renaissance' entries ripe for rejection have been non-prescriptive. Contributors have been encouraged to treat those often unhelpful terms of reference with sufficient elasticity to ensure that nothing of interest or significance has been set aside as inadmissible on merely chronological grounds. At times we have been blatantly pragmatic and almost certainly inconsistent, but we believe that we have encompassed at least those documents essential to achieving as complete a picture of the medieval theatrical scene as is possible within the scope of the publishers' brief and our own awareness.

NOTES

1. *Procopius*, trans. H. B. Dewing, Loeb Classical Library, 7 vols., London and New York, 1914, vol. II, p. 257.
2. *Letters*, Book I, II (to Agricola), 9. I acknowledge the kindness of my former colleague John Ellis Jones in translating this passage.
3. On this issue, see Sister Mary Marguerite Butler, *Hrotswita: The Theatricality of her Plays*, New York, 1960; Silvio D'Amico, *Storia del teatro drammatico*, vol. I, Milan, 1968; Gustavo Vinay, *Alto medioevo latino*, Naples, 1978, pp. 483–554; and Ferruccio Bertini, *Il 'teatro' di Rosvita*, Genoa, 1979; see also **A29**.
4. One of the best attempts to provide an overview of the various scholarly positions taken in the several debates on liturgical drama is C. Clifford Flanigan, 'Medieval Latin music-drama', in Eckehard Simon (ed.), *The Theatre of Medieval Europe*, Cambridge, 1991, pp. 21–41.
5. Compiled at the behest of St Æthelwold (*c.* 908–84), bishop of Winchester, as part of his drive to impose conformity on English Benedictine monasteries (see **B9**).
6. Karl Young, *The Drama of the Medieval Church*, 2 vols., Oxford, 1933, vol. II, p. 542; see **C64**.
7. See David L. Jeffrey, 'St Francis and Medieval Theatre', *Franciscan Studies* 43 (1983), pp. 321–4. For a more specific focus see Fernando Ghilardi, 'Le origini del teatro italiano e San Francesco', *L'Italia francescana* 30 (1955), pp. 341–51; 31 (1956), pp. 81–7; *Il francescanesimo e il teatro medievale. Atti del Convegno Nazionale di Studi San Miniato, 1982*,

Castelfiorentino, 1984; Ronald E. Surtz, 'The "Franciscan Connection" in Early Castilian Theater', *Bulletin of the* Comediantes 35 (1983–4), pp. 141–52.

8. For a fuller account of Kolve's position, see *The Play Called Corpus Christi*, Stanford and London, 1966, pp. 8–32.

9. See Konrad Eisenbichler, 'Confraternities and Carnival: the Context of Lorenzo de' Medici's Rappresentazione di SS Giovanni e Paolo' in *Medieval Drama on the Continent of Europe*, ed. Clifford Davidson and John H. Stroupe, Kalamazoo, 1993, pp. 128–39.

10. For an authoritative treatment of the whole topic, see Miri Rubin, *Corpus Christi: the Eucharist in Late Medieval Culture*, Cambridge, 1991; inevitably, this account of Corpus Christi drama requires supplementation from other sources.

11. *French Theatre in the Neo-Classical Era, 1550–1789*, Theatre in Europe: A Documentary History, ed. William D. Howarth *et al.*, Cambridge, 1997, p. 63; see also **E95**.

12. *Staging*, pp. 259–62. For extracts from the Seurre records, see **E23, 26, 64, 81**.

13. See Nerida Newbigin (ed.), *Nuovo corpus di sacre rappresentazioni fiorentini del Quattrocento*, Bologna, 1983, p. 109.

14. Gordon Kipling in *Enter the King*, Oxford, 1998, suggests that the medieval triumph drew heavily on the liturgy for its concepts and modes of expression.

15. Peter Denley in *The Oxford Illustrated History of Medieval Europe*, ed. George Holmes, Oxford, 1988, p. 285.

Section A
The inheritance

Edited by NICK DAVIS

Introduction

The performing traditions of early medieval western Europe were, no doubt, sparse in comparison with those of the later Roman Empire. Public shows in a wide variety of genres – the Roman *ludi*, which term covers games, contests, stage entertainments, fights, spectacles in general – had held a central place in Roman town life as an interest which most were capable of sharing, and a form of conspicuous expenditure which conferred status on its patrons. Some attempt was made to sustain this culture in Italy under Gothic rule during the early decades of the sixth century [**A2**]. But over the following centuries urban populations shrank still further or were swept away (towns which survived often being little more than military centres), while the politically ascendant Christian Church continued to condemn *ludi* as being of diabolic origin and nature. From the later sixth century few groups in western Europe possessed the means or will to mount lavish performances in the Roman style. The Roman itinerant performer was, however, a hardy species. Among the very few Romans known to have crossed the continent of Asia were jugglers, a troupe of whom was courteously received at the Chinese capital of Chang'an in AD 120 (an official delegation had failed to get through two decades before).[1] In medieval perception a definitive Fall of Rome and loss of continuity with classical civilisation had never occurred: the cultures of the period commonly saw themselves as maintaining, with some suitable Christian revision, rather than replacing the traditions of a still much-admired classical world.[2] Moreover, archaeological investigation has produced more evidence of town life during Europe's 'Dark Ages' than the historical record might have led one to expect.[3] A fair number of the Roman performing traditions must have survived, adapting themselves to new circumstances. With the vanishing of the Roman shows' support structure, performances will typically have taken place on a smaller scale and/or in private venues.

Although few, if any, of the later Roman *ludi* were plays in the ordinary modern sense, many had a theatrical component. The modern circus, with its penchant for clown routines, magical transformations, depictions of heroism, acrobatics in role, and other forms of quasi-theatre, probably conveys something of the shows' nature and appeal. Noticeably popular in the later Roman period were the more-or-less theatrical genres of pantomime, and mime (both terms also naming a kind of performer). Pantomimes were spectacular musical and balletic performances, usually on Greek mythological themes, centering on skills of expression through the medium of dance; accomplished dancers attracted a cult following.[4] The mimes were versatile, also fairly disreputable, itinerant performers, among whose expected skills were dance, music-making and caricatured impersonation [see **A1**, **A8**]; they performed solo or in small groups, sometimes in association with other entertainers such as bear-wards, jugglers and rope-dancers. The tradition of the *mimus* certainly continued and developed in the medieval period.

Educated culture in early medieval Europe had, broadly, three forms of dealing with Roman and contemporary *ludi*. First, scholar-historians, the most influential of whom was Isidore of Seville [**A21**], transmitted a vivid if partly inaccurate image of this aspect of Roman civilisation. Second, the writings of the comic dramatists Terence and, sometimes, Menander and Plautus were copied and studied in the schools as literary monuments and exemplars of rhetoric. At times performance, perhaps in the form of impersonated reading, supplemented study [see **A9**]. As early as the tenth century, in a fragmentary dialogue for performance [**A28**] and in the play-texts of Hrotswitha [**A29**], the schools' interest in Roman comedy can be seen to have borne fruit in the invention of original drama. A neo-Roman comic drama, dedicated now to entertainment rather than instruction, was to flourish in France and England in the second half of the twelfth century [**A31**, **A32**]. Third, from the Roman period onwards officials of the Christian Church attempted to regulate or, where possible, put an end to Christian involvement with games and shows, whether as onlookers or participants. Churchmen of the Middle Ages often wrote against such involvement, especially on the part of the clergy; and edicts went on being framed to prohibit or curtail it [see **A3–6**]. Some of this material repeats Roman Christian condemnation verbatim, and is of doubtful value as current evidence. The items included here do, however, seem to be concerned directly with contemporary performances or kinds of performance. We should note that the leaders of the early church treated the profession of the performer as being incompatible with Christian faith,[5] to be followed in this respect by most senior churchmen of the early Middle Ages.

The early medieval period sees the invention of new dramatic and quasi-dramatic forms. There has survived from the eighth century the opening sequence of a text for singing which narrates the Harrowing of Hell [**A26**]. Liturgical ceremony from the late tenth century began to incorporate short sequences of impersonated performance [see **Section B**]. Hrotswitha's Christian plays make a considered reappraisal of the resources of drama. Some twelfth-century clerical communities possessed substantial Latin plays. From the same century we have the monumental Tegernsee *Antichristus* [**C19**, **36**, **43**], and the Anglo-Norman *Mystère d'Adam* and *Seinte Resureccion* [see **Section C**]. The rise of Christian dramatic traditions and the independent twelfth-century recovery of classical learning across a broader spectrum produced a change in principled attitudes towards theatre [see **A30**, **31**]; Aristotle's *Ethics*, circulating in a full translation from the mid-thirteenth century, provided authoritative support for selective cultivation of the performing arts [see **A37, 38**]. In the twelfth and thirteenth centuries the moral status of drama became, for the educated, a matter of debate rather than of inherited certainty, and drama benefited from the shift of intellectual climate.

NOTES

1. Simon Holledge, *Xi'an*, Hong Kong: China Guides Series Ltd., 1984, p. 47.

2. Suggestive in this context is the *Cena Cypriani*, originally a Latin prose work attributed to St Cyprian, the martyred Bishop of Carthage (*c*. 200–258). In the ninth century it was notably remodelled in Italian verse by John the Deacon, possibly for representation in the Lateran Palace before Pope John VIII, occupant of the Holy See from 872 to 882. In this lively comic pantomime a wide range of biblical characters appear as guests at King Joel's wedding banquet, where they are seated, dressed and fed in wittily appropriate ways. The favoured method of performance may well have been that conceived of as Roman, whereby a recited narrative was expounded by means of mimed actions.

3. For a cautious review of the evidence, see N. Christie and S. T. Loseby (ed.), *Towns in Transition: Urban Evolution in Late Antiquity and the Early Middle Ages*, Aldershot, 1996.

4. See J. P. V. D. Balsdon, *Life and Leisure in Ancient Rome*, London, 1969, pp. 247–9.

5. See E. K. Chambers, *The Mediaeval Stage*, 2 vols., Oxford: 1903, vol. I, pp. 10–16, esp. p. 12, n. 5, and Werner Weismann, *Kirche und Schauspiele*, Würzburg, 1972, pp. 104–10. The First Council of Arles (314), for example, ruled that performers in the public *ludi* (*agitatores, theatrici*) were not to receive communion during periods of performance; see *Concilia Galliae* AD 314–AD 506, ed. C. Munier (Corpus Christianorum, Series Latina, vol. 148; Turnholt, 1963, p. 11). The council held at Carthage in 397, taking a harsher line, classified players (*histriones*) with apostates, who could be received into the church on the condition that they converted to or returned to the faith; see *Sacrorum conciliorum* [. . .] *collectio*, ed. J. D. Mansi, 31 vols., Florence/Venice, 1759–98, vol. III, col. 885.

I.   Continuities

A1   Statuette of a female mime, late second century

Art Museum, Princeton University. Bequest of Professor Albert Mathias Friend, Jr., Class of 1915. Photo: Clem Fiori

The bronze figure, 7.5 cm in height and found in Syria, is described thus by Margarete Bieber: 'The most characteristic costume of the mime is the *centunculus*, a dress composed of many different coloured patches . . . [The statuette of a female mime] combines this clown's costume with the high-peaked fool's cap. She wears a jacket with a frilled collar, scallops hanging down on hips and back, and a belt from which eight straps hang down over the tunic. The *mima* is at the same time dancing, gesticulating, and accompanying herself with music. She holds clappers in both lifted hands, throws back her head, beating the rhythm with the *scabellum*, the footclapper, under her left foot. She also accompanies her dance with bells, seven attached to her cap, three to the lowest points of the scallops of her jacket, eight to the ends of the flaps over her skirt, and four to the strips ornamenting the buskin to the clapper is attached. Her other foot is bare.'[1] This versatile female mime in her fool's cap and motley clown's costume seems to be a recognisable ancestress to medieval professional entertainers with their multifarious skills.

[1] *The History of the Greek and Roman Theatre*, Princeton, 1961, p. 249.

CASSIODORUS

Flavius Magnus Aurelius Cassiodorus (*c.* 485–*c.* 580), kinsman of Boethius, a Catholic Christian and a Roman senator, was chancellor (*quaestor*) to the Ostrogothic king Theodoric between *c.* 506 and *c.* 512, and an influential politician thereafter. Cassiodorus' writings constitute, among other things, the most extensive surviving record of Roman culture in the period. The *Variae*, a selection from the letters and documents which he composed on behalf of his Gothic masters, contains a number of references to the Roman games and shows. The population

of Rome was by now much depleted, partly as a result of the recent Gothic siege; its buildings and monuments were evidently crumbling. Grandiloquence in the *Variae* might be seen as standing in an inverse relation to disposable economic power.

A2   Roman shows under Gothic rule, *c.* 510

Cassiodorus, *Variae* (i) IV.51, ed. and trans. S. J. B. Barnish; (ii) VII.10, ed. Å. J. Fridh

(i) [King Theodoric, addressing the patrician Symmachus, commissions maintenance work on the Theatre of Pompey, considered to have been Rome's first permanent theatre (55 BC).]

[. . .] I might perhaps have neglected the building, if I had not happened to see it: those arched vaults, with their overhanging stonework and invisible jointing, are so beautifully shaped that you would suppose them the caverns of a lofty mountain, rather than anything made by hands. The ancients made the site equal to so great a population, intending those who held the lordship of the world to enjoy a unique building of entertainment.

[There follows a brief history of the origins of theatre, tragedy, comedy, pantomime and mime.]

The succeeding age corrupted the inventions of the ancients by mingling obscenities; their headlong minds drove towards bodily lusts an art devised to give decent pleasure. As with other observances, the Romans uselessly imported these practices to their state, and founded that building – the fruit of lofty thought, and a marvellous greatness of soul. From it, we suppose, Pompey was really called the Great, and not undeservedly.

And therefore, whether such a fabric should be held together by socketed rods, or whether it should be renewed and reconstructed, I have taken care to assign you expenses from my treasury. Thus you may gain reputation from [executing] so excellent a work, while, in my reign, antiquity is fittingly renewed. (pp. 79–82)

(ii) [Formula for the appointment of a Tribune of Pleasures]

Although the slippery arts [*artes lubricae*] are far from honest living, and the wandering life of the performer [*histrio*] seems likely to be overwhelmed in dissoluteness, antiquity nevertheless established the place for a mediator, so that these people do not become entirely lost to us; since even these [feminine] require the offices of a judge. For the display of pleasures must be arranged within a certain regime of order. [. . .] [In these dealings] laws will be tempered by practical concerns, with the effect that decency commands the indecent, and that these people who do not know the way of right behaviour live by laws. For their concern is not so much with their own pleasures as with the delights of others, in the crooked circumstances where they yield up power over their own bodies and are compelled to gratify better spirits. [. . .] Your position may be defined precisely as that of a tutor to these hordes of people. (pp. 270–71)

Five of the six items that follow, including the two passages from the letters of Alcuin, represent attempts made by senior officials of the Church, to enforce the Church's traditional condemnation of professional entertainment and of Christian countenancing of the same. Their particular concern is with members of the clergy and/or educated classes who found themselves drawn to it. **A6** suggests that some players mocked the rituals or customs of the Church, as they are known to have done in the Roman period.

A3   A warning to the clergy, *c.* 572

Edict of Bishop Martin of Braga; *Sacrorum conciliorum* [. . .] *collectio*, ed. J. D. Mansi, 31 vols., Florence/Venice, 1759–98, vol. IX, p. 856

No priest or member of the clergy whatsoever is to attend any of the shows [*spectacula*] presented at a wedding or feast; but they must, before these same shows enter the room, get up and then leave.[1]

[1] This echoes an Eastern Church edict of 416.

A4   Entertainers of the clergy, 679

Councils and Ecclesiastical Documents, ed. A. W. Haddan and W. Stubbs, 3 vols., Oxford, 1869–71, vol. II, p. 133

[Edict of a council dealing with English church affairs, held in Rome.]
[Bishops and other members of the clergy] are not to take up arms, nor maintain *cithara* players[1] or other musicians, nor permit jests or shows [*joci vel ludi*] of any kind to be presented before them.

[1] The *cithara* was a harp or similar stringed instrument, often played solo.

A5   Entertainments at monasteries, 747

Councils and Ecclesiastical Documents, ed. A. W. Haddan and W. Stubbs, 3 vols., Oxford, 1869–71, vol. III, p. 369

[Edict of the Council of Clovesho (England, location unidentified).]
Let bishops see to it [. . .] that monasteries do not become receptacles for the frivolous arts [*artes ludicras*]; which is to say, those of poets, *cithara* players, musicians, and buffoons.

A6   Players ridicule the clergy, 789[1]

Sacrorum conciliorum [. . .] *collectio*, ed. J. D. Mansi, 31 vols., Florence/Venice, 1759–98, vol. XVII, supplementary volume, col. 244

[The edict was issued under Charlemagne.]
If anyone from among the players shall dress in a priestly or monastic garment, or that of a nun [*mulieris religiosiae*], or any kind of ecclesiastical dress whatsoever, let him undergo corporal punishment or be condemned to exile.

[1] Allardyce Nicoll, *Masks, Mimes and Miracles: Studies in the Popular Theatre*, London and New York, 1931, pp. 148–9, argues for this interpretation of the edict.

ALCUIN

Alcuin of York (*c.* 730–804), scholar and churchman, was the leading figure in the first phase of the Carolingian cultural revival. Passage (i) is from a letter addressed to his friend Angilbert ('Homer'), a court official and poet; passage (ii) to one of his students going on a pilgrimage to Italy.

A7   Alcuin on contemporary patronage of mimes, *c.* 800

Epistolae Karolini aevi, ed. Ernestus Dümmler, Berlin, 1895, vol. II, p. 291; p. 439

(i) I fear that Homer is angry about the decree prohibiting shows and devilish feignings [*spectacula et diabolica figmenta*]; which all the holy scriptures [can be taken to] prohibit, in as much as I have read the following statement by Saint Augustine: 'A man who introduces players, mimes and dancers into his home does not know how great a crowd of unclean spirits follows them.'[1] But let it not be the case that the Devil has power in a Christian home. (Letter 176)

[1] This text has not been found in Augustine's writings.

(ii) Be sober in your eating and drinking, setting your mind on a greater source of well-being than fleshly delight, or the most ostentatious human praise which is of no advantage if your actions are displeasing to God. It is better to please God than players, better to concern yourself with the poor than with mimes. (Letter 281)

A8   Epitaph of Vitalis the Mime, *c.* 800[1]

Anthologia Latina, ed. F. Buecheler and A. Riese, 2 vols., Leipzig, 1906, part 1, vol. II, pp. 38–9 (item 487a)

[Original in verse. Extract.]
    Using movements and words, I gave pleasure to everyone in adopting a tragic voice, bringing happiness to sad hearts by divers means. [And] I used to counterfeit the face, manner and speech of those talking, so that you would have believed that many people were speaking out of one mouth. The one whom my portrayal

twinned to the eye felt horror to find his/her existence transposed into my faces. O, how often a woman, seeing herself imitated in my gesture, turned red, utterly embarrassed. Thus, as many human forms as appeared in my body were snatched away with me by the frightful day [of death].

[1] G. Gougenheim argues for this dating – which does, however, remain somewhat conjectural, in 'Le mime Vitalis', *Mélanges . . . offerts à Gustave Cohen*, Paris, 1950, pp. 29–33; the epitaph may be of Carolingian provenance.

A9   Performance in the study of the classics, *c. 825*

Epistolae Karolini aevi, ed. Societas Aperiendis Fontibus, vol. IV, p. 142

[From a letter of Paschasius Radbertus of Corbie, influential teacher and theologian, to a fellow monk.]

It puzzles me that they do not wish to investigate the mystic sacraments of God with the diligence with which they sweat over the mournful stuff of tragedies and feignings of poets, seeking to call forth the praises of men through the theatrical feats of mimes [*per teatralia mimorum*].

A10   A contemporary structure called a theatre, ninth century

Altsächsische Sprachdenkmäler, ed. J. H. Galleé, Leyden, 1894, vol. I, p. 344

[From the fragment of an Old High German glossary once in the abbey of Werden.] A theatre may be of wood [and is a place] where men play and make shows [*spectacula*].

A11   Rules governing sports, games, performances and performers, ninth century

'Penitential of Theodore, Archbishop of Canterbury', in B. Thorpe (ed.), *Ancient Laws and Institutes of England*, 2 vols., Commissioners on the Public Records of the Kingdom: London, 1840). This penitential, a Frankish compilation ascribed to the English Archbishop (668–90), was used in later Anglo-Saxon England. Wulfstan, bishop of Worcester and archbishop of York, issued an English version of item (i) in the early eleventh century; see *Wulfstan's Canons of Edgar*, ed. Roger Fowler, EETS (OS 266); Oxford, 1972, pp. 6–7, no. 18.

(i) They [the secular clergy] should not presume to make disports [*jocationes*], and leapings, and races, or shameful and lustful songs, or devilish games/performances [*lusa diabolica*[1]], neither in [. . .] churches, nor in homes, nor in open spaces, nor in any other place, since this remains from the usage of the pagans. (cap. 38; p. 46)

[1] Wulfstan translates this phrase as 'deofles [g]amena'.

(ii) Players and performers [*scenici et histriones*] and other people of this kind are not to be denied reconciliation [with the Church]. (cap. 41; p. 49)

A12   A holy man encounters a mime; saint's life of *c.* 850

Poetae Latini aevi Carolini, vol. III, *Monumenta Germaniae Historica*, Berlin, ed. L. Traube, 1896, p. 600

[The passage is from Milo's *Life of St Amandus*. Amandus, already facing problems while preaching in Gascony, encounters special hostility from a mime. Original in verse.]

One there who was idle, light-witted, slippery and proud, shameful and vile in his whispering of insulting jokes, rightly called by the people 'Mimmus', confronted the saint unhappily with his stupid abandoned laughter. [On which, a devil tore him apart.]

A13   Assumed content of mimes' performances, tenth century

Sermon of Bishop Attone of Vercelli; pr. Jacques Paul Migne (ed.), *Patrologia cursus completus: series latina*, Paris, 1841–64, vol. 134, col. 844

They do not delight in theatres, like the players [*scenici*]; nor in wedding-songs or sung tales [*cantilenae*], like the mimes; nor in dancers and the circus, like the physical performers [*histriones*] or worshippers of idols. What, indeed, could be more demeaning to the old, shameful to the young, or damaging to the immature, than to sing of the debauching of virgins and the pleasures of prostitutes[1] in shameful gesture and smooth voice, so that their spectators are themselves incited to corrupt behaviour by such trickery.

[1] Compare **A21** Chapter 46 (Isidore of Seville on the content of Roman comedy)

A14   Mimes publicise monastic scandals, *c.* 961

Cartularium saxonicum, ed. W. de G. Birch, 3 vols., 1885–99, vol. III, p. 573

[King Edgar complains to the English bishops and heads of monasteries that dissolute behaviour has reached the point where] the homes of the clergy are thought to be salons for prostitutes, gathering-places for performers [*histriones*]. There is dice-playing, there is dancing and singing, there are vigils drawn out to the middle of the night in loud noise and wildness. [. . .] This the soldiers shout, the people murmur to themselves, the mimes sing and dance[1] in public places [*in triviis*].

[1] J. D. A. Ogilvy, '*Mimi, scurrae, histriones*: Entertainers of the Early Middle Ages', *Speculum* 38 (1963), pp. 603–19, suggests that 'saltare' may convey the sense of 'acting out' monastic shortcomings.

A15   Terence in performance, *c.* 1000

Universiteitsbibliotheek, Rijks Universiteit, Leiden, MS Voss. Lat.Q.38, fo. 50 recto

The image comes from a manuscript of Terence's *The Eunuch*; it is vividly imagined, and may reflect contemporary performing styles. In the scene illustrated – for which, see *Plays of Terence*, ed. G. P. Goold, trans. John Sargeant, 2 vols., London, 1912, pp. 332–6 – the tricky female servant Pythias convinces the comic slave Parmeno that his cunning is about to get him into severe trouble: his disguising of a young man of rank so that he can gain access to the girl whom he has been pursuing looks likely to get the young man castrated.

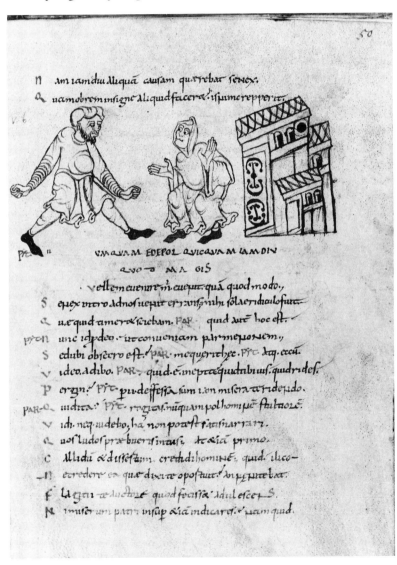

A16   Abbot Poppo breaks up a court entertainment, early eleventh century

Johannes Bollandus, *Acta sanctorum*, ed. Jean Carnandet, 61 vols., Paris, etc., 1863–83, vol. III [January], p. 257

[From the life of St Poppo (later Pope Damasus II); the monarch is Emperor Henry II ('the Good').]

It happened that the imperial courtiers were occupied out of doors with entertainments offered by professional players [*ludi histrionum*], and with a spectacle of a kind that had been chosen by the king and his companions. A certain naked man who had his member smeared with honey was displayed to bears; at which many took fright at the danger in which he stood if these same bears, having consumed the honey, arrived at his bones. [But the emperor was too captivated by the spectacle to care.] Whereat the blessed Poppo confuted the king, arguing the amusement's great unsuitability for a Christian, and soon drew the king and the nobility from the show. Then indeed he freed the man from the danger of the bears and, lest he did more of such things, repeated his judgement, arguing and pleading.

A17   Histrionic singing in church, c. 1150

Ethelred of Rievaulx, 'Speculum charitatis', II, 33; *Patrologia Latina*, vol. 195, col. 571

[The Cistercian abbot of Rievaulx condemns the kind of performance given by certain singing men in choirs.]

Meanwhile the whole body is agitated by actorly movements; the lips are twisted, the shoulders turn and play, and the fingers move in response to certain individual notes. [. . .] The crowd stands looking on [. . .] not without laughter and derision, so that you would think they had gathered not at a place of prayer but at a theatre, not to pray but to watch a show. [. . .] Thus, what the Holy Fathers instituted to incite the weak in faith, love and piety is pressed into the service of unlawful pleasures.

A18   Professional and other entertainments, c. 1165

R. S. Loomis, 'Some Evidence for Secular Theatres in the Twelfth and Thirteenth Centuries', *Theatre Annual* (1945), pp. 33–43

[From an Anglo-Norman commentary on the Psalms.]

Here he blames those in the habit of attending theatres to see shows [*gius*] and marvels, for there they make enchantments, taking no account of the church or of the service of God, although they can hear spoken and sung in church finer miracles and higher adventures than they will see in the theatre, or in the round dance,[1] or in tournaments. For it was a much finer thing that St Peter walked on the sea that that a jongleur [*juggler*] walks on a rope playing an instrument; and yet this seems to them to be a very great feat (p. 36).

---

[1] Quasi-theatrical dancing games were popular in the period; see Richard Axton, *European Drama of the Early Middle Ages*, London, 1974, pp. 47–60.

A19   Performers' non-vocal forms of expression, later twelfth century

Giraldus Cambrensis, *De rebus a se gestis*, ii.5, *Giraldi Cambrensis opera*, ed. J. S. Brewer, J. F. Dimock and G. F. Warner, Rolls Series 21, 8 vols., London, 1861–91, vol. i, p. 51

[After returning from Flanders, Gerald dined with the monks of Canterbury, and noticed two things in particular,] the excessive use of signs and the large number of the dishes. For the prior kept on gesturing to the monks serving at table, to him [Gerald], and down to the lower tables; and those to whom the dishes were brought kept on signalling their thanks, by gestures of the hands and arms and by means of hissing or whistling [*sibilis*], instead of with words, expressing themselves with unsuitable ease and freedom, which seemed to him almost the same as was done among actors [*ludos scenicos*] or between physical performers [*histriones*] and *joculatores*.

A20   Snares and temptations of London, *c.* 1190

Richard of Devizes, *The Chronicle of the Time of King Richard the First*, ed. and trans. John T. Appleby, London, 1963, p. 65

[A Jew warns a Christian boy against staying in London. The passage is influenced by the opening of Horace, *Satires*, 1.2. One might compare its account of London with the very favourable one given shortly before by William Fitzstephen [**A34**], a hyperbolic exercise of a different kind.]

Whatever bad or wicked thing that exists in any part of the world you will find in that one city [. . . London offers] a life of dice and gambling, theatre and tavern. [. . .] Players, filthy jesters, smooth-skinned boys, Moors, flatterers, catamites, effeminates, musical tarts, quacks, hip-thrusters, witches, extortioners, night prowlers, magicians, mimes, beggars, buffoons – all the houses are filled with this kind of person.

II Memories and reflections

ISADORE OF SEVILLE

Isidore of Seville's *Twenty Books of Etymologies or Origins* was the most influential encyclopaedia of the Middle Ages. A scholars' reference resource drawing mainly on the classical past, it laid down a stock of valued knowledge and a set of accepted categories for intellectual enquiry. The *Etymologies* gives the Roman *ludi* extensive coverage (roughly half of one book); while firmly repeating the orthodox Christian condemnation of theatre, along with the Roman shows in general, its treatment also stimulated scholarly interest in the phenomenon of theatre. The *ludi* seem not to have flourished or been allowed to flourish in Isidore's Spain under Christian Visigothic rule,[1] and his knowledge was culled mainly from classical texts which he sometimes misinterpreted. Isidore was, on the other hand, in a good position to inspect Roman buildings. His encyclopaedia presented a vivid, indeed lurid, image of classical theatre and spectacle. It began the Chinese Whispers-like medieval transmission of information which had one of its upshots in Chaucer's two 'tragedies', *Troilus and Criseyde* and *The Monk's Tale*.[2]

Chapters 16 and 59 summarise the well-established Christian position on *ludi*. Tertullian had argued in the *De spectaculis* (*c.* 200), a major source for Isidore, that they were invented by devils plotting against humankind, and that even the most innocent-seeming performances remained defiling because of this concealed impurity of origin; a Christian who favoured them went against the baptismal vow to renounce the Devil, practising – however unknowingly – a form of devil-worship [see **D55**]. Building on Tertullian's argument, Augustine's *City of God* (*c.* 420) had given the *ludi*, and especially theatre, great prominence in its portrayal of a Roman civilisation distinguished by much that was good, but founded at critical points on evil and delusion.

1. In Isidore's time King Sisebut prohibited 'performances with bulls' [*ludi theatrii taurorum*] which had taken place in Barcelona with, apparently, the Church's approval (Chambers, *Mediaeval Stage*, vol. I, p. 21).
2. For an invaluable discussion of Isidore's contribution, see Joseph R. Jones, 'Isidore and the Theater', *Comparative Drama* 16 (1982–3), pp. 26–48.

A21   Isidore on the Roman shows, *c.* 620

Isidori Hispalensis Episcopi etymologiarum sive originum, ed. W. M. Lindsay, Oxford, 1911,
book XVIII, caps. 16–59 (no page numbering), trans. Barry Baldwin and Nick Davis

Chapter 16: *On the shows.* [After an etymological discussion,] [. . .] Enough of
origins in words, since the thing itself originates in idolatory [. . .] On this account
the stain of the origins is to be kept in mind, lest you should consider good what
had its beginning in evil [. . .]

[Chapters 17–26: Gymnastic sports. 27–41: Races.]

Chapter 42: *On the theatre.* A theatre is a place which includes a *scena,* semicircular in shape, where all those standing look on. At first its form was round, like
that of an amphitheatre; afterwards a theatre was made out of the middle part of
the amphitheatre. In origin the word *theatrum* has the same meaning as 'spectacle', deriving as it does from [Greek] *theoria* ['looking'], since in a theatre the people
standing above as spectators looked at the shows. Note that 'theatre' has the same
meaning as 'brothel', since after the shows had been performed the whores pros-
tituted themselves there [. . .]

Chapter 43: *On the scena.* A *scena* was a place in the lower part of the theatre constructed in the form of a house with a platform [*pulpitus*] called the *orchestra;* there
comic and tragic poets recited, and players and mimes danced [. . .]

Chapter 44: *On the orchestra.* An *orchestra* was a platform of the *scena* where a
dancer could perform or two [actors] could dispute between themselves. There
comic and tragic poets mounted in competition, and, while they recited, others
produced gestures [. . .]

Chapter 45: *On tragedians. Tragedians* are those who performed in verse before the
people looking on the ancient deeds and lamentable crimes of wicked kings.

Chapter 46: *On comedians. Comedians* are those who performed in words or
gesture the deeds of private people [i.e. not the great], and presented in their fables
the debauching of virgins and the loves of prostitutes.

Chapter 47: *On the thymelici.* The *thymelici* were, however, the stage musicians
who played introductory pieces on pipes, lyres and harps. They are called *thymelici* because they originally performed in the orchestra standing on a platform
which in Greek is called *thymele.*

Chapter 48: *On the performers.* The performers [*histriones*] are those who dressed
in female garb to impersonate shameless women; they also, however, presented
histories and deeds in dance. They are called *histriones* either because this kind of
performance was imported from Histria, or because they presented histories and
fables mixed together – and were in effect '*historiones*'.

Chapter 49: *On the mimes.* Mimes are called this from the Greek, because they
are imitators of human affairs. They had their own writers who proclaimed the
fable before the mimes performed.

Chapter 50: *On the dancers.* Dancers [*saltatores*] are said by Varro[1] to get their
name from Salius the Arcadian, whom Aeneas brought with him to Italy, and who
was the first to instruct noble Roman youths in dance.

[Chapter 51: Bacchus and Venus were held to be the divine patrons of theatre. What else would you expect? Chapters 52–58: amphitheatre sports.]

Chapter 59: *Of the practice of their shows.* Indeed, these spectacles of cruelty and this gazing upon vain things were established not only by the vices of men but also by the commands of devils. On which account a Christian should have no dealings with the madness of the circus, the shamelessness of the theatre, with the cruelty of the amphitheatre, with the atrocity of the arena, with the dissipation of the game. For that person denies God who presumes to do such things, becoming a double dealer with the Christian faith; who seeks again what he/she has already renounced long before – that is, the Devil, his pomps and his works.

---

[1] Prolific Roman writer of the first century BC.

A22   Theatre as a place for the presentation of spectacles, 1053

Papias the Lombard, *Elementarium doctrinae rudimentum* or *Vocabulista*, cited in Mary H. Marshall, '*Theatre* in the Middle Ages', *Symposium* 4 (1950), pp. 1–39, 366–89

[Papias' dictionary, which derives some of its material on the performing arts from Isidore, circulated widely and fed into later compilations. The idea that a theatre was not necessarily a building may have been influenced by contemporary practice.]

Theatre [means] spectacle. There was a place in towns where royal shows [*ioca regalia*] were performed, and where people were beheaded, many of them innocent. The whole population gathered there.

'Theatre' is the word for any place where a spectacle is presented; it comes from *theoro*, meaning 'I see' (p. 22).

A23   Tragedy as recalling the deeds of warriors, *c.* 1100

Honorius of Autun, *Gemma animae*, book 1, chapter 83, *Patrologia Latina*, ed. Migne, vol. 172, col. 570; for the succeeding lines see **B1 (b)**

It is known that those who recited tragedies in the theatres represented the acts of fighting men to the people by means of gestures.

HUGUCCIO

Developing on Isidore and his tradition and, perhaps, contemporary dramatic practice, the encyclopaedist Huguccio (Hugutius) of Pisa offered an account of classical theatre which was widely received as authoritative in the later Middle Ages.

A24   Theatre as recitation and dumb-show, *c.* 1200

Hugutius, *Magnae derivationes*, cited from Bodl. MS Laud 626 in Marshall, '*Theatre* in the Middle Ages', p. 25

From [Greek] *skenos*, meaning 'shadow', comes the word [. . .] *scena,* meaning [. . .] a place in a theatre which is sheltered and closed off by means of curtains, like the booths of merchants which are covered by curtains on posts; and accordingly it may take its name from *skenos* meaning 'house', since a *scena* was constructed in the form of a house. That sheltered place hid people in masks who came out at the voice of the reciter to act in dumb-show [*ad gestus faciendos*]. [. . .] The *scena* included the *proscenium,* or place in front of the *scena* where they performed.

A25   Imagining the nature of a classical performance, early fourteenth century

The Dominican friar Nicholas Trevet, commenting on Seneca's *Hercules furens*; cited in Marshall, '*Theatre* in the Middle Ages', p. 27

The *theatrum* was a semi-circular open space in the middle of which was a small house called the *scena,* in which there was a pulpit where the poet stood to recite his works. Outside the house were the mimes, who acted with their bodies while the poems were being recited, adapting themselves to whatever character the poet was speaking of.

III   Reinventions, new starts, shifts of attitude

THE BOOK OF CERNE 'HARROWING OF HELL'

This intriguing and tantalising text is found in an Anglo-Saxon miscellany whose contents date from the eighth and ninth centuries, and were copied out probably between 818 and 830. The 'Harrowing' seems to have formed part of a group of texts organised under the direction of Bishop Aethiuald, former abbot of Melrose, who held the see of Lindisfarne from *c*. 730 to *c*. 740. It consists of alternating sections of narration, and speech in role. The narrative sections, shifting between past and present tenses and written unlike the rest in red ink, may have been sung by a soloist, or are perhaps stage directions in the modern sense. The speech in role was more certainly sung by a choir of the 'ancient just' (*antiqui justi*) and by soloists representing Adam and Eve, bound in and then released from Hell. (The narrative derives ultimately from the apocryphal Gospel of Nicodemus.) We seem to be dealing with a liturgical performance of dramatic conception which predates by two centuries the Winchester *Visitatio sepulchri* (**B9(b)**). Some scholars urge caution, however, arguing that the work is no more than a passage designed for private devotional reading.[1]

1.   For a judicious viewpoint see *Nine Medieval Latin Plays*, trans. and ed. Peter Dronke, Cambridge, 1994, pp. xxvi–xxviii.

A26   A sung performance of the liberation of the just from Hell, *c*. 800–*c*. 825

David Dumville, 'Liturgical Drama and Panegyric Responsory from the Eighth Century', *Journal of Theological Studies* 23 (1972), pp. 374–406. Original in Latin verse

[Narration:] This is the speech of the countless number of the holy who were held captive in Hell. With tearful voice and in earnest supplication they beseech their Saviour, saying as He descends to the lower world:

[The just:] You have come, Redeemer of the world; You have come, whom we have hoped for every day in longing. You have come, whom light and the prophets announced to us. You have come in living flesh bringing forgiveness to the sinners of the world [. . .] Help us, God of our salvation; for the honour of Your name, Lord, free us, and be gracious to our sins for Your name's sake.

[Narration:] But there was heard at once, after the request and entreaty of the countless prisoners, the voices of all the ancient just rejoicing in the Lord, their bonds released without any delay at the order of God the saviour, clustered about the knees of the Lord and Saviour, inexpressibly joyful, crying out in humble supplication:

[The just:] Lord, You have torn apart our bonds; to You we offer a sacrifice of praise, who have not treated us according to our sins, nor punished us according to our crimes.

[Narration:] But Adam and Eve are not yet freed from their bonds. Then Adam cried out to the Lord in a tearful and wretched voice, saying:

[Adam:] Have pity on me, God, have pity on me in your great mercy, and in the greatness of Your compassion blot out my crime, since I have sinned directly against you and done evil in Your sight. I went astray like a sheep who was lost. Free me from my bonds, You who made me with Your hand and formed me. Do not abandon my soul in Hell, but have pity on me, and lead me, free, from the house of imprisonment and the shadow of death.

[Narration:] Then, when the Lord took pity, Adam, freed from his bonds, [said this] clasping the knees of Jesus Christ:

[Adam:] Give blessing to the Lord, my soul, and may all that is in me bless His holy name; who dealt graciously with my crimes, who brings a remedy for all my sorrows, who redeems my life from destruction, who sates my longing with goodness.

[Narration:] Eve still continues to weep, saying:

[Eve:] You are just, O Lord, and Your judgement is right, in that I suffer this deservedly; for I, when I possessed honour, had no understanding: I behaved like the foolish beasts of burden, and now I have become like them. But, Lord, forget the faults of youth, forget my follies. Do not remove from me the face of Your compassion, do not turn away in anger from Your handmaiden.

[Here the text breaks off. The homily from which it derives continues with the freeing and thanksgiving of Eve, and concludes with a chorus of praise by the liberated souls (pp. 376–7).]

AN ANGLO-SAXON DIALOGUE OF JOSEPH AND MARY

This is not a play, but a lyric of strongly dramatic conception found in the Exeter Book, the period's largest collection of Anglo-Saxon poetry. Like other medieval treatments of Joseph's response to the discovery of Mary's pregnancy (well-known examples being found in the English cycle plays), it has its germ in Matthew 1.19: 'But Joseph her husband, because he was a just man unwilling to hand her over to the law, wanted to send her away in secret.' Mary speaks first.

A27   Mary comforts the troubled Joseph, tenth century

Adapted from Jackson J. Campbell, ed. and trans., *The Advent Lyrics of the Exeter Book*, Princeton, 1959, pp. 58–61. Original in Old English verse

'O my Joseph, son of Jacob, descendant of David the great king, must you now sever a firm affection, reject my love?' 'Of a sudden I am deeply disturbed on your behalf, despoiled of honour, for I have heard many words, many sorrowful things and hurtful speeches, much harm, and they confront me with many insults. Saddened in heart, I must shed tears. I must shed tears, hoping that God may easily relieve the inner pain of my heart, comfort me in my wretchedness. O young girl, Mary the virgin!' 'What are you bewailing, why do you cry out in sorrow? I have never found any guilt, failing or wrongdoing in you, and yet you speak these words as if you were filled with every kind of sin and crime.' 'I have received too much evil from this pregnancy. How will I be able to refute the hateful talk, or find an answer to my enemies? It is widely known that I willingly received from the bright temple of God a pure virgin, free from stain – and yet, now she is changed by I know not what. It does me no good either to speak or keep silent. If I tell the truth, then David's daughter will die, killed with stones. Yet it is worse that I should conceal the crime. A perjured man, hateful to all people, would be held vile for ever after.' Then the girl revealed the true mystery, and spoke thus: 'The truth I utter through the Son of God, Saviour of Spirits. [Mary speaks eloquently of the Annunciation and Conception.] Now I am made his spotless temple, the Spirit of Comfort has come to dwell in me, so now you may completely relinquish your bitter sorrow. Say eternal thanks to the great Son of God that I have become his mother, while still a virgin, and that you are counted his father by the reckoning of the world. It was necessary for prophecy to be truly fulfilled in him.'

'TERENCE AND THE HECKLER'

This fragmentary piece, preserved in a manuscript of *c.* 1000, takes the form of a staged argument between Terence and his young disparager, self-consciously figures of Age and Youth. The actor playing Terence is, it seems, about to deliver one of the dramatist's works in solo recital.

A28   A Terence prologue, tenth century

E. K. Chambers, *The Mediaeval Stage*, vol. II, pp. 326–8. Original in Latin verse

[Terence, positioned perhaps above in a pulpit, prepares to recite. Heckler [*delusor*], a member of the audience, speaks up:]

Stop sifting through your musty relics, Terence. No more of this; just go away, old poet. Go away, old poet, because I'm not interested in your poems. Now, I'm saying, keep your stories to yourself, oldest of old men [. . .] Lying back here, I feel extremely bored. I don't even know whether the stuff is prose or verse [. . .]

[Terence, furious, steps down to confront his opponent. Heckler now declares himself; there follows a heated argument, which pits the wounded dignity of the playwright against the youthful cynicism of his challenger. The piece breaks off while this is still in progress.]

HROTSWITHA

Hrotswitha (*c.* 935–*c.* 1002) was a nobly born woman of extensive learning who spent most of her life as a member of the Benedictine community at Gandersheim (in what is now Lower Saxony); she did not, however, take the vows of a nun. She was the most prolific poetic writer of her century. Among her works are six plays on Christian themes; two depict martyrdoms, and four, conversions of the sinful. Her stated intention was to imitate Terence's sweetness of speech [*dulcedo sermonis*] and *elegantia*, while rejecting his subject matter [see **A29**(**a**)]. Hrotswitha sometimes writes in short scenes, combining spare dialogue with vivid action [**A29**(**b**)]. As modern productions have shown, her plays are eminently performable within a fluid staging convention. They may have been performed in the community at Gandersheim, though one cannot be certain; some scholars take the view that her dialogues are lyrical, rather than dramatic. One of Hrotswitha's concerns is with the violent and/or comic nature of male sexual passion. In passage (i), from *Dulcitius*, the Roman governor of that name attempts to rape the three Christian virgins whom he has imprisoned but, miraculously deceived, blunders into the adjacent kitchen. In (ii), from *Callimachus*, the hero is enamoured of the virtuous, married Drusiana, who has prayed for and been granted death in order to escape his desperate attentions. Now, incited by her slave Fortunatus, he enters her tomb in order to possess the body that she withheld from him when alive.

A29   Hrotswitha's experimental Christian drama, later tenth century

(a)   Her purpose in writing

The Plays of Roswitha, trans. Christopher St John, London, 1923, p. xxvi

There are many Catholics, and we cannot entirely acquit ourselves of the charge, who, attracted by the polished elegance of the style of pagan writers, prefer their works to the holy scriptures. There are others who, although they are deeply attached to the sacred writings and have no liking for more pagan productions, make an exception in favour of the works of Terence, and, fascinated by the charm of the manner, risk being corrupted by the wickedness of the matter. Wherefore I, the strong voice of Gandersheim, have not hesitated to imitate in my writings, a poet whose works are so widely read, my object being to glorify, within the limits of my poor talent, the laudable chastity of Christian virgins in that self-same form of composition which has been used to describe the shameless acts of licentious women.

(b)   Extracts from the plays

The Plays of Hrotswitha of Gandersheim, trans. Larissa Bonfante, New York, 1979 (i) p. 44, (ii) pp. 63–4. Original in Latin verse; modern stage directions and lineation omitted

(i) [The girls' singing is interrupted.]

AGAPE   What was that noise outside the door?

IRENA   That wretched man Dulcitius is coming.

CHIONE   May the Lord help us and keep us safe!

AGAPE   Amen!

CHIONE   Why is he clattering so around the pots and pans?

IRENA   Let me see. Oh, hurry, come, look through this crack!

AGAPE   What is going on? What is he doing?

IRENA   Look at him, the fool. He's completely out of his mind! He thinks he is embracing us!

AGAPE   What is he doing now?

IRENA   Now he is fondling the pots, and hugging the frying pans to his eager breast, giving them all long, sweet kisses!

CHIONE   It's the funniest thing I have ever seen!

IRENA   His face and hands and clothes are filthy, all covered with soot from the pots he's hugging.

[When Dulcitius re-emerges his soldiers mistake him for the Devil.]

(ii) FORTUNATUS   There's the body – she looks asleep. Her face is not that of a corpse, nor are her limbs corrupt – use her as you will.

CALLIMACHUS   Oh, Drusiana, Drusiana, how I worshipped you! What tight bonds of love entwined me, deep in my inmost heart! Yet you always ran from me. You always opposed my desires – now it lies within my power to force you, to bruise you and injure you as much as I want.

FORTUNATUS   Watch out, Callimachus! A dreadful snake! It's coming after us.

[The snake bites him.]

CALLIMACHUS   Damned Fortunatus, why did you lead me into this temptation? Why did you urge me to this detestable deed. See, now you die from the wound of this serpent, and I die with you from holy fear.

[St John the Apostle prays successfully for the lives of Callimachus, Drusiana and – at Drusiana's entreaty – Fortunatus to be restored. Fortunatus says, however, that he prefers death to seeing Callimachus converted to Christianity, Drusiana alive, and both 'overfull with the power of Grace' (p. 75); at St John's entreaty he dies once again.]

HUGH OF ST VICTOR

Hugh (1096–1141) was a scholar and teacher at the Abbey of St Victor in Paris. His *Didascalicon*, a key text of its period, sets out a modern curriculum for the acquisition of knowledge reflecting the Victorine ambition to unify learning, theology and religious practice. Pointedly revising Augustine (see *On Christian Doctrine*, I.B.1), Hugh groups the arts of theatre – that is, of performance and entertainment in general – with his other approved 'mechanical arts': fabric-making, armament, commerce, agriculture, hunting and medicine [see **A30**]. (In Hugh's scheme the purpose of the mechanical arts is to serve higher forms of study and contemplation by repairing the physical weakness which humankind sustained in the Fall.) This warming of educated feeling towards theatre was probably connected with the twelfth-century recovery of classical learning as well as with the flourishing and spread of drama in clerical communities. The *Didascalicon* became an important point of reference in learned argument, pro and con, concerning the moral status of drama and the performing arts.

A30   Humane approval of Roman plays, sports and games, c. 1127

Didascalicon, II.7; trans. Jerome Taylor, New York, 1961, p. 79

The science of entertainments is called 'theatrics' from the theatre, to which the people once used to gather for the performance: not that a theatre was the only place in which entertainment took place, but it was a more popular place for entertainment than any other [. . .] In the theatre, epics were presented either by recitals or by acting out dramatic roles or by using masks or puppets; they held choral processions and dances in the porches. In the gymnasia they wrestled; in the amphitheatres they raced on foot or on horses or in chariots; in the arenas boxers performed; at banquets they made music with songs and instruments and chants, and they played at dice; in the temples at solemn seasons they sang the praises of the gods. Moreover, they numbered these entertainments among legitimate activities because by temperate motion natural heat is stimulated in the body and by enjoyment the mind is refreshed; or, as is more likely, seeing that people necessarily gathered together for occasional amusement, they desired that places for such amusement might be established to forestall the people's coming together at public houses, where they mght commit lewd or criminal acts.

JOHN OF SALISBURY

The humanist and philosopher John of Salisbury (*c.* 1115–*c.* 1180) studied in Paris with Abelard and was, like Hugh, a major participant in the twelfth-century revival of learning and the arts. The *Policraticus*, dedicated to his friend Thomas à Becket, is a large-scale exposition of political philosophy which is replete with classical allusion and reference [see **A31**].

A31   Humanistic discussion of drama and the idea of theatre, 1159

Frivolities of Courtiers and Footprints of Philosophers [selection from *Policraticus*], trans. Joseph B. Pike, Minneapolis, 1938

(i) [The classical era] possessed more respectable actors than ours, if we may apply the word 'respectable' to that which is regarded as unworthy of any gentleman [...] There were once actors who by the magic of gesture, of language, and of voice reproduced vividly for the audience both factual and fictional narratives. These were the contemporaries of Plautus and Menander and such as were intimate with our favourite Terence. Subsequently comedy and tragedy disappeared, since frivolity held universal sway. The actors of the legitimate drama were consequently forced into retirement [...] Our own age, descending to romances and similar folly, prostitutes not only the ear and heart to vanity but also delights its idleness with the pleasures of the ear and eye [...] Tedium steals upon unoccupied minds and they are not able to endure their own company unless they are pampered by the solace of some pleasure [...] Hence the procession of mimics, jumping or leaping priests, buffoons, Aemilian[1] and other gladiators, wrestlers, sorcerers, jugglers, magicians, and a whole army of jesters. They are in such vogue that even those whose exposures [of parts of the body] are so indecent that they would make a cynic blush are not barred from distinguished houses [...] However, the wise man's mind detects what is fitting or helpful in cases as they occur, nor does he shun fables, stories, or spectacles in general, providing that they possess the requirements of virtue and honourable utility. You must be aware that by the authority of the Christian Fathers the Holy Sacrament is denied to actors and mimes as long as they follow their wicked occupations [...] (pp. 36–9)

1.   Horace mentions an Aemilian school for gladiators.

(ii) It is a proof of levity and vileness to follow the profession of actor, dancer, or that of other panderers of the sort. To find one's pleasures in those fields leads sometimes to idleness and sometimes to dishonour. Modestly pursued for purposes of recreation, they are excused under the licence of leisure; but if for dissipation, they fall under the head of crime. (p. 373)

(iii) Almost the entire world, according to the opinion of our friend Petronius [see *Satyricon*, section 80], is seen to play the part of actor to perfection, the actors gazing as it were upon their own comedy and what is worse, so absorbed in it that they are unable to return to reality when occasion demands [...] So this comedy of the age affects the thoughts of even great men. To lend an attentive ear to the fantasies of the gentiles, all life comes to an end in tragedy; or if the name of comedy be preferred I offer no objection, provided that we are agreed that [...] almost all the world is playing a part [...] It is surprising how nearly coextensive with the world is the stage on which this endless, marvellous, incomparable tragedy, or if you will comedy, can be played; its area is in fact that of the whole world. (pp. 172–76)

TWELFTH-CENTURY NEO-ROMAN COMEDY

Between 1150 and 1175 the schools of the Loire valley produced three rewritings of Roman comedy: Vitalis of Blois' *Geta* and *Aurularia*, and William of Blois' *Alda*. Soon afterwards an unknown writer developed ideas and motifs from Ovid's poem *The Art of Love* into the widely distributed *Pamphilus*. It seems likely that the new comic drama influenced the Beauvais *Daniel* of *c.* 1175, differing as it does in important respects from Hilarius' *Daniel* of *c.* 1140 [see **B37**]. *Babio* (*c.* 1150–85), influenced by *Geta* and *Pamphilus* and, like *Geta*, written partly in mockery of the scholar Abelard, is a brutal farce which climaxes in the castration of its hero; it was probably performed at the court of Henry II of England, and may have been written by the cleric and courtier Walter de Map (*c.* 1140–*c.* 1209) [see **A33**]. In the following scene from *Pamphilus* [**A32**] the bawd delivers the hesitant Galathea into her would-be lover's arms.

A32   A bawd's strategem (from *Pamphilus*), later twelfth century

Seven Medieval Latin Comedies, trans. Alison Goddard Elliott, New York, 1984, pp. 20–1. Original in verse; modern stage directions and lineation removed

BAWD   You are alone at the moment; come to my house and enjoy yourself awhile. See, Galathea, at my house there are apples and nuts for you. My garden is hardly ever without fruit; look, you can enjoy whatever you wish. But now someone – I don't know who it is – bangs at my door. Was it a man or was it the wind? I think it was a man. It is a man! [. . .] It's Pamphilus! I recognise his face. By skill and by force, little by little, he's pulling back the bolt on the door. He's coming in. Does he think I'll stand for this without a word? Why so furiously break down my door, Pamphilus? You've broken the new bolt that I just bought [. . .]

PAMPHILUS   O Galathea, my only hope of salvation! after such long delays, give me a thousand kisses; but my thirsty ardour is unquenched, unsatisfied by kisses; it grows hotter, fed by such mild pleasures. Look, I embrace all my joys [. . .] This place contains all that I love best.

BAWD   I hear my neighbour calling me; I'll go talk to her, then come right back [. . .]

PAMPHILUS   Look how sweet love, blooming youth, and opportunity all urge us, Galathea, to feed our hearts with sport. Lascivious Venus compels us to taste her joys, orders us now to go on [. . .]

GALATHEA   Pamphilus, take your hands off me! [. . .] Alas, how little strength we women have; how easily you hold fast my hands [. . .] What are you doing? It's wrong to take my clothes off! Oh poor me, when will that treacherous woman return? [. . .] You've conquered me, however strongly I resisted, but all hope of love is shattered between us – forever!

PAMPHILUS Now then, we should both rest a bit, as when a horse, his race completed, breathes deeply.

A33   Tricky servant cuckolds ineffectual master (from *Babio*), c. 1150–85

Free trans. William Tydeman from *Babio*, ed. A. D. Fulgheri, Gallizi, 1980, lines 261–300.
The dating is suggested by Ian Lancashire, *Dramatic Texts and Records of Britain*, p. xiv.
Original in verse

[Fodius, farmhand to the surly Babio, is having an affair with his master's wife
Petula; Babio resolves to assert himself.]
[Fodius comes out of the house and Babio lassoes him with a length of rope.]

BABIO Fodius! These are your last moments! Stop there! This rope's going to stay
on your shoulders!

FODIUS And why should I die, pray?

BABIO I'm really too angry to answer.

FODIUS But where are you dragging me off to?

BABIO To hang from the top of an ash tree.

FODIUS I think I'm allowed to hear reasons; reasons should come before hanging.

BABIO You louse, you've been screwing Petula; don't think I don't know about it!

FODIUS No, it's not true!

BABIO Shall we find out by using the fire test?

FODIUS Very well, I agree; you're welcome to use fire or water.

BABIO You stinking adulterer!

FODIUS No, I'm asking for legal protection! No law court would dare set aside
legality's process.

BABIO Do you reckon that 'trustworthy Fodius' deserves such favourable treatment?

FODIUS Pomegranates don't grow from the willow; I'm *not* having it away with
Petula!

BABIO Give me your hand if you're honest; that gesture will quite reassure me.

FODIUS Let's do that then, Babio; give me your hand if you trust me.

[They shake hands, then Babio goes off towards his fields.]

Oh what a genius I am! What dangers my wits get me out of! Babio's got a
brain like an ox – he can't tell his arse from his elbow. In exchange for the
moon, Babio, I've sold you a pan to fry onions! 'I'm not making out with your
wife' – but that doesn't mean that I *haven't*! They're wrong to say courage
can't lie – the courage is all in the timing.

THE NEW TROY

William Fitzstephen, a former member of Thomas à Becket's entourage and
witness to his martyrdom in 1170, prefaced his life of the saint with a highly lau-

datory description of twelfth-century London, the 'New Troy': in London the classical world flourishes again, but an important change has overtaken one of that world's central institutions [see **A34**].

A34   Pious 'representations' in place of pagan shows, *c.* 1175

Materials for the History of Thomas Becket, ed. J. C. Robertson and J. B. Sheppard, 7 vols., London, 1875–85), vol. III, p. 9

In place of theatrical shows, in place of stage plays [*ludi scenici*], London has holier performances, representations of the miracles which have been performed by holy confessors [of the faith], or representations of sufferings in which the constancy of martyrs shone forth brightly.

A35   Kinds of professional performer, *c.* 1220

(i) Helen F. Rubel, 'Chabham's *Penitential* and its Influence in the Thirteenth Century', *Publications of the Modern Language Society of America*, 40 (1925), pp. 225–39; pp. 232–3;
(ii) Chambers, *Mediaeval Stage*, vol. II, p. 262

[Thomas of Chabham, or Chobham, was a subdean of Salisbury Cathedral. His penitential manual was written partly to flesh out the edicts of the 1215 Lateran Council. See also **I4**, **J69**]

(i) When prostitutes or performers [*histriones*] come to confession they are not to be given penitence unless they entirely give up such occupations, since otherwise they cannot be saved [. . .] It is to be noted, however, that there are three kinds of performers. Some indeed transform and transfigure their bodies by means of shameful dances or shameful gestures, or by shamefully stripping their bodies naked, or by putting on shameful masks; on which [grounds] all such can be considered damned unless they give up their occupations. There are also other performers who do not have an occupation of this kind, but still act reprehensibly. Having no fixed home, they haunt the courts of the great, saying indecent and disgraceful things of those who are not present; all such can be considered damned, because the Apostle forbids us to eat food with such people. And such buffoons [*scurre*] are called vagrants [*vagi*], since they are good for nothing except devouring food and speaking evil. There are, moreover, performers of a third kind, who carry musical instruments to give people delight. But these are of two types. Some frequent public drinkings and licentious gatherings, where they sing licentious songs which incite people to indecent behaviour; and such are to be considered damned, like the rest. But there are others called *ioculatores* who sing of the deeds of princes and of the lives of saints, and who bring comfort to people; and such can well be tolerated.

(ii) [A slightly later version adds] And these do not create shamefulnesses without number, as do the male and female dancers, and others who take part in indecent performances [*in imaginibus inhonestis*], and make it seem as if kinds of illusion [*fantasmata*] appear, by means of incantations or in some other way.[1]

[1] See **D66**.

The English *Dame Sirith* and *Interlude of the Clerk and the Girl*, like the Flemish *Le Garçon et l'Aveugle (The Boy and the Blind Man)* [see **Section E**] are small-scale comic pieces in the mime tradition which probably belonged to the repertoire of professional entertainers, and would have been very suitable for performance at feasts. All devolve on trickery and misunderstanding. The English plays' handling of amatory matters resembles that of the previous century's secular Latin drama [see **A32**]. Drama in both traditions is closely related to that of storytelling in the *fabliau* genre, which typically offers an ingeniously plotted treatment of bawdy material. The story of 'The Weeping Puppy' which underlies the two English plays is found in the *Disciplina clericalis* of Petrus Alfonsi (early twelfth century), a very widely circulated story collection. The *Interlude* (incomplete) may have required three performers, Girl, Clerk and Bawd. *Dame Sirith*, with a similar plot, was probably written for a solo performer skilled in mimicry and assisted by a trained dog. At first the young wife Margeri contemptuously rejects the advances of the clerk Willekin. The resourceful Dame Sirith, however, approached for help by the clerk, feeds her dog with mustard and pepper. Assuming a distraught manner, she presents the weeping animal to Margeri as her daughter, vengefully transformed by a clerk whose love she refused. Her ruse is successful.

A36   Theatrical routine for a minstrel and his dog (from *Dame Sirith*), thirteenth century

J. A. W. Bennett and G. V. Smithers (eds.), *Early Middle English Verse and Prose*, Oxford, 1966, pp. 77–95. Original in verse

[SIRITH'S VOICE] Ah, any young housewife is throwing her life away if she doesn't give in to a clerk who asks for her love!

[MARGERI'S VOICE] Ah, Lord Christ, what am I to do! The other day a clerk came here and propositioned me; and I wouldn't listen to him. I know he's going to change me into something. Old granny, how do you think I can escape?

[SIRITH'S VOICE] May God Almighty grant that you don't change into a bitch or a puppy-dog! My dear, if a clerk makes advances to you, do what he says and quickly become his lover – that's my advice. And if you don't, you're being stupid.

[MARGERI'S VOICE] Lord Jesus, I'm in a torment thinking the clerk left before he had his way with me. I'd give anything for him to have lain down with me and

got to work quickly. I'll be your servant forever if you fetch that Willekin, the clerk I'm talking about.
[Dame Sirith obliges] (pp. 92–3).

ARISTOTLE

The full Latin translation of Aristotle's *Nicomachean Ethics* which became available for study in the mid-thirteenth century includes an account of the moral virtue of *eutrapelia* (see 2.4, 4.8). In medieval discussion, *eutrapelia* 'entails not only an ability to give a witty turn to conversation and action, but also a moral decency that involves using proper language, participating only in licit entertainments, and observing the proper circumstances (time, place, etc.) that limit the acceptability of any act of play' (Glending Olson, 'The Medieval Fortunes of *Theatrica*', *Traditio* 42 (1986), pp. 265–86; p. 275). Later medieval interest in this hitherto-unfamiliar virtue strengthened the hand of those who believed that dramatic performance might – depending on its nature and occasion – be an acceptable and even a morally valuable activity.

A37 Study of Aristotle provides a defence of drama, later thirteenth century

The anonymous *Apprehension and the Kinds of Apprehension*, in Albertus Magnus, *Opera omnia*, ed. A. Borgnet, 38 vols., Paris, 1890–9, vol. v, p. 631

[One of the mechanical arts [cf. **A31**] which improves the body internally is 'theatrics',] a knowledge of games directed by the principle of *eutrapelia*; its name comes from 'theatre', a place where the people gathered for purposes of playing.

AQUINAS (*c.* 1225–74)

Thomas Aquinas' comprehensive (though unfinished) presentation of theology for students, the *Summa theologiae*, includes a weighing of the question of whether there can be virtue and vice in our outward bodily actions; the sequence of argument includes discussion of the merits and demerits of theatre. Aquinas is particularly concerned with the moral condition of professional performers.

A38 Aquinas synthesises Christian and classical views, 1265–74

Thomas Aquinas, *Summa theologiae*, 2a2ae.168, ed. and trans. T. Gilby, 60 vols.; London, 1964–6, vol. XXXIV, pp. 210–27

(i) Moral virtue consists in this, that human doings are governed by reason. Clearly our outward motions are included, for our bodily members are set in motion by the command of reason. And so it is evident that our carriage and gestures come into the field of moral virtue.

How they should be composed is determined by what is befitting, first, the person, and, second, the company, the business, and the place [. . .] External motions are signs of inward disposition, above all in respect to the passions of the soul. (p. 213)

(ii) As bodily tiredness is eased by resting the body, so psychological tiredness is eased by resting the soul. As we have explained in discussing the feelings, pleasure is rest for the soul [see 1ae2ae.2,6; 4,1 and 2]. And therefore the remedy for weariness of soul lies in slackening the tension of mental study and taking some pleasure [. . .]

There can be moral virtue about playing. Aristotle gives it the name *eutrapelia*, and a person who has it is called a *eutrapelos*, a pleasant person with a happy cast of mind who gives his words and deeds a cheerful turn [cf. **A37**]. And inasmuch as this virtue restrains us from immoderate amusement it comes under modesty. (pp. 217–19)

(iii) [On the question of whether playing too much is a sin] Also, actors [*histriones*] above all seem to be excessive about playing, since their whole lives are dominated by it. Were it wrong they would all be in a state of sin, and not them alone but also those who employ them or pay them, for they would be accomplices. This would seem to be false. We read in the *Lives of the Desert Fathers* that it was revealed to the blessed Paphnutius that a certain comedian would be his partner in the life to come [. . .][1]

Playing is necessary for humane intercourse, to the service of which lawful employments can be deputed. Accordingly the acting profession, the purpose of which is to put on shows for our enjoyment, is not unlawful in itself. Nor are actors in a state of sin provided their art is temperate, that is, they do not labour with indecent phrases and actions, and play is not intruded into unfitting times and occasions. And though they may have no other occupation in terms of human affairs, nevertheless in the sight of God they have other serious and virtuous activities, such as praying, composing their feelings and deeds, and on occasion relieving the poor with almsdeeds. So also those who support them in due season do not sin, but rather act justly by rewarding them for their services. It is wrong, however, to dissipate oneself in playing, or to contribute to the support of indecent plays, for this is encouraging sin. Augustine holds that giving your property away to actors is no virtue, but very wrong.[2] Unless, we may add, an actor is in dire need, for then he must be assisted. (pp. 220–25)

---

[1] See Cassian's text in *Patrologia Latina*, ed. Migne, vol. 73, col. 1170. St Paphnutius was an Egyptian bishop who died *c.* 360.

[2] See *Patrologia Latina*, ed. Migne, vol. 35, col. 1891.

Section B
Latin liturgical drama

Edited by PETER MEREDITH

Abbreviations

Chambers	E. K. Chambers, *The Mediaeval Stage*, 2 vols., Oxford 1903; various reprints
Churchwardens' Accounts	*Churchwardens' Accounts of S. Edmund & S. Thomas, Sarum, 1443–1702*, ed. Henry James Fowle Swayne, Wilts Record Society, Salisbury, 1896
Coleman	*Philippe de Mézières' Campaign for the Feast of Mary's Presentation*, ed. William E. Coleman, Toronto, 1981
Donovan	Richard B. Donovan, CSB, *The Liturgical Drama in Medieval Spain*, Toronto, 1958
Ecumenical Councils	*Decrees of the Ecumenical Councils*, ed. Norman P. Tanner, SJ, 2 vols., London and Washington DC, 1990.
'Inventories'	C. Wordsworths 'Inventories of Plate, Vestments etc. belonging to the Cathedral Church of the Blessed Mary of Lincoln', *Archæologia* 53 (1892–3) pp. 1–82
London City Church	*The Medieval Records of a London City Church (St Mary at Hill)* AD *1420–1559*, ed. Henry Littlehales, 2 vols., EETS OS 125, 128, London, 1904, 1905
Processionale	Richard Pynson, *Processionale ad usum Sarum, 1502*, facsimile reprint, Clifden, 1980
REED *Bristol*	Records of Early English Drama, *Bristol*, ed. Mark Pilkington, Toronto, 1997
REED *Devon*	Records of Early English Drama, *Devon*, ed. John Wasson, Toronto, 1986
Rites	*Rites of Durham being a Description or Brief Declaration of all the Ancient Monuments, Rites & Customs Belonging or being within the Monastical Church of Durham before the Suppression written 1593*, ed. J. T. Fowler, Surtees Society 107, Durham, 1902
Sarum Missal	*Missale ad usum insignis et præclaræ ecclesiæ Sarum*, ed. Francis Henry Dickinson, AM, Burntisland, 1861–83
Sekules	Veronica Sekules, 'The Tomb of Christ at Lincoln and the Development of the Sacrament Shrine: Easter Sepulchres Reconsidered', in *Medieval Art and Architecture at Lincoln*

	Cathedral, British Archæological Association Conference Transactions 1982, VIII, Leeds, 1986
Smoldon	*The Play of Daniel: a Medieval Liturgical Drama*, ed. W. L. Smoldon, rev. David Wulstan, Plainsong and Mediæval Music Society, Sutton, 1976
Symons	*Regularis concordia*, ed. Dom Thomas Symons, London, 1953
Warren	*The Sarum Missal in English*, trans. Frederick E. Warren, 2 vols., Library of Liturgiology & Ecclesiology for English Readers, London, 1911
Young	*The Drama of the Medieval Church*, ed. Karl Young, 2 vols, Oxford, 1933

Introduction

Liturgical drama is the theatrical action growing out of and to an extent remaining within the annually recurring services of the Christian Church, the liturgy. This is not the place to pursue the debate about the point at which ritual action becomes theatrical action, and, in turn, drama. Dialogue, costuming, impersonation, movement, gesture, lighting and many other elements and approaches have been considered a basis for making the distinction.[1] For some, as for Honorius of Autun [see **B1(b)**], the Mass itself will be drama; others will even hesitate to see theatrical action in the Palm Sunday procession. What is ruled out and what is included is up to a point a matter of personal response. Intention on the part of writers or performers, or reaction on the part of audiences, is clearly important but both are difficult to determine. A priest may well have perceived himself as denoting Christ when stretching his arms wide at the Mass; to an observer he may have seemed simply a performer of ritual gesture. What is certainly true is that theatrical action exists to varying extents within or on the edges of the liturgy.

Most evidence for liturgical drama has survived within church service books.[2] Texts of 'plays' are therefore presented as constituting what should or might be rather than what was. In this, it could be said, they do not differ much from most other play-texts; both rubrics and stage directions are usually statements of what should or might be. Normal rubrics, besides specifying the liturgical pieces to be used (antiphons, responsories, psalms etc.), are also concerned with costume (the appropriate liturgical vestment and its colour or any deliberate variation from that prescription), positioning, movement, timing (the appropriate number of liturgical pieces to cover a processional movement), in fact many elements that are, in effect if not in intention, essentially theatrical. Only very occasionally is there full information for mounting a production: Philippe de Mézières' *Presentation of the Virgin* from fourteenth-century France is exceptional in providing staging evidence of all kinds [see **B35(a)–(f)**].

The church services of the western Church were in Latin (with occasional Greek) and frequently sung; in part by one or more individuals, in part by one or more choirs.[3] They were performed by the clergy, monastic and secular, and not the laity. Experience of monastic services was to a certain extent confined to the monastic clergy; access to the services of the secular clergy, in cathedrals and parish churches, was largely open to the laity – though the buildings themselves could create obstructions (especially altars and the *pulpitum*, for example, but pillars and, later, tombs and chantry chapels as well), though these could in turn have been exploited by the organisers or performers.

Liturgical celebrations of the events of Christ's life, often attempting to create emotional responses or to satisfy emotional needs, frequently re-enacted those events physically or symbolically. Such elements exist from at least the fourth century in Jerusalem[4] and from there develop within the rites of the western Church. Most important, certainly from the tenth century to well beyond the Reformation in the sixteenth century are those which centre on the events of Christ's death and resurrection.

Hundreds of texts of these survive from all over Europe, most frequently in the form of what has come to be known as the *Quem queritis* trope or the *Visitatio sepulchri*. A trope is a verbal and musical expansion of a part of the designated liturgy. *Quem queritis* is the *incipit* or opening words of a particular trope, and the visit to Christ's tomb of the three Maries (the *Visitatio sepulchri*) is the subject matter of that trope.[5] Though this is by far the most numerous of the forms of the liturgical drama, there are a large number of other subjects treated and forms existing, from momentary impersonations to extended plays.

NOTES

1. For some discussion of these matters see Young, vol. I, ch. 3; Rosemary Woolf, *The English Mystery Plays*, London, 1972, chs. I and 2; C. Clifford Flanigan, 'The Fleury Playbook, the Traditions of Medieval Latin Drama and Modern Scholarship', in *The Fleury* Playbook: *Essays and Studies*, ed. Thomas P. Campbell and Clifford Davidson, Early Drama, Art, and Music Monograph Series 7, Kalamazoo, 1985, pp. 1–25, especially pp. 1–4; O. B. Hardison, Jr., *Christian Rite and Christian Drama in the Middle Ages*, Baltimore, 1965, especially ch. 2. There are useful surveys of modern scholarship in C. Clifford Flanigan, *Research Opportunities in Renaissance Drama* 18 and 19 (1975 and 1976), pp. 81–102, 109–36, and *The Theatre of Medieval Europe: New Research in Early Drama*, ed. Eckehard Simon, Cambridge, 1991, pp. 21–41.

2. The earliest service books to record liturgical drama are of the tenth century [see **B9 (a)**, **(b)**] but since these books record regularly recurring elements of the liturgy, it is often difficult to date the first occurrence of a particular element at all precisely. Young gives the dates (as accepted before 1933) of the manuscripts or printed books which he used for his texts, and these have been followed here in extracts derived from Young. They should not, however, be taken as indications of the earliest dates of the ceremonies but rather as dates at which they were established elements in the liturgy of a particular diocese, town or church.

3. The musical element of the liturgical ceremonies has rightly been stressed. Some manuscripts include musical notation but many do not and the Latin word *dicere*, 'to say', is often used for the delivery of a text. It should not be assumed that 'saying' excludes 'singing', however.

4. E. D. Hunt, *Holy Land Pilgrimage in the Later Roman Empire, AD 312–460*, Oxford, 1984,

especially ch. 5. *The Itinerarium Egeriæ* is translated (as 'The Pilgrimage of S. Sylvia of Aquitania') in *The Pilgrimage of S. Sylvia of Aquitania to the Holy Places*, translated by John H. Bernard, Palestine Pilgrims' Text Society, London, 1891; see pp. 57–70 for ceremonies of Easter–Pentecost.

5.   The fullest edition of the *Quem queritis/Visitatio sepulchri* texts is *Lateinische Osterfeiern und Osterspiele*, ed. Walther Lipphardt, 6 vols., Berlin, 1975–81.

I   Symbolic drama

The earliest, and in many respects fullest, attempt to see the liturgy as a presentation of the life of Christ is that of Amalarius, bishop of Metz, in the ninth century (see particularly the *Liber officialis*, *Patrologia Latina* vol. 105, cols. 815–1360) [see **B1(a)**]. This has been extensively investigated by Hardison (*Christian Rite*, pp. 35–79). Honorius of Autun, writing at the beginning of the twelfth century, developed some of Amalarius' ideas [see **B1(b)**]. It remains drama of the imagination rather than actualised theatre, however.

B1   The Mass as drama
(a)   Amalarius of Metz, *Liber officialis*, 821–35

Young, vol. 1, p. 81

The sacraments ought to have some likeness to those actualities of which they are sacraments. Therefore the priest should be like Christ as the bread and wine [*liquor*] are like the body of Christ. Thus the sacrifice of the priest at the altar is up to a point like the sacrifice of Christ on the cross.

(b)   Honorius of Autun, *Gemma animae*, c. 1100

Young, vol. 1, p. 83

It should be realised that those who recited tragedies in theatres were representing to the people by their actions [*gestibus*] the acts of those in conflict. Thus our tragic actor represents to Christian people by his actions in the theatre of the church the conflict of Christ and demonstrates the victory of his redemption to them. So when the priest says, 'Pray', he expresses for us Christ in his agony when he advised the apostles to pray. Through the silence of the Secret [prayer], he signifies Christ as a lamb led in silence to the slaughter. Through the stretching out of his hands he depicts the stretching of Christ on the cross. Through the singing of the Preface, he expresses the cries of Christ hanging on the cross. For he sang ten psalms, that is *Deus meus respice* [My God, look upon me] to *In manus tuas commendo spiritum meum* [Into thy hands I entrust my spirit], and so died. Through the Secret [prayer] of the Canon [of the Mass] he indicates the silence of [Easter] Saturday. Through the kiss of peace and the exchanging [of it] he shows the peace given after the resurrection of Christ and the communication of joy. The sacrament completed, peace and communion are given to the people by the priest, because, [with] our accuser [i.e. Satan] prostrate through the fight with our champion [i.e. Christ], peace is announced by the judge to the people invited to the feast. Then he tells them with 'Go, the Mass is ended' to return with joy to their own business, and they happily give thanks to God and joyously return to their homes.

II   The ceremonies of Holy Week

Rather than present the *Visitatio sepulchri* as an isolated instance of a complete drama, it seems best to attempt to embed it in the context in which it existed. A major part of that context is the commemoration in the liturgy of the chief events of Christ's Passion in the week leading up to Easter Sunday (Holy Week), beginning with the entry into Jerusalem (Palm Sunday) and continuing through the washing of the disciples' feet at the Last Supper (Maundy Thursday) to the Crucifixion (Good Friday), to culminate in the Resurrection (Easter Sunday).

What follows is an extended series of excerpts from the ceremonies for Holy Week in the Sarum (Salisbury) missal. The missal provides instructions for the daily performing of the Mass and for associated Offices for special feast days. The Mass is common to the experience of monastic and regular clergy, as well as laity, and the associated services, especially Matins and Vespers, provide most of the enduring examples of liturgical drama and much of the dramatic ceremony. Missals vary according to the particular form of the services followed in any one place (the Use), and no one form was employed throughout Europe. In England a large number of churches, though not by any means all, followed the Use of Sarum. For the use of 'V' and 'R' in the missal texts, see Glossary under 'responsory'.

PALM SUNDAY

The services for Palm Sunday in the missal begin with the blessing of the flowers and branches [see **B2(a)**, **(b)**] which is followed by the procession around the outside of the church [**B2(c)**]. In some places (e.g. Winchester, Tours) the procession went out of the church precinct and the town and back through the town gates making the parallel with the entry into Jerusalem more distinct. The procession made four stops or 'stations'. At the first, the secondary procession carrying the sacrament and relics in a shrine (the feretory), and representing Christ, met and joined the main procession. This sometimes, as at Winchester, gave rise to dialogue between the two, one group representing the disciples of Christ. At the second station, choirboys representing the children of the Hebrews were placed on a high scaffold or the roof of the church porch [**B2(c)**] to sing the hymn of welcome and praise, *Gloria, laus et honor*. At the third station the versicle quoting the high priest Caiaphas' words was sometimes sung by a boy dressed as a prophet [cf. **B2(c)**]. In some continental services, especially in what is now Germany, the feretory carrying sacrament and relics was replaced or accompanied by a *Palmesel*, or wheeled, life-size model of Christ on the ass, which was taken in procession and brought into the church [**B2(d)**; **B8(a)**].

The antiphons, responses and versicles used in the Palm Sunday service are almost all quotations or adaptations from the Gospels and form a loose narrative sequence. This narrative is told in full through the reading of John's description of the entry into Jerusalem (12.12–19),[1] and the ideas lying behind the 'procession' are reflected upon in the lesson from Exodus (15.27; 16.1–10) [**B2(b)**]. The two together imaginatively link the Palm Sunday procession with the Old Testament wandering of the chosen people and the events of Christ's life. The reading from Matthew's Gospel at the first station also links Palm Sunday with the coming of Christ at Advent.

The rubrics, sometimes with accompanying diagrams [**B2(a)**], act as stage directions for the event, describing, often in great detail, costume, positioning, props, movement, gesture, timing. They are given here in full. Sections of the prayers are also included here to give a sense of the imaginative and emotional content of the service and hence the potential for individual, internalised drama.

The Mass which follows the procession contains premonitions of the Passion mainly through the singing of Psalm 21, always interpreted as referring to the Passion, beginning as it does with the words of Christ on the cross: 'My God, my God, look upon me: why hast thou forsaken me', and the Passion Gospel of Matthew which takes the narrative up to Christ's death.

The Passion from Matthew's Gospel was sung at the Palm Sunday Mass, that from Mark's on Tuesday, Luke's on Wednesday and John's on Good Friday. Besides the variation of 'voices'[see **B3**], each has its own 'staged' moment, whether it is simply the singer breaking off and bowing or prostrating himself at the words 'yielded up the ghost' (Matthew and Mark), the dropping of the curtain suspended in front of the high altar at 'the veil of the temple was rent in twain' (Luke) or the stripping away of the two white cloths from the altar at 'They parted my raiment among them' (John), [**B5(a)**].

1.   All biblical references are to the *Douay-Rheims* translation of the Latin Vulgate, which produces variations of one or two in the numbering of the psalms between numbers 10 and 146 but little variation in the New Testament.

B2   Palm Sunday ceremonies

(a)   Diagram from a Sarum Processional (1502) – the 'station' for the blessing of the palms on Palm Sunday

Processionale, fo. 38

Printed processionals and occasionally missals sometimes contain diagrams of certain of the processional 'stations'. They are not usual in manuscripts though British Library MS Additional 57534, a manuscript missal, has a series of them. This diagram shows the position of the officiating priest (the tonsured head with vestment) between an acolyte on his right and a deacon on his left (both shown just as tonsured heads). In front of them is the gospel book and beyond that the altar with the 'palms with flowers' for the clergy. To their right, on the altar steps, are the 'palms' for others. Below these is the *aspergillum* for sprinkling holy water. Behind the deacon are a cross representing the cross-bearer, two candles representing the candle-bearers and an incense-burner, censer or thurible, representing the *thurifer* [incense-bearer]. The 1502 Sarum *Processionale* contains twelve diagrams, six relating to Easter ceremonials [see **B6(b)** for the blessing of the Paschal Candle].

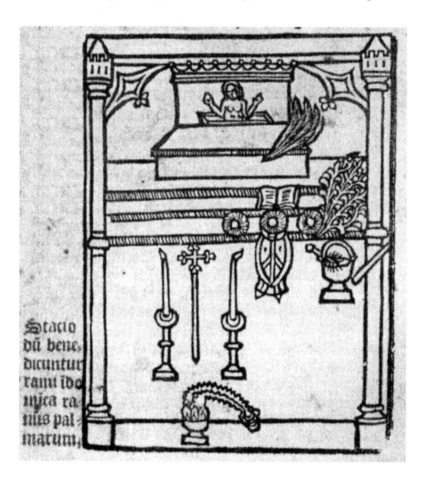

(b)   The Blessing of the Palms

Sarum Missal, cols. 253–8

After the sprinkling of holy water, this lesson with its title shall be read by an acolyte vested in an alb, at the altar step, on the south side, over the flowers and leaves.

Lesson from the book of Exodus [15.27; 16.1–10]

In those days the children of Israel came to Elim [. . .] and, lo, the glory of the Lord appeared in the cloud.

And the Gospel shall follow immediately; and it shall be read where the gospels are read on ferial [non-festival] *days, by a deacon turning to the east, in the manner of a simple feast, after receiving the blessing.*

According to John [12.12–19]

At that time a great multitude [. . .] behold the whole world is gone after him.

The Gospel ended, the blessing of flowers and leaves shall follow [given] *by a priest, vested in a red silk cope,* [standing] *on the third step of the altar, turned towards the south; palms with flowers for the clergy having first been placed on the altar, but for others on the step of the altar on the south side.*

I exorcise thee, O creature of flowers or leaves, in the name of God the Father almighty, and in the name of Jesus Christ his Son our Lord, and in the power of the Holy Spirit. Henceforth all power of the adversary, all the host of the devil, all the strength of the enemy, all assaults of demons, be uprooted and transplanted from this creature of flowers or leaves, that thou pursue not by subtlety the footsteps of those who hasten to the grace of God. Through him who shall come to judge the quick and dead, and the world by fire. R. Amen.

Then prayers shall be said without: The Lord be with you, *but only with*: Let us pray.

Prayer.

Almighty everlasting God, who in the outpouring of the flood didst announce to Noah thy servant the restoration of peace to the earth by a dove bearing an olive branch in her mouth, we humbly beseech thee, that thy truth may sanctify this creature of flowers and leaves, and branches of palms, or leaves of trees, which we offer before the presence of thy glory, so that thy devout people taking them in their hands may be worthy to obtain the grace of thy benediction. Through Christ [. . .] etc.

[There are three further prayers asking God to bless the palms and other branches and recalling Christ's entry into Jerusalem. After the second the 'flowers and leaves are sprinkled with holy water and censed'.]

This done, the palms shall be distributed at once; and meanwhile the following antiphons shall be sung, the cantor beginning the antiphon: The children of the Hebrews, carrying olive branches, went to meet our Lord, crying out and saying, 'Hosanna in the highest'.

Another antiphon.

The children of the Hebrews spread their garments in the way, and cried saying, 'Hosanna to the son of David; Blessed is he that comes in the name of the Lord'.

(c)   The Procession

Sarum Missal, cols. 258–62

While the palm-branches are being distributed a shrine with relics [the feretory] *is to be prepared, on which the Body of Christ* [i.e. the host or consecrated wafer] *should hang in a pyx. It is borne by two clerks of the second rank, who shall go to meet the procession at the site of the first station, not following the procession. There should be no change of vestments. A lighted lantern, with an unveiled cross, and two banners should precede it* [i.e. the feretory]. *Then the procession shall go to the place of the first station. The ministers in the procession shall be vested in girded albs, without tunicles or chasubles. The priest is to wear a red silk cope, the choir following him without any change of vestment.* [As they go they sing two antiphons, one recalls the arranging of the Passover meal and the other Christ's entry into Jerusalem.]

If these two antiphons are not sufficient to fill up the time taken to reach the first station then the following antiphons shall be used:
[Three antiphons follow, likewise recalling Christ's entry and the rejoicing of the children of Israel.]

Here the first station shall be made, that is to say, at the extreme east of the north side of the church, and this Gospel shall be read: When Jesus drew nigh [. . . Hosanna in the highest. Matt. 21.1–9.] *(Look for this Gospel in the first Sunday in Advent.) It is to be read by the deacon, vested for the procession, not close to the cross, but in front of the priest* [. . .] *The deacon is to face to the north, and* [the Gospel] *is to be read as on a simple feast of nine lessons, the benediction having been previously received in the usual manner.*

The Gospel being ended, three clerks of the second rank, without changing their vestments, having turned to the people, and standing in front of and on the west side of the great cross, shall sing together the following verse:
Behold, thy king comes [unto thee, O Sion, mystical daughter, sitting on beasts, of whose coming the prophetic lesson has now foretold.]

After each verse the officiating priest, turning to the relics, shall begin the antiphon:
Hail, [thou whom the people of the Hebrews bear witness to as Jesus, coming to meet thee with palms shouting words of salvation.]

The choir shall take it [the antiphon] *up, kneeling and kissing the ground; the officiating priest himself kneeling first, with the choir. The clerks* [standing] *before the relics* [shall sing] *the verse:*
Behold thy king [etc].

The senior [clerk] *shall say the antiphon:* Hail, thou whom, [etc.,] *the choir rising and taking it* [up at the words]: bear witness to.

Then shall the clerks, before the relics, without change of position, say the verse:
This is he that comes from Edom, [with dyed garments from Bozrah; this that is glorious in his apparel, travelling in the greatness of his strength; not on war horses, nor in lofty turrets.]

Then the senior [clerk], *without change of position, shall say the verse:*
Hail, light of the world, [king of kings, glory of heaven, with whom abides dominion, praise and honour, now and for ever.]

The choir rising, and taking it up at: king of kings. *Then the clerks, in front of the relics, without changing their position, shall say the verse:*
This is he [that comes from Edom etc.]

Then the senior [clerk], *without changing his position, shall say the antiphon:*
Hail, our salvation, [our true peace, our redemption, our strength, who of thine own free will didst submit to the dominion of death on our behalf.]

The choir rising and taking it up at the point: our true peace.

Then shall the procession go to the place of the second station; and the feretory, with the receptacle for relics, together with a light in a lantern, shall be carried between the subdeacon and the thurifer [incense-bearer], with the banners on either side of them, the cantor beginning the antiphon:

Thou art worthy, O Lord [our God, to receive glory and honour.]

[*And*] *antiphon:*

The multitudes come [to meet the Redeemer with flowers and palms, and give due reverence to the triumphant conqueror. The Gentiles proclaim with their mouths the Son of God, and their voices praising Christ resound through the skies with Hosanna.]

If these two antiphons do not suffice [to bring] the procession to the place of the second station, then shall one or both of the following responsories be sung:

Responsory.

The Lord Jesus [six days before the Passover came to Bethany, where Lazarus had died, whom Jesus raised from the dead.]

V. [But] there assembled [there many of the Jews, that they might see Lazarus, whom Jesus raised from the dead.]

Responsory.

[But the chief priests] consulted [that they might put Lazarus also to death, because that by reason of him many came and believed on Jesus.]

V. Testimony, [therefore, the people bore who were with him, when he called Lazarus out of the grave, and raised him from the dead.]

Here the second station shall be made, that is to say, on the south side of the church, where seven boys, from a very elevated position, shall sing together:

> Glory, laud, and honour
> To thee, Redeemer, King,
> To whom the lips of children
> Made sweet Hosannas ring.

The choir is to repeat this stanza after each verse.

Thou art the King of Israel [. . .]¹

This station ended, the procession is to go through the middle of the cloister on the right hand side as far as the west door of the church, singing the responsory:

Then gathered [the chief priests and the Pharisees in council and said, 'What do we? for this man does many miracles. If we let him thus alone, all men will believe on him. And perhaps the Romans will come and take away both our place and nation.']

Here the third station is made, in front of the aforesaid door, where three clerks of the upper rank, standing in the doorway itself, without changing their vestments, shall turn to the people, and sing this verse:

V. But one [of them, named Caiaphas, being the high priest that same year, prophesied, saying, 'It is expedient for you that one man should die for the people, and that the whole nation perish not; lest the Romans shall come and take away both our place and nation'.] [*And*] *a repeat [of]:* lest [the Romans etc.]

This done, they shall enter the church by the same door, passing under the feretory and the receptacle for relics which shall be raised over the doorway, singing:
Responsory.

As the Lord was entering [into the holy city, the children of the Hebrews with branches of palms, proclaiming the resurrection of life, cried out: 'Hosanna in the highest'.]

Here the fourth station is to be made, namely before the cross in the church. And at this station, after the cross has been now unveiled, the officiating priest shall begin the antiphon: 'Hail' and the choir will respond at: 'our King' kneeling and kissing the ground.
Antiphon.

[Hail our King, Son of David, Redeemer of the world, whom the prophets have proclaimed to be the Saviour of the house of Israel that is to come. For thee the Father sent into the world to be the saving victim whom all the saints expected from the beginning of the world, and now expect. Hosanna to the son of David. Blessed is he that comes in the name of the Lord. Hosanna in the highest.]

And the officiating priest is to commence the above antiphon, [by repeating Hail] three times, in a louder voice each time, he and the choir kneeling. After the third repeat the choir shall take up the rest of the antiphon standing at the same station. This done, they shall enter the quire. All the crosses throughout the church are to be unveiled until after Vespers. At the entrance of the quire:
Responsory.

[Lying men] compassed me about; [they scourged me without a cause. But do thou, O Lord, my defender, avenge me.]

V. Deliver me [from mine enemies, O Lord:] R. And [defend me] from them that rise up [against me.]
Prayer.

Almighty and everlasting God [etc.]
All being now finished in connection with the procession, Mass [shall begin.]
[. . .]

---

[1] For the hymns, slightly adapted versions of older translations have been used. This is the translation of *'Gloria, laus et honor'* by J. M. Neale, 'All glory, laud and honour' [See also **B5(c)**].

(d)   The Palmesel

Courtesy of the Victoria and Albert Museum, A.1030–1910

The *Palmesel* is a carved wooden figure of Christ on the ass which was taken round as part of the Palm Sunday procession. It is common in Germany and appears occasionally elsewhere in Europe. The earliest reference to such a figure seems to be late tenth-century (*Lexicon* 3 p. 365, s.v. PALMCHRISTUS, PALMESEL). The *Palmesel* pictured here is from Swabia and dates from the first quarter of the sixteenth century. It is now painted grey, but traces of earlier pigmentation survive on Christ's face, and of gold on the border of his robe. The bridle and wheels are missing but there are slots in the base for the latter and a hole at the front for pulling the image along. The *Palmesel* is 4 ft 10 in (147.2 cm) high. (Information from Michael Baxandall, *South German Sculpture, 1480–1530*, London 1974, p. 34.)

Young (vol. I, pp. 94–7) gives a ceremony from a fourteenth-century ordinary from Essen where the image is drawn into the collegiate church, placed in the middle of the church facing east, with carpets around it, and greeted with the singing of *Gloria, laus et honor* and a series of antiphons. He includes a photograph of the *Palmesel* from Steinen in Switzerland (plate II), with Christ holding a book in his left hand, his right raised in blessing. [See also **B8(a)**].

B3   Singing the Passion at Holy Week Mass
Sarum Missal, col. 264

[. . .]

The Passion follows. And it should be observed that it is to be sung or delivered in three voices – namely a high voice, a low, and a middle, because all the contents of the Passion are either the words of the Jews or the disciples, or the words of Christ, or the words of the Evangelist who tells the story. Therefore understand that where you find the letter (a), the words are those either of the Jews or the disciples, which are to be given in a high voice; where you find (b), the words are of Christ, which are to be delivered in a low voice; where you find the letter (m), the words are of the Evangelist, which are to be read or sung in a middle voice. This rule is to be observed in all the recitations of the Passion.
[. . .]

MAUNDY THURSDAY

Maundy Thursday, four days after Palm Sunday, is the usual English name for the Thursday of Holy Week, derived from *Mandatum* the opening word of the first antiphon before the washing of the feet. In Latin it is most frequently *Cena Domini*, 'the Lord's Supper', in the Romance languages 'Holy Thursday' (It. *Giovedi Santo*, Fr. *Jeudi Saint*). The ceremonies of the day began with the first of the *Tenebræ*, which took place after midnight on the mornings of Maundy Thursday, Good Friday and Holy Saturday. This involved the gradual extinguishing of all the candles in the church during Matins and Lauds, the first services of the day, until a single one was left which was then taken away and hidden, leaving the church in total darkness.

Later in the day those excluded from the church at the beginning of Lent were readmitted as penitents. They gathered outside the west door and the bishop or officiating priest on the inside physically readmitted them. The penitents were then 'restored to the bosom of the Church' one by one by the officiating priest. The rest of the ceremony dwells on the seeking of mercy and ends with the absolution. The Mass which followed does not contain one of the major Passion sections from the gospels but instead the less emotionally charged narrative of the washing of the disciples' feet at the Last Supper [**B4(b)**]. The communion itself is a commemoration of the institution of the sacrament. Since the sacramental wafer, the host, is not consecrated on Good Friday, three are prepared at this service [see **B4(a)**].

Vespers follows on from the Mass and both finish together. The ceremony of the washing of the altars follows, beginning with ten responsories which recall the terror of Christ's doubt, his betrayal and capture on the Mount of Olives and the first incidents of his Passion.

This is followed by the ceremony of the washing of feet [**B4(b)**]. Elsewhere the ceremony involves the laity far more. In an early Besançon text, for example, the feet of sixty poor men are washed [Young, vol. I, pp. 98–9]; at Durham, of thirteen poor men [*Rites*, pp. 77–8].

B4   Maundy Thursday observances
(a)   Preparations for the sepulchre ceremony

Sarum Missal, col. 303

Three hosts should be placed by the subdeacon for consecration; of which two should be reserved for the following day, one to be received by the priest, the other to be deposited with the cross in the sepulchre.
[. . .]

(b)   The washing of feet

Sarum Missal, cols. 311–12

Then the sermon is given. Which being done, the two priests aforesaid shall rise up, and beginning with those of highest rank shall wash the feet of all, one on one side of the quire, and the other on the other; and [lastly] they shall wash each others' feet. Meanwhile, the following antiphons with their psalms shall be sung by the whole choir sitting:

Antiphon.

A new commandment [*Mandatum novum*] [I give unto you, that ye love one another, as I have loved you, says the Lord.]

Psalm.[66]

God be merciful unto us [and bless us, etc.]

[Four antiphons with psalms follow.]

After the washing of feet, the sermon having been given, they shall partake of the loving-cup. And when all has been duly performed, one priest shall say the prayers thus
[. . .]

GOOD FRIDAY AND HOLY SATURDAY

The Latin name for Good Friday is *Parasceve* (*Dies Parasceves*, *Feria Sexta in Parasceve*), in Romance languages 'Holy Friday' (It. *Venerdi Santo*, Fr. *Vendredi Saint*). Holy Saturday is usually *Sabbatum Sanctum* in Latin and similar forms exist in the Romance languages. The Good Friday liturgy is dominated by the death of Christ, that of Holy Saturday by preparation and renewal. Both days began with the putting out of the lights one by one, *Tenebræ*, at Matins and Lauds [see above, MAUNDY THURSDAY]. At Mass on Friday the final Passion, that of John, is sung followed by prayers for all manner of people. Most striking of the Friday ceremonies are the *Improperia*, or Reproaches [**B5(b)**], and the Adoration of the Cross [**B5(c)**; **B8(b)**].

In the former, two priests holding the cross between them speak the words of reproach put into the mouth of Christ (the *Improperia*), punctuated by the repetition of the cry for mercy from the choir. Then comes the 'adoring' of the cross, often called the 'creeping to the cross', first by the clergy then by the people, and finally its burial in the sepulchre [see **B5(b)**, **(c)**, **(d)**; **B7(iv)**]. The services of Holy Saturday are dominated by the blessing of the new fire and of the Paschal candle and its lighting from the newly kindled flame, and finally by the ceremonial blessing of the font [see **B6(a)**, **(b)**, **(c)**, **(d)**].

B5   The Ceremonies for Good Friday
(a)   The Passion
Sarum Missal, cols. 319–24

The Passion shall follow without The Lord be with you, *and without title, thus:*
[John, 18 and 19.1–37]
[The first part of the Gospel is sung as described in **B3**, up to the following verse:]
(*m.*) That the scriptures might be fulfilled, saying: They have parted my garments among them
Here two ministers in surplices shall approach, one at the right, the other at the left side of the altar, and shall take from it two linen cloths, which were placed upon the altar for that purpose.
and upon my vesture they have cast lots. [The next section continues until interrupted at:]
(*m.*) And he bowed his head and gave up the ghost; *there shall follow*: Our Father, Hail Mary, Into thy hands [etc.]
[The Gospel is then continued to the end, followed by solemn prayers.]

(b)   The Reproaches
Sarum Missal, cols. 328–30

[. . .]
The prayers being ended, the priest shall take off his chasuble, and place himself in his own seat by the altar, with the deacon and subdeacon. Meanwhile, two other priests of higher rank, barefoot, and vested in albs, without apparels, solemnly holding up between them in their arms the veiled cross [shall place themselves] behind the high altar, on the right side, and sing these verses:
O my people, [what have I done unto thee, or wherein have I afflicted thee? Reply to me. Because I brought thee up out of the land of Egypt, thou hast prepared a cross for thy Saviour.]
Two deacons of the second rank, in their black copes, standing at the step of the quire and facing the altar, shall say:
Agyos [O Theos, Agyos Iskyros, Agyos Athanatos, eleyson ymas.]
The choir, genuflecting, and kissing the benches thrice at each response, and each time rising again, shall respond:
Holy God, [Holy and Strong, Holy and Immortal, have mercy upon us.][1]
The priests holding the cross behind the altar and the deacons at the steps of the quire saying Agyos are to remain standing. Then the priests, without changing position, shall say the verse:
Because I led thee [through the wilderness forty years, and I fed thee with manna, and brought thee into a land sufficiently good, thou hast prepared a cross for thy Saviour.]
Deacons. Agyos [O Theos, etc.]
Choir. Holy God, [Holy, etc.]

Then the Priests, place unchanged, shall say the verse:

What could I have done more [unto thee that I have not done? I planted thee indeed, O my vineyard, with fair fruit, and thou art become very bitter unto me; for thou gavest me to drink in my thirst vinegar mingled with gall, and piercedst thy Saviour's side with a spear.]

Deacons. Agyos [O Theos, etc.]

Choir. Holy God, [Holy, etc.]

Then the priests uncovering the cross by the altar on the right side, shall sing this anti-phon:

Behold the wood [of the cross, on which hung the salvation of the world. O come, let us adore.]

The choir genuflecting, and kissing the benches, shall respond with the antiphon:

Thy cross, [O Lord, we adore, and we praise and glorify thy holy resurrection; for, lo, by the cross joy hath come to the whole world.]

   Psalm [66] God be merciful unto us [and bless us; etc.]

The whole psalm is to be said by the whole choir, without Glory be to the Father [etc.] *and after each verse the antiphon shall be repeated in the same way by the whole choir, genuflecting. And meanwhile the cross shall be solemnly placed on the third step of the altar, the aforesaid priests being seated close to it, one on the right side, the other on the left.*

[1]   This line translates (in Latin) the preceding Greek 'Agyos [O Theos . . . ymas]'.

(c)   The Adoration of the Cross

Sarum Missal, cols. 330–1

Then shall the clerks proceed barefoot to adore the cross, beginning with those of highest rank.

 When the psalm, with its antiphon, is finished, the following hymn is to be sung by the two priests, seated all this time close to the cross in the manner above-mentioned. Hymn: Faithful Cross. *The choir, sitting meanwhile, shall repeat this [verse] after each [succeeding] verse.*

[PRIESTS	Faithful cross, above all other
	One and only noble tree,
	None in foliage, none in blossom,
	None in fruit thy peer may be;
	Sweetest wood, and sweetest iron,
	Sweetest weight is hung on thee.
CHOIR	Faithful cross etc.]
PRIESTS	Sing, my tongue, [the glorious battle;
	Sing the last, the dread affray;
	O'er the cross, the Victor's trophy,
	Sound the high triumphal lay,
	How, the pains of death enduring,
	Earth's Redeemer won the day.
CHOIR	Faithful cross etc.][1]

[. . .]

When the hymn is finished, the cross shall be carried through the middle of the quire by the two priests aforesaid to where it may be adored by the people before some altar; and in the mean time this antiphon following, with its verse, shall be sung in the quire by the whole choir, seated. The cantor shall begin the antiphon:

While the maker [of the world suffered the punishment of death upon the cross, and crying with a loud voice gave up the ghost, lo! the veil of the temple was rent, and the graves were opened, for there was a great earthquake, because the world cried aloud that it could not endure the death of the son of God.

V. Therefore, the side of the crucified Lord, having been opened by a soldier's spear, there came forth blood and water, for our redemption and salvation.]

V. O admirable [price! by the weighing of which the captivity of the world has been redeemed, the infernal gates of hell have been broken asunder, and the door of the kingdom [of heaven] has been opened unto us.

V. Therefore the side of the crucified Lord

Having been opened [etc.]

When the cross has been adored, and the aforesaid antiphon and its verse are finished, the aforesaid priests shall carry the cross back again to the high altar, through the middle of the quire, with the same reverence with which they carried it out.

Then all the clerics shall come together from the quire to the altar, and the priest shall again put on the chasuble, which he had previously taken off, and approach the step of the altar with deacon and subdeacon, and say the Confession, *and* [Almighty God] have mercy [etc.], *and the Absolution with the prayers and the Collect,* Take away from us, O Lord, [we beseech thee etc.] *in the accustomed manner, but the kiss of peace is not to be given here.*

---

[1]   This is the eighth verse of *Pange lingua gloriosi.* Compare the translation, again by J. M. Neale, 'Sing, my tongue, the glorious battle.'

(d)   The Burial of the Cross

Sarum Missal, cols. 332–3

[. . .]

After Vespers are finished the priest shall take off his chasuble, and taking with him one of superior rank, both being in surplices and barefoot, shall place the cross in the sepulchre, along with the Lord's Body in the pyx, himself alone beginning the Responsory, kneeling with his companion:

I am counted [as one of them that go down into the pit: and I have been even as a man that has no strength, free among the dead.

V. Thou hast laid me down in the lowest pit, in a place of darkness, and in the deep. I have been even etc.]

Once this is begun, they immediately rise. Let the same be done in the Responsory, The Lord being buried. *The choir shall take it up with its verse, kneeling continually to the end of the service.*

When the sepulchre has been censed and the door shut the same priest shall begin the responsory, Being buried. *The choir shall sing it with its verse.*

[The Lord] being buried, [the sepulchre was sealed: rolling a stone to the door of the sepulchre: setting soldiers to watch it.

V. Lest peradventure his disciples should come and steal him away, and say unto the people, He is risen from the dead.

Setting soldiers etc.]

At each of these [following] three antiphons the two aforesaid priests shall kneel continually. The priest shall begin the antiphon:

In peace, [in the same, I will lay me down and take my rest; for it is thou, Lord, only that makest me dwell in safety.]

The choir shall take it up at: in the same

Also the priest, the antiphon:

In peace is made [his place, and his dwelling in Sion]

Also the priest, the antiphon:

My flesh [also shall rest in hope]

The choir shall take it up at: shall rest in hope

When these antiphons are finished and prayers have been said in their own time [ad placitum] *by all, secretly, with genuflection, all others shall go back, as they please, in no fixed order; [but] the priest shall put on his chasuble again and leave in the same order in which he went up at the beginning of the service, with the deacon and subdeacon, and the other ministers of the altar.*

From that time one wax candle at least shall burn continually before the sepulchre, until the procession which is made at the Lord's Resurrection on Easter Day, except that it shall be extinguished while the Psalm, Blessed [be the Lord God of Israel etc.], *and the rest which follows it, is sung on the following night. In the same way it is to be extinguished on the vigil of Easter, while the new fire is blessed, until the Paschal candle, thirty-six feet long, is lighted.*

B6   The Ceremonies for Holy Saturday
(a)   The Blessing of the New Fire

Sarum Missal, cols. 334–71

First of all, the blessing of the fire shall be performed, by the officiating priest, vested in his sacerdotal vestments, with a silk cope, the deacon being vested in a dalmatic, the subdeacon in a tunicle, and the other ministers of the altar in albs and amices, and without light and candles, without cross, without fire in the censer. Also someone of the first rank, vested in a surplice, bearing an extinguished wax taper upon a spear, preceding the procession, walking after the bearer of holy water, shall go processionally through the midst of the quire for the blessing of the new fire, the members of the choir following him without change of habit. They shall proceed to a pillar on the south side of the church, close to the font, where the officiating priest shall bless the fire which is there to be kindled, in the middle between two columns. On the way there the Psalm, The Lord is my light [etc.], *is to be said, without note, and without* Glory be to the Father [etc.]

[. . .]

After the blessing of the incense a censer shall be filled with coals together with incense, and the new fire shall be censed. Then the taper of the spear alone shall be lit from the new fire, the other lights in the church having been first extinguished. Then the procession shall return to the quire in the accustomed order. While returning, two clerks of the second rank in surplices shall sing this Hymn, Thou leader kind, *etc. The first verse is to be repeated by the choir after each verse. While the aforesaid clerks sing their verse they are to be standing still, while the choir moves on; and while the choir is singing the first verse the clerks are to be moving forward. The same rule is to be observed when* Thou, the holy angels' king *is sung with its verses.*

(b)   Diagram from a Sarum Processional (1502) – the 'station' for the Blessing of the Paschal Candle

Processionale, fo. 70

This diagram, also from the Sarum *Processionale* of 1502, shows the positions of deacon (right) and subdeacon (left) (tonsured heads) on the steps of the quire,

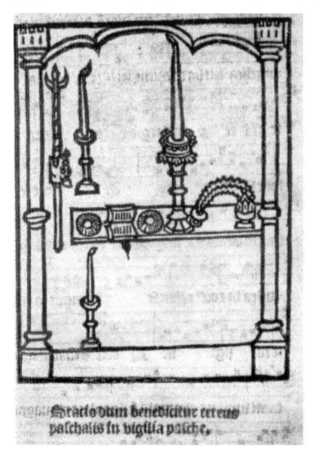

facing each other with the gospel book between them. On either side of them are the candle-bearers; behind the subdeacon is the candle carried on the decorative processional 'spear' and behind the deacon is the Paschal Candle on its stand and the *thurifer* [incense-bearer] (position marked with a censer).

(c) The Blessing of the Paschal Candle

Sarum Missal, cols. 337†–42

Then shall follow the Blessing of the Paschal Candle by the deacon, vested as for a procession, facing north, and standing at the step of the quire, accompanied by two candlebearers, one to his right, the other to his left, [both] turned towards him, and [holding] unlighted candles. The subdeacon shall stand opposite to him, and close to the bearer of the spear, turned [towards him] in the same way. The thurifer [incense-bearer] shall stand behind the deacon, while the deacon chants as follows:

Now let the angelic host of heaven exult, let the divine mysteries be celebrated with exultation, and let the trumpet of salvation sound for the victory of so great a King.

Let the earth rejoice, irradiated with so great brilliancy, and illuminated by the splendour of the eternal King, let it perceive the darkness of the universe to have been done away.

[. . .]

This is the night of which it was written, 'And night shall be light as the day', and, 'And night shall be light in my pleasures' [Ps. 139, 12 and 11].

Therefore, the hallowing of this night puts wickedness to flight, washes away sins, and restores innocence to the fallen, and joy to the sorrowful; it banishes hatred, and prepares peace, and makes sovereignties yield.

Therefore, in favour of this night, receive, O holy Father, the evening sacrifice of this incense,

Here the deacon shall put incense into the candle or into the candlestick in the form of a cross; and in the same way into the small candle, the bearer approaching [with it].

Which the holy church offers to thee by the hands of her ministers in this solemn oblation of wax, the work of the bee.

But now we know the praise of the pillar, which the glowing fire kindles to the honour of God.

At this point the candle shall be lit from the new fire, and not be extinguished till after Compline on the day following. And the Paschal candle shall burn continuously throughout Easter week at Matins, and at Mass, and at Vespers; and likewise on the Octave of Easter. But on all Sundays from the Octave of Easter until the Ascension of the Lord it shall be lit at Mass only, as well as on the feasts of St Mark the Evangelist, and SS Philip and James the Apostles. On the Annunciation of the Blessed Mary, and on the Invention of the Holy Cross it shall be lighted as on the Octave of Easter.

Here the candle-bearers shall light their candles throughout the church.

(d)   The Blessing of the Font

Sarum Missal, cols. 353–4

Wherefore, I bless thee, O creature of water,[1] by the living ✠[2] God, by the true ✠ God, by the holy ✠ God, by the God who in the beginning did divide thee by his word from the dry land, whose Spirit moved upon thee, who made thee flow out of paradise, and commanded thee to water the whole earth in four rivers:

Here shall the priest cast water with his hand out of the font in the form of a cross into the four quarters.

Who, when thou wast bitter in the wilderness, infused sweetness into thee, and made thee fit to drink, and brought thee forth from the rock for the thirsty people.

I ble✠ss thee through Jesus Christ, his only son, our Lord, who in Cana of Galilee by a wonderful miracle through his own power changed thee into wine.

Who did walk upon thee with his feet, and baptized in thee by John in the river Jordan. who did bring thee forth out of his side together with blood, and commanded his disciples that believers should be baptised in thee saying, 'Go ye, teach all nations, baptising them in the name of the Father, and of the Son, and of the Holy Spirit'. *Here he shall change his tone, as if reading.* Do thou, almighty and merciful God, be present with us as we keep these precepts; do thou graciously breathe upon us. *Here he shall breathe upon the font three times in the form of a cross.* Do thou with thy mouth ble✠ss these clear waters, that beside their natural cleansing power over the bodies which may be washed therein, they may also be effectual to the purifying of souls [*mentibus*]. *Here he shall cause drops from the candle to fall into the font in the form of a cross, and then say:* Let the power of the Holy Spirit descend into the fulness of this font, and make the whole substance of this water fruitful in regenerating power. *Here he shall dip the candle into the middle of the font, making the sign of the cross, and then proceed*: Here let the stains of all sins be blotted out; here let nature, formed after thine own image, and reformed to the honour of its author, be cleansed from all the filthiness of the old man; *here the candle shall be taken out of the font with these words*: that every man that approaches this sacrament of regeneration may be born again into a new infancy of true innocence. Through our Lord Jesus Christ, thy Son. Who lives and reigns with thee, in the unity of the Holy Spirit, God. For ever and ever. Amen.

[. . .]

[1.] What follows gathers together a wide-ranging number of references to water in Old and New Testaments: the creation of the world, the feeding of the Israelites in the desert, the miracle at Cana, the walking on the water and the Crucifixion.

[2] At this and subsequent points in the Blessing the sign of the cross is made.

PROPS AND COSTUMES

The majority of costumes used in the Holy Week ceremonies are liturgical vestments and the majority of props, ceremonial items in normal church use. Both help to formalise and aggrandise the ceremonies, most of all those which are central to Christian belief, like the cross, or are sacramental mysteries, the host. The colour of vestments is usually determined liturgically – throughout western Europe red, for instance, is the usual colour for Good Friday and white at Easter, though there are local variations. Sometimes simply the best vestments are called for, regardless of colour. Candles, censers, crosses, processional banners are all in general use, but the sepulchre, the 'setting' for the burial of the cross and for the Easter ceremonies, is a specific construction [see **B11(a)**, **(b)**]. Sometimes it is a permanent building within the church (as at Aquileia and Konstanz) or an ornamented recess (Lincoln), sometimes a structure made for the occasion, almost invariably consisting of a wooden frame and curtaining but occasionally involving carved figures and banners, metalwork and decorative features and possibly even stonework. References to props and costumes appear throughout the various instructions for the services. These references can be filled out sometimes by existing objects or structures, sometimes by allusions in wills, accounts etc. [see **B7(i)**, **(ii)**, **(iii)**, **(iv)**, **(v)**].

B7   Accounts for preparations: Palm Sunday and Good Friday

(i) Accounts for Palm Sunday preparations: St Mary at Hill, London

London City Church, pp. 130, 198, 354, 382

1487–8	Item, for box, palm, flowers and consecrated wafers used on Palm Sundays	8d.
1493–4	Item, for Parys and another man for making the churchyard clean and setting up the scaffold over the porch on the eve of Palm Sunday	6d.
1530–1	Paid for paper for the prophets on Palm Sunday in their hands	1d.
	Paid for cloths [elsewhere 'cloths of Arras'] for the tower on Palm Sunday	12d.
	Paid for wigs, beards and costumes on Palm Sunday	12d.
1539–40	Paid for bread and drink for the prophets on Palm Sunday	1½d.

(ii) Accounts for Good Friday preparations: St Edmunds, Salisbury

Churchwardens' Accounts, pp. 9–10, 11

1462–3	And in making 32 lbs of staples and bars of iron for the sepulchre of the Lord from true iron	2s 8d.
	[. . .] And to a carpenter for making the post of the sepulchre, including [cost of] timber for it	6d.
	[. . .] And for painting various necessary [things] related to the sepulchre	4d.
	And for washing four albs, two cloths and one linen sheet for the sepulchre, and mending one torn alb,	7d.

1468–9   And in candles bought and used in the work of the aforesaid
sepulchre   1d.
[...] And to John Rush, turner, for making forty-seven pegs of
beech and ash for the stand above the sepulchre for wax burning
there   18d.
And to William Eglys, mason, for his work on the sepulchre   6d.
[...]

(iii) Accounts for Good Friday preparations: St Mary at Hill, London

London City Church, pp. 63, 233–4, 296; 51; 343; 53

1426–7   First, paid for the sepulchre for diverse nails and wires and glue   9½d.
1498–9   Item, for mending the monstrance for the sacrament   16d.
Item, for watching the sepulchre and the church, to four men   12d.
Item, for bread and ale to them that watched   Sum 6d.
1517–18   Paid for a wainscot for the sepulchre   10d.
Paid for a new board and nails for the sepulchre   4d.
1553   [Inventory of church goods surrendered or still in the church]
Handed over: a painted cloth that went around the sepulchre
[an earlier entry, 1527–8, records: paid for an ell of fine linen
to mend the sepulchre cloth where it had been eaten by rats,   12d.]
[...]
Item, more in the rood loft; a long chest with the frame of the
sepulchre in it.

(iv) Good Friday: St Stephen, Coleman St., London

Pamela Sheingorn, *The Easter Sepulchre in England*, Kalamazoo, 1987, p. 237

1466   Item, the Resurrection of Our Lord with the device in his chest to put
the sacrament in
[...]
Item, 1 canopy painted with a sun of gold to hang over the sepulchre
at Easter
Item, 1 sepulchre gilded over, with 1 frame to be set up with 4 posts, and
cresting with it
[...]
Item, 4 angels to be set on the posts with 4 censers, 2 gilded and 2 not
gilded
Item, 4 great angels to be set up on the sepulchre with various small
angels
Item, 2 cloths painted with the apostles and prophets, embroidered in
gold, with the Creed
Item, 8 banners embroidered in gold [thread] to be put around the sep-
ulchre, with various small pennons
Item, 4 knights to be set on the posts in front of the entrance

Item, 1 angel to be put at the entrance
[. . .]

(v) The Image of Christ at Lincoln

'Inventories', p. 4

Item: 1 image of Christ of silver-gilt with an opening or cavity [*aperta seu vacua*] in the chest for placing the sacrament at the time of the Resurrection, standing on 6 lions; and it has 1 beryl and 1 halo at the back of the head and a cross in its hand, by weight 37 ounces.

COMMENTS OF A SIXTEENTH-CENTURY REFORMER

The Protestant reformers' comments sometimes clarify or expand the information contained in texts or records, albeit reflecting the latest versions of the ceremonies and from an extremely biassed point of view. The German Thomas Kirchmayer or Kirchmair was the author of a virulent attack on Catholic ceremonies, the *Regnum papisticum* of 1553. It was translated into English by Barnaby Googe as *The Popish Kingdome, or reigne of Antichrist*, 1570. Some of the comments on the ceremonies of Palm Sunday and Good Friday are printed below in modernised spelling from Googe's translation [see above **B2(d)** for the *Palmesel*; see also **B34**, **J11**, **J33**, **J47**, **J61**].

B8   A Protestant testimony
(a)   Palm Sunday – the *Palmesel*

Young, vol. 1, p. 532

Here comes that worthy day wherein our Saviour Christ is thought
To come into Jerusalem on ass's shoulders brought;
Whenas again these papists fond [foolish], their foolish pageants have
With pomp and great solemnity and countenance wondrous grave.
A wooden ass they have, and image great that on him rides,
But underneath the ass's feet a table broad there slides,
Being borne on wheels, which ready dressed [prepared], and all things meet
    therefore,
The ass is brought abroad [into the open] and set before the church's door.

(b)   Good Friday – Adoration and Burial of the Cross

Young, vol. 1, p. 534

Two priests, the next day following, upon their shoulders bear
The image of the crucifix about the altar near,
Being clad in cope of crimson dye, and dolefully they sing.
At length before the steps his [the cross's] coat plucked off they straight him
    bring,
And upon turkey carpets lay him down full tenderly,

With cushions underneath his head and pillows heaped high.
Then flat upon the ground they fall and kiss both hand and feet
And worship so this wooden God, with honour far unmeet [quite inappropriate].
[. . .]
And after them the simple souls, the common people, come
And worship him with diverse gifts, as gold and silver some,
And others corn or eggs again to poll-shorn [shaven-headed] persons sweet.
[. . .]
Another image do they get, like one but newly dead,
With legs stretched out in length and hands upon his body spread,
And him with pomp and sacred song they bear unto his grave,
His body all being wrapped in lawn [fine linen] and silks and sarcenet brave
    [showy soft silk]
The boys before with clappers go, and filthy noises make,
[. . .]
And lest in grave he should remain without some company
The singing-bread [the host] is laid with him, as falleth to his turn,
And frankincense and sweet perfumes, before the bread doth burn [. . .]

III   The ceremonies of Easter Week

The liturgical ceremony which expanded most and which was repeated through-out western Europe, lasting in places well beyond the medieval period, was that representing the discovery of Christ's Resurrection on Easter Day, the *Visitatio sepulchri.* The earliest texts date from the tenth century, and from the latter part of that century come some of the fullest instructions for the ceremony. One of these, the *Regularis concordia,* a monastic rule from tenth-century England, contains a description of the *Visitatio* [**B9(b)**], and also incorporates a description of the burial of the cross on Good Friday, thus giving some information about the nature of the sepulchre [see **B9(a)**].

The basic interchange between the angel(s) and the Maries was expanded in a variety of ways by the addition of new scenes and characters: the Harrowing of Hell, the informing of Peter and John and their race to the sepulchre, the non-scriptural episode of the spice merchant (*unguentarius/mercator*) from whom the Maries buy their ointments to anoint Christ's body, the appearance of Christ himself to Mary Magdalene and the other two Maries, and the setting of the sol-diers to watch the sepulchre. There is no simple chronological expansion here in content or in staging; some quite complex sequences are early, some simple dia-logues occur late in the period.

The position(s) of the angels in relation to the sepulchre depend to some extent on the position of the sepulchre itself – one at the head, one at the foot of the tomb; one at the left, one at the right of the altar; one behind the altar so that the dia-logue takes place across it. The sepulchre may be anything from a full-sized struc-ture capable of being entered [**B11(b)**] to a construction of books on the altar, as at Narbonne [**B14(iii)**]. The Maries may be played by women if the ceremony is under the auspices of a nunnery or a double-monastery [**B10**]. The angels may have wings [**B12(iv)**, **B13(iv)**, **(v)**]; the costumes may cease to be liturgical; the congregation may join in [**B15**].

The series of ceremonies from Barking Abbey, a Benedictine house of nuns, is important for its 'staging' information [see **B10**]. It also illustrates a planned group of events (devised by Katherine of Sutton, the abbess of Barking from 1363 to 1376) centring on the sepulchre, and demonstrates some of the developments of the basic *Quem queritis* exchange that took place at various times, early and late, in the Middle Ages. The major addition here is the prelude to the *Visitatio sepulchri*, the Harrowing of Hell, but there are also developments within the *Visitatio* itself: the somewhat compressed appearance of Christ to both Mary Magdalene and the three Maries together, and the conversation with the disciples (the development of the sequence *Victime Paschali*). There is, however, no running of Peter and John to the sepulchre, or any buying of ointments from the spice merchant, or a setting of the watch.

Notable in the burial section is the detachable image of Christ, which is taken from the cross, and the washing of the wounds [**B10**; cf **B7(iv)**].

Though much of the text used is from the Holy Week and Easter liturgy, some parts are from elsewhere and some were apparently freely composed.

B9   Passages from the *Regularis concordia*
(a)   The Good Friday *Depositio*
Symons, pp. 44–5

Now because on that day we celebrate the burial of the body of Our Saviour, we have laid down in this way the practice of certain religious [which is] worthy of imitation for strengthening the faith of unlearned lay people and neophytes, to be followed in a similar manner if the show is to be made for them or such a thing be thought appropriate.

To one side of the altar, where there is room, let there be a sepulchre-like struc-ture and a curtain stretched around it in which, when the holy cross has been adored, it may be placed in this way. Let the deacons come who have previously carried it and wrap it in fine linen in the place where it was adored; then let them carry it singing the antiphons [. . .] until they come to the place of the monument. Once the cross is laid down there, like the burial of the body of our Lord Jesus Christ, let them sing [. . .]. In that same place let the holy cross be guarded with all reverence until the Lord's night of the Resurrection. And at night let two or three or more brothers be chosen, if the community is large enough, who may keep faithful watch, singing psalms.

(b)   The *Visitatio sepulchri*
Symons, pp. 49–50

While the third lesson is being said, let four brothers dress themselves, one of whom, dressed in an alb, as if for another purpose, shall enter and secretly go to the place of the sepulchre and there, holding a palm in his hand, sit quietly. And while the third respond is being spoken the remaining three shall follow, all dressed in copes, having censers with incense in their hands, and hesitantly, as if seeking something, shall come to the place of the sepulchre. These things are done in imi-tation of the angel sitting in the monument, and of the women coming with spices to anoint the body of Jesus. When, therefore, the one sitting there shall see the three as it were wandering and seeking something, he shall begin in a low voice to sing sweetly: 'Whom do you seek [*Quem queritis*] [in the sepulchre, companions of Christ?'] When this is sung to the end, the three shall reply with one voice: 'Jesus of Nazareth [the crucified one, O heavenly being.'] To which he [replies]: 'He is not here. He has risen as He foretold. Go, announce that He has risen from the dead.' At the sound of this command the three turn to the choir, saying: 'Alleluia. The Lord has risen.' This said, he who is sitting, as if calling them back, says this anti-phon: 'Come and see the place [where the Lord was laid, alleluia.'] Saying this, let him rise and lift up the covering and show them the place, with no cross, but with the linen cloth there in which the cross had been wrapped. When they have seen this let them put down their censers which they brought into the sepulchre, and pick up the linen cloth and open it out before the clergy and, as if showing that the Lord had arisen and was no longer wrapped in it, they sing this antiphon: 'The Lord has arisen from the sepulchre [he who hung for us on the wood [of the cross], alleluia!]

When the antiphon is finished let the prior, rejoicing in the triumph of our King, that having overcome death, He had risen, begin the hymn *Te Deum laudamus* [O God, we praise thee]; at the beginning of which all the bells shall ring together.

B10   The Easter ceremonies from Barking Abbey

Young, vol. I, pp. 164–6, 381–4, and plate x; *Staging*, pp. 226–9

When, however, the holy cross has been adored, the priests, raising the cross from the aforesaid place, shall begin the antiphon 'Above all the cedar trees [you alone excel on whom hung the life of the world, on whom Christ was victorious and death overcame death.]', and with the choir following they shall all sing it together, the cantrix [female cantor] beginning. They shall carry the cross to the high altar and there, as though they were [*in specie*] Joseph and Nicodemus, taking down the image from the cross [*de ligno*], they shall wash the wounds of the Crucified [*crucifixi*] with wine and water. While they are doing this, the convent shall join in the responsory 'Behold how the just [man] dies [and no one feels it in his heart: the just men are killed and no-one heeds it: the just man is killed by the working of evil and his memory shall be in peace.]' the priest beginning, the cantrix replying and the convent joining them. After washing the wounds, they shall bear it [the image] with candles and censer to the sepulchre, singing these antiphons: 'In peace itself [I shall sleep and rest.]'; 'He shall dwell [in your taber-nacle: he shall rest in your holy mountain]'; 'My flesh [shall rest in hope]'. And when they have placed it reverently in the aforesaid place, fittingly decorated with a covering of hangings, with a pillow also [*tapetum palleo auriculari quoque*], and with most beautiful linen cloths, the priest shall close the sepulchre and begin the responsory 'The Lord being buried [the sepulchre was sealed]'. And then the abbess shall offer a candle which shall burn continually in front of the sepulchre, and shall not be extinguished until the image, taken from the sepulchre after Matins on the night of Easter with candles, incense, and procession, shall be put back in its place. And so, these things being done, the convent shall return to the quire and the priest to the vestry.

[. . .]

Note that according to an ancient ecclesiastical custom the Resurrection of the Lord was celebrated before Matins and before any ringing of a bell on Easter Day. And since the congregation of the people in those times seemed to cool in devotion, and human torpor greatly increasing, the worthy lady, lady Katherine of Sutton, then being responsible for their pastoral care, desiring to get rid of the said torpor completely and the more to excite the devotion of the faithful towards such a renowned celebration, ordered with the unanimous consent of the sisters that immediately after the third responsory of Matins on Easter Day the celebration of the Lord's Resurrection should take place; and the procedures were established in this way.

First the lady abbess shall go with all the convent and with certain priests and clerks dressed in copes, and with each priest and clerk carrying in his hand a palm and an unlit candle. They shall enter the chapel of St Mary Magdalene, signifying the souls of the holy Fathers descending into Hell before the coming of Christ; and they shall shut the door of the aforesaid chapel on themselves. Then the officiating priest, dressed in alb and cope, coming to the said chapel with two deacons, one carrying a cross with the Lord's banner hanging from the top, the other carrying a censer in his hand, and with other priests and clerks with two boys carrying candles, approaching the door of the said chapel, shall begin three times this antiphon: 'Raise your gates, [princes, and be lifted up, you eternal gates]'. This priest indeed shall represent the person of Christ about to descend to Hell and break down the gates of Hell. And the aforesaid antiphon shall be begun at each repetition in a louder voice which the clerks repeat the same number of times, and at the beginning, each time, he shall beat with the cross at the aforesaid door, signifying the breaking down of the gates of Hell. And at the third knock, the door shall open. Then he shall go in with his ministers.

Meanwhile a certain priest being inside the chapel shall begin the antiphon 'From the gates of hell, [O Lord, rescue my soul]', which the cantrix shall take up, with the whole community: 'O Lord, rescue etc.' Then the officiating priest shall lead out all those who were inside the aforesaid chapel, and in the meantime the priest shall begin the antiphon 'O Lord, thou hast taken out [my soul]', and the cantrix shall follow: 'From hell'. Then all shall go out from the chapel, that is, from the Limbo of the Fathers, and the priests and clerks shall sing the antiphon 'When the king of Glory' in a procession through the middle of the quire to the sepulchre, each one carrying a palm and a candle, signifying victory recovered from the enemy, with the lady abbess, the prioress, and all the convent following, as if they are the early Fathers [sicut sunt priores].

And when they have reached the sepulchre, the officiating priest shall cense and enter the sepulchre, beginning the verse 'He rises'. Then the cantrix shall follow with:

> 'Christ from the tomb,
>> [The victor returns from the pit
>> Thrusting down the tyrant in chains
>> And unlocking Paradise']
>
> The verse: 'We ask, creator [of all,
>> In this joyous Easter,
>> From every attack of death,
>> Defend your people'.]
>
> The verse: 'Glory be to thee, Lord,
>> [Who has arisen from the dead,
>> With Father and Holy Spirit,
>> World without end']

And meanwhile he shall carry out the body of the Lord [the host] from the sepulchre, beginning the antiphon 'Christ rising' in front of the altar with his face turned to the people, holding the body of the Lord enclosed in crystal in his hands. Then the cantrix shall join in with 'from the dead'. And with the said antiphon they shall make a procession to the altar of the Holy Trinity in solemn state, namely with censers and candles. The community shall follow singing the aforesaid antiphon with the verse 'Let them say now', and the versicle: 'Say to the nations'. Prayer: 'God, who for us your son'. And this procession shall signify [*figuratur*] in what way Christ proceeded after the Resurrection into Galilee with his disciples following.

These things having been performed, three sisters selected by the lady abbess shall come forward, and, having taken off their black vestments in the chapel of the Blessed Mary Magdalene, they shall put on most beautiful surplices, snow-white coverings being placed on their heads by the lady abbess. Thus prepared, therefore, and bearing silver jars in their hands, they shall say their confession [*Confiteor*] to the abbess, and, absolved by her, they shall take their stand in the appointed place with candles. Then she who represents the person [*speciem pretendit*] of Mary Magdalene shall sing this verse: 'At one time of God'.[1] And when that is finished, the second who signifies [*prefigurat*] Mary Jacobi shall reply with the second verse: 'Drawing near, therefore, alone'. The third Mary, having the part [*vicem optinens*] of Salome, shall sing the third verse: 'I am allowed to go with you'. After proceeding to the quire, they shall sing these verses together, with weeping and humble voice: 'Alas [how many sighs beat on] the hearts within us [for our consoler, of whom we miserable ones are deprived; whom the cruel people of the Jews gave over to death]'. These verses ended, Magdalene alone shall say [*dicat*] this verse: 'Alas, miserable one, [why has it happened [that we] see the death of the

saviour?]' Jacobi shall reply: 'Alas, our consolation, [why did he suffer death?]'
Salome: 'Alas, redemption of Israel, [why did he wish to undergo such things?]'
In the fourth verse they shall all join together thus:

> 'Now, now, lo, [now let us hasten to the tomb,
> The chosen ones anointing the most holy body.]

Then the Maries going out from the choir together shall say [*dicant*]:

'Alas, who has rolled away [the stone for us from the mouth of the monument?']

When, however, they have come to the sepulchre, a clerk dressed in a white stole
shall be seated before the sepulchre, representing [*gerens figuram*] the angel who
rolled the stone from the mouth of the monument and sat upon it, who shall say
this: 'Whom do you seek [*Quem queritis*] in the sepulchre, O companions of Christ?'
The women shall reply: 'We seek Jesus of Nazareth'. The angel shall answer' 'He is
not here, he has risen'. And when he has said, 'Come and see', they shall go into
the sepulchre and kiss the place where the Crucified one was laid. Mary Magdalene
meanwhile shall take the sudary [napkin] which was over his head, and shall
carry it with her. Then another clerk in the person [*in specie*] of the other angel
sitting in the sepulchre shall say to Magdalene: 'Woman, why do you weep?' She
shall answer [*subiungat*]: 'Because they have taken my Lord away.' Then the two
angels joining together shall say to the women: 'Why do you seek the living among
the dead, etc.'

Then they still doubting the Resurrection of the Lord shall say mourning to
each other: 'Alas, misery etc.' Then Mary Magdalene sighing shall join in with: 'I
sigh for you etc.' Then on the left-hand side of the altar the *Persona*[2] shall appear,
saying to her: 'Woman why do you weep, whom do you seek?' She, thinking him
to be a gardener, shall reply: 'Lord, if you have carried him away etc.' The *Persona*
shall answer: 'Maria.' Then she, recognising him, shall prostrate herself at his feet
saying: 'Raboni.' The *Persona*, however, drawing back shall say: 'Do not touch me,
etc.' When the *Persona* has disappeared, Mary shall communicate her joy to her
companions with joyful voice singing these verses: 'Rejoice and be happy etc.'
When these are ended the *Persona* shall appear to the three women together on the
right of the altar saying: 'Hail, do not be afraid, etc.' Then, prostrate on the ground,
they shall hold his feet and kiss them. Which done, one after another they shall
sing these verses, Mary Magdalene beginning: 'Jesus the Nazarene etc.' These
verses being finished, the Maries standing on the step before the altar turning to
the people shall sing this response: 'Alleluia, the Lord has risen from the sepulchre',
with the choir replying to them.

When these are ended, priests and clerks representing [*in figuram*] the disciples
of Christ shall come foward saying: 'O people hard-hearted.' Then one of them
shall approach and say to Mary Magdalene: 'Tell us Mary etc.' She shall reply: 'The
sepulchre of Christ [living and the glory of the risen one I have seen], Angelic witnesses, [the sudary and the clothes]'. With her finger she shall point out the place
where the angel was sitting, and shall hold out the sudary for them to kiss, adding

this verse: 'Christ our hope has risen, [he has preceded us into Galilee.]' Then these final verses shall be added by the disciples and choir: 'It is to be believed [rather by the truth of Mary alone than by a crowd of Jews.'] and 'We know Christ [has truly risen from the dead; pity us, victorious king!']³

Then Magdalene shall begin 'Christ rising', with the clergy and choir joining in at the same time. These ended, the hymn 'O God, we praise thee' [*Te Deum laudamus*] shall be solemnly chanted, the priest beginning. And meanwhile the aforementioned priests putting their ordinary clothes on again in the chapel, crossing through the quire with candles, shall approach the sepulchre to give thanks and make a short prayer there. Then they shall return to their station [*stacionem*] until the abbess shall order them to go out to rest.

¹ Where the *incipit* is not expanded the verse is, according to Young, not known from elsewhere and may have been composed especially for the Barking Abbey ceremony.

² *Persona* not *Jesus* or *Christus* is used for Christ throughout. Given the care with which words are chosen to describe taking a part in this ceremony, it is possible that the word was chosen specifically to identify the performer as 'mask' or 'presenter' of Christ. But it may simply refer to Christ as one of the 'Persons' of the Trinity. Engelberg (fourteenth-century ms) uses '*Dominica persona*'; Rouen (fourteenth-century ms), '*sacerdos canonicus in persona Domini*' to describe the role but '*sacerdos*' as a speaker's name; Mont St Michel (fourteenth-century ms) uses '*Deus*' for both purposes; and Cividale (fourteenth-century ms) '*Yhesus/lhesus*'.

³ From 'Tell us, Mary, etc.' onwards the Latin pieces are all part of the Easter sequence *Victime Paschali* [see also **B15(iii) Diessen** and **B17 Palma**].

B11 The Easter Sepulchre
(a) Tomb of Christ in Lincoln Cathedral, *c.* 1300
The Conway Library, Courtauld Institute of Art; pr. Sekules, plates XXIVC and XXVA

The elaborately sculptured monument to the north of the high altar in Lincoln Cathedral is the earliest of the large structures in Yorkshire, Lincolnshire and Nottinghamshire now usually referred to as Easter Sepulchres. It forms part of an arcaded recess of six bays; the western three are a tomb (perhaps that of the founder of the Cathedral, St Remigius), and the eastern three form the Easter Sepulchre, with the sleeping figures of three soldiers carved beneath. It is impossible to be certain how the sepulchres were used in the Easter ceremonies but it seems likely that they played a supporting role to the temporary structures of wood and cloth, perhaps representing the 'shelf' of the sepulchre in Jerusalem on which Christ's body was said to have been placed. Some may have doubled as elaborate 'houses' for the reserved host which needed secure storage, and therefore through their decoration served as reminders throughout the year of the risen Christ (Sekules, pp. 118–31). That at Hawton (Nottinghamshire), for example, besides being elaborately decorated with Ascension images, and containing Resurrection figures, has also an inner cavity, an 'aumbry', in which the reserved host could have been placed.

This at Lincoln, however, contains no inner cavity and seems to have served simply as a sepulchre. In the records of the cathedral there is listed, besides the image of Christ [see **B7(iv)**]: 'a white cloth of damask silk for the sepulchre painted with the Passion and Resurrection of Our Lord' (Inventories, p. 38).

(b)   The Easter Sepulchre at Konstanz, late thirteenth century

The Conway Library, Courtauld Institute of Art

The Easter Sepulchre (*heilige Grab*) at Konstanz is a free-standing, sandstone building in the middle of the chapel of St Maurice (*Mauritiuskapelle*), itself a rotunda built in the tenth century in imitation of the Holy Sepulchre in Jerusalem. Some traces of vivid colour and gilding survive. It is twelve-sided with an entrance on one side. Around the top, between the crocketted gables, are figures of the apostles. Below them, scenes from the Annunciation to the Nativity appear. On the top of the conical roof, now empty, stood the figure of a prophet (as shown in Young's Plate VIII), possibly replacing an earlier angel. Inside there are two scenes: the three Maries with the spice merchant, and the three Maries with the soldiers at the tomb.

The sepulchre is first mentioned in 1317 and stylistically seems to date from the late thirteenth century. A later Konstanz liturgy shows that, at least at that time, it was used during the Easter ceremonies for the burial of the Host. An indulgence for those visiting the image of Christ in his tomb on Good Friday and Holy Saturday dating from the thirteenth century possibly suggests that there was an early wooden tomb and effigy of Christ.

PRESENTING THE EASTER CEREMONIES

The presentation of the *Visitatio sepulchri* varies according to place, time and individual choice. The variation in the form of the sepulchre [see **B11(a)**, **(b)**, **B14(iv)**], the layout of the church, the auspices – monastic or secular clergy; cathedral, monastery or parish church – all affect the form the ceremony took. Sound is clearly important, but light too, bearing in mind the earliness of the hour of performance, can be used to striking effect. Costume is mainly liturgical but special costumes are sometimes indicated for the soldiers who guard the sepulchre (e.g. 'four armed clerics' in fifteenth-century Coutances, Young, vol. i, p. 408), for the Maries, the angels, and for Christ at Mont St Michel [**B13(vi)**]. There are also considerable differences in the use made of the consecrated host [**B10**, **B12(v)**, **(vi)**]. The following are some examples from a wide geographical area illustrating this variety.

B12   Easter ceremonies: special effects, setting and movement

(i) Udine, fourteenth century

Young, vol. I, p. 298

All the bells ring together as in the peal for the dead; but in the end they do not remain together but [ring] as in other feasts. One peal finished, let clergy and people be ready in the church for making the Easter procession [*ad processionem albam faciendam*] with surplices [and] albs [or 'with white surplices'], each holding a candle burning in his hand [. . .] And when the procession, formed up, shall enter the church, let there be two boys hidden in some high place within the church and let them sing this verse in a high register: '*Quem queritis.*'

(ii) Coutances, fifteenth century

Young, vol. I, p. 408

Which done, two boys dressed in rochets shall come to the monument carrying two stripped rods [*duas virgas decorticatas*] on which should be ten candles burning; and immediately when they shall have drawn near to the sepulchre, the aforesaid soldiers shall fall down as if dead, and they shall not rise until *Te Deum* is begun.

(iii) Tours, thirteenth century

Young, vol. I, p. 439

Then an angel shall come and shall throw lightning at them; the soldiers shall fall to the earth as if dead.

(iv) Padua, thirteenth century

Young, vol. I, p. 294

[. . .] the bishop shall stand next to the monument in the body of the church. And, the responsory being at an end, the Master of scholars or the cantor goes down from the altar of the Holy Cross and leads three scholars dressed like women, who signify the three Maries coming to the sepulchre of Christ with ointments and spices [. . .] And they cross singing through the quire of the clergy till they come before the altar of St Daniel. And two scholars like angels, with wings and with lilies ready in their hands, stand above near the sepulchre of Christ [. . .] And then the said Maries go up by steps/ladders [*scalis*] on the south side to the sepulchre of Christ. The angels descend by steps/ladders on the north side. And the said Maries, diligently lifting the covering, searching here and there in the sepulchre, and not having found the body of Christ, take the covering as testimony of Christ's resurrection, and descend with the said covering by the steps/ladders by which the angels descended and come to the entrance of St Daniel, next to the chancel; and holding up the covering, shall sing this antiphon.

(v) Parma, no date

Young, vol. I, p. 300

Before the beginning of Matins two *guarda-chorii* [? leaders of the choir] and two cantors with copes [*pivialibus* for *pluvialibus*] shall reverently enter the sepulchre of the Lord with censers and incense, two candles being placed before the mouth of the sepulchre. And, censing the sepulchre, they seek for the body of Christ [the host] (which the sacrist on watch, before this happens, should have removed from there and shut away reverently in the appointed '*sacrarium*') and they touch the clean linen cloths, in which it was wrapped. Not finding it, they return to the mouth of the sepulchre, not however going outside, but, turning towards the high altar near which shall be certain clerks, they say: 'Whom do you seek?' [*Quem queritis.*]

(vi) Soissons, late twelfth century – early thirteenth century

Young, vol. I, pp. 624–5

When the gospel is finished, a subdeacon should take it [the Gospel book] and, as if secretly, carry it under his chasuble (as if in his breast) to the sepulchre, a young clerk going in front with incense. And they shall both return after placing it on the altar which is in the sepulchre.

[. . .]

Very early in the morning all the bells shall ring; then two by two. Finally they all ring together again. Meanwhile the floor of the presbytery and choir shall be strewn with ivy and with other green foliage, and the church shall be decked, throughout, from top to bottom, with lighted candles. The high altar, with an increased number of candles, shall be surrounded in light. The number of candles around and in front of the altar should be eighty, and a cord be stretched overhead [*a capite usque ad pedes*] on which an iron ring with seven candles in it shall hang above the entrance to the sepulchre. This ring, which is called by us 'the star', represents the true Lucifer, who rose in the morning. In addition ten candles shall burn around the crucifix. At the beginning of all these [ceremonies] a clerk in a surplice appointed for the purpose, shall carry the Body of the Lord reserved on Maundy Thursday in a small container, with the utmost honour to the sepulchre, placing it on the altar.

B13   Easter ceremonies: costume

(i) St Blaise monastery, fourteenth century

Young, vol. I, p. 260

[. . .] Meanwhile two priests [representing the Maries] dress themselves in copes, taking two censers, and place amices over their heads [. . .]

(ii) Fritzlar, fifteenth century

Young, vol. i, p. 257

Then three scholars, dressed in silk copes or in women's costume, coming near the sepulchre with censers and candles lit, reply singing: [. . .]

(iii) Fécamp, fourteenth century

Young, vol. i, p. 264

One [of the Maries] in a red cope shall carry a censer between two others, and the other two on either side of her in white dalmatics shall carry containers like boxes.

(iv) Narbonne, fifteenth century

Young, vol. i, p. 285

There should be two boys above the altar [as the angels], dressed in albs and amices with violet stoles and red gauze over their faces, and wings on their shoulders, who say: 'Quem queritis.'

(v) Besançon, St John Evangelist, fourteenth century

Young, vol. i, p. 290

Three canons or three members of the community [. . .] for playing [faciendum] the Maries [. . .] ought to have head-coverings on their heads so that they cover their foreheads, and white dalmatics and carrying in their hands gold or silver vials [. . .]

Meanwhile two boys should be got ready, led to right and left of the altar, with amices and albs and having wings on their shoulders, and over their shoulders, red stoles in the manner of deacons, holding (circumdantes) the wings on.

(vi) Mont St Michel, fourteenth century

Young, vol. i, pp. 372–3

At Matins of Easter before Te Deum laudamus the brother who shall be God [i.e. Christ] shall have a white habit stained as if with blood, with a halo [cum dyademate] and beard, and with bare feet. With a cross he shall pass through the quire at the end of the responsory and return to the vestry.

After the last responsory, the three who shall be the women, dressed in white dalmatics, having amices over their heads in the manner of matrons, carrying alabaster [jars], coming through the lower part of the quire towards the altar, shall sing: 'Who has rolled away?' He who shall be the angel shall be above the altar dressed in a white cope, holding a palm in his hand and having a crown on his head [. . .]

Two brothers in the sepulchre, who shall be the two angels, dressed in red copes, shall say: [. . .]

(vii) Fleury, thirteenth century

Young, vol. I, p. 394

To them an angel shall reply sitting outside at the head of the sepulchre, dressed in gold-adorned alb, head covered with a mitre without bands [*deinfulatis*] holding a palm in his left hand [and] a full branch of candles in his right.

B14   Easter ceremonies: the Sepulchre

(i) Châlons-sur-Marne, thirteenth century

Young, vol. I, p. 279

Two boys dressed in white clothing sitting by the altar, one to the right, the other to the left, like the two angels at the sepulchre of the Lord . . . the boys removing the white cloth like the *sudarium* from the altar, reply: 'He is not here' [*Non est hic*].

(ii) Metz, no date

Young, vol. I, p. 261

[Two deacons, as the Maries, 'dressed in white dalmatics', and carrying censers in their right hands and palms in their left approach the altar. The *Quem queritis* is spoken by two priests in chasubles behind the altar.] The two deacons standing by the 'horns' [front corners] of this altar meanwhile ought to cense the front part of the altar [– *Non est hic* etc. follows –] And meanwhile they [the priests] reveal a silver relic case which is on the altar by raising a *levamen* [? light cover] with two rods.

(iii) Narbonne, no date

Young, vol. I, p. 285

[After *Non est hic* etc.] They [the angels] raise with a cord a cloth which is over some silver books on the altar representing (*in figura*) the sepulchre.

(iv) Bamberg, sixteenth century

Young, vol. I, p. 323

Where it is to be noted that a place convenient for representing the sepulchre of Christ ought to be designed as a temple (or 'in the church' [*in templo*]), closed in with tapestry or hangings, in which, amongst other things, a linen cloth should lie, or a fine white *sudarium* [shroud], representing the grave-cloth [*sindone*] in which the dead body of Christ was wrapped, because he rose again, living, from the sepulchre leaving the grave-cloth there.

B15   Easter ceremonies: the people's part

(i) Nuremberg, thirteenth century

Young, vol. I, p. 401

[...] Here, returning from the sepulchre with the procession, they [Peter and John] go to the quire singing this antiphon: 'He has risen as the Lord said [...]', with the people meanwhile proclaiming '*Crist ist erstanden*' [Christ is risen].

(ii) Essen, fourteenth century

Young, vol. I, p. 334

[...] Then one of the apostles shall go up to the organ and facing the assembly shall call out thus: 'Thanks be to God.' He shall call this three times, first low, second higher, third very high and the convent shall reply to him the same number of times in the same way. When this is done the people shall sing the German song of the Resurrection.

(iii) Diessen, fifteenth century

Young, vol. I, p. 359

After this the organist begins: 'To the Easter sacrifice[...]': When the verse is completed let two cantors, raising the image [of the risen Christ], sing: '*Crist ist erstanden* [...].'[1] The organist 'sings': 'The Lamb redeems [...]'; the choir comes in with: 'Death and life'. The people sing, the cantor beginning: 'Alleluia, alleluia!' Organist: 'Tell us, Mary, [...]'; choir: 'Angelic [...]'; the people: 'Kyrieleyson'; organist: 'Believing [...]'; choir: 'We know Christ [...]';[2] the people: '*Wär er nit erstanden, die welt di wär zergangen.*' ['Had he not risen, the world would have been lost.']

[1] '*Crist ist erstanden*' is a vernacular German hymn found as early as the twelfth century.
[2] All the Latin *incipits* represent verses of the Easter sequence *Victime Paschali* a piece frequently incorporated into the *Visitatio* representing, as it does, a questioning of Mary Magdalene about her experience of the risen Christ.

(iv) Sixteenth-century Germany

Young, vol. I, p. 643

[After 'The Lord is risen from the sepulchre' etc.] And the trumpeters shall play the best song [*canticum*] they know, twice.

EASTER WEEK

The ceremony of the *Peregrinus* or *Peregrini* ('Pilgrim'/'Pilgrims'), which derives from the gospel reading at Matins and Mass on Easter Monday (Luke 24.13–35), was the commonest of the ceremonies of the week after Easter. It tells the story of the meeting between two disciples and the risen Christ on the way to Emmaus and their failure to recognise him. They address Christ as *'peregrinus'* (literally 'stranger' but in the Middle Ages usually 'pilgrim'), hence the title of the ceremony. Examples survive from all over western Europe, usually performed during Vespers on Easter Monday or Tuesday. The use, in some instances, of the host for bread and the altar for the table at the inn complicates the meaning.

The most obviously theatrical moment is the disappearance of Christ as he breaks the bread for the disciples and their subsequent realisation of his identity [**B16**]. The fullest indications of staging are provided in the Fleury collection [**B16(vi)**], where the episode is continued into later meetings with all the disciples.

From Palma Cathedral, Majorca, there comes a quite different ceremony on Easter Tuesday which centres on Mary Magdalene and the sequence *Victime Paschali*, and is accompanied by some remarkable stage effects [**B17**]. The manuscript from which it comes is early sixteenth century but the ceremony clearly existed at an earlier date, apparently with less elaborate stage effects. The director of the ceremony is called by various names, *ragent*, *custos*, *sacrista*, but appears to have been one and the same person.

B16   Staging the *Peregrinus*
(i) Bayeux, thirteenth century
Young, vol. 1, p. 690

In returning to the font [at Vespers on Easter Monday] a station is made in the middle of the church, and when all have settled down there a representation is made of how the Lord appeared to the two disciples going to Emmaus, who are called the Pilgrims [*Peregrini*]. When it is over the fourth antiphon shall be started again as before [. . .]

(ii) Rouen cathedral, thirteenth century
Young, vol. 1, pp. 461–2

[The procession to the font singing the psalm *In exitu* [Psalm 113] comes to a halt in the middle of the church.] Towards the end of the psalm two clerks [. . .] wearing tunicles and copes on top of them crosswise [*in transversum*], carrying staffs and wallets like pilgrims, shall enter the church by the right-hand west door and slowly come up to the procession. [They sing the hymn *'Jesu nostra redemptio'* ['Jesus, our redemption']]. And when they have sung as far as this place, *Nos tuo vultu saties* ['Content us with thy face'], then a priest dressed in alb and amice, barefoot, carrying a cross in his hands, shall enter the church through the left-hand west door and coming up to them with head bent shall suddenly stand between them. [When they reach 'Emmaus'] the priest steps back pretending to go on, and the pilgrims hurriedly following stop him as if inviting him to the inn, and, pointing out the town [*castellum*] with their staffs, [. . .] they lead him to the structure [*tabernaculum*] in the middle of the nave of the church made to look like the town of Emmaus. When they have gone up into it they shall sit at the table laid there, and the Lord, sitting between them, shall break the bread for them. In breaking the bread they recognise him and suddenly drawing back he vanishes from their sight [. . .]

(iii) Sicily, twelfth century

Young, vol. i, p. 460

And thus, holding the Pilgrim between them, they shall come to the altar. And there let a meal be prepared with bread and wine; and they shall sit, and he shall break the bread and give it to them, and after that he shall vanish from their sight. Then the disciples shall say: 'Were not our hearts burning within us when he spoke to us about Jesus on the way? [. . .] Why has our reason left us? Alleluia!'

(iv) Saintes, fourteenth century

Young, vol. i, p. 454

Then they sit and the Lord divides the host between them. And afterwards he vanishes from their sight, going into the concealed place [*opertum locum*]. And the pilgrims get up saying: 'Were not our hearts [. . .] Alleluia!'

(v) Padua, thirteenth century

Young, vol. i, p. 482

Here the pilgrims go out of the upper sacristy [*secrestia*], and Christ himself joins up with them, as is said here. And then two of the disciples of Christ, Cleophas and a certain other, go out of the upper sacristy dressed in cloaks, slavins [pilgrims' tunics] and carrying staffs like pilgrims; and the master of the scholars or cantor is with them, who keeps them safe from the pressure of the people. And then the Christ joins them, with slavin, staff and small wine-jar [*barisello vini*] like a pilgrim. And the disciples wish to go to the town called Emmaus and they do not recognise him, and go along lamenting, talking to each other about the achievement and death of Christ. And the Christ says to them: 'What are these discourses that you hold one with another?' And they follow the words of the gospels until they come to [the altar of] St Daniel. And then the Christ makes as if to go further. And they make him stay with them, because the day is drawing to a close. And he enters, and eats and drinks with them at (*supra*) the table prepared there, and they recognise him at the breaking of bread. And he vanishes from their sight. And then wafers are thrown down from the roof of the church and all who can catch them.

(vi) Fleury, thirteenth century

Young, vol. i, pp. 471–2

In making the likeness of the Lord's appearance in the form of a pilgrim, which is made on the third *feria* of Easter [Easter Tuesday] at Vespers, two dressed only in tunicles and copes (with their hoods concealed to look like cloaks), having hats on their heads and carrying staffs in their hands, shall come forward and sing in a lowish voice: 'Jesus, our redemption' [. . .]. while they are singing this another shall approach, like the Lord, carrying a wallet and a long palm, appointed just like a pilgrim, having a hat on his head, dressed in tunic and cloak, barefoot. He shall follow behind them secretly. [Their conversation follows.] These said, they shall go and sit in the seats prepared for this [ceremony], and water shall be offered them for washing their hands; the table then well prepared, upon which there shall be placed uncut bread and three wafers and a cup with wine. Taking the bread [and] raising it in his right hand he blesses it and breaks it into individual pieces singing: 'My peace [. . .]'. Then he gives the cup to one of them and says: 'These are the words [. . .]' These said, as they eat the wafers he leaves them secretly, as if they did not know. After a moment or two, [each] turning to his neighbour and not finding [Jesus] between them, they rise as if sad and leaving the table begin to search for him and walking slowly they say these verses in a high voice: 'Were not our hearts [. . .]'

AN EASTER TUESDAY CEREMONIAL FROM MAJORCA

One of the most detailed and graphic descriptions of an Easter Tuesday practice survives in a *consueta* from Palma Cathedral in Majorca dating from 1511, a more succinct version being preserved in an earlier manuscript. The ceremony incorporates the traditional angel at the tomb, who appears with a dramatic explosion, burning candles adorning his wings, but the principal focus is on the figure of Mary Magdalene and on the six or more choirboys representing the resurrected dead, who emerge from beneath the high altar and tumble down its steps. Mary's part includes lines from the Easter sequence *Victime Paschali laudes* employed elsewhere [see **B10**, **B15(iii)**].

B17   The Palma Mary Magdalene ceremony, sixteenth century

Donovan, pp. 133–4; *Staging*, pp. 263–4

In the morning, before the Hours begin, the sacristan [*ragent*] is to have all the *inproperis* [symbols of the Passion] of Jesus Christ brought to the high altar, as noted in the *consueta* [instructions for the ceremony] of Mary. And he is to have a costume for Mary made ready in the sacristy, that is an alb with apparels, and a dalmatic of green velvet, and a cloak made from a cope of crimson velvet. And the part of the said Mary is to be taken by a priest, chosen by the sacristan [*custos*], who is to give him a *cruat* for his pains. And the said sacristan is to choose a boy [*un fedri*] for the angel and give him one *sou*.

And when the priest goes to the altar to say Mass, the subdeacon is to bring the Veronica and the deacon is to bring the Gospel-book. And when the Mass has begun, Mary is to dress himself, and the angel likewise, [and] the angel is to make his way to the Chapel of the Trinity so that when it is his turn to sing he will be high in the galleries [*corradors*] on the Saint Gabriel['s Chapel] side. And when the Epistle is finished, the sacristan [*ragent*] with the said Mary and two altar-boys [*fedrins del altar*] in surplices, with the large silver candlesticks with white candles lit, shall leave the sacristy to go to the quire. And they are to leave the cathedral by the Mirador [entrance]. They are to enter the Cathedral [*la Seu*] by the doorway on the seaward side and stop near the entrance to the quire so that they cannot be seen from the quire. And the candles are to be relit if they have gone out. And as they are finishing the *Alleluia angelus Domini* [Alleluia, the angel of the Lord], the sacristan [*custos*] and Mary, with the boys in front, are to enter the quire. And at the top of the steps leading to the quire, between the seat of the Lord Bishop and [that] of the archdeacon, the Mary is to sing *Victime Paschali laudes* [Praises to the Easter sacrifice], and the choir is to take it up, and the said sacristan and the Mary with the others are to go through the quire on the Bishop's side. And they are to walk towards the high altar past the Chapel of St Eulalia. And before the high altar there is to be placed a stool [*escabell*] on which Mary is to stand, her face turned towards the choir. And the sacristan is to stand on Mary's right side, to read the *consueta*, and to hand the symbols [of the Passion] to the said Mary. And at one corner of the altar, on the side on which the sacristan [*sacrista*] is standing, there shall stand a boy [*escola*] to give the symbols to the sacristan. And the said sacristan shall give them to the Mary. And at the other corner of the said altar, there shall stand another boy to receive the said symbols from Mary's hand. And just inside the entrance to the quire shall stand the 12 priests with copes and staffs, who are to question the said Mary. And the sacristan [*custos*], reading the *consueta*, is to give the symbols to the said Mary as the *consueta* requires.

And when the point is reached where the Mary is to sing of the resurrection of the dead, there are to be beneath the high altar seven or eight boys, or as many as desired, dressed in albs and their heads covered with amices. And when the moment of the resurrection comes, they are to come out from under the altar, and roll down to the bottom step, and go to the sacristy.

And the angel is to be in the gallery. When the time for him to sing comes, he is to have his wings full of lighted candles. And when he comes out, there will be an explosion [*una bombarde*], or some such noise, to signal his appearance. And when he has sung, he is to withdraw, and after the ceremony [*consueta*] is over, the Mary with the sacristan [*ragent*] and the boys are to return to the sacristy to change. And they are to come down from the altar on the side of the Chapel of St Gabriel. And the Office is to continue.

IV   The ceremonies of the Christmas season

INTRODUCTION

The Christmas season provides a focus similar to Easter for a number of ceremonies with theatrical developments. *The Prophets* derives from a sermon thought in the Middle Ages to be by St Augustine, part of which appears as a reading at Matins during the seasons of Advent and Christmas. The section of the sermon used is that which calls upon the prophets (who include Virgil and the Erythræan Sibyl) to prove the godhead of Christ to the Jews.[1] The appearances of the prophets sometimes develop into short self-contained scenes (e.g. Balaam, Nebuchadnezzar) [see **B18(a)**, **(b)**, **(c)**]. In Catalonia, exceptionally, the Sibyl plays a major part, repeating the whole of her prophecy and often appearing outside the confines of *The Prophets* on Christmas Eve.[2]

The Shepherds [see **B19 (a)**, **(b)**] parallels and most probably derives from the *Visitatio* in its adaptation of the *Quem queritis* text, and centres on the visit of the shepherds to the new-born Christ in the crib, a prop which sometimes, particularly after the institution of the ceremony of the *presepe* by St Francis in 1223 **[B19(c)]**, develops a life of its own.

The most fruitful of the Christmas ceremonies were those at Epiphany (6 January) concerned with the visit of the Magi [see **B20(a)**, **(b)**, **B21**] and in particular with Herod and his wild rages **[B22(a)**, **(b)]**, together with the Slaughter of the Innocents **[B23]**. Also associated with the Christmas season were the ceremonies of topsy-turvydom. The best documented of these is the ceremony of the Boy Bishop (*episcopellus* in Latin) **[B24(a)**, **(b)**, **(c)**, **(d)]** who was often elected on St Nicholas' Day (6 December) but whose 'reign' is usually on Holy Innocents (28 December), starting on the vigil. It is one of a series of upsettings of hierarchy between Christmas and Epiphany.

The Benediktbeuern Christmas play [see **C14**] links together *Prophets*, Annunciation, Magi, Herod, *Shepherds* and the Slaughter of the Innocents, all, indeed, of the typical liturgical pieces, though it is unlikely that the whole was itself liturgical. Included here are excerpts from the *Prophets* section **[B18(c)]**.[3] Though the feast of the Annunciation is celebrated later in the year (25 March), the *Aurea*

Missa or Golden Mass celebrating that feast, which developed in a number of French churches, was attached to the beginning of Advent [**B25(a)**, **(b)**, **(c)**, **(d)**].

1.   The relevant part of the sermon is given in full in Young, vol. II, pp. 126–31.
2.   For discussion of the place of the Sibyl in the Iberian peninsula see Donovan, pp. 165–7 and elsewhere.
3.   For a brief description of the Benediktbeuern manuscript see Young, vol. I, pp. 686–7. The new edition he mentions (Mikla and Schumann) has now been completed by Bernhard Bischoff (Heidelberg, 1970).

THE PROPHETS

B18   The presentation of the *Prophets*
(a)   A costume list from Laon, thirteenth century
Young, vol. II, pp. 145, 150

Isaiah: bearded, dressed in a dalmatic, a red stole hanging down the middle at front and back.

[...]

Moses: with a dalmatic, bearded, carrying tables of the law.

David: in a regal costume.

Habakkuk: bearded, stooping, hump-backed.

Elizabeth: in a female costume, pregnant.

[...]

Virgil: with ink-horn and reed-pen, crowned with ivy, holding a piece of writing.

Nebuchadnezzar: in a regal costume, with a proud walk.

Sibyl: in a female costume, hair unbound, crowned with ivy, looking wild.

[...]

Balaam: on his ass, stooping, bearded, holding a palm, urging on [his ass] with spurs.

[...]

Here the angel shall come with a sword. Balaam strikes the ass, and, when it does not move, angrily says: 'Why do you delay, ass, obstinate creature? Now the spurs shall tear your sides and flanks!' The boy [concealed] in the ass replies: 'An angel with a sword, whom I see stand in front, prevents me from moving on. I'm afraid I'll be killed.'

(b)   Rubrics for the *Festum asinorum* at Rouen Cathedral, fourteenth century
Young, vol. II, pp. 154–65

After Terce has been sung, with the prophets prepared according to their instructions [*ordo*], [and] a furnace of linen and tow in the middle of the nave of the church arranged, the procession shall move out of the cloister and two clerks of the second rank in copes shall rule the procession: [. . .] Then the procession stops in the middle of the church. And six Jews are ready there and on the other side six Gentiles, and the summoners (*vocatores*) thus call all the people: 'All people [. . .]' The summoners [call] first Moses, saying thus: 'You, Moses, law-giver, come near and relate the worthiness of Christ!' Then Moses, holding the tables of the law open, dressed in alb and cope, and with horned face, bearded, holding a rod in his hand, shall say: [. . .] This said, the summoners shall lead him beyond the furnace saying [. . .]

Aaron, vested in pontifical vestments and mitre, bearded, holding a flower, shall say: [. . .]

Daniel, dressed in a green tunicle, having the face of a young, man, holding an ear of corn, shall say: [. . .]

Habakkuk, an old man, lame, dressed in a dalmatic, having roots [or 'radishes'] in a bag, and having long palms with which he strikes the people, eating, shall say: [. . .]

Then Balaam, costumed, sitting on an ass, having spurs shall hold the reins and strike the ass with the spurs. And a young man having wings, holding a sword, shall get in the way of the ass. Someone inside the ass shall say: [. . .]

Meanwhile Nebuchadnezzar, dressed as a king, pointing to an idol, shall say to two armed men: [. . .]. Then the armed men shall point to the idol saying first: [. . .] Meanwhile they shall show the idol to the three boys saying: [. . .] Then the boys rejecting the idol shall say: [. . .] Then the armed men leading the boys to the furnace saying: [. . .] Then they shall put the boys into the furnace and it shall be lit. But they, released, shall say: [. . .] The king hearing this shall say, wondering: [. . .]

(c)   Benediktbeuern, thirteenth century
Young, vol. II, pp. 172–90

First the seat of Augustine is placed in [or 'towards the'] front of the church, and Augustine shall have Isaiah and Daniel and the other prophets on his right side, and Archisynagogus [the spirit of Judaism] and his Jews on his left side. [The attestations of the prophets follow. After Balaam and his ass] Archisynagogus with his Jews shall shout out vehemently against these prophecies they have heard and [he] shall speak to his companion poking him, moving his head and his whole body, and beating the ground with his foot, with his staff imitating the manner of the Jew in everything; and he shall say to his companions indignantly:

Tell me, why does a whitewashed wall preach?

Tell me, why does truth decayed make assertions?

Tell me [. . .]

[He is responded to by the Boy Bishop [see **B24**]. After a heated debate the prophets either withdraw or go to their seats and the Annunciation follows. Later Archisynagogus becomes Herod's adviser.]

THE SHEPHERDS AND THE CRIB

The earliest Shepherds ceremonies date from the eleventh century. They existed throughout western Europe in simple and slightly more developed forms. The text is largely derived from a trope used on Christmas Day, itself probably based on the *Quem queritis* Easter trope. *The Shepherds* normally appears at the beginning or, in the case at Rouen, end of Matins on Christmas Day [see **B19(a)**, **(b)**]. Later records from Spain frequently describe the shepherds dancing up to or around the crib but it is difficult to tell how early this distinctive element developed. The shepherds also appear in some Magi ceremonies.

The celebration of Christ's birth inaugurated by St Francis in 1223 centred on the creation of a stable scene to 'excite devotion among the townspeople of Greccio'. There are no shepherds and no imitated actions. It is described by Bonaventure and by Francis' follower and biographer, Thomas of Celano [see **B19(c)**].

B19   The Shepherds and the Crib
(a)   Rouen, fourteenth century
Young, vol. II, pp. 14–16

When *Te Deum laudamus* is finished the Office of the Shepherds is performed in this way, following the use of Rouen. A stable/crib [*presepe*] is to be prepared behind the altar and the image of Saint Mary is to be placed in it. First, a boy in a high place in front of the quire, representing [*in similitudinem*] the angel announcing the birth of the Lord to the shepherds, five canons [. . .] or their substitutes from the second bench. The shepherds enter by the main doorway to the quire passing through the middle of the quire, dressed in tunicles and amices, saying this verse: 'Fear not for behold' up to 'in a manger'. There are to be more [elsewhere: seven] boys in the roof of the church, as if angels, who shall sing in a high voice: 'Glory to God in the highest' up to 'of [good]will'. Hearing this, the shepherds shall go to the place where the *presepe* is prepared singing this verse: 'Peace on earth' – the whole piece. When they have entered, two priests of higher rank, in dalmatics, as if [they were] the midwives who were in the stable, shall sing: *'Quem queritis'* [Whom do you seek] up to 'say'. The shepherds shall reply: 'Christ the Saviour' up to 'angelic'. Next the midwives, opening a curtain, shall reveal the child, saying: 'Here is the little one' up to 'Isaiah the prophet said'. Here they shall show the mother of the child saying: 'Behold, the virgin' up to 'who is born'. Then, having seen this, let them adore the child on bended knees and salute [them] saying: 'Hail, matchless virgin' up to 'born, to enjoy the sight [of him]'. Then going away, let them turn to the choir saying: 'Alleluia, alleluia! Now we know indeed' up to 'with the prophet saying'. This finished, the Mass is started and the shepherds rule the choir.

[. . .]

The Mass over, [. . .] the archbishop or another priest turning to the shepherds shall say: 'Whom did you see, shepherds, say? Tell us, who has appeared in the lands?' The shepherds shall reply: 'We saw the newborn' etc. and they shall complete the whole antiphon.

(b)   Rouen, thirteenth century

Young, vol. II, pp. 16–17

[. . .]. Then the shepherds shall go up through the quire as far as Christ's crib, carrying staffs in their hands and singing the verse: 'Let us go to Bethlehem [. . .]'.

(c)   St Bonaventure's account of St Francis' *presepe* at Greccio, 1223

Young, vol. II, p. 430

[. . .]

Having sought and obtained a licence from the Pope, he had a crib [*presepe*] prepared, had straw brought, [and] ox and ass led to the place. The brothers were summoned, the people came, the wood rang with voices, and this venerable night was made resplendent and solemn with many bright lights and with tuneful and harmonious songs of praise. The man of God stood before the crib, full of holiness, bedewed with tears, filled with joy. The solemnities of the masses were celebrated over the crib with Francis, the deacon of Christ, singing the holy gospel. Thereafter he preached, to the people standing round about, of the birth of the king of the poor, whom, when he wished to name Him, he called, for the tenderness of love, 'the child of Bethlehem' [. . .] John of Greccio claimed to have seen a child, wondrously beautiful, sleeping in that crib, whom the blessed father Francis, embracing in both his arms, seemed to rouse from sleep.

THE MAGI AND HEROD

Sometimes referred to as the *Officium stellæ*, from its most prominent stage property, the ceremony of the coming of the Magi takes place on 6 January, Epiphany. Elements of the ceremony appear in the Mass itself (at the Offertory, Limoges [see **B20(a)**], at the reading of the gospel, Besançon [**B20(b)**]) but further developments take place before the Mass (Rouen, fourteenth century) and during Matins, especially in the establishment and expansion of the role of Herod [**B22(a)**, **(b)**]. Quite lengthy versions already existed in the eleventh century. Gerhoh of Reichersberg (1093–1169) refers to Nativity and Magi ceremonies in his attack on 'theatrical spectacles shown in the church of God' [**B26**].

Usually it is Herod whose presentation is developed but in the twelfth-century Montpellier ceremony the Magi are given gibberish speeches to characterise their foreignness [**B22(a)**]. Not only did the Magi ceremony in some instances encompass the raging Herod but occasionally also the victims of his rage, the Innocents. This sometimes appears as a separate piece, referred to as the *Ordo Rachelis*, the archetypal mother or the church weeping for her dead children (Matthew 2.16–18) [see **B23**].

B20   The Magi at Mass
(a)   Limoges, no date
Young, vol. II, pp. 34–5

When the offertory has been sung, before they go to make the offering, three choristers dressed in silk garments, each having a gold crown on his head and in his hands a gilded cup or other precious treasure, in the likeness of the three kings who came to adore the Lord, shall enter by the great door of the quire, moving with dignity, singing the following prose: 'O how worthy is this day [. . .]' The first raising his cup says: 'Gold, first.' Then the second says: 'Frankincense, second.' And the third: 'Myrrh, for giving third.' In the aforesaid order, the first says; 'Gold, a king'; the second: 'Frankincense, a heavenly being'; the third: 'Ointment denotes dying.' Then standing round the middle of the quire, one of them raises his hand pointing at the star hanging by a cord, which goes ahead of them, singing in a high voice: 'This is a sign of a great king'. Then the three together go towards the main altar singing: 'Let us go, let us ask about him and offer him gifts: gold, frankincense and myrrh.' And they go to the offering, handing over their treasures there. After this a boy sings behind the main altar, in likeness of an angel; he sings, addressing the kings: 'I bring a message to you from on high: Christ is born, Ruler of the world, in Bethlehem of Judea, thus indeed the prophet foretold.' Astonished at this sight the kings return, marvelling, by the door which leads to the sacristy singing the antiphon: 'In Bethlehem is born the King of heaven.'

(b)   Besançon, no date
Young, vol. II, pp. 37–40

At Mass, before the Gospel, a procession of the three Kings takes place. They are dressed in amices, apparelled albs, stoles and tunicles of different colours. Also copes are placed on their shoulders, they are given caps with crowns and, to each one, servants who carry the chalices [*phialas*]. When the Prose is finished they come out of the vestry preceded by candles, a censer and two choristers, the junior of whom goes in front with his staff [and] the senior follows the Kings. The Kings go as far as the altar of the blessed Mary singing; 'Of a new begetting [. . .]'. When they reach the altar of the blessed Mary, turning in front of the quire the three Kings say together: 'We, in respect of grace [. . .]' When they have come to the middle they sing together; 'We see whose star [. . .]' When they have processed a little further, they say together: 'We give such gifts [. . .]' At the entrance to the quire they say together: 'The right of Kings, in gold; of priests, in frankincense; myrrh, the third gift, is an indication of death.' When they have gone up onto the pulpitum, they shall read the Gospel each one his verse in this manner: [The gospel is divided between the cantors, Kings together and Kings individually. One division, towards the end, is] Cantors: 'They gave him gifts'; 1 King: 'Gold'; 2 King: 'Frankincense'; 3 King: 'And myrrh' [. . .] In the same place [the pulpitum] the first King says, pointing out the star to the others: 'Behold the star!'; 2 King: 'Behold the star!'; 3 King: 'Behold the star!' [They then descend, offer their gifts and crowns at the main altar and depart each in a different direction.]

B21   The Office of the Three Kings, Rouen, fourteenth century
Young, vol. II, pp. 43–5

On the day of Epiphany, when Terce has been sung, three from the upper bench dressed in the manner of kings [. . .] should meet together from three directions in front of the altar with their household servants dressed in tunicles and amices, carrying the gifts of the Kings [. . .] The middle one of the three Kings, coming from the East, pointing out the star with his staff shall say loudly; 'A star shines with a great brightness.' The second King, on the right side, shall reply: 'Which tells that the king of kings is born.' The third king, on the left side, shall say: 'Whose coming the prophets long ago signified.' Then the Magi shall kiss each other before the altar, and together sing: 'Let us go [. . .]' [. . .] The procession drawn up in the nave of the church shall make a 'station'. When the procession is about to enter the nave of the church the crown [of lights], hanging in front of the cross in the manner of a star, shall be lit, and the Magi pointing out the star shall go to the image of St Mary previously placed on the altar of the Cross [. . .] At Mass the three Kings rule the choir [. . .]

B22   The Herod element
(a)   Montpellier, twelfth century
Young, vol. II, pp. 69–72

[. . .] The messenger preceding the Kings and pointing with his staff announces [them] to Herod: 'Behold the Magi are coming, and, led by a star, they are looking for him [who is] born king of kings. They carry their gifts together to the royal child [*insonti?* for *infanti*]'. When this has been said, let the middle king say to Herod: 'Greetings, powerful king of this people and ruler of the world; what would you learn from us?' Let Herod kiss him, making him sit on his right side. Let the second [king], on the right, say to Herod: 'Ase ai ase elo allo abadac crazai nubera [. . .] ravidete qui adonay moy.' Kissing [him] let Herod order him to sit next to the first. Let the third, on the left, say to Herod: 'O some tholica lama ha osome tholica lama ma chenapi ha thomena.' Let Herod act with him as with the previous ones, to whom let Herod say: 'The king whom you seek, by what sign did you learn he had been born?' [Herod seeks information from his scribes about the prophecies of Christ's birth.] When he has heard them, let Herod, looking into the book of prophecy, angered throw it down. [After learning that the Kings have tricked him.] Herod receives a sword, brandishes it and hands it back to the person who gave it him.

(b)   Padua, thirteenth century

Young, vol. ii, pp. 99–100

The Representation of Herod on the Night of Epiphany. When the eighth lesson is finished, Herod with his chaplain comes out of the upper sacristy, and they are dressed in the poorest, skimpy chasubles. And he has a wooden spear in his hand, which with the greatest fury he hurls towards the quire and, with as great a fury, climbs up into the pulpit, and two scholars hold candles in front of him and with the same fury he begins the ninth lesson. And meanwhile his ministers, with great fury, go around the quire beating bishop, canons and scholars with inflated bladders, and also men and women standing in the church. And sometime or another they carry away Herod's spear which he hurled through the church. When the lesson is finished Herod descends with his ministers and with the aforesaid fury again goes round the quire beating them as before. When the responsory is finished, a deacon dressed in a dalmatic goes up into the pulpit with Herod and his chaplain, and the chaplain carries a censer, with two scholars, with candles, in front. And meanwhile the bishop begins the antiphon: 'In Bethlehem of Judea.' And afterwards the deacon says the Gospel namely: 'The genealogy of the Lord', and when it is finished the bishop begins the *Te Deum laudamus*. And Herod carries the gospel book and the chaplain censes the bishop and canons with the censer, and they kiss the gospel book which Herod brings them; and afterwards the scholars are censed without the book. And the choristers take up the antiphon of Lauds: 'The head' as above. And then one of the scholars, above at the altar of St Michael, sings the first verse of the hymn, namely: 'A message to you.' When that is finished he shows a burning candle, representing the star, which he throws towards the quire – and the choir continues the hymn.

B23   The Slaughter of the Innocents, Fleury, thirteenth century

Young, vol. ii, pp. 110–12

For the Killing of the Children let the Innocents be dressed in white stoles [or 'stoles [and] albs'] and, rejoicing through the monastery, pray to God saying: 'O how glorious [. . .]' Then let the Lamb, coming unexpectedly [*ex improviso*], carrying a cross, precede them here and there and let them following sing: 'Send down, O Lord, your lamb [. . .]' [Joseph is warned by the angel to escape and goes with Mary and the child 'unseen by Herod', who is seated on his throne.] Meanwhile let a soldier, announcing that the Magi have returned by another route, first salute the king and afterwards say: [. . .]. Then let Herod, as if a broken man, having seized a sword, make as if to kill himself; but he is prevented by his people and quietened. [Herod agrees to the slaughter.] Meanwhile, with the murderers approaching, let the Lamb be drawn away secretly and as it goes the Innocents salute it: 'Hail, Lamb of God, hail, who bears the sins of the world, alleluia!' Then the mothers pray to the murderers as they kill: 'We beg you spare the tender lives of our children.' Afterwards, the children lying still, let the angel summon them from heaven, saying [. . .] Then let Rachel be brought forward with two women consoling her and standing over the children let her weep, at times falling [to the ground], saying 'Alas [. . .]'

THE BOY BISHOP AND RELATED CEREMONIES

The ceremony of the Boy Bishop, which appears throughout western Europe, is one of a series of celebrations involving the upsetting of ecclesiastical hierarchy that follow directly after Christmas. John Belet [Johannes Belethus] in the late twelfth century lists four: St Stephen (26 December), taken over by the deacons; St John the Evangelist (27 December), by the priests; Holy Innocents (28 December), by the choirboys; and Circumcision (1 January) – or Epiphany (6 January) or the octave of Epiphany (13 January) – by the subdeacons. Only those of the boys and the subdeacons are distinguished by their own titles, *festum puerorum* etc. and *festum stultorum* (Feast of Fools) [see **I12–14**, **J14**, **J17**] etc.

Each ceremony involves an overturning of the hierarchy inasmuch as the services for the day are ruled by the lower orders of clergy. Though these inversions of order were planned and regulated by the Church, they clearly allowed the tensions between rule and licence to surface. Numerous prohibitions have survived in bishops' registers and elsewhere forbidding the excesses of the feasts, and often the celebrations themselves [**B28(a)**, **(b)**]. Innocent III's condemnation of incidents in the province of Gnesen in Poland (1207) [**B27(a)**] was absorbed into Gregory IX's *Decretals* (1234) as a part of canon law [**B27(b)**].

The descriptions of the Boy Bishop make it clear that in intention the celebration is mainly a role-reversal inspired by the concept of the child martyrs, the Innocents, and explored in a variety of ways [see **B24(a)**, **(b)**]. Occasionally an additional element of representation, such as that of the Flight into Egypt [**B24(c)**], is intruded. It was supported financially by the Church or by individuals in the Church *ex officio*. The services of the day emphasise children and in many places the verse of the *Magnificat* at Vespers on the vigil, 'He has put down the mighty from their seats' ['*Deposuit potentes de sede*'], was used as the moment for the changing of position, choirboys etc. taking over the higher stalls from the upper clergy [**B24(a)**, **(b)**].

B24   Instituting the Boy Bishop
(a)   Salisbury, early sixteenth century

Ceremonies and Processions of the Cathedral Church of Salisbury, ed. C. Wordsworth, Cambridge, 1901, pp. 52–3

On St John's Day. At Vespers, after the memory of St Stephen, the procession of the boys shall go to the altar of the Innocents, or of the Holy Trinity and All Saints [. . .], in silk copes with candles lit and burning in their hands singing, the Bishop of the Boys, dressed in full pontificals, [. . .] beginning the responsory. The Bishop of the Innocents alone, if present, representing the child Christ, true and everlasting bishop, shall begin [. . .] And thus the procession shall enter the quire by the west door [. . .]. And all the boys, from both sides of the choir, shall take themselves to the upper stalls; and from this time until after the procession on the next day following no clerk by custom goes up into the upper stalls, of what rank soever he be.

(b)   Role reversal, Tours, fourteenth century

Chambers, vol. I, p. 347

[At vespers on St John's day] when the *Magnificat* is sung, the choirboys shall come into the quire with [their] bishop having candles burning appropriately. And when '*Deposuit*' is sung, the cantor of the boys receives the staff [of office], and then the boys go up into the stalls and the others come down.

(c)   The *Episcopellus* at Padua Cathedral, thirteenth century

Young, vol. I, pp. 106–9

Here the Little Bishop goes to the house of the bishop. In the evening the Little Bishop, dressed in cope and mitre, goes with the canons, preceded by choirboys with candles and censer, to the bishop's house, and at the entrance the antiphon 'Unless you become as little children' is sung. And then the Little Bishop and the old bishop and the canons and clerks and choirboys and also the laity who are present are censed and all sit. And then the Little Bishop questions the other bishop about his good administration of the goods of the church and many other jests are made there [. . .]

At Mass. After Prime a priest says the Mass of the Little Bishop at the altar of the Holy Cross, and there the Little Bishop in cope and mitre is placed on the right of the altar with his chaplains. Office: 'Out of the mouth of infants' [Psalm 8.3]. Epistle. 'I beheld [. . .] upon Mount Sion' [Revelations 14.1–5].

The person who says [the Epistle] is dressed poorly and holds a wooden spear in his hand which he throws towards the people. And there are armed men who follow the spear and go round the church seeking the child with its mother, that is Christ with the Blessed Virgin Mary. And there is someone dressed like a woman who is sitting on an ass, holding a child in her arms, and someone, who represents Joseph, leads the ass fleeing through the church, signifying the flight of the Virgin with her child into Egypt as an angel of the Lord warned Joseph in a dream.

[. . .]

How the Little Bishop goes on a visitation after supper [. . .] After supper he mounts a horse in cope and gloves, ring and mitre. His chaplains likewise in copes mount horses and some of the canons, scholars and members of his household. And he goes around the town blessing men and women and visiting the monasteries under his jurisdiction [. . .] and at some of these monasteries he dismounts with his clerks and household. And then he is received worthily by abbots and priors [etc.] with copes, incense and holy water, and then he shall enter the church and prostrate himself in prayer before the altar, and afterwards he blesses everyone and they enter the monastery. And the Little Bishop calls for wine to be brought and all drink. [If they refuse he puts them under an interdict.]

(d)   The Boy Bishop on St Nicholas' Day, Bristol, 1478–9
REED, *Bristol*, p. 9

Item, on the eve of St Nicholas similarly the Mayor and Sheriff and their brethren walk to St Nicholas' Church to hear their evensong there, and in the morning to hear their Mass and make offering and hear the [Boy] Bishop's sermon and have his blessing. And after dinner the said Mayor, Sheriff and their brethren are to assemble at the Mayor's Counter there to await the coming of the Bishop, playing dice meanwhile (the Town Clerk to provide the dice and have a penny from every game). And when the Bishop has arrived, his chapel is to sing there and the Bishop is to give them his blessing. And then he and all his chapel are to be served there with bread and wine and so depart, the Mayor, Sheriff and their brethren to hear the Bishop's evensong at St Nicholas' church aforesaid.

THE *AUREA MISSA*

The fullest information about the *Aurea Missa* or Golden Mass of the Annunciation is from Tournai, early sixteenth century and St Omer, first half sixteenth century [see **B25(a)**, **(b)**, **(c)**, **(d)**]. That at Tournai was founded by Pierre Cotrel, a canon of the church and that at St Omer by Robert Fabri, a cantor of the collegiate church (who died in 1535). The masses were performed on the Wednesday of the fourth week in Advent (*Quattuor temporum*). Both involve the lowering of a dove from the church roof, at St Omer described as 'a dove of wood covered in white damask' (Young, vol. II, p. 483). The directions from Tournai demonstrate a meticulous concern for the smooth-running and timing of the descent [see **B25(c)**, **(d)**].

There are other versions on the day of the Annunciation itself (25 March) at Padua and Cividale (Young, vol. II, pp. 247–50), both fourteenth century, and at Parma during the Mass a figure of the angel Gabriel is lowered through the roof to a position above the *pulpitum* from which the gospel was being sung (Young, vol. II, pp. 245 and 479). The representation does not seem to have had the universality or frequency of the other Christmas celebrations but being specifically endowed by individuals, the details of the descriptions of performances at Tournai and St Omer are greater.

B 25   Staging the Golden Mass
(a)   The two 'stages': Tournai
Young, vol. II, pp. 480–1

[On the Tuesday after Vespers the carpenter of the church sets up . . .] in the places now arranged for this [ceremony], opposite each other, two 'houses' [*stallagia*] made for this purpose which shall be enclosed with curtains and silk cloths [one near the bishop for the Virgin Mary, the other near the dean for Gabriel.]

(b)   The two 'stages': St Omer
Young, vol. II, p. 483

[. . .]
In primis, 244. Eight curtain hangings and two lengths of white linen for the two 'tabernacles', decorated with the arms of S. Fabri.

245. Two 'heavens' of the same, each sewn with a central sun and several stars of taffeta.

246. Eight *coupettes* of gilded wood to attach to the pillars of the two 'tabernacles'.
   [. . .]

(c)   The action: Tournai
Young, vol. II, pp. 480–2

[. . .] Item, after the singing of the seventh lesson at Matins the two young people shall come, namely those representing Mary and the Angel, thus prepared in the aforesaid treasury. They enter the quire by the large door of the said quire, two lighted torches preceding them, Mary to the side of the lord bishop, carrying in her hands a beautiful book of hours, and the Angel to the side of the lord dean, carrying in his right hand a silver-gilt sceptre. And thus they shall progress with their directors solemnly to the high altar, where on bended knees they begin a prayer to the Lord. [They then go to their 'houses', where they remain concealed within the curtains.]

Item, when the celebrant shall come to the high altar for beginning the Mass, and before *Confiteor*, immediately the curtains around the oratory of the Virgin only shall open, the Virgin herself intently praying, and on her knees with her book open on a cushion provided for the purpose, with the Angel still remaining enclosed in his 'house'.

Item, *Gloria in excelsis Deo* shall be sung, then the curtains of the 'house' in which the Angel is [stationed] are opened. In the 'house' the said Angel shall stand upright, holding in his hands his silver sceptre, and doing nothing else until the time of the singing of the Gospel. Nor shall the Virgin, meanwhile, make any sign of having seen the said Angel, but with eyes downcast she shall always be intent on prayer.

Item, when the time for singing the said Gospel shall be near, the deacon and the subdeacon, with the boys with the candles and cross preceding, shall go to the place prepared for them in the sacristy and shall sing the Gospel 'The angel Gabriel was sent', and Mary and the Angel shall sing their parts, as it is ordered and noted in the book prepared for this.

Item, when the Angel shall sing these words of the Gospel '*Ave gratia plena Dominus tecum*' he shall make three salutations to the Virgin: first, at the word '*Ave*' he shall make a obeisance with head and body, afterwards solemnly raising himself; and at the words '*gratia plena*' he shall make a second obeisance, half bending his knees, afterwards raising himself; and at the words '*Dominus tecum*', which he shall sing with gravity and solemnity, he shall make then a third obeisance kneeling on the ground, and when the phrase is finished he shall rise, the Virgin meanwhile not moving. But when the Virgin Mary shall sing 'In what manner may this be' she shall rise and turn her face slightly towards the Angel with gravity and modesty, not moving otherwise. And when the Angel shall sing: 'The Holy spirit shall come upon you' etc. [The descent of the dove follows, see **B25(d)**. After that Mary returns to her kneeling prayer and the Angel to standing still – except at the Elevation of the Host – until the end of the Mass.]

(d) The lowering of the dove: Tournai

Young, vol. II, pp. 480–2

[. . .] on the same day [the Tuesday] the one deputed [to arrange] for the descent of the dove on the following day shall go to the 'tabernacle' placed in the high *carolis* [?galleries]. He shall put the cords in place and prepare the appointed apparatus [*instrumentum . . . munitum*] with its candles by which the Holy Spirit shall descend in the form of a dove at the time of the singing of the Gospel [. . .] And he shall be careful to lower the cord of the bell and arrange it at the Angel's 'house' for the ringing of the bell at the appropriate time on the following day, as will be said afterwards.

[. . .]

And when [at the Mass on the Wednesday] the Angel shall sing 'The Holy Spirit shall come upon you' etc., then the Angel shall turn his face in the direction of the dove to indicate it and immediately it shall descend from the place prepared in the high *carolis*, with candles burning around it, in front of the 'house' or oratory of the Virgin, where it shall remain until after the final *Agnus Dei*. When that has been sung it shall return to the place whence it descended.

Also the singing-master [*magister cantus*] who shall be in the 'house' of the Angel should be very careful about the right time to strike the bell in the high *carolis*, reacting at the beginning of the Gospel so that he who shall be in charge of the lowering of the dove shall be forewarned and get everything necessary ready and light the candles. And he shall be very careful a second time to strike the said bell so that exactly at the word 'Holy Spirit' he shall lower the dove, decorated with lighted candles, to the Virgin. And it shall remain where it descends until the last *Agnus Dei*, as has been said. And then the same singing-master shall again strike the same bell for the third time so that the dove shall return from whence it descended. And the one placed or deputed to lower the said dove shall be well warned about the above-said three ringings, and what each shall signify, lest there be any mistake in that.

V   *The Church's view of theatrical activity*

The Church's attitude to performance *per se* was by no means hostile. It is frequently praised and advocated as a means of increasing devotion on the part of clergy and laity [**B9(a)**, **(b)**, **27(b)**]. There are individuals, however, for whom any kind of intrusion of play into the seriousness of worship is obnoxious [**B26**]; but in most cases it is particular examples of excessive rowdyism, leading to civil unrest or to disruption of the church's services, or bringing the church into disrepute that provoke ecclesiastical censure [see **B27(a)**; **28(a)**, **(b)**; **29**; etc.]. Even then it is often expressed as restriction rather than prohibition. It is not until the parting of the ways of Catholic and Protestant that performance becomes an embarrassment, though even then the Catholic Church is far from absolute in its condemnation.

B26   The opposition: Gerhoh of Reichersberg (1093–1169)
Young, vol. II, pp. 524–5

Of theatrical spectacles shown in the church of God. And priests, so they say, now do not dedicate themselves to the ministry of church or altar but to exercises of avarice, idleness and of shows, so that they turn the churches themselves, the houses of prayers, into theatres and fill them with feigned spectacles of plays.

[. . .]

Why, indeed, may the devil not make use in earnest of things exhibited to him in idle play, as the Lord Jesus also converted into seriousness the ridicule with which he was afflicted in his passion before the Jews and Pilate?

[. . .]

What wonder, therefore, if these also now acting Antichrist or Herod in their plays, do not pretend in play, as is their intention, but show in reality, seeing that their behaviour is not far from the disordered behaviour of Antichrist?

[. . .]

And who can tell whether the rest of the Antichrist performance, his portrayal, the masks of devils, the Herodly madness, are not shown in reality?

[. . .]

They show also by images [*imaginaliter*] the cradle of the infant Saviour, the crying of the child, the motherly manner of the child-bearing Virgin, the flaming of the star like a heavenly body, the killing of the children, the motherly weeping of Rachel. But God above and the true face of the church abhors theatrical shows; it does not deal in idlenesses and false madnesses (indeed not false but true madnesses) in which true men reduce themselves to women as if ashamed that they are men, clerks to soldiers, men transfigure themselves in the masks of demons. And they hurry themselves to such vanities and insanities in places and at times for celebrating the sacraments of devils, as if the abomination of desolation is to be seen in the holy place.

B27   A papal response to licence

(a)   Pope Innocent III's condemnation of excesses in Poland, 1207

Chambers, vol. I, p. 279

From time to time theatrical entertainments are put on in these same churches and not only are masked shows introduced into them as playful spectacles but also in three feasts of the year which follow directly after the Nativity of Christ, deacons, priests and subdeacons in turn, exercising their scandalous stupidities, through the obscene revellings of their behaviour, make clerical dignity worthless in the sight of the people.

[The church authorities must put a stop to such things.]

(b)   The gloss on the *Decretals* entry of Innocent's words, c. 1263[1]

Young, vol. II, pp. 416–17

[...]

By this, however, it is not forbidden to represent the stable [*presepe*] of the Lord, Herod, the Magi, and how Rachel wept for her children [i.e. the Slaughter of the Innocents] etc., which are associated with these feasts about which mention is made here, when such things lead men rather to devotion than to licentiousness or sensual pleasure – as at Easter, the sepulchre of the Lord and other things are represented for the exciting of devotion.

[...]

---

[1] The *Decretals* are papal letters collected together for use as authoritative pronouncements on particular matters of importance. Innocent III's letter was included in the collection made by Pope Gregory IX (1227–41), published 1234. Later in the thirteenth century this comment or 'gloss' was added to the letter drawing a clear distinction between acceptable and unacceptable ceremonies.

B28   Suppression of clerical excesses

(a)   Bishop Grandisson's censure of Exeter Cathedral, 1333

REED, *Devon*, pp. 6–7

[. . .] We have learnt that certain vicars and other ministers of the said church, to the offence of God and the notable hindrance of divine service and the scandal of this our church, are not afraid damnably to perform dissolute actions, mockery, loud laughter and other insolences, irreverently, and, furthermore, masked, within the solemn ecclesiastical services and especially on the celebrated feast of the Holy Innocents; through the lewd madnesses of their behaviour they degrade clerical dignity in the sight of the people [. . .][1]

---

[1] This document also appears in a later section as **J14**.

(b)   Further problems at the collegiate church of Ottery St Mary, 1360

REED, *Devon*, pp. 12–13

[. . .] it has come to our notice that [. . .] on the very holy feasts of the Lord's Nativity and of Saints Stephen, John the Apostle and Evangelist, and the Innocents, when all the faithful in Christ are expected to devote themselves to divine worship and the offices of the Church more devoutly and more peaceably, [. . .] some [. . .] ministers, with the boys, have rashly presumed by the pernicious example of certain churches, not only at Matins and Vespers and other hours but, what is most detestable, within the solemnity of the Masses, to get together to take part in entertainments unsuitable and harmful and unbecoming clerical dignity – nay, rather detestable mockeries of divine worship – within the same church, setting aside the fear of God, polluting vestments and other ornaments of the church, namely through the manifold scattering of dirt and filth, much to the harm and dishonour of this our church and us. From the mocking behaviour and jeering laughter of which, the people, by universal custom coming together in church most particularly at these times for the sake of devotion, are much more distracted and also dissolved in disorderly laughter in improper enjoyment, and divine worship is mocked and the office wrongly hindered. And thus what was first devised for rousing and increasing the devotion of the faithful, from such insolences is converted or rather perverted (not without the offence of blasphemy) into irreverence and contempt for God and the saints [. . .]

(c)   A Catalan prohibition on post-Christmas processions, Vich, 1360

Donovan, p. 96

It is decreed that in the processions on the feasts of Saints Stephen and John the Evangelist no animals are to be introduced into the new cloister, namely horses, nags, mules, asses, cattle or the like, on the occasion of certain entertainments which are accustomed to be held in the cloister on these feasts.

B29   William of Wadington's condemnation of 'miracles', thirteenth century

Young, vol. II, p. 417

Foolish clerks have devised another clear folly which are called 'miracles'. These mad ones have disguised their faces in masks, which is forbidden by [church] decree; so much greater is their sin. They may make representations – but let it be done reverently in the office of holy church when one performs the service of God – as when Jesus Christ the son of God is placed in the sepulchre, and the Resurrection, in order to increase devotion.[1]

[1] Wadington appears to have written his *Manuel des Pechiez* in Anglo-French during the reign of Edward I; it was freely translated c. 1303 by Robert Mannyng of Brunne (c. 1288–c. 1358) as *Handlyng Synne* [see **C33**]. (For further allusions to unsanctioned masked performers, see **C65** etc.)

B30   'On not performing spectacles in churches'
(a)   Council of Basel, 1435

Ecumenical Councils, vol. I, p. 492

Shameful indeed is that abuse, carried on in certain churches, in which at certain annual celebrations, with mitre, staff and pontifical vestments, they give blessings in the fashion of bishops, [with] others dressed as kings and lords, which in certain areas is called the Feast of Fools, or Innocents, or Boys. Others [put on] masked and theatrical pastimes; others, arranging dances and entertainments of men and women, attract people to spectacles and buffoonery; others prepare feasts and banquets in the same place [i.e. the church]. The Holy Synod detests these [activities], and decrees and orders that both ordinaries and deans and rectors of churches, under pain of suspension of all ecclesiastical revenues for the space of three months, do not permit any longer these or similar abuses to be carried on (or, furthermore, markets or conducting business deals in church, which ought to be a house of prayer, or, indeed, in the cemetery), and that they do not fail to punish transgressors through ecclesiastical censure and other remedies of the law.

(b)   The local council of Sens quotes the Basel decree, 1460

Young, vol. ii, pp. 418–19

[. . .] we forbid the holding of games [*ludos*] and dances and such improprieties in holy Church and other places. Although, if they seem to be putting on something as a remembrance of feasts and in veneration of God and the saints, according to the customs of the church, at the Nativity of the Lord, or Resurrection, let this be done with decency and peaceably without extending, hindering or cutting short the service, [without] masking and blackening of the face, by special permission of the ordinary and with the good will of the ministers of that same church, so that the improprieties of [these] games, especially around the Feast of the Innocents, prohibited in other of our provincial statutes (which prohibition we renew), may be contained, observing the order of the sacred council of Basel. And in this our present statute we have had it inserted, of which the argument follows and is thus: 'Shameful indeed is that abuse [. . .]'.

VI   Other calendar ceremonies

Theatrical elements appear in the liturgy of other seasons as well, for example Ascension Day [see **B31(i)**, **(ii)**; **B32**; **B33**; **B34**]. In most cases the evidence is similar to that of the ceremonies already discussed. But two are very different, de Mézières' *Presentation of the Virgin* (1372) and the Elche *Assumption of the Virgin* [see **I19**; **I53(a)**, **(b)**; **I62**]. The one is part of what has been called a campaign for the establishment of the feast and the other is still performed in the present-day town of Elche in south-eastern Spain. The genesis and aim of Mézières' ceremony is made clear in his preface – devotion to the Virgin Mary and a desire to rouse that devotion in others – and his descriptions of preparations and action are minutely detailed [**B35**].

THE ASCENSION

B31   Flying mechanisms for the Ascension
(i) Moosburg, fourteenth century
Young, vol. I, pp. 484–5

A tent or little house of wood enclosed in beautiful cloths is prepared and located in the middle of the monastery within the paved area below the opening, high in the roof, to represent Mount Sinai [*sic*]. And in this little house there should first be placed an image of the Saviour dressed in appropriate vestments, viz. humeral, a girded tunic [*sarrocio*] or alb, with stole and cope or something similar according to what seems appropriate, carrying a banner in its hand. A thin cord shall be let down through the opening in the roof and so end at the head of the image of the Saviour, so that it is possible by those means for it to be raised aloft. There should be two circlets decorated with flowers hanging from two other cords, and in one circlet there should be an image of a dove, in the other circlet an image of an angel. There should also be a third circlet, hung round with silk cloths, which should hang stationary at the mouth of the opening in the roof, through which the afore-said cords may pass in descending and the image of the Saviour pass in ascending, as if into heaven.

(ii) Berlin, sixteenth century

Young, vol. 1, pp. 696–7

[An image of Christ is placed on a platform in the middle of the church and held up by the dean and cantor. The others taking part form a circle. After repeated ceremonies of leave-taking, at which 'the trumpeters in the roof play an artfully composed song',] the angels with candles ought to be slowly lowered from the roof [. . .] Afterwards two appointed prelates shall skilfully and carefully tie the image [of the Saviour] with the cords, turning the face of the image to the east, and allow it to be raised upwards with the angels flying around it, one at the head, the other at the feet. Meanwhile the trumpeters should play their instruments. And all the people in the circle should look up, their faces turned to the image, [their backs] to the west. Then the *prepositus* [bishop or officiating priest], dean, cantor and schoolmaster [*scolasticus*], in reverence for the Ascension of the Lord and to provide against danger from the falling of the image (which the Lord avert) shall hold a gold cloth firmly in their hands directly under the image and the opening in the roof, as long as they can see the image. When the image has been drawn up, wafers are thrown down from the roof and a drum is struck to represent thunder [. . .] And thereupon two boys with high voices shall sing alone above the roof the whole antiphon: 'Men of Galilee, why are you looking up into heaven ?' etc [. . .]

B32   Costumes for the apostles, Moosburg

Young, vol. 1, p. 485

The apostles ought to be barefoot and vested in chasubles or copes girded from left shoulder to right side, as deacons are normally girded, and have on their heads 'shields of victory', which we call 'haloes' [*diademata*] with their proper names written [on them]. And if not all, at least some should hold their attributes in their hands, viz. Peter, a key, John, a book, Andrew, a cross, Bartholomew, a knife, and Thomas, a lance, and so for the others.

B33   The climax and its dangers, Moosburg

Young, vol. 1, pp. 487–8

And be warned lest the noise and unsightliness of the image of the devil, with abominations of fire, of sulphur and of pitch, or mixed coloured waters and other irreverences and dialogues of whatsoever kind, prohibited by Holy Mother Church, become mingled with this devotion, through which not only the holy places, consecrated to divine service, and the house of God, where sanctity is proper through the length of days, are profaned, but also the devotion of the people is often provoked into wantonness and ridicule, and at times riot. But after the image of the Saviour has entered the roof, then large wafers [. . .] are sent down from above with roses, lilies and flowers of various kinds. And small children coming from the school, dressed poorly, according to our custom, collect the wafers and the flowers in their hands, praising the heavens and singing 'Holy, holy holy' or 'Come, Holy [Spirit]'. By the little children in poor clothing are understood the humble, not seeking worldly possessions, of whom the Lord says: 'Unless you become like one of these little ones, you shall not enter into the kingdom of heaven'. They collect the flowers of various kinds, that is the varied gifts of the Holy Spirit. By the wafers is understood the presence of the body of Christ, which is with us in form of bread until the end of the world.

B34   The reformer's view: Barnaby Googe, 1570

Young, vol. II, p. 537; [for Googe see **B8(a)**, **(b)**, **J11**, **J33**, **J47**, **J61**]

Then comes the day when Christ ascended to his father's seat,
Which day they also celebrate, with store of drink and meat [food].
Then every man some bird must eat, I know not to what end [why],
And after dinner all to church they come, and there attend.
The block [image] that on the altar still, till then was seen to stand
Is drawn up high above the roof, by ropes, and force of hand;
The priests about it round do stand, and chant it to the sky
[...]
Then out of hand [suddenly] the dreadful shape of Satan down they throw,
Oft times with fire burning bright, and dashed asunder tho [apart then].
The boys with greedy eyes do watch, and on him straight [at once] they fall,
And beat him sore [hard] with rods, and break him into pieces small.
This done, they wafers down do cast, and singing – cakes [hosts] the while,
With papers round amongst them put, the children to beguile [entertain].
With laughter great are all things done, and from the beams they let
Great streams of water down to fall, on whom they mean to wet.
[...]

THE PRESENTATION OF THE VIRGIN, 1372

Philippe de Mézières' theatrical ceremony for the *Presentation of Mary* is part of a complete and new liturgical Office and Mass for the establishment of the feast on its traditional date of 21 November. It was first performed at Avignon on that date in 1372. The feast had been celebrated in the Eastern Church from at least the eighth century. There were signs of it in Anglo-Saxon and later England but it was not generally celebrated in the West. It was an individual act of homage to Mary as the foundation upon which the whole of Christianity stood.

The theatrical ceremony does not simply fit into or latch onto a pre-existing liturgical practice but is created as part of a new one, containing a sermon, an explanatory letter, an account of a related miracle, the Office, a Mass and the ceremony. The whole survives in a manuscript which was Mézières' own.

Details of the staging are remarkable. The information is divided into (*Staging*, pp. 207–8):

a list of *dramatis personæ* [**B35(a)**]
a description of costumes and accessories [**B35(b)**]
a description of the layout of the playing area [**B35(c)**]
the procession and its ordering [**B35(d)**]
the action of the piece [**B35(e)**]
the action within the Mass and the later ceremonies: progress, meal, sermon.
  [**B35(f)**]

Contained within this are the dimensions and positioning of the stages and their use, details of costumes, crowd control, audience reaction, gesture, script.

As with other instructions, these legislate for what should be. There is a brief description of an actual performance in 1385 [**B36**] which shows considerable differences.[1]

---

1.   For a complete translation of the Presentation see *Staging*, pp. 207–25.

B35   Staging de Mézières' *Presentation of Mary*
(a)   The *dramatis personæ*
Coleman, p. 85; *Staging*, p. 208

First, there shall be a young and most beautiful girl [*virgo*], about three or four years old, who shall represent Mary, and with her, two other most beautiful girls of the same age. Then there shall be Joachim and Anna, and also two angels, Gabriel and Raphael. Then there shall be nine angels representing the nine orders of angels. After that there shall be a most beautiful woman, aged about twenty, who shall be called *Ecclesia* and who shall represent the Church. Then there shall be a woman of advanced age who shall be called *Synagoga*, and who shall represent the law of Moses and the Old Testament. Also there shall be two young men playing instruments. Then there shall be the Archangel Michael and Lucifer. Finally there shall be a bishop with a deacon and a subdeacon.

(b)   The costumes and properties
Coleman, pp. 85–9; *Staging*, pp. 208–10

Having given the names of the people who shall put on the performance [*representatione*], it is necessary to speak of their costumes and accessories. Mary shall wear a pure white tunic of sendal [fine silk] without any unnecessary decoration, with a narrow hem encircling the lower edge of the tunic, visible on the outside of the tunic. And the tunic shall be loose-fitting everywhere except the sleeves which shall be tight; nor shall she have a girdle around the tunic. Over that she shall have a cloak, also pure white, of sendal or silk cloth open in front the whole length of the body, with a cord of gold embroidery for fastening the cloak over the breast, in the manner of a bridal cloak. And around the neck of the tunic and all along the opening of the cloak there shall be put a narrow strip of gold embroidery; and encircling the lower edge of the cloak there shall be a hem, visible on the outside of the cloak. Mary's head shall be bare and her hair hanging loose behind over the shoulders. She shall have, however, on her head a golden circlet of silver gilt, the width of the middle finger, with a halo of fine silver gilt, of a moderate width, fixed to the circlet at the back of her head. This shall be the ornament for Mary's head. She shall have no rings, nor a girdle, nor anything else on her but of white or gold, showing the innocence and virginity of Mary and the purity of her love.

The two girls accompanying Mary: one shall be dressed in green silk or sendal representing the humility of Mary, and the other in the colour blue or azure [celestino] representing Mary's faith and hope, for according to the apostle, 'Our dwelling-place' (but even more so that of Mary) 'is in heaven.' These two girls shall not wear cloaks as Mary does, but shall have loose-fitting tunics with hems at the lower edge as is said above. Nor shall they have girdles around their tunics. But on their bare heads, they shall wear circlets of silver without the halo, of the width previously mentioned, and hair let down loose behind, as above for Mary.

Joachim, Mary's father, shall be dressed in the alb of a priest, girded like a priest, with a stole around his neck and coming down over the breast in the form of a cross, as a priest, and over that an ancient but not torn cope. And he shall have on his head a covering of fine material, fairly long and, if it may be managed, decorated in some way, with which he shall cover his head and neck. And the two ends of the covering shall hang down the length of two hands-breadths and a bit more over the shoulders, on top of the cope to the right and to the left. He shall have a long, full, and white beard coming down over his breast, and shall hold in his hand, outside the cope, a smallish glass vessel full of red wine.

Anna shall be dressed in white linen, both body and head, in the manner of an old honourable matron, and shall carry in her hand a round loaf, pure white and reasonably large.

The two angels Gabriel and Raphael are to be dressed in girded albs with amices, with stoles around their necks and crossing over the breast. On their heads they shall wear hats close-fitting to the head above the ears, and around the head at the top they shall have a triangular or rectangular shape, not too broad, with two lappets behind as on the mitre of a bishop. And these hats shall be of white sendal or silk cloth or paper or parchment with a border [frizello] around the hat, painted in some way and covered with flowers painted on top of the hats. And whoever wants to may put narrow fringes of silk of various colours around the hats. The two angels shall have two wings of some kind, and shall carry in their right hands a red rod of some sort.

The nine angels shall be dressed like Gabriel and Raphael except that the three who shall represent the higher order of angels (namely cherubim, etc.) shall have their hats, as described, painted red; the three of the second order of angels shall have blue hats, or of azure colour, and the three of the third order of angels white hats. All nine shall have a lily on a slender rod of a green colour; and the lily of the first order shall be gilded, and the lily of the second order of an azure colour, and the third of a silvery colour.

Ecclesia shall be a very handsome young man about twenty years old, without a beard and dressed completely in gold in the costume of a deacon, with the most beautiful hair of a woman extending over his shoulders. And on his head he shall wear a gold crown with lilies and precious stones. Against his breast shall be fixed with a cord a silver gilt chalice without paten, which chalice shall signify the New Testament. And in his left hand he shall carry a long cross, along the upright and cross-piece of which shall be a red rod the width of the thumb, and the cross shall be gilded throughout without any decoration. In his right hand he shall carry a round apple, all gilt, signifying the universal rule of the Church.

Synagoga shall be dressed in the manner of an aged woman in an ankle-length ancient tunic made of some cloth of a plain colour and a cloak black and torn. Her head shall be dressed as an old woman's with some covering of a dark colour, and in front of her eyes and face she shall have a black veil through which, however, she can see. In her left hand she shall carry a red banner the black pole of which shall appear broken, the banner leaning on her shoulders. On this red banner shall be written in letters of gold SPQR, which are the arms of the Romans. And in her right hand she shall carry two tables of stone tilted towards the earth, on which stone tables shall be written letters like Hebrew letters signifying the law of Moses and the Old Testament.

The two young men who play soft instruments shall be dressed as the angels except that they shall not wear stoles or wings, but good hats of a green colour.

Then there shall be the Archangel Michael, who shall be dressed in the finest armour from foot to head, and on his helmet or bascinet or barbute he shall have a gilded crown, sign of a victorious soldier and sign of Christ triumphant. In his right hand Michael shall hold a naked sword, shining and raised towards heaven; and in his left hand he shall hold an iron chain with which Lucifer, following behind Michael, is bound around the neck.

Lucifer shall be costumed [*ornetur*] in such a way as befits that most vile and abominable [character] with horns, teeth, and a hideous face. And with his right hand Lucifer shall hold a crook or hook of iron carried over his shoulder, and with his left hand he shall hold the chain, as if he wished to rebel against Michael.

(c)   The stages and layout

Coleman, pp. 89–91; *Staging*, pp. 210–12

How the place [*locus*] is laid out for putting on the performance. In the church between the great west door and the door of the canons' or brothers' quire, in the middle of the church but somewhat nearer to the door of the quire than to the west door so that it can the more clearly be seen from all parts of the church, a structure of wood or a stage [*stacio*] is to be erected, six feet in height. On top it shall be boarded in the manner of a platform [*solarii*], and this platform shall reach across the church – namely, from north to south, ten feet in length, and from east to west the platform shall be eight feet in width. And against the middle of the platform towards the west door there shall be as many steps as are necessary from the paved floor of the church to the platform; and likewise there shall be similar steps opposite the door of the quire for descending from the platform, so that any step is about three feet in length and hence it takes up as little of the platform as can be managed. And these steps are to be enclosed on both sides with boards or planks so that no one can go up except in the proper way for the performance.

On the platform in the space between the two flights of steps, the way shall be level. But on the north side there shall be a bench for sitting on, extending across the platform from west to east. And this bench shall be long enough for Joachim and Anna to be able to sit down at either end and Mary in the middle, but so that Mary's seat is raised just enough that, with the three sitting down, the head of Mary sitting in the middle shall be on a level with her father and mother. And between the bench and the edge of the platform towards the north a space is left for Gabriel and Raphael who shall stand on their feet there behind Mary. On the south of the platform, beyond the way between the steps, there shall be two seats as high as the aforesaid bench upon which Joachim and Anna shall sit. One of these seats shall be placed to the east of the platform and the other to the west, on which *Ecclesia* and *Synagoga* shall sit looking at Mary, so that anyone mounting the platform by going up the steps can pass freely between *Ecclesia* and *Synagoga* to the edge of the platform towards the south. At the four corners of the platform there shall stand, at the northern corners Gabriel and Raphael, and at the southern the two young men playing instruments. The platform is protected all round by a narrow board at a height above the platform of two feet, in the manner of a railing, so that the said platform may appear more fitting for a performance and so that those who are on the platform may not easily fall off it. This platform, the bench, and the seats shall be covered with carpets. Let the structure or platform [*edificium seu solarium*] be made of very strong planks and well joined together, lest because of the pressure of people standing around it should somehow be possible for it to collapse.

Furthermore, between the seats of the canons or brothers and the high altar, to the north against a wall or pillar in a prominent position shall be constructed another platform of large timbers, but a small one, namely, in height seven or eight feet. The platform shall be six feet square at the top, and all around this square it shall be protected with a narrow board, one foot above the platform. And the platform shall be covered with carpets; and on the carpet almost in the middle of the platform shall be placed a small stool covered with some fine silk cloth, with a small silk cushion for Mary to rest upon [*ad apodiandam*] while hearing Mass. And directly in the middle of the platform shall be placed on the carpet a large silk cushion for Mary to sit on; and the aforesaid stool immediately in front of Mary.

It shall be arranged for some place near the church, as for instance a ground-floor room of some house near the church adequate for this, sufficient to hold all the people getting ready or dressing for the performance – which place could perhaps be the chapter-house of the brothers, but shut off in front with curtains – in which our most sweet Mary with her company shall get ready and, prepared and arrayed as is declared above, await the procession.

(d)   The ordering of the procession

Coleman, pp. 92–4; *Staging*, pp. 212–14

[. . .]

After the musicians shall follow the two young girls walking together. And the one dressed in green shall carry in her right hand a green candle, three-quarters of a pound [in weight], and the other young girl a similar candle of an azure colour. Immediately after the two young girls, our most sweet Mary shall follow carrying in her right hand a candle similar in weight but pure white, and in her left hand she shall carry a pure white dove at her breast. And on the right side of Mary, Gabriel shall walk with his red rod raised, and on the left side of Mary in the same way Raphael walking reverently step by step with Mary, not coming too near the person of Mary but always looking at her. After Mary, Gabriel and Raphael, Joachim and Anna shall walk together, looking continually at Mary, and carrying the bread and wine, as is stated above. And after them, Michael the Archangel shall come, in armour, with his sword gleaming upright in his right hand and with his left, with the chain a yard long, he shall drag Lucifer, roaring and at times howling and as if going along unwillingly.

[. . .]

When Mary goes out from the chapter house with her company, certain strong young men shall be appointed who shall hold in their hands the shafts of spears bound one to another with rope crosswise all along the procession from the bishop to Lucifer inclusive, and walking processionally in this double row so that Mary with her costumed company going between the spears shall not be annoyed by the press of people and shall have a clear path in so far as the men holding the spears in their hands shall walk opposite each other outside the spears on the side of the people, holding back the people on either side with the spears. Nor shall anyone be allowed to go between the two rows of spears except Mary and her company, apart from two, three, or four sergeants or officers of the law [*servientibus aut clientibus justicie*] who may be within the spears to ease the press of people, lest Mary and her company become oppressed by the crowd.

[. . .]

And note that the procession must begin very early in the morning, about sunrise, because the ceremony of the performance [*misterium representationis*] is long and very devout, and at that time [of year] the days are short.

(e)   The performance
Coleman, pp. 94–104; *Staging*, pp. 214–21

Of the performance and the Praises of Mary. The performance is thus: Gabriel and
Raphael with Mary, Joachim, and Anna, and with the two musicians playing and
leading, shall go quickly to the foot of the steps of the platform, with the other
angels, *Ecclesia*, *Synagoga*, Michael, and Lucifer standing fast in their places and
waiting. The ascent of the steps of the platform is to be guarded carefully by the
sergeants-at-arms and the officers [*servientes . . . armorum seu clientes*] so that no
one may presume to go up except those so ordered for taking part in the performance [*ad representationem fiendam ordinati*]. Then Gabriel first shall go up onto the
platform, and with his rod, turning himself to all sides (with a gesture not with a
word), he shall impose silence upon all with his rod. And straightaway, Mary, alone
without any help, shall go up on to the platform by the steps, with a joyous expression. And if she shall not be able to carry her candle in going up, Raphael shall
carry the candle. And Mary shall in going up carry her dove in front of her breast,
with the instruments playing. And when Mary is on the platform, with her face
raised to the high altar, immediately Raphael shall go up, and together with
Gabriel they shall place Mary in her seat, referred to above, towards the northern
end.

[. . .]

And at once *Synagoga* first and after her *Ecclesia* shall go up, and they shall sit
upon the stools previously indicated, namely *Synagoga* on the east side, and
Ecclesia on the west side, looking towards Mary and holding in their hands,
Synagoga banner and tables, and *Ecclesia* cross and apple, as is stated above.

[. . .]

Then *Ecclesia* shall rise from her stool, and, standing on her feet looking at Mary,
she shall sing in a loud voice these words [*dicens*]:

> 'Let the heavens rejoice and the earth be glad!
> Behold our redemption approaches; behold the
> gathering of the sons of God approaches.'

And indicating herself with her right hand, in which she holds the golden apple,
she shall say:

> 'Behold the new mother, full of the fruitfulness not
> of the Law, but of Grace; not of fear, but of love;
> not of bondage, but of freedom. For behold this
> virgin,'

pointing at Mary –

> 'who shall conceive and bear a son, who shall save
> His people from their sins. Glory be to the Father

> and to the Son and to the Holy Spirit; as it was in
> the beginning, is now and always, and for ever and
> ever.'

And all the angels shall reply: 'Amen.' And *Ecclesia* shall remain in her place sitting on her stool, as before. And after some music, *Synagoga* shall rise to her feet, standing in her place with her face inclined to the left. As if sorrowful, she shall turn to all sides and shall sing, as if weeping, these words;

> 'Who shall give a spring of tears to my eyes so that
> I may bewail my wretched desolation? Behold her'

indicating Mary –

> 'through whom this truth shall be brought to pass:
> When the holy of holies comes, your anointing shall
> cease.'

And then suddenly Gabriel and Raphael shall come and, as if in anger, drive off *Synagoga* from the platform by the western steps. And then *Synagoga* going down shall throw away banner and tablets to right and to left in the temple off the platform; and thus she shall flee out of the church, upright, weeping and complaining; and she shall not appear again. And Gabriel and Raphael shall not go down from the platform but shall return to their places. And the instruments shall play for a short while and until the people have quietened their laughter at the expulsion of *Synagoga*.

To the sound of an instrument, Michael shall go up onto the platform and shall lead Lucifer with him, as if advancing unwillingly and howling. And after Michael's bow to Mary, he shall place himself where the angels shall sing their songs. And Lucifer shall be near Michael, but when he shall cross in front of Mary he shall pretend to be [*finget se*] fearful and trembling and shall let himself fall on his face. And Michael shall drag him as if by force to the place aforesaid, namely where the angels have spoken their verses. Then Michael, with his face towards Mary, holding his shining sword aloft and holding in his left hand the chain of the kneeling Lucifer, shall say in a loud voice:

> 'Hail, lady most high, whom the heavens, earth,
> sea, the abyss, and all creatures obey! Command
> and I shall obey you!'

And with the point of his sword indicating Lucifer, he shall say:

> 'Behold the rebel against God, the scandal of angels
> the enemy of human nature! You, indeed,
> have received from God the power of treading
> underfoot, of overcoming and tormenting him on

behalf of God Almighty. He is placed under your
sentence, is given over to your will, and is bound
under your feet.'

And then Michael shall place Lucifer bound thus and howling under Mary's feet,
and she shall beat with her feet upon him and drive him away from her. And at
once he shall be pushed from the platform by Michael, Gabriel, and Raphael down
the western steps to the ground; and he shall not appear again in the celebration
[*in festo*]. And the instruments shall play and Michael shall place himself where
Synagoga was, looking always at Mary.
    [. . .]
    One thing is to be noted, that when Mary with her company has come before the
altar and the angels divide, as has been said, those strong young men who shall
carry the spears in a double line shall make one large rectangle with their spears
in front of the altar, in which rectangle Mary and her company shall be safe from
being crushed. Nor shall the sergeants-at-arms permit any persons to enter unless
they are of the company of Mary, in order, that is, that the ceremony [*misterium*]
of the Presentation of Mary can be seen by all without obstruction.
    [. . .]

(f) The Mass

    Coleman, pp. 104–6; *Staging*, pp. 222–4

[. . .]
    Joachim and Anna shall pray for a short time with their heads bowed to the
ground, Mary remaining on her feet. And presently they shall rise and lead Mary
holding her candle and her dove in front of the bishop and, kneeling, they shall
present her to him. Then the bishop shall say in a loud voice, in the person of God
the Father:

        'Come, my friend, come, my dove, because there is
        no blemish on you. Come from Libanus, chosen from
        eternity, so that I may receive you as the chosen
        bride of my beloved Son.'

And then the bishop shall receive her in his arms, turning to right and left, and
shall make her kiss the altar, and shall put her down on the ground. Joachim and
Anna shall offer on the altar the bread and wine, kissing the altar, leaving Mary in
front of the altar with the two young girls, who shall also kiss the altar, and shall
go down to the angels.
    Then Gabriel and Raphael shall lead Mary between them on to the platform set
up between the altar and the seats of the quire on the north side, as stated above.
And the two young girls shall go up also on to the platform with Mary; on which
little platform no one shall stay except Mary and the two young girls, with Gabriel

and Raphael behind Mary, remaining standing, with their rods upright as if guarding Mary. In front of Mary's little stool, on which she shall rest herself while hearing Mass, there shall be three candlesticks in which the candles of Mary and the young girls shall be placed. And on the stool shall be a beautiful little book, the pages of which Mary shall turn as if saying her hours, at the time when she shall be sitting on the large cushion and the young girls near her on the carpet. At the Gospel, Mary and the young girls shall rise and hold their candles in their hands; and Mary shall bear herself in a grown-up way and devoutly at the Mass, Gabriel and Raphael instructing her. When the Mass has begun Mary shall let her dove fly away. And let it be noted that when Mary is on this small platform, Joachim, Anna, *Ecclesia*, Michael, the nine angels, with the musicians playing, each in his position shall process out with the instruments playing: the angels first, with *Ecclesia*, the musicians, Joachim and Anna, and Michael walking behind, bowing their heads in front of the bishop and the altar, and afterwards deeply before Mary, and they shall go to the place where they got ready and shall leave their costumes and accessories [*vestimenta sua et ornamenta*], all which accessories shall be carefully looked after for performance in a future year.

[. . .]

When the Mass is finished, Mary with her angels and young girls shall go down from the platform, and, kissing the altar, she shall offer her candle, and the young girls also. And immediately the musicians who withdrew shall come forward, and with them preceding and playing, Mary, between Gabriel and Raphael, the young girls falling back, accompanied by a great crowd of noble ladies, especially of girls and boys of every kind, shall be carried to the house where she will eat by some man of high stature; or else riding on a horse, and the angels also upon two horses with Mary between, making a short progress through the city if the weather is fine. At the meal Mary shall be placed in her costume in a higher place on a royal throne, accompanied by as many young girls as possible at the table, Gabriel and Raphael serving attentively, punctiliously, and with profound reverence until the end of the meal.

[. . .]

And let it be noted that the songs above-written for the praises of the Virgin, which shall be sung or spoken in a loud voice by the angels and the other people above-mentioned, are most religious and are, chiefly for the faithful who understand Latin, sure to move them to tears because of their devotion. But because the common people do not understand Latin, if it shall seem expedient, and our most sweet Mary inspires the hearts of her faithful through grace, these often-mentioned songs may be translated into the vernacular, and they may be delivered in the same way in the vernacular. Doing or not doing this, I leave to the faithful piously reading the present ceremony [*representationem*] of the spotless Virgin.

B36   An account of the performance of the *Presentation* at Avignon, 1385

Coleman, pp. 110–11; *Staging*, pp. 224–5

At the solemn Mass in praise of the Virgin and through the devotion of her faithful followers, a certain ceremony [*representacio*] was performed by fifteen young girls of three or four years of age, the best-looking of whom represented Mary accompanied by the said young girls. And thus diversely costumed in a most devout procession in which Joachim and Anna were represented [*figuratis*], and with angels preceding and following the Virgin, she was led with instruments of music to the altar. And there she quickly climbed the fifteen wooden steps leading to the altar and was presented in figure [*figuraliter*] by her parents and devoutly received by the high priest of the law of the Old Testament, dressed in the costume of the high priests of the Jews.

When she had been presented at the altar with praises and psalms, delivered in a loud voice by the angels, Joachim and Anna and Mary herself, she was led into the midst of the choir and cardinals onto a higher place, as has been mentioned, with her company, and there she waited until the end of the celebration of the Mass [. . .]

VII The plays

Besides the many theatrical ceremonies which remain more or less closely integrated with the liturgy, there are a number of fully developed plays whose precise connection with it is difficult to discover. It is impossible to categorise them as liturgical or extra-liturgical since they may be (and, indeed, may have been) either. Only of the Hilarius *Daniel* (early twelfth century) is it specifically stated: 'when this is finished, if it is performed at Matins, Darius shall begin the *Te Deum laudamus*, if at Vespers, the *Magnificat anima mea Dominum*' (Young, vol. II, p. 286). The simple presence of a concluding *Te Deum* has led to the assumption that certain plays were intended for Matins. It may be so, but there is no reason why the *Te Deum* should imply exclusively a liturgical context. The evidence suggests that the plays were sung throughout; the language is mainly Latin but with an admixture of vernacular.

There are Old Testament plays (*Isaac and Rebecca* [see **C45**], *Daniel* (two), *Joseph* [see **C13**] (Young, vol. II, pp. 258–306), episodes from miracles of the saints (especially St Nicholas) (Young, vol. II, pp. 307–60), a play of the wise and foolish virgins (the *Sponsus*) [see **C18**, **C52(i)**], and plays of Antichrist [**C19(i)**, **C36**, **C43**] (Young, vol. II, pp. 361–96).[1] There are also extended New Testament episodes (Lazarus [**C17**], St Paul, the Crucifixion), or sequences of episodes (Young, vol. I, pp. 411–50, 492–540; vol. II, pp. 199–24).

Though the scope of these plays is considerable – the Beauvais *Daniel* play contains feasts, battles, processions, special effects: the handwriting on the wall, the lions' den [see **B37(a)**, **(b)**, **(c)**] – their stage directions and information generally on staging is slight. One exception to this is the Cividale *Planctus Mariæ et aliorum* (fourteenth century) which contains a remarkable series of instructions for expressive gesture [see **B38**].

There are two collections of plays, as opposed to the usual appearance of texts singly in service books. The Benediktbeuern manuscript collection (thirteenth century), possibly from the Tyrol, which includes the *Carmina Burana*, contains two Passion plays (a shorter and a longer) [**C16(i)**], a Christmas play [**C14**], a Resurrection play, a *Peregrinus* and a fragmentary play on the fall of the idols in Egypt at the coming of the Holy Family.[2] The Fleury play-book (thirteenth century) possibly from Fleury or its neighbourhood, contains four miracle plays of St Nicholas [see **C27**, **C28**], a conversion of St Paul [**C38**], a resurrection of Lazarus [**C37**] and four, more conventional, theatrical liturgical ceremonies.[3] Both collections may have been made for performance in the liturgy, but it is perhaps more likely that they were gathered together for the purposes of performance whatever the context.

1.   There is an English translation of Young's text of the Tegernsee play in *The Play of Antichrist*, trans. John Wright, Toronto, 1967. For additions to his bibliography see Flanigan, *RORD* 19 (1976), pp. 134–5.

2.   The Benediktbeuern plays are edited by Young, vol. I, pp. 432–7, 463–5, 514–16, 518–33, vol. II, pp. 172–90, 463–8. There is a new edition: *Die Trink-und Spielerlieder: die geistlichen Dramen*, ed. Bischoff. The two-part manuscript which incorporates them is housed in the Bayerische Staatsbibliothek in Munich (Clm 4660; Clm 4660a).

3.   For an extensive discussion of the Fleury play-book see *The Fleury* Playbook: *Essays and Studies*, ed. Campbell and Davidson.

B37   The Beauvais *Daniel*, thirteenth century
(a)   The making of the play
Smoldon, p. 1

In your honour, O Christ, this play of Daniel was devised in Beauvais, and the young men [?of the song school] devised it.

(b)   The writing on the wall
Smoldon, p. 5

Meanwhile a hand [*dextra*] shall appear in the sight of the king [Belshazzar] writing on the wall: 'Mane, Thechel, Phares'. Seeing it, the king amazed shall call out: 'Call the astrologers [. . .]'

(c)   Daniel in the lions' den
Smoldon, pp. 22–5

[. . .]
   Then the king's officers [*satrapæ*] shall seize Daniel and he, looking at the king [Darius], shall say: 'Alas, alas [. . .]' And the King, powerless to release him, shall say to him: 'God, whom I know you worship faithfully [. . .]' Then they shall throw Daniel into the pit. And immediately an angel holding a sword shall threaten the lions so that they do not touch him, and Daniel entering the pit shall say: 'I am not guilty of this crime, [. . .]' In the meantime another angel shall tell Habakkuk the prophet that he should bring the dinner which he was carrying to his harvesters to Daniel in the pit of lions, saying: 'Habakkuk, [. . .]' Then the angel, holding him

by the hair of his head, shall lead him to the pit and Habakkuk, offering Daniel the dinner, shall say: 'Rise now [. . .]' This done, the angel shall lead Habakkuk to his place. Then the King, descending from his throne, shall come to the pit, saying mournfully: 'Do you think [. . .]?' And Daniel to the King: 'O King, live for ever! [. . .]' Then the King joyfully shall cry out: 'Release Daniel [. . .]' When they [the satraps] have been stripped and have come to the pit, they shall cry out: 'Justly do we suffer this [. . .]' When they have been thrown into the pit, at once they shall be devoured by the lions [. . .]

B38   Instructions for gesture, Cividale, fourteenth century

Young, vol. I, pp. 507–12; *Staging*, pp. 178–80

[. . .]

MAGDALENE

Here let her turn to the men with arms outstretched
  'O brothers'
Here to the women
  'and sisters,
  where is my hope?'
Here let her strike her breast
  'Where is my consolation?'
Here let her raise her hands
  'Where all salvation,'
Here, with head bowed, let her place herself
[sternat] *at Christ's feet*
  'O my master?'

MARY THE VIRGIN

Here let her strike her hands [together]
  'O misery!
  Alas, misery!
  So wherefore,'
Here let her indicate Christ with open hands
  'dear son,
  do you hang thus,
  when you were alive,'
Here let her strike her breast
  'existing before time [was]?'

JOHN

Here, with hands outstretched, let him indicate Christ
  'Celestial king,
  on account of evil men'
Here, throwing himself forward [projiciendo],
let him indicate the people
  'you absolve penalties
  foreign (to you),
  Lamb without sin.'

MARY JACOBI   *Let her indicate the cross with open hands*
                    'Pure flesh, precious to the world,
                        why do you wither on the altar of the cross,'
                Here let her strike her breast
                    'a sacrifice for sins?'

[. . .]

MAGDALENE   *Here on bended knees before the cross*
                    'O benign Father,
                    O glorious master,'
                Here let her indicate herself
                    'do not abandon me:'
                Here let her strike herself
                    'behold a sinner,
                    you who have saved me!'

MARY THE VIRGIN   'O Mary'
                Here let her indicate Magdalene
                    'Magdalene,'
                Here let her indicate Christ
                    'sweet disciple of my son,'
                Here let her embrace Magdalene around the neck with her two arms
                    'complain with me, my sister,'
                Here embracing Magdalene let her turn in another direction
                    'complain passionately with me'
                Here let her indicate Christ
                    'the death of my sweet son,'
                Here let her indicate Magdalene
                    'and the death of your master,'
                Here let her indicate Christ
                    'his death who'
                Here let her indicate Magdalene
                    'so loved you,'
                Here let her indicate Magdalene
                    'who all your sins'
                Here let her stretch out her hands downwards [relaxat . . . deorsum]
                    'has released [*relaxavit*] from you,'
                Here, embracing Magdalene as she did at first,
                let her finish the verse:
                    'most sweet Magdalene.'

[. . .]

Section C
Extra-liturgical Latin and early vernacular drama

Edited by LYNETTE R. MUIR

Abbreviations

Anglo-Norman Adam	*Le jeu d'Adam (Ordo representacionis Ade)*, ed. Willem Noomen, Paris, 1971; trans. Lynette R. Muir, *Adam, a Twelfth-Century Play*, Leeds Philosophical and Literary Society, 1968
Beverley	Diana Wyatt, 'Performance and Ceremonial in Beverley Before 1642', D.Phil. thesis, University of York, 1983
Cyprus Passion	*The Cyprus Passion Cycle*, ed. August C. Mahr, Notre Dame, Indiana, 1947
D'Ancona	Alessandro D'Ancona, *Origini del teatro italiano*, 2 vols., Florence, 1877; reprinted Rome, 1981
EETS	Early English Text Society publications
Fleury *Lazarus*	Young, vol. II, pp. 199–208
Fleury *St Nicholas*	Young, vol. II, pp. 351–7
Fleury *St Paul*	Young, vol. II, pp. 219–22
Jeu de St Nicolas	Jean Bodel, *Le jeu de Saint Nicolas*, ed. F. J. Warne, Oxford, 1951; reprinted 1968
Jeu de Ste Agnes	*Le jeu de Sainte Agnès, drame provençal du XIVe siècle*, ed. Alfred Jeanroy, Paris, 1931
Loomis	R. S. Loomis, 'Chivalric and Dramatic Imitations of Arthurian Romance', in *Medieval Studies in memory of A. Kingsley Porter*, ed. Wilhelm R. W. Koehler, Cambridge, Mass., 1939, pp. 79–97
Maastricht *Passion*	*Mittelniederländisches Osterspiel*, ed. J. Sacher, *Zeitschrift für deutsches Altertum* 2 (1842), pp. 303–50
Miracle de l'enfant ressuscité	ed. Graham A. Runnalls, Paris and Geneva, 1972
Miracle of a Woman whom Our Lady Saved from being Burned:	*Un miracle de Nostre Dame comment elle garda une femme d'être* brulée, *Miracles de Nostre Dame par personnages*, ed. Gaston Paris and Ulysse Robert, Société des Anciens Textes français, 8 vols., Paris, 1876–83, vol. IV, pp. 175–236 (play 26)
Muir, *Biblical Drama*	Lynette R. Muir, *The Biblical Drama of medieval Europe*, Cambridge, 1995

Mystères inédits	*Mystères inédits du quinzième siècle*, ed. Achille Jubinal, 2 vols., Paris, 1837; reprinted Geneva, 1977
Neumann	Bernd Neumann, *Geistliches Schauspiel im Zeugnis der Zeit. Zur Ausführung mitteralterlicher Dramen im deutschen Sprachgebiet*, Münchener Texte und Untersuchungen zur deutschen Literatur des Mittelalters 84, 85, Munich and Zurich, 1987
Orvieto *laude*	Vincenzo De Bartholomaeis, *Laude drammatiche e rappresentazioni sacre*, 3 vols., Florence, 1943, vol. I
Paschon Christos	*La Passion du Christ de Grégoire de Nazianse*, ed. André Tuilier, Paris, 1969
Play of Isaac and Rebecca	Young, vol. II, pp. 259–64
Perugia *laude*	*see* Orvieto *laude* above
REED	Records of Early English Drama
REED York	Records of Early English Drama, *York*, ed. Alexandra F. Johnston and Margaret Rogerson, 2 vols., Toronto, 1979
Rubin	Miri Rubin, *Corpus Christi: the Eucharist in Late Medieval Culture*, Cambridge, 1991
Seinte Resureccion	*La Seinte Resureccion*, ed. Thomas A. Jenkins *et al.*, Anglo-Norman Texts 4, Oxford, 1943
Sponsus	*Le 'Sponsus', Mystère des Vierges sages et des vierges folles*, ed. Lucien-Paul Thomas, Paris, 1951
Young	[see General Bibliography]
ZDA	*Zeitschrift für deutsches Altertum*

Introduction

The material included in this section has been selected on two principal grounds: the date or occasion of the plays and performance records on the one hand, the language and subject matter of the plays on the other. For the vernacular plays the problem is to define 'early', and the cut-off point will be seen to vary with the different language groups; with very few exceptions nothing is included that is post-1400.

The Latin plays present a more difficult challenge since the word 'extra-liturgical' is not susceptible of exact definition. Here the decisions, as worked out between the editors of **Sections B** and **C**, have been arbitrary but fairly logical, though it has been necessary to split collections such as those in the Fleury or Benediktbeuern manuscripts between the two sectors. All miracle and saints' plays have been included in **Section C**, whereas for the biblical material the division generally depends on the number of liturgical festivals represented in the play. If Christmas and Epiphany, or the Passion and the Resurrection, are dramatised in one play, they cannot strictly be performed on a correct liturgical occasion for both. An additional criterion is the presence in a play of one or more members of the three persons of the Trinity. There are no extant plays earlier than the twelfth century which introduce God on the stage and even then only the Risen Christ appears in such liturgical dramas as the *Peregrinus* [see **B16**] or the *Noli me tangere* scenes between Christ and Mary Magdalene. However, a number of plays in the twelfth century dramatise the life and ministry of Jesus and especially the Passion; there are also plays of the Creation and Fall of Man and plays from eschatology ('the last things'). By the end of the thirteenth century God the Father and God the Holy Ghost have made their dramatic debuts in Latin or vernacular plays, thus presenting God in his triple credal role of Creator, Redeemer and Judge.[1] It is indeed this move towards more and more complex play sequences and eventually complete cycles that is the informing principle of the period and has been used to define the layout of the biblical material in this instance: from Easter play to Passion cycle. There are few morality plays from the earliest period, the only one of note being Hildegard of Bingen's *Ordo Virtutum* [The Play of the Virtues] (*c.* 1150–5), in which Anima (the Soul), brought up by the Virtues, is tempted by the Devil (the only spoken/male role) and rebels against her limited life. Eventually she repents and returns to the fold. The play has few directions and not much action, most of the effect depending on the music.[2] At around the same time appears the earliest known vernacular play, the Castilian *Auto de los reyes magos* (the Play of the Magi Kings), probably staged in Toledo Cathedral at Epiphany.[3] It lacks stage directions, but in that it seems not to rely on music, it is a lively forerunner of plays to come [see **C32(ii)** note 1].

Even when the Latin dramas were moved out of the liturgy, they remained within the Church and even within the Office: the Lazarus play by Hilarius may be performed at either Matins or Vespers [see **C17**]. Moreover, many plays, both Latin and vernacular, were performed by the clergy, some of them being subject to criticism as unsuitable for priests to perform [see **C32**, **C33**]. There is also evidence of lay actors performing plays presumably in the vernacular in churches – a custom which continued, in Spain and Italy at least, right through to the sixteenth century and beyond.[4]

Though Latin drama held its own in the thirteenth century, the fact that these plays were normally *sung* almost certainly contributed to their replacement in the following century by spoken vernacular texts, though some German plays retained a bilingual structure with speeches being first sung in Latin, then spoken in German [see **C56**]. As the laity became more involved, the proportion of vernacular drama also increased, encouraged by the use of vernacular in preaching, growing literacy especially in towns, and the increased availability of native paraphrases and translations of the Bible: a Bible in French, authorised by the Sorbonne, was completed in 1260.[5]

Since there are few examples of associated records and play-texts, such as are found later, the religious material has been separated into two divisions: 'Play texts and stage action' and 'Performance references and records, including examples of royal festivities'. The small group of Greek plays and references from the Orthodox East (which run well into the fifteenth century) has been kept together in section III [**C66–C70**], with the exception of two Passion plays [see **C5(i)**, **(ii)** and **C6(i)**, **(ii)**] included in section I.[6]

Section IV [**C71–C80**] is dedicated to the Feast of Corpus Christi and its drama, separated from the other religious material because, although the feast was established within the given dates, there are very few early plays: the evidence of early Corpus Christi dramatic celebrations has been arranged country by country.

Section V [**C81–C90**] gathers together the small amount of secular drama surviving from this period.

NOTES

1.   God the Father first appears in the Perugia Annunciation *lauda* [**C24**], the Holy Ghost in the Purification *lauda* (Perugia *laude*, p. 94).

2.   For text and commentary on Hildegard's *Ordo* see *Nine medieval Latin Plays*, trans. and ed. Peter Dronke, Cambridge, 1994, pp. 147–84.

3.   See Winifred Sturdevant, *The 'Misterio de los reyes magos': its Position in the Development of the Medieval Legend of the Three Kings*, Baltimore, 1927; reprinted New York, 1973.

4.   For example, the plays in S. Annunziata and S. Maria della Carmine in fifteenth-century Florence [see **G20** and *Staging*, pp. 243–7], and the Elche Assumption play [see **I53**].

5.   See 'The vernacular scriptures' in *The Cambridge History of the Bible*, vol. II, ed. G. W. H. Lampe, Cambridge, 1969, pp. 338–491.

6.   Items **C67–C69** in this section were selected, translated and edited by Professor Barry Baldwin.

I Play-texts and stage action in the religious drama

Of the wide range of texts to be considered in this section, many survive only as unattached plays composed for an occasion we cannot pinpoint and a purpose we cannot divine: floating masterpieces in a world of ordered form. Nevertheless, from dialogue and stage directions it is possible to recreate what may be called 'stage action' – the theatrical flavour of the work. The biblical material is arranged, as far as possible, chronologically to show the evolution and development that took place between 1100 and 1400 as the Christmas and Easter liturgical plays evolved into the great Passion cycles of the fifteenth century. The miracle and saints' plays, however, are grouped by protagonists. No attempt is made to separate the Latin from the vernacular plays, for it may be argued that the only major difference between the two in content and performance is that one group was sung and the other spoken.

FROM EASTER PLAY TO PASSION CYCLE

Easter plays continued to be written, performed and developed throughout the medieval period. Some churches continued to use the simple forms of the *Visitatio* [see **B9(b)**], but others introduced more and more stage action or vernacular dialogue, making provision for the three Maries to purchase spices or ointments from one or more merchants. The earliest dialogue between the *mercator* and the women appears to be that found in the Ripoll troper from Spain (*c.* 1100).[1] The play from the convent of Origny-Sainte-Benoîte (*c.* 1284) has all its rubrics and some of its dialogue in French [see **C1(i)**], and a number of German texts elaborate the scene with the merchants into a substantial play, such as is also found in the fully vernacular German *Osterspiel* (Easter play) from Innsbruck [see **C1(iii); F14**].[2]

1. See Young, vol. i, pp. 678–81.
2. For details of the Origny and German plays, see Young, vol. i, Chapter 14.

C1 The Maries buy ointment from the merchant

(i) The merchant at Origny also believes in Jesus

Young, vol. 1, p. 414

Here Mary Magdalene shall stand still and the other two Maries shall go up to the Merchant [. . .] In this same place the two Maries say:[1] Tell us, good, true and loyal merchant, if you are willing to sell this ointment, tell us quickly the price you want for it. Alas! We shall never see him again!

The Merchant says: If you greatly desire this ointment, you will have to give five gold bezants[2] for it; otherwise you cannot take it away. [They buy it.]

Maries: Do you want to come to the place where his sacred body was laid? Alas! We shall never see him again!

Merchant: Sweet ladies, do not ask that again. Certainly I want to go after Jesus. Those who do not follow him are fools.

[1] All the dialogue in this scene is in French.
[2] The bezant, a gold coin of Byzantine origin, apparently equated to the Roman *solidus*.

ii) Details of the purchase are given at Tours

Young, vol. 1, p. 440

[. . .] *Another merchant says to them: What do you seek? [quem queritis? See B9(b)]*

The Maries at once reply: We have come to buy perfumes or unguents, if you have what we need.

The Merchant replies: Tell me what you want.

Maries: Balsam, frankincense and myrrh, silaloe [?] and aloes.

Merchant: Behold all these things are already before you; tell me, how much do you want to buy?

Maries: About a hundred pounds will be sufficient. Tell us how much it costs, sir.

Merchant: You can have them for a hundred *solidi* [. . .] *Then the Maries give him the money and receive the ointment and they go to the sepulchre.*

(iii) The merchant engages an assistant, Innsbruck, 1391

Das Innsbrucker Osterspiel , ed. and trans. Rudolf Meier, Stuttgart, 1962, pp. 46–8

Rubin [to the Merchant] I'm a right good fellow, and know all the service of women. If you will reward me for it I'll go to Franconia with you; escort your wife to church; help her to weed the flax and moreover rub hair as one does with young women![1] I have lied all over Franconia, tricked people all over Bavaria. If you want to travel with me through the regions, we'll both end up in disgrace.

Merchant: You seem to me a well brought up lad, just right for my service [. . .] Tell me, dear Rubin, how low are your wages?

Rubin: Five shillings, sir. That's my charge.

[Two hundred lines later[2] the Maries enter and are met by Rubin] *He precedes them singing* [in Latin]:[3] Here are the three ladies, three ladies, they seek Jesus, Jesus, Jesus. Maria Magdalena, Maria Jacobena, and Salomena, you have called them the three ladies, give me the money, I'll give you sal- sal- salve for it. [He then speaks to the merchant] Sir, I have carried out what you sent me for; they can easily make us rich and we can have a good laugh.

[1] This remark, like many in this episode in German and in Czech, has a lewd double meaning.
[2] Out of a total play of 1300 lines, more than 500 are given to this scene.
[3] The play is mostly in spoken German but there are frequent sung speeches in Latin as well, on the same theme as the German but not exact translations.

RECORDS OF EARLY PASSION PLAYS

C2   Plays at Hagenau, 1187

Neumann, p. 38

The citizens of Hagenau,[1] with the permission of the magistrates and for the increase of religion and devotion to the mystery [*mysteria*] of the Lord's Passion and its most sacred instruments· instituted comedies, dramas and processions which drew spectators and pilgrims from the populations of all the neighbouring cities, towns, hamlets [*pagis*] and estates [*villis*].

[1] In 1135, the emperor, Frederick Barbarossa, had built in the Alsatian town a church to hold relics of the Passion: 'part of the Crown of Thorns, the Lance and a Nail'; these are three of the Instruments of the Passion which feature in many paintings and also in plays.

C3   A Passion play at Padua, 1244

D'Ancona, vol. 1, p. 88

That year, at Eastertide, there was a solemn and orderly representation of the Passion and Resurrection of Christ in Prato Vallis [Prato della Valle, a suburb of Padua].[1]

[1] The play is reported in similar terms in two other chronicles.

C4   A boy represents Christ on the cross, Siena, 1257

D'Ancona, vol. 1, p. 90

[From the council records of 7 April] Item, if it may please you that in reverence to Jesus Christ [something shall be given] to the boy [*puero*] who was placed on the cross in place of the Lord on Good Friday.[1]

[1] The council's answer is not recorded. The use of a boy implies a mimed rather than a speaking role.

THE FIRST PASSION TEXTS

There are no extant dramatisations of the Passion before 1100, for even the oldest, the Greek *Paschon Christos*, though attributed in the fifth century to Gregory of Naziansus, only survives in a twelfth-century manuscript. The latest editor of the text suggests that the date, though not the authorship, may be correct. The play shows a strong influence of Euripides, with the use of a chorus, messengers and descriptions rather than representations of stage action [see **C5**, **C6**]. The thirteenth-century Greek *Passion* from Cyprus is known only from a director's copy [see **C53**]. At this date Venice ruled Cyprus and the author may have been influenced by the traditions of the Venetian Latin church. Latin Passion plays first appear in the twelfth century with the oldest originating in Montecassino.[1] It covers the events of Holy Week from the Last Supper and betrayal by Judas to the death and burial of Jesus. Two other Latin Passions are found in the thirteenth-century Benediktbeuern manuscript; one is very short [*Passione breve*] but the longer one is substantial and involves a number of locations and a large number of characters; a series of scenes from the Ministry lead up to Palm Sunday and all the events of Holy Week. The earliest extant vernacular Easter play, the Anglo-Norman *Seinte Resurreccion* includes the death of Christ, and the episode with Longinus, followed by the deposition and burial.[2]

In all these plays the Crucifixion is shown but not the actual nailing; the main emphasis is on the *planctus* or lament of the Virgin Mary over the body of Jesus [**see B38**]. All the plays include the Resurrection [**see C1**].

---

[1] There is also a fourteenth-century actor's role for the Fourth Soldier from Sulmona which is textually related to the Montecassino *Passion*.

[2] The play is incomplete and does not actually include the Resurrection scene.

C5   The Crucifixion in the early plays

(i) Mary comments on the appearance of the crucified Christ

Paschon Christos, pp. 183–5

Let us then go and witness the suffering of my Son. O wretched me! No longer can I recognise my Son's glorious face. He has lost His glory and His exceptional beauty. O you who are the salvation for all men, Son whom I so longed for, why do you suffer thus? [. . .] How can I look at you crucified with thieves?[1]

---

[1] Throughout this text the action is described rather than shown but there is no question of a statue being used for Christ, since He speaks to Mary and John.

(ii) The Crucifixion in the *Cyprus Passion*

Cyprus Passion

[. . .] *and, having laid the cross on His shoulders, they shall lead Him away to crucify Him. And forthwith they shall take the Two Thieves out of the prison, and having laid upon each his cross, they shall walk with Him. And as they have come out a little, they shall press into service Simon and lay the cross on him [. . .](p. 191).*

And when they arrive at the place, the Gipsy Smith[1] shall come and crucify Him, and the Two Thieves, on the right hand, and on the left. (p. 193)

[1] Several different folktales connect the Gipsies with the Crucifixion. See *Cyprus Passion*, pp. 61–5.

(iii) The Montecassino *Passion*

Montecassino *Passion*, pr. Sandro Sticca, *The Latin Passion Play: its Origin and Development*, Albany, N.Y., 1970, pp. 66–78

Then the armed men [loricati] [. . .] shall lead Him to the place where He is to be crucified [they lay the cross] on His shoulders [. . .] The Lord Jesus shall kneel down and raise His hands to Heaven praying for the crucifying Jews [crucifixoribus Judeis], and shall say in a loud voice: [. . .] and the soldiers [. . .] place [ponant] Him on the cross and the two thieves.[1] (p. 76)

[1] The Latin text is very corrupt and incomplete.

(iv) The Benediktbeuern Crucifixion

Young, vol. I, p. 529–30

Then let Jesus be led to be crucified [. . .] Then let Jesus be hanged on the cross, and let there be a title: Jesus of Nazareth, the king of the Jews [. . .] Then let the Mother of our Lord come, lamenting, with John the Evangelist, and, approaching the cross, she looks upon the crucified one: 'Alas, alas, woe is me today and evermore! Alas, how I now look upon the dearest child that ever any woman in this world brought forth.'

C6   Longinus pierces Christ's side

(i) The Mother of God addresses the chorus

Paschon Christos, p. 213

Alas, young women! I see one of the wretches who have broken the thieves' legs cast his lance into my son's entrails [. . .] Look, see the blood which pours from the pierced body. See, see the two streams which spread out for blood and water gushed out from His side as soon as the sword of this young Roman of an enemy race, had struck the corpse [. . .] But the man who struck is himself afraid! With loud cries he proclaims that 'this dead man is truly the Son of God'.[1]

[1] This text equates the soldier who pierces Christ's side with the centurion who declared Jesus was the Son of God (Matt. 27:54).

(ii) The Captain declares Jesus is the Son of God before the centurion pierces him

Cyprus Passion, p. 199

Thereupon the Captain shall say: Truly this man was the Son of God, *But the centurion shall pierce His side with a spear and [the Captain] ready beneath shall catch the blood and the water.*

(iii) The soldiers bribe the blind beggar Longinus

Seinte Resurreccion, pp. 9–12

The soldiers [. . .] said to blind Longinus:[1] [. . .] Would you like to earn some money? [. . .] You shall have twelve pence for piercing this fellow's side. [. . .] *When they arrived at the cross, they put a lance in his hands [and said]*: Thrust upwards hard without failing, so it goes in as far as the lungs, then we can be sure whether he's dead or not. *He took the lance and thrust it into the heart. Then blood and water flowed down onto his hands; he wet his face with them and as soon as he put it to his eyes, that very moment he could see and then said:* O Jesus, O worthy Lord! [. . .] You have shown me such mercy that now I can see with eyes that saw not. I yield myself to you, I cry you mercy.

[1] The tradition that Longinus was blind was widespread in the Middle Ages. In the *Semur Passion* he appears with a boy as guide.

(iv) Blind Longinus explains his actions

Perugia laude, vol. i, p. 233

I am Longinus [. . .] who was deprived of light; I heard that everyone was saying that Jesus was nailed to the cross. 'He will not return to earth,' they said, 'unless you should pierce him in the side' [. . .] But Jesus, Lord of pity, whom I should not even touch, let fall a little of His precious blood on my face and gave me back my sight completely and so I confess He is truly God.

THE EVOLUTION OF THE CYCLIC PLAY

At the end of the thirteenth century, when the vernacular had almost (but not quite) replaced Latin for the extra-liturgical drama, performances of the first biblical cycle play are recorded – in Latin, by clerks [see **C7(i)**, **(ii)**]. About this time, too, a major new development took place: the beginning of the Italian sung vernacular *laude* [praises], hymns composed and sung by groups of flagellants [*disciplinati*] in Perugia *c.* 1260 and then in many Italian towns from the late thirteenth century. Each group of flagellants was centred on a church, and the *laude* were performed on Sundays and feast days during and after the use of the discipline. Being newly composed in the vernacular, they do not include the traditional chants and hymns which feature in the liturgical plays. Many *laude* are lyrical but others include dialogue, impersonation and dramatic action.[1] The fourteenth-century Perugia *laudario* containing the full sequence of texts begins, like the Church calendar, at Advent, with the subject of each *lauda* being taken from the gospel of the day. The sequence begins with an Antichrist and Judgement play (one of the normal themes for Advent)[2] and continues with the Annunciation through the Christmas, Lenten and Easter seasons to the Ascension followed by a number of saints' plays.[3] [For further references to the *Lauda*, see **C9**, **C19**, **C24**, **C47**, **C72**; **section G**.]

[1] For a confraternity costume list see **C47**.
[2] See Muir, *Biblical Drama* pp. 148–53.
[3] The dramatic *lauda* attains its zenith with Jacopone da Todi (*c.* 1236–1306), whose *Queen of Heaven* (*Donna de Paradiso*) represents the masterpiece of the form.

C7   Clerks present cycle plays at Cividale, 1298, 1304

Young, vol. II, pp. 540–1

(i) Of the representation of the play of Christ [*Ludus Christi*] AD 1298: [. . .] On Pentecost and the two following days there was a performance of the Play of Christ: that is to say the Passion, Resurrection, Ascension, coming of the Holy Spirit and the coming of Christ at the Judgement [. . .] in Friuli, in honourable and praiseworthy manner by the clerks of the city.

   (ii) In AD 1304 a play was performed by the clerks, or rather the Chapter of the city, and the following incidents were presented: first the Creation of the First Parents, then the Annunciation to the Blessed Virgin, the Nativity and many others; then the Passion and Resurrection, Ascension, coming of the Holy Spirit and of Antichrist and other matters and lastly the coming of Christ at the Judgement. And the aforesaid matters were done with solemnity in the *curia* of the Lord Patriarch on the feast of Pentecost with the two following days in the presence of the Patriarch of Aquilegia, [. . .] and many other lords of the city and the castle of Friuli.

CREATION TO ANNUNCIATION

The several episodes of the Christmas season were collected within one general seasonal play early in the twelfth century.[1] This celebration of the Incarnation was soon preceded by numerous plays of the Annunciation, which in turn were prefaced by Old Testament prophets and occasionally plays of the Fall – the cause of the Incarnation. Latin Prophet texts date from the twelfth century,[2] as does the important vernacular Anglo-Norman *Adam* play with its three sections: the Fall, the murder of Abel and a procession of prophets looking forward to the Redemption. The only other Latin Old Testament plays, both incomplete, the thirteenth-century

Ordo de Ysaac et Rebecca from Austria and the Laon *Ordo Joseph* are mainly interesting for staging details [see **C12**, **C13**] and the use of allegorical glosses in the former.[3] The prophets also appear in the Perugia Christmas *laude*. The earliest Italian Fall play, from the 1405 Orvieto collection, includes the first vernacular play of the Fall of the Angels [see **C9**].

[1]   Plays of the Purification were not included in the cycles before the fifteenth century.
[2]   For Latin Prophet and Daniel plays, see **B12**, **B35**.
[3]   The allegories are interspersed in the action and sung by the *pueri*. For example, Jacob as younger brother superseding Esau, the elder, is an allegory of the New Law and the Old Law (Young, vol. II, p. 260).

THE FALL OF THE ANGELS AND OF MAN

C8   A Creation and Prophet play, Regensburg, 1194

Young, vol. II, p. 542

In AD 1194 there was celebrated the *Ordo* of the Creation of the angels and the fall of Lucifer and his followers, the Creation and Fall of Man and the Prophets, during the papacy of Celestinus III and the reign of the ever-august Emperor Henry and his contemporary, Bishop Conrad.

C9   God the Father orders that Lucibello be expelled from Heaven

Orvieto *laude*, p. 341

God the Father says: Cherubim, Rafael, soldiers [*milizie*] and armies [*eserciti*] and other Thrones, put Lucibel[1] in the Hell with the other demons. And there crown him with serpents for greater despite. Let his seat be of fire and for ever to darkness we condemn him.

[1]   The name Lucibel(lo) is found also in other Italian and Breton plays. (See Muir, *Biblical drama*, p. 204 n.13).

C10   Lucifer reigns over Hell

Das Wiener Passionsspiel, in *Das Drama des Mittelalters*, ed. Richard Froning, 3 vols., Deutsche National-Litteratur 14, Stuttgart, 1892, vol. I, pp. 305–6

Then the Lord [dominica persona] *casts him out with his followers*: Go hence Lucifer to Hell with all your fellows [. . .] *Then let Lucifer be made ready in the form of a devil and he is led by devils to his seat in the midst of all in silence and the devils go into Hell.*

   [After the Expulsion Adam and Eve lament] *and let there be demons ready who first drag Adam before Lucifer* [. . .] *after this they lead in Eve and she stands before Lucifer and says*: O woe is me, wretched woman [. . .] *and she is led to Hell.*[1]

[1] These opening scenes in the Vienna play are followed by the worldlinesss of Mary Magdalene [see **C16**]. At the beginning of the incomplete manuscript are the words: *Ad materie reductionem de Passione domini. Incipiet ludus pascalis.* (For the reduction of the Passion of the Lord. Here begins the Easter play.)

CII   Stage action in the Anglo-Norman *Adam*

Anglo-Norman Adam

(a)   Adam and Eve have to leave Paradise

Then Adam [takes] a spade and Eve a hoe and they begin to cultivate the earth and sow corn. After they have sowed they go and sit down, at a little distance, as if worn out with toil and gaze frequently towards Paradise, beating their breasts and weeping. Then comes the Devil and plants thorns and thistles in the cultivated ground and then he goes away. When Adam and Eve return to their plot and see the thorns and thistles, they prostrate themselves in violent grief, beating their breasts and their thighs and showing their grief in their gestures. (pp. 181–2)

(b) Cain murders Abel and is taken to Hell

Then Abel genuflects to the East. And he shall have a pot hidden in his garments which Cain shall strike as if killing Abel. Then Abel shall lie down as dead [. . .]

Then the Figure[1] goes to the church and the demons come and lead Cain to Hell, with many blows; Abel, however, they lead more gently. (p. 188)

[1] In this play God is referred to once as the Saviour [*Salvator*, see **C46(i)**] but otherwise as the Figure [*Figura*] probably from Hebrews 1:3 where the Son is the '*figura substantiae*' of the Father (see L. R. Muir, *Liturgy and Drama in the Anglo-Norman Adam*, Oxford, 1973, p. 15).

C12   Esau goes hunting

Play of Isaac and Rebecca, p. 261

Soon Esau shall go out, with his companions, with a bow and arrows, blowing the horn in the manner of a huntsman. Then they shall pursue a goat or other animal, seeking to kill it with arrows.

C13   Potiphar's wife tries to seduce Joseph

Laon *Ordo Joseph*, pr. Young, vol. II, p. 270

Then the wife of Potiphar, enamoured of Joseph, calls him secretly. Joseph does not accept her proposal, and when he tries to leave she seizes his cloak. Joseph abandons it and flees. She hurriedly casts blame on the innocent man and coming to the front of her house [domum] *carrying the cloak with her raises a cry in these words:* [. . .] (p. 270)

PLAYS OF THE CHRISTMAS SEASON

A number of Latin Christmas plays are set inside the church and make great use of liturgical pieces, including not merely the Nativity, with the Shepherds, but also the Kings and even the Slaughter of the Innocents and the Flight into Egypt. Since they cannot therefore be linked with a specific liturgical occasion but belong to both Christmas and Epiphany, they are treated in this section with the extra-liturgical plays. The cult of the Christmas crib was greatly developed in the thirteenth century by St Francis of Assisi and his recreation of the Nativity at Greccio [see **B19(c)**].[1] The most elaborate Christmas play is that from Benediktbeuern [see **C14**] which begins with a prophet scene [see **B18(c)**] and includes a brief Annunciation and Visitation, the Kings with Herod, the annunciation to the Shepherds (who are tempted by the devil not to obey the angels and go to Bethlehem); the adoration of the Shepherds and a meeting with the Kings on their return; adoration of the Kings and Slaughter of the Innocents.[2]

There are not many vernacular Nativity plays before the fourteenth century. The Perugia Christmas *laude* sequence[3] begins with Joseph's doubt and dream, and includes the journey to Bethlehem followed by the Nativity and Adoration of the Shepherds. A mime play appears to have been staged during the Council of Constance in 1417 [see **C15**].

[1] The relics of the manger were preserved in Santa Maria Maggiore in Rome, and Mass was celebrated in the chapel every Christmas (see Young, vol. II, p. 25).
[2] A corrupt play which follows in the manuscript includes the Flight into Egypt; see Hansjürgen Linke, 'Der Schluss des Weihnachtsspiels aus Benediktbeuern.' *Zeitschrift für Deutsche Philologie* 94 (1975), Sonderheft: pp. 1–22.
[3] This sequence of *laude* contains almost no stage directions and little stage description.

C14   The Benediktbeuern Christmas play
Young, vol. II, pp. 172–90

(a) The birth of Jesus

Mary replies: My soul magnifies the Lord. *Then Elizabeth goes away for this character no longer has a place* [amplius non habebit locum]. *Then Mary, who has already conceived by the Holy Spirit, goes to her bed and gives birth to the Son. Beside her sits Joseph in decent clothes and an abundant beard* [prolixa barba]. *The Boy being born, the star shall appear and the choir begin this antiphon*: [. . .] (p. 180)

(b) The Adoration of the Shepherds and the Kings

Then the Shepherds go to the manger singing this antiphon [. . .] *Having sung it, they worship the Boy. Then the Shepherds are returning to their work* [officia sua] *when they are met by the three Magi who say*: Shepherds, tell us what you saw and the news of

Christ's Nativity? *The Shepherds reply*: We saw a child in swaddling clothes and a choir of angels praising the Saviour. *Then the Kings go to the manger and after worshipping the Boy they offer their gifts: the first gold, then frankincense, the third myrrh. Then they go a little way and then sleep; and the angel appears to them in sleep saying*: Do not return to Herod etc. *Then they do not go back to Herod.* (p. 188)

C15   A Christmas play at the Council of Constance, 1417

E. K. Chambers, *The Mediaeval Stage*, 2 vols., Oxford, 1903, vol. I, p. 101

On the 24th day of January [. . .] the bishops from England: the bishop of Salisbury, bishop of London, and five other English bishops invited the councillors[1] of Constance with other honest citizens of the same, to Walter Burchardt's house [. . .] and gave them a huge and splendid meal i.e. two successive courses of eight dishes each [. . .] During the meal, between the courses, they made [*machten*] tableaux and dumb-shows [*bild und geberd*] such as Our Lady bearing her Child, Our Lord and also God, with very elaborate materials and clothes. And they showed Joseph with her, and the holy Three Kings bringing gifts to Our Lady. And they had made a bright gold star which went in front of them on a fine metal wire. And they did King Herod, and how he sent after the Three Kings and how he slew the little children. All this was done with very rich clothes and with great belts of gold and silver.

[1] It is not clear from this eye-witness account whether these are the city councillors or those gathered for the Church Council.

THE MINISTRY OF JESUS

Not many scenes from the Ministry are dramatised before 1300 though the worldliness of Mary Magdalene and her anointing of Jesus' feet appear in the Cyprus and the Benediktbeuern *Passions* [see **C16**].[1] The latter scene also appears in the Fleury *Lazarus* and the *Cyprus Passion*. There is also a play of the raising of Lazarus by Hilarius [see **C17**]. These two episodes together with other scenes from the Gospels are found in the early vernacular Passions. The Magdalene scene is particularly popular in German texts.

1.   The latter play opens with brief scenes of the calling of the Apostles and the conversion of Zaccheus followed by the entry into Jerusalem.

C16   The worldliness and repentance of Mary Magdalene
(i) Mary buys perfumes from the merchant

Benediktbeuern *Passion*, pr. Young, vol. I, pp. 514–33

Mary sings: The world's pleasure is sweet and agreeable, [. . .] I'll lay down my life for worldly enjoyment and serve the cause of temporal pleasure. I'll pamper my body, caring for nothing else; I'll deck it out in many colours. *Now let Mary go with* [*her*] *young women to the merchant, singing*: Salesman, bring me your [very best] wares and I'll give you much money in return. And some perfumes, too, if you have them [. . .]

Let the merchant sing: [. . .] These are sweet-smelling; if you try them, you'll surpass all other fleshly desire.

Mary Magdalene: Merchant, give me colour to redden my cheeks, That I may entice young men with the thoughts of love [. . .] Look at me, you young men. Let me give you pleasure. (pp. 520-1)

(ii) The repentant Mary Magdalene anoints Jesus' feet

Cyprus Passion, pp. 141–7

Prepare the supper-table [in the house] of Simon, and there the Master and His Disciples shall sit down, and Simon shall wait upon them. Thereupon the Harlot shall enter and shall weep and cry out: [. . .]
This completed, she shall betake herself to the Vendor of Ointments to buy the ointment, speaking to the Vendor of Ointments [. . .] until, at last, she takes the ointment, that is to say, a vessel full of extract of roses, [. . .] and having received the ointment, she shall run and pour it over the feet of Jesus, saying nothing, but merely wiping the feet of Jesus with her hair.

(iii) Martha rebukes Mary for her worldly life

Maastricht *Passion*, p. 331

Martha to Magdalene: Mary, I tell you [. . .] your pleasure is not good when it is so uncontrolled. It is sinful and impure and also very common [*gemeine*]!

C17   The raising of Lazarus

Hilarius *Lazarus*, pr. Young, vol. II, pp. 212–18

First, as Lazarus is becoming faint, the two sisters, Mary and Martha, with the four Jews, will come forward, stricken with grief, and, standing beside his bed, they will sing these verses: O God, have mercy on him whom you can heal. *The Jews will say to console them*: Dearest ones, leave off weeping, nor provoke to tears those who are standing by; rather, address your supplications to God, and beg health for Lazarus. [. . .]

Then He [Jesus] will say to the dead man: O Lazarus, come forth [. . .]

Then when Lazarus has arisen, Jesus will say: Behold, he lives! Now unbind him and allow him to depart without bonds.

Lazarus, having been unbound, will say to those standing by: Behold, the mighty works that are of God [. . .] *When this is finished, if it has been performed at Matins, let Lazarus begin the Te Deum, but if at Vespers, the Magnificat.*

PLAYS FROM ESCHATOLOGY

Antichrist and the Last Judgement episodes are mentioned in the Cividale cycles [see **C7**], but the Judgement was never part of the cyclic Passion as it was for the later Corpus Christi cycle play. The *Sponsus* [Bridegroom], *c.* 1100, from Limoges, dramatises the parable of the Ten Virgins which was always linked with the Judgement [see **C18**]. About one-third of this sung Latin play is in the Provençal vernacular, including the lament of the Foolish Virgins: 'Ah woe to us wretches, we have slept too long' (p. 178). The twelfth-century Tegernsee *Antichrist* is an elaborate play with detailed staging directions [see **C36**]. The only vernacular eschatological plays from this period are a *lauda* from Perugia and the Besançon *Jour du Jugement* which emphasises the role of Antichrist, here equated with the schismatic pope, Benedict XIII (reigned 1394–1417), but includes also the angels with the phials of the wrath of God from Revelation, Chapter 16 [see **C20**]. One strong response to the uncompromising implications of such pieces comes from early fourteenth-century Thuringia [see **C21**].

C18   The Foolish Virgins are rejected by the Bridegroom

Le '*Sponsus*', *Mystère des Vierges sages et des vierges folles*, ed. Lucien-Paul Thomas, Paris, 1951, p. 186

Christ: Go, wretches, go cursed ones, for you are condemned to eternal torments and now to Hell you will be taken.[1]
Then the demons seize them and they are cast [precipitentur] *into Hell.*

[1] This part of Christ's speech, like many other sections of the play, is in sung vernacular not Latin.

C19   Antichrist and the Judgement

(i) Antichrist is struck down by God

Tegernsee *Antichrist*, Young, vol. II, p. 387

A burst of thunder suddenly explodes above Antichrist's head and he collapses, and while all his followers are rushing out in headlong flight, Ecclesia says: Behold the man who did not choose God as his helper!

(ii) God orders Gabriel to kill Antichrist

Perugia *laude*, vol. I, p. 38

Christus: Go, Gabriel, thrust your sword into Antichrist and give him a great beating [*flagello*] [. . .]
The Angel kills Antichrist with a flaming sword, saying: Your glory is taken from you because that is the will of the Eternal Father. Satan! you and your followers, lead him away and torment him strongly!
Satan with other demons leads him to Hell.

C20   The angels pour out the phials of the wrath of God

Le Jour de Jugement, Mystère français sur le grand schisme, ed. Emile Roy, Paris, 1902, pp. 240–1

(a)   The First Angel destroys the followers of the Beast

First angel with phial [a fiole]:[1] I shall pour mine out without delay on those wicked ones [. . .] who have adored the vile Beast.

[1] Cf. Revelation 16.2.

(b)   The Fourth Angel's phial is for Antichrist

Fourth angel with phial: And I shall empty mine on Antichrist who called himself Son of God and thus insulted the true God of all creation [. . .] This sun will be so hot that it will stifle by great excess of heat those who followed him.

C21   A violent reaction to a parable play, Eisenach, 1322

Neumann, p. 307

In 1322 [. . .] the people of Eisenach on the Sunday evening two weeks after Easter, [. . .] presented a beautiful play of the Ten Virgins, five of them wise and five foolish, about whom Christ preached in the gospel [Matt. 25:1–13].[1] And Landgrave Frederick the Joyful [. . .] saw and heard how the five foolish Virgins, despite grief and repentance and good works, were shut out from eternal life and that Mary and all the saints begged in vain that God would change his verdict. Then he fell into doubt and was moved to great anger and said: 'What is this Christian faith? Will God not have mercy on us at the intercession of Mary[2] and all the saints?' [. . .] And after that he suffered a stroke as a result of the prolonged anger so that he was confined to bed for three years. Then he died at the age of fifty-five.

[1] There are three separate accounts of this incident in the chronicles, one in Latin and two in German. I have translated from the third (Neumann, no. 1483) [cf. **F28(i)** for a slightly different account of the incident].

[2] Mary appears in most later Judgement plays but has limited success as intercessor.

THE COMPLETION OF THE PASSION CYCLE

In addition to the Latin cycle plays [see **C7**] and the Italian *laude*, there are also, by the end of the fourteenth century, performance records from Avignon and London suggesting substantial Passion or cycle plays [see **C22**, **C23**] and texts are extant from this period in German, French and Dutch. The play-text of the Frankfurt Director's script (*Dirigierrolle*) begins with the Prophets and includes substantial scenes of the Ministry before the Passion, Resurrection and, finally, the Ascension [see **C56**]. The St Genevieve manuscript (*c.* 1380) includes a series of plays from the Creation to the Resurrection which could be played as a cycle.[1] The three-day Cornish *Ordinalia* (*c.* 1375) includes Old Testament material, a Passion sequence ending with Christ's entry into Heaven, and a Death of Pilate play [see **D11**].

The late fourteenth-century Maastricht *Passion* [see **C16(iii)**] is the only extant play-text of the period to contain a full Passion cycle beginning with the Creation and Fall of the Angels and Man. The incomplete text breaks off at Jesus' Arrest.[2] A scene peculiar to these great cycle-plays is the Debate on the Redemption or Trial in Heaven,[3] which first appears in a scene between the angels, God the Father and the Son in the Perugia Annunciation *lauda* [see **C24**]. A similar episode but one where the angels are replaced by the personified virtues, Justice and Mercy, is included in the Maastricht *Passion* [see **C25**].

1. The St Genevieve Nativity play and the Resurrection play are both preceded by Fall plays. This may reflect a variety of possible performance combinations.
2. Preserved till the eighteenth century in the convent at Maastricht, the play is written in a dialect of the Lower Rhineland found in both Germany and The Netherlands.
3. The concept goes back originally to Psalm 85.11 [Vulgate numbering]. One of the most often used sources of this scene is the fourteenth-century volume of *Meditationes* attributed to St Bonaventure.

C22   An Italian merchant describes a Passion play at Avignon, 1400

Gustave Cohen, 'Mystères sacrés et profanes à Avignon au quatorzième siècle', in *Etudes d'histoire du théâtre en France au moyen âge et à la Renaissance*, Paris, 1950, pp. 164–5

I have nothing new to tell you [the eye-witness is writing to his patron] except that on the 7th of this month many of the tradesmen of Avignon at their own expense put on a play on the three days of Whitsun; which was the Passion of Our Lord when he was crucified. (Three months ago they acted a play of the siege of Troy, like the one the Duke of Anjou attended, where there were many towers with barbicans and banners.) Let me tell you about the three outstanding things: Firstly, two hundred actors were needed to stage the said play [the Passion] with, in addition, so many costumed players and armed men that no one could count them.[1] Secondly, many scaffolds were set up outside the Dominican monastery, which were occupied two days running by men and women, and decked with so many banners, carpets and painted cloths that the King of France could not present a finer array; never was there such a royal and magnificent spectacle which attracted between ten and twelve thousand spectators. Thirdly, the town ordered a guard for the fortress of three hundred of the most important burgesses and merchants, commanded by a marshal and a vice-marshal, with three hundred pennants with the arms of the Church,[2] all on horseback, armed from head to foot riding through the city to keep guard there – a fine sight to see. Thus for two days they rode around while the play was on and a man was put on the cross just as Our Lord was. It is said the play cost more than a thousand ecus. It is ten years since they last did the play and they took care to guard the town lest there should be any trouble.

We suffered loss by it for we had to lend a lot of armour without recompense and it was damaged.[3]

[1] The scale of this performance and the choice of the three days of Pentecost suggests something more than a simple Holy Week play.
[2] Avignon was papal territory at this date.
[3] The writer, Tieri di Benci, was agent for the house of Datini.

C23   Scriptural plays at the Skinners Well, London, 1390–1409

John Stow, *A Survey of London*, ed. Charles Lethbridge Kingsford, 2 vols., Oxford, 1908; reprinted 1971, vol. 1, pp. 15–16

[. . .] the said church [of Clerkenwell] took the name of the well, and the well took [the] name of the parish clerks in London, who of old time were accustomed there yearly to assemble, and to play some large history of Holy Scripture. And, for example, of later time, to wit, in the year 1390, the fourteenth of Richard II, [. . .] the parish clerks of London, on the eighteenth of July, played interludes at Skinners' Well near to Clerks' Well, which play continued three days together; the king, queen and nobles being present.[1] Also in the year 1409, the tenth of Henry IV, they played a play at the Skinners' Well, which lasted eight days, and was of matter from the Creation of the World.[2] There were to see the same the most part of the nobles and gentles of England.

[1] In 1391 Richard II donated £10 to the clerks for a play on the Passion and the Creation of the World which suggests a cyclic play.
[2] An eight-day play is not recorded anywhere else from England and again the reference suggests some form of cycle.

C24   God the Father and God the Son plan Man's redemption

Perugia *laude*, vol. 1, pp. 98–9 (*Annunciation*)

The angel begins [*speaking*] *to the Trinity*: O great Trinity, have mercy on Man who was your creation; for whose wicked act all are deprived of the kingdom [. . .]

God the Father: Man has broken the commandment, and his wife also. No one can be found who could make amends [*penetenza portasse*] for him [. . .]

The Son to the Father: If by my suffering Humankind could find salvation [. . .] I wish to bring about this redemption [. . .]

[The Father sends Gabriel to the Virgin Mary]

C25   The debate in Heaven in the Maastricht *Passion*

Maastricht *Passion*, pp. 306–7

Our Lord addresses Mercy [. . .] Hear, for Justice sake, and, daughter, for the sake of Mercy,[1] what I shall now ask you.

   Mercy speaks: I was ever and shall ever be your daughter and you are my father. I am called Mercy and you know my name [. . .]

     Our Lord to Truth: Daughter, for Justice sake, give me advice and counsel [. . .]

     Truth answers: I am called Justice, the name of your Godhead is given to me [. . .][2]

---

[1]   In this first debate of the Virtues, there is some confusion of the roles.

[2]   The equation here of Truth and Justice is unique. At the end of the debate God sends Gabriel to the Virgin Mary and the cycle continues.

MIRACLE PLAYS

The earliest miracles to be dramatised were those of St Nicholas, who was a popular subject for Latin plays in the twelfth and thirteenth centuries. With Rutebeuf's *Miracle de Théophile* (*c.* 1280), however, the role of miracle worker was taken over by the Virgin Mary. There is also a little-known collection of Miracles of St Genevieve, patron saint of Paris, composed towards the end of the fourteenth century. There is a fragment of a miracle play of St James of Compostella in Provençal and another is recorded in the accounts for 1324–5 from the Confrérie St Jaques in Paris: '[the sum of] £13 *par*. which the pilgrims who performed the play on the day of the meeting collected from the tables at dinner'.[1] Miracle plays were often performed at guild meetings [see **C26**].

   Saints' plays from this period include a Provençal play of St Agnes [see **C48**], and some *laude* from Perugia.

1.   Robert A. Clark points out that the members of the Confrérie are referred to as *pélerins* [pilgrims], which suggests the actors were themselves part of the group. (See 'The "Miracles de Nostre Dame par Personnages" of the Cangé Manuscript and the Sociocultural Function of Confraternity Drama', UMI Dissertation services, 1994, p. 136.)

C26   Plays for an Amiens confraternity at their annual meeting, 1393

Graham A. Runnalls, 'Medieval Trade Guilds and the *Miracles de Nostre Dame par personnages*', *Medium Aevum* 39 (1970), pp. 257–87

A remarkable literary society was founded [at Amiens] in 1393, under the title of Confrérie du Puy.[1] The members of this *confrérie* were almost all the rhetoricians[2] of Amiens who met on the principal feasts of Our Lady at the house of one of their number, called the master of the *puy* [for a poetry competition]. On the feast of the Purification [2 February], the *confrérie*'s feast day and [. . .] the day assigned for the election of the Master for that year, the latter had a great feast at his house and during the dinner the Master had a *mystère* performed and gave a green hat and a copy of the *mystère* to each of those present.[1] (p. 271)

[1] This account is quoted from a history of Amiens (1832) based on the unpublished *confrérie* records. The term *mystère* is used for any kind of serious, usually religious, play.
[2] For rhetoricians' groups see **Section H**.

ST NICHOLAS PLAYS

Four different miracles of St Nicholas survive in eight Latin play-texts,[1] five from France and three from Germany: the *Tres filiae* [Three daughters] tells how the saint threw three balls of gold into their house to be the girls' dowries;[2] there are two versions of the miracle of the resuscitation of three students murdered by an innkeeper.[3] Less well known is the miracle of the son of Getron [see **C27**]. In the *Iconia* stories (two Latin texts and one French) the statue of the saint is used to protect treasure. The earliest vernacular play, the French *Jeu de St Nicolas* by Jean Bodel of Arras, was composed in about 1205.

1. Young, vol. II, ch. 26, gives the texts of all eight plays, from various locations, including Fleury and the works of Hilarius.
2. Texts from Hildesheim and Fleury. The story is commemorated in the pawn-brokers' sign of three gilded balls.
3. Texts from Hildesheim, Einsiedeln and Fleury.

C27   The Fleury St Nicholas rescues Getron's son who has been carried off by invaders

Fleury St Nicholas play[1]

(i) The boy is carried off to a far land

Meanwhile let Getron and Euphrosina set off with their son and a number of clerks for the church of Saint Nicholas, as if to celebrate his feast day. And when they see the king's armed men coming to that place, let them flee into the city, forgetting their son in their fear. Then let the king's attendants seize the boy and take him to the king. (p. 351)

[1] This is the longest and most elaborate of the plays with extensive stage directions. Unfortunately no music has survived for any of the Nicholas plays.

(ii) King Marmorinus is feasting. St Nicholas appears and carries the boy back to his parents

[*Then*] *let water be brought and the king wash his hands, and as he begins to eat let him say*: I was hungry and now I'm thirsty; let wine be brought to me as quickly as possible by my [slave], Getron's son.

Meanwhile let one in the likeness of Nicholas appear, take hold of the boy clutching the freshly poured cup of wine, [. . .] and put him back in his place outside the gates [of his city] and let him withdraw, apparently unnoticed. (p. 356)

C28   A play of the statue of St Nicholas

Jeu de St Nicolas

(i) The town crier announces the news

Oyez, oyez, gentlemen all! Come along, give me a hearing! On the King's behalf, I have to tell you that henceforth his treasure will not be locked-up. You'll find it all laid out openly as far as I can see. If anyone can steal it, let him do so. For he has only got it guarded by a single horned mommet[1] – dead apparently – he doesn't move. (pp. 23–4)

[1] St Nicholas' statue in its mitre (worn at this date with the division in the front) is referred to as an idol or Mahomet, from which comes the English 'mommet'.

(ii) In a tavern, three thieves learn about the treasure

RASOIR   [. . .] A mommet lies on top, made of stone or wood – I don't know which. The King won't get even a whisper from him if somebody steals or carries off the lot. We'll go together all three, this very day, when we are sure it's the right moment.

PINCEDÉS   So help you God, is this true?

RASOIR   Is it true? Yes, by St John, I heard the proclamation [. . .] Let's see if we can get credit on that.

CLIQUET   Go on, Pincedés, pour him a drink. Good news deserves a tankard full.

PINCEDÉS   There you are, Rasoir. You can collect the winnings next time you see me gambling [. . .] That reminds me, who's for a game?

CLIQUET   Shall we toss for heads or tails?

PINCEDÉS   No, let's dice, the three of us. (p. 33)

(iii) St Nicholas orders the thieves to return the treasure

ST NICHOLAS   You wretches, I am Saint Nicholas, I who put wanderers back on the road. Go back the way you came and take the treasure back to the King! You have committed a crime in even thinking of theft. With my statue laid on top the treasure should have been well protected. Make sure it is put back again: as you value your lives, when you have replaced the treasure put the statue back on top! (p. 58)

MIRACLES OF OUR LADY

Rutebeuf's *Miracle de Théophile* (c. 1280) has only a few stage directions but the scene is easily reconstructed from the lively dialogue [see **C29**]. The forty plays in the collection of *Miracles de Nostre Dame* (preserved in the fourteenth-century Parisian Cangé manuscript) were composed for the annual meeting of a confraternity of the goldsmiths' guild in Paris.[1]

[1] Probably the Confrérie Notre-Dame-de-l'Annonciation, founded in 1353, see Clark, *Miracles*, pp. 110–14.

C29   Théophile sells his soul to the devil

Rutebeuf, *Le Miracle de Théophile*, ed. Grace Frank, Paris, 1975

(i) Salatin conjures up the devil

Here Théophile comes to Salatin who talked to the devil whenever he liked [. . .] *Here Salatin speaks to the devil*: A Christian has come to me for help and I've taken much trouble with him for you are no enemy of mine! Are you listening, Satan? He'll come tomorrow, so be waiting for him [. . .]

Salatin shall conjure up the devil [An incantation in gibberish] *Now the devil shall come, having been conjured, and say*: You spoke the formula correctly, he who taught you didn't forget a word. (p. 6)

(ii) Théophile signs a pact with Satan

Here Théophile shall go to the devil in great fear, and the devil shall say to him: Come this way! Quickly then [. . .]

THÉOPHILE   I've come to pray and beseech you to help me in my need [. . .]

THE DEVIL   Then clasp your hands together, and become my vassal [*mes hon*] and I shall help you [. . .] Now, since we're agreed, you should know that I must have a charter from you [. . .] For many people have cheated me because I did not take their charters, that's why I like them done properly.

THÉOPHILE   Here it is, I've written it out. *Then Theophile hands his deed to the devil.* (pp. 9–11)

(iii) Our Lady forces the devil to return the deed

[Théophile repents and prays] *Here Our Lady shall speak to Théophile and say*: Who are you, walking about here?

THÉOPHILE   Have mercy on me, Lady. I am the wretched Théophile [. . .] whom the devils trapped and caught [. . .] Once you looked on me as a son, fair queen!

OUR LADY   I am not interested in your flattery, Go away! Get out of my chapel!

THÉOPHILE   I dare not, Lady. Flower of eglantine, lily, rose, in whom dwells the

Son of God [. . .] Honoured Lady, I know my soul will be devoured and I shall dwell in Hell [. . .]

OUR LADY Théophile, I once knew you, and you served me long ago. Now, be assured I will reclaim the deed that you handed over in ignorance. I'll go and fetch it.

Now Our Lady shall go for Théophile's charter.

OUR LADY Satan, where have you hidden yourself? [. . .] Give me the deed you took from my clerk.

SATAN SPEAKS Give it back to you? I'd rather they hanged me!

OUR LADY Then I shall trample on your belly!

Now Our Lady shall carry the covenant back to Théophile. (pp. 23–4)

C30   Guilty women are saved by the Virgin

(i) The bailiff is suspicious at the sudden death of a young man

Miracle of a Woman whom Our Lady Saved from being Burned, lines 578–84; 593–600

The bailiff hears the news: I'm astonished, and wonder how he can be dead [. . .] I think he has been wounded by someone. Yes, I'm sure of it. His death is so sudden.[1] [He visits the house to see the corpse and certify the death]: Uncover the bier for me quickly and unstitch speedily part of his shroud so that I can see him as far as the thigh so as to be the more certain. I will complete my investigation before he is buried.[. . .] Uncover his face for me, completely, so I can see his throat and chest [. . .] Hey there! Seize the mother, the daughter and the father. They cannot deny that it looks as if he has been murdered. It's obvious. See how black his throat is. Someone, whoever it may be, has strangled him.[2]

[1] The woman has had her son-in-law murdered because he was trying to seduce her.
[2] The mother-in-law admits her guilt and is condemned to death but because of her penitence the Virgin intervenes. The woman spends the rest of her life in a nunnery.

(ii) A woman accidentally drowns her newborn child

Miracle de l'enfant ressuscité, pp. 20–32

LADY Mother of God, Mother of God, how shall I bear this agony? Mercy, sweet Mother of God. O God, my back! O God! [. . .] Agnes, my loyal friend I'm sure that no woman born has ever endured such waves of pain as I am doing!

MAID This is nothing yet, madam, be sure of that. When it comes to the birth there won't be a single vein of yours that does not burst – except the little finger.

[. . .]

MAID Madam, the bath is all ready for you to get in when you want to. I'm sure it will do you a lot of good; so get in.

LADY I quite agree, Agnes. But I cannot get in by myself. You'll have to help me

until I have got in [. . .] Now go and fetch my child. I want to hold him in this
bath. [. . .] Now I must rest here and sleep. I am so tired I must just shut my
eyes until she comes [. . .]

MAID She's asleep,I think. Where's she put the child? [. . .] Alas! Her baby's
drowned![1]

[1] The woman is condemned to death for infanticide but the husband prays to the Virgin, and the child
is brought back to life.

MIRACLES OF ST GENEVIEVE

A sequence of plays on the life and miracles of the patron saint of Paris, composed
about 1380 probably for a confraternity of St Genevieve, is preserved in the library
of the abbey of St Genevieve in a manuscript, compiled about 1440 which also
includes biblical and saints' plays [see **C50**].[1] An extract from one of the St
Genevieve pieces apears as **C31**.

1.   The only complete edition of the manuscript dates from 1835; for more recent editions
of individual plays see Runnalls, *Etudes sur les mystères*, Paris, 1998, *Bibliographie*.

C31   Angels and devils quarrel over the soul of an unbaptised child

Mystères inédits, vol. 1, pp. 238–44

JESUS Gabriel, Raphael, Michael. Leave Heaven and go down and take the soul
which the devils are holding and put it back into the body, willy nilly.[. . .]
Genevieve [. . .] begs for it and I do not want to refuse her.

ANGELS We shall do that, most powerful Lord [. . .]

ST MICHAEL (*to the devils*) Now then, wretches arguing there. Hand over that
soul, come on.

DEVILS Go to the other door, you're beaten, Master Michael. You'll get nothing.

ST MICHAEL Yes, I shall, slavering tumblers, for it's God's will [. . .]

RISOUART [a devil] Now listen, Sir. Whoever has original sin [. . .] even if he's got
no other faults is damned if he dies in this state. The sentence is unchange-
able.

ST MICHAEL Risouart, God who is the master of the law, wants him restored to
life.

[A long legal argument follows. Satan joins them]

SATAN Devil take it! This wretched Genevieve has so bewitched him that she's
made God mad.

THE ANGELS (*taking the image*) Come on, hand over!

SATAN (*hanging on tightly to the image*) I won't! Help! Help! Here, here!

THE OTHER DEVILS HELPING HIM Michael, Michael You shan't have it!

ST MICHAEL (*to the other angels*) Go on, hit these wretches.

THE ANGELS (*hitting out*) Take that! And that!

THE DEVILS Leave it, it's ours.

ST MICHAEL (*seizing the soul from him while the others are hitting them*) We'll have him, in spite of you. Go on, get out of here [. . .] [The devils flee]. *Then St Michael takes the soul and says to St Genevieve* [. . .]

II *Performance references and records*

A number of early play-texts include specific descriptions of stages, decor, costumes and properties to be used for the performance and there are also a few examples of cast lists, actors' roles, and director's play-texts. The picture they give is full of gaps, particularly on the identity of the actors and the nature of the audiences, but it does provide some idea of the general principles of theatrical production in the period before 1400. In each of the following sections, the texts are arranged as far as possible in chronological order. Details of the plays concerned can be found in the first section.

THE AUTHORITIES AND THE PLAYS

The explosion of drama inside and outside the church in the twelfth century inevitably led to trouble with the authorities in every country on both moral and practical grounds [see **C32**; with **C32(ii)** compare **B27(b)**]. In addition to what they tell us about the attitudes of the authorities at this period, these references provide information on the number and scale of performances of different kinds of plays.

C32   Alfonso X of Castile lays down guidelines for church drama, *c.* 1260

Alfonso X el Sabio, *Primera Partida*, ed. Juan Antonio Arias Bonet, Valladolid, 1975, trans. Louise M. Haywood [for Alfonso see **I28**]

(i) Priests who perform or watch unsuitable plays are condemned

Nor should priests stage plays of mockery in order to lure the people [to church] to watch them, and if other people do these things, the priests should not go to see them, nor should they be allowed to perform in the churches, but rather they should be expelled from the churches remorselessly because Our Lord said in the Gospel that his house was for praying in and should not become a den of thieves. (p. 161)

(ii) Some performances are acceptable and should be encouraged

But there are plays that the clergy may stage, like the birth of Our Lord Jesus Christ, which tells how the angel came to the Shepherds and told them Jesus Christ was born, and, besides His birth, how the three Kings came to worship Him,[1] and also His Resurrection, which shows how He was crucified and arose on the third day. They may stage these [plays] which incite the people to good deeds and religious devotion in order that the people may recall through [them] that these things happened in fact. But this must be done very properly and devoutly, and in the large cities, where archbishops or bishops are present and with authorisation[2] from them or from others, acting in their name, and they must not do this in towns or disreputable places or in order to earn money (p. 162).

[1] The earliest extant text from Castile, and its only example of Christmas drama, the incomplete, late twelfth-century *Auto de los reyes magos* [Play of the Wise Kings], has unfortunately no stage directions.

[2] The curé in Bayeux who, in 1351, was fined by the Cathedral chapter for putting on a Nativity play in his church, may have failed to ask permission *(Mystères inédits,* vol. II, p. 3).

C33   Clerks are warned against profane plays, *c.* 1303

Robert of Brunne's 'Handlyng Synne', ed. F. J. Furnivall, EETS (OS), vols. 119, 123 (1901), (1903), pp. 154–6

[A clerk] is forbidden [. . .] to make or see miracle plays[1] [. . .] If you [clerks] act plays by highways, or in graveyards, [. . .] they [*sic*] break the vow they took, and renounce God and Christendom if they put on for anyone such miracles and bawdy devices, or expensive tournaments. These are the vanities you forsook, when you embraced the Christian life [. . .] If priest or clerk lends a vestment that has been hallowed by sacrament, he is to blame more than a layman; such sacrilege will blight his name and the offence will be his ruination: a just punishment for his action. Dances, carols, summer games all encourage shameful behaviour; you do not please God when you undertake to organise these; moreover you will be accountable for all whom you cause to sin in such ways.

[1] Christmas and Easter plays are allowed. Robert [usually known as Mannyng] is here translating from William Wadington for whose *Manuel des Pechiez,* see **B29**.

C34   Performance of plays causes environmental damage, 1301

Public Record Office, London; pr. 'Plays at Clerkenwell', W. O. Hassall, MLR 33 (1938), pp. 564–7

To our Lord the King [Edward I]. The unfortunate Prioress of Clerkenwell prays that he take action to provide and order a remedy from the damage which the people of London cause with their frequent miracle plays and wrestling-matches, devastating and destroying her corn and grass. The result is that she derives absolutely no profit from her crops, nor can she obtain any unless the King mercifully takes her side against them. They are savage folk, and we cannot resist them or bring them to justice through the law. Thus, Sire, we beg you to have pity on us.[1]

[1] In his response dated 8 April 1301 Edward ordered the mayor and sheriffs of London to redress the prioress's grievance.

C35 A fight breaks out during a clerks' play, 1346

REED, *Cumberland/Westmorland/Gloucestershire:*, ed. Audrey Douglas and Peter Greenfield, Toronto, 1986, pp. 63–4, trans. pp. 147–8

[. . .] at Carlisle the Monday before the Feast of St Michael the Archangel, 29 September, 1346 [Certain named men] swear on oath that on Sunday, the Vigil of St Peter ad Vincula [1 August], just as the clerks began to perform a certain miracle play[1] in Carlisle marketplace at the centre of the city, Edward Walays (of the Bishop's household) struck Walter Cole of Scalby three times on the head with a large stick, and Walter grabbed him by the hood.[2] [A general uproar followed].

[1] Another account of the incident has simply: 'when the clerks performed a certain play in the marketplace of the said city of Carlisle'.
[2] This clash, arising from a long-running feud between the castle garrison and the citizens of Carlisle, led to a series of violent incidents.

STAGES AND DECORS

Nearly all the early stages described involve a multiple set. Many were probably performed in church using the open areas of the church as was done in the liturgical plays but the twelfth-century Antichrist play may have been intended for a court performance [see **C19, 36**].

C36 An elaborate setting for the Tegernsee *Antichrist*

Young, vol. II, pp. 371–87

The temple of God and seven royal stations must first of all be arranged in the following order: in the East the temple of God; near it should be placed the station [*sedes*] of the king of Jerusalem and that of Synagoga. In the West the station of the Emperor of Rome, and near it the stations of the king of the Teutons and of the king of the Franks; to the South, the station of the king of the Greeks; to the North, the station of the king of Babylon and that of *Gentilitas*.[1] (p. 371)

[1] There is no English equivalent for this collective word for the Gentiles.

C37   Changing use of locations in a Latin Lazarus play

Fleury *Lazarus*, p. 201

Then Jesus with his disciples shall leave there and go away as if to Galilee and let there be prepared for them on the other side a place [locus] where they can remain. Afterwards the Jews shall go away into some other place as if in Jerusalem so that from there they may come to a suitable place to console the sisters. The house itself, of the said Simon, can serve for Bethany (he having gone away) and then Martha shall be put there. Lazarus shall then begin to be ill.

C38   Multiple staging for the *Conversion of St Paul*

Fleury *St Paul*, p. 219

In order to stage the conversion of the blessed apostle Paul, let a seat for the chief priest be prepared in a suitable place representing Jerusalem. And let another seat be prepared, and upon it a young man representing Saul; and let him have armed attendants with him. And in another place a little way away from these seats, as if in Damascus, let two seats be prepared, on one of which a man named Judas shall be seated, and on the other the chief [priest] of the synagogue of Damascus. And between these two seats let a couch be prepared on which a man representing Ananias should lie. When these things are prepared in this way, let Saul say to his attendants: [. . .]

C39   Rubrics for the sets for the Anglo-Norman *Adam*

Anglo-Norman Adam

(i) Paradise shall be constructed on a raised place, with curtains and silk hangings surrounding it at such a height that the persons who are in Paradise can be seen from the shoulders upwards; there shall be ferns and sweet scented flowers and varied trees with fruit hanging from them, so that it appears a very pleasant place. (p. 166)

(ii) [Cain and Abel] go to two large stones which shall be placed ready for this purpose. The stones shall be set apart from each other, so that when the Figure comes, Abel's stone is on his right and Cain's on his left. Abel offers a lamb and incense, from which the smoke rises. (p. 186)

(iii) Then the prophets shall be ready in a special private place, suitable for them. Then shall be read in the choir the reading: 'You it is I now invoke, O Jews.' And the prophets shall be called by name and shall enter in proper order and speak their prophecies loudly and clearly. Abraham shall come first [. . .] Seated on a stool[1] he shall begin his prophecy in a loud voice. (p. 188)

---

[1] All the prophets sit to prophesy except Balaam who is on horseback [*equens*].

C40   Verse prologues describe the set for the late twelfth-century *Seinte Resurreccion*

Seinte Resurreccion pp. 1–2; trans. *Staging*, pp. 6–7

[MS C:[1] *If you have the devout intention of presenting the Holy Resurrection in honour of God and reciting it before the people, arrange that there shall be room to make a very large acting area and also you must make proper provision how you set out the places, and that the mansions* [maisuns] *which belong to it shall be properly provided for. First of all the crucifix and after that the tomb, the men at arms who will keep watch there, and the Marys who will come there.* [P: *And on the platforms* [estals] *first of all Pilate with his vassals (he will have six or seven knights); Caiaphas will be on the next, and the Jews* [la Juerie] *will be with him, then Joseph of Arimathea; in the fourth place shall be Lord Nichodemus* {C: *and Longinus the blind beggar*}; *each of them shall have his men with him. In the fifth the disciples of Christ; the three Maries shall have their place in the sixth.*] *The disciples on their platform should behave in a prudent way. David's tower and Master Bartholomew and a jail shall be put there to incarcerate the prisoners. Let Hell be put on one side there, in which will be the devils together with the patriarchs who shall be held there in bonds. You must not forget Heaven where the angels must dwell. Let it be arranged that they make Galilee in the middle of the playing area, and Emmaus, a little castle, where the pilgrims will take their lodging. And when everyone is seated and there is quiet on every side, Joseph of Arimathea shall come and say* [. . .]

---

[1] The two manuscripts of the *Seinte Resurreccion* are both incomplete with some overlapping. A staging prologue in verse precedes each and is particularly important as showing what locations would have been included. The one from manuscript C is given here with interpolations from manuscript P, where they give fuller information.

C41   An Annunciation play for the Feast of St Mark, Venice, 1267

D'Ancona, vol. I, pp. 92–3, note 3

Be it known to you, my lords, that the last day of January[1] is the double feast and procession [of St Mark] in which, after the boys and the clergy, there came [. . .] a clerk dressed in women's clothes all in gold. And the said clerk was seated on a richly draped chair carried on the shoulders of four men, with banners of gold before it and on each side. He represented the Virgin Mary and when he came past the Doge he bowed to him, and he returned the courtesy. Then there followed another clerk in the guise of an angel, who was seated on a richly draped chair carried on the shoulders of four men. And when he reached the place where the Doge was, he bowed to him and our Lord the Doge returned his courtesy. And after that the procession went on [. . .] until it came to the church of Our Lady St Mary; and when the clerk dressed like an angel came into the church and saw the other dressed to represent the Virgin Mary, he rose up and said 'Hail Mary full of grace, blessed art thou among women and blessed is the fruit of thy womb, Jesus' [. . .] After these words every one left the church and returned to their homes. [1378 it was decreed that] Mary and the Angel in the Feast of St Mark in Scolis, for the honour of the most glorious [lady] and the feast, should not rise from their seats when they pass in front of the Doge.

---

[1] This is the feast of the translation of the relics of St Mark to Venice. His usual feast day is 25 April. [See **section G** for further Italian material.].

C42   Sets for different episodes in the life of St Genevieve

Mystères inédits, vol. 1

(i) Stones represent a well

Then she takes the pot and goes to where [. . .] there are stones like the mouth of a well. Then she leans her elbows on them and weeps. (p. 178)

(ii) St Genevieve's oratory in Paris

Then she stands in front of Paris, a little downstage [*un pou avant ou champ*]. And in that place there shall be a small altar on which is a statue of Our Lady and in front of the altar a small bench [*fourmete*] where she can kneel to pray and nearby her bed, made of a table upside down [*? en hault*] and a thin coverlet on it and a wooden pillow. (p. 181)

COSTUMES AND PROPERTIES

The use of rich and striking costumes was a feature of the church drama from the start [see **B13**, **17**, **32**, **35(b)** etc.]. Often church vestments might be used [see **C46**], sometimes with disastrous results [see **C44**].

C43   Costumes for the Tegernsee *Antichrist*

Young, vol. II, p. 372

Then Ecclesia, in the garb of a woman and wearing a breastplate and crown, shall come forward supported, on her right, by Mercy with the oil and at her left, by Justice bearing scales and the sword, both dressed as women also. (p. 372)

C44   A disaster with costumes in Dunstable, c. 1110

Young, vol. II, p. 541

Geoffrey [of Gorham] [. . .] settled at Dunstable, awaiting the mastership of the school of St Albans, promised to him once again. Here at Dunstable he staged a certain play of St Katherine – which we call in the vernacular a 'miracle play' – in order to beautify which, he requested the Sacristan of St Albans that copes worn by the choir should be made available for his use, and he obtained them. And this play of St Katherine took place [. . .] Then, through a catastrophe which occurred on the following night, the schoolmaster's house caught on fire, and was burnt down, along with Geoffrey's books and the copes already mentioned. Therefore, not knowing by what means he should compensate for such damage suffered by both God and St Albans, he gave himself to God amid the holocaust, adopting the religious habit in St Albans Cathedral. And this was the reason why, later promoted to Abbot, he displayed so much diligence in order to make reparation for the choir's costly copes.

C45   Set and costumes for the play of Isaac and Rebecca

Play of Isaac and Rebecca

(i) The play requires three separate locations

Three separate mansions [tabernacula] *shall be set up with beds and other accessories as are suitable, one for Isaac, the second for Rebecca and Jacob and the third for Esau. Kitchens for Esau and Jacob, where fine meals should be laid out* (lit. 'visible'), *with bread and wine. A roebuck* (or 'wild goat') *if this is possible. Two kids. Hairy covering for the hands. A hairy skin to cover the neck. Jewish garments for Isaac and his two sons in various colours* [. . .] *Bow with arrows.* (p. 259)

(ii) Rebecca disguises Jacob as his brother

The mother covers Jacob's hands and neck with hairy skins and she clothes him in the best, perfumed clothes left in Esau's dwelling. (p. 263)

C46   Costumes for the Anglo-Norman *Adam*

Anglo-Norman Adam

(i) Costumes for God

Then shall come the Saviour wearing a dalmatic. (p. 166)
      The Figure approaches, wearing a stole. (p. 178)

(ii) Adam and Eve wear garments of glory in Paradise

Adam and Eve shall take their places before him, Adam wearing a red tunicle,[1] but Eve in the white garments proper to a woman, with a white silk headdress. (p. 166)

---

[1] We are also told that Cain wears red garments and Abel, white (p. 183). For the significance of these
   costumes, see Lynette R. Muir, *Liturgy and Drama in the Anglo-Norman Adam*, p. 35.

(iii) Adam changes garments after the Fall

[Adam] bends down so that he is hidden from the people and takes off his solemn vestments and puts on poor garments sewn with figleaves. (p. 176)

(iv) Other garments prescribed for the play

An angel comes, wearing an alb and carrying a flaming sword.[1] (p. 181)
Abraham, an old man with a long beard wearing flowing garments. (p. 188)
Balaam, an old man in flowing garments, seated on an ass. (p. 191)
Daniel, young-faced but dressed as an old man. (p. 192)

[1] It is interesting that the costumes of the devils are the only ones not described.

C47   Costumes lent out by the Perugia confraternity, 1339

Ciro Trebalza, 'Una Laude umbra e un libro di prestanze', in *Scritti vari di Filologia dedicati a Ernesto Monaci*, Rome, 1901, pp. 188–9

These are the objects lent by the confraternity of St Dominic for the play of the dead [. . .]. Pietro Pavolo de Francesco and Bartolomeo de Pavolo de Nato came to fetch them.

First, the cloak, scythe, hour-glass, the hands [gloves?] of Death.
And for the play of the Passion:

4	short surplices [*tonecelle*]
1	yellow cope
2	shirts without tails [*fondo*] with the amice, returned but torn [*schagnate*]
10	wigs, five in good condition and five middling: returned the five good ones and three middling
7	beards
1	flesh-coloured garment with stockings
	Another pair of flesh-coloured leather stockings
7	yellow angels' crowns

C48   Costume references in the play of St Agnes

Jeu de Ste Agnès

(i) Agnes' nakedness is miraculously covered by her hair

Christ tells the Archangel Michael to go and visit Agnes and take her a garment of hair[1] [. . .] Then the angel gives Agnes the garment of hair and places it on her head [. . .] and he tells the harlots they should leave [the brothel] and the angel throws their clothes out [saying:] Cast away these garments which are foul and stinking and go into Agnes who is truly the bride of the Son of God, Jesus Christ, as I tell you. (pp. 17–18)

[1]   The fourteenth-century Provençal play follows very closely the *Vita* of St Agnes, which tells how when Agnes insults the Roman gods she is put, naked, into the brothel: by a miracle her hair grows and covers her.

(ii) God sends Gabriel with garments for Agnes

Gabriel, go and unbind my daughter and clothe her with this garment for she is still naked [. . .] *Then Gabrel puts the garment down beside Agnes but does not speak to her and Agnes puts on the garment God has sent her.* (p. 21)

C49   Properties for a Resurrection play in Cambrai Cathedral, 1376

Mystères inédits, vol. II, p. 5

For putting the sepulchre ready on Easter Eve, for the nails, the ropes, and workmen-actors [*compagnons ouvriers*] who worked on this: 13s.

Item for the *mystère* of the Resurrection,[1] for preparing Jesus, that is to say for a pair of shoes and gloves, and artificial thunder: 7s.

Item as a reward [*gratification*] for the actors who played the parts in the said *mystère* of the Resurrection: one *mouton royal* worth 30s.

[1]   Although apparently performed in the cathedral on Easter Day this can scarcely be called liturgical since the performers are paid working-men.

C50   Costumes in a miracle of St Genevieve

Mystères inédits, vol. I, p. 187

Here St Peter stands up, wearing an alb and dalmatic with a splendid cope over them and a cowl(?) [*cocuche*] on his head; then St Paul wearing an alb, tunicle, cope or crimson cloak thrown over his shoulder, holding a sword; then St John wearing an alb with a white or green dalmatic and holding a palm branch; then St Denis, wearing alb, dalmatic and crimson chasuble, holding a scroll.[1]

[1]   These are the normal church vestments often shown in pictures of the saints, see Glossary.

MUSIC IN THE PLAYS

In addition to the Latin plays which were mostly sung throughout, music played an important role in the vernacular spoken plays: the *Sponsus* and some other Latin plays include music for speeches in vernacular, while the Italian vernacular *laude* are entirely sung.

Some plays, like the *Anglo-Norman Adam*, included a separate choir singing liturgical pieces, elsewhere such items were sung by the characters as in the Provençal St Agnes [see **C48**]. Music was particularly used in the representation of Heaven.

C51   Singing angels mentioned in many plays

(i) Angels sing at the birth of St Genevieve

Mystères inédits, vol. I, p. 170

Here the angels sing *Virginis prolet* or some other piece without leaving Paradise;
then the maid stands up holding a swaddled infant and says [...]

(ii) Singing angels regularly escort Our Lady to earth

Miracle de l'enfant ressuscité, pp. 60–1

OUR LADY   Rise up now John and you, Eloy; you too, Agnes. All of you come down
there with me [...]
SECOND ANGEL   [...] Let us all go together singing – this seems good to me – this
fair sweet rondeau.[1]

[1]   A similar scene, including a rondeau, occurs in most of the *Miracles de Nostre Dame*.

(iii) An angel sings even in Hell

Jeu de Ste Agnes, p. 35

*Then the angel goes to Hell and finds the soul [...] which the devils are beating. And the
angel laments* [facit planctum] *to the tune* [in sonu] *of Veni Creator Spiritus [...]
Afterwards the angel speaks to Agnes to the same tune:*[1]

[1]   There are sixteen sung items in this play, not limited to the heavenly host but sung by many different
characters to older melodies, both religious and profane, many of them written out in the manuscript.

C52   Noise and devils for Hell and damnation

(i) The Foolish Virgins are damned

Sponsus, p. 186

CHRIST TO THE FOOLISH VIRGINS [*Fatuas*]   [...] Go, wretched ones, go
accursed! You are condemned to everlasting torment and now you shall be
taken off to Hell.
At once demons shall seize them and they shall be cast into Hell.[1]

[1]   The implications of this direction for the staging of the play are interesting [see **C18**, **C19(ii)**; **F28**,
F29, **F30**].

(ii) Adam and Eve are dragged off to Hell

Anglo-Norman Adam, p. 183

Then comes the Devil with three or four demons carrying iron chains and fetters,
which they put round the necks of Adam and Eve. Some push and some pull them
towards Hell. Others come to meet them, rejoicing in their damnation. Some point
at them, then throw themselves on them and drag them into Hell. A great smoke
rises and there are noisy rejoicings and a clattering of pots and pans so that it can

be heard outside. After a time the demons come out and run about but others stay in Hell.

DIRECTING THE PLAY

Two important examples of director's prompt-copies are extant: the mid-thirteenth-century Greek *Cyprus Passion* and the early fourteenth-century Frankfurt *Dirigierrolle* [see **C53**, **C54**, **C56**]. The former is particularly interesting since it begins with instructions to the director on how to set about his task. Within the body of the script there are also detailed directions on how to set the stage, dress the actors and arrange their movements. The *Dirigierrolle* is more of a working copy with stage directions in Latin and *incipits* of the Latin or German speeches in between.

C53   The duties of the director

Cyprus Passion, p. 125

Be merciful to us, our Lord Jesus Christ, Son of God, and be not angry with us that wish to represent in a play Thy life-giving sufferings, through which Thou hast graced us with tranquillity:

You, who are master of the present production and are going to direct the others, must before the beginning of the action organise in proper order the things such an enterprise requires and have them all ready, so that when it is needed each thing is at once ready and prepared. Furthermore you must make individual contact with each actor and costume each according to the character he is to represent, from Christ and the Apostles to the other men and women. And similarly for the Jews and everyone else. The performers must be selected, choosing those who are suitable to perform and present the types of characters. In addition they must be able to ask and answer in writing.[1] And instruct them to play their part in such a way as not to excite laughter and mockery, but with piety and great attention in the fear of God. Let them take heed not to interrupt each other or cut in so that confusion follows, but let each one, as you wish it, ask or reply in proper form. Further let them not make any alteration nor say anything which might make the spectators laugh. But let all things be done to arouse awe or fear.

---

[1] This suggests a literate and possibly clerical cast.

C54   Setting the scene and positioning the actors

Cyprus Passion

(i) The raising of Lazarus

Place Christ and His Disciples before the grave of Lazarus at a goodly distance therefrom, but Martha and Mary, the sisters of Lazarus, and a few Jews, place nearer to the grave;

and he that plays dead Lazarus, within the grave, bound with graveclothes, and his face bound about with a napkin.

Thereupon see you send someone unto Jesus. (p. 127)

[. . .] *And he that was dead shall come forth, bound with graveclothes, and his face bound about with a napkin.* (p. 135)

(ii) The washing of feet

Keep in readiness stools, a basin, and a towel. The Disciples shall sit down in their right order. (p. 151)

[. . .] *Now, having washed their feet, He shall lay aside the towel and put on His garments again and, sitting down again, He shall say unto them* [. . .] (p. 153)

C55   Directing the actors how and where to stand
Anglo-Norman Adam

(i) *And they shall both stand before the Figure, Adam however nearer, with a calm expression and Eve more humbly.* (p. 166)

(ii) *Then both come forward and stand before the Figure, not quite upright, but somewhat bowed under the weight of their sins.* (p. 178)

C56   The Frankfurt Director controls the performance
Die Frankfurter Dirigierrolle in *Das Drama des Mittelalters*, ed. Richard Froning, 3 vols., Deutsche National-Litteratur 14, Stuttgart, 1982, p. 354

(i) In the Garden of Gethsemane

Here Jesus with his disciples will go to the Mount of Olives where green trees have been placed to form a garden, there Jesus will say to his disciples: [In Latin, then in German][1] *Wait here and pray. Having said this he will withdraw a little from them, sorrowfully, and pray. Judas, however, will not be with the disciples but remain behind them and run to the Jews saying to them* [. . .]

[1]   Only the first line of each speech is given.

(ii) The play ends with the Ascension

Here the said disciples as prearranged [ex preordinacione] *shall have a table and table-cloth* [mensale], *bread, wine and fish, roast meat, even eggs and wafers* [tortas]. *When they have sat down the Lord* [dominica persona] *shall break, distribute and eat* [the bread] *with them. The meal being quickly over, they shall rise and the Lord shall sing: I am ascending to my Father and your Father, alleluia!* [. . .] *This being ended, the Lord leads the disciples to [Earthly] Paradise,*[1] *and having received the banner* [vexillo] *he shall summon the Souls and lead the way to the place where he is to ascend. The souls, who have put on white garments, shall follow the Lord singing: [. . .] until they come to the stairway by which they must ascend. Let there be also a throne where God in Majesty is seated, splendid and high and wide enough to receive all the Souls comfortably, having also a stairway convenient for ascending to this height.*

[1] It is unusual for the Souls left in Earthly Paradise after the Harrowing of Hell to be brought into the Ascension scene. (cf. Muir, *Biblical Drama*, p. 139.)

C57   A confraternity is founded to organise and control the York Paternoster Play, 1388–9

REED *York*, pp. 6–7, trans. p. 693.

First, as to the cause of the founding of the said fraternity, it should be known that after a certain play on the usefulness of the Lord's Prayer was composed, [. . .] and was played in the city of York [. . .] very many said: 'Would that this play were established in this city for the salvation of souls and the solace of the citizens and neighbours!' Wherefore, the whole and complete cause of the foundation [. . .] of the same fraternity was that that play be managed at future times for the health and reformation of the souls, both of those in charge of that play and of those hearing it. And thus, the principal work of the said fraternity is that the play should be managed to the greater glory of God, the deviser of the said prayer, and for the reproving of sins and vices [. . .] Item, they are bound, whenever the play of the said Lord's Prayer is shown in the form of a play in the city of York, to ride with the players of the same through certain principal streets of the city of York (and to be dressed in one livery, to give greater ornament to their riding) [. . .] until the said play be completely finished for the peaceful managing of the said play.

ACTORS

Actors seem to have come from a variety of backgrounds. Many of them must have been literate [see **C58**] and able to speak and sing Latin, especially in the twelfth and thirteenth centuries. By the fourteenth century actors may be members of guilds and confraternities or simple citizens [see **C59**]. Sometimes these actors were rewarded by the town for their plays [see **C60**].

C58   The actors must speak the verse correctly

Anglo-Norman Adam, p. 166

And let Adam be carefully instructed when he is to speak, that he reply neither too soon nor too late. Not only he, but all the actors shall be so taught that they speak calmly and with gestures suited to what they are saying. And in the verse they shall neither add nor omit a syllable but pronounce everything clearly and say in proper order what they have to say.[1] Whoever names Paradise shall point to it with his hand.

[1] This is almost a transposition of the rubrics from the liturgical books, some of which date back to the early centuries of the church: 'Moreover, great care must be taken not to spoil the sacred melodies by unevenness in the singing [. . .] Neither are those to be imitated who hurry the chant thoughtlessly or who drag out the syllables heavily.' (See Muir, *Liturgy and drama* p. 43).

C59   Citizens of Cahors act in a Limoges churchyard, 1290, 1302

Mystères inédits, vol. II, p. 2

A play of the miracles of blessed St Martial[1] [was performed by] some citizens of Cahors in the St Martial's cemetery, near the stone cross in the said cemetery [on the eve of the Ascension].

[1] The church of St Martial of Limoges was an important centre for early drama including the oldest extant *Ordo prophetarum* and the *Sponsus* [see **C18, C52**].

C60   Deventer pays a number of different acting groups

Neumann, pp. 271–5

1339	Item to the scholars for their play £2 by order of the echevins [*iussu scabinorum*].[1]	
1357	Item [on 2 January] to the scholars of the town for their play by the echevins	£2
	Item on the same day to the maidens [*virginibus*] of the town for their play from the echevins	16ss.[2]
1366	To the young ladies [*joncvrouwen*] for their play	15ss.
	To the boatmen [*schijmmans*] for their play	20ss.[3]
1380	To the young ladies for their play	£2 8ss[4]
	" to the clerks [*cleriken*] "	£2
	" to the bowmen [*schutten*] "	£2
	" to the young men [*basselierres*] "	£3

[1] Similar payments occur in 1340, 1347, 1348, 1355, 1356. At this time, Deventer was noted for its schools, some of which were run by the Brethren of the Common Life, [see **H2(a), (b)**].

[2] In subsequent years they are both given money, the scholars always receiving £2, the girls varying but lesser amounts. In 1361 the scholars are simply described as youths [*juvenibus*].

[3] The records changed to vernacular in 1362. These boatmen did plays in winter to earn some money when the weather prevented their working.

[4] From 1394 onwards the references are all to men.

C61   A cast list for a Christmas play in Toulon, 1333

Revue des Sociétés savantes, série 5e, vol. VIII (1874), p. 259 [see also *Mystères inédits*, vol. II, p. 3]

The list[1] includes] Mary as a child and grown-up [*in magna etate*]; Joachim and Anna; Isacaar guardian of the Temple maidens; Abiatar [high priest]; Joseph; Anastasia [the midwife]; Angels and Shepherds; three Kings each with a body-guard [*miles*]; Herod, his son Arthaleus, six soldiers [*milites*] and twelve armed men [*armati*]; let there be the disputation of Wisdom;[2] a boy, the son of Mary. Messengers, devils, scoundrels and butchers [*ribaldi et carnificies*].[3]

[1] The list, preserved in a lawyer's register gives not merely the list of the cast but the names of the sixty-nine actors – all male and from the leading families in Toulon. It is clear from the *dramatis personae* that the play includes the early life of Mary and the full Christmas sequence.
[2] This may be the Debate in Heaven [see **C25**].
[3] These are surely for the Slaughter of the Innocents.

C62   The parish clerk performs, *c.* 1400

Geoffrey Chaucer, *The Miller's Tale*, pr. *The Riverside Chaucer*, ed. Larry D. Benson, Oxford, 1988, pp. 70, 71.

He could trip and dance in twenty different styles, after the school of Oxford, throwing his legs to and fro [. . .] Sometimes to demonstrate his sprightliness and skill, he plays the role of Herod up on a high scaffold.[1]

[1] It is interesting to note that in the Prologue to the tale we are told that the drunken Miller spoke 'in Pilate's voice' (p. 67). [see **D40**]

AUDIENCES AND THEIR REACTIONS

Many plays include a command or entreaty to the audience to listen quietly; sometimes the character speaking threatens those who misbehave [see **C63**]. References in prologues suggest some of the audience were seated. One presentation is commemorated by the performance of a miracle [**C65**].

C63   Prologues address the audience in various ways
(i) The prologue tells the audience the story of the play and begs their attention (*c.* 1205)

Jeu de St Nicolas [see **C28**] p. 1

Good sirs, don't be overmuch astonished if you see some curious business here, for whatever you see us doing will be a faithful attempt at presenting the miracle on the stage just as I've described it. The legend of Saint Nicholas is the theme and story of our play: Give us some peace and you will hear it!

(ii) The audience is warned to behave itself (*c.* 1300)

The Cambridge Prologue, pr. *Non-Cycle Plays and Fragments,* ed. Norman Davis, EETS (SS)1, Oxford, 1970, p. 114–15

Now sit still and all pay attention, to make sure that nothing unpleasant happens to you here! Sit apart from each other, so that folk can pass between you. You who are gathered together in this crowd, don't talk too loudly – it would also bring great disgrace on you to impede our entertainment. Moreover, I swear by this day and by the law of Mohammed[1] that if anyone is so bold as not to keep the peace the emperor commands his men to seize and hang him, unless it be a child or a lunatic – and he has ordered that even he shall be tied up and soundly thrashed [. . .] Now sit still, that is my advice! Amen.

[1] The speaker is evidently a member of a pagan emperor's court. There are two versions of this text, one in Norman French (translated here) and one in English. They are similar but not identical.

(iii) The prologue to the Play of the Martyrs urges good behaviour (*c.* 1380)

Cycle de mystères des Premiers Martyrs, ed. Graham A. Runnalls, Geneva, 1976, p. 65

Good people, listen a little, quietly, without making a fuss. You'll have less trouble, I assure you, if you consent to be silent a while than if you jostle one another or make an uproar or disturbance. Now sit down and listen and you'll hear what I am trying to say.

(iv) A mixed audience for an outdoor play (early fifteenth century)

The Pride of Life, pr. *Non-Cycle Plays and Fragments,* ed. Davis, pp. 90–105

Silence ! And listen, all of you that are here – rich and poor, young and old, men and women: both learned and unlettered, strong and bold. Lords and gracious ladies, listen in kindly mood to the way our show will start and end [. . .] Now stand still and be courteous, and abide what the weather brings, and before you depart you shall be glad that you came here.

C64   An audience is frightened by the fighting, Riga, 1204

Young, vol. ii, p. 542

This winter [1204] a prophet play (in the manner which the Latins call comedy) was performed in the middle of Riga, that the rudiments of the Christian faith should be visually shown to the Gentiles. Which play [. . .] was expounded most carefully both to the neophytes and the pagans who were present. However, when the army of Gideon was fighting with the Philistines, the pagans, afraid of being killed, began to flee but were called back [. . .] For in this play were wars, such as those of David, Gideon and Herod and the doctrines of the Old and New Testament to convert the Gentiles and instruct them in the doctrines of the Old and New Testaments that they might come to true peace and eternal life.

C65   A miracle during a Resurrection play, Beverley, *c.* 1220

Beverley, pp. 412–13

It happened that one summer, within the graveyard of the church of the Blessed John, on the north side, the Resurrection of the Lord was presented by masked persons (as usual) in both words and action. A great crowd of both sexes flocked thither, drawn by various desires, namely for enjoyment, or in wonder, or with the holy purpose of arousing devotion. But when the access they wanted was blocked to many people, particularly short ones, by the very thick circle of people standing there, a large number went into the church, either to pray, or to look at the paintings, or to beguile the tedium of the day with some kind of recreation or amusement. And so some small boys who had entered the church happened by chance to find half-open a certain door from which steps led up to the upper parts of the walls. The little boys ran lightly to it and climbed up step by step to the vaulting of the church above the walls, intending, as I suppose, to see more easily, through the high windows of the turrets or through any holes there might be in the glass of the windows, the actors' costumes and action, and to concentrate more easily on hearing their dialogue – thus imitating Zaccheus who because he was of very small stature climbed a sycamore tree in order to see Jesus. But just then the sextons discovered what the boys were doing; and presumably afraid lest the boys, in their eagerness to see the actors performing the said show, should carelessly make holes in the glazed windows or somehow damage them, they ran after the boys; and [. . .] forced them to return by boxing their ears hard. Now one of the boys [. . .] afraid of falling into their pursuers' hands, retreated upwards until, climbing very rapidly, he reached the great cross which at that time was placed at the end of the altar of the Blessed Martin. And standing there looking down, he put his foot carelessly on a block of stone which, loosened and falling from the wall, crashed on to the stone pavement and despite its hardness was smashed into fragments. The boy, losing his foothold and shocked by the terrible crash, fell to the ground, and lay there for some considerable time senseless and apparently dead.

[. . .] His parents wailed and tore their hair, [. . .] not knowing that soon, by divine dispensation, sorrow would be turned to joy, and lamentation into laughter. For God [. . .] wishing to bear witness to the truth which was at the same time being shown in the representation of His Resurrection [. . .] raised the apparently dead boy, so completely unharmed that no injury was to be seen anywhere on his body. And so it was brought about that those who, because of the crowds of people, could not be present at the representation outside the church, were able to see a miraculous token of the Resurrection inside the nave [. . .]

III   Biblical plays from Byzantium and the Orthodox East

INTRODUCTION

The Eastern Orthodox liturgy did not encourage the development of a liturgical drama but there are some indications of dramatic activity in references from the writers of the later period. Some scholars have suggested that a group of homilies, preserved in manuscripts of the ninth to eleventh centuries, but dating back to the period before the iconoclastic controversy,[1] contain the relics of dramatic scenes and dialogues. The essential characteristic of all these 'dramas' is their theological and dogmatic emphasis. The three episodes most commonly so treated are the Annunciation [see **C70**], the Baptism and the Harrowing of Hell. John Damascene (c. 675–c. 749), who defended icons because they represented the incarnate Godhead[2] is also said by Eustathius (died 1194) to have composed a play of Susanna [see **C67**]. Other surviving plays or references include a Fall play by Ignatius the Deacon [see **C66**], and records of performances of a 'play' of the Burning Fiery Furnace [see **C69**]. The texts cited here are arranged according to biblical chronology. The *Paschon Christos* and the director's copy of the twelfth-century *Cyprus Passion* were considered earlier with the other early Passion plays [see **C5(i), (ii), C6(i), (ii)**].

1. Controversy over the veneration of icons ravaged the Byzantine Church in the eighth and ninth centuries. Officially settled by the Seventh Council of Nicea in 787, the controversy flared up again temporarily between 814 and 842.
2. 'I make an image of the God of matter who became matter for my sake.' See *St John Damascene on Holy Images, followed by three sermons on the Assumption*, trans. M. H. Allies, London, 1898, p. 15.

C66   A Greek Fall play of the eighth century

Trans. Joseph S. Tunison, *Dramatic Traditions of the Dark Ages*, Chicago and London, 1907, pp. 257–9

The Serpent comes to Eve, raising his crest and saying:[1]

SERPENT   What, then, woman, did the Creator say? Not to touch this plant only, lest you become gods? Surely He said this in envy.

EVE   He said we were to eat of every tree. But of this tree we were to avoid even the taste, lest we procure for ourselves death instead of nourishment.

SERPENT   And do you believe that? For He knew that, if you were to taste this fruit, you would become clear-sighted as gods.

EVE   Have you spoken to Adam, my husband and my master? Or did you, impudently, come to me first though you know I was created second to him?

SERPENT   Adam has no will of his own. He will follow your advice whatever it is, and will eat, if you eat.

EVE   You come to me as if in fear, and would prevail on me with wiles. But suppose he eats this, there will be all the rest for me.

SERPENT   Trouble not the man. First try; first eat. Thus you will win easily, for you are a woman.

EVE   You have prevailed on me to eat and to persuade my husband to eat. But, friend, pledge me that what you have promised shall be fulfilled.

SERPENT   Be not slow to act if you expect swift fulfilment. Delay gathers little favour.

EVE   How sweet is the fruit of this tree, husband. Take, eat, and become a god.

ADAM   Divine is the gift offered by a friend. But how will tasting make one a god? For he who requires food is no god.

EVE   Do you seek a better thing than knowledge? Eat of this, and you shall know all the bounds of good and evil [. . .]

ADAM   Lo, woman, I have eaten, and what I have learned is my own misery.

EVE   And I, too, writhe with pain, misled by the wicked serpent.

ADAM   Alas, woman, look! We are naked. How shall we hide our shame? Where is there covering for modesty?

EVE   We will clothe ourselves in these rough fig leaves. Henceforth life will be harsh for us.[. . .]

ADAM   Do you not hear the voice of God, woman? How I dread His justice for what we have done.

EVE   I hear His footsteps. How frightful the thunder is! Friend, let us conceal ourselves.

ADAM   Where can I hide? No place is without God. But follow me, woman [. . .]

GOD   O you! weaker than woman, you shall till the ground among the thorns, with sighs and pain and the sweat of your brow. And you, woman, shall suffer in childbirth. You both shall live in toil and care till you return to the earth, whence you came. (pp. 257–9)

---

[1]   The serpent 'raising his crest', the 'rough fig-leaves' and the 'thunder' all suggest a dramatic performance. Some of the language of Tunison's translation has been modernised.

C67   A play of Susanna by John Damascene (*c.* 675–*c.* 749)

Eustathius, *Proemium* to *Interpretatio hymni Pentecostalis Damasceni, Patrologia Graeca*, vol. 136, cols. 507–8

He did not just leave pages of regular poetry, but also wrote plays. We know this at first-hand, having come across his play, written on the virtues of the Blessed and chaste Susanna noted in the margins as being the work of John Mansur [i.e. John Damascene, (died 749)][1] [. . .] The play is entirely Euripidean in style.[2] Susanna genealogises herself and bewails that she fell into such great evil and violence within the garden.[3] Then having compared the place to the garden in which the first mother [Eve] was deceived by the devil, she sweetly says that 'The serpent, the architect of all evil, has sent me forth to wander like a second Eve.'[4]

[1] Eustathius' language may imply that, in his day, this text was obscure and its authorship disputed.
[2] A credible claim. The *Paschon Christos* begins, 'Now shall I tell of the sufferings of the Saviour of the World in the manner of Euripides.' [see **C5**]
[3] The Greek words here used for violence and garden can comport the double meaning of 'rape' and 'vagina'. Such verbal plays do occur, e.g. in the poems of the Byzantine hymnographer Romanos. Thus, they may here reflect the text of the original.
[4] Eustathius refers elsewhere to the 'author of the play *Susanna*, I think the Damascene' (*Commentary on Dionysius Periegetes*, p. 976).

C68   A play (?) to celebrate the assumption of Elijah

Liutprand of Cremona, *Relatio de legatione constantinoplia*, pr. Samuel Baud-Bovey, 'Sur un "Sacrifice d'Abraham de Romanos"', *Byzantion* 13 (1938), pp. 321–34

The 20th of July, the day on which the flippant Greeks celebrate the snatching-up of the prophet Elijah with stage performances.[1] (p. 330)

[1] Liutprand's Latin is *ludis scaenicis celebrant*. There has been much unresolved argument over just what this implies, with interpretations ranging from fully-fledged liturgical drama to mere sarcastic metaphor for the Eastern Church service.

C69   Representations of the Burning Fiery Furnace
(i) A defence of traditional liturgical ceremonies, 1429

Symeon of Thessalonica (d. 1429), '*Dialogue Against the Heretics*', *Patrologia Graeca*, vol. 155, cols. 33–176

If the Latins reproach us for the furnace of the three children, they should not congratulate themselves. For we light up candles and lights rather than a furnace, and we offer incense to God according to custom. We do not send a man, we use a representation of an angel. We also use three boys, as pure as those children, to sing their song according to tradition.[1]

[1] Again, some take this all at face value, others in a non-literal sense. For details of this and other 'plays' see Samuel Baud-Bovey, 'Sur un sacrifice d'Abraham de Romanos', pp. 321–34.

(ii) A westerner attends the ceremony, 1432

Le voyage d'Outremer de Bertrandon de la Broquière, ed. Charles H. A. Schefer, Paris, 1892, pp. 154–6

I waited all day [17 December 1432] to see how they performed the mystery of the three children whom Nebuchadnezzar put into the furnace.

C70   The Virgin Mary questions Gabriel's message

St Germanus [eighth century], *In Annunciationem, Patrologia Graeca*, vol. 98, trans. Leslie Barnard

THE ANGEL   Listen, glorified one; hear the secret words of the Highest. 'Behold, you will conceive in your belly and you will bring forth a son and you will call His name Jesus.' Be ready finally for the appearance of Christ [. . .]

MOTHER OF GOD   Go away from my city and go away from my country, man, and leave in haste my dwelling place. You who speak to me, withdraw a long way from my doors and do not bring such good tidings to me in my lowliness.

THE ANGEL   In wanting to fulfil His plan of old and to pity erring man, God consented to become a man, [. . .] from the goodness of His love for mankind. Why finally do you not accept my welcome, you who have found favour? [. . .]

MOTHER OF GOD   I am afraid and I quake at such words as these from you and I make reply that you have appeared to lead me astray like another Eve [. . .]

THE ANGEL   I announce to you a message of joy; [. . .] I announce to you the presence of the high King which is beyond telling [. . .]

MOTHER OF GOD   When you announce these events to me [. . .] I do not believe such an announcement of yours because you came to set at nothing my maidenly worth and to grieve the one who is to marry me [. . .]

THE ANGEL   To what end, why and for what purpose have you distrusted so much my good news, you who are glorified? How far are you disobedient towards the angel sent to you from heaven? I am not the one who misled Eve, I am not![1]

---

[1]   This literal translation of an extract from this Greek sermon-play was made some years ago by the late Leslie Barnard of Leeds University.

IV   The Feast of Corpus Christi and the plays

INTRODUCTION

The original intention behind the institution and celebration of the Feast of Corpus Christi was twofold: to encourage greater veneration of the Eucharist with more frequent communion by both clergy and laity, and to emphasise the true importance of the Sacrament whose institution on Maundy Thursday was over-shadowed in the Holy Week liturgy by the Johannine emphasis on the Washing of Feet and the beginning of the Passion.

A special celebration in honour of the establishment of the Eucharist was first urged in Liège by Blessed Juliana of Cornillon. A feast of the Eucharist was estab-lished in that diocese in 1240 and subsequently spread into Germany by the Dominicans.[1] Meanwhile, Jacques Pantaleon, a former archdeacon of Liège, was elected pope in 1261, taking the name Urban IV. He had already supported the feast in Liège and in 1263 the Bolsena miracle of the bleeding Host [see **C72**] is alleged to have so impressed him that in 1264 he formally established the feast for the whole church by the bull *Transiturus de hoc mundo* [Preparing to leave this world] [see **C71**].[2] It was celebrated in a number of churches in France and Germany in the last years of the thirteenth century, but the death of Pope Urban the year after the bull was promulgated, delayed universal acceptance of Corpus Christi, and it was only in 1317 that Clement V's decree from the Council of Vienne (1311–12) was officially promulgated by John XXII, who ordered that on that day the Sacrament should be processed publicly with great solemnity. The Thursday after the Octave of Pentecost (which might fall between 21 May and 24 June) was fixed on for the celebration of the new feast. In the course of the fourteenth century cos-tumed figures, tableaux and later plays were added to the compulsory procession [see **C76**, **C77**] though in Bohemia *ludos theatrales* were actually banned from the procession in 1366.[3] However, the only actual play-texts extant from before 1400 are sacrament plays [see **C72**, **C77**].

[1] See Miri Rubin, *Corpus Christi: the Eucharist in Late Medieval Culture*, Cambridge, 1991. pp. 164–81.
[2] See J. N. D. Kelly. *The Oxford Dictionary of Popes*, Oxford and New York, 1986, p. 196. The role of the

Bolsena miracle in the establishment of Corpus Christi is still a subject for scholarly debate but for the Church the miracle was (and still is) the foundation of the feast [see **C74**].

[3] J. F. Veltrusky, 'Medieval Drama in Bohemia', *Early Drama, Art and Music Review* 15 (1993) p. 51.

C71   Extract from the bull establishing the Feast of Corpus Christi, 1264

Bullarum diplomaticum et privilegiorum sanctorum Romanorum pontificum, Editio Taurinensis, vol. III (1181–1268), Rome, 1858

This glorious commemoration fills the souls of the faithful with joy in their salvation [. . .] at this most holy commemoration, therefore, there comes to us joy and tears of sweetness. Whereby we rejoice in our sadness and weep in our joy. (p. 706)

On this Thursday, therefore, let the devout throng of the faithful crowd eagerly into the churches [. . .] then from the hearts and wills of all, there may resound hymns of joy at man's salvation; then faith sings psalms [*psallat*], hope dances, charity exults. (p. 707)

THE FEAST IN ITALY

Italy was the only country in Europe that did not accept the Liège origins of the feast, preferring to ascribe it to a miracle that took place in Bolsena, near Orvieto, in 1263–4 [see **C73**]. A play based on this miracle dates from the late fourteenth century [see **C72**].

C72   The Pope declares a miracle at Bolsena, 1360

Orvieto *laude*

This representation is performed for the solemn feast of the Body of Christ [Corpo di Cristo]. [*Telling*] *how a foreign priest having serious doubts* [*about the Real Presence*] *a miracle occurred while he was celebrating* [*the Mass*]: *the host on the corporal turned crimson and became flesh and blood.* (p. 368)[1]

The Pope says to Thomas [*Aquinas*]: Thomas, we have a great miracle of the Body of Christ [*Corpo di Cristo*] and we see truly that it is flesh and blood. So I intend to make a sacred Office and solemn Feast. (p. 380)

[Thomas is asked to prepare the office]

Thomas to the Pope: O my lord, holy father, here is the Office which I have found [*trovato*]; let it [the feast] be made known to all for it is worthy to be venerated (p. 381).[2]

[1] Heading to the text of the play.

[2] The Office for Corpus Christi is traditionally ascribed to Thomas Aquinas who died in 1274 and was canonised by John XXII in 1323. For discussion of the likelihood of Aquinas' authorship, see Rubin, pp. 185–9.

C73   The miraculous corporal from Bolsena
Orvieto Cathedral authorities

The cloth is preserved in the Chapel of the Corporal in Orvieto Cathedral which dates from *c.* 1360. The cathedral was specially built to house the relic.

C74   Pius II confirms the Bolsena miracle as the origin of the feast, 1460

Pope Pius II (Aeneas Sylvius Piccolomini)], *Commentarii rerum memorabilium . . .* (Rome, 1584), trans. F. A. Gragg and L. C. Gabel, Smith College Studies in History 22, 25, 30, 35, 43, Northampton, Mass., 1936–57, vol. xxx, p. 378

This miracle was authenticated by Urban IV and therefore was instituted the feast of the most Holy Body of Christ which is celebrated yearly with the profoundest solemnity and devotion by the nations of the entire Christian world.

THE FEAST IN ENGLAND

In England an extensive drama eventually developed in connection with the feast, but only after 1400 [see **Section D**]. There were a number of early Corpus Christi confraternities[1] and in 1353 the one in Cambridge 'used some entry fines, paid by a married couple, towards expenses "in ludo filiorum Israel" [for the play of the children of Israel]'.[2] The most important early records of Corpus Christi guild plays are from Beverley and York. It is noteworthy that the earliest indication that the pageant wagons in York carried *plays* rather than tableaux is from 1394 [see **D2**].

1. See Rubin, pp. 238–9.
2. See ibid., p. 240. In the context of the feast it is probable that this was a play of the giving of the manna in the desert – a well-known prefiguration of the Eucharist.

C75   An early English reference to Corpus Christi celebrations, *c.* 1335

Robert Holcot, *Super librum Sapientiae* [Upon the Book of the Wisdom of Solomon], lectio 174; pr. Siegfried Wenzel, 'An Early Reference to a Corpus Christi Play', *Modern Philology* 74 (1977), pp. 390–4

St Thomas [Aquinas] distinguishes, moreover, three types of play. One is undoubtedly the vile and dishonourable piece which is essentially the cause of ignominious things being done. And that kind of play the pagans perform in the presence of their gods in places of assembly [*theatris*] and in temples. And for Christians that is frankly beyond the pale, as with such types of performance in other places too. The second type of play is the play of devotion and spiritual joy, *such as Christians perform on Corpus Christi Day,*[1] and such as David performed before the Ark of the Lord.[2] The third is the play intended for human consolation.

1. The italicised words are Holcot's addition. Aquinas' connection with the feast [see **C 72**] explains Holcot's expansion of Aquinas' reference to plays 'which proceed from the joy of devotion' and 'are not to be avoided, but praised and emulated' (Aquinas, *Commentary on the Sentences* book 4. 16.2.1.).
2. David *danced* before the Ark (2 Samuel 6.21–2) so that the allusion may refer to no more than a mute processional pageant; however, the term *ludus* may suggest a dramatic performance (cf. Rubin, p. 273).

C76   Early Corpus Christi records from York

REED, *York*, pp. 689–92

(i) From the Bridgemasters' accounts, 1376

For one building in which three Corpus Christi pageants are housed per annum 2s (trans. p. 689)[1]

1. These Latin entries are quoted here in the REED translations. For later references see **Section D**.

(ii) From the Tailors' accounts, 1386–7

Item the said four searchers will collect each year within the city the proper amount from each man of the said guild for the support of their pageant of Corpus Christi and will make all the expenditures to sustain and maintain the said pageant and will give account each year the third Sunday next after the said feast of Corpus Christi without any more delay, on pain of 10s to pay, one half to the four searchers aforesaid and the other half to the Council Chamber on Ouse Bridge in York. (trans., p. 690–1)

(iii) A dispute over housing the pageants, 1387

Memorandum that although a certain dispute recently had been moved between Robert de Waghen, carpenter, on the one hand, and John de Duffeld, skinner, John de Catton, baker, and Robert de Halton, dyer, and men of their own three crafts, on the other hand, about the building and repair of a certain house on the Tofts for housing their Corpus Christi pageants, nevertheless they came to an agreement under this form, viz, that the said Robert de Waghen will undertake competently to build and repair the said house for housing the three said pageants. (trans., p. 691)

(iv) The Fletchers shall not work on Sundays, 1388

First, that no fletcher of this city will work henceforth any Sunday [. . .] on pain of 40d to pay, one half to the Chamber and the other to their pageant of Corpus Christi, and this each time that they [. . .] shall be convicted. (trans., p. 692)

THE FEAST IN GERMANY

Although Germany, like England, had many guild plays for Corpus Christi in the fifteenth century, the only early one is sacramental not biblical. The *Fronleichnamsspiel* [Corpus Christi play] from the Innsbruck codex[1] includes thanksgivings for the Sacrament from Adam and Eve; a Creed play, with each apostle's item being followed by two prophets (who sing their prophecies in Latin and then gloss them in German); speeches by John the Baptist and the three Kings and finally a sermon by 'a pope'. There is no information on who performed it, or how it was presented.

1.   The play is named for the location of the manuscript (codex 960), but the dialect is from further east near the modern Czech border.

C77   A play to teach the faithful, Innsbruck codex, 1391

Fronleichnamsspiel, pr. *Altteutsche Schauspiele*, ed. Franz Joseph Mone, Quedlinburg and Leipzig, 1841

(i) Preface to the play and its title

Here begins the play useful for the devotion of the simple, for performing [*peragendus*] on Corpus Christi day or during the Octave, for making known [*intimandus*] the Catholic faith. Composed by literate persons and suitable for them. Here begins the play of the Body of Christ. (p. 145)

(ii) The play is performed in the presence of the Sacrament

Adam says: On the third day he [Christ] rose up truly from the bonds of death. That is true and no lie. I see him there with my eyes and we shall soon go to him and take him into us [*innclichen*] with great joy. (p. 146)

The Pope says: Hear my counsel, dear friends, for you have already heard the laments of Adam who was deceived by the devil [. . .] but God's wisdom [. . .] did not forget the race of men and has given us a food that will bring us back again to eternal life, [. . .] the holy body of God [*froner lichnam*]. Now all whom God has gathered here fall down upon your knees and raise your hands and beg him for a good ending [. . .] (p. 163)

Here ends the book of Corpus Christi the year of Our Lord 1391. (p. 164)

THE FEAST IN SPAIN

In 1300 the *reconquista* of Spain was not complete and drama is rare in Castile and unknown in Andalucia. In Catalonia, however, which had had a flourishing liturgical drama since the eleventh century, the feast was eagerly adopted and celebrations are recorded from, among others, Gerona and Barcelona, both in the 1320s, and over the border in Valencia (1355).[1] The earliest processions featured tableaux on floats [*rocas*] with figures and walking groups, and by the end of the century there were actual dramatic elements in Barcelona and Valencia but with no indication of plays with speaking roles. The full elaboration of the Spanish Corpus Christi drama did not develop until the fifteenth (and in the case of Castile the sixteenth) century [see **Section I**].

1.   See N. D. Shergold, *A History of the Spanish Stage from Medieval Times to the Seventeenth Century*, Oxford, 1967.

C78 Edicts for keeping the feast in Barcelona

Agustí Duran i Sanpere, *La fiesta del Corpus*, Barcelona, 1943

(i) The establishment of the feast, 1320

[The ordinances of the Councillors and the guild masters [*prohombres*] in the streets of Barcelona] record the ordinances given by the Holy Father so that, for the honour and glory of God and the exaltation of the Christian faith [. . .] there shall be celebrated throughout the world and in perpetuity a feast dedicated to the holy and precious Body of Our Lord Jesus Christ. [They record also] that the Holy Father has authorised many and great indulgences to each person who shall attend Mass, Vespers and the other Hours and the Office on the appointed day and also Vespers on the day before. Therefore the Councillors etc. have ordained that all the citizens, both men and women, should come together in the morning at the cathedral to attend the Office and then take part in the procession which will be celebrated with great solemnity. [Moreover] it is ordained that everyone shall keep the feast with great joy and devotion as for Easter and Christmas; that the work-shops and the commercial shops shall not be open nor any market held of any kind [. . .] on pain of paying ten *dineros.* (pp. 13–14)

(ii) Jews must keep off the streets

That Jews and Jewesses shall not dare to come out from the Cal' [Jewish quarter] on Corpus Christi day. (p. 14)

(iii) Preparations for the procession, 1323

Those who wish to take part in the religious procession must gather very early in the morning at the cathedral, to accompany the Host [*Santissima*] carrying tapers and candles. The streets shall be barricaded off and the ground covered with rushes; the scaffolds and the gates decked with branches. (p. 15)

(iv) Characters involved in the procession, 1391

The four evangelists; the Innocents wearing crowns; three bishops; Jacob, with the ladder of his vision and an angel; St Helena with a cross, a crown and some nails; St Nicholas with the three balls of gold;[1] St Martin accompanied by a beggar; [and several of the lesser saints. There were also two floats:] the paradise, with Adam and Eve with a fig-tree and the serpent; Noah's Ark with a dove (p. 16).

---

[1] See the introductory paragraph to **C27, C28.**

C79   The processional route must be clear of stands, 1394

Manuel Milá y Fontanals, *Orígenes del teatro catalán*, in *Obras completas*, 8 vols., Barcelona, 1888–96; vol. VI, p. 368; trans. *Staging*, p. 67

[It is forbidden to] make or have made any structure or scaffold [*bastiment ò cadafal*] on the streets through which the procession is to pass. This is so that the streets [of Barcelona] may not be obstructed; neither are fireworks, including exploding fireworks, to be set off, on pain of a fine of *20s* for each offence.

C80   Details of the procession in Valencia, 1400–08

John E. Varey, 'Minor Dramatic Forms in Spain with Special Reference to Puppets', Doctoral thesis, Cambridge University, 2 vols., 1950, Appendix I, p. 329

(i) Payments for costumes and properties

[1400] money was paid for] bread, wine and veal for the angels, apostles, patriarchs, prophets, virgins, and other saints who walked, playing and singing, in the said procession [. . .] A mask [*testera*] for Moses, painted with red and gilt; twenty-four beards of horsehair [*cerdes*] for prophets and patriarchs [. . .]

   Payment for the two men who were lions and 8 skins were bought to cover their clothes.

(ii) Additional floats added in 1407, 1408

[1407] and for four pairs of wings which were made new for the angels at the tomb. And for carrying and decorating the *roca* of St Francis.

   [1408] the *roca* [. . .] of the martyrdom of St Vincent and the gateway [*porta*][1] of Jeremiah.

---

[1] Jeremiah's messianic prophecy refers to the gates of the Temple (Jeremiah 7.2–3).

(iii) Much repainting done in 1408

[. . .] and to paint the serpent and the withered tree and the tree called 'of Life'; St George's lance and the king of the East's sceptre [*la verga del rey d'Orient*]; [. . .] and to make [*tornar*] Adam, Eve and Mary of Egypt and blood for the Innocents.

V   Secular theatre

The flowering of vernacular drama in the town of Arras in the thirteenth century included a miracle play of St Nicholas [see **C28**] and *Courtois d'Arras*, a version of the parable of the Prodigal Son (*c.* 1225) [see **C81**]. Both plays have religious subjects but the emphasis in the treatment is on the scenes of contemporary life which reached their perfection in the works of Adam de la Halle, a notable poet and musician, known also to his contemporaries as Adam le Bossu or Adam d'Arras.[1] He attended the Sorbonne but later entered the service of the Count of Artois as a *jongleur* (a professional poet and musician) and travelled with him to Sicily where he died about 1285–9 [see **C85**]. In addition to poetry and music, he wrote two plays [see **C83, C84**].

There is little specifically secular drama from the fourteenth century, apart from the Dutch *Abele spelen* [see **section H**]. In French, the Arras tradition is continued by one farce, a pastoral and the *Estoire de Griselidis*,[2] but scenes of contemporary life feature in many of the miracle plays [see **C28–C30**]. From England, there is only the interlude *De Clerico et Puella*.[3] For court festivities and royal entries before 1400 see **C86–C88**.

1. For Adam's life and works see Jean Dufournet, *Adam de la Halle à la recherche de lui-même*. Paris, 1974.
2. See G. Cohen, *Le théâtre français en Belgique au moyen âge*, Brussels, 1953, pp. 63–75.
3. See **A36** and Ian Lancashire, *Dramatic Texts and Records of Britain*, Cambridge, 1984, p. 5.

C81   The establishment of the *Confrérie des jongleurs et des bourgois d'Arras* (end of the twelfth century)

Dufournet, *Adam de la Halle*, p. 223

This charity is held from God and Our Lady [. . .] It was not established for lechery or foolishness [. . .] This charity is founded by the *jongleurs* and the *jongleurs* are the masters or it and he whom they admit is admitted and he whom they reject cannot remain except with their permission, for there is no authority above the *jongleurs*.

C82 *Courtois d'Arras*: a parable play

Courtois d'Arras, Jeu du XIIIe siècle, ed. Edmond Faral, Paris, 1911

(i) Courtois demands his share of the estate and leaves home

COURTOIS To the devil with this slavery! I'm going to leave you, but before I set out I'll have whatever is due to me [. . .] and give me mine in coinage, not less than my share is worth!

FATHER Be at peace, dear son Courtois, eat up your bread and peas,[1] and give up this foolish plan.

COURTOIS Father, this is a miserable way to live. There's nowhere on earth I could do worse. God owes me my income [*rente*] of bread and peas.

FATHER My son, you're talking like a fool. All the same I've sixty sous and [. . .] you shall have them on one condition. That you give up your right to anything else and call it quits between us. (pp. 2–3)

---

[1] In this version of the parable of the Prodigal Son (Luke 15:11–32) the evolution of the plot is expressed in changes of food and clothing.

(ii) In the tavern, Courtois is left to pay the bill, but his purse has been stolen by two girls

COURTOIS You're foolish to worry about that for they will soon come back. If you're doubtful about me, take my cloak.

TAVERNER That's well said – now you owe less. But I must have your jacket too.

COURTOIS How can I go away without? I never heard of such an idea.

TAVERNER In faith, Courtois, you'll have to do it. And your breeches, if they're clean. Hurry up, unlace your sleeves; we've got other things to see to.

COURTOIS Here you are [. . .] Now, I must seek some way to sort myself out unless I want to die of hunger [. . .]

TAVERNER [. . .] There's an ancient smock inside,[. . .] You can have it if you like, so you won't be quite naked. (pp. 13–15)

(iii) Courtois gets a job herding pigs

CITIZEN Now take your herder's stick in your hand – it'll make you look more used to the job.

COURTOIS Now I've everything I need. Get up there! I don't think this flesh was fattened up on acorns: [. . .] My master will very soon be able to cut you into bacon! Oh, God! What time can it be now? I know I ought to eat something, but my bread is as hard as biscuit [. . .] It must be made of oats or barley [. . .] I would rather die of hunger – I could never eat it! [. . .] Now I'm so hungry it makes me groan [. . .] I wonder about those peapods that the pigs are trampling in the mud, perhaps they would [. . .] ease this awful pain [. . .] If only God would grow me some fresh peas [. . .] These are bitter and rotten, every one! I shan't get very fat on them. They would have tasted better hot – shelled and mashed, and cooked with bacon. Now I know I shall die of hunger. (pp. 17–19)

(iv) Courtois returns home to his father's delight

FATHER   He has no fur-lined mantle now! Indeed, as you can imagine he's not had much to eat or drink. Let's have a new gown made for him [. . .] and kill and flay our fatted calf (p. 23).

THE PLAYS OF ADAM DE LA HALLE

The *Jeu de la Feuillée* [The Play of the Leafy Bower] (*c.* 1276) has been described as a mixture of *A Midsummer Night's Dream* and a student revue. Adam portrays himself, his father and many other known Arras personalities. There are scenes with a doctor, a fool, a madman, and a monk collecting money with relics. Morgan le Fay and two companions come on stage for a fairy play, and the play ends in the tavern. There is no record of public performance but it might have been presented at a meeting of the Arras *Confrérie des jongleurs* [see **C81**]. *Robin et Marion*, a pastoral which includes songs and dances, was probably written later than the *Feuillée*, perhaps after Adam entered the service of the Count of Artois.

C83   Scenes from the *Jeu de la Feuillée*

Adam le Bossu, *Le Jeu de la feuillée*, ed. Ernest Langlois, Paris, 1911; reprinted 1965

(i) The doctor plies his trade

DOCTOR   In faith, I know quite well what's the matter with you, Maistre Henri [. . .] You have the disease that's known as Avarice. If you'd like me to cure your ailment, you must talk to me privately. I'm a doctor with plenty of custom; I've people up and down the country whom I shall cure of this disease. I've more than two thousand here, in this very town [. . .]. Have you brought a urinal?

HENRI   Yes, Doctor, I've one right here.

DOCTOR   Did you pass water while fasting?

HENRI   Yes.

DOCTOR   [. . .] Good Sir, you have Saint Leonard's disease, I don't need to see any more [. . .]

DAME DOUCE   Please, good sir, advise me too. and here's my money. My stomach is so swollen that I can't walk. I've come three leagues on foot to bring this sample of my urine.

DOCTOR   This comes from lying on your back, madam, that's what the urine says.

DAME DOUCE   You're lying, you filthy-minded brute! I'm not that kind of lady! I've never been in that profession, not for promise or reward (pp. 8–10).

(ii) The fays come to the table that Adam has prepared

GILLOS I can hear Hellekin's people; if I am right, he's their leader. Lots of little bells are ringing. I'm sure they must be close at hand [. . .]

RAINELÈS Oh, God! It is dangerous here. I wish I was safe at home at this moment.

ADAM Silence! There is nothing wrong. They're ladies, beautifully dressed.

RAINELÈS No, in God's name, sir, it's the fays. I'm going! [. . .]

[The three fays go to the table][1]

MORGAN [. . .] Now, Maglore, come over here, and Arsile, you sit next to her. I myself shall take this place between you, at the end of the table.

MAGLORE Look, I'm sitting at the end where they haven't put a knife.

MORGAN I've got a splendid one.

ARSILE So have I.

MAGLORE Then what does it mean that I have none? Am I the worst? By God, they didn't think much of me, who arranged for me to be the one without a knife! [. . .]

MORGAN Sweet friend, see how fine and bright and clean it all is.

ARSILE I think we should give a fine present to those who took the trouble to decorate this place.

MORGAN Yes, indeed. But we don't know who it is.

CROKESOS Madam, [. . .] it was two clerks who did the work [. . .] Rikier Auri is one, the other, Maistre Henri's son, was in a [clerk's] gown.

ARSILE It's proper to reward them for it. Each fay should contribute a gift [. . .] I wish that he may be charming and gay and a wonderful writer of poems and songs. (pp. 24–8).

---

[1] This is a unique example of the inclusion of an Arthurian character in a medieval French play but see **C86–C87**. The episode with the knife is found in French versions of the Sleeping Beauty.

C84 Staging *Robin et Marion*

(i) Costumes and properties referred to in the text

Adam le Bossu, *Le Jeu de Robin et Marion*, suivi du *Jeu du pèlerin*, ed. Ernest Langlois, Paris, 1924; reprinted 1958

Marion sings: Robin bought me a fine and handsome scarlet jacket, a petticoat and a little girdle [. . .]

 He gave me this little basket, my shepherdess's crook and my knife.[. . .] He brings me a portion of his cheese: I have some here in the front of my dress and a good big piece of bread he brought me for my dinner.[1] (pp. 2–4)

---

[1] The knight has tried to seduce Marion but she remains devoted to Robin who has given her such presents.

(ii) A Robin and Marion play in Angers, Whitsun 1392

Sieur Charles Du Fresne Du Cange, *Glossarium mediae et infimae Latinitatis cum supplementis integris D. P. Carpenterii, et additamentis Adelungii et aliorum digessit G. A. L.,* *Henschel*, 7 vols., Paris, 1840–50; vol. v, p. 784, under '*Robinetus*'

Jehan le Begue and five or six other students, his companions, went round the town of Angers, masked (*deguisiez*), to perform a play called 'Of Robin and Marion' as is customarily done each year during the Whitsuntide fair by local people, whether students, burghers' sons or other groups.[1]

---

[1] From a letter of remission of 1392. For a fuller account see **J57**.

C85   A pilgrim describes the fame of Adam de la Halle

Jus du pèlerin, pr. Adam le Bossu, *Robin et Marion*, pp. 70–2

THE PILGRIM   [. . .] I have returned via Apulia where there is much talk of a clerk, fair and subtle, gracious and noble – the non-pareil of the world; he was born in this town. He was called Master Adam le Bossu and Adam of Arras.[The peasant interrupts him]

Now quiet please, good sir. This clerk I am telling you about is loved, appreciated and honoured by the Count of Artois and I will tell you truly the reason for it: this Master Adam could compose poems and songs and the count was searching for such a man [. . .] Now Master Adam is dead, God have mercy on him. I have been to his tomb (on whom Jesus have mercy); thanks be to the count who showed it to me when I was there last year.

[The peasant again interrupts and threatens the pilgrim but is checked by Rogaus.]

ROGAUS   Be quiet, Warnier, he is talking about Master Adam, the honoured clerk, the fair one, the generous giver who was full of virtues. The whole world should mourn him for he had many good qualities and above all knew how to compose fine poems and was a finished singer of them. [The characters then discuss and quote Adam's poems.][1]

---

[1] This rather pedestrian farce was written after Adam's death, by an unknown and inferior poet.

COURT CELEBRATIONS AND ROYAL ENTRIES

Kings and nobles often took part in or were entertained by feasts and festivals of all kinds, including events presented between two courses of a meal [see **C87**]; or to celebrate a royal visit [see **C90**]. In the thirteenth century, especially, tournaments were often organised round themes from the romances of King Arthur.[1] The fighting in a tournament held at Figueras in 1286, for example, is described by the chronicler as 'the finest feats of arms that had ever been done in a tournament since the time of King Arthur'.[2] A few of these 'Round Tables', as they were called, included genuine dramatic elements: the *Tournoi du Hem-sur-Somme* was held by

'Queen Guinevere', most of the characters had Arthurian names and only the Chevalier au Lion is explicitly identified as the Comte d'Artois (the patron of Adam de la Halle) [see **C88**].

1. Loomis, 'Chivalric and Dramatic Imitations of Arthurian romance' quotes many examples, see **C85**, **C86**. See also Ruth Huff Cline, 'The Influence of Romances on Tournaments of the Middle Ages', *Speculum* 20 (1945), pp. 204–11.
2. Ramón Muntaner *Crònica*, ed. E. B., 9 vols., Barcelona, 1927, 1951–2, vol. V, p. 27

C86   A festival in Acre, 1286

Loomis, p. 80

When the king[1] came to Acre he held a fortnight's festival [. . .] with jousting and tourneys [*d'envissures et de behors*] and they imitated the Round Table and the queen of Femenie: that is to say the knights dressed as ladies and jousted together [. . .] And they played at being Lancelot and Tristan and Palamedes with many other fine games [*jeus*].

[1] Henry II of Cyprus, who was crowned King of Jerusalem.

C87   An Arthurian play for an English royal wedding,

Lodowijk van Velthem, *Continuation of the Spiegel Historiael 1248–1316*, ed. Hermann Vander Linden, Willem de Vreese *et al.*, 3 vols., Brussels, 1906, vol. I, pp. 314–15; trans. Elsa Strietman

[At the wedding feast following Edward I's marriage to Margaret of France, a Round Table of knights and squires was organised].[1] Then according to custom a play [*spel*] of King Arthur was performed [*gemaect*] [. . .] The best were chosen and named after the knights of the Round Table. (pp. 299–300)

[A banquet followed the tournament. After the first two courses, squires, apparently wounded or bound, bring challenges to the 'knights' who accept them. After the third course a hideous damsel enters][2] [. . .] her nose was clearly a foot long and more than a palm's width. Her ears were, God knows, just like those of an ass; she had plaits in front and behind [. . .] hanging down to her girdle, that seemed as coarse as a horse's mane, or coarser; on her long red neck was a goitre as large as a goose egg [. . .] her teeth, some black and some white were as long as a finger [. . .] She rode on a small thin, red, limping horse. (pp. 314–15)

[She gives quests to both 'Perceval' and 'Gawain']

When the lady had left the room [. . .] she soon escaped and divested herself of her adornments. This lady [. . .] was one of the king's servants and the king had this [. . .] mask and this head made in secret [. . .] so that it seemed to be a lady. (p. 318)

1   This lengthy verse chronicle is summarised by Loomis pp. 91–2. He points out that at the date given
    in the text, 1254, Edward I was not yet king. 1299 seems a more reasonable suggestion.
2   This was a common motif in Arthurian romances.

C88   The Chevalier au Lyon, with his lion, at Ham, 1278

Sarrasin, *Le Roman du Hem [1278]*, ed. Albert Henry, Les belles lettres, Paris, 1938, lines
1444–50

The count, who had captured the castle[1] set off joyfully [. . .] with the maidens [he
had rescued] [. . .] and ordered his lion to accompany him, which it did not hesitate to do [. . .] All seven of them came to the palace [. . .] there were many torches
burning there and all the knights of the court gazed eagerly at them. And the lion
ran along still in front of them by their horses' hooves [. . .] He who was leader of
the group came up to the queen's dais and the lion, who was well-mannered [*courtois*], stood quietly before the queen without moving, his muzzle on the table.

1   It is not clear if the middle section of this long account, the freeing of the ladies, was narrated or
    staged. Certainly this final scene, with the lion, describes a real event. 'The comic part of the lion was
    probably filled by some thirteenth-century Snug the Joiner in a lion's skin' (Loomis, p. 95), or by a
    squire [see **C87**].

C89   The burghers of Magdeburg stage a tournament, 1281

Loomis, pp. 84–5

There were at this time constables [*kunstabelen*][1] who were the sons of the wealthi-
est burghers; they were accustomed to put on plays [*spel*] at Whitsun, such as
Roland, the shield-tree,[2] round tables and other plays [. . .] One of them, Brun von
Sconebeke, was a man of learning and his companions, the constables, asked him
to compose and organise a joyful play [*vreidig spel*].[3]

1   This seems to be an honorary title.
2   Knights would hang their shields on a tree as an invitation to others to challenge them.
3   Brun's 'play' is a tournament, with a grail [*gral*] which here is clearly 'a tent or bower of love'
    (Loomis, p. 85). Invitations are sent to neighbouring towns to compete for the beautiful '*vrow Feie*'.
    The lady is won by a merchant from Goslar.

C90   Scenes for a royal visit to Paris, 1313

La Chronique métrique attribuée à Geffroy de Paris, ed. Armel Diverrès, Strassburg, 1956,
pp. 184–6

The burghers made such celebrations that the royals[1] thanked them [. . .] Among
the other marvels [*faërie*] there, they saw God [the child Christ] smiling at his
mother; Renard, doctor and physician; [. . .] Our Lord eating apples and Our Lady
close by with the three Kings of Cologne [the Magi]; and the angels in Paradise,

some ninety of them, and the souls singing within; and I can assure you that Hell there was black and stinking, the souls being thrown and cast down. There were more than a hundred devils who all sallied forth to attract souls to them, to whom they then did evil things. There they seemed to be tortured and could be seen lamenting. On Wednesday there was a strong wind which rent and tore the curtains but they were quickly repaired and set up again. Our Lord in judgement was there and the Resurrection [. . .] Herod and Cayphas in his mitre and Renard chanting the Epistle and Gospel could be seen with crosier [. . .] and Hersent spinning and on the other side Adam and Eve and Pilate washing his hands [. . .] all this was the work of the weavers. The cordwainers also with great care and attention counterfeited the life of Renart [. . .] who was seen as bishop, pope and archbishop, in every kind of disguise as his life tells: on a bier, on a cross, and with a censer.[2]

---

[1] Edward II of England and his queen, Isabeau of France, were visiting Paris for the knighting of the Dauphin Louis, son of Philip the Fair.

[2] If Arthur was the ideal of chivalry, Renart, the cunning fox, was the hero of much social satire, especially against the Church.

Section D
England, Ireland, Scotland and Wales

Edited by WILLIAM TYDEMAN

Abbreviations

BL	British Library
Chester	*The Chester Mystery Cycle*, ed. R. M. Lumiansky and David Mills, EETS (SS 9), 2 vols., Oxford, 1974–86
Dawson *Kent*	*Records of Plays and Players in Kent, 1450–1642*, ed. Giles Dawson, Malone Society Collections, London, 1965
Digby	*The Late Medieval Religious Plays of Bodleian MSS Digby 133 and E Museo 160*, ed. Donald Baker, John L. Murphy and Louis B. Hall Jr, EETS 283, Oxford, 1982
EETS	Early English Text Society publications
HMC	Historical Manuscripts Commission
Kahrl *Lincs*	*Records of Plays and Players in Lincolnshire, 1300–1585*, ed. Stanley J. Kahrl, Malone Society Collections 8, Oxford, 1969
Macro	*The Macro Plays*, ed. Mark Eccles, EETS 262, Oxford, 1969
MES	*The Medieval English Stage: Corpus Christi Pageants and Plays*, Alan H. Nelson, Chicago and London, 1974
METh	*Medieval English Theatre*
MPS	*Medieval Plays in Scotland*, Anna Jean Mill, St Andrews University Publications 24, Edinburgh and London, 1927
NCP	*Non-Cycle Plays and Fragments*, ed. Norman Davis, EETS (SS 1), Oxford, 1970
Norfolk and Suffolk	*Records of Plays and Players in Norfolk and Suffolk, 1330–1642*, ed. David Galloway and John Wasson, Malone Society Collections 11, Oxford, 1980–1
N-Town P	*The Passion Play from the N. Town Manuscript*, ed. Peter Meredith, London, 1990
PRO	Public Record Office
REED	Records of Early English Drama
REED Newsletter	*Records of Early English Drama Newsletter*
RS	Rolls Series publications
Sharp *Dissertation*	Thomas Sharp, *A Dissertation on the Pageants or Dramatic Mysteries Anciently Performed at Coventry*, Coventry, 1825; reprinted Wakefield, 1973

Survey	John Stow, *A Survey of London*, reprinted from the text of 1603, ed. Charles Lethbridge Kingsford, 2 vols., Oxford, 1908; reprinted 1971
ThN	*Theatre Notebook*
Towneley	*The Towneley Plays*, ed. Martin Stevens and A. C. Cawley, EETS (SS 13, 14), 2 vols., Oxford, 1994

Introduction

By contrast with those of the French- and German-speaking areas, the surviving corpus of plays in medieval English is not extensive, and what remains by way of scriptural episodes and sequences, morality pieces, saints' plays and other genres may be unrepresentative of what once flourished. The dramatic texts we have disclose relatively little about stage conditions or performance techniques, and we are therefore highly dependent on drawing inferences from archival materials, which are contributing increasingly to a fuller picture of theatrical activity. In England at least the evidence of play-making appears initially to be significant if not abundant. Since Elizabethan times generations of 'retrievers of forgotten things from oblivion' (in John Aubrey's phrase) – antiquarians, bureaucrats, chroniclers among them – have salvaged a wealth of documentary material for posterity's perusal.[1] At certain English urban centres, records chiefly relating to staging communal religious plays are quite extensively preserved, and documents from such important medieval cities as York, Chester and Coventry necessarily loom large in any general analysis. Sadly, testimony from Ireland, Scotland and Wales only survives in frustratingly irregular pockets: almost nothing exists from Ireland prior to the Dublin Corpus Christi list of *c.* 1498 [see **D10**], and Wales is merely represented by two biblical interludes, the earliest manuscript of which is dated 1552.[2] In Scotland, though Lindsay's *Satire of the Three Estates* (*c.* 1540)[3] survives, only Aberdeen retains anything substantial by way of pre-1500 records.[4]

While much of this material has been known for several centuries, only in the last few decades has it been systematically sifted, arranged and disseminated in accordance with best scholarly practice. In this development, editors of the Malone Society's collections of dramatic data led the way,[5] and now the Toronto-based Records of Early English Drama project (REED), by tracking down, transcribing and reprinting all extant documentation concerning dramatic, ceremonial and minstrel activity up to 1642, is currently ensuring that at least what exists today will in future remain untouched by Time's rude hand. The present section draws heavily on REED material, and its editor owes the team directed by Professor Alexandra F. Johnston an immense debt of gratitude.

Nonetheless, surviving documentation still carries us only a short way towards establishing the true nature and extent of dramatic performance in these islands during the later Middle Ages. Record research has until recently been concentrated in the main on the copious archives of major cities, from two of which (York and Chester) survive almost complete texts of the cycles of vernacular scriptural episodes that form the central part of the Middle English repertoire. Consequently, attention has generally been directed towards atypical, large-scale productions of biblical sequences often set forth processionally in city thoroughfares, and on the functions exercised by the organs of local government and religious, craft or trade guilds in sustaining them. This balance is now being redressed, especially with the exploration of more modest parish drama. Popular secular theatre, however, is far more of a closed book. Only the lavish pageantry deployed in the streets of London and other cities, and the private entertainments enjoyed by English and Scottish royalty and their aristocratic accolytes is documented in any detail.

But not all medieval presentations were mobile, urban, or prestigious as several other sections of the present work demonstrate. In many parts of England alternative production concepts, sites and conditions prevailed, as with the three late fourteenth-century Cornish scriptural plays known as the *Ordinalia*, the lengthy Towneley Cycle often associated with the Yorkshire town of Wakefield, and the assemblage known as the 'N-Town Plays'. The epic requirements of the early fifteenth-century East Anglian morality play *The Castle of Perseverance*, presented under uncertain auspices, also dictated full deployment of the considerable resources of so-called 'place-and-scaffold' staging [see **D14**]. In several instances elementary stage plans assist speculation as to *mise en scène* [see **D11**, **D12**, **D14**], but *Everyman*, the best-known morality piece in the English language (despite being adopted from the Dutch), evades almost all attempts to establish its mode of performance. Precisely because information relating to these and other similar presentations is at a premium, much of our knowledge of early dramatic performance in these islands remains conjectural.

The documents are divided according to the following plan:

I   material dealing with the performance of religious drama within the local community, namely:
  • mobile presentations predominantly in processional form, with documentation emanating from York, Chester, Coventry, Norwich and Dublin
  • static presentations set forth on some designated open space where one more platforms or 'scaffolds' might be erected, evidence for which derives mainly from Cornwall and East Anglia
  • information regarding the administrative and financial arrangements underpinning community productions
  • items relating to performance in its several aspects, including acting, costumes and properties, special effects

II a selection of extracts typifying reactions both general and specific to dramatic presentation

III documents referring to secular activities (e.g. varieties of street performance;

royal entertainments at the English and Scottish courts; the emergence of household troupes towards the end of the fifteenth century.

1. Early examplars include Robert Rogers and William Dugdale [see items **D6**, **D8**], and such early nineteenth-century pioneers as William Hone, Thomas Sharp [see **D21**, **D49**], and the notoriously unreliable John Payne Collier.

2. See Gwenan Jones, *A Study of Three Welsh Religious Plays*, Aberystwyth, 1939.

3. See Anna J. Mill, 'Representations of Lyndsay's "Satyre of the Thrie Estaitis"', *PMLA* 47 (1932), pp. 636–51; John MacQueen, '*Ane Satyre of the Thrie Estaitis*', *Studies in Scottish Literature* 3 (1966), pp. 129–43; Robert Potter, *The English Morality Play*, London, 1975, pp. 81–8; *Four Morality Plays*, ed. Peter Happé, Harmondsworth, 1979, pp. 56–61.

4. Documentation for the city's *ludo de ly haliblude* (Corpus Christi play) goes back to 1440; some form of Candlemas celebration on 2 February is recorded from 1442 onwards. (See *MPS*, pp. 115–23).

5. See, for example, Dawson *Kent*, Kahrl *Lincs*, and *Norfolk and Suffolk*.

I   *Communal religious theatre*

INTRODUCTION

Documents surviving from the late 1300s onwards [see **C76**] illustrate the sundry ways whereby mounting religious drama involved committing the resources of entire medieval communities to a corporate venture. Performances took place not only in such notable cities as Beverley, Chester, Coventry, Dublin, Ipswich, King's Lynn, Norwich and York, but in more rural regions where performances were less susceptible of regulation by organisational statutes and ordinances. Yet from not one venue to date has there emerged a completely unequivocal description of the exact manner in which these communal dramas were presented before an audience.

Although the error no longer persists that performances mounted on the wheeled pageant wagon associated with the lengthy sequences of scriptural plays known (often inaccurately) as 'Corpus Christi plays' were the norm, it still needs to be affirmed that even at locations where evidence exists for an annual processional parade featuring carts, it is not axiomatic that dramatic performances (let alone complete cycles) took place on them as they passed through the streets. Floats may have carried no more than biblical tableaux or miming characters, as in some continental countries; alternatively, presentations may only have taken place on one or more platforms, where a single static performance formed a climax or sequel to the street parade.

Nevertheless, strong evidence indicates that at some locations at least, including York, Chester, Coventry, and probably Norwich, Beverley and Newcastle, live performances on wagons *were* staged at intervals along a processional route. Assertions that the enactment of all the episodes in a cyclic drama was confined to some culminating finale in such places of public assembly as the Pavement at York or the Roodee at Chester have been vigorously resisted. Certainly the notion of a single concluding performance within doors has won little support.[1]

1.   The York debate was chiefly developed by Alan H. Nelson in 'Principles of Processional Staging: York Cycle', *Modern Philology* 67 (1970), followed by his *The Medieval English Stage: Corpus Christi Plays and Pageants*, Chicago and London, 1974. Competing contributions include those of Martin Stevens, 'The York Cycle: from Procession to Play' and

Margaret Dorrell, 'Two Studies of the York Corpus Christi Play', *Leeds Studies in English* 6 (1972), pp. 37–61, and pp. 63–111.

MOBILE PRESENTATION

York

Among all the cities of medieval England, York possesses the most impressive set of documents relating to the mounting of community drama. Not only do its archives contain a rich array of documents dealing with every aspect of theatrical operations, but it is also the home of the York Cycle,[1] the fullest Middle English sequence of plays or pageants whose forty-eight episodes cover biblical history from the Creation to the Day of Judgement. The day selected for its presentation through the city streets by the trade and religious guilds was Corpus Christi (the second Thursday after Whitsun). York also staged two processional plays no longer extant: a Paternoster play first mentioned in 1388–9 and presented by the religious guild of that name [see **C57**], and a Creed play (*c.* 1446) which belonged to the Guild of Corpus Christi [see **D26**(i), **28**].[2]

1. A single unique text of the cycle survives as British Library MS Additional 35290; it has been edited as *The York Plays* by Richard Beadle, London, 1982.
2. See Alexandra F. Johnston, 'The Plays of the Religious Guilds of York: the Creed Play and the Pater Noster Play', *Speculum* 50 (1975), pp. 55–90.

A York pageant wagon

The exact manner in which processional performances of the York Cycle evolved is still a matter for speculation, but some form of annual parade of pageant wagons was in place by the final decades of the fourteenth century [see **C76**]. At whatever point in time these 'pageants' came to serve as stages for spoken performances at intervals during their progress through the streets, details of their lavish embellishment leave no doubt that they represented a salient feature of the drama at centres where they were employed. The description of the wagon on which by 1443 the York Mercers presented their play of Doomsday and its accoutrements [see **D1**] conveys something of the importance of a pageant's physical appearance for a guild's prestige, while the Norwich Grocers' inventory of 1565 [see **D9**] offers a useful comparison.

D1   The York Mercers' indenture, 1433

Merchant Adventurers' Archives, York: D 63 (Mercers' Pageant Documents), 11 June 1433; pr. REED, *York*, pp. 55–6

[The Master and Constables of the York Mercers' Company and the four members currently serving as pageant masters[1] agree that they have received into their safe keeping the 'pageant gear' detailed below.]

[. . .] First, a pageant with four wheels; Hell-mouth; three garments for three devils; six devils' faces in three masks [i.e. with a face on each side]; array for two Evil Souls (that is to say, two shirts, two pairs of hose, two masks and two wigs); costumes for two Good Souls (that is to say, two shirts, two pairs of hose, two masks and two wigs); two pairs of angels' wings with iron in the ends; two trumpets of silver plate and two gold [red]; four albs for four Apostles; three diadems with three masks for three Apostles; four diadems with four wigs of yellow for four Apostles; a cloud and two pieces of rainbow of timber; array for God [i.e. Christ], that is to say, a slit [wounded][2] shirt, a diadem with a gilded mask. A great painted hanging of red damask for the rear of the pageant; two other smaller hangings for two sides of the pageant; three other hangings of linen broad-cloth for the sides of the pageant; a little hanging, four-square, to hang at the back of God; four iron supports to bear up Heaven; four end-bolts (?) [finale coterelles] and an iron pin; a grid-framework (?) [brandreth] of iron that God shall sit upon when He shall ascend up to Heaven, with four ropes at four corners; a Heaven of iron with a pulley (?) [naffe] of wood; two pieces with red clouds and stars of gold belonging to Heaven; two pieces with blue clouds painted on both sides; three pieces with red clouds with sunbeams of gold and stars for the Highest of Heaven, with a long narrow border of the same material; seven great angels holding the [symbols of the] Passion of God (one of them has a pennant of brass and a gilded cross of iron on its head); four smaller gilded angels holding the [symbols of the] Passion; nine smaller angels painted red, to run about in Heaven; a long slender cord to make the angels run about; two short rollers of wood to put forth the pageant [. . .]

Endorsed: Item, one banner of red fabric [buckram] embossed with gold, with the Trinity and with ostrich feathers and with one long streamer; item, four small rose-coloured banners with the Trinity on them [. . .]

---

[1] Each guild appointed pageant masters to supervise its arrangements; see **D18** etc., and REED *York*, p. 104.

[2] The term 'wounded' used may mean that Christ's robe was stained red, rather than merely slit to represent the traditional wound in the side.

Regulating processional performances

The complexities of presenting communal drama in the processional mode called for a considerable degree of organisational skill from the civic authorities: the ideal of order and structure needed to be imposed to prevent the spirit of *laissez faire* overwhelming the proceedings. The York authorities had to establish the route taken by the procession and confirm the pageants' stopping-places or 'stations' [**D2, D3**]; issue firm injunctions concerning the timing and sequence of the performances [**D4**]; negotiate with private citizens eager to benefit financially from the location of the stations on the processional route [**D5(i), (ii)**].

D2   Establishing the stations, York, 1394

North Yorkshire County Library, York: E 20 (A/Y Memorandum Book), fo. 17 verso (28 April 1394); pr. REED, *York*, p. 8; trans. p. 694

[. . .] On the same day it was agreed that all the Corpus Christi pageants shall play in the places assigned to them in ancient times and not in others, but exactly as prearranged by the Mayor, the Bailiffs and their officers, so that if any pageant does differently, the members of the craft staging the said pageant shall pay six shillings and eightpence for public works into the Mayor's Chamber.

D3   Confirming the processional route, York, 1399

North Yorkshire County Library, York: E 20 (A/Y Memorandum Book), fo. 19 verso; pr. REED, *York*, pp. 10–12; trans. pp. 697–8

To the honourable men, the Mayor and Aldermen of the city of York, the Commons of the same city plead that, given that they incur great expense and costs in connection with the plays and pageants of Corpus Christi Day, which cannot be played or performed on the accustomed day as they should be, because the aforesaid pageants are presented in so many several places at considerable loss and discomfort to the said Commoners and strangers who have travelled to the said city on the very day for the same purpose, that it may please you to reflect that the said pageants are maintained and supported by the Commons and craftsmen of the same city to honour and reverence our Saviour Jesus Christ and for the glory and benefit of the same city, that you ordain that the aforesaid pageants are played in the places to which they were limited and assigned by you and by the aforesaid Commons previously [. . .]

[A list of twelve 'stations' follows.]

D4   Some rules laid down, York, 1415

North Yorkshire County Library, York: E 20 (A/Y Memorandum Book) (1415), fos. 252 verso–255; pr. REED, *York*, pp. 24–5

Ordo paginarum ludi Corporis Christi [. . .]

[. . .] We command on behalf of the king and the Mayor and Sheriffs of this City [. . .] that men who bring forth pageants [. . .] play at the places assigned for that purpose and nowhere else, on pain of forfeiting [. . .] forty shillings [. . .] And that all types of craftsmen who bring forth their pageants in order and sequence [course] by good players well turned out and speaking clearly and audibly [openly], upon pain of losing one hundred shillings to be paid to the Chamber without any pardon. And that every player that shall play be ready in his pageant at convenient time, that is to say at the mid-way point between four and five in the morning, and then all other pageants fast following [i.e. 'sticking close'] each one after the other as their course is, without delay, under penalty of making over to the Chamber six shillings and eightpence [. . .]

D5   Renting out the stations, York, 1417, 1478

(i) North Yorkshire County Library, York: E 20 (A/Y Memorandum Book), fos. 187 verso – 188 (7 June 1417); pr. REED, *York*, pp. 28–30; trans. pp. 713–14

[. . .] [it is] ordained that all those who, because of the scaffolds which they erect in the previously mentioned locations before their doors on what is public ground, receive money from those sitting on them, shall pay to the Chamberlains of the City for the use of the said Commons, the third penny of any money so received. And if they shall refuse to pay a third penny or agree some other sum honourably in this way with the Chamber, that then the play shall be transferred to other places as the Mayor in office at the time and the Council of the Chamber of the City dispose and desire, no one speaking against this ordinance, apart from a few owners of scaffolds in Micklegate.

[1] On 12 June 1417 it was agreed that the stopping-places in future would only be sited where tenants of scaffolds agreed to pay for the privilege, and that in future stations would be located where the most generous contributors had their holdings.

(ii) North Yorkshire County Library, York: E 20 (A/Y Memorandum Book), fo. 331 verso (2 September 1478); pr. REED, *York*, pp. 119–20; trans. p. 781

[. . .] Know ye that we [the Mayor and Commons] have assigned and made over in return for rent-money to Henry Watson and Thomas Dicinson, sellers of pike, the play or performance of Corpus Christi annually presented in High Ousegate between the buildings now in the said Henry's and Thomas's tenure, that is to say at the east end of Ouse Bridge; the said play or performance to be held and kept there from the Feast of Corpus Christi Anno Domini 1478 to the end of the next full twelve years to follow, for an annual return from thence to us, the aforesaid Mayor and our successors, that is, into the hands of the Chamberlains in office at that time, eleven shillings of legal English tender annually, for public works in the said city throughout the said period, that is, within the six days following the aforesaid Feast of Corpus Christi under pain of losing the said play (the present lease in no way withstanding), that is to say, so that the said play or performance shall not be played at that location at all [. . .]

Processional performances

Many cities and towns do not possess York's wealth of documentation relating to the finer points of processional presentation. In two instances, the principal evidence derives from two relatively late and therefore undependable sources. For Chester there is Archdeacon Robert Rogers' so-called Breviary dating from 1609 [see **D6**]; for Coventry one must rely on William Dugdale's monumental *Antiquities of Warwickshire*, published in a handsome folio of 1656 [**D8**].[1] Both, though unreliable in varying respects, nonetheless appear to draw on recent testimony for their main conclusions.

¹ Dugdale (1605–86), schooled in Coventry, compiler of the *Monasticon anglicanum* and *The Baronage of England*, ended his career as Garter King-of-Arms.

Chester

While Chester's earliest dramatic records are sparse, after 1500 they are extensive enough to provide a considerable amount of valuable information on processional performances through the city streets by its guildsmen. The Chester plays ultimately consisted of twenty-four biblical episodes¹ mounted on 'carriages' and presented on the three days following Whitsunday, but this practice seems only to have evolved between 1519 and 1531. Prior to that a single static presentation of a Passion play, preceded by a religious procession, appears to have sufficed to mark the Feast of Corpus Christi, a custom local clergy continued until *c.* 1548 when it was suppressed. During the doctrinal upheavals of the sixteenth century the cycle underwent a number of changes, a final single static presentation being confined to Midsummer Day 1575.

1.   The cycle plays are principally preserved in six late sixteenth- and early seventeenth-century manuscripts copied by local antiquarian scholars; see R.M. Lumiansky and David Mills (eds), *The Chester Mystery Cycle*, EETS (SS 3, 9), 2 vols., Oxford, 1974, 1986.

Archdeacon Robert Rogers

The most familiar account of English processional presentation derives from the late sixteenth-century reminiscences of Archdeacon Robert Rogers of Chester, who died *c.* 1595 and whose antiquarian notes or 'Breviary' were written up around 1609 by his son David. As a staunch Protestant, Rogers Senior was self-declaredly hostile to the performances, and the accuracy of his account of Chester's 'Whitsun plays' may be contested, yet it commands attention as being based on apparent eye-witness evidence. Moreover, it is supported in some measure by such documents as the list of pageants (the so-called 'Early Banns') dating from 1539–40 [see **D7**].

D6   Robert Rogers' account of Chester's Whitsun Plays, 1609

Chester City Archives: unnumbered MS (Archdeacon Rogers' Breviary); pr. REED, *Chester*, pp. 238–9 [see also *MES*, pp. 154–69]

Now of the plays of Chester called the Whitsun Plays, when they were played, and what occupations bring forth at their charges the plays or pageants.

    [. . .] The manner of which plays was thus: they were divided into twenty-four pageants according to the companies of the city, and every company brought forth their pageant, which was the carriage or place which they were played in. And before these plays there was a man which did ride (as I take it) upon St George's

Day [23 April] through the city and there published the time and the matter of the plays in brief.

They were played upon Monday, Tuesday and Wednesday in Whitsun week. And they first began at the Abbey Gates, and when the first pageant was played at the Abbey Gates, then it was wheeled from thence to Pentice[1] at the High Cross before the Mayor, and before that was done the second came, and the first went into the Watergate Street, and from thence unto the Bridge Street, and so one after another till all the pageants were played appointed for the first day, and so likewise for the second and the third day.

These pageants or carriage[s] was [sic] a high place made like a house with two rooms being open on the top; [in] the lower room they apparelled and dressed themselves, and the higher room they played [on], and they [the wagons] stood upon six wheels, and when they had done with one carriage in one place they wheeled the same from one street to another, first from the Abbey Gate to the Pentice, then to the Watergate Street, then to the Bridge Street through the lanes and so to the Eastgate Street. And thus they came from one street to another, keeping a direct order in every street, for before the first carriage was gone from one place, the second came and so before the second was gone the third came, and so till the last was done, all in order without any staying in any place, for word being brought how every place was near done, they came and made no place to tarry till the last was played [. . .]

[1] On the south side of the church of St Peter.

D7   Chester pageants, *c.* 1539–40.

British Library: Harley MS 2150, fos. 85 verso–88 verso; pr. REED, *Chester*, pp. 31–3

[. . .] These be the crafts of the city, the which crafts bear the charge of the pageants in [the] Play of Corpus Christi [. . .] and were the ancient Whitsun plays in Chester set out at the charges of these occupations, yearly played on Monday, Tuesday and Wednesday in Whitsun week [. . .]

Barkers or Tanners	The Falling of Lucifer
Drapers and Hosiers	The Creation of the World
Drawers of Dee and Waterleaders	Noah and his Ship
Barbers, Wax Chandlers and Leeches or Surgeons	Abraham and Isaac
Cappers, Wiredrawers and Pinners	King Balaak and Balaam with Moses
Wrights, Slaters, Tilers, Clothes-menders [Daubers] and Thatchers	Nativity of Our Lord
Painters, Needleworkers [Broderers] and Glaziers[1]	The Shepherds Offering
Vintners and Merchants	King Herod and the Mount Victoriall
Mercers and Spicers	Three Kings of Cologne [Magi]

These nine plays and pageants above written be played on the first day

Goldsmiths and Masons	The Slaying of the Children of Israel by Herod
Smiths, Polishers [Furbours] and Pewterers	Purification of Our Lady
Butchers	The Pinnacle [i.e. The Temptation] with the Woman of Canaan
Arrow- and Parchment-makers	The Rising of Lazarus from death to life
Corvisers or Shoemakers	The Coming of Christ to Jerusalem
Bakers and Millers	Christ's Monday when He sat with His Apostles [i.e. The Last Supper]
Bowyers, Fletchers, Stringers, Coopers and Turners	Scourging of Christ
Ironmongers and Ropers	Crucifying of Christ
Cooks, Tapsters, and Hostelers and Innkeepers	The Harrowing of Hell

These nine plays or pageants above written be played upon the second day

Skinners, Cardmakers, Hatters, Pointers and Girdlers	The Resurrection
Saddlers, Saddle-tree Makers [Fusters]	Castle of Emmaus and the Apostles
Tailors	Ascension of Christ
Meat-dealers [Fleshmongers]	Whitsunday; the Making of the Creed
Shearers of Cloth [Shearmen]	Prophets before Doomsday
Dyers and Bellfounders	Antichrist
Weavers and Fullers [Walkers]	Doomsday
Played upon the third [day]	

On Corpus Christi Day the colleges and priests bring forth a play at the assentment of the Mayor [. . .]

---

1 The Painters etc., Bowyers etc., and Skinners etc. shared a common wagon on successive days, as did the Vintners etc., Goldsmiths etc., and Dyers etc.

Coventry

Awareness of medieval Coventry's full theatrical importance is blunted not only by the severe losses its original records have sustained through fire and enemy action, but also by the survival of no more than two of its pageant sequence of ten plays in texts dating from *c.* 1535. In any case, the complete work they represent may well have differed from the scriptural cycles in that it possibly constituted a dramatisation of the tenets of the Apostles' Creed.[1] It is certainly a notable feature of what remains[2] that several biblical episodes are concentrated within the confines of a single pageant.

Coventry's records still offer the interested reader a formidable body of information relating to the mounting of plays in the city from the late fourteenth century onwards [see **D21**, **D38(ii)**, **D45**, **D49**, **D51**]. Sir William Dugdale's account of processional staging in the city [**D8**] forms a useful adjunct to the testimony of Chester's Archdeacon Rogers [**D6**], although it should be remembered that Dugdale believed Coventry to be the home of the N-Town Plays, which are unlikely to have been presented processionally [see **D8**, note 2].

[1] See Alexandra F. Johnston, 'What if No Texts Survived? External Evidence for Early English Drama', in *Contexts for Early English Drama*, ed. Marianne G. Briscoe and John C. Coldewey, Bloomington and Indianapolis, 1989, pp. 1–9.

[2] See Hardin Craig (ed.), *Two Coventry Corpus Christi Plays*, EETS (extra series) 87 (1957); reprinted 1967.

D8   William Dugdale on the Coventry Plays, 1656

William Dugdale, *The Antiquities of Warwickshire Illustrated* [. . .] London, 1656; revised edn, 1730, p. 116

Before the suppression of the monasteries [*c.* 1536–9], this city was very famous for the *Pageants* that were played therein, upon *Corpus Christi Day*; which, occasioning very great confluence of people thither from far and near, was of no small benefit thereto. Which *Pageants* being acted with mighty state and reverence by the friars of this house [the Franciscan monks of Greyfriars][1] had theatres [i.e. stages] for the several scenes, very large and high, placed upon wheels, and drawn to all the eminent parts of the city, for the better advantage of spectators. And contained the story of the New Testament, composed into old English rhyme, as appeareth by an ancient *MS* entitled *Ludus Corporis Christi*, or *Ludus Coventriae*.[2]

I have been told by some old people, who in their younger years were eye-witnesses of these *Pageants* so acted, that the yearly confluence of people to see that show was extraordinary great, and yielded no small advantage to this city.

[1] Dugdale misunderstood an entry in the city annals for 1493, stating that Henry VII 'came to see the Plays acted by the Grey Friars', assuming that the words referred to the performers, rather than the site, of the presentation. A station in Grey Friars' Lane is advocated by Nelson, *MES*, p. 149.

[2] Dugdale, like many others, is mistaken as to the link between Coventry and the text bearing the title 'Ludus Coventriae' (BL MS Cotton Vespasian D.8), which is in fact of East Anglian provenance, and now usually referred to as the N-Town Play or Plays [see **D17**, **D42** etc.].

Norwich

The citizens of late medieval Norwich enjoyed a wide range of frequent processional displays, including one held on the Feast of Corpus Christi incorporating a parade of pageants. A list of 1527 names eight pageants on Old Testament, and four on New Testament subjects, but of these only that of the Fall of Man (the Expulsion of Adam and Eve from Paradise) as presented by the Grocers' Guild survives, albeit in three variant versions. Dramatic presentation appears to have been originally associated with Corpus Christi, but by 1527 the plays had transferred to

Whit Monday and Tuesday [see **D36(v)**]. Some argue that the pageants merely processed as tableaux, with live performances only mounted subsequently at a stationary site, but the words 'when the Grocers' Pageant is played without any other going before it . . .'[1] (which precede one of the two alternative Prologues of 1565) suggest otherwise. Whatever the context, a Grocers' Guild inventory of 1565 offers some graphic details of its presentation of 'Paradise' [see **D9**].

[1] John Kirkpatrick's transcription (c. 1720), Norwich Record Office, MS 21 f (11), no. 68. See *NCP*, pp. xxvi–xxx; Joanna Dutka, 'The Lost Dramatic Cycle of Norwich and the Grocers' Play of the Fall of Man', *Review of English Studies* 35 (1984), pp. 1–13.

D9   The Norwich Grocers' inventory, 1565

Norfolk Record Office, Norwich: 21. f (Grocers' Guild Records), fo. [8] (1565); pr. REED, *Norwich, 1540–1642*, pp. 52–3

Inventory of the particulars appertaining to the Company of the Grocers, AD 1565
A Pageant, that is to say, a house of wainscot painted and built on a cart with four wheels
A square top to set over the said house
A gilded griffin with a pennant to set on the said top
A bigger iron pennant to set on the end of the pageant
Forty-three small pennants belonging to the same pageant
A rib coloured red
A coat and hose with a bag and a cap for Dolour,[1] stained
Two coats and a pair of hose for Eve, stained
A coat and hose for Adam, stained
A coat with hose and a tail for the serpent, stained, with a white wig
A coat of yellow fabric [buckram] with the Grocers' arms for the flag-bearer
An angel's coat and over-hose of apes' skins
Three painted cloths to hang about the pageant
A mask and wig for the Father
Two wigs for Adam and Eve
Four neck-halters of broad linen tape [inkle] with knobs and tassels
Six horse-cloths, stained, with knobs and tassels
Item. Weights etc.[2]

[1] A personification of Sorrow who accompanied Adam and Eve from Paradise into exile.
[2] In 1570 the Grocers' wagon was sold off to pay rent long overdue on their pageant house.

Allocating the pageants

The basis on which local authorities, guild officials or pageant masters determined to which group each scriptural pageant should be allocated is a matter of conjecture. In some instances the assignment is entirely appropriate – Butchers play Torturers, Goldsmiths the Magi – but no doubt tradition, prestige, and willingness to take pains were other factors influencing decisions reached. The list from Dublin [**D10**] may be compared with that of Chester [see **D7**]. Almost every entry concludes with the words 'pain [[i.e. penalty] for any failure to satisfy the authorities] forty shillings'; these are omitted in transcription, though they demonstrate the importance attached to corporate commitment. Dublin's mixture of secular and sacred subjects and the terminology employed make it unlikely that the pageants listed in 1498 took the form of acted dramas as they did at York, Coventry or Chester: the parade may well have constituted no more than the kind of mimed dumb shows or tableaux from which spoken processional drama could have evolved elsewhere.

Dublin

The city of Dublin possesses little by way of early drama in English, although an incomplete and now destroyed morality piece *The Pride of Life* [see **C63(iv)**] predates *The Castle of Perseverance* [see **D14**] by at least half a century. While it is clear that by the late fifteenth century a procession of mingled sacred and profane pageants 'made by an old law' was being mounted to mark Corpus Christi Day [see **D10**], there is no evidence that it made up a series of even disconnected dramatic episodes.

D10   Corpus Christi pageants at Dublin, *c.* 1498

Dublin City Archives C1/2/1, (The Chain Book), fos. 56 verso–57 recto [I am most grateful to Dr Alan J. Fletcher for allowing me to use this recent transcription from his *Drama and the Performing Arts in Pre-Cromwellian Ireland*, Toronto, forthcoming]

The pageants of Corpus Christi Day made by an old law and confirmed by an assembly [. . .] [on 20 July 1498].

Glovers: Adam and Eve with an angel following bearing a sword [. . .]

Shoemakers [Corvisers]: Cain and Abel with an altar and their offering [. . .]

Mariners, Vintners, Ships' Carpenters, and Salmon-takers: Noah with his ship costumed appropriately [. . .]

Weavers: Abraham [and] Isaac with their altar and a lamb and their offering [. . .]

Smiths, Shearmen, Bakers, Slaters, Cooks and Masons: Pharaoh with his host [. . .]

Skinners, House Carpenters and Tanners and Needleworkers [Browderes]: For the body of the camel and Our Lady and Her child well costumed with Joseph to lead the camel and Moses with the Children of Israel and the porters to carry the camel [. . .]

(The Stainers and Painters to paint the head of the camel [. . .])

Goldsmiths: the three kings of Cologne [Magi] riding worshipfully with their offering, with a star before them [. . .]

Hoopers: the shepherds with an angel singing *Gloria in excelsis Deo* [. . .]

Corpus Christi Guild:[1] Christ in His Passion with three Marys and angels bearing large candles [serges] of wax in their hand[s] [. . .]

Tailors: Pilate with his fellowship and his lady and his knights smartly turned-out [. . .]

Barbers: Annas and Caiaphas well turned out in appropriate clothing [. . .]

City Accountants (Auditors?) [Conpteours]: Arthur with [his] knights [. . .]

Fishers: the twelve Apostles [. . .]

Merchants: the Prophets [. . .]

Butchers: six Tormentors with their garments well and neatly painted [. . .]

The Mayor of the Bullring and bachelors of the same: the Nine Worthies riding worshipfully with their followers in appropriate fashion [. . .]

The Stack-yard men [Hagardmen] and the Husbandmen to bear the dragon and to repair the dragon [for] St George's Day and Corpus Christi Day [. . .]

[1] It is noteworthy that members of the Corpus Christi Guild appear alongside the trade and craft guildsmen.

OPEN-SPACE PRESENTATION

In parts where pageant-wagon presentation was not an option, the most frequent alternative was to select some suitable open space in town or country, delineate a playing area (the 'place' or *platea*), and designate within it one or more *loci* (usually free-standing platforms known as 'scaffolds' or 'stages').[1] Such a system with its unlocalised arena and basic scenic units with specific identities could be flexibly employed, although not every variation is satisfactorily documented. Too little is known, for example, about productions at London's 'Skinners Well', where, according to John Stow [see **C23**], plays performed on scaffolds by London's parish clerks attracted large audiences. Equally shadowy is the presentation of the Passion Play at New Romney in Kent, although records state that 'stages' were built there [see **D32**]. However, it is clear that 'place and scaffold' staging was the principal method employed to set forth much of the medieval English repertoire.[2]

1. In around 1390 Chaucer alludes to a parish clerk appearing as Herod 'upon a scaffold high' [see **C62**].
2. See Alan H. Nelson, ' Some Configurations of Staging in Medieval Drama' in Jerome Taylor and Alan H. Nelson (eds.), *Medieval English Drama: Essays Critical and Contextual*, Chicago, 1972, pp. 116–47.

'Theatre-in-the-round'

By far the best-documented static staging convention is the 'theatre-in-the-round' format, also frequently encountered across the English Channel [see **Section E**]. Some physical evidence for the existence of such performance venues survives [see **D13**], but awareness of the circular mode derives chiefly from diagrammatic staging plans linked to three play-texts: (a) the Middle Cornish scriptural sequence known as the *Ordinalia* [see **D11**]; (b) the later Cornish piece based on the career of the Breton saint Meriasek [see **D12**]; (c) the most ambitious of the Middle English moralities *The Castle of Perseverance* [see **D14**]. Each drawing shows a circular playing arena with certain areas assigned to different dramatic characters or locations, for most of which one assumes scaffolds were erected either within the arena itself or set into its circumference. The sketches may perhaps replicate practicable layouts for performance, but equally they may be no more than notional. Particularly controversial has been establishing the site of the water-filled ditch or moat shown in *The Castle* plan, which rival scholars have positioned at the base of the central tower, between *platea* and spectators, and around the entire auditorium [see **D14**].[1]

1.   See Richard Southern, *The Medieval Theatre in the Round*, London, 1957; 2nd edn, 1975; Natalie Crohn Schmitt, 'Was there a Medieval Theatre in the Round? A Re-Examination of the Evidence', *ThN* 23 (1968–9), pp. 130–42; 24 (1969–70), pp. 18–25; Catherine Belsey, The Stage Plan of *The Castle of Perseverance*, *ThN* 28 (1974), pp. 124–32; Pamela M. King, 'Spatial Semantics and the Medieval Theatre', in *Themes in Drama*, vol. IX, *The Theatrical Space* (ed. James Redmond), Cambridge, 1987, pp. 45–58.

Cornwall

Apart from a few fragments, drama in the Cornish language survives in three texts: the three-part *Ordinalia* preserved in Bodleian MS 791 and associated with the Collegiate Church at Glasney; the mid-sixteenth-century *Gwreans an Bys (Creacion of the World)*[1] copied down in 1611, and the two-day *Beunans Meriasek* contained in MS Peniarth 105 at the National Library of Wales, and connected with the parish of Camborne.

The *Ordinalia*'s scriptural material is divided into three epic-scale dramas – *The Creation of the World*; *The Passion of Christ*; *The Resurrection of the Lord* – which perhaps once formed parts of a lengthier sequence. The texts are in Middle Cornish, the stage directions in Latin [see **D11**(i), (ii), (iii)]. The episodic (though not amorphous) *Beunans Meriasek* draws for its subject matter on the lifelong piety and miracle-working powers of the Breton saint and incorporates a number of popular hagiographic motifs. In the text Middle Cornish dialogue is interspersed with stage directions in English [see **D12**(i), (ii)].

1.   This text, sometimes known by the Cornish title *Gwreans an Bys* is the first play of a lost sequence; it was edited and translated by Paula Neuss (New York and London, 1983) [see **D53**(i)].

D11   Plans for three days' performances of the Cornish *Ordinalia*, c. 1375

Bodleian Library, Oxford, Bodley MS 791, fos. 27 recto; 56 verso; 83 recto; text trans. Markham Harris, *The Cornish Ordinalia. A Medieval Dramatic Trilogy*, Washington, 1969

Each of the texts which makes up the *Ordinalia*'s three parts is succeeded by a circular stage plan, identifying eight separate locations on the rim of the playing area. On all three days Heaven (*Celum*) is sited to the east; on Days 1 and 3 Hell (*Infernum*) occupies the northmost scaffold.

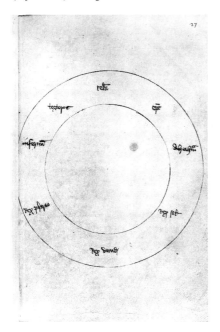

DII (i)

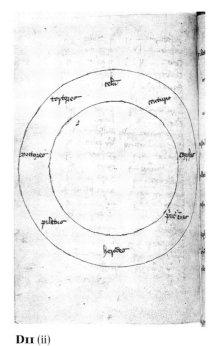

DII (ii)

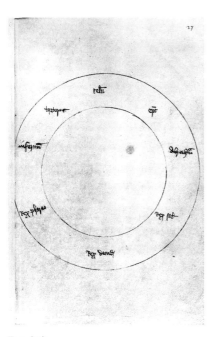

DII (iii)

D12   Plans for *Beunans Meriasek*, c. 1504

National Library of Wales, MS Peniarth 105, pp. 98, 180; text trans. Markham Harris, *The Life of Meriasek. A Medieval Cornish Miracle Play*, Washington, 1977

The action of the play is spread over two days and its scaffolds are not firmly identified with a principal occupant, but assigned to several figures in conjunction. On Day 1 a scenic feature denoting a chapel occupies the centre of the *platea*, much as the castle provides the focal point for *The Castle of Perseverance* [see **D14**].

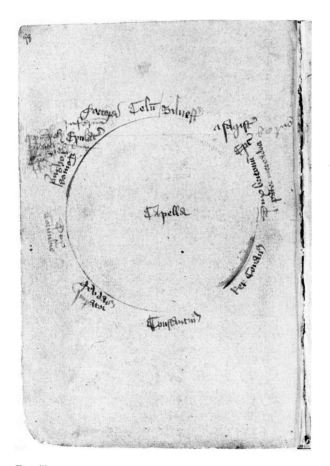

D12 (i)

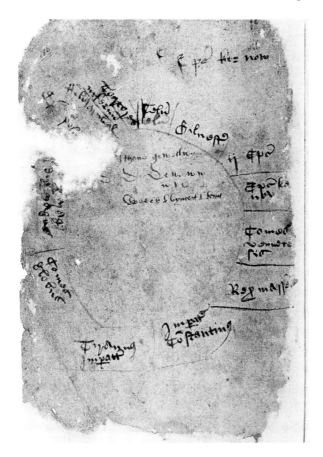

D12 (ii)

The Plen an Gwary

Whether or not the Cornish 'rounds' known as *plenys an gwary* were earthworks designed for other purposes or specially constructed for theatrical ends, a number of local antiquarians record their existence and possible use [see **D13(i)**, **(ii)**, **(iii)**]. Certainly Richard Carew in 1602 [**D13(i)**] speaks as if they were currently being constructed and employed for play performances, but his reliability as an authority on present practice must remain in doubt. Remains of two Cornish *plenys an gwary* can still be inspected at St Just-in-Penwith and at Perran Round, near Perranporth, and while there is no positive evidence that medieval presentations took place in them, many scholars consider it highly probable.[1]

---

[1] Scepticism is expressed by Schmitt, 'Was there a Medieval Theatre in the Round?', and by Treve Holman, 'Cornish Plays and Playing Places', *ThN* 4 (1950), pp. 52–4; Brian O. Murdoch in *The*

Cambridge Companion to Medieval English Theatre, ed. Richard Beadle, Cambridge, 1994, pp. 211–39, and REED, *Cornwall*, Toronto, 1999, adopt a more positive view.

D13   Cornish 'rounds' as performance sites, 1602–1758

(i) *The Survey of Cornwall, written by Richard Carew* [. . .]

London, 1602

[. . .] The Guary miracle, in English a miracle play, is a kind of interlude, compiled in Cornish out of some scripture history, with that grossness which accompanied the Romans' *vetus Comedia* [Old Comedy]. For representing it they raise an earthen amphitheatre in some open field, having the diameter of his enclosed plain some forty or fifty foot. The country people flock from all sides, many miles off, to hear and see it; for they have therein devils and devices to delight as well the eye as the ear [. . .] (pp. 71–2)

(ii) William Borlase, *Observations on the Antiquities, Historical and Monumental, of the County of Cornwall*

Oxford, 1754(?), 2nd edn revised, 1769

Book III. Chapter VII. 'Of Circular Monuments [. . .]'

Among the most ancient British monuments, the Circles of Stones-erect may justly claim a place [. . .] We find the number of Stones erected on a circular plain various; some Circles consisting of twelve, others of more, the most which have reached my notice, seventy-seven [. . .] (p. 191)

Where these Stone inclosures are semi-circular, and distinguished by seats and benches of like materials; there is no doubt but they were constructed in that form, out of regard to and for the convenience of the spectators, at plays, games and festivals [. . .] (p. 207)

[. . .] these are called with us in Cornwall (where we have great numbers of them) *Plan an guare*; viz. the level place, or Plain of sport and pastime. The benches round were generally of Turf [. . .] (p. 207)

We have one whose benches are of Stone, and the most remarkable Monument of this kind which I have yet seen; it is near the church of St Just, Penwith, now somewhat disfigured by the injudicious repairs of late years; but by the remains it seems to have been a work of more than usual labour and correctness [. . .] It was an exact Circle, of 126 feet diameter; the perpendicular height of the bank, from the area within, now seven feet; but the height from the bottom of the ditch without, ten feet at present, formerly more. The seats consist of six steps, fourteen inches wide, and one foot high, with one on the top of all, where the Rampart is about seven feet wide. The Plays they acted in these Amphitheatres were in the Cornish language; and the Subjects, taken from Scripture History [. . .] (p. 208)

(iii) William Borlase, *The Natural History of Cornwall*

Oxford, 1758

[. . .] The places where they were acted were the *Rounds*, a kind of amphitheatre, with benches either of stone or turf. Of the former sort that exhibited in the *Antiquities of Cornwall* [i.e. St Just] [. . .] served this purpose; but a much larger one of higher mound, ditched [fossed] on the outside, and very regular, is the amphitheatre in the parish of *Piran-sand* [. . .] A, the area of the amphitheatre, perfectly level, about one hundred and thirty feet diameter. B, the benches, seven in number, of turf, rising eight feet from the area [. . .] (pp. 297–9)

East Anglia

A high proportion of the surviving English play repertoire stems from East Anglia. It includes the scriptural dramas of the N-Town group, the two contrasting moralities *The Castle of Perseverance* and *Mankind*; the sole example of a native miracle play *The Croxton Play of the Sacrament*; the so-called 'Digby Plays' – *Mary Magdalene, The Killing of the Children, The Conversion of St Paul* from Bodleian MS Digby 133 – and the esoteric morality fragment *Wisdom*. Most of these seem designed with presentation at sites within a specific region in mind, and it is reasonable to assume that in some instances their performance may have involved the use of the 'place-and-scaffold' system as in the case of *The Castle of Perseverance*.

The Castle of Perseverance

D14   Plan for *The Castle of Perseverance*, c. 1400–25

Folger Shakespeare Library, MS V.a. 354 (the Macro manuscript), fo. 191 verso

This heavily annotated sketch plan indicates the presence of a centrally positioned 'castle' and five scaffolds located on the periphery of a circular playing space. It is less clear in identifying audience accommodation (though spectators are specifically forbidden to occupy the castle and it seems unlikely that they would have congested the vital *platea*), and in establishing whether the ditch or moat surrounds the central structure, the playing area, or the entire arena. The scaffolds are allocated to the World, the Flesh, and the Devil (Belial), to Heaven, and to Covetousness, the Deadly Sin which has a pivotal role in the action.

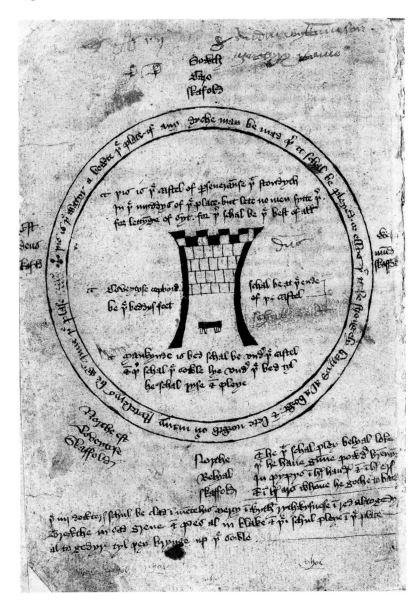

John Capgrave

Capgrave, an Augustinian friar of King's Lynn, went on pilgrimage to Rome in 1450, and later wrote up his visit to benefit other travellers to the Holy City. In discussing Roman theatres, which he only understood imperfectly – he thought the Colosseum a temple – Capgrave seems to show personal familiarity with English theatres-in-the-round [**D15**].

D15   John Capgrave and 'places all round', *c.* 1450

John Capgrave, *Ye Solace of Pilgrimes*, ed. C. A. Mills, Oxford, 1911, pp. 17–18

These [Roman] emperors also had certain places which they called *theatra*, and that signifies in our language a place in which men stand to see plays or wrestling or other such exercises of mirth or of solace. Some of these places were called *ampheatrum* – that was a place all round such as we have here in this land; some were called *theatrum* and that was a place like half a circle, of which there were seven in Rome [. . .]

The East Anglian 'game place'

Evidence for the use of 'game places' as popular East Anglian venues for all forms of recreation including drama is of relatively late provenance, but throws interesting light on what were possibly custom-built structures intended for mounting plays among other pastimes.[1]

1.   See Richard Beadle, 'The East Anglian "Game-Place": a Possibility for Further Research', *REED Newsletter* 1 (1978), pp. 2–4.

D16   East Anglian 'game places', 1538/9–*c.* 1577
(a)   The game place, house and garden, Great Yarmouth, 1538/9

Great Yarmouth Assembly Minutes, 15 March 1538/9, pr. *Norfolk and Suffolk*, pp. 12–13 (see also David Galloway, *ThN* 31 (1977), pp. 6–9)

[. . .] the said bailiffs and chamberlains [. . .] have granted, conveyed and rented to the same Robert Copping and to his assigns a certain garden lying on the south side of the parsonage garden, extending in length by the same parsonage wall 36 feet and in breadth 21 feet, and it abuts upon the town wall against the east side, together with a certain house called the Game-place House with the whole profit of the ground called the Game-place, to have and to hold the said garden, house and game-place to the said Robert Copping and to his assigns from the Feast of St Michael the Archangel [29 September] last past before the date of these presents, unto the end and term of thirty years, yielding and paying therefor yearly to the said bailiffs and chamberlains and to their successors to the use of the common profit of the town of Yarmouth aforesaid five shillings yearly during the said term [. . .]

[1]   The house may have served as a kind of 'pavilion' to the game-place.

(b)   A Suffolk game place, Walsham-le-Willows, *c.* February 1577

University of Chicago: Bacon MS 969 (Field Book of the Manors of Walsham-le-Willows and Walsham Churchhouse), fo. 59 verso; pr. Kenneth M. Dodd, 'Another Elizabethan Theater in the Round', *Shakespeare Quarterly* 21 (1970), pp. 125–56

The said game place in the tenure of divers men to the use and benefit of the said town of Walsham aforesaid is customary ground[1] held of the said manor of Walsham, and a place compassed round with a fair bank cast up on a good height and having many great trees called poplars growing about the same bank;[2] in the midst a fair round place of earth with a stone wall about the same to the height of the earth, made of purpose for the use of stage plays [. . .]

[1] i.e. sanctioned by custom rather than legal right.
[2] For purposes of protection and shelter.

The 'place-and-scaffold' convention

A number of dramatic texts further our understanding of 'place-and-scaffold' presentation. The 'place' or *platea* served to identify unspecified locations or journeys [see **D17(i)**], while one or more 'scaffolds' offered more precisely localised scenic components [see **D17(ii)**]. Deployed in a variety of ways (even in linear formation), to suit the terrain or the script's requirements, scaffolds might be elevated well above the *platea* and approached by ladders, ramps or steps to facilitate dramatic ascents or descents [see **D17(iii)**]. They were often fitted with hangings or curtains to conceal or reveal characters within, thus enabling continuity of action as often in the N-Town Passion Play [see **D17(iv)**].

D17   'Place-and-scaffold' staging in action

[See *Macro* (for *The Castle of Perseverance*); *NCP* (for *The Play of the Sacrament*); *Digby* (for *Mary Magdalene, The Conversion of St Paul, The Killing of the Children*); *N-Town P* (for the N-Town Passion Plays I and II)[1]

(i) The use of the 'place'

Here shall the leech's man come into the place (*Sacrament*, 524 s.d.)

Here Saul rides forth with his servants about the place, out of the place (*Conversion*, 140 s.d.)

Here the ship goes out of the place (*Magdalene* 1445, s.d.; 1922 s.d.)

Here the knights and Watkin walk about the place till Mary and Joseph be conveyed into Egypt (*Killing*, 232 s.d.)

Here Christ rides out of the place if he wishes to [and he will] (*N-Town P* I. Appendix 1, 43 s.d.)

Here a messenger shall come into the place, running and crying 'Tidings! Tidings!', and so round about the place [. . .] (*N-Town P* II. 89 s.d.)

Here Satan enters into the place in the most horrible manner. And while he performs, they shall put on Jesus's clothes, and on top of the rest a white garment, and lead him about the place, and then to Pilate by the time his wife has performed (*N-Town P* II. 486 s.d.)

(ii) Employing scaffolds

Here the prince of devils shall enter on a stage, and Hell underneath that stage (*Magdalene* 357 s.d.)

Here Satan shall go home to his stage, and Mary shall enter into the place alone [. . .] (*Magdalene* 563 s.d.)

By the time that the procession [of characters] *has entered the playing-area, and Herod has taken his scaffold, and Pilate, and Annas and Caiaphas their scaffolds also* [. . .] (*N-Town P* II. Opening s.d.)

(iii) Ascents and descents

Here HUMANUM GENUS *ascends to* MUNDUS [i.e. on his platform] (*Castle,* 614 s.d.)

Here they [the Four Daughters of God] *ascend all together to the* BAD ANGEL [. . .] *Then they ascend to the throne* [of God] (*Castle,* 3585 s.d., 3593 s.d.)

Here Annas goes down to meet with Caiaphas (*N-Town P* I. 280 s.d.)

And here Pilate shall come down from his scaffold with Caiaphas and Annas and all their retinue [meinie], *and shall come and look on Christ* (*N-Town P* II. 866 s.d.)

(iv) Revelations and concealments

Here Annas shall show himself on his stage [. . .] (*N-Town P* I. 164 s.d.)

[. . .] *and in the meantime the council house mentioned before shall suddenly unclose, showing the bishops, priests and judges sitting in their estate* [appropriate rank] *as if it were a convocation* [synod] (*N-Town P* I. 518 s.d.)

[. . .] *And then the place that Christ is in shall suddenly unclose round about, showing Christ sitting at the table and his disciples each in his proper place* [degree] (*N-Town P* I. 662 s.d.)

Here the devil shall go to Pilate's wife, the curtain drawn as she lies in bed; and he shall make no din, but soon after he has come in she shall make a pitiable [rewly] *noise, coming and running off the scaffold* [in] *her smock* [shirt], *and her gown* [kirtle] *in her hand* [. . .] (*N-Town P* II. 543 s.d.)

1   The N-Town Plays (British Library Ms Cotton Vespasian D. viii) represent a curious phenomenon
    among the major extant scriptural cycles, being an amalgam of several independent biblical and
    apocryphal dramas, dove-tailed together to form a whole, yet on closer examination bearing only a
    superficial impression of unity. Its highlights include a unique play on the early life of the Virgin, and
    two linked Passion Plays remarkable for their detailed stage directions. (See *The Mary Play from the
    N. Town Manuscript*, ed. Peter Meredith, London and New York, 1987; revised edn, Exeter, 1997; *The
    Passion Play from the N. Town Manuscript*, ed. Peter Meredith, London and New York, 1990.) The name
    by which this text is usually known derives from its 'banns' (or trailer) which suggests that provision
    was made for all or part of the play to be presented at a variable location, indicated by the words 'N.
    Town'. The script could probably be hired for performance: the appropriate place name could then
    be introduced to replace 'N'.

ORGANISATION, CONTROL, AND FUNDING

The financial, legislative and logistical arrangements required to mount medieval
community theatricals differ widely: procedures adopted at one centre were not
necessarily replicated at another. Even in English cities and towns where craft,
trade, and religious guilds exercised power, and the local authorities' ability to delegate responsibility for the performances and to control participants produced a
measure of similarity in matters of organisation, funding and control, it must
never be mistaken for uniformity of practice.

Taking responsibility

In the case of the presentation of scriptural sequences chiefly undertaken in large
towns and cities rather than in more modest surroundings, the burdens of sponsorship and administration rested on the shoulders of the community's governors
and officials, who in turn transferred responsibility to such citizens and guild
members as were willing or duty-bound to execute the relevant tasks. A document
of *c.* 1496 from Plymouth makes the chain of command clear [see **D18**], while a
memorandum emanating from Lincoln indicates that here the religious guild of St
Anne controlled proceedings, albeit with city council backing [see **D19**].[1]

1.   See Kahrl *Lincs*, p. vii.

D18   A Plymouth guild's responsibilities defined, *c.* 1496

West Devon Record Office, Plymouth: W 46 (Black Book 1535–1707), fos. 62–3 (1535–6);
pr. REED, *Devon*, pp. 226–7

[. . .] we [the Mayor of the Borough and others] have given and granted unto the
brethren and craft of Tailors of the same Borough, full authority and power to elect
these and make Masters of their occupation and craft. And they so made and
chosen by them of the same occupation [. . .] shall have full authority and power
to rule and correct all things belonging to the said occupation and craft so fixed,
made and established. They shall make or cause to be made at the cost and charge

of the said craft a pageant yearly unto Corpus Christi Guild for the wealth and profit of the same Guild on Corpus Christi Day. And the same they shall keep and maintain for ever at their cost and charge, for the which pageant the said brethren may be entreated for ever in the same Guild [. . .][1]

[1] This document, copied from the old Town Ledger of Plymouth into the so-called ' Black Book' in 1535–6, is dated 1496 by J.C. Jeaffreson, *HMC Report* (1883), p. 274.

D19   The guildsmen of St Anne empowered, Lincoln, 1520

Lincoln Archives Office L 1/1/1/1 vol. 1 (Lincoln Common Council Minutes 1511–41), fo. 115 (27 June 1520); pr. Kahrl *Lincs*, p. 48

[. . .] proclamation shall be made through this city that every occupation under the supervision of the Gracemen[1] shall prepare and make ready their pageants to be employed as they have been accustomed to do on previous occasions against St Anne's Day, and on that day every occupation is to bring forth their pageants upon penalty of forfeiting to the Common Chamber every one of them that defaults ten shillings. And that every Constable give their attendance upon the pageants in procession upon St Anne's Day upon pain of forfeiting each of them six shillings and eightpence. And if any of the occupations lack a graceman then two of the most honest men and men of ability are to be charged to bring forth their said pageants [. . .]

[1] Gracemen were the guild's senior officials.

'Directors' and 'producers'

It is unlikely that the concept of 'artistic director' in the present-day sense of the term would have been recognised during the Middle Ages. Yet in the light of warnings and fines relating to poor presentation [see **D33**], it is hard to believe that performances were left to chance or that nobody took charge of proceedings. Organisers certainly sought out individuals or groups prepared to assume responsibility for the practical arrangements staged performance involved, a task closely corresponding to that of today's 'producer'. Some of these figures were apparently prepared to pay for the privilege [see **D20**]; others were handsomely rewarded for their involvement [see **D21**], though not always very expeditiously [see **D22**]. At York colleagues seem to have acted in concert [see **D23**], while at Lincoln a priest made a commitment as part of his prescribed duties [see **D24**]. Occasionally someone with expertise in one or more related spheres may have assumed a producer's function [see **D25**]. During the sixteenth century the term 'property player' begins to occur, notably in documents from the south-east [see **D39**], indicating the introduction of a professional employed to arrange the production, purchase costumes and properties, provide the script, and no doubt appear in the leading role, in short, acting as a forerunner of the actor-manager.[1]

[1] See John C. Coldewey, 'That Enterprising Property Player: Semi-Professional Drama in Sixteenth-Century England', *ThN* 31 (1977), pp. 5–12. It is interesting to note parallel developments on the Continent [see **E88**, **E89**, **E90** for the career of Pierre Gringore, and **I73**, **I74** for early Spanish actor-managers].

Delegation of duties

D20   An undertaking at Beverley, 1391

Beverley: BC/II/3 (Great Guild Book), fo. 13; pr. A. F. Leach, *Beverley Town Documents*, p. 37

John of Arras Hairer[1] came before the twelve Keepers of the town of Beverley in the Guild Hall, and undertook on his own behalf and that of his colleagues of the same craft to perform a certain play called 'Paradise' competently, (that is to say, every year on Corpus Christi Day when the other craftsmen of the same town perform), during the lifetime of the said John of Arras at his own personal cost, accepting and granting that he will pay ten shillings to the community of the town of Beverley for every error in the aforesaid play, Nicholas Falconer acting as his surety. And he also undertook at the end of his life to return to the twelve Keepers of the town then in office all the needful items belonging to the aforesaid play then in his possession, under a penalty of twenty shillings, that is, one pageant wagon [car]; eight hasps; eighteen staples; two masks; two wings for an angel; one spar of fir-wood [firsparr]; one serpent [worm]; two pairs of linen half-boots; two pairs of shirts; one sword.

[1] Worker in horsehair.

D21   'Ruler of the pageant', Coventry, 1453

Sharp *Dissertation*, p. 15; pr. REED, *Coventry*, pp. 27–8

[. . .] accorded and agreed on Monday next before Palm Sunday Anno Henry VI 31 [19 March 1453], that Thomas Colclow skinner from this day forth shall have the rule of the pageant until the end of the twelve years next following, he to find the players and all that belongs to the pageant all the said term, except that the Keeper of the craft shall have the pageant wagon brought out, and provide the cloths that go around the wagon and the rushes.[1] And every Whitsun week those that are Keepers of the craft shall dine with Colclow, and every master shall lay down four-pence, and Colclow shall have yearly for his labour forty-six shillings and eight-pence.[2] And on the next Sunday after Corpus Christi Day he is to return to the Master the Original [the master copy of the script].[3] and fetch his seven nobles .[4] And Colclow must return at the latter end of his term of office all the garments that belong to the pageant in as good a condition as they were when delivered to him [. . .]

[1] For the floor of the pageant.

[2] Colclow seems to have acted in a similar capacity in 1449 and 1451; on these occasions the Smiths paid him 43/4.

[3] See **D26**, **D27**.

[4] i.e. he received his promised 46/8, a noble being valued at 6/8.

D22   The petition of William Coursey, Kilkenny, 1603

Kilkenny Corporation Archives: pr. Alan J. Fletcher, 'The Civic Drama of Old Kilkenny', *REED Newsletter* 13. 1 (1988), pp. 12–30

[20 September 1603]

To the worshipful the Mayor and Aldermen of the City of Kilkenny: Showing that where your suppliant was promised to have as much this last year for setting forth of [the] Corpus Christi Play as he had any other year, whereupon your suppliant bestowed his labour and pains in setting forth the same in the best manner he could the last Corpus Christi Day, not doubting of performance of that promise, he having had thirty shillings sterling the year before for the like service. And whereas your suppliant was allowed fifteen shillings sterling yearly for keeping safe and preserving the clothes and other ornaments belonging to the comedy [stage-play] of the Resurrection, whereof your suppliant was paid for several years, but for five years past your suppliant has not been paid thereof, although he has carefully kept and preserved the said clothes and ornaments. The premises considered, it may therefore please your worships to take or choose for satisfying your suppliant was well of the said thirty shillings for setting forth the said last Corpus Christi Play, as of the arrears of the said fifteen shillings for the said five years last past for keeping the said ornaments, amounting to £3 15s sterling [. . .][1] (p. 24)

[1] Coursey apparently appears in the records first in 1584 as an actor and trumpeter. In 1602 and 1603 his name occurs as the 'setter-forth' of the Corpus Christi play. The Kilkenny performances continued well into the seventeenth century.

D23   Shared responsibility, York, 1484

North Yorkshire County Library, York: B 5 (House Books), fo. 24 (28 April 1484); pr. REED, *York*, pp. 133–4

[. . .] William Robinson Innholder, Robert Shirley Glazier and Innholder, and Andrew Blyth Weaver and Adam Siggeswick Barber came before Thomas Wrangwysh, then being Mayor of this City of York, and by the assent of all the Innholders of this said city took upon them to bring forth yearly during the term of eight years then next following, the pageant of the Coronation of Our Lady pertaining to the said Innholders and also to repair the said pageant [. . .] and that also the said William Robinson, Robert Shirley and Andrew Blyth have yearly of the Chamber of this City during the said eight years for bringing forth of the said pageant according to the ordinance thereof made, that is to say yearly two shillings.[1]

[1] The Innholders' pageant was unusual in that it was partly funded by the city authorities.

D24 A priest in charge, Lincoln, 1517

Lincoln Archives Office: Lı/ı/ı/ı vol. ı (Lincoln Common Council Minutes, 1511–41), fo. 75 (22 September 1517); pr. Kahrl *Lincs*, p. 45

[...] it is agreed that Sir Robert Devnas of Lincoln Priest shall have, use and fill the post [occupy] and be St Anne's priest in the City of Lincoln during his life, to sing for the brethren and sisters and for all the benefactors of the same Guild, and he is [to] have yearly (as long as that he may occupy and sing Mass and help to bring forth and prepare the procession and pageants of the same Guild in the City of Lincoln yearly) five pounds of good and lawful money of England to be paid by the hands of the Graceman[1] of the same Guild yearly for the time being [...]

[1] Senior guild official [see **D19**].

D25 A general factotum, Edinburgh, 1554

Extracts from the Records of the Burgh of Edinburgh 1528–1557, Scottish Burgh Record Society, Edinburgh, 1871, vol. ıı, pp. 198– 9; pr. Sarah Carpenter, 'Walter Binning: Decorative and Theatrical Painter (fl. 1540–1594)', *METh* 10. 1 (1988), pp. 17–25

12 October [1554] The Provost, Baillifs and Council ordains the Treasurer Robert Grahame to content and pay to Walter Binning the sum of five pounds for the making of the play equipment and painting of the banner and the players' faces; provided always that the said Walter make the play gear written below available to the town when they have need for it, which he has now received, namely eight play hats, one king's crown, one mitre, one fool's hood, one sceptre, one pair of angel's wings, two angels' wigs, one chaplet of triumph.[1]

[1] Carpenter suggests that Binning carried out this work for the Edinburgh presentation of Sir David Lindsay's *The Satire of the Three Estates*. One may usefully compare the role played at Bozen by Vigil Raber [see **F19**, **F20**].

Texts and scripts

As **D21** indicates, at centres where a performance in dialogue featured, it was customary for a master copy of the play's text, often known as the 'Original' or Register, to be fairly written and lodged for safe keeping with a responsible official or institution [see **D26(i)**, **(ii)**]. Such a precious document could then be produced when required, particularly where loaned out for players' parts (referred to at some centres as 'billets', at others as 'parcells') to be copied and distributed [see **D27(i)**, **(ii)**; **D28**; **D34**].

D26   The York Creed Play text, 1446, 1455

(i) Borthwick Institute of Historical Research, York: Probate Register 2 (Codicil to will of William Revetour, deputy civic clerk of York, 11 August 1446), fo. 138 verso; pr. REED, *York*, p. 68; trans. p. 746

[. . .] Item, I leave to the Fraternity of Corpus Christi in York a certain book entitled the Creed Play with the books and banners belonging to the same, and to the Guild of St Christopher a certain play of St James the Apostle compiled in six pageants [. . .]

(ii) North Yorkshire County Library, York: B 7 (House Books), fo. 137 (12 September 1455); pr. REED, *York* pp. 87– 8; trans. pp. 764–5

[Be it known that] this book was begun, being made afresh and written anew, in accordance with the aged and worn-out copy which William Revetour, formerly chaplain of St William's Chapel on Ouse Bridge, conveyed and bequeathed to the aforesaid fraternity in his will, being made at the request of John Foxe, executor of this same William Revetour. However, on condition that this incomparable play shall in future be made public every ten years at various locations of the said City of York before an appropriate audience for the sake of their spiritual welfare. Therefore those who live in these places must pay and provide adequately for the costs and expenses of the play.

D27   Scripts and the original, Wakefield, 1556, 1559

(i) Private collector: Wakefield Burgess Court rolls, pr. 'References to the Corpus Christi Play in the Wakefield Burgess Court Rolls: the Originals Rediscovered', A. C. Cawley, Jean Forester and John Goodchild, *Leeds Studies in English* 19 (1988), pp. 85–104[1]

[. . .] Item a penalty is laid down that every craft and occupation do bring forth their pageants of Corpus Christi Day [1557] as has been heretofore used, and to give out the speeches of the same in [the] Easter holidays with a penalty that everyone not doing so is to forfeit forty shillings [. . .][2]

(ii) Source as for (i) above; pr. in as above

1559. Item a penalty is laid [down] that Giles Dolleffe shall bring in or cause to be brought the Original [master copy] of Corpus Christi play between this and Whitsunday [. . .]

---

[1] Wakefield has frequently been associated with the sequence of thirty-two biblical plays now more usually referred to after the one-time owners as the Towneley Cycle (Huntington MS HM 1). Not all the pageants are complete and several entire episodes may be missing from the original set. The most striking of the existing plays are six generally attributed to the so-called 'Wakefield Master'; of the rest there are at least five and possibly more borrowed from the York repertoire. That Wakefield was the venue for performances of the Towneley plays is suggested by local place names in the text, from the prohibition of performances in the town in 1576, and in the documents cited under **D27**, but none provides conclusive evidence that the Towneley texts were presented in Wakefield. However, the EETS editors of the plays argue that 'there remains little room for doubt that the Towneley plays were performed in Wakefield' (*Towneley*, p. xxii).

[2] For a signal failure to obey such an order, see **D34**.

D28   Preparing the players' scripts, York, 1568

North Yorkshire Library, York: B 24 (House Books), fo. 104 verso (13 February 1567/8); pr. REED, *York*, pp. 352–3

[The city has decided to present the York Creed Play rather than the Corpus Christi Play.]

[. . .] first the Original or Register of the said Creed Play is to be obtained from the Master and Brethren of St Thomas' Hospital who have the custody thereof, and after expert and suitable [meet] players have been selected for the skilful handling of the said play, then every one of them is to have their parts fairly written and delivered to them, so that each person may have leisure to con his part. And the said Chamberlains are further to see all manner of the pageants' playing gear and necessaries is provided in readiness, and as occasion shall require, to ask advice and aid about the same [. . .]

Problem-solving

While some trades and crafts were highly cooperative [see **D29**], not all of them appear to have been anxious to play their part in the proceedings, and in 1490 the Canterbury Burghmote insisted that no craft was exempt from contributing to and participating in the city's reinstated Corpus Christi Play [see **D30**]. At Chester in 1421 the Ironmongers and Carpenters haggled over their right to the assistance of five other craft guilds; at York in 1431–2 the city's Goldsmiths, responsible for two pageants, had their burden reduced when the Masons took over their play of Herod. It is apparent that the authorities were usually successful in resolving disputatious issues, but there were doubtless intractable cases too.

D29   Speeding the flow of performance, York, 1422

North Yorkshire County Library, York: E 20 (A/Y Memorandum Book) (31 January 1422), fo. 247; pr. REED, *York*, p. 37; trans. pp. 722–3

[. . .] the entire community laments that the Play on Corpus Christi Day in this city, which was instituted in ancient times for the mighty cause of [stimulating] devotion and the extirpation of vice and reformation of behaviour, is alas hampered more than usual through the multiplicity of pageants, and unless a swifter and better system is provided, it is to be feared that it will be hampered even more in a very short passage of time. And the craftsmen of the Painters, Stainers, Pinners and Metal [Latten]-workers of the aforesaid city, formerly assigned to two separate pageants in the aforesaid Play, namely one on the stretching and nailing of Christ on the Cross, and the other in fact the Raising of the Crucified [One] on the Mount [Calvary], realising that the matter of both pageants could be shown combined in a single pageant, so more conveniently shortening the Play for the people hearing the sacred words of the performers, consented on their own behalf and their other co-workers in future that one of their pageants from now on should be omitted and the other retained, in accordance with what the Mayor and the Council of the Chamber wished to decree [. . .].

D30   No craft to be exempted, Canterbury, 1490

Canterbury Cathedral Archives and Library: REG A 1, Record Book of the Burghmote; pr. 'The Records of the City of Canterbury', ed. J. Brigstocke Sheppard, HMC *Ninth Report*, London, 1883, vol. 1, p. 174 (col. a); pr. *MES*, p. 203

[. . .] where before this time there has been, by the most honourable and worshipful [of] the City of Canterbury, used and continued within the same city a play called Corpus Christi Play, as well to the honour of the same, as to the profit of all victuallers, and other occupations within the same; which play before this time was maintained and played at the costs and charge of the crafts and mysteries within the same city; and whereas now of late days it has been left and laid apart, to the great hurt and decay of the said city, and for lack of good ordering of certain crafts within the city not corporate. Wherefore it is enacted, ordained and established, that from henceforth every craft within the said city, being not corporate for the non-sufficiency of their craft, be associate, incorporate, and adjoining to some other craft most needing support, if they will not labour to be corporate within themselves [. . .] And if any craft be obstinate or wilful, and will not make suit to the Burghmote [the citizens' court] for the reformation of the premises, by the said Feast of St Michael [29 September] next ensuing, to forfeit to the Chamber twenty shillings, and their bodies to be punished furthermore at the pleasure and discretion of this court [. . .]

Provincial arrangements

If large towns and cities provide abundant evidence, our knowledge of the administrative and practical arrangements for mounting plays of local provenance in less urbanised settings is far less copious. However, at some provincial centres, arrangements for delegation appear to have resembled those in larger communities [see **D31**], and certainly at New Romney [see **D32**] regulations defining participants' obligations were as stringent as those of any major city.

D31   Organisers to be selected, Stamford, 1465–6

Stamford, Lincolnshire: Hall Books (town council enactments) (1. 1461–1657); pr. Kahrl *Lincs*, pp. 87–8

These are the names of all manner of Crafts set together in pageants which shall among themselves choose themselves Wardens for to search and oversee all manner of points belonging to the same Crafts that they be chosen of, for the welfare and worship of this said town and borough. And if any Warden so chosen find any manner of default within his Craft or in the master or servant of the same that will not be amended by him, he shall then complain to the Alderman that he and his brethren and council may therein take a due correction and reformation. [Forty-two guilds plus 'all other hammermen' are named, grouped into eleven units.]

New Romney

Records of a Passion and Resurrection play staged by the townspeople of New Romney in south-east Kent go back to at least 1428, and those relating to presentations proposed for 1556 and 1560 throw invaluable light on the agreements entered into by the would-be participants, both performers and technical staff.[1]

1.　See James M. Gibson, '"Interludum Passionis Domini": Parish Drama in Medieval New Romney' in *English Parish Drama*, ed. Alexandra F. Johnston and Wim Hüsken, Amsterdam, 1996, pp. 137–48.

D32　Building the stages, New Romney, 1560

Kent County Archives: New Romney NR/JB 7/ fos. 67 verso–68 (13 May 1560); pr. Dawson *Kent*, p. 206

[. . .] Master Bailiff and all the Jurats [aldermen] and commoners except John Parker being assembled together in the Common Place, have fully and wholly agreed, ordained and decreed that every man that is here appointed to build the stages neglecting and not doing his duty in building the same at such time as shall be appointed by Master Bailiff and Jurats, shall lose, forfeit and pay to the use of the town twenty shillings to be forthwith levied by Master Bailiff's sergeant. And further that all other labourers and inhabitants of the town failing and not doing such things as they have granted and shall be assigned to do by Master Bailiff and Jurats shall lose, forfeit and pay to the use of the town two shillings to be forthwith levied of the goods of the offender and offenders for every default.

　　And they grant that all men shall have their money again that have paid any money.

CONTROLLING THE PRESENTATION

Though offering evidence of dedication, good order and cooperation, documents also preserve instances of indifference, dissension, mutual antagonism and disruption. The displeasure of administrators in such cases was marked by at least a rebuke, if not a fine. Notable are the levies exacted for various breaches of discipline at Beverley [see **D33**], and accounts of intriguing offences survive from Exeter and Bungay [see **D34**, **D35**].

Beverley

Whether participants in the communal plays at Beverley were unduly slack or the municipal authorities exceptionally strict in punishing offenders, the town records include numerous instances of errors and omissions for which fines were speedily exacted, even though frequently remitted. (I am greatly indebted to Dr Diana Wyatt for use of the fresh transcripts made for her York Ph.D thesis (1983), 'Performance and Ceremonial in Beverley before 1642: an Annotated Edition of Local Archive Materials'.)

D33   Various misdemeanours, Beverley, 1392–1521

(i) The Smiths fail to perform, 1392

Beverley: BC/II/3 (Great Guild Book), fo. 13; pr. *Beverley Town Documents*, ed. Arthur F. Leach, Selden Society 14 (1900), p. 36

[. . .] Because Thomas Lorimer, Robert Marshall, John Lorymer beside the Cuckstole Pit, John Lorymer above the Smith's Row and their colleagues defaulted in their play[1] on the Feast of Corpus Christi in the year of Our Lord 1392, it was therefore considered by [. . .], Keepers of the Town of Beverley, that they should pay forty shillings to the Beverley town community [. . .]

[1] The Smiths' play was that of the Ascension.

(ii) The Fishers' pageant not ready on time, 1450

Beverley: BC/II/7/I (Governors' Minute Book I), fo. 106; pr. *Report on the Manuscripts of the Corporation of Beverley*, HMC London, 1900, p. 134

[10 June 1450] [. . .] Robert Galt, Thomas Couton, Robert Potager, Thomas Haddif and William Gelle, Fisher, are here instructed to lay down forty shillings for the good of the community, because they did not have their pageant[1] ready for performance on Corpus Christi Day this year [4 June], according to the town's custom and in contradiction of the penalty laid down [. . .]

[1] The Fishers performed the play of Simeon (Christ's Presentation in the Temple).

(iii) Fines for lines, 1452

Beverley: BC/II/7/I (Governors' Minute Book I), fos. 117 and 117 verso

[. . .] Henry Couper Weaver [Webster] did not know his part on Corpus Christi Day in contradiction of the fine proclaimed by the common bellman; [fined] six shillings and eightpence forfeit to the community, and in the name of the said fine laid down three shillings and fourpence to the common good, being as he is a poor man [. . .] Robert Thornskew Alderman was instructed here on 16 June in the year written below to lay down six shillings and eightpence because the players of the Carpenters' craft[1] did not know their play [i.e. lines] [. . .]

[1] The Carpenters played the episode of the Resurrection.

(iv) Falling standards, 1520–1

Beverley: BC/11/6/18 (Town Account Rolls), membrane 4

[. . .] And [the accountants return this account] of two shillings received of Richard Trollopp Alderman of the Painters because their play of *The Three Kings of Cologne* [the Magi][1] was badly and chaotically presented, disgracing the entire community in the presence of outsiders. And [. . .] of twelve pence received from Richard Gaynstang Alderman of the Tailors, because their play of *Sleeping Pilate* was badly played in breach of the ordinance made on that subject. And [. . .] of two shillings received from William Patson alderman of the Drapers because their play[2] was badly played. And [. . .] of fourpence received from the same craft because their pageant was not covered with decent draperies [. . .]

[1] Formerly undertaken by the Goldsmiths.
[2] By this date the Drapers were assigned the play of 'Demyng Pilate' (Pilate sitting in judgement).

D34   Exeter Skinners defy their mayor, 1414

Devon Record Office: Exeter City Accounts: MCR 1/2 Henry V (Mayor's Court Roll), membrane 38d (18 June 1414); pr. REED, *Devon*, pp. 82–3; trans. pp. 357–8.

[. . .] Although by ancient custom a certain play has traditionally been performed annually at the Feast of Corpus Christi in the City of Exeter right up until a short time ago, for the reason that the Mayor and the Commons of the same City, by unanimous agreement and assent among themselves, have ordained for the greater convenience and honour of the same City, that the aforesaid play should be presented annually on the Tuesday of the week of Pentecost [Whitsun], and although the Mayor and Commons now in office had settled on and fixed in advance the Tuesday of Whitsun week just past as the day for the play to be performed, and that from each craft of the same City two, three or four representatives should be assigned agreed portions of the said play called 'pageants', and that they should find players in sufficient numbers to set forth the aforesaid plays at their own expense, and although fixed player's parts and speeches taken from the Original [master copy] of the aforesaid play were delivered in written form to John Benet and William French and to others (in their capacity as Chief Masters of the Skinner's craft) by Peter Sturte, Mayor at the time with the agreement of the said Commons, in order that they should present the said play according to the allocation and execution of the said parts and speeches, nevertheless, on the same Tuesday and before that, the same John Benet approached several players of the Skinners' craft and of the other crafts allocated the said portions and speeches of the pageant, and procured and encouraged them not to perform their parts.

And on that day itself the same John retained in his own hands the various parts of the play (in other words speeches) allocated to the said Skinners and placed in the custody of the said John in order for the said play to be set forth. Wherefore two episodes and their dialogue required for performance that same day from the said Skinners' craft were left out, to the reproach of the whole city and in contempt of the Mayor and the entire Commons aforesaid, and contrary to the aforesaid ordinance.

And immediately, on the same day, with the said performance still not completed, the said Mayor spoke with the said John Benet concerning the aforesaid default, and tried to find out from him why he obstructed the said play in this way and brought such shame on the Mayor and Commons. He responded to him scornfully with a face full of mockery, turning his back on him, saying 'By God, no man is going to be hanged without the chance to defend himself!' And so contemptuously and derisively he left him [. . .]

[A public outcry forced Benet to submit himself to the mayor's mercy before the full city court on 24 June.]

D35 An affray at Bungay, 1514

PRO: Star Chamber Proceedings, STAC 2/7, fo. 194 (16 June 1514); pr. *Norfolk and Suffolk*, pp. 140–1.

[In a letter to Cardinal Wolsey the inhabitants of Bungay claim that the town bailiff Richard Wharton and others] arrayed as rioters and in riotous manner at Bungay aforesaid at eleven of the clock on the Friday at night next after Corpus Christi Day, in the sixth year of the most noble reign of King Henry [VIII] that now is; and at that time the said Richard Warton, Thomas and John broke and threw down five pageants of your said inhabitants, that is to say, Heaven pageant; the pageant of all the world; Paradise pageant; Bethlehem pageant; and Hell pageant[1] the which were ever wont formerly to be carried about the said town upon the said day in the honour of the Blessed Sacrament. And since that time the said Richard would have compelled your said orators to have them [the pageants] built against their costs and charges [. . .]

[1] Alan H. Nelson points out (*MES*, p. 183) that since each of the pageants takes its name from 'sacred geography', they may have served as settings for a stationary dramatic presentation which followed their tour of the town.

FUNDING THE PRESENTATION

Surviving documentation sheds useful light on the manner in which the costs of mounting medieval English drama were met, levied, collected and recovered. A variety of methods was devised for funding performances, particularly in country districts, where fewer established organisations facilitated the collection of contributions: in cities and large towns guild members were at least accustomed to the imposition and levying of financial subscriptions for a range of purposes.

Statutory levies

The general pattern in large towns and cities appears to have been for members of religious, trade and craft guilds to make such financial contributions to the presentation of their pageants as their own regulations or those laid down by the civic or municipal authorities stipulated [see **D36(i)**, **(ii)**, **(iii)**, **(iv)**]. But appropriate levels of funding were adjusted as the relative prosperity of individual guilds fluctuated or trade in general declined, and crafts suffering financial hardship might find their burden eased by having the expense of mounting a prestigious display divided among their associates [see **D36(v)**].

D36   Requirements from city guilds, 1467–1568

(i) Chester Coopers' Records: loose papers, 12 March 1467–8; pr. REED, *Chester*, p. 12

This script and composition made by all the Masters and brethren of the craft of Fletchers and Bowyers within the City of Chester [. . .] that every Master and journeyman shall be contributory to pay for the sustaining and furtherance of the light of Corpus Christi, and other charges that shall [accrue] to the Play of Corpus Christi and other charges belonging thereto, upon pain of thirteen shillings and fourpence to be levied by way of distress or imprisonment of the person that so offends or by levy of his goods by the Steward of the said crafts at their election. And that every person that shall be made a Brother in any of the said crafts shall pay at his entry, to the sustaining of the said light and other charges twenty-six shillings and eightpence, and that no person be received into the same brotherhood in none other wise [. . .]

(ii) North Yorkshire County Library, York: A/Y Memorandum Book Y: E20, fo. 27 (1471) (Coopers); pr. REED, *York*, pp. 102–3

[. . .] it is ordained that every hired man of the same craft, be it by year or by week, that has been apprentice[d] in the same craft within the said City shall yearly pay to the Searchers [supervisors] of the same craft for the sustaining of their pageant fourpence. And if he were not apprentice[d] within the said City, yearly he is to pay to the same Searchers for the same purpose sixpence.

(iii) Lincolnshire Archives Office, Lincoln: Monson 7/2 (Accounts of the Holy Trinity Guild, Louth), fo. 238 verso (1527–8); pr. Kahrl *Lincs*, p. 80

It is agreed by the whole body of the Town of Louth that the pageant yearly of Corpus Christi Day shall be brought forth, as the custom is, at the costs and charges of Trinity Guild: 6s 8d; Corpus Christi Guild: 6s 8d; St Peter's Guild: 6s 8d; St Michael's Light [Peter of Louth's chantry]: 6s 8d. And the rest of Our Lady's Guild, how much soever it cost.

(iv) North Yorkshire County Library, York: B24 (House Books), fo. 104 verso (13 February 1568); pr REED, *York*, p. 353

[. . .] it is further agreed by the said presents that all such the crafts and occupations of this City as are charged with bringing forth the pageants of Corpus Christi shall gather every [one] of them their accustomed pageant money and pay it to the Chamberlains' hands towards the charges of bringing forth the said Creed Play, and warning be given to every one of them accordingly.[1]

---

[1] Due to Reformist pressures, the projected performances never took place.

> (v) Norfolk and Norwich Record Office, Norwich Assembly Proceedings 1491–1553, fos. 129 verso – 130 recto (21 September 1527); pr. *NCP*, pp. xxvii–xxviii

[. . .] that where yearly for a long time past the said Guild of St Luke[1] till now has been accustomed to have kept and held within the aforesaid City on the Monday in Pentecost Week, on which day and the one following many and varied disguisings and pageants both of the lives and martyrdoms of many and various holy saints and of many other frivolous [light] and feigned figures and pictures of other persons and beasts, the annual sight of which disguisings and pageants, both on the said Monday in Pentecost Week in time of procession then going about a great circuit of the said City and on the Tuesday in the same week serving the lord called the lord of Misrule at Tombland[2] within the same City, has been and still is so greatly desired particularly by the people of the region [. . .] the Brethren and Sisters of the same Guild alone are yearly sorely charged with repairing, funding [finding], and setting forth the said pageants and disguisings [. . .] in such a way that for lack of brethren and sisters of substance [. . .] the Guild is almost ruined and unlikely to remain in anything but a state of decay unless your favourable minds and comfortable aid and assistance are extended to the said Alderman and Brethren [of the Guild] and to their successors [. . .] Wherefore may it please your discreet wisdoms [. . .] to enact, ordain, and establish by the authority given to you that every occupation within the said City shall annually at the said procession upon the Monday in Pentecost Week set forth one pageant, by your discreet wisdoms to be assigned and appointed, at their own cost and charge [. . .][3]

---

[1] A guild of painters, braziers, plumbers and other crafts.
[2] The site of the annual Pentecost Fair in the vicinity of the cathedral.
[3] The request was granted.

Other methods

Where established facilities for imposing and collecting statutory levies were not in place, presenters had to depend on rather more *ad hoc* arrangements to defray costs, relying in many communities on the fact that productions were frequently staged in aid of local good causes. Money could sometimes be ploughed back: in 1477 at Leicester takings from at least one previous presentation appear to have been made available to its successor [see **D37(i)**]. At New Romney in Kent in 1497 and 1505 private loans funded the Passion play; in 1503 the town chamberlains themselves made monies available to the play wardens. At Bassingbourn, Cambridgeshire, in June 1511 twenty-seven neighbouring parishes contributed varying sums to support a play of St George, and the 1535 production at Boxford,

Suffolk in aid of the church was backed financially by twenty-eight nearby villages [see **D39**]. The New Romney organisers for 1560 not only received gifts from neighbouring Lydd and Ivychurch to be added to the actual takings [see **D37(ii)**], but also sent 'bann criers' advertising the play into neighbouring villages and towns where collections were also taken up. At other locations too a pre-performance collection or 'gathering' features in the accounts: in Perth on 13 June 1520 five shillings and eightpence was 'gadderit about the toun to furneis the play affoir the processioun'; at Holbeach in Lincolnshire sixteen pence was 'Gaderett in the churches upon Corpus Christi Day' in 1539. At Louth the local schoolmaster seems to have made a loan to the players at a moderate rate of interest [see **D37**(iii)].[1]

---

[1] Of general interest here is J. Charles Cox, *Churchwardens' Accounts from the Fourteenth Century to the Close of the Seventeenth Century*, London, 1913, pp. 270–4; for specific regions see *English Parish Drama* ed. Johnston and Hüsken.

D37   Defraying expenses, 1477–1558

(i) Leicester: the Hall Book of the Corporation, 26 March 1477; pr. *MES*, p. 188

The players, who played the Passion Play the year immediately preceding, brought in a bill which concerned certain duties of money, and [requested] whether the Passion [Play] shall be put to crafts to be bound or not. And at that time the said players gave to the pageants their money which they had acquired in playing the said play ever prior to that day, and all their costumes with all other manner of stuff that they had at that time. And at the same Common Hall by the advice of all the Commons, were chosen these persons named after this, to have the guiding and rule of the said play [. . .][1]

---

[1] The names of nineteen people and two 'beadles' follow.

(ii) Kent County Record Office, Maidstone: New Romney Chamberlains' Book 1528–80 (Teichman-Derville no. 33), 1560; pr. Dawson *Kent*, p. 207

Item received of the gift of the parish of Ivychurch towards our play	3s	4d
Item received of the gift of the town of Lydd towards our play	10s	
Item received gathered at our play on Whitsun Tuesday	£12 5s	6d
Item received the money gathered at the second play	£6 10s	9½d
Item received gathered at the third play day	£4 9s	
[. . .] Item received gathered at our fourth play day	47s	6½d

(iii) Lincolnshire Country Archives; Louth Grammar School Records B III/1, pp. 16, 29; pr. Kahrl *Lincs*, pp. 83–4

1555–6
Item paid to Mr Goodall [the schoolmaster] for money laid forth by him at the plays   13s   3d

1557–8

Item paid to Mr Goodall for certain money by him laid forth for the
furnishing of the play played in the Market stead on Corpus Christi
Day the year before my entering (i.e. 1556–7)   16s

Expenditure

To detail comprehensively here the nature of the expenses incurred in mounting
drama in Britain and Ireland is clearly impracticable. The readiest expedient has
been to reprint two typical expense sheets, one for Perth in Scotland recording
payments to players [see **D38(i)**], the other a more miscellaneous list from the
Coventry Drapers, who were charged with staging the pageant of the Last
Judgement [see **D38(ii)**].

D38   Typical expense lists, Perth 1518; Coventry 1566

(i) *The Perth Hammermen Book 1518 to 1568*, ed. Colin Hunt, Perth, 1889, fo. 2; pr. *MPS*,
pp. 271–2

22 April 1518

The players on Corpus Christi Day and what money shall be paid to them, that is
to say: Item imprimis to Adam 6d and Eva 6d. Saint Eloy 6d. The mermaiden 8d.
The devil 8d. His man 4d. The angel and the clerk 6d. Saint Erasmus 8d. The cord-
drawer 8d. The king 12d. The three tormentors 3s. The best banner 12d. The other
6d. The stool-bearer and the harness 5d. The devil's chepman [?] 8d. To Robert
Hart for vestments 4d. Item for [. . .] 2d. Item to the minstrel 2s.[1]

---

[1] Nelson (*MES*, p. 201) concludes that here we have an apparent conflation of a Corpus Christi play on
the Fall, a pageant or play of the martyred St Erasmus (whose intestines were removed by the 'cord-
drawer'), and a pageant of St Eloy or Eligius, renowned for skilled metalwork and the Hammermen's
patron saint. The role played by the mermaid seems less clear.

(ii) Coventry Record Office: Acc 154, fos. 65–6; (Drapers' Accounts 1566); pr. REED,
Coventry, pp. 237–8

Payments for the pageant

Imprimis for three rehearsals	6s	
Item for setting forth the pageant		6d
Item for setting in the pageant		6d
Item for driving the pageant	2s	6d
Item for keeping of the wind[lass]		6d
Item for dressing of the pageant and opening and shutting the doors		6d
Item for keeping Hell mouth and the fire		10d
Item paid to four angels	2s	
Item paid to the two demons	3s	4d
Item paid for fetching and keeping the ladder		2d

Item paid to the three black souls	5s	
Item paid for blacking the souls' faces		6d
Item paid to the worms of conscience		16d
Item paid to the three white souls	5s	
Item paid to Robert Crow[1] for [playing] God's part	3s	4d
Item paid for playing the Prologue		8d
Item paid to the three patriarchs		18d
Item paid to Robert Crow for three worlds	3s	8d
Item paid to James Hewit for small organs [rignalls]		12d
Item paid to the trumpeter	2s	
Item paid to the singing men	2s	
Item paid to the pageant players for their supper	4s	
Item paid to Robert Crow for his gloves		2d
Item paid for laces [points] for the souls and the demons		14d
Item paid for rushes and soap		5d
Item paid for resin, candles and packthread		4d
Item paid to Thomas Nicols for setting a song		12d
Item paid to two carpenters for mending the pageant		14d
Item paid to Mr Pyxley for thirteen yards of cross-braces [ledges]		13d
Item paid for three yards and two feet of boards		7d
Item paid for nails and hooks for pageant		12d
Item paid to the players to drink	2s	
Item paid to Mr Brown for bottles of drink		16d
Item for five yards of fabric [buckram]	3s	11d

Sum [total]   £3 0s 12d

[1] Robert Crow contributed signally to the proceedings, not only playing the role of God but also fabricating the three worlds set alight in the Doomsday episode.

Rendering up the accounts

Methods employed to wind up proceedings with a final statement of accounts are unremarkable. Of most interest here is perhaps the entry in the Boxford churchwardens' accounts for 1535 which records how matters stood, once the 'property player' (a professional or semi-professional 'actor-manager' employed at several south-eastern centres including Chelmsford and New Romney) and the players from outside the district had been rewarded [D39].

D39   The final reckoning, Boxford, 1535

Ipswich and (East) Suffolk Record Office: FB 77/E2/2: Boxford Churchwardens' Accounts, pp. 33–4 (1535); pr. *Norfolk and Suffolk*, pp. 137–8

And it is to be remembered that all the persons of the town beforesaid (which brought in money to the profit of the play) found all the township's meat and drink at their proper cost and charge[1] without any manner of allowance made to them for any manner of charge, by which means there is no manner of allowance [expenditure due] out of this play, but only thirty shillings to the property player and fifteen shillings to divers players which came out of strange [non-local] places. So that there was made from the same play to the clear profit of the church – £18 19s 5½d [...]

Item received of Peter Fenne in part payment of 26s 8d which he received at the play: 6s 8d. And so he still owes 20s which he has promised to pay at Midsummer nest coming.[2]

[1] i.e. 'out of their own pockets'.
[2] Fenn did not clear his debt until some time in 1538.

PERFORMERS AND PERFORMANCES

Performers

British documents offer few glimpses of that shadowy figure, the medieval actor. If *The Canterbury Tales* reveals the technique evidently customary in one role [see **D40**], play-texts contain few overt clues as to histrionic requirements. An *N-Town* prologue and the epilogue from the 'Reynes Extracts' suggest what actors may have felt themselves capable or incapable of [see **D41(i), (ii)**], but even the unusually plentiful and expansive rubrics of the N-Town Passion cannot be relied on as evidence for the demands performance made on its exponents, since they may not relate to practical expectations [see **D42**].

D40   'The voice of Pilate', *c.* 1400

Geoffrey Chaucer, *The Miller's Tale*, in *The Riverside Chaucer*, ed. Larry D. Benson, Oxford, 1988, p. 67

[...] The Miller, who was all pale from drinking so that he could scarcely stay on his horse, would not remove his hood or his hat, nor defer courteously to anyone, but loosed a shout in the voice of Pilate,[1] and swore ' By God's arms, by His blood and bones! I know a damn good story with which I shall now cap the Knight's tale [...]'

[1] Pilate was popularly identified as a ranting tyrant akin to Herod, which is certainly the character he bears in the Towneley sequence.

D41   Possible inadequacies, *c.* 1475

(i) BL MS Cotton Vespasian D.VIII; pr. *The N-Town Plays*, ed. Stephen Spector, EETS (SS 11–12), 2 vols., Oxford, 1991, Play 8 (*Joachim and Anna*)

CONTEMPLATIO Christ preserve this congregation from perils past, present and to come, and also the people performing here, that their speech may be bold and confident, and no lack of clarity make their subject matter obscure, but that it may profit and please everyone present from start to finish, and thus continue, so that Christ and those He has created rest content with the project. (lines 1–8)

(ii) Bodleian MS Tanner 407: 'the Reynes Extracts 1', fo. 44 verso; pr. *NCP*, p. 123

[. . .] it was indeed our intention to acquit ourselves well, and if any faults were found therein, our negligence was responsible; the short period we had to prepare was a further cause, and we certainly had little time to learn our parts. Moreover, not everyone is enough of an expert in eloquence to address you confidently in public [. . .] (lines 14–19)

D42   Stage directions, the N-Town Passion Play, c. 1475

BL MS Cotton Vespasian D.VIII; pr. *N-Town P*

(i) The conspiracy to take Christ

Here the bishops [i.e. the High Priests] *separate in the playing-area, and each of them takes his leave in dumb-show* [by countenance], *each man resorting to his place with his retainers* [meinie] [. . .] (Passion Play 1. 662 s.d.)

(ii) The taking of Christ

Here Judas kisses Jesus, and immediately all the Jews gather round Him and lay hands on Him, and pull Him about as if they were mad, and make a great outcry against Him all at once [. . .]

   Here the Jews lead Christ out of the playing-area with great clamour and noise, some pulling Christ forward and some backwards, and so leading Him out with their weapons raised and lights burning [. . .] (Passion Play 1. 988 s.d.; 1032 s.d.)

(iii) The Crucifixion

Here they [the Jews] *shall drag Jesus out of His clothes and lay them together. And there they shall pull Him down and lie Him along the cross, and after that nail Him to it* [. . .] *Here they shall stop* [erecting the cross], *and dance briefly around the cross* [. . .] (Passion Play 11. 746 s.d.; 774 s.d.)

The actor's role

The general paucity of evidence makes an entry in the York House Book for 3 April 1476 invaluable, for it supplies one of the few English references to processes of auditioning and casting [see **D43**]. From this it seems clear that pains were taken to ensure that parts were competently played, and that those privileged to perform were prevented from spreading their abilities too thinly by the decree that they should only take two roles in the course of the sequence, a condition met with at other centres. Controls elsewhere appear to have been equally stringent: a document from New Romney [see **D44**] indicates that players often had to enter into recognisances when chosen for a particular role, and so seriously was the responsibility taken, that one Coventry religious dissident was even released temporarily from gaol to take up his part [see **D45**].

D43   Auditioning and casting, York, 1476

North Yorkshire County Library, York B 1 (House Book), fo. 14 verso (3 April 1476); pr. REED, *York*, p. 109

[. . .] yearly in the time of Lent there shall be called before the Mayor currently in office, four of the most skilful, discreet and able players within this city, to search [for], hear and examine all the players and plays and pageants throughout all the artificers belonging to Corpus Christi Play. And all such as they shall find adequate in presence [person] and skill [cunning] to the honour of the City and prestige of the said crafts, to admit and empower, and all other persons inadequate either in skill, voice or presence to discharge, remove and send away.

And [. . .] no player that shall play in the said Corpus Christi Play [shall] be directed and retained to play more than twice on the day of the said Play. And [. . .] he or they so playing play not over twice the said day upon pain of forty shillings to forfeit to the Chamber as many times as he or they shall be found at fault in the same.

D44   Players' recognisances, New Romney, 1555

Kent County Archives NR/JB 6, fos. 215–16 (27 December 1555); pr. Dawson *Kent*, pp. 202–3

[. . .] where the above bound parties have taken upon them to be players in the stage-play at New Romney aforesaid, to be played (by the grace of God) at the Feast of Pentecost [Whitsun] next coming, and have received players' speeches or parts in the said play, that is to say [. . .] [a list of fourteen names and a blank follows] [. . .][1]

If they and every [one] of them learn before the said Feast of Pentecost their parts before specified, and are ready then to play the same, and further at every time of the rehearsal of the said play come to Romney aforesaid and rehearse their said parts without any secret deception (God, the King and Queen's Majesties,[2] and no reasonable cause preventing them), that then this present recognisance shall be void, or else shall abide in all his full strength and force.[3]

---

[1] Two similar entries list the players for another thirty named roles, making a total of at least 45 participants.

[2] i.e. Mary Tudor and her husband Philip of Spain.

[3] After these preparations the New Romney play was not presented in the summer of 1556.

A Protestant martyr in performance

The compendious pages of John Foxe's monumental *Ecclesiastical History, containing the Acts and Monuments . . .*, popularly known as 'Foxe's Book of Martyrs', secrete at least one dramatic pearl, the account of John Careles, a Coventry Weaver, arrested with three other citizens in November 1553 for 'lewd and seditious behaviour' probably in connection with the proposal to restore the Mass in England from 21 December, Mary I having succeeded to the throne on 19 July. It is a striking comment on the complexities of religious belief and observance at this period, that Careles gave his services to maintaining a tradition that many of his fellow Protestants abhorred, Coventry long being a centre for popular religious dissent. Careles ultimately died in London's Fleet prison on 1 July 1556.

D45   Released from prison to perform, Coventry, 1553–5

John Foxe, *Acts and Monuments*, vol. II (1583), pp. 1920, column b–1921 column a; pr. REED, *Coventry*, pp. 207–8

It appears from the examination of the aforesaid John Careles that he spent the space of two whole years as a prisoner, having a wife and children. During his captivity, being initially in Coventry Gaol, his credit with his gaoler was so good that upon his word of honour he was let out to play in the pageant around the city with others of his companions.[1] And that done, keeping his word with his keeper, he returned again into prison at his appointed hour.

[1]   Presumably in the Weavers' pageant of Christ's Presentation in the Temple, for which the text survives. (See Hardin Craig, ed., *Two Coventry Corpus Christi Plays*, EETS (ES 87), 2nd edn, Oxford, 1952, pp. 33–71.)

Playing the part

Although individual idiosyncracies could hardly be suppressed, a degree of histrionic stylisation must have prevailed at such locations as York, where a sequence of different players would all have been required to portray (say) God or Christ. But this did not necessarily make performances unconvincing. The concept of 'putting on an act' was obviously understood, as the celebrated account of the Duke of Suffolk's Herod-like tirade in a Norfolk manor court makes clear [see **D46**]. Thomas More, too, touches on the same notion in his *Life of Richard III* [see **D47**].

D46   The Duke of Suffolk in performance, 1478

BL Add. MS 27446, fo. 13 (letter from J. Whatley to Sir John Paston II, 20 May 1478); pr. *Paston Letters and Papers of the Fifteenth Century*, ed. Norman Davis, 2 vols., Oxford, 1976, vol. II, p. 426

[. . .] as for Hellesdon, my lord of Suffolk was there on Wednesday in Whitsun week [13 May], [. . .] while he was there that day nobody playing Herod in the Corpus

Christi play performed better and more to his pageant's satisfaction than he did [. . .][1]

---

[1] John de la Pole, duke of Suffolk, laid claim to Paston's estates at Hellesdon and Drayton, the former having been sacked, 'hall, lodge, church and village' in October 1465. Suffolk was evidently arguing his case before a manor court (see Davis, *Paston Letters*, vol. I, p. 510).

D47   Thomas More uses a dramatic analogy, *c.* 1513

The History of King Richard III, ed. Richard S. Sylvester, *The Complete Works of St Thomas More*, New Haven and London, 1963, pp. 80–1

[. . .] men must sometimes for the sake of appearances not acknowledge what they know [. . .] in a stage play all the people know perfectly well that he who plays the Sultan is in fact a cobbler.[1] Yet if someone should be so crass as to demonstrate at an inopportune moment how well acquainted with him he is, and call him by his own name while he stands in his majesty, one of his henchmen[2] might well break his head open, and deservedly so, for spoiling the dramatic effect [. . .]

---

[1] Sylvester argues (p. 259) that More probably adopted this image, invoked elsewhere in his writings, from Lucian's *Menippus*, but the context seems essentially contemporary.
[2] The original reads 'tormentors', the generic term applied to attendants on such a figure as Herod in the cycle sequences; however, the term also appears in *Menippus*.

Costumes and properties

On an essentially non-illusionistic stage, dress and properties are apt to assume even greater significance than where elaborate scenery claims a more dominant role. In many instances 'modern dress' was worn to complement the contemporary setting of the action, yet several stage directions in the Passion Play of the *N-Town* manuscript [see **D48**] suggest that costume might occasionally be employed to create more exotic effects. Companies' requirements in matters of clothing were often spelt out in considerable detail, as records from the Coventry Smiths' accounts make clear [see **D49**]. On occasion an outfit could be hired from another guild (the Coventry Smiths paid tenpence to the Tailors and Shearmen for a gown in 1579), but for financial if not aesthetic reasons, other means of acquiring appropriate ready-made garments for use or adaptation were attractive. Well-wishers could lend properties or costumes [see **D50**] or public-spirited guildsmen might thoughtfully bequeath clothing for theatrical use [see **D51**]. At certain centres participants were obliged to furnish themselves with appropriate apparel or be fined for non-compliance [see **D52**].

D48   Dressing the High Priests, the N-Town Passion Play, *c.* 1475

BL MS Cotton Vespasian D.VIII; pr. *N-Town P*

Here Annas shall show himself on his stage arrayed like a bishop of the Old Law[1] in a scarlet gown, and over that a blue tabard furred with white, and a mitre on his head in the style of the Old Law; two doctors standing by him in furred hoods, and an individual in front of them with his staff of office; and each of them with a furred cap on his head, with a huge tassel [knop] on the top; and someone standing in front dressed like a Saracen, who shall act as Annas's messenger [. . .] (Passion Play 1. 164 s.d)

Here the messenger goes forth, and in the meantime Caiaphas reveals himself on his scaffold, dressed like Annas except that his tabard shall be red, furred with white; two doctors with him dressed in furred cloaks following the old style, and with furred caps on their heads [. . .] (Passion Play 1. 208 s.d.)

[1] It is often claimed that this is an instruction to 'naturalise' the High Priests by dressing them like contemporary bishops, but mention of 'the Old Law' suggests Old Testament costume, and iconographically 'knops' on headgear characterised Jewish figures (see *N-Town P*, pp. 26–7; 171–2).

D49   Typical costumes and properties, Coventry, 1452–90

Coventry Smiths' Accounts (now lost, but preserved in Sharp, *Dissertation*, pp. 26, 33); pr. REED, *Coventry*, p. 25

1452

Item paid for six skins of white leather for God's garment	18d
Item paid for making the same garment	10d
Item paid for making four gowns and four hoods for the tormentors and the stuff that went into them	24s 10½d

(i) Sharp, *Dissertation*, p. 30; pr. REED, *Coventry*, p. 69

1488

Item to reward to Mistress Grymesby for lending her gear for Pilate's wife	12d.

(ii) Sharp, *Dissertation*, pp. 15–17; pr. REED, *Coventry*, pp. 73–4

1490

[. . .] these are the garments that were newly repaired against Corpus Christi Day

Imprimis, four jackets of black fabric [buckram] for the tormentors with nails and dice upon them

Item, [an]other four for tormentors in another style with damask flowers

Item, two of fabric [buckram] with hammers crowned

Item, two parti-coloured jackets of red and black [. . .]

Item, a crest for Herod

Item, a broad curved sword [fawchon] for Herod

Item, a hat for Pilate

Item, a hat for Pilate's son
Item, two mitres for the bishops [. . .]
Item, a poleaxe for Pilate's son
Item, a sceptre for Herod
Item, a mace
Item, a sceptre for Pilate's son
Item, four scourges and a pillar
Item, two gilded wigs [cheverels] for Jesus and Peter
Item, the Devil's head [i.e. mask ?]
The sum of all the costs and workmanship and colours adds up to fifteen shillings.

D50   Borrowing costumes in difficult times, Lincoln, 1515–21

Lincoln Archives Office: L1/1/1/1, fo. 42 verso, fo. 132; pr. Kahrl *Lincs*, pp. 43, 49

1515 [. . .] it is agreed that where divers garments and other adornments are borrowed in the district yearly for the embellishment of the pageants of St Anne's Guild, now the knights and gentlemen are scared by the plague, so that the Graceman [the Guild's Chief Officer] can borrow no such garments; wherefore every Alderman shall prepare and set forth in the said array two good gowns; and every Sheriffpeer [former Sheriff] one gown; and every Chamberlainpeer one gown; and the persons with them are to wear the same. Also it is agreed that the Chief Constable shall command in Mr Mayor's name every Under-Constable to wait upon the array in procession, both to keep the people from the array and also to take heed of such as wear garments in the same [. . .]

1521 [. . .] George Browne, one of the Aldermen of this city, who has been elected in the place of the Graceman of St Anne's Guild, complains that where the plague is reigning in this city, so that he cannot get such garments and other adornments as should be [worn] in the pageants of the procession of St Anne's Day. Wherefore it is agreed that Mr Alanson shall be instantly desired to borrow a gown from my Lady Powes for one of the Maries, and the other Mary[1] to be dressed in the crimson gown of velvet that belongs to the same guild.

[1] Probably Mary Magdalene, given the crimson gown considered appropriate.

D51   A bequest of costumes, Coventry, 1518

PRO PROB 11/ 19, fo. 67 verso–68 verso (the will of William Pisford, 2 March 1518) pr. REED, *Coventry*, pp. 112–13[1]

[. . .] Also I bequeath to the pageant of the same craft I am of myself [the Tanners] my lined scarlet gown without fur and my scarlet cloak, to be kept to serve them in their said pageant [at] the time of the plays. And I bequeath to the Craft of Tanners my lined crimson gown not furred, to the same use [. . .]

1   Pisford was a prosperous citizen who rose to be Coventry's mayor in 1501–2. The precise scriptural
    episode with which the Tanners were associated is unknown; Caiaphas and Annas, to whom
    Pisford's clothes might seem best suited appear in the *Smiths'* play of Christ's Betrayal, Trial and
    Crucifixion.

D52   Providing suitable wear, Lincoln, 1523

Lincoln Archives Office: L 1/1/1/1 vol. 1 (Lincoln Common Council Minutes, 1511–41), fos.
159, 169; pr. Kahrl *Lincs*, pp. 51–2

28 May 1523

[. . .] Also it is agreed that every Alderman of this city shall (according to an old
act formerly made) have a gown for preparing of the Kings in St Anne's Guild,
either of his own as it is previously ordained or else to borrow one gown for that
day upon pain of ten shillings to be forfeit of every person that does the contrary
and paid; and every Sheriffpeer [former Sheriff] to have one person arrayed in an
honest gown of cloth going among the Prophets in [the] procession of the same
guild, upon pain of twenty shillings.

Special effects

Medieval theatre was largely compelled to conform to the principles of non-illu-
sionism, but never repudiated entirely the use of localised devices to create effects
which if limited in scope maximised a play's impact on its spectators' senses [see
E57–E62]. Visual spectacle was an integral part of the dramatic experience, and
stage directions feature a notable range of *coups de théâtre* [see **D53**]. Aural effects
also played a central role: instructions for minstrels to play or for hymns to be sung
attest to the importance attached to musical embellishment in enhancing theatrical presentation [see **D53(ii), (iii), (vi)**].[1]

1.   See JoAnna Dutka, *Music in the English Mystery Plays*, Kalamazoo, 1980; John Stevens,
      'Music in Medieval Drama', *Proceedings of the Royal Musical Association* 84 (1958), pp.
      81–95.

D53   Spectacular aspects of performance

[For abbreviations of certain titles see **D17**.]

(i) 'The heavenly sphere'

*And first in some high place – or in the clouds, if it is possible – God speaks to Noah stand-
ing outside the ark with all his family* (Chester Noah's Flood, opening s.d.)

Here shall heaven open, and Jesus shall show himself (Magdalene, 1348 s.d.)

The Father must be in a cloud and when He speaks [out] *of heaven, let the leaves open*
(Cornish *Creacion*, opening s.d.)

(ii) Descents and ascents

Here the Holy Spirit descends upon Him [. . .] (*N-Town Baptism*, 92 s.d.)

Then Jesus shall ascend, and in ascending, he shall sing [. . .] *When, however, Jesus has completed the hymn, he shall pause mid-way as if standing above the clouds* [. . .] (*Chester Ascension*, 104 s.d., and s.d. [b]).

(iii) Fire and lightning

Here shall come a cloud from heaven, and set the temple on fire [. . .] (*Magdalene*, 1561 s.d. [b])

Here comes a flash of lightning [fervent] *with great tempest, and Saul falls down off his horse* [. . .] (*Conversion*, 182 s.d.)

Then God shall send forth the Holy Spirit in the form of fire, and while it is being sent, two angels shall sing the antiphon 'Accipite Spiritum Sanctum [. . .]' *And as they sing they shall throw fire upon the apostles* [. . .] (*Chester Pentecost*, 238 s.d.)

(iv) Devils

And he that shall play Belial look that he have gunpowder burning in pipes in his hands and in his ears and in his arse when he goes to battle (*Castle of Perseverance* stage-diagram [see **D14**])

Here a devil [Belial] *is to enter with thunder and fire* [. . .] (*Conversion*, 411 s.d.)

Here they [Belial and Mercury] *shall vanish away with a fiery flame, and a tempest* (*Conversion*, 501 s.d.)

(v) Horses and other animals

[. . .] *King Balaack shall come riding near the mountain* [. . .]; *Then Balaam and the Knight shall ride together* [. . .]; *Then Balaam shall climb on an ass and ride with the Knight; and the Angel of the Lord shall encounter them with his sword drawn; and the ass, not Balaam, sees him and throws herself to the ground* [. . .]; *Then Balaam shall beat his ass. And here someone should be transformed into the likeness of an ass, and when Balaam beats her, the ass should say:* [. . .] (*Chester Moses/Balaam* 95 s.d.; 199 s.d.; 215 s.d.; 223 s.d.)

Here they shall descend from their horses and go into the mountain[s]

[. . .]; *Then* [they] *go down to the beasts and ride about* (*Chester Three Kings* 48 s.d.; 112 s.d.)

Then comes the first King, riding [. . .] *Here the Kings alight from their horses* (*Towneley Offering of the Magi*, 84 s.d.; 504 s.d.)

The Centurion shall come like a knight, riding (Towneley Resurrection, 44 s.d.)

Then Noah shall go into the ark with all his family, his wife excepted, and the ark must be boarded round about. And on the boards all the beasts and fowls hereafter rehearsed must be painted, so that their [i.e. the actors'] *words may agree with the pictures.* (Chester Noah's Flood 160 s.d.)

(vi) Miscellaneous

Here the idol [mament] *shall tremble and quake* (Magdalene, 1553 s.d.)

Here a ship shall enter with a merry song (Magdalene, 1394 s.d.)

Here the oven must split asunder and bleed out of its crannies, and an image [of Christ] *appear out of it with wounds bleeding* (Play of the Sacrament, 712 s.d.)

II   Reactions and responses

Few native documents survive recording drama's impact on observers and commentators, let alone any investigatory responses to the notion of theatre in the abstract. Where expressions of opinion exist, they stem predominantly from hostile clerical sources: sadly, the 'native of Malmesbury' does not specify what theatrical activities Walter Reynolds had been allegedly involved in when preferred to the See of Canterbury in 1313 [see **D54**].

Impious and subversive behaviour associated with all forms of theatre certainly invoked the wrath of medieval clerics. No doubt antipathy was sometimes provoked by their eager imitation of patristic vehemence, as may be the case with John Bromyard who censures performers and spectators as depraved [see **D55**]. Yet even if genuine antagonism was spontaneously generated through first-hand acquaintance, there were many who saw drama as an effective means of inculcating sound Christian beliefs and values in the laity. In particular, the controversy which surrounded religious play-making stemming from Lollard opposition [see **D56**], led to spirited debate as to its legitimacy as a supplement to worship [see **D57**, **D58**]. Certainly what seems the undeniable impact of live presentation may be gauged from a scrap of testimony which survives from as late as the English Civil War period [see **D59**].

D54   An archbishop as a presenter of plays, *c.* 1313

Vita Edwardi monarchi cuiusdam Malmesberiensis [The Life of King Edward by a native of Malmesbury], ed. and trans. Noel Denholm-Young, London, 1957, pp. 45–6

On the death [11 May 1313] of the Primate [Robert Winchelsea], the Prior and Convent of Christ Church, Canterbury, proceeded to an election, and by a unanimous vote chose Mr Thomas de Cobham, a nobleman, and a doctor of Canon and Civil Law, who at once set out and crossed the sea to prosecute his cause [. . .] [However,] the King of England [Edward II] sent to the Pope [Clement V] praying him that he should see fit to promote his clerk the Bishop of Worcester [Walter Reynolds] to the archiepiscopal see.

O what a difference there was between the elect and the 'preferred'! For the elect was the very flower of Kent, of noble stock; he had lectured in arts and on Canon Law, and was a Master of Theology; a man eminently fitted for the See of Canterbury. The bishop, on the other hand, had recently been a mere clerk and was scarcely literate, but he excelled in theatrical presentations, and through these obtained the King's favour [. . .][1]

[1] This account may be justified or the result of prejudice. Reynolds, said to be the son of a Windsor baker, was made Royal Treasurer on Edward II's accession in 1307, Bishop of Worcester in 1308, and Chancellor in 1310. Later declaring for Edward III, whom he crowned on 29 January 1327, he died later the same year.

JOHN BROMYARD

John de Bromyard, an Oxford-educated Dominican friar and a keen opponent of the teachings of John Wycliffe, lectured in theology at Cambridge, becoming the university's Chancellor in 1383. In the course of his principal work, the *Summa praedicantium* – 'that great monument of Dominican preaching' (G. R. Owst) – unpublished until 1485, he repeats the traditional patristic charge that the activities of theatrical performers should be shunned as tainted by diabolic associations [see **A7**, **B26**, **J5**, **J71**, etc.].[1]

D55   Entertainers, robbers, devils: some analogies, *c.* 1360

John Bromyard, *Summa praedicantium*; parts trans. G. G. Coulton, *Five Centuries of Religion*, vol. I, *1000–1200*, Cambridge, 1923; 2nd edn, 1929, pp. 535–6 [see also G. R. Owst, *Literature and Pulpit in Medieval England*, Cambridge, 1933]

[Bromyard finds resemblances between popular entertainments and unhallowed rites] [. . .] there are two kinds of men who wear masks, that is, actors and robbers. For those who perform in those plays called in the vulgar tongue *miracles* employ masks, beneath which the players are disguised; in the same way demons, whose sport it is to destroy souls and ensnare them through sin, employ masks – that is, fascinating decorative devices – in *their* play, as do dancers whose feet are swift to seek out evil. What is more, robbers use masks as a disguise, and so do these devils who are robbers of men's souls. Again, dancers are like that dancing daughter of Herodias [Salome], through whom John the Baptist lost his head; thus, through dancers, many lose their souls [. . .][1]

[1] Cf. John Wycliffe's allusion in his *Ave Maria* to 'he that knows best how to play a pageant of the devil is held to be the best sport [*muriest mon*]' (*English Works of Wiclif hitherto unprinted*, ed. F. D. Matthew, EETS (OS 74), 1880, p. 206). For use of masks see **C65**.

A TREATISE

Undoubtedly the most substantial English indictment of clerical encouragement of, and lay exposure to, popular religious drama is the *Treatise of Miraclis Pleyinge*

(*c.* 1400) [see **D56**]. Owing something to patristic tradition as represented by
Bromyard, the *Treatise* represents one facet of the divergent assaults on features of
late fourteenth-century religious practices which John Wycliffe and his followers
found incompatible with their view of Christ's original teachings.

For students of theatre, the *Treatise*'s principal interest lies in its vehement dem-
olition of the arguments endorsing current scriptural dramas, though whether
unauthorised clerical *miracula* [see **B29, C65**] or embryonic plays in cycle form is
never clear. Its author (possibly Nicholas Hereford of Merton College, one of
Wycliffe's early disciples) challenges those who defend live presentation of incidents from scripture, on the grounds that every representation, however pious in
intention, can only travesty the divine events on which it is based. In order to make
sacred history graphic and meaningful for a lay audience, too many concessions
to popular taste and human indiscipline have to be made, diverting audiences from
the very truths playwrights claim to disseminate and validate.

D56   *A Treatise on playing miracles, c.* 1400

BL Add. MS 24202 (the Tenison MS), fos. 14–21; pr. *A Middle English Treatise of the Playing
of Miracles*, ed. Clifford Davidson, Washington, 1981; reprinted Kalamazoo, 1993[1]

[. . .] this performing of miracle plays overthrows Christ. Firstly, by making entertainment out of the very thing He treated most earnestly. Secondly, by devoting to
miracle plays our fleshly or earthly desires and our Five Wits (which God dedicated
to bringing us to an understanding of His bitter death, to teaching us to do
penance, to fleeing from indulging our senses, and to mortifying them). And thus
it is that the saints frequently note that in Holy Writ we never read of Christ laughing but of His frequent penitence, His tears and shedding of blood, thereby causing
us to understand that all our actions on earth should consist of doing penance, dis-
ciplining the flesh, and in suffering the penance of adversity. And therefore all the
things we do which contravene these three points utterly overturn Christ's works.
And that is why St Paul says that 'If you escape the chastening process in which
all good men are made participants, then you are heretics and not the sons of God'
[Hebrews 12.8]. And the performing of miracle plays overthrows the practice of
penance, since they are played with great pleasure and set forth with great enjoyment, while by contrast penance is performed in deep and heartfelt mourning, and
is ordained to be undergone in great sadness [. . .]

[. . .] since no man may serve two lords at once, as Christ says in His gospel
[Matthew 6.24; Luke 16.13], nobody can effectively hear the voice of Christ our
master and that of his own desires simultaneously. And since playing miracles
arises from fleshly desires and bodily enjoyment, no one can effectively heed them
and the voice of Christ at the same time, since Christ's voice and that of the flesh
are those of two mutually opposed rulers. And so playing miracles subverts discipline, for as St Paul says: 'Without doubt discipline at the time is not a matter for
joy but for mourning' [Hebrews 12.11]. Also the practice forces people to watch
vain costumed spectacles, where men and women of poor self-control dress up,

either inciting each other to lecherous deeds or to squabbling, since most quarrels arise from most forms of bodily indulgence, because this kind of pleasure makes a man less inclined to restrain himself, and facilitates gluttony and other vices, by which means it fails to permit a man to observe clearly God's scourge above his head, but makes his thoughts run on all those things that Christ through His Passion bade us forget. Wherefore these miracle performances override Christ's commands and His own deeds in matters of penance, true discipline and restraint [. . .]

---

[1] For a critical review of Davidson's edition, see Nicholas Davis, *METh* 4.1 (1982), pp. 48–55. See also the same author's invaluable '*The Tretise of Myraclis Pleyinge*: on Milieu and Authorship', *METh* 12 (1990), pp. 124–51.

CONTRASTING VIEWPOINTS

By contrast with *A Treatise*, an extract from *Dives and Pauper* (*c.* 1410), a lengthy prose dialogue expounding the Ten Commandments, invokes orthodox tenets of faith to vindicate the effectiveness of the comedic and ludic approach to religious instruction, by defending the Church's strategy in saving souls through human recreational experience [see **D57**]. Reginald Pecock, in exonerating his profession from the charge that it is prepared to sanction idolatry, also provides a traditional defence of devotional aids which he believes can rightfully support the Church's evangelising mission. But he firmly rejects the view that a fallible and spiritually compromised human actor can represent Christ as effectively as a graven image [see **D58**].

DIVES AND PAUPER

This lengthy prose dialogue between a rich yet devout layman and an indigent preacher, composed during the first decade of the fifteenth century, follows Augustinian precept in approving the presentation of stage-plays on scriptural themes. V. A. Kolve has employed *Dives and Pauper* to support his identification of laughter and game as furthering the instructional purposes of the English cyclical sequences, quoting Pauper's claim that manifestations of joy and celebration, which may include play performances even on the Sabbath, are divinely sanctioned activities anticipating the pleasures awaiting Christian souls in heaven.[1]

---

1.   See V. A. Kolve, *The Play Called Corpus Christi*, Stanford and London, 1966, pp. 131–4.

D57   *Dives and Pauper, c.* 1410

University of Glasgow Library: Hunterian MS 270, fos. 106–7 verso (Precept Three, cap. xvii); pr. *Dives and Pauper*, ed. Priscilla Heath Barnum, EETS (OS 275) 1976, pp. 293–5

[In the course of justifying to Dives the import of the Third Commandment – that Sunday should be kept as a holy day – the orthodox Pauper draws a clear distinction between legitimate Sabbath activities and those which the Church deplores and condemns [see **B27(a)**, **B27(b)**; **C32**(ii)].]

DIVES Miracles, plays and dances undertaken on great feast-days and on Sundays, are these not legitimate?

PAUPER Miracles, plays and dances done principally for reasons of devotion and honest mirth, to teach men to love God more deeply, without ribald purpose and not interspersed with bawdry or falsehoods, are legitimate, so long as the people are not prevented from serving God or from hearing God's word as a result, and there is no falsehood mixed in with such miracles and plays against the faith of Holy Church nor against the statutes of Holy Church, nor against righteous living. All other types are forbidden both on holy days and workdays [. . .] [But] to represent in performance at Christmas Herod and the Three Kings and other gospel narratives, both at that season and at Easter and at other times also, is lawful and commendable.

REGINALD PECOCK

Pecock, born in Wales *c.* 1395, became a fellow of Oriel College, Oxford, and in 1444 bishop of St Asaph. He was subsequently translated to the see of Chichester from 1450–8, dying *c.* 1460. Pecock lived through the troubled years of the Lollard heresies, which he set out to combat in a number of notable polemics, for which he himself was later charged with heresy in setting the principles of reason above the authority of the Church.

In *The Repressor of Over Much Blaming of the Clergy*, Pecock attempts against a background of Lollard scepticism to vindicate six orthodox priestly practices, including the advocacy of the spiritual benefits accruing from sacred images and participation in pilgrimages. But he is scornful of the belief that an actor in live performance can more effectively represent Christ (although he claims the practice is 'seldom met with and in few regions') than can a carved or sculpted image [**D58**].

D58 Reginald Pecock on religious images, *c.* 1449

Cambridge University Library MS Kk.iv.26, pr. Reginald Pecock, *The Repressor of Over Much Blaming of the Clergy*, ed. Charles Babington, RS 19, 2 vols., 1860, vol. I, pp. 221–2 (part II, Chapter 12)

The Second Part. Vindication of Images and Pilgrimages.

[. . .] it is obvious that nothing can be truly an image of another thing if it does not observe these three conditions [that it should *resemble* the other thing, that it was made *for no other purpose*, and that it was not designed *to be anything else*] [. . .] But it is a fact that no Christian man now living fulfils these three criteria with regard to the person of Christ in His manhood, in the same way as does a block of wood or a stone fashioned into the likeness of Christ hanging on a cross naked and wounded, with other appropriate accessories. (As is evident enough to every man who takes a good look and assesses how far it satisfies all these three conditions at one and the same time.) However, there is the case of arranging for a living man in a play to be hanged naked on a cross and to be apparently wounded and scourged. Yet this happens very seldom and in few places or regions. Wherefore no man living and walking on earth and going about his business and being involved with other men, as they live and walk and busily attend to their livelihoods, is so perfect and so complete an image of Christ crucified or of Christ performing this miracle or that miracle, as is a wooden block or a stone shaped for that purpose [. . .]

A BACKWARD GLANCE

Eye-witness testimony to the effectiveness of medieval-style performance is rare: one graphic first-hand account derives from the mid-seventeenth century when communal religious theatre was mostly a mere memory [see **D59**]. Yet in the recollections of the man from Cartmel, even as cited to demonstrate what the Puritan narrator deplores as his spiritual ignorance, we surely hear the authentic tones of an archetypal spectator gripped by a powerful stage image whose imprint he retained for life.[1]

1.   This view is challenged by Henk Gras, *METh* 11 (1989), pp. 175–86, n. 15.

D59   An eye-witness account, Cartmel, 1644

BL Add. MS 4460 ('The Life of John Shaw'), fos. 7–7 verso; pr. REED, *Cumberland/Westmorland/Gloucestershire*, p. 219

[. . .] I went to Cartmel about the later end of April 1644, and about the beginning of May following my wife came to me to Cartmel, where I found a very large spacious church, scarce any seats in it; a people very ignorant, yet willing to learn [. . .] One day an old man, about 60, sensible enough in other things, and living in the parish of Cartmel but in the chapelry of Cartmel Fell, coming to me about some business [. . .] I told him that the way to salvation was by Jesus Christ God-man who as He was man shed His blood for us on the cross etc. 'Oh sir', said he, 'I think I heard of that man you speak of, once in a play at Kendal called *Corpus Christi play*, where there was a man on a tree and blood ran down etc.' And after, he professed that though he was a good churchman – that is, he constantly went to Common Prayer at their chapel – yet he could not remember that ever he heard of salvation by Jesus Christ except in that play [. . .][1]

[1]   The antiquarian John Weever in his *Ancient Funeral Monuments* (1631), p. 405, attests to the continuing popularity of the Kendal play 'in the beginning of the reign of King James [I]' (*REED Cumberland/Westmorland/Gloucestershire*, p. 219), but the northern ecclesiastical commission would appear to have suppressed it after 1605 (ibid., pp. 17–18).

III Secular theatre

INTRODUCTION

With the exception of *Dame Sirith, The Interlude of the Clerk and the Girl* [see **A37**], and a few Robin Hood play fragments [see **J58**, note 3], no popular secular play-texts survive from British sources. Yet some English and Scottish records document aristocratic pleasures both public and private which demonstrate a strong theatrical bias: participants in jousts and tournaments frequently disguised themselves in elaborate costumes and masks [see **D60(a)**, **(b)**, **(c)**], while the wealth of visual pageantry generated by the tournament conceivably influenced the staging of those communal religious dramas which form the subject of section I.[1]

1. See Glynne Wickham, *Early English Stages, 1300–1660*, 3 vols., London, 1959–81, vol.
    I, on street theatre; Steven I. Pederson links with tournament convention *The Castle of Perseverance* [see **D14**], in *The Tournament Tradition and the Staging of 'The Castle of Perseverance'*, Ann Arbor, 1987. On the whole topic see Richard Barber and Juliet Barker, *Tournaments: Jousts, Chivalry and Pageants in the Middle Ages*, Woodbridge, 1989.

CHIVALRIC THEATRE

D60 Pre-joust processions, London, 1331–74
(a) Aristocrats in chains as Tartars, 22 September 1331

BL MS Cotton Otho B. 3, pr. *Chronicles of the Reign of Edward I and Edward II*, ed. Williams Stubbs, RS 76, 2 vols., London, 1882–3, vol. I, pp. 354–5

In this year [1331] a famous tournament was proclaimed in the centre of the city of London (namely Cheapside) by Lord William of Montacute, a most dynamic soldier who handled the many and varied expenses [. . .] Precisely at the time laid down for the tournament, the king [Edward III], his earls and barons, with all the royal knights, assembled in London; and on the Lord's Day, that is the day after the Feast of St Matthew the Apostle [21 September], the aforesaid William, who managed these ceremonies on the king's behalf, together with the king and other chosen knights, all of them dressed in splendid array and in masks to resemble Tartars, also processed with these and a number of the nobler and lovelier of the king's ladies, who were dressed in gowns of red velvet and cloaks of white came-line [supposedly camel-hair cloth] [. . .]

(b)   Challengers as Catholic clergy, 1343

Raphael Holinshed, *Chronicles of England*, 6 vols., London, 1807–8, vol. ii, p. 627

This year about Midsummer, there were solemn jousts proclaimed by the Lord Robert Morley, which were held in Smithfield, for which challengers came forth, one apparelled like the Pope, bringing with him twelve others in garments like cardinals [. . .]

(c)   The 'Lady of the Sun', 1374

Survey, vol. ii, pp. 29–30

In the forty-eighth year of Edward the Third [1374], Dame Alice Perrers (the King's concubine) as Lady of the Sun, rode from the Tower of London, through Cheap[side], accompanied by many lords and ladies, every lady leading a lord by his horse's bridle, till they came into West Smithfield, and then began a great joust which lasted for seven days after [. . .]

PUBLIC DISPLAY

It is a truism that the medieval psyche responded positively to all forms of display, and in England most major cities exploited the opportunities provided by great national events to mount elaborate parades and tableaux in honour of the occasion. Londoners, in particular, seem to have committed themselves to devising such impact-making spectacles [see **D61**, **D62**, **D63**].

D61   London celebrates the Battle of Falkirk, 1298

Survey, vol. i, p. 96

[. . .] in the year 1298,[1] for victory obtained by Edward I against the Scots, every citizen, according to their several trades, made their several shows, but especially the fishmongers, which in a solemn procession passed through the city, having, amongst other pageants and shows, four gilded sturgeons, carried on four horses; then four salmon of silver on four horses; and after them six and forty armed knights riding on horses, made like pike [luces] of the sea; and then someone representing St Magnus, because it was upon St Magnus' Day,[2] with a thousand horsemen, etc.

---

[1] Stow dates the engagement erroneously in 1293; the Battle of Falkirk against the Scots under William Wallace took place on 22 July 1298. The 'victory parade' was presumably held the following month.

D62   Pageantry for Richard II's coronation, 1377

Thomas Walsingham, *Historia Anglicana*, ed. H. T. Riley, RS 28, 2 vols., London, 1863–4, vol. i, p. 331; pr. and trans. Wickham, *Early English Stages*, vol. i, pp. 54–5

[. . .] a kind of castle with four turrets had been constructed in the upper part of the street called Cheapside where goods are sold, and from two of its sides wine flowed in abundance.[1] Moreover, on its turrets four extremely lovely young girls of the same stature and age as the King, had been positioned, dressed in white clothing – one girl to each turret. At the King's distant approach they scattered golden leaves in his path, and as he came nearer they showered both him and his horse with imitation gold florins. Furthermore, when he arrived at the foot of the castle, they took gold cups and, filling them with wine from the outlets the said castle provided, offered them to the King and his attendant lords. At the summit of the castle, raised in such a way that it stood between its four turrets, a golden angel was stationed, holding a golden crown in its hands. This angel had been so skilfully contrived that as the King arrived it lent forward and offered him the crown [. . .].

[1] i.e. from the 'great Conduit of sweet water' on the east side of 'West Cheaping' (Cheapside), built of stone *c.* 1285 and later replaced.

D63   Henry V returns from Agincourt, 1415

Gesta Henrici Quinti [The Deeds of Henry the Fifth] trans. Frank Taylor and John S. Roskell, Oxford, 1975, pp. 103–11. By permission of Oxford University Press

[. . .] When the tower at the entrance of the bridge was reached, there was seen placed high on top of it, and representing as it were the entrance into the city's jurisdiction, an image of a giant of astonishing size, who, looking down upon the king's face, held, like a champion, a great axe in his right hand and, like a warder, the keys of the city hanging from a baton in his left. At his right side stood a figure of a woman, not much smaller in size, wearing a scarlet mantle and adornments appropriate to her sex; and they were like a man and his wife who, in their richest attire, were bent upon seeing the eagerly awaited face of their lord and welcoming him with abundant praise [. . .]

And when, further on, the tower of the conduit in Cornhill was reached, that tower was found to be covered over with crimson cloth stretched out, like a tent, on staffs wrapped in similar cloth [. . .] And under an awning was a company of prophets with venerable white hair, in tunicles and golden copes, their heads wrapped and turbanned with gold and crimson, who, when the king came by, released, as an acceptable sacrifice to God for the victory He had conferred, a great flock of sparrows and other tiny birds, of which some descended on to the king's breast, some settled upon his shoulders, and some circled around in twisting flight [. . .]

A CONTINUING TRADITION

Mounting elaborate spectacles in streets and public places did not abate with the waning of the Middle Ages. Indeed, Renaissance aesthetics imbued dramatic pageantry with renewed life, not least by importing literary and scenic devices drawn from classical history and mythology. The need to create visual expressions of political, financial and social dominance remained imperative until the period of the English Civil War. When Protestant officialdom condemned communal religious drama as idolatrous and heretical in the 1570s and 1580s, the continuing existence of processions, pageants and parades seems never to have been challenged.

PRIVATE DISPORT

Although their actions may occasionally have been ill-judged [see **D64**], hired professionals were doubtless entrusted with providing most forms of private court entertainment [see **D66**, **D67**, **D68**]. However, the citizens' mumming visit of 1377 [see **D65**] demonstrates that performances could also involve aristocratic participation. The nature of every type of courtly festivity is impossible to chart: the example cited in the memoir of Henry VI once attributed to John Blacman [see **D67**] was probably atypical, and mummings devised by John Lydgate for the young king probably represent the genre more accurately [see **D68**]. But all court entertainments in fifteenth-century Britain were probably modest in scope: more opulent forms would only develop with the arrival of the later Stuarts in Scotland and the early Tudors in England.[1]

1.   See, for examples, Sydney Anglo, *Spectacle, Pageantry, and Early Tudor Policy*, Oxford, 1969; W. R. Streitberger, *Court Revels 1485–1559*, Toronto, 1994.

D64   Death among the dancers, Jedburgh Abbey, 1285

The Chronicles of Scotland, compiled by Hector Boece, translated into Scots by John Bellenden, 1531, ed. Edith C. Batho and H. Winifrid Husbands, Scottish Text Society 3rd series, 10, 15, (1935–41), vol. II, p. 244

[. . .] The thirty-fourth year of his [Alexander III's] reign was the first coming of the plague in Scotland, to the great mortality of people. In the triumph and second marriage of King Alexander [on 14 October], when every man was processing in the dance along with his wife, dancing with all the gladness that might be devised, there appeared before their eyes an image of a dead man, devoid of skin and flesh with his bones all bare, as a result of which the king and the remainder of the people were so amazed that they quitted the masquerade with great dismay and displeasure.[1]

[1] For a fuller Latin version see *MPS*, p. 48. Alexander's second marriage was to Yolande de Dreux, his first wife Margaret having died ten years before; he was himself killed in March 1286, when his horse fell over a cliff in darkness.
[For the apparition of Death on another festive occasion see **I49**.]

D65   A mumming for Prince Richard, Kennington, 1377

Survey, vol. 1, pp. 96–7

[. . .] One other show, in the year 1377, made by the citizens for disport of the young prince Richard, son to the Black Prince,[1] in the feast of Christmas, in this manner. On the Sunday before Candlemas [2 February][2] in the night, one hundred and thirty citizens, disguised and well horsed, in a mummery, with sound of trumpets, sackbuts, cornets, shawms, and other minstrels [*sic*], and innumerable torchlights of wax, rode from Newgate, through Cheap[side] over the bridge, through Southwark, and so to Kennington beside Lambeth, where the young prince remained with his mother and the Duke of Lancaster his uncle [John of Gaunt], the Earls of Cambridge, Hertford, Warwick, and Suffolk, with divers other lords. In the first rank did ride forty-eight in the likeness and habit of esquires, two and two together, clothed in red coats and gowns of fine serge or rich silk [say or sendal] with comely visors on their faces. After them came riding forty-eight knights in the same livery of colour and weave; then followed one richly arrayed like an emperor; and after him some distance, one stately attired like a pope, whom followed twenty-four cardinals,[3] and after them eight or ten with black visors, not amiable, as if they had been legates from some foreign princes. These maskers, after they had entered the manor of Kennington, alighted from their horses, and entered the hall on foot; which done, the prince, his mother, and the lords came out of the chamber into the hall, whom the said mummers did salute, showing by a pair of dice upon the table their desire to play with the prince, which they so handled that the prince did always win when he cast them. Then the mummers put up as stakes to the prince three jewels, one after another, which were a bowl of gold, a cup of gold, and a ring of gold, which the prince won at three casts. Then they set to the prince's mother, the duke, the earls and other lords, to every one a ring of gold, which they did also win. After which they were feasted and the music sounded, the prince and lords danced on the one part with the mummers, which did also dance. Which jollity being ended, they were again made to drink, and then departed in order as they came [. . .]

[1] The future Richard II who was to succeed to the throne later in the year, on 22 June [see **D62**].
[2] The church festival commemorating the Presentation of Christ in the Temple, or the Purification of the Virgin Mary.
[3] See **D60(b)**.

D66   Banquet entertainments, *c.* 1400

Geoffrey Chaucer, *The Franklin's Tale* in *The Riverside Chaucer*, ed. Larry D. Benson, Oxford, 1988, p. 183

[Aurelius, frustrated in his love for Dorigen, a virtuous married woman, appeals for assistance to his brother who recalls the reputed ability of 'tregetours' to conjure up marvels of the type described.]

'[. . .] I am certain that occult sciences exist through which people create various false appearances like the ones these skilful "tregetours" present. I have heard it truly said that frequently at feasts illusionists have introduced a stretch of water into a spacious hall, and a barge in which they rowed up and down. Sometimes it's seemed that a fierce lion entered, and sometimes flowers sprang up as if in a meadow; sometimes a vine with white and red grapes; sometimes a castle all made of lime and stone, and when they chose, they removed it immediately. That's how it appeared to everybody's sight [. . .]'[1]

[1] Robert Lindsay of Pitscottie's account of an Edinburgh banquet entertainment in May 1508 speaks of demonstrations of the 'craft of Igramancy which caused men to see things appear which was not' (*MPS*, p. 77). The household accounts of the Courtenays, earls of Devon, for 1395 contain a payment of 16d given 'au Tregatour & au harper' (REED, *Devon*, p. 307).

D67   Henry VI shuns an erotic entertainment, *c.* 1422–5

Collectarium mansuetudinum et bonorum Regis Henrici VI (attributed to John Blacman), pr. *Henry the Sixth. A Reprint of John Blacman's Memoir with Translation and Notes*, M. R. James, Cambridge, 1919, pp. 29–30[1]

His modesty [. . .]

Another example

[. . .] it happened once that at the time of Our Lord's birth, a certain great lord pre-sented in his presence a dance or display of young women with bare breasts who he proposed should dance before the king in that unclad state, perhaps to test him or to ensnare his youthful mind. But that king was not taken unaware, nor did he fail to recognise the devilish trick, and spurning the deception and averting his eyes in considerable anger, turned his back on the company, and went off to his room, saying 'Fie, fie, for shame! Forsooth, you are to blame!'

[1] Blacman, a Fellow of Merton College, Oxford, and of Eton, was Henry VI's confessor; what purported to be his memoir of the king was first printed by Robert Copland in 1510, but present-day historians query its authenticity along with Blacman's authorship (see Bertram Wolffe, *Henry VI*, London, 1981, pp. 4–21).

JOHN LYDGATE

Lydgate (*c.* 1370–*c.* 1450), composed at least seven semi-dramatic mummings during his lengthy poetic career, dating from *c.* 1425–30 when the poet was fre-quently employed at the court of the youthful Henry VI. Unlike the Kennington visitation of 1377 [see **D65**], these pieces doubtless featured trained professionals since they relied in part on authored speeches, though amateur participants may have mimed roles while a presenter spoke on their behalf. Two introductory rubrics convey the flavour of Lydgate's work: perhaps the liveliest piece is the Hertford mumming probably presented before Henry VI at Christmas 1427 [see **D68(a)**] in which six rustics petitioned the king, accusing 'their fierce wives' of multiple forms of maltreatment, to which the women vigorously responded in kind.

The mumming at Windsor [**D68(b)**] draws on the legend that the Frankish King Clovis I (*c.* 465–511), converted to Christianity under the influence of his wife St Clotilda, was presented with a shield bearing the triple lily and was anointed at baptism from oil from a golden ampulla delivered by a holy dove. Lydgate's piece was addressed to Henry as alleged true successor to the French crown.

D68   Preambles to John Lydgate's mummings, *c.* 1425–30

MS Trinity College Cambridge R.3.20. 40– 8, 71– 4; pr. Henry Noble MacCracken (ed.), *The Minor Poems of John Lydgate*, part II, EETS (OS 192) (1934), pp. 668–701 [see also Wickham, *Early English Stages*, vol. I, pp. 191–207]

(a)   A mumming at Hertford

Now follows here the style of a petition by way of supplication put to the King holding his noble feast of Christmas in the Castle of Hertford as in a disguising of the rude country folk complaining of their wives, with the forceful answer of their wives, devised by Lydgate [. . .]

(b)   A mumming at Windsor

Now follows next the device of a mumming before the King Henry the Sixth, being in his Castle of Windsor the Feast of Christmas holding there, made by Lydgate Dan John, the Monk of Bury; how the ampulla and the *fleur de lys* came first to the kings of France by miracle at Rheims [. . .]

PLAYERS AT COURT

We have no direct evidence that acted drama formed part of the repertoire of the late medieval minstrel; perhaps its presentation was one of the multiple skills perennially expected of trained professionals [see **Section A**], but fifteenth-century allusions suggest that their repertoire by then was predominantly musical.[1]

It is therefore uncertain precisely who would have performed, for example, Lydgate's mummings [**D68(a)**, **(b)**]. Perhaps professional or semi-professional entertainers were imported to handle these specialised dramas, recruited in the same way as the enigmatic 'Jack Travaill and his companions' who performed unspecified acts at the boy-king Henry VI's court in 1427 [see **D69(a)**]. But the establishment of even a part-time troupe of English court players cannot be dated

much before 27 May 1494, the date of the first documented record of their existence [see **D69(c)**]. In this respect the Scottish court may have anticipated its
English counterpart [see **D69(b)**], though Patrick Johnson's precise status seems
difficult to determine.[2]

In England by the 1490s Henry VII's treasurer was sanctioning payments to visiting groups attached to the households of some of the king's nobility [see
D69(d)], though what form their repertoire took remains unclear (see 'Household
Players' below). Payments were also made to the king's own company, who under
John English contributed to the entertainments forming part of the programme of
festivities designed to mark the marriage of James IV of Scotland to Henry VII's
daughter, Margaret Tudor, on 8 August 1503 [see **D69(e)**].

1. The minstrel class originally included acrobats, jugglers, conjurors and jesters. For an
    account of minstrels active at a Whitsun feast held by Edward I on 22 May 1306 to
    mark the knighting of the future Edward II, see Constance Bullock-Davies,
    Menestrellorum Multitudo, Cardiff, 1978.
2. Anna J. Mill (*MPS*, pp. 57–8) points to the possibility that he may have been one of the
    Clerks of the Chapel or the leader of a 'drama group' in Linlithgow, rather than a pro-
    fessional player.

D69   Players at the English and Scottish courts, 1427–1509
(a)   Eltham Palace, Christmas 1427

Thomas Rymer, *Foedera, conventiones, literae . . .*, 20 vols., London, 1704–35, vol. x, p. 387

To Jack (*Jacques?*) [Jakke] Travaill and his companions putting on [*feisans*] various
entertainments [*diverses jeuues*] and interludes,[1] during the feast of Christmas,
before our said lord the king   £4
    And to other players [*jeweis*] of Abingdon, putting on other interludes during
the said feast of Christmas   20 sol[2]

[1] 'Interludes' was a highly elastic term, and given that Henry VI was only just six at Christmas 1427,
    in this instance they are unlikely to have been straight plays. They may have been no more than
    games in which the boy took part.
[2] A unit of coinage, roughly equivalent to a penny.

(b)   A playing troupe at the Scottish Court, 1475–89

Exchequer Rolls of Scotland VIII. 333, 404, 512; Accounts of the Lord Treasurer of
Scotland, vol. I, 91, 118; pr. *MPS*, pp. 311–14

1475–6   [. . .] in payment made to Patrick Johnson at the lord King's
           command, for his plays at the time of Christmas and
           Shrovetide, and expenses incurred thereon   £6
1477   [. . .] in payment made to the said Patrick (Johnson) for certain
           pastimes [*joccis*] and plays presented in the King's presence   £6

1477–8	[. . .] in payment made to the said Patrick Johnson for certain plays and interludes presented at the time of our Lord's Nativity in the King's chamber and palace [. . .]	£6
1488	[. . .] to Patrick Johnson and the players of Linlithgow that played to the King [on 5 August]	£6
1489	[. . .] to Patrick Johnson and his fellows that played a play to the King at Linlithgow	£3 12s.

(c)   Recognition of the Players of the King's Interludes, 1494

PRO E 36/131, p. 73 (see W. R. Streitberger, *Court Revels 1485–1559*, Toronto, 1994, pp. 48–9; 320)

27 May [1494] to John English, Edward Maye, Richard Gibson, and John Hammond, *Lusoribus Regis*, in other words, in the English language, the Players of the King's Interludes, as their fees five marks per annum [. . .][1]

---

[1] F. Devon, *Issues of the Exchequer*, p. 516, gives similar payments for Michaelmas 1494 and Michaelmas 1503; in the latter the names of William Rutter and John Scott appear, increasing the troupe's personnel to six. For Richard Gibson, Yeoman Tailor and Porter of the Great Wardrobe, see W. R. Streitberger, 'The Development of Henry VIII's Revels Establishment', *METh* 7 (1985), pp. 83–100, and *Court Revels*.

(d)   Selected payments to players at Henry VII's Court, 1492–1509

Sydney Anglo, 'The Court Festivals of Henry VII: a Study Based Upon the Account Books of John Heron, Treasurer of the Chamber', *Bulletin of the John Rylands Library* 43 (1960–1), pp. 12–45

1 Jan. 1492	Item to my Lord of Oxon's[1] players in reward	20s
7 Jan. 1493	Item to my Lord of Northumberland's[2] players in reward	20s
6 Jan. 1494	Item to the King's players for a reward	53s 4d
3–8 Jan. 1496	Item to the King's players in reward	13s 4d
12 Jan. 1498	Item to my Lord of Oxon's players	13s 4d
2–4 Jan. 1499	Item to my Lord Prince's[3] players in reward	13s 4d
5–11 Jan. 1499	Item to my Lord of Essex's[4] players	13s 4d
7 Jan. 1502	To John English[5] the player	10s
1 Jan. 1506	Item to my Lord Prince's[6] players that played in the hall upon New Year's Even	10s
16 Jan. 1507	Item to the King's four players that played before the King upon Twelfth Day at night	40s
2 Jan. 1509	Item to my Lord of Buckingham's[7] players that played in the hall at Greenwich in reward	6s 8d

[1]   John de Vere, thirteenth earl of Oxford (1442–1513).
[2]   Henry Algernon Percy, fifth earl of Northumberland (1478–1527) [see **D71**].
[3]   Arthur, Prince of Wales (1486–1502).
[4]   Henry Bourchier, second earl of Essex (c. 1472–1539).
[5]   One of the four King's players [see **D69(c)** and **(e)**].
[6]   The future Henry VIII (1491–1547).
[7]   Edward Stafford, third duke of Buckingham (1477–1521), made High Constable of England on 23 June 1509.

(e)   English players at the Scottish Court, 1503

John Leland, *De rebus Britannicis collectanea . . .*, 6 vols., London, 1774, pp. 299, 300

[11 August 1503] After supper, the King and Queen being together in their Great Chamber John English and his companions played, and then each one went his way.

[13 August 1503] After dinner, a Morality[1] was played by the said Master English and his companions, in the presence of the King and Queen, and then dances were danced.

[1]   Probably a complimentary piece with didactic import featuring allegorical characters.

HOUSEHOLD PLAYERS

In some fifteenth-century noble households places were found for personnel partly employed to entertain their superiors, even if one apparent reference to a servant being retained as an actor is now felt to be ironic [see **J58**]. Yet evidence that troupes of such men travelled the country performing plays to entertain the community is far from conclusive.[1] The problem is largely one of terminology: few of the allusions in city and town records to visits from this or that lord's *histriones* or *lusores* tell us anything about the nature of the fare provided, given that the customary term *histrio* is not used exclusively to denote 'actor' but often 'variety performer' or (especially) 'musician'. Even the occurrence of the vernacular term 'player' in some Kentish records of the late 1400s [see **D70**], does not in itself certify that great lords' retainers were presenting acted plays. On the other hand, two early Tudor account-books [see **D71**] certainly give support to the importance of both visiting and residential performers for a noble household of the early 1500s.[2]

1.   See Peter Meredith, 'The Professional Travelling Players of the Fifteenth Century: Myth or Reality?', in *European Medieval Drama 1997*, Tempo di Spettacoli, ed. Sydney Higgins, Camerino, 1997, pp. 25–40.
2.   See also Suzanne R. Westfall, *Patrons and Performance: Early Tudor Household Revels*, Oxford, 1990.

D70   Household players in East Kent, 1477–*c.* 1509

Dawson *Kent*, pp. 26–32, 149–51

Dover

1477–8	Item paid the 24 January to players of my lord of Arundel[1]	5s
1478–9	[. . .] to players of my lord of Arundel	5s
1479–80	[. . .] to players of my lord of Arundel 3s 4d and in wine	18d
1483–4	[. . .] to players of my lord of Arundel	6s 8d
1489–90	[. . .] to players of my Lord Cobham[2]	2s 8d
1494–5	[. . .] to players of my Lord Warden[3] playing before the Mayor and Jurats [aldermen]	6s 8d
1498–9	[. . .] to my lord of Oxford's[4] players	2s
1503–4	[. . .] to the King's players	10s

Sandwich

1497–8	And paid in reward to my lord of Oxford's players which played before the Mayor and divers of his brethren	5s
1508–9 (?)	And paid to my lord of Arundel's players, showing sport to Mr Mayor and his brethren	2s
	And paid to the King's players showing the mayor, his brethren and the commonalty sport in the Fishmarket openly	10s

[1] Thomas Fitz Alan, twelfth earl of Arundel (1450–1524), at the time Constable of Dover Castle and Lord Warden of the Cinque Ports.
[2] John Brooke, second Lord Cobham (d. *c.* 1513).
[3] The future Henry VIII, aged one!
[4] John de Vere, thirteenth earl of Oxford (1442–1513) [see **D69(d)**].

D71   Plays and players in the Percy household, 1511–*c.* 1525

The Regulations and Establishment of the Household of Henry Algernon Percy, fifth Earl of Northumberland [ed. Thomas Percy], London, 1827

(i) The first household book, 1511–*c.* 1525

REWARDS TO PLAYERS

[. . .] to be paid [. . .] for rewards to players for plays played in [the] Christmas [season] by strangers in my house [here]after 20d every play[er] [. . .] (p. 22)

My lord's chaplains in household [number] 6 Viz. the Almoner and if he be a maker of interludes[1] then he [is] to have a servant to the intent for writing of the parts [. . .] (p. 44)

[. . .] My lord useth and accustometh to give yearly when his lordship is at home to every earl's players that comes to his lordship betwixt Christmas and Candlemas, if he be his special lord and friend and kinsman   20s

[. . .] My lord useth and accustometh to give yearly when his lordship is at home to every lord's players [. . .]   10s (pp. 340–1)

[. . .] My lord useth and accustometh to give yearly if his lordship keep a chapel and be at home them of his lordship's chapel if they do play the Play of the Nativity upon Christmas Day in the morning in my lord's chapel before his lordship 20s

[. . .] My lord useth and accustometh to give yearly when his lordship is at home in reward to them of his lordship's chapel and other his lordship's servants that doth play the Play before his lordship upon Shrove Tuesday at night yearly in reward 10s (p. 345)

[A similar entry [p. 345] refers to 'the Play of the Resurrection upon Easter Day in the morning' for which the reward is 20s]

[. . .] My lord useth and accustometh yearly to give him which is ordained to be the Master of the Revels yearly in my lord's house in Christmas for the overseeing and ordering of his lordship's plays, interludes, and dressing [up?] that is played before his lordship in his house in the twelve days of Christmas. And they to have in reward for that cause   20s (p. 346)

[. . .] My lord useth and accustometh to give every of the four persons that his lordship admitted as his players to come to his lordship yearly at Christmas and at all other such times as his lordship shall command them, for playing of plays and interludes before his lordship in his lordship's house for every of their fees for a whole year   [left blank] (p. 351)

[1] These 'interludes' do appear to be secular acted dramas performed by members of the Percy household.

(ii) The second household book, *c.* 1515

Ian Lancashire, 'Orders for Twelfth Day and Night circa 1515 in the Second Northumberland Household Book', *English Literary Renaissance* 10 (1980), pp. 6–45

[. . .] That it be ordered the said night that there be either play[ed] as an interlude a comedy or tragedy,[1] to be played before the lord and lady before the disguising come into the said hall.[2] (p. 10)

[1] One of the earliest references to these terms; see Lancashire, 'Orders for Twelfth Day and Night', p. 34, note.
[2] The reference makes it possible that household players presented 'interludes', while nobility and gentry appeared only in the more costly 'disguisings'. Again, one must stress the elasticity of the term 'interlude'.

Section E
France

Edited by LYNETTE R. MUIR

Abbreviations

Amboise — Graham A. Runnalls, 'Le Mystère de la Passion à Amboise au Moyen Age: représentations théâtrales et texte', *Le moyen français* 26 (1990), pp. 7–86

Angers — Célestin Port, *Documents sur l'histoire du théâtre à Angers*, *Bibliothèque de l'Ecole des Chartes* 22 (1861), pp. 69–80

Bouchet *Epistres* — Jean Bouchet, *Epistres morales et familieres du traverseur*, Poitiers, 1545; reprinted New York, 1969

Bourges *feintes* — *Extraicts des fainctes qu'il conviendra faire pour le mistère des Actes des Apostres*, ed. Auguste-Théodore de Girardot, *Annales Archéologiques*, Paris, 1854, pp. 8–24

Bourges *monstre* — Jacques Thiboust, *Relation de l'ordre de la triomphante et magnifique monstre du mystère des Saints Actes des Apostres faite à Bourges, 1536*, Bourges, 1838

Châteaudun — *Compte du mystère de la Passion: Châteaudun 1510*, ed. Maurice Couturier and Graham A. Runnalls, Société Archéologique d'Eure-et-Loir, 1991

Comédiens — Louis Petit de Julleville, *Les comédiens en France au moyen âge*, Paris, 1885

Dauphiné — Jacques Chocheyras, *Le théâtre religieux en Dauphiné du Moyen Age au XVIIIe siècle*, Geneva, 1975

Dijon — Louis de Gouvenain, *Le théâtre à Dijon (1422–1790)*, Dijon, 1888

Draguignan — 'Régistre des ordonnances . . . de Draguignan', *Revue des sociétés savantes* 6.3, 1876

Issoudun — *Zimmerische Chronik*, ed. Karl A. Barack, Bibliothek des Litterarischen Vereins 91–4, Tübingen, 1869, vol. III, pp. 226–8

Michel *Passion* — *Le 'Mystère de la Passion' de Jean Michel* [Angers 1486], ed. Omer Jodogne, Gembloux, 1962

Modane — Louis Gros, *Etude sur le mystère de l'Antéchrist et du jugement de Dieu, joué à Modane en 1580 et 1606*, Chambéry, 1962

Mystères	Louis Petit de Julleville, *Histoire du théâtre en France. Les Mystères*, 2 vols., Paris, 1880; reprinted Geneva, 1969
Provençal Director's Notebook	Alessandro Vitale-Brovarone, *Il quaderno di segreti d'un regista provenzale del Medioevo: Note per la Messa in scena d'una Passione*, Alessandria, 1984
René *Comptes*	*Extraits des comptes et mémoriaulx du roi René*, ed. [Richard] A. Lecoy de la Marche, Paris, 1873
Romans	*Mystère des Trois Doms représenté à Romans en MDIX . . . avec . . . des documents relatifs aux représentations en Dauphiné du XIVe au XIVe siècle*, ed. Ulysse Chevalier and Paul-Emile Giraud, Lyon, 1887
Rouergue *Judgement*	*Le Jugement Dernier (Lo Jutgamen General): Drame provençal du XVe siècle*, ed. Moshé Lazar, Paris, 1971
Roy	Emile Roy, *Etudes sur le théâtre français du XIVe et du XVe siècle*, reprinted Geneva, 1975
Saint Laurent	*Le Mystère de saint Laurent*, ed. W. Söderhjelm and A. Wallensköld, Helsinki, 1891
Seurre	*Andrieu de la Vigne: Le Mystère de Saint Martin*, ed. André Duplat, Geneva, 1979
Staging	see General Bibliography
Vigneulles *Chronique*	*La Chronique de Philippe de Vigneulles*, ed. Charles Bruneau, 4 vols., Metz, 1927–33
Vigneulles *Gedenkbuch*	*Gedenkbuch des Metzer Bürgers Philippe von Vigneulles aus den jahren 1471–1522*, ed. Heinrich Michelant, Bibliothek des litterarischen Vereins in Stuttgart XXIV, 1852

Introduction

The surviving body of theatrical material from medieval France is enormous. Not only are there about a million lines of biblical and hagiographic *mystères*, with more than 300 shorter moralities, farces and *sotties*, but detailed sets of accounts and numerous performance records and details. One of the problems in handling this great body of material is distinguishing between the different play types and names – *mystère*, *moralité*, farce, *sottie*, miracle – which are used interchangeably by the medieval authors and printers. I have, therefore, followed here the 'distinction by subject matter' suggested by Alan Knight[1] by which plays are divided into historical and fictional genres, the former being plays on biblical, historical or hagiographic themes for which I have used the common term *mystères*, and the latter, the farces, moralities and *sotties* which include material from epic, romance or contemporary life. Miracle-plays may belong to either genre.

Play texts, especially for Passion plays, were widely copied and from about 1480 printed versions could be bought in Paris, Lyons and some other major cities. The best-known authors of Passion texts were Arnoul Gréban and Jean Michel – the latter made use of much of Gréban's material but expanded it considerably. Alternatively, a town might commission a known *fatiste* to write a play on a chosen topic – usually the life of a local saint. The length of plays varied greatly from the 10,000 lines of the Semur *Passion*, which includes the Creation and other Old Testament material, to the 60,000 of the composite Passion presented in Paris in 1506 which included material on the early life of the Virgin Mary, the Nativity and the Ministry of Jesus as well as the Passion and Resurrection. French Passion plays did not include the Last Judgement, which is only found as a separate play. Some manuscripts survive in the form of an actor's *rollet*, a narrow strip of paper or parchment which could be wound round the finger and containing just the cue words and one character's lines [see **E24**]. (For a director's copy see Mons in **Section H**.) Many editions are very old and a number of plays have never been published at all.

As in most parts of Europe at this period, plays were mostly performed in towns, with many places in certain areas having one or more performances recorded, while in other regions almost none is known. This is partly the result of the lack of study of the records, but also of the history of the period. In the fifteenth century, conditions in France were constantly changing, as the king, the dukes of Burgundy, the Emperor and the English fought and squabbled over the different towns and provinces. For the purposes of the present study, the towns included are those which, at the time of their plays, were a part of France, including Burgundy itself. Not included here is the drama of the French-speaking Burgundian territories in the Low Countries – Hainault and part of Flanders round Lille *Flandre gallicante*[2] – whose plays are treated with their Dutch contemporaries in **Section H**. Also included are some of the provinces in the south-east, such as Dauphiné and Provence, which only became part of France at the end of the century, and the independent but French-speaking duchy of Savoy. The Breton *mystères*, based on French originals, do not include any performance references and have been omitted.[3]

Much of the material in the records was first printed in the nineteenth century, especially in the great collections published in the 1880s by Louis Petit de Julleville [see Bibliography], who collected records of play performances from the work of even earlier scholars or from correspondents who sent him information from their own researches. Much of the material has not been investigated since and up-to-date manuscript references are not available. More recent publications include a number of carpenters' contracts for building stages and lists of the *feintes* [special effects] required for particular productions. The most important new material is the set of accounts for the performance in 1510 at Châteaudun, published by Couturier and Runnalls in 1991.

The typical form of staging found in provincial France is the multiple-set established in an enclosed location such as a cloister, churchyard or town square. Part at least of the audience was seated and everyone had to pay for admission although the play at Autun specifically mentions that the seats were free [see **E74**]. A modest amount of street theatre is recorded, mainly for royal or princely entries with only rare references to plays for Corpus Christi or other festivals [see **E95**].

Except in Paris, the big *mystères* were normally a cooperative venture of a whole town, including the merchants and the craftsmen, the patriciate and the church – many major roles including that of Christ are regularly played by clerics. Members of the legal profession also played a considerable role in both the urban *mystères* and the satirical *sotties* and farces staged by the clerks of the *Parlements*, the judicial bodies of the major cities. The surviving records of a few of these plays give details of the costs of staging the plays as well as the income derived from patronage, admission charges and civic funds. The actors were amateur, but there are payments for wine and/or food for rehearsals. By 1520 women were playing a range of roles in these plays.

The section has been organised into: 'The theatre of the *mystères*', 'Farces, *sotties* and moralities', 'Processional and street theatre' and 'Drama in the bilingual cities: Metz'.

NOTES

1. Alan E. Knight. *Aspects of Genre in Late Medieval French Drama*, Manchester, 1983, p. 91.
2. For *Flandre gallicante* and *Flandre flamigante* see Richard Vaughan, *Philip the Bold*, London, 1962, p. 26.
3. For the Breton *mystères* see Lynette R. Muir, *The Biblical Drama of Medieval Europe*, Cambridge, 1995, p. 21.

I   *The theatre of the* mystères

The two discrete dramatic genres, the historical and the fictional described in the introduction, almost never overlap in performance and will be considered separately, beginning with the plays of the historical genre or, as they were often called in the Middle Ages, the *mystères*. The term is equally used for plays or tableaux on biblical, hagiographic or historical subjects.[1] From the end of the fourteenth century through to the late sixteenth, scores of *mystères* were performed in France with the material falling into two distinct parts: the origin and development of the Confrérie de la Passion in Paris and the civic theatre from other parts of France.

1.   With the exception of Millet's *Siege of Troy*, the subject matter of the historical plays is all drawn from the Roman period.

PARIS

Before 1402

By the end of the fourteenth century a flourishing community drama seems to have existed in the Paris area which led to the development of the most celebrated religious confraternity in the history of French drama – the Confrérie de la Passion. The existence of Passion plays in the Paris area is confirmed in a series of legal documents, many of them from the archives of the Châtelet, the headquarters of the law-enforcement arm of the Paris Parlement. The material includes exonerations from negligence in accidents [see **E1**], incidental remarks in a deposition in a case of attempted assault, and a police report of the interrogation, under torture, of a woman accused of witchcraft who claimed to have seen the devil [see **E2(a)**]. She was subsequently convicted and burnt. Despite the efforts of the authorities to ban these plays, they continued as can be seen by two of these documents from 1398. One reads: 'By order of our lord the king we prohibit all those inhabitants and dwellers in the town of Paris, Saint-Maur and all towns around Paris from acting or performing any plays [*jeus de personages*][1] such as farces, lives of saints or any other without the permission of the said lord or of us, on pain of the king's displeasure and being guilty of an offence against him.' The very next document describes the reading of this interdict in St Maur and concludes:

284

'[Nevertheless] after this was done there were some who acted a play of the Passion of Our Lord.'[2]

1.   Literally a play with characters. Used for a play with live actors, rather than mimes or tableaux.
2.   *Mystères*, vol. I, pp. 414–15.

E1   Two fatal accidents with cannon, 1380, 1384

Antoine Thomas, 'Note d'histoire littéraire: Le Théâtre à Paris à la fin du XIVe siècle', *Romania* 21 (1892), pp. 606–11; trans. *Staging*, pp. 191–2

(a)   Death of an assistant

[In 1380, during the plays] in the honour and remembrance of the Passion of our Lord Jesus Christ in our good city of Paris by some of the burghers and other good people of the same [. . .] [Guillaume Langlois was asked to attend in order] to fire the cannons at the proper time so that their parts might be better performed. [Jehan Hemon joined Guillaume Langlois as assistant] and they prepared and set in order these cannons to fire and make a noise at the moment of ordering of the Crucifixion as it is customary to do in the said plays in remembrance of the death and Passion of our Lord Jesus Christ; and because [. . .] a hot ramrod was put and thrust into a cannon that was in that place, the wad of this cannon flew out from the explosion [. . .] Hemon was accidentally struck by the said wad on one of his legs and injured and the said Guillaume also was burnt and scorched by the explosion of fire.[1]

[1]   Jehan died of his injuries but had previously signed a declaration before witnesses totally exonerating Guillaume.

(b)   A by-stander killed at Aunay-les-Bordy

[1384. The king, Charles VI, having] been notified by the kinsmen of Fremin Severin [. . .] that the inhabitants [of Aunay] had undertaken on the Sunday after the Nativity of St John Baptist [24 June] to present [. . .] the Miracle [. . .] of Théophile, in which play [. . .] someone had to fire a cannon [. . .] On the Sunday before the said Feast of St John [they] were in the church [. . .] to rehearse their parts; the said Fremin who had to take care of the said cannon had filled the barrel of the said cannon with paper only, without any fire or wood being there, and [. . .] this Fremin had said to the people who were there 'stand back, you run a great risk in being so near'. Nevertheless, the late Perrier le Roux by chance stood in front of the said cannon when it was let off so that [. . .] the paper which was in the barrel of the said cannon struck him in the eye; which late Perrier le Roux died the following Friday.[1]

[1]   Fremin was duly exonerated.

E2   Items taken from the records of the Châtelet

Roy, p. ccxiii; p. ccxiv

(a)   A condemned witch describes the devil

[. . .] and then there appeared to her the devil in the form and appearance of the devils who appear in the plays of the Passion save that he had no horns[1]

[1] The mention of the horns is particularly convincing.

(b)   An indoor performance in 1399

On Sunday afternoon, the 3rd May, [Laurens Desmarés[1] went] to see certain plays of the Annunciation to the Virgin Mary and the Nativity of Our Lord Jesus Christ, which were being performed in the house of our dear and well beloved brother, the duc d'Orléans, in the said parish of St André-des-Arts, to which many people went.[2]

[1] Desmarés had been accused of theft on his way to Paris.
[2] Roy suggests that since the spectacle was obviously public it is more likely that the performance was by a group who may even be the future Confrérie de la Passion who had rented the place, rather than by the duke's private players. This house was one of a number owned by the duc d'Orléans in Paris.

E3   A reference to a scaffold for a play in Chelles

Gustave Cohen, 'Le théâtre à Paris et aux environs à la fin du quatorzième siècle', in *Etudes d'histoire du théâtre en France au moyen âge et à la Renaissance*, Paris, 1956, pp. 169–78

[Jehan Martin deposed that he went to Chelles] to see a celebration [*feste*] which was to take place there the following day in commemoration of the Passion of Our Lord. [He met up with several others in an inn, two of whom subsequently] slept that night, fully clothed, on the scaffold which had been erected for the said celebration.[1]

[1] This Passion may be linked up with those held at St Maur but the use of the term *feste* may suggest a different kind of celebration.

The founding of the Confrérie de la Passion

At the beginning of the fifteenth century, a group of actors in Paris apparently appealed to the king, Charles VI (who must have attended some of their performances), for support – presumably against the officers of the law. In 1402 the king granted to the Confrérie de la Passion their celebrated charter. This important document in the history of French theatre is, unfortunately, virtually all we know about the Confrérie till the beginning of the next century.

E4   The charter of the Confrérie de la Passion, 1402

Mystères, vol. i, pp. 417–18; trans. *Staging*, pp. 36–7

We, Charles etc., make it known to all present and to come, that we have received the humble supplication of our well beloved brothers, the Masters and Governors of the Confrérie of the Passion and Resurrection of our Lord, based on the Church of the Trinity in Paris, setting out that for the performing of [. . .] the play of the Passion which they have recently begun and prepared to perform before us, as they have done previously, which they have not been able properly to continue because we were not then able to be present; for which performance and play the said Confrérie has laid out and spent much of its goods as have also the *Confrères* each one in proportion; saying further that if they played publicly to the community [*en commun*] it would be to the profit of this Confrérie, which they may not properly do without our leave and permission, they request our gracious granting thereof. We who will and desire the welfare, profit, and advantage of the said Confrérie and the rights and revenues thereof to be increased and augmented with favors and privileges so that everyone as an act of devotion may and should join them and be of their company; to those Masters, Governors, and *Confrères* of the said Confrérie of the Passion of Our Lord, we have given and authorised, give and authorise with special favour, power, and royal authority, this time for all time and always in perpetuity, by the tenor of the present letters, authority, leave, and permission to perform and play any play at all, be it the said Passion and Resurrection or any other of saints both men and women, that they shall select and put on whenever and as often as they please either before us, before our commons, or elsewhere either in rehearsal [*en recors*] or otherwise and to meet, unite, and assemble in whatever place or space lawful for this purpose which they find either in our town of Paris or in the surrounding districts in the presence of three, two, or one of our officials as they select, without thereby committing any offence against us or justice. And these Masters, Governors, and *Confrères* above-mentioned and each one of them during the days on which is performed the said play that they are playing, either before us or elsewhere, either in rehearsal or otherwise, thus and in the said manner may go, come, pass, and return peacefully, dressed, garbed, and equipped each one of them as the case shall require and as is appropriate, according to the ordering of the said play without let or hindrance;[1] and for the greater confirmation and surety of our most abundant favour we have taken these *Confrères*, Governors, and Masters under our protection and safeguard during the course of the said plays and while they are playing only, without any harm to them nor to any one of them on this occasion or otherwise however it may be to the contrary.[2]

---

[1] This reference to costuming would protect the players from being arrested for wearing women's clothing which was illegal.

[2] This monopoly did not affect the performance of saints' plays by the trade guilds, at their annual meeting.

The Confrérie's final years

Although they are known to have performed regularly at the Hospice de la Trinité, we only have certain knowledge of one of their texts: at the end of the manuscript of the *Vie de Saint Louis* in three days[1] are the words: 'This book belongs to the Passion of Our Lord Jesus Christ' i.e. to the Confrérie de la Passion. However, since the Confrérie had a monopoly of Passion plays in Paris, it may also be assumed that the texts of Michel's *Passion*, published in Paris and citing performances in 1490, 1498, 1507, refer to their activities.[2] As for their playing place, however, we learn from the legal documents of the sixteenth century that in 1539 they lost their theatre in the Trinité and moved into the Hôtel de Flandres where in 1539 they performed the *Sacrifice of Abraham* in the presence of Francis I, who had confirmed their privileges in 1518 and went on to stage the *Acts of the Apostles* in 1541 [see **E5**, **E6(i)**]. The edict of 1548 [see **E8**] was the end of Passion plays in Paris but not yet the end of the Confrérie itself, which built itself new premises on the site of the Hôtel du Bourgogne [see **E7**] and thus still retained possession of its theatre and monopoly, so that seventeenth-century classical tragedies and comedies were performed in the theatre still owned by the Confrérie de la Passion.[3]

[1] *Le mystère de Saint Louis*, ed. Francisque Michel, Roxburghe Club, 1871.
[2] For details of these editions, see G. A. Runnalls, 'La circulation des textes des *mystères* à la fin du moyen âge', *Etudes sur les mystères*, Paris, 1998, pp. 413–44.
[3] For details of the Confrérie in the seventeenth century, see W. D. Howarth (ed.), *French Theatre in the Neo-Classical Era, 1550–1789*. Theatre in Europe: a Documentary History. Cambridge, 1997.

E5   A call for actors for the *Actes des Apôtres*, 1541

Mystères, vol. 1, p. 365

Time urges us in our brief life to turn to biblical discourse [. . .] and for this honest occupation for catholics be it known by public sound and *cri*[1] that a *mystère* is being prepared in Paris representing the acts of the apostles [. . .] Come, city, town, university; [. . .] come men of valour, solemn censors, magistrates, politicians, take part in the play of truth, by performing the deeds of the apostles. We summon there poets, orators true teachers and lovers of eloquence to be directors of this holy enterprise.[. . .] The time is fixed when the session will be held [. . .] to choose the most expert on the stage with requisite gesture and voice for the theatre [. . .] We want only at this time to learn and judge each person and see who can play them properly so that the roles can be distributed.

[Then followed a prose announcement that those who wanted to act in this play should attend] on the feast of St Stephen in the hall of the Passion [where they would find those] charged and deputed to hear everybody's voice [. . .] the said sessions will continue every day until the completion of the said *mystère*.[2]

[1] The *cri* is several stanzas long and was published widely both orally and in writing. For large-scale plays the Confrérie obviously needed additional actors.
[2] The performances on Sundays and feast days lasted eight months and were extremely successful.

E6   Problems for a production of the Old Testament, 1542

Mystères, vol. I, pp. 423–5

(i) The procurator-general attacks the company and the play

Both the organisers and the actors are ignorant people, men who work with their hands, knowing neither A nor B, who have never been trained or rehearsed to perform such actions in theatres and public places; moreover they do not know how to speak, nor [use] proper language and decent pronunciation nor [have] any understanding of what they say, to such a degree that often they make of one word, three; have a pause or stop in the middle of a proposition; [utter] incorrect speech or sense, making a question into an exclamation; or use gesture, emphasis or accent contrary to what they are saying which often gives rise to derision and public outcry in the theatre itself, so that instead of edifying, their play is turned to scandal and ridicule. These uneducated men without understanding in such matters, of low condition – cabinet-maker, usher, weaver, fishmonger – prolonged their performance of the Acts of the Apostles [in 1541] by adding apocryphal material and mingling at the beginning and end of the play lewd farces and low comedy [*momeries*], so that their play lasts for six or seven months whence resulted and continues, the ending of divine service, a coldness towards charity and alms-giving, endless adultery and fornication, scandals, derision and mockery. [. . .] While the plays lasted, the common people by eight or nine o'clock in the morning on feast days abandoned their parish Mass, sermons and vespers to go to keep their place for the said plays and stayed there till 5 o'clock in the evening. Preaching ceased for the preachers would have had no one to listen to them. On their way back from the said plays they made fun of the actors' performance loudly and publicly in the streets, imitating the poor speaking they had heard in the play; or other failure – shouting derisively that the Holy Spirit had refused to come down and other mockery. And often, the parish priests, so that they could amuse themselves at the plays, failed to say vespers or said it all alone at midday, not at the customary time; and even the cantors and chaplains of the Sainte Chapelle of this Palace [the *Palais de Justice*], as long as the plays were on, said vespers on feast days at midday and said them unthinkingly and on the move in order to get to the said plays.

[The performance of the Old Testament should be banned because] there are certain matters in the Old Testament which it is not expedient to declare to the people who are ignorant and stupid and who might from lack of understanding make this a reason to go over to the Jewish faith. (pp. 423–4)

(ii) The performance is allowed but on strict conditions

[. . .] They shall charge each person only 2s admission to the theatre; only charge 30 escus for the rent of each box for the duration of the said *mystère*; there shall be performances only on feast days that are not Solemn Feasts; they shall begin at one hour after midday and finish at five; they shall ensure that there is no scandal or riot; and since the people will be attracted away from Divine Service and this will diminish the alms-giving, they shall pay to the poor the sum of a thousand pounds, unless a larger sum is ordered.[1] (p. 425)

[1] The popularity and box-office success of the performances is clearly shown by the fact that the Confrérie accepted these stringent conditions.

(iii) Special performances are sometimes authorised

[On the 13th June] the duc de Vendôme [. . .] asked for permission to be given to the organisers of the Old Testament to play after dinner today as he wants to see the play and is in haste to set off on a mission for the king. The said Court[1] has not only given permission but has ordered, on behalf of the said duke, the organisers to arrange a performance for this afternoon (p. 425).

[21 June] For this once only [the Parlement will allow a performance on a Wednesday] because the Court appreciates that next Friday, the feast of St John there will be no performance because of the solemnity of the day. (p. 425)

[1] The Court is the Cour de Justice, not the royal court.

E7   The Confrérie acquires part of the Hôtel de Bourgogne for its future home, 1548

Mystères, vol. 1, p. 429

[The masters] explained and declared to the said dean and *confrères* that they had no longer a place or hall where they could carry on the business of the Confrérie since the hall [. . .] in the Trinité which they used to occupy had been taken away from them by order of the Court[1] and since that time they had had to rent and would henceforth have to rent a room and large space for a large sum of money each year [. . .] and might be forced to leave it at the end of the lease and move elsewhere and often change location and place which they could not easily find that was large, spacious and convenient enough for their needs [. . .] [they therefore suggest acquiring part of the Hôtel de Bourgogne, namely] an area 17 *toises* long and 16 *toises* broad[2] which seems to them suitable for constructing and making the large hall and other buildings necessary [. . .] at a rent of 100 gold ecus per year or a total payment of £4500T in instalments [. . .] [The Confrérie would also pay the taxes and the seller would have] a box of his choice for him, his family and friends, for life, without any charge.

[1] The Confrérie had applied to the Parlement to use the Hôtel de Bourgogne because 'three years previously the hall of the said Confrérie, called the hall of the Passion, had been taken over [. . .] and used as a poor house' (p. 427).
[2] For money and measurements, see glossary above.

E8   The Parlement bans all religious plays, 1548

Mystères , vol. i, p. 429

[The Parlement] prevent and forbid the said petitioners[1] from playing the *mystère* of the Passion of Our Lord or any other sacred *mystère* on pain of summary fine, allowing them, however, to perform secular *mystères*, decent and proper ones; [. . .] and the said Court forbids all others to perform or present henceforth any plays or *mystères* either in the town, suburbs and surrounding districts of Paris except in the name of the said Confrérie and to its profit.

[1]   After signing the contract for the Hôtel de Bourgogne, and extensive building work, the Confrérie had applied to the Parlement for permission to begin performances.

PERFORMANCES OF *MYSTERES* IN OTHER PARTS OF FRANCE

However regularly the Confrérie may (or may not) have performed in Paris during the early fifteenth century, there was little encouragement for other towns, particularly in the north, to put on large-scale plays while France was still in the throes of the Hundred Years' War and the civil strife between the Burgundians and the Armagnacs. However, from about 1450 onwards, a very large number of plays are recorded from all parts of France ranging from brief references, to complete accounts of the preparations, performance and aftermath. It is noticeable, that in provincial France, as in Paris, financial matters play a large role in planning the plays and we often collect the evidence for a play from account books. In the following sections, different aspects of theatre will be considered in turn, with examples from a wide range of texts and records. Within each section or subsection the material is arranged as far as possible in chronological order. It is noticeable that some towns had a tradition of regular performances – Amiens[1] performed the Passion eight times between 1413 and 1501 – while elsewhere only a single play is recorded. Plays from two towns in particular are fully documented with civic records and accounts which enable us to reconstruct the performance in every detail: the *Passion* from Châteaudun on the Loire performed in 1510 and the play of the *Trois Doms* [<*dominus*: lord see **E19**] staged in 1509 in Romans in Dauphiné, for which there is also an extant text. Texts could be either specially commissioned or, for the Passion, purchased from Paris or other large town. It is not surprising in view of the popularity of *mystères* that rules for their composition should be laid down in such books as the late fifteenth-century *Fleur de Rhetorique* [see **E13**].

1.   The early plays were presented by the Confrérie du Saint Sacrement, the local equivalent of the Paris Confrérie, but the later performances were organised directly by the town council. [see **E9**]

ORGANISING AND FINANCING THE CIVIC PLAYS

The reason for performing a play might be thanksgiving for safety from plague or a good harvest, but many of them seem to have been for the sheer satisfaction of performance. The organisation and especially the finance might come from several sources. Usually the civic authorities would bear the whole cost themselves, though they always sought to recoup a part of the outlay through admission charges [see **E69**]. Sometimes the local overlord or the church was involved financially and also personally.

The town as organising unit

E9   Plays in Amiens, 1413–1501

Mystères, vol. II

(i) A performance of the Passion in Amiens in 1413

[1413. To the Confrérie of the Saint Sacrement] 40sP[1] to help them pay for the great expenses they have had to bear to put on at the feast of Pentecost just passed [. . .] the Passion of Jesus Christ and his Resurrection, specifically for the cost and expense of the stages on which were accommodated the noble Bailiff, mayor, aldermen and some councillors of the said town. (p. 9)

[1] See glossary.

(ii) The town prepares to stage the Passion without the cooperation of the church, 1500

[Some priests and the *maistre des enfants* [master of the choristers] [. . .] presented today to the echevins a request pointing out that the *mystère* of the Passion [. . .] had not been performed in that town of Amiens for a long time, and that there were some respectable *compaignons*[1] and people of rank who would be very willing to take part in such a performance [. . .] and for these reasons the aforenamed asked us to grant permission for them to perform or have played the said *mystère* of the Passion [. . .] on the field where we were accustomed to perform the *mystère*; to allow actors to run about as devils [*faire courir les personnages des diables*] [. . .] and, with the help of God, they offer [. . .] to edify the people and the inhabitants of this town and of other places who would come to see the said *mystère*. [The council met on 3 February and two members] reported on the interviews they had had with the king's officers about the [. . .] Passion [. . .] which it was planned to perform this year; they had responded favourably but as for the lord bishop and the chapter, it seemed from their excuses and criticisms that they were not favourably disposed nor wished to contribute. Having debated the matter, the councillors decided that if the royal officials are in favour of the performance, without further discussion with the aforesaid bishop and chapter they will have the Passion [. . .] performed at the forthcoming feast of Whitsuntide. (pp. 77–8)

[1] *Compaignons* may be used for younger members of the craft guilds or for groups of performers.

E10   Seurre decides to stage a play of St Martin, 1496

Seurre, pp. 117–18, trans *Staging*, pp. 259–60

In the year 1496, the ninth day of May, the vigil of the Ascension, there assembled in the room of Maistre Andrieu de la Vigne[1] [a group of leading citizens] for the said Seurre, who made a deal with him to make and compose for them a text which should set out and declare *par parsonnaiges* the life of my lord St Martin so that on seeing it acted the common people would easily be able to see and understand how the noble patron of the said Seurre lived a holy and devout life. And this text was made and completed as it appears five weeks after that date. And [. . .] would have been acted on the next feast of St Martin[2] had it not been for the rumour of war and the great number of soldiers [*gendarmes*] who came to the said town of Seurre, so that the matter was put off for a time.

[1] This discussion is part of a lengthy account preceding the text of the play and written by the author, Andrieu de la Vigne, a well-known poet.
[2] July 4th. St Martin had two feast days in the Middle Ages, the other was 11 November. The play was finally performed on 11 October, after delays for bad weather, harvest, fighting and more rain.

E11   Civic rivalry and the hope of financial gain

Issoudun; trans. *Staging*, pp. 39–40

(a)   A successful performance in Issoudun, 1534

Some rich citizens of a small town called Issoudun, ten French miles from Bourges, decided to put on a Passion play. For this purpose they built a proper theatre [*theatrum*], just as we read that the Romans did down to the days of Pompey the Great. The costumes were also made expensively from all kinds of silks. The nobility with their womenfolk rode from great distances to see it. The organisers profited greatly as did the citizens of Issoudun in general, for the play attracted enormous crowds and everyone wanted to see it, for nothing like it had been seen in France in many years and it was therefore valued for its rarity.[1] The Passion [. . .] could scarcely have been finished before it was known that the citizens there had done such good business that several thousand francs were left, over and above all expenses, besides the praise which had accrued to them. (p. 226)

[1] The German author of this account was escorting two youths of the family of the counts of Swabia who were travelling in France.

(b)   Bourges prepares to go one better, 1535

The leading citizens of Bourges held a meeting and decided that, since everything had gone off so well and so profitably at such a small place as Issoudun, all that could well be put on with great honour and magnificence at Bourges, and that besides they had space for a theatre and other possibilities in every way better than those at Issoudun [. . .] They decided that not only they who were meeting the costs would benefit from it greatly, but that all the citizenry would derive great profit from it. And when they had requested and obtained from the court permission and privilege they began serious preparations with the intention of putting on the *Acts of the Apostles* [. . .] The extent of their expenditure on the costumes and other items can well be judged from the fact that several of them were almost ruined by the expense, for the simple reason that immediately after Easter [. . .] war broke out between the Emperor Charles and the King of France, so that the greater part of the nobility was called on to perform feudal service, and in addition there were all kinds of trouble in France. This proved a great hindrance to this play, so that they could not make so much money from it as would have been the case otherwise. (p. 228)

E12   Individuals could purchase copies of play-texts

(i) Abbeville buys a play text from Paris, 1452

F.-C. Louandre, *Histoire d'Abbeville et de la Comté de Ponthieu jusqu'en 1789*, 2 vols., Paris and Abbeville, 1844–5, vol. I, pp. 237–8

[Guillaume de Borneuil was reimbursed for] the sum of 10 gold ecus which he had paid for a copy of the play of the Passion in Paris from Master Arnoul Gréban.[1]

---

[1] Gréban's *Passion* was probably the best known of all the medieval French plays. Originally written about 1440 it survives in many manuscripts but the whole text was never printed.

(ii) Modane has a play-book of the Judgement, 1580

Modane, p. 6

Certain individuals from Modane [. . .] have paid out a certain sum of money to have and acquire the text of the *mystère* of the Judgement, [. . .] and seeing this *mystère* not being set forward, have called on [. . .] officers of Modane to inform them whether the community of the said Modane intend to play it or not [. . .] if they are informed that the said community want to play the said *mystère*, they will offer the said text to this community, on their warranty for the money employed to acquire the said text without asking for expenses. Otherwise they have been asked to hand over the said books elsewhere, which they will do. To which the said officers did not wish to give any reply without having first heard the will of the people of the said Modane [. . .] [who] agree and are of the opinion that, with divine help and all being done devoutly and for the instruction of the people, the community of Modane should perform this *mystère* and to this end retain the said texts, have them corrected and generally carry on as the matter requires until any other decision be taken by the community.

E13 On compiling *mystères*: a verse treatise on writing plays, 1501

Pro misteribus compilandis, reprinted Graham A. Runnalls, *Etudes sur les Mystères*, Paris, 1998, pp. 32–4

To make a notable chronicle or history or fair *mystère* which will be pleasing to people, after making a complete translation of the subject matter according to the facts without rhyme or prose style, one must with various ornaments [. . .] treat a noble subject.

If it is intended to make a play of it [*en personnnaiges*] one must consider and note down how many characters should be depicted without overcrowding or being inadequately supplied, then consider what form it is appropriate to give to each as is suited to them.

Item it is necessary to consider the deeds and status of lords [. . .] and give them servants, also to the ladies and the maidens and to all according to their rank, such as belongs to each lady or gentleman [. . .] for it is quite wrong if they are left without attendant squire or servant. That is the level of a mere common hack writer.

Item: everyone's speech should be suited to the person; if he belongs to the church he must speak like a churchman; let his speech be of wise things or rational argument or some other appropriate matter.

[Nobles should speak of chivalry, honour, tournaments and arms.]

If he is a burgess or a merchant he should speak of profit, trading in many lands [. . .] in order to enrich himself.

For labourers and tradesmen of town or suburb, be they masons or carpenters, smiths or silversmiths, let them speak in favour of their tools and their trades at all times.

If sailors come into the play it is right to have them mention stretches of water, and many places, and the winds of the sea. Being knowledgeable in the items used in boats, ships and barges; naming for example the anchor, mast, sails, oars and rigging.

ROYAL AND NOBLE PATRONS OF THE PLAYS

René d'Anjou, patron of the theatre

Unlike the English charter boroughs or the free towns of the Empire, French towns were closely linked with the local religious and secular authorities. A number of examples survive of tax rebates, or gifts of money or wood by local overlords towards the performance of plays. Especially noted as a patron of the theatre was René d'Anjou (1409–80), cousin and brother-in-law of Charles VII. He had inherited a claim to the kingdoms of Sicily and Aragon (though he never actually controlled them) and was often known as *le bon roi* René or the *roi de Sicile*. Throughout his long life he organised, encouraged and financed plays in all parts of his extensive territories, especially in Anjou and Provence.

E14   Payments for a play of the Resurrection, 1456
Angers, p. 75

To master Jehan Daveluys the sum of 8 gold ecus [...] for having made a clean copy of the text of the Resurrection with some additions [...]

To Pierre de Hurion the sum of ten gold ecus [...] for having costumed the characters for the Resurrection [...]

To Jehan Duperier, called Leprieur, the sum of 100 gold ecus [...] to be employed and expended on the *feintes*[1] and expenses for the *mystère* of the Resurrection of Our Lord, which the said *roy de Sicile* intended to have played at Pentecost ...

[1] *Feintes* or *secrets* are both commonly used for the special effects which were so important in *mystères*.

E15   A performance of the Passion at Saumur, 1462
René *Comptes*, p. 328

The *roy de Sicile* [...] desiring to have played the *mystère* of the Passion [...] to arouse his subjects' hearts to devotion, and considering that this could not be done without great layout and expense, has made a gift to the said burghers, merchants, inhabitants and dwellers of the said town of Saumur of the sum of £600T[1] [...] for making the scaffolds, special effects and proper and suitable costumes for the people of the said town.

[1] The money was in the form of a tax rebate to be paid in two instalments over successive years.

E16   Problems in raising money from the townsfolk, after René's death, Angers, 1486
Angers, pp. 78–9

[On behalf of the actors it is pointed out that] to help pay for the *feintes* of the said *mystère* it had been formerly granted the sum of only £100T with the intention and hope that the said actors or their deputies would collect and receive such sums as it might please the worthy burghers, merchants and others of the town to pay and contribute to provide the balance necessary for the said *feintes* [...] but despite all their efforts they had only managed to collect the sum of about £125 16s 7d, which

was quite inadequate to pay for the said *feintes* [. . .] In order that the *mystère* should
not be left unfinished which would have been a great scandal for the town, it was
agreed to give the actors [. . .] a further sum of £100T.[1]

[1] René had died in 1480 so the town had lost its patron.

Châteaudun and its overlord

Châteaudun was the capital of the Dunois region. The family name is used for the
duke, the region and the inhabitants. The accounts for the performance of 1509
survive but not the text, though it is probable from the references that it was a
Passion play of the Gréban/Michel group.[1] Larrivé who played the role of God is
described as an *ecuyer* in the duke's service [see **E33**].[2] Since he was sent to
Amboise to collect the play-text and had paid for one of the scaffolds in the auction,
he was evidently a man of some status.

1. A full discussion of the play can be found in the introduction to the edition of the
    accounts.
2. The *ecuyers* ranked below the chamberlains but above the heralds and domestic ser-
    vants, see George Small, *Georges Chastelain and the shaping of Valois Burgundy*,
    Woodbridge, 1977, p. 55.

E17   The duc de Longueville decides to have a play performed, 1509

Châteaudun

(i) The duke writes to the town of Amboise, 1509

I am told that you have the book of the [. . .] Passion which was staged in Amboise
and is said to be the finest that could be found. Therefore, since it is my intention
to have the *mystère* performed in our town, I ask you to kindly send me the book by
the hand of the servant who brings this letter, and I will see it is returned and sent
back to you.[1] (p. 69)

[1] The council preferred to have a copy made for the duke at their expense (p. 69).

(ii) The townsfolk agree to undertake the play

A general assembly was summoned by public proclamation at the sound of the
trumpet at all the crossroads of the said town and in the outlying districts, that all
the inhabitants and dwellers thereof should come to the marketplace of the said
town where was assembled [. . .] Jehan de Villexis, representative of the bailiff of
Dunois[1] [and other notables. It was agreed] to undertake a performance in the
town of Châteaudun of the [. . .] Passion [. . .] and that the costs [. . .] should be
advanced from the common fund of the town.[2] (p. 88)

1   The bailiff was the duke's representative.
2   To help persuade the Dunois to do the play, the duke renewed his previous concession to the town of
    the tithe on the retail of wines and beverages. This was to be farmed out to the highest bidders and
    brought in a total of £699 5s 1d. The duke also contributed 100 ecus (pp. 88–9).

(iii) Auctioning control of the audience seats

Further money [was] received by the said procurator from the high boxes [*chambres*] on the scaffolds, which rooms were advertised by the cryer in the town and suburbs to be offered to the last and highest bidders, according to the location and quality of the said boxes [. . .] £150 10dT. (p. 93)

JOINT VENTURES BY TOWN AND CHURCH

The play of the *Trois Doms* at Romans is the most notable example of a joint venture recorded [see **E19**]. A century earlier in Bar-sur-Aube a charter gave permission to the clergy of St Maclou to stage the life and miracles of their patron [**E18**]. Elsewhere the association was less formalised.

E18   Cooperation between the church and the laity

(a)   Clergy and townsfolk perform together, Bar-sur-Aube, 1408

Bibliothèque de l'Ecole des Chartes, series A, vol. III, ed. Vallet de Vireville, Paris, 1841, pp. 450–1

[The bishop of Langres to the dean and canons of St Maclou:] You, together with some of the burghers and inhabitants of the said Bar [. . .] on the two ferial days after Trinity or as soon as possible afterwards in a suitable and decent place or places [*platea seu plateis*] within or outside the town, in either French or Latin [*lingua Latina o materna*][1] with a variety of actors and suitable costumes [. . .] are permitted to set forth and recite the life and miracles of this noble confessor [. . .] on condition that it shall cause no scandal nor harm to the Catholic faith.

1   The choice of language permitted is particularly significant when linked to the warning about causing 'scandal' to the faithful.

(b)   Permission to play in the churchyard in Rouen, 1476

Edouard Gosselin, *Recherches sur les origines et l'histoire du théâtre à Rouen*, Rouen, 1868, p. 23

[The chapter of Notre Dame decided] that the said brothers [the Confrérie of St Romain] should set themselves up in front of the church and in the graveyard and they would be responsible for any damage done to the buildings or other things[1] belonging to the church. [It was ordered] to give to the brothers to perform the *mystère* of St Romain, the Bête de la Gargouille[2] which was kept in the church in a certain place in the care of the master of the fabric.

[1] The 'things' included vestments, regalia and tapestries.
[2] Apparently a local monster, possibly the dragon used in the Rogationtide processions.

E19   A joint venture at Romans, 1509

Romans, pp. 599–600

In the year 1508 [. . .] there gathered together the gentlemen of the Cathedral Chapter, the gentlemen of the Chapel of St Mary, of the church of my lord St Bernard and the merchants of the town of Romans with some of the inhabitants of the said town, where it was agreed and they decided all together to have the book made to perform the play of the *Trois Doms*[1] with the agreements written and declared hereafter; and the worthy Canon Pra of Grenoble was given the responsibility of making the said book, and the accounting of the money [was placed] in the hands of Master Escoferius, secretary of the gentlemen of the Chapter. And firstly it was said that the gentlemen of the Chapter and those of St Mary's will pay half of all the cost and expense which will be made, both for making the book and for the production of the said play. That is to say that the gentlemen of the Chapter will pay two thirds of the half and the gentlemen of the Chapel of St Mary's will pay one third of the half; thus the town will pay the other half of the said expenses.

[1] Namely the local saints: Severinus, Exuperius and Felicianus.

PREPARING THE PERFORMANCE

Play directors, auditions and actors

Having decided on their play and obtained a text, the town then had to select and rehearse the actors. Plays might be directed by a chosen group of townsfolk or by one individual. The director's role included casting, rehearsals and 'holding the book' or acting as prompter during the play. A separate technical director, often a painter, was used in the big plays, and might be brought in from another town [see **E28**, **E57** and compare **D25**].

E20   An organiser of a play at Vienne in 1400

Dauphiné, p. 39

To master Jean Gorio alias Galaot, organiser of the play [*istorie*], 40 florins as had been agreed plus 10 for a robe because we have been satisfied with his services and he has done most of the work.[1]

The Passion was performed at Pentecost in the cemetery of St Peter's Abbey and partly paid for by using income from the wine tax.

E21   A director and his assistant at Châteaudun, 1510

Châteaudun, p. 162

[To Francois Souef] for having been present at each and every rehearsal, acted as prompter and held the book every day that the *mystère* [. . .] was performed, the sum of six gold ecus.

[To Pierre Jahan, his assistant who] had made the general list of the roles in the *mystère* and the names and numbers of the actors so as to summon them on each rehearsal day, had been present at each rehearsal, correcting the text according to the views of the actors, copied and added in several additions offered by the said actors, had several times acted as crier at the crossroads in the town and outlying suburbs to advertise the *mystère* and let the general public know the days on which it would be acted [. . .] had been present on each performance day as prompter and guided the actors from the beginning to the end.[1]

[1] For all his services he received 10 gold ecus.

E22   The martyrdom of St Apollonia from Fouquet's miniature in the Heures of Etienne de Chevalier, *c.* 1460

Musée Condé, Chantilly

The scene represents the torture of St Apollonia.[1] The circular arrangement of the scaffolds with their mixture of audience and actors, might be compared to those at Autun or Bourges [see **E48**, **E49**] and there is a fool and a man who 'holds the book' whose staff may indicate his directorial function. However, there is considerable debate as to whether this is a reproduction of an actual performance.[2]

[1] A play of the martyrdom of St Apollonia is mentioned in a Tours bookseller's catalogue but has not survived. See Runnalls, *Etudes sur les mystères*, Paris, 1998, p. 405.

[2] For recent discussions of this vexed issue, see Philip Butterworth, '"The Martyrdom of St Apollonia" and " The Rape of the Sabine Women" as Iconographical Evidence of Medieval Theatre Practice', in *Essays in Honour of Peter Meredith*, ed. Catherine Batt, Leeds Studies in English 29, Leeds, 1998, pp. 55–68, and the debate between Gordon Kipling and Graham Runnalls which occupies pp. 26–120 of *Medieval English Theatre* 19 (1997) [see bibliography].

E23   Careful preparations at Seurre, 1496

Seurre, p. 117

Then the roles were made and set out by the said Maistre Andrieu, and the following worthy persons were appointed to distribute and give these out to people
proper to perform them: [the mayor, and three leading citizens] who after careful
and mature deliberation distributed the said roles to each person as the situation
required, receiving from the players the oath required in such case to be prepared
to perform as soon as the right moment should come. After which each one individually took care to study his role and to go to the church of the said lord St

Martin or to St Michael's when it was necessary to see the rites and ways of doing things for when they would perform in public.[1] [When the date of performance was finally fixed] the said players carried out their duty of providing suitable clothes and accessories.[2]

---

[1] The play calls for St Martin to say Mass on the stage. A direction specifies that 'He can say the whole Mass but will not consecrate. Then when he reaches the elevation of the Host, it must be chest-high only' (p. 473).

[2] The costumes mentioned in the stage directions include many church vestments.

E24   The Prologue describes a performance of a St Nicholas play

'Le Miracle de St Nicholas; prologues', ed. Charles Samaran, *Romania* 51 (1925), pp. 191–7

Shame would urge me to silence so that I might not offend anyone, but I have great desire in my heart [. . .] to make known the enterprise of my companions who have put all their efforts [. . .] to show you now *par personnages* a miracle of my lord St Nicholas,[. . .] protesting, nevertheless, that if we say anything blameworthy we submit it to the correction of wise men who speak with authority. And we beg you not to take it amiss or rebuke us from envy but patiently pardon our ignorance and let not our play offend anyone.[1] We beg you to excuse our youth for it is not by arrogance that we have bound ourselves together but for the love we have for St Nicholas, whom we serve and of whom we are parishioners, for he is honoured in this place.[2] (pp. 191–2)

---

[1] Compare the defensive tone of other prologues, e.g. **C63(i)**, **D41**.

[2] The play is probably being performed in the churchyard.

E25   Controlling the actors at Chalon-sur-Saône, 1497

Mystères, vol. II, p. 74

[. . .] Also it has been agreed that [the organising committee] shall attend all the rehearsals that are held and that if they decide any actors are not competent to play the roles allotted to them, they can make changes and give other roles to those whom they consider appropriate or do all that they consider proper within reason. [Thirty inhabitants] swore on the gospels [. . .] to accept willingly the roles offered them in the Play of St Sebastian and to perform them and costume themselves at their own expense and cost; each as is appropriate and necessary to the character portrayed.[1]

---

[1] Failure to do so incurred a fine of 10 escusT.

E26   The playwright praises the actors at Seurre

Seurre, pp. 120–1

[During Lucifer's speech] the man who played Satan, when he prepared to enter through his trapdoor underground, his costume caught fire round his buttocks so that he was badly burned. But he was so swiftly succoured, stripped and reclothed that without giving any sign [of pain] he came and played his part, then retired to his house. [Inspired by his courage and] with the help of my lord St Martin who took the matter in his hands, things went a hundred times better than expected. After this the father and mother of St Martin with their attendants came onto the said playing area and made such a lively beginning that everyone – both actors and audience – was very surprised and indeed, abolishing this former fear, the said actors were filled with such confidence and boldness that no lion in his den nor murderer in a forest was more bold and confident than they were when they performed.

COSTUMES AND PAYMENTS FOR ACTORS

Normally actors were not paid but occasionally priests might be paid for playing God and a few examples occur of help with expenses especially for the costumes which each actor had to provide at his own cost (with the result that the accounts rarely include information about them). Amboise also paid to obtain 'from the Bishop of Tours or his vicar, dispensation for the clergy who have roles in the play to let their beards grow' (*Amboise*, p. 14). A single example of an understudy is recorded, who was paid for his time.

E27   Some costumes are prescribed in Michel's *Passion*

Michel *Passion*

(i) Satan disguises himself for the temptations

Here Satan comes to Jesus in a hermit's robe to tempt him. (p. 35)

Satan takes off his hermit's robe [. . . and] puts on a doctor's robe. (p. 36)

(ii) Working costumes for the apostles

St Peter and St Andrew [. . .] follow Jesus in their fishermen's clothes until the Second *Journée*[1] when they appear in apostles' dress.[2] (p. 53)

St Thomas follows Our Lord in his carpenter's clothes but leaves all his tools behind. (p. 55)

The twelve Apostles in their secular dress follow Jesus. (p. 66)

---

[1] A *journée* was one day's playing-time but might be of very varied length from two to eight or more hours.

² The apostles' dress seems to have been a mantle (at Mons, which follows Michel's text, it is red [Michel *Passion*, p. 292]). After the arrest, St John drops his mantle and flees naked (ibid., p. 295) but is given a white silk robe by Martha at Bethany (ibid., p. 299).

E28   A costume subsidy in Châlons-sur-Marne for a good actor, 1507

Mystères, vol. II, p. 91

[. . .] Several wealthy men from the said Châlons who are not taking part have offered and promised to costume at their expense the man who is playing the role of Lucifer because he is poor and a good player.

E29   An expensive robe for Christ at Châteaudun

Châteaudun, p. 157

Paid [. . .] the sum of £8 15sT for five ells of red taffeta at 35sT per ell [. . .] by commandment of Monseigneur ¹ [. . .] which was used to make the robe for him who played God² when he was led before Pilate dressed in purple [*pourpre*].³

¹ The duc himself paid for this robe.
² Larrivé, the *duc's ecuyer*, see **E33**.
³ The biblical 'purple' is crimson, not violet. For other 'purple' robes, see Lynette R. Muir, 'Playing God in Medieval Europe', in *The Stage as Mirror*, ed. Alan E. Knight, Woodbridge, 1997. pp. 25–50.

E30   Jean Bouchet advises the citizens of Issoudun, 1534

Bouchet *Epistres*, p. XCII

Assign your roles to people of the right ages and do not use borrowed costumes (even if they are of gold) unless they are appropriate to the characters being portrayed. It is not good that learned doctors, Pharisees or councillors should be dressed the same as Pilate.¹

¹ Bouchet had been asked to direct the play but declining because he was too busy with his legal work, sent a letter of good advice.

E31   People in Modane disagree about who should pay for the costumes, 1580

Modane, p. 8; trans. *Staging*, p. 36

And the said Benedict Nuer and Jean Jordain, butchers, have protested that they understood the costumes of the actors were to be provided or undertaken at the expense of the community¹ [. . .]

Mathe Valloyre [. . .] does not consent to the costumes being provided in common at the expense of the same community [. . .]

François Lanfrey, Mathe Pinet and Claude Torne said that if they were eligible to take parts [*ils seront capables faire personnages*] they had no power to undertake [their costumes, but two townsmen] said they were ready to support all the expenses [of the costumes] on their account but did not wish to play a part [. . .]

Master Michel Replat, the ducal notary, agreed to act, but did not agree that the said costumes should be provided by the community.

Claude, son of the late Pierre Coct, said he had enough to pay without that and did not consent to it [. . .]

The said current officers declared themselves in agreement with the majority of the above voices first declared.[2]

[1] The play of *Antichrist* at Modane in 1580 is one of the latest for which we have such details.
[2] It is not clear which way the majority had voted.

E32   Priests are paid to play God at Amboise, 1494, 1507

Amboise

[1494] To Michel Laloue, £9 for his trouble and effort both in studying the role given him for the *mystère* [. . .] which had been planned for performance in the said town, for which he had toiled for more than half a year, and for having attended and cooperated in several rehearsals made with the other players. (p. 10)

[1507] To Messire Jehan Baudeau, priest, who had the role of Our Lord to play in the Passion, has been allotted and paid the sum of £8T for his efforts and recompense in having rehearsed the said role for four months ending on 15 March 1507 which is a rate of 10sT per week. (p. 13)

E33   Payment for an understudy at Châteaudun, 1510

Châteaudun, pp. 139–40

And because they feared that some problem of illness or other problem might affect Larrivé who was playing God, it was ordered by the said abbot that the said procurator should make Fleurentin Boucher rehearse the role and for this he would receive £7 on the understanding that if any mishap befell the said Arrivé, the said Boucher would play God.

REHEARSALS

Rehearsals are often mentioned in the accounts of the big civic plays. They might be held in the town hall or other suitable building since the set was not available till nearly the time of the performance. They were normally taken by the director or his assistant. The entries usually refer to either heating or refreshments.

E34   Rehearsals at Romans, 1509
Romans

(i) Paid 23rd December for coal to take to the Cordeliers [religious house where play was staged] for the rehearsals, amounting to 9 liars.[1] (p. 603)

[1] Similar entries for wood for 5th January, 11th January, 17th February.

(ii) Paid the 18th March[1] for collation made at the Town Hall [*officiala*] while holding a rehearsal, 7s 9dT. (p. 609)

[1] Similar entries for 9th April, 14th April, 15th April, 21st April, 29th April, 7th May.

E35   Special refreshments for women at Châteaudun
Châteaudun, pp. 115–16

For the rehearsals attended by several men and women acting in the said Passion, for collation [*gouster*]: 6sT for twelve pints of wine de la Bruyere; 10d for small cakes and 1s 3d for Cappandu apples for the women.[1] Total paid 8s 1d.

[1] Refreshments for other rehearsals do not mention the women (p. 119).

WOMEN IN THE PLAYS

In Paris there is no evidence of women acting in plays before 1600, but the presence of women in the cast is a feature of the later French provincial civic plays. Sometimes their presence is only indicated by references in the accounts [see **E35**] but sometimes lists of names and status indicate that women from the best families could join in these plays.

E36   Many women listed among the cast at Romans, 1509
Romans, pp. 593–7

Silence: Claude, wife of maistre Joffrey Vache and daughter of Girard Chasteing.[1]
   Asia: Suzanne Alexe, daughter of Jehan Alexe [. . .]
   Dame Jullie, the emperor's wife: Noble Jehanne de Boysson, wife of noble Pierre Varse [. . .]
   Severinus' sister: Alis, wife of maistre Jehan Bonniaud
   Felicien's mother: the woman Arniere, wife of Ponson Luc.[2]
   Our Lady: Jaquemine, wife of aforesaid Jehan du Boys.[3]

[1] She also played Poudrefine the torturer's tart. All the women's roles were played by women. With two exceptions they were married, many of them to men of rank and importance.
[2] The description of '*femme Arniere*' suggests a lower social class than many of the others.
[3] Proserpine, Queen of Hell, one of the devils, an obvious 'drag' role, was played by a man.

E37   The director coaches one of the actresses

Châteaudun, p. 162

To the venerable and discreet messire Francois Souef,[1] monk of the [abbey of] the Madeleine of Châteaudun for having directed, coached and instructed the wife of Jehan Roussel who played the role of Mary Magdalen in the *mystère*.

[1] Souef was the director of the play [see **E21**].

E38   Women acting at Valence in 1526

Dauphiné, p. 28

[In the play of the *Trois Martyrs*] all the principal clergy and citizens took part, to the number of twenty-two persons, including the wife of Monsieur de Dorne who portrayed Our Lady and Suzanne de Genas who represented Holy Dove.[1]

[1] This was almost certainly a 'Holy Spirit' role

E39   A woman plays the Mother of God in Grenoble, 1535

Mystères, vol. II, p. 127

Françoise Buatier, who played the role of the Mother of Christ, excited general admiration by her gestures, voice, pronunciation and delivery which charmed all the spectators. In her grace and beauty were allied to fine speaking.

MUSICIANS IN THE PLAYS

Although the actors were all amateurs, the musicians were normally professionals and had to be paid. Music played an important role in the plays. In addition to professional instrumentalists, such as those mentioned at Romans and Châteaudun [see **E40**, **E41**], most plays included singers for the music of Heaven and there are many examples of songs by shepherds and other groups on earth. Court scenes also required music and sometimes dances are specified as they are for Salome who dances before Herod.

E40   Trumpeters are employed at Romans

Romans

Paid on 23rd April to Maitre Perdigon for an authorisation given to Andrieu du Boes, alias of Paris, to go to Vaureas to sign up the trumpets 1s. (p. 614)

Paid 9th May for the breakfast of the four trumpeters because they will play in the morning (*firont les obades*) the day of the parade (*montra*) 3s.6dT. (p. 618)

Primo. 30th day of May 1509. I have paid to Honorat Barnaut, trumpeter of Vaureas, for the remainder of the 50 florins which were owed to the 4 trumpets of which he was part: 40 florins 9s. (p. 623)

E41   The music at Châteaudun proves very expensive

Châteaudun

(i) The first players want too much money

18th May. For three trumpet players who came and played this morning on the scaffold in the presence of my lord the abbot, by order of my lord the lieutenant, to see if they played well and if they would come for the performance of the *mystère* of the Passion and what salary they would ask for this [. . .] and the said performers came back after dinner on the same day to the said scaffold and asked too high a salary. They were paid 5s. (pp. 127–8)

(ii) Three other players are hired

26th May [. . .] to Guillaume Chasteau and two of his fellow musicians the sum of 4 gold ecus for salary and expenses for that they had worked for two days playing their instruments[1] at the said *mystère* (including the day of the parade) £7. (p. 130)

5th June [. . .] to Guillaume Chasteau, musician, and two of his companions the sum of £10 10s for salary and expenses for the three days they played their instruments for the Nativity of the said *mystère*.[2] (p. 138)

[1] Their instruments are not mentioned but we may assume they were also trumpeters.
[2] They received in all for twenty days £69 (p. 63). The total paid for the music for this Passion is the highest recorded from France.

(iii) Liveries provided for all the musicians

3rd July paid [. . .] to sire Jehan Berthran, burgess and merchant of Châteaudun, the sum of £20 6s 3d for 12½ ells of green and violet taffeta at 32s 6d the ell, which was used to make the costumes for the five musicians[1] who played each day of the Passion so that they might have a livery as had been promised them when the contract was made.[2] (p. 147)

[1] A drummer and his son were also hired. They received £12 15s for playing on seventeen days (p. 150).
[2] The payments for special livery remind us that the play was initiated by and performed in the presence of the duc de Longueville.

STAGES, DECORS AND SPECIAL EFFECTS: SCAFFOLDS AND STAGES

The commonest form of staging for the civic *mystères* involved one or more scaffolds in a fixed location, with seats for the audience and often a surrounding fence.[1] This temporary 'theatre' might be constructed in a variety of places including a churchyard, the courtyard of a religious house, a marketplace and a filled-in town moat.[2] The arrangement of the stages varied considerably from town to town and information about these scaffolds also comes from a variety of sources, including prologues to play-texts, contracts with carpenters, financial records, and audience descriptions.

[1] *Echafaud* [scaffold] is the usual term in French. See Graham A. Runnalls, '"Mansion" and "Lieu": Two Technical Terms in Medieval Staging?', *Etudes sur les mystères*, pp. 467–78.
[2] A number of these locations with much other staging detail is described in Henri Rey-Flaud, *Le cercle magique: essai sur le théâtre en rond à la fin du moyen âge*, Paris, 1973.

Stage descriptions taken from the play texts

Several saints' plays begin with a prologue describing the locations for the different characters in what is obviously a multiple stage set [see **E42**]. From the St Louis play we learn that the scaffolds are surrounded by curtains which enable the actors to change their costumes between entrances.[1] The Rouergue Last Judgement play which has a similar prologue is one of a group of fifteenth-century biblical plays in a dialect of the Languedoc, from the Rouergat region round Rodez, Aveyron. No other records survive about their performance. Staging references within play-texts often merely describe the location of the scaffolds rather than their construction and use. The scaffolds at Seurre are mentioned in the long preliminary description but without reference to construction, dimensions or use; we are also told that the actors were responsible for decorating them. They may have been separate units as at Châteaudun, perhaps with actors and audience mixed on the scaffolds [see **E50**].

1.   See *Staging*, pp. 77–8, 123.

E42   Prologue to the play of St Laurent, 1499
Saint Laurent, p. 1; trans. Staging, p. 77

I want to show you the characters, the actors and the stages too, so that you can understand what we want to make known to you. This construction [*habitacle*] here shows Paradise and represents it. There is the one called God: it is right that the place should be beautiful. The angels are around him. Philippe the Roman Emperor who holds all men under his rule is seated in his high place. Beside him is his son Philippe and round them are their knights [. . .] Lo, there is a great king of Gaul [. . .] and here is the defender of Rheims [. . .] Beyond you see the domain of the great country of Spain [. . .] Decius is on this side [. . .] and in this place are also seated four wicked men, torturers [. . .] In this place lives and dwells the wise provost Ypolite [. . .] You can see in this dwelling [*repaire*] Sixtus, the holy father of Rome [. . .] The good widow in this stand [. . .] See the goldsmith in this low place [. . .] On this side is Hell [. . .] My division is finished.

E43   The Last Judgement play from Rouergue

Rouergue *Judgement*, p. 58; trans. *Staging* p. 87

And first our Lord should be seated on a well-adorned throne and shall display all his wounds, in the presence of everyone, all gilded. Next there should be four angels, two on each side, one carrying the cross, the next, the column with the rope fastened to the column, the next the nails and the scourge, and the next the lance and sponge. And there shall be a well-adorned throne for Our Lady to sit on at the appropriate time on her Son's right hand. And there should be two angels, each with his trumpet and in Paradise should be St Michael and a great number of angels with him. And the saints should be on the other scaffold [*escadafal*] each in his place arranged on benches. And St Peter should wear his tiara as pope and the emperor and kings as becomes their condition, dressed according to their estate, in garments of green and black and squirrel-fur [*mosa*]. And there shall be emperors and kings and churchmen and women dressed according to their estate; the Jews shall be together and the others similarly and shall approach when summoned by the angels. The devils shall be at the side [*apart*] when they have come from Hell and been before Eternal God and heard their sentence. Our Lady, richly dressed, shall be all alone in her place [*son loc*] on the large scaffold and shall be there until it is time to approach. Justice and Mercy and Life shall be all together on the large scaffold. Death shall be in its place on the scaffold. The Jews shall be at the side of the large scaffold [. . .] the idolaters shall be at the side of the scaffold [. . .] [also] the bad Christians [. . .] the members of religious orders: Bernardines, Carmelites, Augustinians, Dominicans, Cordeliers, Minorites [. . .] [God summons angels who sound their trumpets and call on the dead to rise] [. . .] and after [. . .] the dead shall rise, some from the tombs and the others from secret places and shall all come before God and kneel in silence. After which, the saved shall move on to a scaffold lower than Paradise, on the right-hand side and the damned shall remain on the large scaffold on the left-hand side.

E44   An unusual stage layout from Rouen in 1474

Le Mystère de l'Incarnation et Nativité de Nostre Saveur . . . Jésus-Christ représenté à Rouen en 1474, ed. Pierre le Verdier, 3 vols., Rouen, 1884–6, frontispiece

The incarnation of our Saviour and Redeemer Jesus Christ which was performed as is written down hereafter in the year 1474 at Christmas[1] in the town and city of Rouen in the new marketplace. And the scaffolds [*establies*] were set up in the southern side of it from the hostelry of the Crowned Axe to the hostelry of the sign of the angel according to the order described at the end of the codicille. But the scaffolds for the six prophets were away from the rest in different parts and areas of the said new market [. . .] To avoid tedium we will not describe the locations; you can recognise them by the notice [*escritel*] which you see above them.[2]

[1] The Rouen *Nativity* survives only in an early printed version which includes the brief stage layout description. It was unusual to have a major outdoor play in mid-winter.

[2] The scaffolds were apparently labelled.

Stage descriptions from records and contracts

A number of carpenters' contracts have survived with details of the arrangement of the scaffolds and the seating for the audience. For example, the very detailed accounts of the play at Romans [see **E46**] make it clear that that stage was rectangular, with towers at each corner and various other buildings on it. The audience sat round each of the four sides but were separated from the acting stage by palings [see **E22**]. There was space under the stage by which actors could move from place to place and emerge from the trap doors. Information about wood and other materials also appears in the accounts.

E45   Compensation for damage to the stage at Amboise, 1496

Amboise, p. 10

To Mathurin Prunelle for supplying two hundred beams of firwood to make the scaffolds on which the Nativity of Our Lord was performed before the king on Christmas night, and for the loss he suffered in that about a hundred of the beams were stolen and the others were split and spoilt by the nails used for the said scaffolds. £11 15s.[1]

[1] This Christmas performance was prepared for Charles VIII and his queen, Anne of Brittany [see **E97**].

E46   A carpenters' contract from Romans, 1509

Romans, pp. 797–8

30 December 1508. Firstly, the afore-named carpenters shall be required to make a platform, 30 paces long and 15 paces wide, at 2 paces to the *toise*, which platform shall be raised on pillars to the height recommended by the commissioners [. . .] secured by strong beams and morticed joints [*clevellees*].

Item. The said carpenters will undertake to enclose the said platform from the top downwards with planks well joined together so that no one can see underneath the said platform, and from the platform upwards to supply an enclosure of squared poles in the manner of stakes with nets and double-painted cloths to form a trelliswork [*pour trelisser*] with the said poles inside to the height of four feet or thereabouts.

Item. The said carpenters shall undertake to make within the said platform, turrets, castles, towns of wood and stakes and canopies as necessary, with portals

and openings for the *feintes* and steps. And change them from day to day according to the requirements of the *mystère* [. . .] Item the said carpenters shall undertake to make Heaven and Hell in wood with carpenters' work [. . .]

Item. The above-named said carpenters shall undertake to construct all round
the said platform sloping tiers [*pantes couches en deppendent*] six *toises* in width
approximately which shall be made of large pieces of wood, good and strong, set
closely side by side, each four pieces being held by a beam, furnishing the four
angles of the said slopes with wood and beams in the form of right-angled brackets [*en maniere d'arpie*] and between each beam shall be provided pieces [of wood]
called planks good and proper for the work and for seats appropriate to it as the
commissioners require and they shall make two gates to the said slopes for going
in and out and shall make a privy [*ungz retraitz*] in the said platform if it is needed.[1]

---

[1] This privy was for the actors rather than the audience, who had theirs at the ends of the rows of
boxes on top of the raked tiers of seats [see **E68**].

E47   Two-storey scaffolds for the Vienne *Passion*, 1510

Mystères, vol. II, pp. 100–1

The *mystère* of the glorious Passion [. . .] was performed in the great garden of St
Peter's abbey where the finest scaffolds were built, two stories high not counting
the space below for the common people. And there were 96 boxes each locking
with a key and each was rented at 4 ecus soleil and everyone who entered for the
play paid 2 liards [farthings]. The awnings overhead were of lengths of serge
stitched to one another, and stretched on ropes coloured black and white. They
looked more beautiful to see than ever such scaffolds had been seen.[1]

---

[1] Records of performances survive from many towns in Dauphiné from 1398 to the late seventeenth
century. See Table in Jacques Chocheyras, *Le théâtre religieux en Dauphiné . . .*, Geneva, 1975, pp.
149–52.

E48   A theatre to hold 80,000 at Autun in 1516

Catalogus gloriae mundi, Bartolomeus Cassaneus, Frankfurt, 1597, part 12, section 66;
Latin text in *Staging*, pp. 280–81; trans., p. 63

We, the people of Autun in the year of the Lord 1516 constructed an excellent and
magnificent amphitheatre in the field of St Lazarus, which is in the middle of our
city. It was made of squared timbers constructed with extraordinary skill at the
expense of the church and the citizens. There was nothing comparable in France.
It had two hundred and forty boxes in the upper parts, all divided by wooden partitions covered in panelling. There the churchmen, nobles, senators, knights, gentlemen, and dignitaries of the city had their places. In the acting area [*cavea*] or
lower part, the tiers [*gradus*] and seats were so arranged that the circuit increased
in size as it rose up where the people were sitting together under linen awnings

which protected the spectators, both sitting and standing, from the rain. The actors were also covered by these in the middle of the acting area [*theatralis scenae*] and were separated from the people by a ditch full of water and other barriers.[1] In this amphitheatre, eighty thousand people could be easily accommodated[2] and as the performance had been publicised in the neighbouring districts the spectators poured in in almost endless numbers.

[1] The use of a ditch to separate the stage from the audience recalls the English stage plan for *The Castle of Perseverance* [see **D14**].
[2] This is obviously an exaggeration but it is not certain how much. The Roman Colosseum could seat between forty and fifty thousand.

E49   Bourges erects its theatre in a ditch

Issoudun, vol. III, p. 228; trans. *Staging*, p. 40

Now at Bourges there was on one side an astonishingly large ditch at a place in the town which was somewhat on an elevation; the old people said that once many years ago a tower stood there[1] [. . .] This ditch or the open space [. . .] the citizens obtained from King Francis as a theatre [. . . and] began to fit it out as an amphitheatre of a pretty good size, in any estimation almost as large as the capacity of the Colosseum at Rome. Also on the ground they had their channels through which they could secretly direct the water into the acting area [*caveam*] and out again.

[1] The ditch was probably in fact an old quarry.

CHATEAUDUN, 1510: A SPECIAL CASE

The structure and dimensions of the scaffolds at Châteaudun are not clear. They were arranged in two facing lines and consisted of a series of different sized scaffolds with boxes [*hautes chambres*] on top which were occupied by both actors and audience. The actors paid to have the use of the boxes for themselves and their families [but see **E51**]. The only indication of how much the rest of the audience paid are the takings recorded for each day. The whole area was enclosed.

E50   Stage arrangements at Châteaudun

Châteaudun

(i) The scaffolds are in two facing lines

From the first scaffold counting from Paradise in the direction of the *Ostel Dieu* [infirmary] of the said town [were twenty-three scaffolds] [. . .] From the first scaffold beginning at Hell and going in the direction of my lord abbott's house [were sixteen scaffolds]. (p. 93)

(ii) The scaffolds and playing area are covered with canvas

The procurator made a bargain with Roullet Macon, mercer, and Colas de
l'Abbaye, goldsmith and merchant, to supply ropes and cloths to cover the playing
areas [*parcs*] and scaffolds as they had been begun in the cemetery of the church
of the Magdalene of Châteaudun [. . .] If they failed to cover the said scaffolds with
cloths well and suitably on the days of peformance they would have the sum of ten
pounds for each such day deducted from the money they were to have for the said
covering of the said scaffolds [. . .] and it was agreed that after the feast of St Rémy
[Oct. 1st], the same Macon and de l'Abbaye could take back their ropes and cloths
and sell them off. The cloths were supported from two tall masts. (p. 105)

E51   Actors might receive rebates on the rented boxes
Châteaudun

The procurator should make punches to make the tokens which would be given
and distributed to the actors in the said *mystère*.[1] Which the said procurator made
in lead and in card, embossed severally and variously with the arms of the duke
and of the town. (p. 152)

[. . .] Francois Chastel [paid £5 15sT but] it was reduced to 70s because he acted
and his tokens were redeemed for 2s 6d each,[2] Value 45s. (p. 93)

[The provost of Châteaudun, Girard Guelet paid £8, but] the whole sum was repaid
because the said Guelet [. . .] his wife and his children acted in the play, and their
tokens were redeemed. (p. 97)

[Jehan Lecomte received a rebate of £5 10s on his £8 5s] because he played several
roles and he is due his tokens. (p. 97)

[Charles de Robeton paid nothing] because the beauty [*la belescee*] who played the
Magdalene occupied this scaffold. (p. 94)[3]

[Jehan Larrivé[4] paid nothing] because he played God and because Georges Souef
who played Annas occupied it. (p. 94)

---

[1] For the auction of the boxes, see **E17(iii)**.
[2] This is the only reference to the value of the token so may be assumed to be a standard.
[3] For the woman who played Magdalene, see **E37**.
[4] For Larrivé see **E33**.

PROPERTIES, DECORS AND *FEINTES*

Having constructed the stage it was necessary to make the properties and decors
needed. Sometimes the sets are described in the play-text, especially in the printed
editions of the *Viel Testament*, and the manuscript and later printed versions of the
Angers *Résurrection* of 1456 [see **E52**; compare the *Adam* Paradise (**C38**)].

Numerous small references to these items survive but the most important are those which refer to the *feintes* or *secrets*, the special effects which were usually made by a professional to a contract [see **E53–E62**]. Often the specialist was imported from a distance [see **E54**, **E55**]. Some of these contracts are very extensive: for the Bourges *Acts of the Apostles* in 1536, the list runs for more than twenty pages. In other towns the requirements were more modest. The late fifteenth-century Provençal Director's Notebook contains specific instructions for making the effects he requires [see **E57**]. Some of the descriptions, including the detailed account of the method of making a fire-breathing devil [see **E60**], are accompanied by small drawings with various details labelled.

E52   A detailed stage direction for Paradise, Angers, 1456

Le Mystère de la résurrection. Anger (1456), ed. P. Servet, 2 vols., Geneva, 1993, vol. 1, p. 318

Here the angel named Seraph, guardian of the Earthly Paradise having red clothing and face and holding a white naked sword in his hand, speaks to the Penitent Thief through a crenelation of the wall to the right of the wicket of the said Paradise. Which paradise should be made of paper and within there should be branches of trees, some in flower, some loaded with fruits of different kinds such as cherries, plums, almonds, oranges, pomegranates, figs, grapes and similar things, artificially made. And other branches of beautiful may blossom, roses etc., which should be newly cut on the day of the said play and the ends put in vessels filled with water to keep them fresh and so that they can be clearly seen through the crenelations of the wall of the said Earthly Paradise.

E53   A flying mechanism for Simon Magus at Aix, 1444

Maurice Raimbault, 'Une réprésentation théâtrale à Aix en 1444', *Revue des Langues Romanes* 67 (1933–6), pp. 263–74; trans. *Staging*, p. 100

Item: within the auditorium, the machine for Simon Magus[1] which can lift up three people, secretly, all safely belted and then descend again equally secretly in such a way that it cannot be seen. (pp. 272–3)

[1] Simon Magus (Acts 9:9–11) appears in several plays of SS Peter and Paul.

E54   Amboise uses a variety of specialists, 1496

Amboise, p. 11

To Jehan Le Noir for thirteen fuses filled with gun powder and a pound of gunpowder used in the play of the Nativity; twelve of the fuses were put into an idol and the other in Paradise whence it was thrown down on the said idol to burn it [. . .] To Anthoine Bryant, painter, for 7 dozens of gilded pewter and two glass platters used to make the suns for the Nativity. [Other items were used] to make the *feintes* such as idols, angels' wings, the emperor's crown, a *tymbre*[1] for God the Father, a lily [*lys*] which carried the angels across the park to bring tidings to the shepherds. [The town paid] for six pounds of glue and a bushel of rye flour used to stick together the paper to make the lily [. . .] for gold leaf to put on a star and for making the said star [. . .]

[1] *Tymbre* may mean a drum, a bell without a clapper or, most likely here, an animal skin, such as ermine.

E55   Châteaudun sends for a painter from Evreux

Châteaudun, p. 104

It was agreed between the said procurator and master Guillaume [Brudeval], the painter, that he should make each and every one of the *feintes* necessary and appropriate [. . .] for the sum of one hundred gold ecus worth thirty five sous tournois apiece [. . .] The town had to provide him with dwelling house, beds, linen, crockery and other household utensils for the period in which he would be working on the *feintes* and other things necessary for the said *mystère* of the Passion.[1]

[1] The town paid fifty sous a month rent for the house they provided for Guillaume and his family, for eight months and eight days. Total cost: £28 12s 6d.

E56   Two men plan a play festival in Athis-sur-Orge, 1542

Wilma S. Deierkauf-Holsboer, 'Les Représentations à Athis-sur-Orge en 1542', in *Mélanges . . . offerts à Gustave Cohen*, Paris, 1950, pp. 199–203; trans. *Staging*, pp. 103–4

Christofle Loyson, painter [. . .] promises Maître Jehan Vinot clerk, of the church of Athis-sur-Orge and Nicholas Temponnet, merchant and innkeeper [. . .] to furnish and hire three devil's costumes, a mask for Death and [for] Envy, four crowns, four sceptres for the kings, a wig, beard and mitre for God the Father, two heads of angels supplied with wings, [. . .] all other devices necessary for the Selling of Joseph, the Judgment of Solomon, and the Rich Sinner [play of Dives and Lazarus] which the said Vinot and Temponnet are putting on this current year in the village of Athis[1] for a period of eight days and a day for the parade [*monstre*]. And also to provide the cannons and flaming fireworks necessary for the said devil-scene all according to his said trade of painter and to provide the materials necessary to make everything as the painters are accustomed to do in such a case [. . .] This contract is made for the sum of £7T [. . .] which the said Vinot and Temponnet promise him and guarantee to supply and pay [. . .] by degrees as he makes the aforesaid devices [. . .] And they promise to feed, during the said nine days, the said painter and his servant.

[1] A privately organised performance on this scale seems to have been a rarity. Athis was not far from Paris so the fact that only the Confrérie could play publicly in Paris itself may be relevant here.

E57   A specialist describes how to create the *feintes*
Provençal Director's Notebook

And to bring forth the bloody sweat, Jesus must wear a wig and when he puts it on he must put underneath it two or three carefully positioned sponges, full of vermilion well diluted and must be careful not to press on the wig until the moment when he wants to sweat blood so that when he prostrates himself on the ground he must put his hand on his head and press firmly so that the sponges spout forth the vermilion that they have absorbed.[1] (pp. 26–7)

For the nails of Jesus, it would be better that a large wooden nail should be made, hollow and filled with vermilion and there should be a small hole at the end so that the blood flows over the hand. (pp. 7–8)

[1] A similar wig was used at Châteaudun where they paid 'at the command of monseigneur [. . .] the sum of £6T to fetch and pay for the trick wig which Larrivé wore to play God, which was brought from Amboise' (see Châteaudun, p. 129).

E58   Dummy bodies and dolls are used for scenes of torture

(a)   The Martyrdom of St Hippolyte in the St Laurent play
Saint Laurent, pp. 162–4

Then they attach two horses to the hands in addition to the two which are at Ypolite's feet. And after he has been dragged on a hurdle across the playing area by the first two horses, he speaks what follows [. . .] And then when he has spoken, the torturers put a dummy, similar to him, in his place, to which they attach the four horses, one to each limb. [Dialogue] Then the torturers exchange and put a dummy in the place of Ypolite under the protection of the scaffold and then they harness the other two horses as well as the first two and do not move. [Dialogue in Paradise. The torturers each mount a horse.] Then each one individually spurs his horse and each drags away his limb of the dummy. [Dialogue.] Then they untie the pieces and leave them in the playing area, and when they have done it they go away, and the angels come to look for the soul among the pieces.

(b)   The tortures of the damned
Rouergue *Judgement*, pp. 164–6

Then shall be prepared the throne of Pride, and the devils come out of Hell leading Pride all dressed in fine clothes and a collar round the neck. And they set her on the throne and secretly they must put there a dummy figure made to look like her. And let him who plays Pride position himself behind the throne, and the devils shall torture the said person in silence, and when they have done so Pride shall speak thus [dialogue between Pride and the devils]. Then Pride shall be put in the pit, and when that is done they shall bring out Avarice [. . .]

E59   An extensive list of *feintes* for Bourges, 1536

Bourges *feintes*

(i) The martyrdom of Stephen

The face of St Stephen must appear radiant as the sun to terrify the false witnesses who testify against him. There must be artificial stones for the stoning of St Stephen. There must be an artificial soul for St Stephen and artificial birds and other artificial creatures to guard his body. (p. 10)

(ii) A miracle for the death of Saint Paul

St Paul shall be beheaded and the head will bounce three times, and from each bounce will spring up a fountain from which will flow milk, blood and water. (p. 24)

(iii) Elaborate arrangements for the Assumption

Jesus Christ must descend from Heaven and come to the deathbed of the Virgin Mary accompanied by a great host of angels and he must bring the soul with him. At the moment that Jesus enters [. . .] there must be a strong scent of different perfumes. There must be a dummy soul.

There must be a crown of twelve stars to crown the said soul in Heaven [. . .] There must be a round cloud shaped like a crown, in which are several artificial angels holding darts and naked swords in their hands and if possible there should be some live ones to sing. (p. 15)

HELL

Many of the special effects mentioned in the contracts refer to devils and Hell and include the use of gunpowder and fire crackers [see **E60–E62**].[1] There were also many devices for making a noise. In some plays a separate Limbo section of Hell was built in the form of a tower or prison for the prophets and patriarchs in the plays of the Harrowing of Hell. The most elaborate Limbo is described in the Paris Resurrection (see *Staging*, pp. 90–1).

1.   For information on the making and use of fireworks in the Middle Ages see Philip Butterworth, *Theatre of Fire. Special effects in early English and Scottish theatre*, London, 1998.

E60   Instructions for making a devil mask that will blow fire

Provençal Director's Notebook, pp. 50-3

The devils' masks must have something in the mouth as in the drawing, for those who want to make fire come out of the mouth, ears and nose. Then it can be even more entertaining to make them blow fire out of their mouths. These masks must include between the mouth of the mask and the face of the person wearing it a place separated off to hold the fire of a dimension adequate to hold 2 or 3 coals and this area must be all covered with mud on the inside so that the fire does not burn the mask. And there must be 30 or 40 goose quills filled with powdered sulphur inside and aqua vita and when you want to make the fire come out you do no more than take a quill in the mouth and blow so that the sulphur comes on to the fire and the flames come, all blue, out of the lips of the devil's mask. (Sketch bears the legend 'fire will come out here'.)

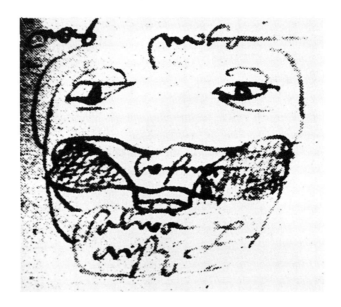

E61   Expenses for the Hell Mouth at Vienne, 1400

Dauphiné, p. 39

To master Jean de Ligio who undertook the construction of the Hell Mouth without charge, and who is a man of honourable rank, because we are satisfied with his services, ten florins; in addition to defray his expenses for himself and his servants at the inn: 10 florins 4 gr.

To two painters from Lyon who spent three days painting the Hell Mouth and the other things needed, 6 florins.

To [. . .] Pierre de Geneve for eighteen linen cloths needed for Hell: 20 gr.

To Colin Boursier who made the eyes for the Hell: 6 gr.

To Jasserand Gros for the wood needed to make the Hell Mouth: 5½ florins.

To Guillaume du Prieuré, for the wood for the great tower,[1] the pillar and the gallows, also his salary and that of his assistants 4 florins.

To a scabbard-maker in Vienne for his days' work and the skins he supplied for the said Mouth: 22 gros

To Jacquemette, widow of Jacques du clos, apothecary, for [. . .] the aqua vita she provided for Hell, 8 florins 10 gros.

To Etienne Brochier, for the small hoops furnished by him for the said Mouth and for the toil and trouble he had to assemble the said hoops, 6 gros.

To Jean Collonge carpenter for the ten days work of him and his assistants in making Hell and for five large hoops and two dozen small hoops he supplied: 3 florins 4 gros.

¹ This is probably the tower used for the Limbo of the prophets. The pillar would be for the flogging and the gallows for Judas.

E62   Contract for *feintes* for the Judgement, Modane, 1580

Modane

(i) The contractors are fireworks experts

[. . .] On the 24th January 1580, master Thomas Mellurin senior of Ouix in Dauphiné and master Thomas Mellurin, inhabitant of Modane being present in person, painters and experts in handling fire with gunpowder, who having been required [. . .] to use their skill in the service of the public performance [. . .] of the *mystère* of the great Judgement of God at the feast of Whitsun next, [have agreed] to serve them in the art of painting and skill with fire necessary to the said representation. (pp. 27–8)

(ii) Fire and cannon for the devils and Antichrist

They shall make and supply fireworks [. . .] for each of the devils every time they emerge from Hell and for Lucifer each time he speaks, each day [. . .] and shall make a great blaze of fire and noise every time the devils take some dead to Hell, every day.

They shall fire cannons and bombards when Gog and Magog greet Antichrist and for the war which is enacted both on the first day with the kings, as on the second against the emperor, with smoke in front in the most skilful way possible [. . .] Then they shall make water boil in the cauldron in which the seneschal is put and do it with fireworks without heating the water.

They will paint Antichrist's pavilion in which he tries to go up to heaven and will make various sorts of blazing fires when he falls to earth [. . .]. (pp. 29–31)

AUDIENCES, SEATING AND ADMISSION CHARGES

Attracting an audience

Many of the plays in France were mounted at great expense, and looked to recoup part at least of their outlay by admission charges. Since the plays might last from three to ten days consecutively with longer plays spread over a number of Sundays and feast days, there was also a general benefit to the town's commerce if it could attract large audiences to see them. Several methods of advertising were used to attract these audiences, including invitations to neighbouring towns and persons of importance. Local nobility also attended with assiduity [see **E63(b)**, **(c)**].

E63   Audiences come from many places to see the plays
(a)   A ten-year-old describes his first play, 1486

Jean Bouchet, *Annales d'Aquitaines*, Poitiers, 1537, p. 296

In Poitiers,[1] at the beginning of the summer I saw acted and set forth by *mystères* and *personnages* the Nativity, Passion and Resurrection of Our Lord Jesus Christ with great success and richness Many gentlemen and young ladies of the Poitou region and the surrounding area were there and it was attended by my Lord Jacques du Fou, seneschal of the said region of Poitou.

[1] Jean Bouchet (1476–c. 1559) [see **E30**] later became a lawyer in Poitiers and continued to watch and help prepare plays all his life, as he describes in the *Annales* and *Epistres*. (See Jennifer Britnell, *Jean Bouchet*, Edinburgh, 1986.)

(b)   An important audience for St Barbe, Laval, 1496

Guillaume le Doyen, *Annales et Chroniques du pais de Laval . . .*, ed. M. H. Godbert and Louis La Beaulière, Laval, 1839, p. 74.

My lord[1] and his noble countess were present all six days [. . .] My lord had sent for the gentlemen of the Parlement of Paris to attend at his cost, to see the deeds of St Barbe. There were tents on the field[2] which would have held a hundred men.[3]
   [Guillaume chronicled the plays in Laval and Maine for forty years.]

[1] Guy, comte de Laval who had taken an active part in the preparations for the play.
[2] Presumably the '*pre de Botz*', where the play was performed.
[3] It is not clear if these were for the Parisians or the audience in general.

(c)   Refreshments for noble visitors, Mézières, 1534

Mystères, vol. ii, pp. 122–3

To Dame Rondeau for 12 pots of wine given at different times to my lord the Comte de Porcien, Mme de Buzancy and others who had come to see the said *mystère*, at 3s 6d the pot, 42s.

(d)   Refreshments for the whole audience at Rheims, 1490

Mystères, vol. ii, pp. 56–7

[The echevins decided] that the noble lords who came to see the *mystère* of the Passion, should be offered goblets of wine from the two puncheons which the procurator[1] had bought for the purpose for £24T [. . .] and there were actors who had dressers loaded with silver ware and all decorated, and they had wine and fruit offered in their name.[2]

[1] Jean Fouquart, the author of the unpublished memoirs from which this account is cited.
[2] Fouquart also says that throughout the performance, women went round offering wine and cakes to the audience and actors.

THE MONSTRE

The parade to display [monstrer] the splendour of the forthcoming production usually took place about two weeks before the performance [see **E64**, **E65**]. Groups of costumed performers marched through the streets in a long procession which always began with the devils and ended with the Heavenly Host. Sometimes tableaux, especially of Hell and Heaven, might be presented on floats. For the Châteaudun monstre it was agreed 'that it would be good to have and make a huge dragon on which the one who played Lucifer would ride and the said dragon would spit fire from all apertures and would be carried by many men' (Châteaudun, pp. 128–9).

E64   A long procession for the *monstre* at Seurre
Seurre, pp. 118–19; trans *Staging*, p. 260

When the day came appointed for the monstre[1] it was proclaimed by a trumpeter that all those who had parts in the said mystère should assemble at midday in Lombardy,[2] each one dressed in his costume [. . .] The said players assembled in the said place and were arranged in order one after the other, mounted, equipped, armed, and adorned so well that it could not have been improved upon. And [. . .] they made such a long procession that when God and his angels left that place riding behind the others, the devils were already beyond the tower of the prison near the Chantblanc gate [. . .] And there was a space of barely two and a half feet between the horses, and a total of around nine score horses.

[1] The Seurre monstre took place only the day before the performance (which then had to be postponed for twenty-four hours because of rain).
[2] The rue des Lombards, which still exists in Seurre.

E65   The account of the magnificent and triumphant *monstre* of the *mystère* of the holy Acts of the Apostles, staged at Bourges, 1536

Bourges *monstre*; trans. *Staging*, pp. 265–7

(i) An eye-witness describes the organisation

Do not imagine, kind readers, that the description hereafter given of the parade is a fairytale, nor that the directors should have wanted anything written but the truth. It is certain that it has been set down from beginning to end as the eye beheld it [. . .] About six o'clock in the morning, the mayor and echevins of the said town, accompanied by the officers thereof, to the number of thirty-six, wearing their red and green gowns; and the said officers on foot, each having a white staff in their hands to keep order and protect the throng of people, made their way to the Abbey and Monastery of Saint-Sulpice of Bourges, in which were already the major part of the townsmen who were to portray the characters of the said *mystère*; all of whom, after having heard Mass, withdrew, each one to the rooms and other places prepared for them to dress and array themselves, in which place they were all, according to their rank, honourably and with goodwill, welcomed by the religious of the said monastery who offered them all food and wine in abundance. Then, about nine o'clock, there came also to the said abbey, the members of the judiciary to give help and support to the organisers of the said *mystère* and see how the parade would be ordered. To this end they sounded the trumpets, drums and pipes, which was the signal given to everyone to present himself ready to be placed in his order [. . . at] the place ordained which was a great open space, surrounded by walls, in which there were three big gates by one of which on the side by the church, all these people entered, and at the other of these gates, giving onto the grounds and gardens of the said Abbey surrounded and enclosed by water-filled ditches so that no one could enter them except through this gate, was someone, appointed to the task, and standing in a high place, holding in his hands the order of the said *monstre*, the number, names and surnames of the characters in it, whom he called out in turn; the said members of the justiciary, mayor and councillors conducted and guided them to the other, third gate of the said area, round a lake which was in the said meadow and gardens, so that it was possible to see the whole of the said procession except the horses and triumphal cars, Paradise and Hell which had remained in the great court [. . .] At eleven o'clock, they began to emerge from the said abbey [. . .] (pp. 16–19)

(ii) One of the floats in the procession

Next came the Eunuch of the said queen of Ethiopia, on another car or chariot, painted to look like red and green porphyry with great scrolls and gilded foliage in the antique style, representing different birds flying in the air, and his coat of arms. The said Eunuch was seated on a chair made in gilded flower-work covered with a silk cloth. He was dressed in cloth of gold and silver and over it a gown of crimson velvet, lined in crimson satin, worked all over in skilled gold work. His doublet was of fringed cloth of silver grey-blue velvet in the Ethiopian style on which hung many clusters [*houppes*] of pearls. He was adorned with chains and rings in great numbers and of great value and worth. In front of him was placed a reading desk on two long supports of gilded scroll-work, on which stood an open book, whose cover was of silver gilt worked in large figures. (p. 60)

ADMISSION COSTS AND ACCOMMODATION

The civic drama, having gone to great pains to attract its audiences also took considerable trouble to house them conveniently – for a consideration. All this involved the construction of seats [see **E17(iii)**] and sometimes the provision of special accommodation for distinguished visitors [see **E66**, **E67**]. Accommodation varied, according to cost, from seats on raked steps to special boxes [**E68**, **E69**].

E66   Payment for making a box for René d'Anjou, 1471

René *Comptes*, p. 329

Perrin le mercier, carpenter, the plaintiff [. . .] said that about three years before, the *mystère* of St Vincent was performed in this town of Angers [. . .] and he made a scaffold for the said *roi de Sicile* twenty-four feet long and thirty wide, all floored with planks dovetailed and fastened with great iron nails, covered with planks and shingles and on the said scaffold was the large room, the privy for the said *roi de Sicile* and between two partitions of planks, places for the chancelry, rooms and secret privies also fastened with great iron nails.[1]

---

[1]   René [see **E14**, **E15**, **E16**] had attended the play in 1471, but by 1474, the carpenter had not been paid for making his box and sued, claiming £25 for supplying the wood and making the scaffold. He was awarded £15.

E67   A three-storey scaffold for the mayoral party, Angers, 1492

Mystères, vol. II, p. 61

[In Angers] on the playing area where the *mystère* of St Catherine had been played [carpenters worked on] the three storeys of the scaffold of my lords the mayor and echevins of the said town.

E68   Special family boxes at Romans

Romans, p. 798

Item, the said carpenters shall undertake to make above the said slopes[1] eighty boxes [. . .] floored with planks so that one cannot see between the beams and between each two of these rooms shall be wattle walls and on the side of the entrance to the said rooms shall be solid timbers in order to put a lock on the door of each room. And on the viewing side they shall undertake to put a barrier to prevent falling and a beam across on account of the small children. [They shall] make on the entrance side of the said rooms a gallery with wooden railings and at each end [. . .] shall make a privy [. . .] and ladders to ascend to the said galleries.

[1] For the construction of the 'slopes' see **E47**.

E69   Admission costs and receipts at Romans
Romans, p. 624

Here follows an account[1] of the money received both for the boxes and for the scaffolds [. . .] for the three days of Pentecost:

First for the seventy-nine boxes rented at 3 florins the box: 252 florins.[2] Item. on the first day of Pentecost at ½s per person, old or young, the scaffolds raised 153 fl 4½ gr. [. . .] Total for the scaffolds, excluding the boxes: 443 fl. 9¾ gr. Total received for the tiers and the boxes: 689 florins 11s 9dT.

[1] Romans has the most detailed accounts and includes all the money taken as well as spent. For money see glossary, above.
[2] There were eighty-four boxes altogether but four were given to those involved in the play and one remained empty.

CONTROLLING THE AUDIENCE

Because of the great numbers who attended the plays, strict security precautions were enforced which might involve doubling the watch, making innkeepers register the names of their guests, and closing some of the city gates [see **E70**, **E71**, **E72**].

E70   Arrangments to keep order at Grenoble in 1398
Dauphiné, p. 37.

[Payment for torches for the watch] the vigil of the Nativity of John the Baptist, when the Passion of Our Lord Jesus Christ was performed: 4 fl. 9 gr.

Item for a quantity of wine and other expenses incurred by those in charge of the watch for two nights during the perfomance of the said Passion play; 16 gros.

E71   A proclamation by the canons of the church of St Pierre, Beauvais, 1452
Mystères, vol. II, p. 23

It is forbidden [. . .] to make trouble, noise, disputes or anything that might hinder the actors or to climb on the stage and scaffold [. . .] without permission and licence [. . .] on pain of punishment or fines such as reason will adjudge.

E72   Special precautions are taken for the performance of Jean Michel's *Passion* at Angers in 1486

(i) Plans to ensure order in the town during the play

Mystères, vol. II, p. 50

To ensure silence at the said play they elected [list of names including] the procurator royal, the regent of the university,[1] the procurator general of the university [. . .] It was agreed that during the play only the gate on one side of the city should be open and that only the wicket but each day the keys should be handed to the constable who can open [the door] if necessary.

[1] The involvement of the university is unusual. They also contributed to the expenses.

(ii) No one allowed in from an area where there is plague

Angers, p. 76

Innkeepers in the town and the suburbs are warned to take care whom they receive in their houses and not to accept anyone coming from Brissac or anywhere where there is plague.

E73   Several devices are used to achieve silence during the Angers *Passion*

(i) Threats to noisy spectators

Angers, p. 77

On pain of prison and fines [. . .] let each person be silent and obey those ordained to ensure the silence for the play.

(ii) Mass might be said on stage

Mystères, vol. II, p. 50

Item and to make a better beginning and achieve silence, if it is thought expedient, Mass will be said at the play on a decently prepared altar.

(iii) An author's suggestion

Michel *Passion*, p. 107

Nevertheless, the Canaanite woman's daughter can begin the session speaking like one possessed until there shall be complete silence.

E74   A perfect performance at Autun, 1516

Catalogus gloriae mundi, Bartolomeus Cassanaeus, Frankfurt, 1597, part 12, section 66; Latin text in *Staging*, pp. 280–1; trans., p. 63

The performance was perfect; given in the honour of St Lazarus [. . .] not for vainglory but in honour of the Divine Majesty and St Lazarus [. . .] And God therefore granted that it was performed with no whistling or uproar among the people or any mockery; also that it rained overnight but all day no finer weather for those days had been seen.

AUDIENCE REACTIONS

In the sixteenth century a number of writers speak of plays they have seen, the most frequent being Jean Bouchet of Poitiers [see **E30**, **E63(a)**]. Like most of his material, his criticisms are contained in the many verse *Epistres* he wrote. Of the Poitiers *Passion* of 1534 Bouchet has many good things to say but also some criticisms [see **E75**]. Other comments are those made by de la Vigne on the play at Seurre [see **E10**, **E23**, **E26**, **E64**], or the account of the Bourges *monstre* [see **E65**]. François de Bonivard (later famous as the Prisoner of Chillon) took part as a young child in the play of St Blaize and was martyred with his mother. His reference to this incident is taken from a treatise Bonivard wrote in 1563 on languages – hardly the most likely place to look for theatrical criticism [see **E76**].

E75   Lack of rehearsal time for the *feintes*

Bouchet *Epistres* xc

If there were defects in the *feintes* and in the covering of the playing area (arranged in the round) complaint must be made to the contractor and the maker of the *feintes*. The painters too, but without being contemptuous for they had neither the space nor the time. God allowed this so that overweening pride should not corrupt the merit of this work.

E76   A soldier or a knight? A linguistic problem

Advis et Devis des Lengues, composé par Bonivard, 1563, Bibliothèque de l'Ecole des Chartes, series B, vol. v (1849), p. 339

In my childhood I was engaged with another child to act in a tragedy of the passion and martyrdom of St Blaise where they needed two children [. . .] and also soldiers who led him to his martyrdom. But as the Latin history used the term *milites* the soldiers who here were merely acting as executioners were dressed as knights which made me think that emperors always used knights as their executioners.

A LAST WORD ON THE VALUE OF BIBLICAL PLAYS

In his old age, Bouchet looks back with pleasure on the *mystères* he has seen and draws from his experience some conclusions on the value of dramatising the Bible [see **E77**]. The last of the *Grands Rhétoriqueurs*, Bouchet was still writing in 1557, but died not long after.

E77   Jean Bouchet regrets not seeing the Acts of the Apostles performed

Bouchet *Epistres* XC

I am content, considering my age, yet, while I say my rosary, I much desire to see the Acts of the Apostles performed, for it is the continuing sweet fruition of the Passion of Jesus Christ. Nay the form and manner in which Holy Church was planted. It is true that I see them written down and hear them preached; [but] the mind is more satisfied by seeing than by hearing; matter that is seen live is more easily apprehended when you hear it.

II   *Farces,* sotties *and moralities*

More than 300 texts are extant of the farces, *sotties* and moralities which, though there are a number of farces combined with the biblical and hagiographic plays [see **E80**], need to be considered separately from the big civic *mystères* with their wide-ranging community appeal. These fictional plays, though not civic, were essentially urban in their outlook and subject matter: the farce portrayed scenes and characters from contemporary society, the morality presented personified abstractions or allegories, and the *sottie* (or *sotie*: both spellings are found) was a peculiarly French type of satirical play performed by actors wearing the headgear of fools (*sots*), the traditional long-eared cap of the jester [see **E88**]. Performances of these genres are generally less well documented and rarely figure among civic financial records. However, some indications of staging, action and even costume can be gleaned from payments in royal accounts and the stage directions of the plays.

A number of texts from the late fifteenth century refer to the practice of having a play, usually a farce, at weddings. The actors were virtually professional and were paid in the same way as the musicians [see *Comédiens*, pp. 330–3]. The performers of monologues [see **E83**] were mostly still amateurs but from them developed the professional farcers who made part of the troupes at the Paris theatres of the early seventeenth century. Despite many attacks, the farce retained its popularity longer than any other medieval genre and some were still being praised in the seventeenth century, especially the most famous of all – the *Farce de Maistre Pathelin* with its refrain *Revenons à nos moutons* [Let's get back to our sheep] which has passed into general linguistic usage.

FARCES AT COURT

A few references in the royal accounts from the end of the fourteenth and early fifteenth centuries show that farces were popular with both Charles VI and Queen Isabeau [see **E78**]. Indeed, a legacy in the king's will (Charles VI died in 1422) left money to 'Jean du Bois dit Mauvisant, farcer' [*farseur*].[1] A number of entries in the accounts of René d'Anjou, *roi de Sicile* also refer to court entertainments [**E79**].

---

1.   This is the earliest known example of the word *farseur* in French.

E78   Farcers at the royal court in Paris, 1388–1422

Roy, p. ccvii

[February 1388] To Jehan de Besceul, player of farces [*joueur de farses*] for money given to him by order of the king, for hay and oats for his horse: 64sP.

[February 1409] To Fatras and his companions, players of farces, for performing before him [. . .]

[April 1415] To Jehannin Cardon, actor [*joueur de personnages*] for him and six of his companions who had played before the said lady [Queen Isabeau] several farces and plays.

E79   René d'Anjou employs many entertainers

René *Comptes*, p. 324

[1447] To Guillaume Bernart [for having paid] two ecus to those who performed a farce before the said lord [in Lyon].

[1448] To Nicolo de Candia who performs tricks on ropes etc. 10 florins [. . .] for having twice displayed his skill before him.

[1449] To the said Dauvergne [cordwainer] for a pair of shoes with long points for the World, when the morality was acted, 5s.

FARCES IN THE CIVIC *MYSTERES*

Farces were sometimes intercalated into the civic plays, such as the farce of the *Boy and the Blind Man* [*Le Garçon et l'Aveugle*][1] found in a number of texts and incorporated into the Semur *Passion* where the blind man is Longinus. Another well-known theme of the fraudulent beggars, the Blind Man and the Cripple, is introduced in the Seurre *St Martin* play with the couple trying to avoid being cured because they will lose their livelihood. When the saint's relics pass by them and they are healed, the Blind Man rejoices but the Cripple still laments his lost income. The admixture of 'lewd farces' with biblical material was one of the criticisms of the *Acts of the Apostles* played by the Confrérie de la Passion [**E6**]. A number of *mystères* had a role for a *fou* or *sot* or *villein* who provided humorous commentaries or interludes in the action. The text was sometimes left blank in the manuscript but usually the censor insisted on seeing it before it was played [see **E82(ii)**]. Details of the problems faced by a group of farcers can be assembled from documents in the Dijon Archives: a farce was inserted in a play of St Eloi performed mainly by Carmelite friars, 'to wake people up and make them laugh', but the writers were accused of having included words and phrases in the verse 'tinged with mockery, reproach or derision against the honour of our lord the king, the Dauphin and their court' [see **E80**].

1.   This farce seems to derive from Tournai in present-day Belgium and dates from *c.* 1280. There is a valuable translation by Jean Dufournet (Paris, 1982).

E80 Trouble for the actors in Dijon, 1447

Dijon, pp. 268–71

[Proceedings were started against] the players of this farce who without permission from the authorities performed this scene, and [it was considered] whether the actors of the *mystère* should be included with those who performed the farce. [One actor explained he had seen the farce performed in Beaune and] having found it very amusing [had produced it when there was a suggestion] of inserting a farce in the play of St Eloy. He added that during the rehearsals no one had noticed in the words used anything derogatory or touching anyone's honour especially not of our lord the King or the Dauphin [. . .] and for his part if he had known or been told by anyone that it was wrong to play this farce [. . .] he would not have joined the group [. . .] but he was no clerk and could only read a little.[1]

---

[1] Unfortunately the end of the story is not recorded.

E81 A farce to amuse a rain-soaked audience, Seurre, 1496

Seurre, pp. 119–29; trans. *Staging*, pp. 260–1

[It poured with rain all day] which was very distressing for the actors and everyone else. And indeed those who had come from the towns round about decided to go away when they saw the weather so changed. When the said mayor and others learned of this they decided, when the weather improved, that they would perform a farce in the playing area [*sur le parc*] to satisfy and please them. So the trumpeter cried that all the players should at once go, ready costumed, to the house of M. le Marquis [. . .]

Then the actors were put in order and they left the house [. . .] following each other so impressively that when they came to the playing area everyone was much astonished. They circled round as was proper, and then each went to his box [*loge*] and the only people who were left in the playing area were the actors in the farce of the Miller[1] [. . .] which was so well acted that everyone was delighted and nothing more was done that day.

---

[1] The farce of *The Miller*, written by the author of the play of St Martin, was certainly a 'lewd farce'.

E82 Fools and comic peasants in the *mystères*

(i) The *sot* ends the session in the Troyes *Passion*

Le Mystère de la Passion de Troyes, ed. Jean-Claude Bibolet, 2 vols., Geneva, 1987, vol. I, pp. 138–9

[After Adam's death] *Le Sot*: We must talk of a different dish: I'm going to have a look in the kitchen. This fasting has gone on too long! I advise everyone to have dinner. *Here dinner will be taken.*

(ii) The censor insists on seeing the Fool's text, Savoy

Mystères, vol. II, p. 560

I have read this except some remarks by the fool [*stultum*] which are not included and the same will not be allowed unless they have been seen first. Provided other corrections or cuts are made as marked it is permitted to perform what has been seen in this book.[1]

---

[1] The text is a fifteenth-century play of St Sebastian that was being performed in 1547.

E83   In a monologue printed in 1530, a farcer describes his repertoire

Comédiens, p. 332

If I am wearing a fool's cap [. . .] I counterfeit a clever talker full of little jokes [. . .] If I am wearing a mourning hat, I fret all by myself, I weep and lament a great deal, sighing with a tear in my eye like a friend of the deceased. If I have a doctor's hood, I counterfeit the orator, and appear from my manner like a very worthy preacher.

E84   Jean Bouchet condemns the farce as unworthy of students

Bouchet *Epistres (Morales)*, I, xiii

[In comedy] one studies subjects that are lewd, wicked and degenerate [. . .] assaults on women [. . .] despicable adulteries [. . .] We call them in the vulgar tongue farces and often criticise the actors of them, and it is right that those who earn their livelihood by such a means should be noted rogues. Scholars should not be tempted by such knowledge.[1]

---

[1] For details of Jean Bouchet see **E63**.

SOTTIES AND THE BASOCHE

The best-known groups of actors of the satirical plays or *sotties* were the *Basochiens* and the *Enfants sans Souci*.[1] The Basoche was the name given in the fifteenth century to the association of law clerks attached to one or other of the Parlements, the legal/administrative body of Paris and other large towns. The Basoches were highly organised, like most medieval confraternities, with a king and ministers having total control over the activities of the group.

The earliest document to mention their activities dates only from 1442, but it is in the form of a decree of the Parlement of Paris condemning the actors to several days in prison for having disobeyed the order forbidding them to perform plays. It is thus certain that such performances were known before this date. The plays were banned again in 1476 [see **E85**].

The Paris Basoche is the best known but they also flourished in many regional capitals where there was a local Parlement. Jean Bouchet of Poitiers, lawyer, and former *Basochien*, summed up the function of these satirical groups in 1536 in a letter to the King of the Basoche in Bordeaux [see **E86**].

1. For a detailed study of these groups see Louis Petit de Julleville, *Les Comédiens en France au moyen âge*, Paris, 1885, especially chapters 5 and 6, and Howard G. Harvey, *The Theatre of the Basoche*, Cambridge, Mass., 1941.

E85   An edict against the *Basochiens*, 1476

Comédiens, p. 101

[The Court of Justice] has banned and bans all clerks and servants both of the Palais and the Chastelet of Paris[1] of whatever condition they may be, from henceforth performing publicly at the said Palais and Chastelet nor elsewhere in public places, farces, *sotties* or moralities [. . .] under pain of banishment from the kingdom and confiscation of all their goods.

[1] The Palais de Justice was the supreme court of Paris, the Châtelet the law-enforcing arm. Each had its own Basoche.

E86   Jean Bouchet to the King of the Basoche in Bordeaux

Bouchet, *Epistres (Familières)*, xxxxii, xxxiv

King bazilical of the illustrious Bordigal Parlement [it is your function] to declare by grave tragedy, rude satire and feigned comedy, the good of the good and the evil of the wicked.

THE *ENFANTS SANS SOUCI*

The *Enfants sans souci* in Paris were a group of actors under the rule of the Prince des Sots (Prince of Fools) and Mere Sotte (Mother Fool). They may have been separate from the Basoche or simply a subgroup: 'It seems safe to assume that the *Enfants sans souci* was an amateur play-acting society recruited largely (or entirely) from the Basoche.'[1] Like the *Basochiens*, the *Enfants* presented plays on a wide range of subjects, in the three major modes of farce, *sottie* or morality. In 1512 a programme of three plays, one of each type, all by Pierre Gringore and based on related subjects, was given in the Place des Halles, the Paris marketplace [*Comédiens*, p. 165]. The *Enfants* also performed their farces and moralities at the theatre of the Confrérie de la Passion both before and after the edict of 1548 [see **E8**]. Similar bodies or *sociétés joyeuses* existed in many other major towns, among the best known are the *Infanterie de Dijon* under Mere Folle and the *Connards* of Rouen and Evreux.[2]

[1] Howard G. Harvey, *The Theatre of the Basoche*, Cambridge, Mass., 1941, p. 26.
[2] In Montferrand in 1536, the consuls gave 42s to the '*Enfants sans souci* who performed [*jouerent*] before the duc and the comtesse d'Alais on both the days they stayed in the town'. (Graham A. Runnalls, 'Le théâtre en Auvergne au moyen age', in *Etudes sur les mystère*, pp. 133–60).

E87   Jean Bouchet sums up the purpose of satire
Bouchet *Epistres (Morales)*, I, xiii

[. . .] Other poets are called satirists for all their verses are attacking public evils and reproving them by their satirical verses which prick them till they draw blood, fearing nothing but with all liberty of speech praising virtue and detesting all vice without sparing any evildoer from fear [. . .] But because it sometimes attacks individuals and causes scandal, satire is said to be a bad thing. In France it is called a *sotie*, because *sots* re-enact on stages in polished language the great follies of high and low society. And this is allowed by kings and princes so that they shall know the disarray of their councils, which no one dares to tell them unless they are warned of it by Satire. The king, Louis XII, wanted them to perform them [*sotties*] in Paris and said that by these plays he learnt of many faults which were hidden from him by over-cautious advisers.[1]

[1] Other writers of the period also mention the king's comment; see *Comédiens*, pp. 106–7.

PIERRE GRINGORE: MERE SOTTE

The most famous actor/author of the period was Pierre Gringore. Although he wrote poetry and a play of St Louis for the Paris Guild of Carpenters and Masons, he was best known for his satirical plays, especially a number of *sotties*. He was also an actor, playing Mere Sotte in many performances. In 1518, Gringore left Paris for a post as *huissier d'armes* at the court of the Duke of Lorraine in Nancy. His post appears to have been more or less honorary and he continued in his real work as court entertainer as can be seen from the accounts, whose entries clearly show that Gringore and Mere Sotte were still considered the same person: the annual salary goes to Gringore, the intermediary gifts go under either name indiscriminately. In 1526, when the municipality of Valence, threatened with a plague, decided to revive their play of the *Three Martyrs*, first performed in 1473 and supposed to be performed every twenty-five years, they invited Gringore to help with the production [see **E90**].

E88   Illustration of Gringore as Mere Sotte with the motto of the *Sots*

Frontispiece to *Oeuvres complètes de Gringore*, ed. Charles d'Héricault and A. de Montaiglon, Paris, 1858–77

The illustration shows the performer set within a border bearing the motto of the *Sots*: 'Raison par tout: Par tout Raison: Tout par Raison' [Reason is everything: Reason everywhere: All things by Reason]. Gringore and his colleagues wear the characteristic *sot*'s cap with large asses' ears attached at either side.

E89   Gringore joins the ducal court at Nancy

Charles Oulmont, *Pierre Gringore*, Paris, 1911, p. 343

(i) Payments to Gringore in 1518

To Pierre Gringore, *Huissier*, the sum of 72 francs money of Lorraine, which my lord the duke has allotted to him for his wages for the year [. . .] 21 November 1518.

To Mere Sotte, composer of farces, as a gift, ten francs [. . .] 4th March 1518.

Pierre Gringore, *huissier d'armes* [. . .] the sum of twenty francs as ordered, 12th September 1518 [. . .] Mere Sotte for the same, six florins.[1]

---

[1] Later entries include the names: 'mersotte' and 'Pierre Mere Sotte'.

(ii) Confusion of names in the accounts of 1519

Mere Sotte, 20 francs, money of Lorraine for expenses incurred for costumes [*accoustrements*] to perform farces before the said lord duke.

[. . .] Maistre Pierre Gringore dit Mere Sotte, 1.fr.50 for a *curtil*.[1]

---

[1] A *curtil* or *courtault* was a musical instrument which provided the bass for the *musette* [bagpipes].

E90   Maistre Meresote is sent for to Valence in Dauphiné

Dauphiné, pp. 11, 25

Following the deliberation and conclusion made by the general council to stage the
mystère of the *Three Martyrs* [. . .] by commandement of Valence and the commissioners, Meresote, *fatiste*,[1] came to present the said play.

[1] The term *fatiste* is often used for an author or adaptor; Gringore probably revised the text as well as
overseeing the performance.

PROBLEMS FOR OUTSPOKEN ACTORS

Gringore's departure from Paris may have been partly due to the attitude of Louis
XII's successor, Francis I, who was much less liberal in his attitude to satirical performances, especially any remarks made against the king or court. Two of the
farcers mentioned here, Seroc and Pontalez,[1] were well known and very popular
actors and could almost be considered as early professionals [see **E91**].

[1] They were both members of the *Enfants sans souci*; see *Comédiens*, pp. 167–83.

E91   Francis I imprisons some actors, 1516

Comédiens, p. 115

[. . .] three prisoners from Paris, Jacques *le Basochien*, Jehan Seroc and Master Jehan
du Pontalez, farcers, were taken before the king at Amboise in chains [. . .] for
having played farces in Paris concerning the nobility; among other things [sug-
gesting that] Mere Sotte ruled the court and was taxing, robbing and pillaging
everyone. The King and the Queen-Regent were very angry about this.[1]

[1] The actors were imprisoned but escaped to Blois and soon after were given a pardon. The incident
emphasises there was no real distinction made between a *basochien*, a *sot* and a farcer.

THE STAGING OF SECULAR PLAYS

There are few details available for these plays, though some indication can be gathered from the woodcuts in the early printed farces. Otherwise we are limited to the
texts themselves and information in the dialogue and rubrics. *The Condemnation of
Banquet*,[1] a morality 'in praise of diet and sobriety for the profit of the human body'
has useful and detailed stage directions [see **E92**]. The theme was popular and a
number of sets of tapestries are known from which further details can be deduced
[see *Banquet*, pp. 31–7].

1. 'Banquet', both in French and English, originally meant the dessert served on a small
bench [*banquet*]. The purpose of the play is to show that dinner and supper are enough
for anyone and that eating between meals can cause many illnesses.

E92   Set and costumes described in a morality play

Nicolas de la Chesnaye, *La Condemnation de banquet*, ed. Jelle Koopmans and Paul Verhuyck, Geneva, 1991

(i) The characters are in place on the stage before speaking

[*After the prologue*] *the doctor retires and goes to sit down until he comes forward to give his sermon. The three repasts* [*Dinner, Supper and Banquet*] *are in their places and Dinner comes forward and speaks* [. . .] (p. 1)

(ii) Bonne Compagnie and her friends prepare to eat

[. . .] 'and in addition [to various wines] bring us two dishes of Damascus plums'. *This first meal will be taken on a round or square table and if it is not the season when plums are available, it will be necessary to use dried ones or make wax ones having the appearance and colour of Damascus ones.* (p. 73)

(iii) Pastime suggests a dance

To be noted that – on the scaffold or on some more elevated location – there will be the different kinds of instruments to play and add variety when it is time. At this present time they can play a fairly short basse-dance then Dinner will speak [. . .] (p. 76)

(iv) The entrance of the Maladies

Note that the Maladies come and show themselves in hideous and monstrous forms, armed with sticks and so strangely dressed that it is difficult to tell if they are men or women. (p. 127)

(v) The Maladies, summoned by supper, attack the company

Then they will make great to-do, knocking down the board and the trestles, the crockery and dishes and not one of the seven [*eaters*] *will avoid being beaten; however, they will finally force their way out, one wounded, another bleeding. And this battle can last the length of a Pater Noster or two. Then, when they have fled, Jaundice speaks* [. . .] (p. 129)

AMATEUR GROUPS STAGE MORALITY PLAYS

Sometimes groups of citizens combined for the purpose of putting on morality plays, joining themselves together by legal contracts agreeing to rehearse and perform at the arranged times on pain of being fined. A group of citizens in Draguignan including local lawyers, apothecaries, and priests signed a pact to perform a morality called *The Earth and Fortune* [see **E93**]. A similar contract with similar players and fines comes from Toulon in 1483, where the play is a morality called *The Lover and the Girl* [*de l'Amoros et de la filha*] (see *Comédiens*, pp. 288–9).

E93   A contract to perform in Draguignan, 1461

Draguignan, p. 509

[It was agreed that] each one would play the character already allocated to him; [. . .] each of us was bound to attend, unless there was a good excuse, at the place and time chosen by the said Master Jacobus de Barbona elected to this task, to learn and rehearse this morality and he who was not present at the rehearsal at the time and place agreed had to pay one gros each time.[1] [. . .] and each of us should, promptly and without making difficulty, assist in the construction of the scaffolds for acting the said morality as was necessary [. . .]

---

[1] Absence without just and acceptable reason on the day of the performance was to be punished by a fine of one ecu.

III *Processional and street theatre*

France has less street theatre than many European countries but a few examples are known of plays performed on wagons or on stages set up in the street. There are also descriptions of tableaux and other set pieces connected with princely entries and celebrations [see **E96**, **E97**]. The account of the St John's Day festivities in Bordeaux was written in 1578, the year the tradition was abolished [see **E94**]. The same parish of St Michael for several years records payments to those who, on Corpus Christi day, 'carried the tabernacle and those who played the Passion' (1487) or 'for those who played the story of the Passion and apostles' (1493). The custom of having a craft guild perform a play for Corpus Christi (the only recorded instance of this in France) may derive from the English tradition, since Bordeaux was under English rule until 1453.

E94 The St John's Day procession and play from Bordeaux

Charles Mazouer, *La vie théâtrale à Bordeaux des origines à nos jours*, vol. 1, Paris, 1985, pp. 27–30

Every year on the Feast of St John the Baptist [24 June], the coopers and other tradesmen of the Parish of St Michael in Bordeaux were accustomed to prepare several raised stages in different parts of the town [. . .] They walked to these sites in solemn procession with torches and flambeaux, cross and banners, some of them dressed for this performance as apostles, as St John and as Our Lord, with wooden trenchers on their heads as big as plates, long hair and wigs which hung down to their waists, barefoot and dressed in albs and church vestments of varying colours. When they arrived at the place where one of these stages [*théâtres*] had been set up, those who represented Our Lord and St John the Baptist climbed on the stage and baptised each other in the sight of the people [. . .] but the others, who acted the roles of the apostles, remained on the ground round the stage. And it should be noted that each carried in his hand the symbol of the apostle he represented: St Peter, the keys; St Paul, the sword; St Andrew, the cross which bears his name, and so on.

CORPUS CHRISTI PLAYS

Corpus Christi plays of any kind are rare in France, though the obligatory procession was of course held. Bordeaux had a Passion play [see **E94**] and in Laval, in
1533, 'the *Sainte Hostie* was performed in front of the churchyard [*la cimetiere Dieu*]
on the feast of Corpus Christi and the feast of St Gervais' (18–19 June).[1] In Dijon it
was apparently the custom to have actors present plays of the martyrdom of
saints, both men and women, on the feast of Corpus Christi, for in 1469 a basket-
maker was paid 100s for repainting the crowns and other properties. The continuation of the plays in the sixteenth century is attested by a reference in 1509 to a
certain Widow Gousset who, on Corpus Christi day, was chased by an apprentice
dyer 'dressed in a devil's costume [when] the plays were performed outside the
Carmelite house'.[2] The most substantial surviving references are from the
Provençal town of Draguignan, first recorded in 1437. Unfortunately the records
for the second half of the fifteenth century are missing, but references to the plays
recur frequently in the sixteenth and seventeenth centuries. The brief entries [see
E95] make it clear that the *moralités*, of which they speak, are biblical plays and
the costumes recorded for 1574 suggest the episodes chosen.

1.   *Mystères*, vol. II, p. 120.
2.   Dijon, pp. 273–4.

E95   Corpus Christi plays in Draguignan, 1437–1574

Draguignan, pp. 464–70

1437 [. . .] to Johannis Morerus on account of the plays which he is accustomed to
put on year by year for the feast of Corpus Christi and which he cannot do without
a subvention, it was ordered to pay therefore 1 florin

1533 [. . .] for the maintenance and repair of the costumes of the Old Testament
for the annual celebration [. . .] 10 florins

1549 [. . .] the play will be acted after the procession

1551 [a local notary was paid for having] composed the Old and New Testaments
done on the feast of Corpus Christi for five years including the present one [. . .]
making these Old and New Testaments suitable for presentation *par personnages*
and with texts composed from the prophets and others.[1]

1553 [. . .] it was ordered that the said play should be done and would begin in
the presence of the Blessed Sacrament, at five a.m. on the market place and from
there they will set off and march as is customary[2] [. . .] All the costumes for the
morality will be brought out from the town hall by those nominated,[3] and those
who have been chosen to act must be in their costumes at the house of the
Dominicans, each ready to act and present his role. The said market place to be surrounded by benches and beams [. . .]

[1555] It has been agreed that the morality of the Old and New Testaments shall be played as usual on Corpus Christi day [. . .] and those who act must only go to the places they know are suitable, and in each place a scaffold shall be erected at the expense of the town for them to perform each in their turn[4]

[1558] The said play will perform [*jora*] with the procession as formerly and as many and as short scenes [*istoeres*] as possible will be involved and will be spoken while on the move [*tout en cheminant*][5] without any performer stopping, so as to avoid prolixity or confusion both of the procession and the play and so that strangers can see it easily

[1560] The story of the Old Testament shall be played on the forthcoming feast of Corpus Christi

[1574] The sum of eight gold ecus formerly paid to the organiser of the play [*l'entrepreneur du jeu*] for his wages and for the costs of staging has been raised to 12 ecus. [the list of the accoutrements includes] the head of Holofernes, six false beards, two wigs, two banners, Herod's staff, the devil's outfit, two masks, [. . .] the brazen serpent, Our Lord's robe, Noah's ark, a crown.

[1] In 1564 the organiser is warned not to have plays performed which might cause any dispute.
[2] In contrast to 1549 it seems that this year the play precedes the procession.
[3] In 1558 the notary is ordered to keep a list of those who receive costumes from the town hall, so as to ensure they are returned afterwards.
[4] Apparently this year the play is separate from the procession and performed at several different locations.
[5] The term used here is unique but seems to imply action on the ground as they move along, rather than on stages as in 1555. There is no mention of the use of wagons.

SECULAR CIVIC PROCESSIONS

Processions with floats and tableaux were regularly organised for secular, civic and national occasions. Joan of Arc's raising of the English siege of Orleans in 1429 was celebrated by an annual procession on 8 May, which was sometimes supplemented by stages bearing tableaux of an appropriate kind: in 1439 Jehan Hilaire was paid £7T for the purchase of a standard and banner to be used in the representation of the attack on the Tourelles when they were recaptured from the English.[1] The most common reason for such processions was a visit by a king or other notable person [see **E96–E100**]. The early tableaux for these entries were usually biblical or hagiographic but in the sixteenth century they became more formalised with allegorical and classical elements in them.

1.   *Mystères*, vol. II, p. 191–2.

E96   English royal entries into Paris, 1420, 1424

(a)   Henry V of England enters Paris with Charles VI of France, 1420

Journal d'un bourgeois de Paris sous Charles VI et Charles VII, ed. André Mary, Paris, 1929, p. 142

In the rue de la Kalende, in front of the Palais [de Justice] there was a lifelike portrayal of the Passion of Our Lord, as it is sculpted around the choir of Notre Dame in Paris and these scaffolds stretched for about a hundred yards [. . .] and there was no one who saw this *mystère* whose heart was not touched by it.

(b)   The Duke of Bedford enters Paris as regent for Henry VI, 1424

Mystères, vol. II, p. 190

In front of the Châtelet there was a very fine *mystère* of the Old and New Testament done by the *enfens*[1] of Paris and was done without words or gestures as if they were figures against a wall. After he had looked at this *mystère* for a long time he went on to Notre Dame.

[1]   These are the *Enfants sans Souci* [see **E86**].

E97   *Mystères* for Queen Anne of Brittany's entry, 1504

Charles Oulmont, 'Pierre Gringore et l'entrée de la reine Anne de Bretagne en 1504', in *Mélanges offerts à M. Emile Picot*, 2 vols., Paris, 1913

(i) Gringore and others prepare the plays

To MM. Regne de Collerie [. . .] Mere Sote [see **E90**] and others, all creators and inventors of the said *mystères* and entertainments [*esbatemens*], the sum of £11 5s, paid [. . .] for having toiled for several days before the said entry in devising *mystères* and versifying the speeches which have been presented in the said places (p. 389).

(ii) The Confrérie de la Passion stage the Transfiguration

[To the] masters and governors of the Confrérie de la Passion et Résurrection [see **E3**] founded at the church of the Trinité in Paris, the sum of £10 allocated to them to cover the costs of the *mystère* of the Transfiguration [. . .] presented by them in front of the said church on the day of the said entry. (p. 391)

E98 Organising the entries

Mystères, vol. II, p. 202.

[1502 Paid to] Jehan Marchant and Pierre Gringore,[1] composer and carpenter, who have staged and composed the *mystère* presented at the Châtelet at the entry of the Lord Legate, directed the actors, dressed and clothed them as is necessary for the said *mystère* and equally for having made the scaffolds needed for this and provided the necessary wood – £100.

[In 1514, at the entry of Mary of England[2] they were paid £115 because they] hired hangings and paid the singers, minstrels and other people needed for the *mystère* [. . .] and because of the large number of actors presenting this said *mystère* whom they had to pay, costume and apparel according to the quality of the characters they represented.

[1] For Pierre Gringore see **E87.**
[2] Henry VIII's sister who married Louis XII of France.

E99 Ducal entries at Dijon

Dijon

(a) A friar composes biblical plays, 1454, 1473

In both years, Friar Gilles, a cordelier, received] for his effort, reward and toil, 100s.T.

[In August 1469 in his cell] were assembled the mayor, echevins and other officers of the town to agree upon and discuss a suitable form for the extracts of Holy scripture to be used for the moralities.

[In the winter of 1469 he was sent a load of coal] for the love of God [because] he was suffering so badly from gout that it was pitiful and he could not look after himself. (p. 246)

(b) Painters paid for making properties, 1454

[To two painters] for having painted [. . .] two huge images of a giant called Goliath with the three heads needed for the statues [one presumably for David to hold up] and two other images of heads for the character of Holofernes [. . .] to be used in the plays presented at the joyous entry of our redoubted lord:[1] 36 frs 1 gr. (p. 243)

[1] Philippe le Bon was then at the height of his power.

E100   Royal entries at Dijon

(a)   A scene of the Shepherds for Louis XI, 1479

Dijon, p. 248

[1 franc 3 gros for Huguenin Guillemin for supplying wooden beams] for the scaffold in front of the hôtel de Morimont,[1] several of which beams have been broken because while performing the *mystère* played on that site, the shepherds did nothing but dance and jump about.

[1] This was the first visit of the King of France to Burgundy after the death in 1477 of Charles le Téméraire, last of the Valois dukes.

(b)   King Louis XII visits Dijon, 1501

Mystères, vol. II, pp. 210–11.

[. . .] Guillaume Flamang[1] was sent for to prepare, at the expense of the town, a joyous *mystère* for the coming of King Louis XII. Robert Vyon, the procurator is comissioned to ask the clerks and men of letters for *mystères* suitable to be played at the king's entry.[2]

[1] Guillaume Flamang was a priest and the author of a play of St Didier performed at Langres in 1482.
[2] A painter was paid for 'six beards for six Roman senators' (p. 251).

(c)   The Queen enters Dijon, 1533

Dijon, p. 257

[It was agreed] to pay the Cordeliers[1] £10T in recompense for having lent their friary to facilitate the *mystère*, and the other matters agreed on for the joyful entry of the queen[2] and the *mystères* remained there three months. Also they lent their copes to dress the scaffolds.

[1] The Franciscans or Cordeliers were very active in France at this period; the Romans performance of 1509 [see **E46**] was given in the quadrangle of the local monastery.
[2] Eleanor of Austria, wife of Francis I and sister to Emperor Charles V.

IV   Drama in the bilingual cities: Metz

A number of cities in the region once known as Lotharingia, including Lorraine and other regions along the upper Rhine and in Switzerland, were (and are) bilingual. As a result, the drama there might be in either French or German, or even both in the same city as in Fribourg/Freiburg in Switzerland from which there survive texts of Epiphany plays in both French and German.[1] The most important of these bilingual cities and the most ambiguous in its drama traditions is Metz, which throughout the Middle Ages was an independent city – a state led by a prince bishop, whose allegiance was to the imperial archbishopric of Trier, and the ruling civic council which included both patricians and bourgeois.

Politically and dramatically, fifteenth-century Metz stood at a crossroads between France, Burgundy, the Empire and the Low Countries, but despite pressure from all sides, it managed to retain its independence until the sixteenth century when the city joined the opposition to the ambitions of Spain and the Emperor Charles V, and in 1552 was reunited to France, under Henry II.[2]

Twenty performances are recorded in Metz, from the *Apocalypse* in 1409 through to the *Sacrifice of Abraham* in 1520 – a spread only equalled by that of Paris itself. The plays are recorded in chronicles, composed in the latter part of the fifteenth century, in French, but there are no surviving play-texts from the town to justify the commonly held assumption that the drama there was all in French. Indeed there is nothing to indicate whether, in this bilingual city, any one play was in French or in German.

Most of the records refer to hagiographic plays staged by the townsfolk for a civic audience but in 1437 there was a performance of the Passion attended by the then bishop, Conrad Bayer de Boppart (described in the chronicle on his appointment in 1415 as 'speaking fluently the three languages, i.e. Latin, French and German'.)[3] It has generally been assumed that the texts of this Passion play, and of the *Vengeance de Jésus Christ* performed later the same year, were the French plays known as the Arras *Passion* and Mercadé's *Vengeance*.[4] Although the latter play performed in the September [see **E103**] may well have been Mercadé's French text, there is no real evidence for the use of Arras or any other French Passion for the July performance, since substantial German Passions already existed at that date and the invited notables for the Passion play are from the mainly German-speaking regions of Lothringia and the Empire [see **E101**].

1.   *Trois jeux des rois*, ed. Yves Giraud, Norbert King, and Simone de Reyff. Friburg, 1985. For the German plays see Rolf Bergmann, *Katalog der deutschsprachigen geistlichen Spiele und Marienklagen des Mittelalters*, Munich and Zurich, 1986, p. 128.
2.   *Histoire de Metz*, ed. F.-Y. Le Moigne. Toulouse, 1986, p. 220.
3.   Vigneulles *Chronique*, vol. II, p. 165.
4.   Stephen K. Wright, *The Vengeance of Our Lord. Medieval Dramatizations of the Destruction of Jerusalem, Studies and Texts* 89, Toronto, 1989.

E101   A Passion play in Metz, 1437

Mystères, vol. II, pp. 12–13

In the said year [1437] in the month of July the play of the Passion of our Lord Jesus Christ was played in Metz in the Place de Change.[1] The *parc* was constructed in a very noble manner, for there were nine tiers of seats like steps all around, and behind were large and long seats [*grands sièges et longs*] for the lords and ladies [. . .] And at that time there were many foreign princes and noble lords and ladies in the city of Metz. First among them was the Lord Conrad de Bayer (then the bishop of Metz), the comte de Vauldemeont, lord Baudoin de Fleville, abbé de Gorze,[2] the comtesse de Sarrebruch and the councillor of Bar and Lorraine [. . .] and many other lords and ladies from Germany [Allemaigne] and other countries whose names I do not know. And for this reason it was ordered that lanterns should be set at night in the windows throughout the city and lights at the gates throughout the play [. . .]

[1] Now the Place Saint Louis; plays were normally performed in this square.
[2] The abbey of Gorze was an important foundation just outside the city.

E102   A narrow escape for two actors in the *Passion*, 1437

Mystères, vol. II, pp. 12–13

And the role of God [i.e. Christ] was played by a priest, *seigneur* Nicolle de Neufchastel en Lorraine who was then the vicar of St Victor's Church in Metz. And this priest was in great danger of his life and nearly died during the Crucifixion, for he fainted and would have died had he not been rescued. And it was necessary for another priest to take his place and finish playing the part of God, which priest was one of the executioners and guards in the said play. Nevertheless they gave his role to another and he played out the Crucifixion for that day. And the following day, the said priest from St Victor was restored to health and played out the Resurrection and performed his part very nobly. And this play lasted four days. And in this play was yet another priest called lord Jehan de Missey who was chaplain of Mairange, who took the part of Judas; and because he was left hanging too long, he also was unconscious and seemed dead, for he had fainted; therefore he was swiftly taken down and carried to a place nearby where he was rubbed with vinegar and other things [*aultre chose*] to restore him.

E103   The *Vengeance* play is performed in September 1437

Mystères, vol. II, pp. 12–13

And 17 September following, the play of the *Vengeance of Our Lord Jesus Christ and the Destruction of Jerusalem* was performed in the same *parc* and the same location as the Passion had been given. And the city of Jerusalem was very well and cunningly constructed and made with the port of Jaffa beside it in the *parc*. And in this play Jean Mathieu I the barrister took part, in the role of Vespasian and the *curé* of St Victor who had been God in the Passion. And the *mystère* lasted four days.

SAINTS PLAYS IN METZ

Of the many hagiographic plays performed in Metz during this century, the play of Saint Catherine in 1468 is the only known example of a play on a newly made saint: Catherine of Siena died in 1380 and was canonised in 1461. Moreover, the play was commissioned and staged by a devout (and obviously wealthy) lady, Catherine de Baudoiche, who founded a chapel dedicated to the new saint in the church of the Dominicans where she herself was subsequently buried. It was in the courtyard of this church that the play was performed on the three festal days of Pentecost, 1468.

E104   An actress stars in the role of St Catherine of Siena, 1468

Chroniques de Metz de Jacomin Husson, ed. Heinrich Michelant, Metz, 1870, p. 103

And the role of St Catherine was taken by a young girl,[1] about eighteen years old, the daughter of Dediet the furrier [. . .] and she did her duty marvellously well to the delight and pleasure of everyone. Although she had twenty-three-hundred lines to speak nevertheless she knew them all perfectly; and this girl spoke in such a lively and pleading way that she made many people cry, and delighted them all. And as a consequence of this the girl made a very good match with a gentleman, a soldier in Metz, called Henry de la Tour who fell in love with her because of his great delight in her performance.

---

[1] Catherine of Siena was a confessor not a martyr, and remarkable as a peace-maker and mediator. Such a character is not inappropriately represented by a girl. This is the earliest reference to a laywoman acting on the stage and the only example of a woman having the starring role.

E105   A barber's apprentice stars as St Barbe, 1485

Mystères, vol. II, p. 48

On the 24th of July a play was performed in the Place de Chambre in Metz of the life and passion of Madame St Barbe. It lasted three days and was the best played and most successful that had been seen for a long time and everyone was pleased with it. A week beforehand the scaffolds were erected in the Place de Vezegnuef, on which they ran through and performed the whole play but without words.[1] Then on the 24th of July the play was acted in the said Chambre and people went to take their places at four o'clock in the morning [. . .] And there was at that time living in Metz a young barber's apprentice called Lionard, a native of Aachen in Germany[2] but who had lived in Metz for a long time in the house of Master Hannes, the barber in Quartaul. He was a very handsome boy who looked like a beautiful girl and he played the role of St Barbe so skilfully and devoutly that many people wept with compassion for he had such good form and carriage, with such good appearance and gesture with his maidens, that he pleased everyone and no one could have done it better.[3]

[1] This is a rare reference to a run-through of a play on the stage.
[2] Aachen was a German-speaking town which may suggest a German-language play here.
[3] Lionard was such a success that a rich widow wanted to make him her heir but a cathedral canon adopted and educated him.

E106   Philippe de Vigneulles declines a role in the play of St Catherine of Sinai, 1486

Vigneulles *Gedenkbuch*, p. 14

[. . .] they performed the play of St Catherine of Sinai in the Place de Chambre, which I had been asked to take part in, and it was due to take place at Whitsun [. . .] and the St Catherine was a young barber's apprentice[1] [. . .] and at that time I looked so like the boy that I was taken for him seventeen times and therefore the boy liked me very much and wanted me to be one of his maidens in the said play. But I had other things in mind and had decided at that time to leave Metz secretly with a companion.[2]

[1] [See **E105**]. The play was less successful for Lionard's voice had already started to break, and 'the characters, language and rhetoric were not so well composed and ornamented as those in the *mystère* of St Barbe' (*Mystères*, vol. II, p. 52–3).
[2] Although only fifteen at the time, Philippe duly set off for Rome and only returned to Metz five years later.

WHITSUNTIDE PLAYS IN METZ

E107   Secular plays on Whit Tuesday 1491

Vigneulles *Chroniques*, vol. II, p. 329

At that time on the third feast day of Pentecost, there was played in Metz a play of Griselda and the play known as '*Correcting the Magnificat*'.[1]

[1]   The first play is perhaps a version of *L'estoire de Griselidis* written in 1395. The second is a *sottie* composed before 1488. The full title is *Sottie des sots qui corrigent le Magnificat a cinq personnages*. (Ed. Eugénie Droz, *Le recueil trepperel. les Sotties*, IX, Paris, 1935). To 'correct the Magnificat' was a well-known saying meaning 'to correct or foolishly criticise those more educated than yourself'.

E108   Philippe describes the special effects for the play of the *Sainte Hostie*, 1513

Vigneulles *Gedenkbuch*, pp. 244–5

On the Monday of Pentecost, a play was acted in the Place de Chambre of the Miraculous Host which [. . .] is in the church of St Mary in Paris.[1] [. . .] The treacherous Jew, wishing to find out if it [the Host] were God, [. . .] struck it with a knife then by a *secret* great abundance of blood came forth and soared up high from the said Host as if it had been a child pissing, and the Jew was all blood spattered and stained by it and acted his part very well [. . .] Then, enraged, he took the host and flung it in a cauldron of boiling water and it rose up in the air in a cloud and became a little child as it rose and all this was done by pulleys and secrets.[2]

[1]   The miracle of the *Sainte Hostie* took place in Paris in the thirteenth century and was commemorated there by an annual procession with tableaux *(Mystères*, vol. II, pp. 574–6). There are interesting parallels between the Metz piece and the East Anglian *Croxton Play of the Sacrament*. See *Non-Cycle Plays and Fragments*, ed. Norman Davis, EETS (SS 1), Oxford, 1970, Play VI.

[2]   On the following two days there were more plays: a miracle of St Nicholas and a morality of *The false tongue* [*La fausse langue*] which included a scene of fire and tortures in hell 'very ingeniously contrived'. The three plays altogether raised twenty-three francs in admission and seat money which Philippe helped to collect.

Section F
The German-speaking area

Edited by JOHN E. TAILBY

Introduction and abbreviations

This section continues the consideration of drama in German in the period from about 1400 to the point where it can no longer be considered medieval. For this reason material from the later part of the sixteenth century has only been included where it seems reasonable to regard it as illustrating the continuation of medieval strands. There is at this time no 'Germany' to put alongside the nation-states of England and France. We can speak only of the 'German-speaking area,' but even this term implies a nonexistent homogeneity, since in order to complete the geographical range of cover the Low German of Lübeck [see **F39**] and Redentin [see **F15**] has been included alongside various High German texts. These also illustrate the changing boundaries of the 'German-speaking area' by the inclusion of German texts from locations which are now in France [see **F2**], Hungary [see **F12**], and Slovakia [see **F28(iii)**, **F42(iii)**]; texts from Switzerland [see **F21**, **F23** and **F24**] and Austria [see **F3** and **F14**] are included as well as those from South Tyrol, always German-speaking and now part of Italy [see **F13**, **F16–F20**, **F31**, **F32** and **F42**].

Scholarship on medieval drama in German distinguishes between 'religious' and 'secular' with considerable justification, since there is very little overlap between the two sets of material [see, however, **F40** and **F41**]. The amount of information easily accessible regarding the religious drama has changed fundamentally in the last decade since the publication of Bernd Neumann's two-volumed *Geistliches Schauspiel im Zeugnis der Zeit* (Munich, 1987). Before these volumes appeared knowledge was also very restricted regarding the large number of places from which records of dramatic performances survive. Neumann records meticulously on p. 64 and note 133 the areas he was not able to cover in his work. We can now see that dramatic performances did occur with varying frequency all over the German-speaking area throughout this period. Neumann lists on pp. 64–97 all the documented performances of religious drama between 1187 and 1607. The following selection of material aims to illustrate this temporal and geographical spread after *c.* 1400.

That the great majority of this 'religious' material is concerned with Eastertide has also been recognised for some time. Modern scholars make the further division between 'Easter plays' which begin with the action of Easter Day and derive ultimately from liturgical sources; and 'Passion plays' in which the Resurrection is preceded by the action of Holy Week from Palm Sunday to Good Friday, sometimes by sections covering the life of Christ, in some cases also by scenes from the Old Testament, usually those felt to have prefigurative significance. These Passion plays appear to begin spontaneously at several points in the German-speaking world in the thirteenth century, and scholars recognise an earlier group dating from the thirteenth and fourteenth centuries and a later group from the fifteenth and sixteenth centuries. In this section Corpus Christi plays, which are processional but deal with the same material, will also be considered besides eschatological plays and performances concerned with saints' lives and deaths.

Scholarship has been bedevilled by problems concerning the names by which plays are known, which frequently related to where they had been discovered and not where they originated from. Attempts to remedy this produced titles such as *The Rhenish Easter Play from the Berlin Manuscript ms. Germ. Fol 1219*. This situation has now been remedied, one trusts definitively, by the production in Cologne of a list which avoids ambiguity and excessive complexity by reducing titles such as the above to *Berlin [Rhenish] Easter Play*. The list is incorporated in Neumann, volume II, pp. 826–68 as '3. *Spieltexte*', i.e. play-texts.

Demonstrating that 'Shrovetide play' is not coterminous with 'medieval German secular play' has been a recurring theme in scholarship for a century and will be covered in the section below on Shrovetide plays.

The following abbreviations are used throughout this section.

Keller   *Fastnachtspiele aus dem fünfzehnten Jahrhundert*, Bibliothek des Literarischen Vereins in Stuttgart, vols. 28–30 (1853) and *Nachlese*, vol. 46 (1858), ed. Adalbert von Keller; reprinted Darmstadt 1965–6 (references are to play number followed by page and line numbers in this edition)

Neumann   Bernd Neumann, *Geistliches Schauspiel im Zeugnis der Zeit*, 2 vols., Munich, 1987 (references are to the item numbers used in this section)

Sterzing   *Die geistlichen Spiele des Sterzinger Spielarchivs*, ed. Walther Lipphardt and Hans-Gert Roloff, 6 vols., Bern, 1980–

I   Religious drama

Planning and permission

The impulse for a performance might come from various sources. From some locations only a single document survives, but contains the evidence that there was a
tradition of presentation. From locations where we know of a performance tradition, documents may record a request and its refusal. Elsewhere the impulse came
from the local authority, either town council or overlord; for performances in
church the authorisation could be ecclesiastical.

The town council of Amberg/Oberpfalz in 1524 announced their intention of
putting on a play after postponement; though this is the only document surviving
from Amberg, it contains the information that there was around this time a tradition of regular performances [see **F1**].

Frequently a group of citizens approached the town authorities asking permission to perform. The following application, of typical length, was made by a group
in Colmar, now in France, in 1534 [see **F2**]. The only two surviving records from
Feldkirch in the Vorarlberg region of Austria are also very valuable as an example
of the overlord as initiator [see **F3**], while at Helmstedt the bishop's authorisation
was essential [see **F4**]. Documents from Frankfurt-on-Main, with its rich and
diverse tradition in medieval drama [see **C56**], and Freiburg im Breisgau, famous
for its Corpus Christi procession and play [see **F25**], illustrate that applications
were scrutinised and liable to rejection, whether the applications were made in
good time or not [see **F5**, **F6**, **F7**].

F1   Council announcement, Amberg/Oberpfalz, 1524

Neumann, item 18

We, the Mayor and council of the town of Amberg make known by this letter, since
the scenes [*figuren*] of the Passion and suffering of Christ, which for some time
usually have been performed around Eastertide here in Amberg, due to the arrival
of the illustrious prince our most gracious lord the Prince Palatine, have hitherto

been postponed and not taken place, that for the most subservient [*unterthenigem*] delight of his grace the prince elector and pre-eminently for the special glory of Almighty God and for the improvement of the sinful lives of us Christian people, these scenes will take place next Sunday and start around midday. Therefore and on account of the devotion, as much as the Christian believer can have from the aforesaid scenes and observations of the suffering of Christ our Saviour, it is our friendly neighbourly request that you and each person to whose attention this letter comes will make this known to your inferiors [*unnderthanen*] and have it made known publicly. We ask this in the name of your friendly and neighbourly good will. Given under our seal attached to the reverse on the Thursday after the Sunday Jubilate [i.e. April 21] a.d. 24.

F2   Citizens petition the town council, Colmar, 1534

Neumann, item 1157

Wise, illustrious, prudent, benevolent dear sirs, you can at all times be sure that our humble, obedient, willing service is readily at your excellencies' disposition. Favourable sirs, we have no doubt but that your excellencies and the greater council still recall well to what extent the Passion Play [*der passion*] was performed with scenes acted out by people [*durch menschliche figuren*] with good purpose three years ago at Eastertide to the praise of Almighty God, for the improvement of the honourable council and the general citizenry, young and old, [which] without any doubt brought many pious people to devotion and moved them to good works, from which the Heavenly Father derived great pleasure in heaven through Christ his only son, who suffered such death and torture for the human race. – Now since we are called Christians and no one can do too many good works and also sadly nowadays young people are not taken to the sermon by their father or mother in order to hear the word of God, but are growing up in all worldly things, through which faith and all the sufferings which Christ underwent for us, are extinguished and we are punished for this, all unknowing why, we have refrained from all Shrovetide plays and with great desire for the agreement of you our benevolent masters, have undertaken to play some Gospels and the Passion according to the clear letter [of the Gospel?], as is done in many places by various nations and per-formed annually in order that the world be found somewhat more adept in the practice of good works. To this end, wise, illustrious, prudent, benevolent dear sirs, we deferential citizens most urgently request your illustrious and wise selves that this same wisdom of yours will not refuse us this intention and desire of ours, and not think that we want the town to incur expense [since there is still so much beau-tiful and expensive equipment [*ristung*] for such a play available] but accept from us our kindly intention that we are heeding the authorities, the town and the common advantage, [. . .] from which many pious people who see and hear such things derive great pleasure. Therefore your honourable and wise selves are asked to grant us permission to perform at the coming Eastertide the Gospel, when it is to be performed more extensively, more perceptively and in more praiseworthy fashion than has been seen previously; and if you, kind sirs, are willing to assist us with the equipping of the trestles [*Pritschen*], [we will] go along with the help and advice of two councillors nominated by your good selves so that the honourable council derives delight, the town derives from all delights profit, and furthermore all spectators will feel praise, devotion and praise towards God, in the good hope that all of us receive the love of God and so live in His will. If however your illustrious wise selves do not approve of our planned intention or consider it problematical, we will nevertheless be your obedient inferiors. So we ask your wise selves for a favourable reply. – Your respectful citizens who have previously put on the Passion Play with the help of good citizens and other people.

[On the reverse is noted in the handwriting of the town clerk] Agreed and granted on the Saturday after the Conversion of Paul [1 Feb.] anno etc. 34.

F3   Overlord's announcements, Feldkirch, Vorarlberg, Austria, 1380, 1390

Neumann, items 1489 and 1490

[i] In 1380 around St George's Day [23 April] Count Rudolff[1] had an Easter play[2] in the churchyard at Feldkirch; it lasted three days, very beautiful, and cost some 500 Fl.

[ii] In 1390 my lord, Count Rudolff, started the second Easter play at Feldkirch and it lasted three days, very beautiful.

[1] Rudolf IV of Montfort; see the entry 'Montfort, Grafen von' in *Neue Deutsche Biographie*, vol. XVIII (1997), pp. 51–4.
[2] We know from well-documented sources such as Lucerne that plays put on around Eastertide were sometimes called 'Easter plays' even though they are what modern scholars call Passion plays. Since an Easter play lasting three days seems highly improbable, these performances were doubtless Passion plays.

F4   Episcopal authorisation for Ascension Day performances in church, Helmstedt, 9 August, 1423

Neumann, item 1946; trans. from Latin by Steven Ryle

John, by the grace of God and of the Apostolic See bishop of the diocese of Halberstadt, sends everlasting greetings in Christ Jesus, who is the true salvation of all, to all Christ's faithful who will hear and see this proclamation.

Our gentle mother the Church, the bride of Christ and virgin without spot (though to her enemies she is always like an army arrayed with banners), must still, when attacked by her enemies, arm herself against them with the weapons of justice and the shield of faith, against which the gates of Hell will not prevail. So that she may always remain undamaged like the seamless robe of Christ, mother church herself, worthy of devout and universal belief from of old concerning the ineffable divine Trinity and undivided unity and the twofold nature of Christ, has duly laid down that their festivals should be permanently observed, lest they should lapse from the memory of the faithful; but because, alas, certain people have taken up again the obstinate belief, long since refuted,[1] of a doctrine that is not catholic, and have not been ashamed or afraid to sow weeds in the field of genuine faith, shamelessly desiring to tear apart and besmirch with their trumperies the unity of the faith and the purity of its vesture. In order, therefore, that the Lord's field, entrusted to us and placed in our care, may not be infected with the diseased wheat of false doctrine, we shall take zealous care to cleanse it of harmful, unproductive seeds, and to make it receptive to good and fertile ones, and by constant attention to make it bear abundant crops; and considering that this will happen more fruitfully through declarations of the articles of the faith, and that the understanding of simple people is given a firm basis and foundation more quickly and easily by means of objects and examples perceived by the senses rather than through words, we have graciously assented to the appeals of our devoted officials of the town of Helmstedt, and we approve, ratify and by these present letters confirm for future times a praiseworthy and catholic custom of representing the ineffable mystery of the Lord's Ascension, enacted and accustomed to be held each year on the feast of the Ascension in the parish church of St Stephen in the aforementioned town, up to now with church songs and catholic praises as well as with consecrated pictures; and nonetheless endorsing the divine worship of the aforesaid parish church, as far as we are able, and urging the whole faithful people of Christ to a blaze of more ardent devotion. In addition to what has been said, we concede, grant and permit by these present letters that in the aforesaid parish church of St Stephen every year in future on the actual day of Pentecost, both clergy and populace, together with the singing of Nones[2] and the other canticles and catholic devotions consistent with this, and with images (as long as they are consecrated) prepared, may solemnly enact and fulfil the visible Sending of the Holy Spirit upon the disciples of Christ by performing the pious office with all the accustomed solemnities. And desiring the people of God, as we are bound to do, to render constant devout observance and attendance at divine worship and particularly at the aforesaid commemorations or representations of the Ascension of the Lord and the Sending of the Holy Spirit (since they are articles of the catholic faith), by attracting them with gifts and spiritual benefits, we mercifully grant to all and sundry who, being truly penitent and having confessed their sins, devoutly participate in the aforesaid offices or any one of them while it or they are performed, deriving from the mercy of Almighty God and relying on the authority of the blessed apostles Peter and Paul and St Stephen the protomartyr, an indulgence of forty days from the penances enjoined on them.

---

[1] As noted by Neumann and his source, around here the writer loses the thread of his Latin sentence.
[2] The traditional monastic Office celebrated daily at the 'ninth hour'.

Deliberation and rejection

F5   Council minutes, Frankfurt-on-Main, 1470

Neumann, items 1502, 1504 [compare **F7**]

Fifth day after St Walburga's day [26 April] Item. As some people have applied regarding putting on the Passion [play] and a fraternity, – we will consider further. [The organisers clearly got wind of this hesitation and submitted a long application on May 3. A further minute dated the same day states] To those who want to play the Passion, not to be authorised or allowed.[1]

---

[1] These applications and decisions seem to have been made at very short notice if we note the 1492 observation that 'in the Whitsuntide holidays a Passion play was performed at Frankfurt' (note the date!). Neumann, item 1509.

F6   Council minutes and petition, Frankfurt-on-Main, 1515

Neumann, items 1544–6

The third holy day after St Kilian's day [10 July]. As some gentlemen from St Leonhart's [church] and Switzer request permission to put on a play about St John on the Frauenberg and for the loan of timber to construct a stage, – refused. [Thereupon the chief organiser made the following submission] To the wise, honourable and prudent Mayor and council of this city of Frankfurt, our well-disposed, friendly masters. – Wise, honourable and prudent sirs, I humbly applied together with several other honourable citizens and fellows [*gesellen*] for permission to perform or put on the stories or legends of the austere life of St John Baptist for the praise of God and to be a devotional pointer for the common people; this request was refused for we know not what reason. Since I am now approached by common people and citizens and exhorted as to why the Passion has been left unperformed for so long, saying it is now after all the tenth year, from which I have noticed and understood the common people to have a longing for the Passion, I have been moved by this and have agreed with the common people, insofar as it is pleasing to your excellencies, that I will perform it next Whitsuntide, as long as God gives me health. Therefore I then began to stage this laudable story of St John as a precursor of the Saviour Jesus Christ our dear Lord, and have now often tried it out and rehearsed it with the performers. They have also met (?) [*sich bestelt*] several times regarding costume, learning the lines and organising the properties – in the hope that your excellencies will not refuse us such a seemly request – for the story is godly and honourable. Also [we] started concerning the Passion, so that the performers in it shall be all the more skilled and selected, and the ineptitude shown previously shall not occur, and only using the stories according to the Gospel, as much as is necessary. And in order that no error in accounting or other matters occur, the society members are prepared to set up a locked box in which the collected money of the society is to be kept and the members of the council assigned to us by your good selves will have the keys and the society the box, which will then be for the saving and spending of the aforesaid money saved in it. And in order that in future we shall perform the Passion in a more seemly and appropriate manner, it is the urgent plea and request of myself and all the society to your good selves that we be granted permission to perform this present story of John the Baptist, and further that on the next Feast of the Purification of Mary [i.e. 2 Feb. 1516] we be authorised to put on a play about Creation and the Fall of the angels, also Adam and Eve together with the Nativity and the Magi, all this drawn from the Gospel and Bible. If I am doubted, all this together with the Passion is to be performed with greater assiduity and devotion than occurred hitherto for previously I gave something to the honourable old gentleman Johan Kolmesser as seemed proper to his age and allowed him to act as he wished; this Mr Johan still has in his possession all the things belonging to the Passion and purchased with difficulty by the society. The society desire to demand these things from him and have them kept in a chest, in case he were to die and permission were given to perform the Passion, lest the society were hindered by his testamentary dispositions, out of which it would be troublesome to get them. As regards the stage I am of the opinion not to make it as previously but by laying pieces of wood one on another and fastening them together at the four corners, as I have often seen done in the Netherlands,[1] so that we do not make many holes as has been done previously. Therefore, sirs, we implore you with humble zeal not to reject this our moderate/seemly request. I together with all the society am ready to be found to deserve this at all times with humble and willing service. Therefore, sirs, we ask for your favourable reply, which we have to obey. Dated [19 July 1515]   Your excellencies' very willing and obedient Peter Seligenstadt, canon of the church of Our Lady, together with other society members belonging there, etc.

[The council minutes for the same date record bluntly] As Peter von Seligenstadt writes and requests to be allowed to do St John's play likewise at the Purification the Nativity and at Whitsuntide the Passion – refused.

---

[1] 'im Niderlande' might also mean in the Low German-speaking north of what is now 'Germany'.

F7   Council minutes, Freiburg im Breisgau, 1551, 1553

Neumann, items 1586, 1587

[i] 1551 Play on Our Lord's [i.e. Corpus Christi] Day: It is agreed again this year to hold the play and the procession on Our Lord's Day; and it is agreed to repay Hans Burger in view of his complaint the money he has spent in the past two years over and above the three pounds which they are [regularly] given; but at the same time that they are in future to be given no more than the three pounds, and they are to proceed accordingly.

[ii] 1553 Play on Our Lord's Day: It is agreed not to hold the play on Our Lord's Day this year on account of inflation, pestilence and war.

Borrowing

Advance planning of a different kind was necessary when organisers intended to borrow texts or properties from elsewhere [see **F8**, **F9**, **F10**].

F8   Town council requests loan of properties, Adorf, Thuringia, 1503

Neumann, item 2

Honourable, wise, particularly well-disposed sirs, good friends and neighbours, our willing service to your honours before all. Well-disposed sirs, we are intending to put on a little play in the coming holy days of Easter, in praise of our Lord God and His holy Resurrection; for this we lack and are in need of several pieces of equipment. Therefore it is our friendly request to you that you lend us a portion of the equipment, as much as our [fellow-]citizen who delivers this letter will indicate. We will return it to you without any harm and unblemished and are confident that as well-disposed sirs, our friends and neighbours, you will do as we ask and not refuse. We are happy to put ourselves in debt to you for the reciprocal or greater case.[1]

[1] Though Neumann quotes an article stating it was to be an 'Easter play' the actual phraseology makes a 'Passion play' at least as likely.

F9   The Abbot of Weingarten Monastery makes conditions, 1557

Neumann, items 3598–602[1]

(i) 24 May to Konrad von Bemelberg

I am this year again willing and intend, to the praise and honour of our Lord God, on the forthcoming feast of Corpus Christi to have the Passion and suffering of Christ acted and performed. Since however I do not have any clothing or garb for Our Lady the mother of Christ, I request you in friendliest fashion with particular urgency [*fleiss*] not to hesitate in again [as has happened previously] lending me the blue satin robe [*mantel*] which belongs to the statue of Our Lady at Ehingen and to send it to me with this servant of mine. Immediately after the celebration I will thankfully send it back to you completely unharmed and I will be at pains to acknowledge my thanks to you, beside God's reward.

(ii) 2 June to Hans Jacob zu Königsegg[2]

[. . .] and I ask you according to your recent offer and agreement made with me that you will send to me with this servant [*frommen*] of mine the clothing for King Herod together with the sabre and other things you have, useful and suitable for this matter, since the play will be rehearsed in costume in the next few days. I will certainly send it all back undamaged with my thanks and I shall look forward to you and your spouse and anyone else you like appearing here very early on Corpus Christi day, if the weather is fine. But if it is not fine but rainy, we shall have to postpone the play to the following Sunday.

(iii) [A different source records]

Anno 1557 June 17 the Passion was performed; [and that there was another performance in 1560] June 13. The Passion was performed at Weingarten.

[1] Weingarten is situated near Ravensburg, just north of Lake Constance. We also have a brief series of notes of performances from the 1540s; in 1540 'the Passion was recited'; in 1541 a play 'about the state of the world' [*de statu mundi*] was performed; and in 1549 a play about St Apollonia.

[2] This text contains several uncertain points of transcription.

F10   Aschersleben's representative's response to a request from the Wernigerode (Harz) town council, 26 March 1539

Neumann, item 35, same as 2772

My devoted friendly service above all. Honourable and wise, especially good friends. I have understood from your esteemed letter that your young citizens [*burgers kinder*] intend to put on a performance at the coming Easter and for this need certain equipment, as stated in a note sent to our preacher Andreas Sachse, requesting us to lend them such items insofar as available here. According to your request I have enquired industriously, what is still available. Now it is largely lost, especially the costumes of Death and Lucifer; I send to your excellencies two masks, one crown, two sceptres, two pairs of wings, one devil's pole [*stange*]; the vestments of God the Father: we used a choir cope from the church for it, together with a grey beard and hair; that too is not available. If there had been anything else obtainable which would have been helpful for your people, I should gladly have sent you it. And I am very pleased and willing to help your good selves in any other ways. [Signed by] Markus Müller, citizen of Asch[ersleben].

The hazards of lending and storing

A number of entries make clear the possible hazards of lending properties or texts. The day after the 1604 performance of the Corpus Christi Play in Freiburg im

Breisgau the council agreed that greater care needed to be taken in looking after things they had paid for [see **F11**]. The only record surviving from Ödenburg, now Sopron in Hungary, just across the border from Vienna, tells a sad tale of the dangers of lending out private property to unscrupulous neighbours [see **F12**]. That this also applies to play-texts can be seen from a note in the hand of the scribe Vigil Raber on the front cover of the 1539 manuscript of the South Tyrolean play about the Rich Man and Lazarus [see **F13** and **F31**].

F11   Care of properties from Freiburg Corpus Christi Play, 1604

Neumann, item 1681

Regarding the costumes belonging to the action of the Passion on the square [. . .] as to where these are now to be stored, it is agreed that although they were previously stored in the warehouse [*chauffhaus*], but an informed [*inwissender*] town clerk has to be troubled and bothered with organising the Passion, that henceforth such costumes and other items – except the large cross, the Mount of Olives and the tomb – are to be kept tidily in a convenient place in the town hall in a box or chest and an inventory of what is present is to be made; nor are such items to be lent to townspeople or students for any other play of theirs without permission from the town council.

F12   Unscrupulous borrowing and misappropriation, Ödenburg [now Sopron, Hungary], 1412

Neumann, item 2339

As I really made clear to you at Ebenfurt regarding Stephen Mautter and my harness, now Mautter has sent me a written reply; and what he writes is not the truth and I am writing to tell you how I acted in this matter. When the king was recently in Ödenburg I had to vacate my accommodation in Gaislein's house. Therefore I took my harness and other possessions of mine that I had at that time up to Stephen Mautter's and was thereafter accommodated there, as you well know, and I gave it to him to keep as trustee. Then Stephen Mautter came to me in the Dreysgkaf [inn ?] and asked me to lend him the harness for a play which they put on in the church. I did so and allowed him to have the harness, on condition that he should let me have it back again in good condition. He promised he would. That is the way things happened and not otherwise.[1]

---

[1] It seems that Stephen is now claiming the harness as his own.

F13   Lost play manuscript, Vigil Raber, Tyrol, 1520–39
Neumann, item 3677

I have copied it out again [*Hab jch wider fur bracht*] since lent out since 1520 and not able to obtain it, copied again.[1]

---

[1] See **F31** concerning this play.

EASTER PLAYS, PASSION PLAYS AND CORPUS CHRISTI PLAYS

Despite headings in manuscripts which do not always agree, scholars recognise the valid distinction between the first two groups of plays. Though, for example, the Lucerne play is called 'Lucerne Easter Play' in publications emanating from that city, since it was performed at Eastertide, it is referred to in other publications as the 'Lucerne Passion Play', given that it is a prime example of one of these plays, covering the whole action of Holy Week, scenes from the Nativity and public ministry of Christ besides prefigurative Old Testament scenes. Passion plays seem to be a spontaneous new development in the thirteenth century, generally thought to derive from the spirituality of that age which concentrated on the suffering Christ. The associated introduction of the Feast of Corpus Christi [see **C71–C80**] led almost universally to processions, but relatively few of these evolved into plays, as seems to have been the case elsewhere, notably in England and on the Iberian peninsula [see **Sections D** and **I**].

Easter plays

Easter plays begin with the action surrounding the Resurrection and stem ultimately from Latin liturgical sources [see **B9(b)**]. Hence derives the great unresolved question regarding the manuscripts of these plays, which turns on the Latin *incipits*, a regular feature at the more liturgical points in the action. Frequently the stage directions say that a person sings in Latin and then speaks in German; almost always the Latin text is confined to a brief *incipit*, even to a single word. Editors react differently to this situation. Earlier in the twentieth century it was standard practice to expand and give the whole Latin text. Recently editors have shunned this procedure, first because it is now perceived as tampering with the manuscript evidence in an unpermissible fashion; and secondly because scholars, now knowing more about the multiplicity of variant Latin texts available, are unwilling to state categorically which Latin version is implied. In some cases we have later manuscripts of the same play which dispense with the Latin entirely. [See **F30** for an example of this difference between two extant versions of a shorter play.]

The following examples [see **F14**, **F15**] from the extreme north and south of the German-speaking area illustrate the variety of treatment of the components of an Easter play besides the varying use of Latin. The originality of the Redentin author has been recognised. Recent scholarship on both linguistic and topographical grounds firmly attributes this play to Lübeck; see several articles in *Leuvense Bijdragen*, vol. 90 (2001), parts 1 and 2.

F14   Outline of the Innsbruck Easter Play of 1391

Das Innsbrucker Osterspiel: Das Osterspiel von Muri. Mittelhochdeutsch und Neuhochdeutsch, ed. and trans. Rudolf Meier, Stuttgart, 1962

[After the entry of Pilate and his soldiers, the Expositor speaks the opening forty lines, telling the audience to] 'sit down and be quiet' (line 5) [and] 'sit and keep quiet' (line 39). [The next Latin stage direction states] next Pilate sings 'Ingress pyl' [which the editor of the most recent edition expands to six lines of Latin beginning *'Post haec ingressus Pilatus'*; the next direction states simply] and speaks [the following six German lines are by no means a close translation of the Latin:] 'I am called Pilate, King in the land of the Jews, and intend to sit here in judgement, so that all Jews will have to sweat; if Jesus is to rise, then we must all die.' [His servant agrees, saying] 'Sir, I will help prevent that, even if I were to die for it. We will send people to the tomb, to prevent the stone being moved away.' [Only then do the Jews appear, singing ten lines of gibberish] 'cantant Judaicum' [the first Jew then sings six lines of Latin, given is the *incipit 'Audi Israhel praecepta domini'*, and speaks eight lines suggesting going to Pilate asking for the tomb to be guarded; the second Jew speaks eight lines agreeing; they then proceed to Pilate singing their standard eight lines. They agree with him that he will send out a messenger to recruit guards; the latter] runs to and fro in the central acting area [*currit hinc et inde in circulo*], [quickly recruits four guards, and as they make their way to Pilate the Jews again sing the eight lines, this time at the end the angels say or sing] *Siletis* [no verb is given. After only brief negotiations on pay, the soldiers go singing on their way to the tomb. On arrival one of them notes that] 'Jesus' disciples intend to come and steal the body from us and say he has risen.' [Nevertheless the next stage direction says] they lie down to sleep. [Despite this instruction the next words are] then an angel striking [them] down appears [*tunc angelus percutiens exiit*] and sings *cantando* '*Exsurge quare obdormis domine*'. [The angel speaks ten German lines and Jesus] sings 'Resurrexi' *et stat ad horam*. [The immediately following stage direction has Pilate send the messenger to check on the guards; though they are asleep he speaks four lines to them and reports back to Pilate who then returns with him to the tomb to catch them asleep. The defence offered fits what the stage direction said] 'Sir, we will swear by our honour as knights, this morning as day broke, great harm befell us: a magnificent angel came from high heaven and struck us [down] as though dead.' [Another states] [. . .] the body has been stolen from us! Jesus' disciples have done this.' [Without further comment from or mention of Pilate they begin fighting one another; the stage direction reads] *Et percutient se modicum ad horam. Quo facto Ihesus et angeli ibunt ad infernum, angeli cantant 'Cum rex gloriae'.* [The action therefore cuts from the fighting soldiers straight to the start of the Harrowing of Hell, where the liturgical basis leads to a series of Latin *incipits* being given, each expanded by the editor. Some time after Adam has sung *Advenisti* he speaks ten lines including] 'Be welcome, dear father Jesus Christ, how long you have been.' [He and Eve recall regretfully the Fall and Jesus says] 'Now come, my dear ones, into my father's kingdom, which is prepared for you eternally.' [A damned soul is prevented from following the saved, then Lucifer laments] 'Alas! Alas! Pride, that you were ever invented! I was a bright angel and shone above all the angelic host.' [. . . We have now reached line 350. The next 150 lines are devoted to Lucifer refilling Hell; he sends Satan and the other devils out to recruit from a long list beginning] pope and cardinal from Avignon, patriarch and legate, [. . .] king and emperor [and including professions such as baker, butcher, weaver, cobbler, shoemaker, drinker, gambler, miller, smith, gossips. He welcomes six souls individually to Hell, but rejects the lover, who he fears will populate Hell with his bastards. – This figure in some other plays is an amorous priest.

The three Maries now appear, sing Latin texts the whole of which are in the manuscript and speak in German; and at line 540 the Mercator enters with his wife and maid. Rubin volunteers to be his servant Their scene ends only at line 1075 and includes both Rubin and Mercator singing in Latin. At this point comes the action associated with the words *quem queritis*. The Third Mary is upbraided by Jesus] in the shape of a gardener [saying] 'Is this appropriate for good women to be running around like servants in this garden so early in the morning?' [to which she replies] 'Why are you shouting at me like this?' [Only at the second meeting is Jesus recognised. The play ends with Peter and John having met Mary only after Jesus has been seen by the initially doubting Thomas.]

F15   Outline of the Redentin Easter Play, 1464

Das Redentiner Osterspiel. Mittelniederdeutsch und Neuhochdeutsch, trans. Brigitta Schottmann, Stuttgart, 1975. (See also A. E. Zucker, *The Redentin Easter Play Translated from the Low German of the Fifteenth Century*, New York, 1966 which has not, however, been consulted here.)

[After the title *De resurrectione* the first stage direction follows immediately. Two angels share the opening, the first beginning] 'Be silent all of you, both rich and poor [and the second] Sit down and rejoice, [ending] Let each one hear and see.' [A Jew then reminds Caiaphas and the others that Jesus] 'claimed to be God's son [and said] he would rise on the third day [so that] we must have the tomb guarded, so that he cannot escape. If his disciples get him away from there secretly, they will say he has risen from the dead.' [Pilate finds the idea absurd but consents to his soldiers being posted as guards:] 'If I want any peace I shall have to send you watch and guard.' [Pilate then goes and supervises the setting of the guard at some length, now agreeing] 'If he were to rise in the third night we should all be disgraced thereby.' [The guards are joined by a watchman, first mentioned in the stage direction 'The watchman sings and after one line says' *Vigil cantat et uno versu finito dicit*: It therefore seems that the text of his song is not included, only his speech which ends] 'If anything happens, I will help you with the sound of my horn.' [Three soldiers in turn respond to his calls, with increasing irritation, the second conversation containing the local allusions which fit Lübeck, the third beginning his reply] 'Watchman, dear kinsman, I will give you all my treasure if I can sleep a little.'

[The next stage directions after his speech are:] Angels: 'Be silent' [*Angeli: 'Silete'*] [and] Raphael above the tomb is to sing 'Sleep!' [*Raphael super sepulchrum cantet: Dormite!*] [Raphael then speaks four lines, the angels sing again – what is not specified – then Uriel sings [?] 'Rise up' *Exurge* [and the fourth angel speaks 18 lines beginning] 'Rise up, God's child, to whom we are subject! Rise up, divine consolation!' [The next stage direction states] then an earthquake occurs [*Tunc fit terre motus*, giving no clue how this is marked. Jesus sings] 'I have risen' [[*Resurrexi*] and speaks] 'Now everything is accomplished, which was previously planned in eternity, that I was to die a bitter death and regain grace for mankind. Therefore I have now risen and am going to Hell to fetch out of it Adam and Eve and all those dear to me who are born to joy, which Lucifer lost through pride.' [As the souls in Hell rejoice we have speeches from Abel, Adam, Isaiah, Simeon, John the Baptist, who is just arriving, and Seth, who speaks 34 lines spanning the period from the death of Adam to the birth of Christ.]

[Satan then reports to Lucifer the great catch who is coming their way, Jesus, for] 'How could He be God's son, since He fears the pains of death?' [Lucifer knows differently:] 'God cannot die, Satan, you poor fellow, He cannot die, He will destroy Hell for us!' [As Jesus approaches Hell, David first speaks then sings] 'O key David' *O clavis David*, [likewise Adam; Eve only speaks. Lucifer resents the interruption:] 'Now see, it not strange, that we cannot remain in peace? We have lived here more than five thousand years without such disturbance.' [Jesus announces He will break the bolts on Hell's doors, then sings and then speaks that He is Alpha and Omega. From the stage directions] He then breaks Hell and seizes Lucifer: . . . [*confringit infernum . . . Et arripit Luciferum*]. [When Jesus begins to lead the saved souls away Lucifer, Tutevillus[1] and Satan try to keep back John the Baptist; then Enoch and Elias have to explain their presence in Paradise, as does the saved thief; the scene ends with an angel leading the souls back to Paradise.

At line 755 we return to the guards being wakened by the watchman, who sings an unspecified song, blows his horn three times and speaks twice, first a parody of a dawn song [*aubade*], secondly saying] 'Are you going to sleep all day? The sun can shine on your backsides. Our townspeople's maids have already fed their pigs. It's no use my blowing on the horn any more for you, you need the bells on the tower ringing.' [Each guard speaks once, including the lines] 'Things have gone disgracefully for us: Jesus is risen [. . .] I don't know what to say. A great earthquake came before daybreak, that caused harm for us all, I could neither sit nor stand. Oh! As I said already, but none of you would listen to me, his disciples have come and taken the man away from us [. . .] We will go to Caiaphas and inform the Jews of these things.' [In reply to the Jews' sarcasm when they report, the fourth soldier retorts:]

'Annas, foolish man, let such statements be! I will tell you an important fact, that Jesus is a great lord. In truth I saw the angel come from bright heaven in shining glory and take the women along with it to the tomb, and speak thus "Jesus of Nazareth is risen and has gone to Galilee." We think nothing of your mockery. If you go and look you will find the tomb undestroyed, the angel lifted the stone away. That cannot have been otherwise. God has overcome the pains of death.'[2]

[Caiaphas after taking advice – silently [*facto consilio*] – bribes the soldiers to keep quiet:] 'If anyone asks where the body is [. . .] you must say the disciples stole it from the tomb.' [Annas agrees the Jews will defend the soldiers against Pilate if necessary. Summoned by him to explain, he threatens then with the thumbscrews and other punishment, so they invoke the Jews' promise and he relents after reading Caiaphas' letter, concluding with the following twenty lines:]

'It seems to me the Jews are disgraced. They can turn it this way or that, I cannot find any truth in their statements. If I have understood the matter correctly, they have acted foolishly, that Jesus died at their hands. They have got themselves eternal heartache. Jesus who had come from God, has risen from the dead. This they would dearly like to cover up. They are all going to get a taste of it. They said so in advance themselves and they will rightly pay the price. I would gladly have seen him live. I said "I will not be guilty of his blood" and they all shouted out loud "That is all a mere nothing to us! Let his blood be on us and our children!" That may well come about to their great harm.'

[The second half of the play, from line 1043 to line 2025, is set among the devils in Hell. It begins, immediately after the above speech by Pilate, with the chained Lucifer on his barrel lamenting, as the stage direction states:] *Tunc diaboli educunt* LUCIFERUM *cathenatum, qui sedens in doleo lamentando dicit.* He thanks his devils for their loyalty and regrets that after five thousand years' stability Jesus has changed things.] 'But we will not be dispirited and never give up. Since we have lost the saints in this way, we must look out for sinners. [After a pause he continues] All be off from here quickly and strive to do my bidding. Teach the people in such a way that they turn away from God.' [Satan] the cleverest among them [is encouraged especially and asks whether any and everyone is welcome to Lucifer, who replies with a long list of likely candidates. It starts with] rich and poor [and continues with a list of thirty-two professions and groups; though it includes] knight and nobleman [the other thirty in the list are people the citizens of Lübeck are more likely to be able to identify with, including usurer, thief, baker, brewer, scribe, ploughman and carter. The passage of time has to be assumed, since immediately after Satan's speech encouraging his fellows as they split up to roam the world, we read] Lucifer calling his people cries out in a loud voice [*Lucifer vocans suos clamat alta voce*]. [After a delay only Satan appears and reports that he was delayed because just about to capture the soul of a usurer; but that the others are all waiting a little distance away because they have drawn a blank. Lucifer encourages them to report to him and Astrot explains what a hard time they have been having . . .] where we knew there were people we had converted to our ways by our evil devices and taught them our works – we had completely lost them all, they have chosen to give us up.' [Lucifer then sends them out again with the special tip to go to Lübeck,] 'where many people are going to die'.[3]

[When Lucifer calls out this time Puk, Lepel and Noitor report a good haul. Baker, shoemaker, tailor, innkeeper, weaver, butcher, peddler, thief, each in a speech of fourteen to sixteen lines reports his tricks and misdeeds which have brought him to Hell; in each case Lucifer and the devil who caught the sinner each speak at considerable length in one or two speeches. Licketappe is reproved for catching only one soul, but it is the thief, who takes some controlling. Funkeldune has caught no souls, apparently because he is lazy.] 'I lay by the fence and listened in all directions, but got no glimpse of a soul, neither layman nor cleric. Then I began to sleep for rage.' [Lucifer dismisses him and banishes him from Hell] 'Go and become a knacker, then you can sleep all day [. . .] You are dismissed, I think I'll get servants. Indeed I will no longer put up with you! Clear off out of my sight. If ever again you come where I am, it will bode you ill.' [Lucifer then notices the absence of Satan and is concerned] 'Satan! Satan! Loyal servant! Alas, I fear he is dead!' [Satan arrives bringing a priest whom he thinks he has captured because] 'You murmured keenly with your mouth, but as far as I could see your heart was never in it.' [But despite the initial confidence of Lucifer and Satan the priest makes things too hot for Lucifer who says] 'O, Satan, you deserve to be hanged! The priest has singed my hair! He achieves that with mere words. If he came into our system, we would not have to wait long before we had to clear out of Hell. [And later] Satan! Let the priest go! I cannot stand the heat any longer!' [Because Satan does not give up on the priest soon enough, Lucifer banishes him and puts him under the power of the priest, whose parting words are] 'If Jesus again comes before your gates, he will destroy the whole of Hell. Of one thing I am certain: that God is more powerful than the devil.'

[Lucifer begins his last speech] 'On account of my pride I am lost [. . .] Pride is the start of all sin.' [He then cheers himself up slightly but finally is so depressed at the prospect raised by the priest of Jesus coming again that his devils have to carry him off to Hell.

The final speech is addressed to the audience by the Conclusor.]

[1] This is commonly used as the name for one of the devils in Easter and Passion plays.
[2] This speech has been quoted in full since it includes the only reference in the whole play to the three Maries.
[3] This may be a comment on the epidemic in Lübeck in 1484.

Passion plays

Among Passion plays, too, the aim here is to present a representative selection from different parts of the German-speaking area. The Lucerne material is best known to English-speaking readers and will therefore not be emphasised. Entries 2031 to 2256 in Neumann come from Lucerne yet cover only material up to the

1571 performance, i.e. he includes none of the material concerning the 1583, 1597 and 1616 performances.

Well-documented but little known is the material from South Tyrol, now in Italy but always German-speaking. The texts were first edited by Wackernell a century ago (*Altdeutsche Passionsspiele aus Tirol*, ed. J. E. Wackernell, Graz, 1897). His edition included much information about the performances, recently repeated more exhaustively and accurately by Neumann; Wackernell's edition followed the conventions of his time and sought to reach the archetype from which the various extant texts had derived.

Performances for which texts survive took place notably in Bozen and Sterzing (now known officially, though not in German-language scholarship on these plays, by their Italian names of Bolzano and Vipiteno) and Hall. As in Lucerne, we owe the survival of such a concentration of material to one individual, in this instance Vigil Raber (died 1552), who deliberately added to the archive bequeathed to him by the schoolmaster Benedict Debs (died 1515). Both were involved in the Bozen parish church performance of 1514, on which we will concentrate, considering archive material in Neumann besides the actual play-texts.

F16 reproduces what Raber wrote at the end of a manuscript of the Palm Sunday play.

F16   Vigil Raber on the performances at Bozen, 1514

Neumann, item 545

This play was copied by me Vigil Raber at Sterzing during Lent and presented to the council at Bozen, where it was performed in the year 1514 together with the whole Passion, and played on seven days, on each day its specific material [*yeds tags ain sundere matheri*], namely on Palm Sunday this play,[1] on Maundy Thursday the Last Supper and Christ's capture, on Good Friday Christ's Passion, on Easter ['Baptism'] Saturday Mary's lament with the prophets, on Easter Day Christ's Resurrection, on the Monday the brethren [going] towards Emmaus, on Ascension Day the Ascension, etc. Such plays first undertaken and *phradgschlagt* [= ?] by the eminent Lienhard Hiertmeier the elder, citizen and provost here in Bozen, also master Benedict [i.e. Debs], schoolmaster, together with me Vigil Raber.

---

[1] i.e. the one to which this note is appended.

The Bozen Palm Sunday Play, 1514

Despite the relative wealth of material from Bozen and Sterzing, there is a less than perfect match between the published surviving texts and the archive entries. The third volume of the Sterzing *geistlichen Spiele* contains both the basic text relating to Bozen in 1514, *Rabers Passion*, which he copied later in the year from the text actually used for the performance; and the *Passion from Hall*, which is generally acknowledged to have been copied for this Bozen performance. But **F16** comes from the manuscript of the *Palm Sunday Play* and we have also the plays for Maundy Thursday and Ascension Day. Typically for Tyrol the plays were performed on a series of non-successive feast days. It is therefore correct to say that the 1514 Bozen performance stretched over the stated seven days and is in that sense the longest recorded play in German; but none of the plays exceeds 2,500 lines of spoken text and therefore they do not add up to as much as the 10,916 lines of the basic Lucerne text in Wyss' edition. The three texts that follow contain many interesting stage directions in Latin showing movement and gesture.

We concentrate on the *Palm Sunday Play*, with its stage plan [see **F17(a)**, **(b)**, **(c)**; **F22**] and besides information from the text we adduce the municipal records [see **F18**, **F19**] and Vigil Raber's own notes [see **F20**]. Not all archive entries relate specifically to an individual play.

F17 Bozen Palm Sunday Play, 1514

Sterzing, vol. IV, pp. 7–95

(a) Latin stage directions on movement and gesture

[After the opening speech by the *Predicator* the play opens with the temptation of Jesus:] With all the persons located in their assigned positions the Saviour walks to and fro in a desert place and prays. Meanwhile Luciper [*sic*!] comes out of Hell and catching sight of Jesus from a distance approaches Hell calling Sathanas. [He tells him to try tempting Jesus dressed] 'as though you were a cleric.' [Consequently] Sathanas soon enters Hell and changes his clothes. Then he approaches Jesus and says in greeting [. . . Later in the temptation] Then they both go to a high place. When he gets to it Sathanas speaks pointing out to Him all the countries of the world saying [. . . The action moves on to a series of healing miracles] And thus the Disciples approach Jesus and He leaves with them and the crowd following towards the Paralytic. The Canaanite woman follows Him shouting out after Him, and two men lead a girl behind them tied up with bonds [*sumibus*], screaming and raging (Matt. 15). The Canaanite woman says [. . . On reaching the Paralytic Jesus asks simply] 'Do you want to be healed?' [He replies at length, then] He takes up his bed across his shoulders and quickly crossing the synagogue is held by the Jews and interrogated as follows. Jesus however goes into the temple.

[The confrontation with the Jews about the Adulteress ends with Jesus' words] 'Indeed, indeed, hear me: before Abraham was, I am.' End of John Chapter 8. And Jesus leaves the temple with these people, He moves off with His disciples because the Jews are picking up stones to throw at Jesus. Pharisees go to their position. But the eight Jews remain in the temple. Jesus walks further. Then the disciples seeing the blind man approaching, Peter says to Jesus: 'Master, who sinned that this man is born blind? Did he do it himself or his parents? You should now make this known

to us'. [Alongside this speech in the right-hand margin is] John 9th 9. [At the start
of the raising of Lazarus Jesus calls for Mary] And thus rising Magdalena quickly
leaves her place and finds Jesus, with the Jews following a long way off. [. . .] Here
Magdalena comes to Jesus. Falling at His feet she says weeping [. . . Then] Lazarus
rises[1] steadily [*continuo*] with his hands and feet bound and a kerchief [*sudarium*[2]]
on his face [. . .] Then Lazarus proceeding in front of Jesus' feet speaks to Him [. . .]

[1] Careful reading of the edition reveals that at the raising the Latin words '*Lazare, veni foras*' have been
    added later in a different hand.
[2] English appears to lack a translation for this Latin word; the German is *Schweisstuch*, i.e. 'sweat cloth';
    it is the word used for the cloth Veronica applies to Christ's face on the way to Calvary and the alter-
    native term in the drama texts is indeed *Veronika*.

(b)   Movement of groups

Then these four Pharisees and Lazarus go with Jesus into the house of Simon the
Leper. Welcoming Jesus and his disciples Simon says [. . .] Then Jesus and Lazarus
sit down to a meal with Simon. Then Magdalena comes and speaks to Simon's
servant [. . .] Then Magdalena enters pouring the ointment on Jesus' head. Then
Judas [I] Scarioth standing before the table sings.[1] [After Judas has approached the
Jews and they have conferred further] Now the Apostles also rise from the table
and stand before the home of Simon until the arrival of the same Malaluel and
Judas. Jesus so far remains seated. Then Annas speaks to Malaluel [. . .] Sinagogue
sings. Then Malaluel proceeds and Judas goes with the Succentor, following, and
when they come in front of Simon's house Malaluel speaks to the disciples as they
are standing in front of that house [. . .] Then Malaluel alone comes to Annas. He
quizzes him. Meanwhile Jesus rises from the meal. The others remain in Simon's
house and He goes out to the disciples. Bartolomaeus speaks to Jesus [. . .] Then
Judas with the Succentor following Jesus furtively come to the Jordan. Lamech in
Bethany says to Mathusalah [. . .] The Sinagogue sings. Thus Jesus and all crossing behind him go along (?) [*secus*] the Jordan and when He has reached His position Jesus takes his disciples aside and says [. . . After the healing of another blind
man, without his being touched] All the populace praise the Lord[2] and Jesus with
His disciples crosses to the Mount of Olives, and as He approaches sends Peter and
John [to get the donkey] So they both cross to the place where the donkeys are
standing and release them (?) [*sollunt illis.*] [. . .] The Sinagogue sings. Jesus sits on
the donkey and rides. The disciples follow and reach the position. A certain youth
exhorting others meets Jesus, saying [. . .] Two cut branches from the trees, and
two lower down pick them up and spread them out. Then the first one spreading
speaks to the riding [Jesus . . .][3]

[1] The only Latin text in this play for which music is provided.
[2] A rare occurrence of the term 'the Lord'; usually Jesus or Saviour [*Salvator*].
[3] From this point onwards the liturgical aspect becomes dominant and Latin singing is frequently indi-
    cated coupled with German speech.

(c)   List of participants

[The castlist shows that the roles indicated by asterisks were played by women; other female parts were undertaken by men.]

Herald; Lucifer; Satan; Saviour; three angels; Gabriel; Canaanite woman; Peter; Canaanite woman's daughter;* Paralytic; Paralytic's servant; first scribe; Sadoch[1] the Jew; second scribe; chief rabbi [? Archisynagogus]; first Pharisee; second Pharisee; Annas; Caiaphas; Caiaphas' first servant; second servant; third servant; fourth servant; Nicodemus; Adulteress; first Jew; second Jew; third Jew; fourth Jew; Man blind from birth; fifth Jew; sixth Jew; seventh Jew; eighth Jew; blind man's father and mother; Rabbi Moses; Rabbi Samuel; the precentor in the synagogue; Timothy [? Thineus]; Lazarus; Martha;* Mary Magdalene;* Martha's [male] servant; Simon the Leper; Thomas; Phillip; Joseph of Arimathea; Sareth the Jew; Tobias; Barnabas; Simon's servant; Judas Iscariot [played by Vigil Raber]; Malaluell the Jew; Lamech the Jew; Mathusalam; Arfarax; Gabin; Blind man along the way; Esrom; John with other disciples;[2] servant of [i.e. with] the asses; a certain young man exhorting; another young man exhorting; first and second young men prostrating themselves in the road; two young men who sing for the first time 'This [. . .]'; two young men who sing for the second time 'This [. . .]'; another two who sing 'How great [. . .]'; another two who sing 'Do not be afraid dau[ghter . . .]'; eight who sing 'Hail King, Crea[tor . . .]'; two bigger ones who sing 'With flashing [. . .]'; two bigger ones who sing 'They run up [. . .]'; two bigger ones who spread out their garments; first, second, third, fourth, etc.,[3] they sing 'Glory, laud [. . .]'; first Jewish buyer; Moss the Jew; second Jewish buyer; Israhel the Jew; third Jewish buyer; Habiatur the Jew; fourth Jewish buyer; Caleph the Jew; fifth Jewish buyer; Varachias the Jew; sixth Jewish buyer; Ozoch the Jew; Andrew; James; first Sadducee; second Sadducee; James the Lesser; Matthew; Simon the Apostle; Taddeus.[4]

[1] Proper names attributed to those playing their usual New Testament roles are given their conventional English form, e.g. John, Judas Iscariot; however, names taken from the Bible but given to 'unbiblical' characters, such as the individual Jews, appear as in the published German text, e.g. Sadoch and Mathusalam.
[2] This entry makes it impossible to state a precise total number of performers.
[3] This entry makes it impossible to state a precise total number of performers.
[4] The stage has to accommodate all these and still leave room for audience/congregation. What changes – if any – were made to it before the next play on Maundy Thursday we do not know. The church and municipal records contain numerous entries about payments made in relation to the plays for this year, but few of them permit assignation to a specific part of the action.

THE BOZEN ASCENSION DAY PLAY, 1517

The manuscript of the *Bozen Ascension Day Play* bears the date 1517 inside the front cover though a nineteenth-century note says 1514. Certainly it is another autograph of Vigil Raber's and it seems highly probable that even if this is the text for 1517 it is very close to the 1514 version. Even before the commissioning of the

Apostles, the play includes the choosing of Matthias at Christ's suggestion. At the commissioning the Apostles with the exception of James the Lesser introduce themselves by name to Jesus and the audience, and they do the same again later when they make contributions to the composition of the Apostles' creed.

The stage directions for the actual ascension are written in a mixture of Latin and German.

F18   Bozen Ascension Play, 1517: stage directions for the Ascension

Sterzing, vol. IV, pp. 257–99

Now Jesus stands in the midst of His disciples and they surround Him beneath the hole of Heaven [*sub foramime celi*]. [What this hole or opening of or in heaven is, we do not know; however the opening stage direction after the Precursor's speech puts the Apostles into two groups:] And then the Apostles enter to the designated place [*locum deputatum*], but Barnabas and Matthias and Thomas to their own place beneath the pinnacle [*sub pinaculo*].[1] [After Jesus' next long speech comes another mixed-language set of directions.] Here musical instruments are played. Then both angels are hooked on at the bottom [*vnden angehengt*]. Meanwhile the first one speaks to the Saviour [twelve lines of text]. Then they are drawn up above [*aufgezognn yberhalb*] singing 'Ascending into a high place'. The second says upwards [*aufwertz*] [six lines] A young man above the hole or the Third Angel [*Vnus juuvenis supra foramina, scilicet Tercius Angelus*] [four lines] The first angel replies to the place of the Saviour above [*Primus angelus respondit loco Saluatoris supra*] [ten lines] Then something is played on the organ or by the pipers [*Hic fiat aliquod jn organis vel per fistulatores*]. Meanwhile the Saviour is also hooked on and the first two hooked-on angels are to stand beside Him, with burning candles be ready to rise up, and the disciples kneel around them together, Mary too. Then the Saviour sings being pulled up: 'I am ascending to my Father and your Father, your God and my God, alleluia!' And as He is being let down again says [six spoken lines] For the second time He is taken up somewhat higher than before, singing [same Latin text] and in being lowered He says [six lines]. For the third time He is drawn up completely singing '*Ascendo*' as above and hanging He says [eight lines]. Then on the organ the horn and the pipers are sounded [*gepraucht*] until He is up. Then the angels sing: 'Men of Galilee, what are you staring at?'

[1] Whether this is the pinnacle of the Temple as on the plan for the Palm Sunday play [see **F22**] and whether this is then Heaven, is uncertain.

F19   Bozen account details, 1514

Neumann, items 548–604

(i) Further, spent on sustenance, food and drink, for the play at Ascension, for the Apostles on the stage [. . .] Further spent for drinking [*vertrinckhen*] on Ascension

Day for the stone masons and the carpenters when they worked above with the pulling up and down. 2h perner[1]

(ii) Paid to master George, carpenter, for 6 days' work when he made the stage for the ascension and the pulleys (?) [*züg*] in church and took it [all] down again. For all this paid 6h perner[2]

(iii) [There are numerous references to payments to Vigil Raber, including] Further paid to Vigil the painter with reference to the Ascension 1h 6kr; Further expenditure, cows' tails for the play, Vigil the painter received 1h 6kr; paid out to Vigil the painter when he wanted to buy beaten gold [=gold leaf?] 6kr

(iv) Paid to Silvester the painter when he played Simon the Leper, when the Saviour and the disciples ate together, they consumed of wine and pretzels and [illegible word] 2h 6kr.

(v) Further to Vigil the painter, when he worked for the play 12 weeks. Consumed 5m 2h 3kr[3]

(vi) Given to Alexius from the school for writing out the play-texts [*reimen puecher*] and for other expenses when he was the Saviour 2m

(vii) spent on eight wooden bowls, to go on the Jews' heads 11kr

(viii) for striped ticking/coarse cloth [*zwilch*] for Jews' caps 2kr

(ix) further spent on tinsel [*rausch gold*]

(x) paid to Michael from the school because he wrote the play lists [*spil register*] 10h; further 2h 6kr. Makes in all 1m 2h 6kr

(xi) Further paid to Master George, carpenter, when he worked at the minster (?) [*Auf der muster*]; and the grave down and back up again 2h; and erecting the stage and dismantling again and clearing away all sticks, wooden blocks and boards and to keep body and soul together and (?) [*vom hungerduch*, compare Modern German *am Hungertuche nagen*] 2h [. . .]

(xii) Further to Sültzner for four timbers (?) [*raffen*] of 6 fathoms [i.e. 6 feet] and for two beams [*träm*], also for the stage-makers 5h

(xiii) Paid to Anndre Tanner, the German schoolteacher, for binding two play-texts [. . .] 1h 4kr

(xiv)   Paid to Peter Paungarter for transporting wood, [. . .] blocks, boards from the minster down to the churchyard 1h 6kr

(xv) Paid to the carpenters on Palm Sunday, Maundy Thursday, Good Friday, Easter eve, Easter Day when they helped with the stage in the church for the plays, which was not covered by their daily wages, given as a tip [*trinckhgellt*] 2h 6kr

(xvi) Paid to Federl the tailor on the Saturday after Holy Cross day [= 6 May] for having made for the play all the caps [or 'copes' ? *Kapen*], slippers [*schlappen*], hoods [*hauben*], devil costume, body stocking and others all adds up to 1m 5h

(xvii) Paid to the rope-maker for 12 fathoms of rope for the clock [*ur*] and 6 fathoms for the cross, when they wanted to lower the Saviour, one into the other (?) [*ains in das annder*], at 9d per fathom, makes 2h 8kr 2d

(xviii) Paid to Hans [illegible name] for two cartloads when he carted wood from the cemetry to the minster for the play, 8kr

(xix) Further paid to Thomas Baker [*Peckhen*] for 24 oak [*ferhen*] timbers for the stage for the Passion [*zuo der pün zum Passion*] 8h perner

(xx) Paid to a scribe who wrote out the play-texts [*die reim piecher*] for 14 days, as payment 9h 4kr

(xxi) Paid to the sacristan from Hall for giving [i.e. providing ?] several texts for the play, as a tip, 2h 6kr

(xxii) Paid to Michl the Joiner for working for the play, all kinds of work according to his enclosed list [which does not survive] as follows: First he made the book for the Jews' school, for that 2h 6kr [. . .] further he made a board to go onto the cross, for that 4kr, a further 8 boards, for that 13kr; further two poles for the coronation [i.e. scourging] 6kr; [. . .] further a bishop's staff 3kr; further 13 [!] staffs for the Apostles, for that 1h; further 20 hoops[4] to go on the Jews' hats; for that 15kr; [. . .] further a Jewish staff, with which they struck on the book, for that 6kr; further a bier on which the calf was carried, for that 10kr; further a sceptre for that 4kr; further the sword and the wings for the angels, for that a pound; and a club for the thieves [*schachern*[5]] and a spear 1h Makes 1m 11kr

(xxiii) Agreed with Lienhart Aufleger, trader [*kramer*], for providing for the Passion Play [*spil des Passion*] linen, ticking [*zwilch*] fustian [*parchat*], taffeta [*zenndl*], and other things according to his enclosed list [which does not survive] as follows: first 16½ ells of linen, at 5kr per ell; further 3 ells of white linen, at 6kr per ell; further two ells of black linen at 8kr per ell, further 3 and one quarter ells of green linen at 9kr per ell; further one ell of blue linen at 9kr; 3 ells of brown linen at 8kr per ell, further 3 ells of harsh (?) [*herbene*] linen for 10kr. Further 3 bales (?) [*prätschen*] of fustian:1h 4kr; further 3 bales of yellow taffeta at 7kr the ell. Makes in total 2m 9kr 4d.

---

[1] Here and elsewhere 'h perner' signifies 'Bernese pounds', 'L' standing for 'Pfund'.
[2] There is a similar reference from Sterzing from 1548, which uses almost identical wording
[3] Compare the former British system of pounds, shillings and pence.
[4] *khüeff*   To do with the word for 'cooper', also means 'runner or rocker on sled or crib'; clearly some long thin pieces of wood.
[5] This word is regularly used for the thieves crucified with Christ.

F20   Vigil Raber's own notes, Bozen 1514

See **F19**

(i) What I had made: by Michael the joiner the song boards [*tafl*[1]], the title to go on the cross, 20 buttons to go on the bowls, the poles for the crowning, the two trestles [*prütschen*] in the synagogue, the bier for the calf, 13 staffs, also the board for the garden and nails, the hangman's club, 8 director's staffs [? *Regentn stäb*], the spear started. – by the locksmith for covering the boards, the bands. From the spurrier, covering the [illegible word] and covering the book also four small hooks[2] to go on the cross, the trinity tacked up [? *drifaltika[i]t auf gheft*] Luciper's mask riveted, a [illegible word] for the hangman's club. – Sigmund Sadler: the belts or harnesses [*gheng*] for the hanging also a handful of [uncertain reading of word] and two straps for the book.

(ii) The tailor took two ells of brown linen 14gr, two ells of green linen 14gr, two ells of black linen 14gr, 1 ell of white linen 7gr for copes [bracketing together these four items]. Also taken 8 ells of linen cloth for devils' costumes at 5kr per ell. The tailor also since, 1½ ells of cloth. Myself also two ells for [illegible]ing the masks at 9gr [. . .] Myself further [. . .] two ells of striped for 2h

(iii) What I have spent or have to organise. A large pot with a flat saucepan [? *tegel* = *Tiegel*] Further two small grey pots. Further two glazed tiles. From the tiler at the minster two small tiles at 8 f[ierer][3] and three large ones for 16f[ierer] – From the tanner cows' tails for 17f[ierer]. Nails for coating the boards 1gr [illegible word] For *loch* and nails 4f[ierer].

(iv) What Schwenn himself gave me money for buying initially. For three books of [uncertain reading, *reall*?] paper, 2h; further 2gr for two small books; further for ink 1gr [uncertain numeral]; further for a book of paper 3gr; further for varnish [*firnis*] 1gr; For a parchment skin [*permet haut*] 7gr; a small ball of binding thread [*ain kleuell pintgarn*] 1gr; For glue from Six Schrefl 2½ [totals] 10gr. Further 2h glue from Lintacher. *Aderwerch* from Chuenrat the sadler [. . .] for tinsel 4gr, for varnish 2gr. From Hans Redorfer for oil 2gr, ink for 3gr, and 1gr nails.

---

[1] This is the word for tablets of law of Moses; also for the boards with the text and music of the Jews' songs in the Lucerne play.
[2] To hang the notice on?
[3] Etymologically = ¼, i.e. 'farthing'.

Rueff's Zurich Protestant Passion Play, 1545

This play is demonstrably the source of text in several subsequent Catholic Passion plays and shows clearly how the same text can be used for reading or for performance. In Rueff's Preface addressed to Ambrosius Blarer, he discusses its use as reading material, and the text at the end of Day One and the start of Day Two gives clear indications of how it could be performed.

F21   Rueff's Zurich Protestant Passion Play, 1545

Das Züricher Passionsspiel: Jacob Rueff: Das lyden vnsers Herren Jesu Christi das man nempt den Passion, ed Barbara Thoran, Bochum 1984

(i) Author's preface, lines 127–45

[. . .] Therefore this booklet can serve and be useful to young people to learn and study from it as well as and better than other booklets which people have and use, such as 'table manners', 'advice of the wise', and whatever other books there are which teach manners and virtue. For from this not only can young people learn to read or write but rather come to a correct regard for and evaluation of the suffering of Christ our Lord as they are growing up and coming to understanding. ¶ Further it can serve and be useful to not only young people that they are taught from it. On which account no little effort has been expended on it, as is made clear in the Herald's opening speech, but particularly also it will suit and be useful for other people who are like children, having less understanding of divine teaching.

(ii) Text, transition from day one to day two

[Scene of the mocking of Jesus, stage direction] now they begin jumping about round Him and one leads the singing with the others following.
Another watchman calls these four towards daybreak and calls out the day [. . .]
Herald. The closing speech of the first day. [lines 2140–247]
End of First Day
[new page]
The start of the second day
Herald: 'Our Lord God Jesus Christ Himself is witness [. . .] For now we want to start with what we omitted yesterday, about which Matthew informs us in Chapter 27. Early in the morning as dawn was rising the matter was arranged by the elders and chief priests how they could dispose of Christ and have Him killed and murdered. To that end they planned cunningly and then led Him as a prisoner to the town hall [! *Radthuss*] with weapons, clubs, staves, judged His innocence falsely. In order that you are informed about these things, look who is present there. Caiaphas has got up from his bed. He will start today's play, he is coming on stage [*ban*] now.'
Caiaphas is now to walk about on the stage [*brügi*] and rub his eyes open as if he had just awakened.
Second Day
Caiaphas steps forward, rubs his eyes as if he has just awakened, looks at the sky and talks to himself [. . .]

STAGE PLANS

Several plans associated with performances of medieval religious drama have survived from the German-speaking area. None is uncontroversial. Reproduced here are two contrasting examples: the Lucerne plans [**F23(i)** and **(ii)**] are well known and contain a great amount of detail. The Bozen Palm Sunday play plan [**F22**] is little known and its 'difficulty' derives from the sparseness of the detail.

The Lucerne town clerk and director of the performance Renward Cysat drew himself a plan of the Weinmarkt square as it would be during the 1583 performance of the Passion play. Indeed, he had several goes; his first attempt survives as Collectanea L, fol. 374 recto, reproduced by M. Blakemore Evans facing page 153. He then produced a large A2–size plan for each of the two performance days; these are now catalogued in the Lucerne Zentralbibliothek as L Sc 1:20 and 21; Evans reproduced them, greatly reduced in size, between pages 140 and 141. An English translation appeared not quite full size as an insert in *Staging*. Alterations are evident especially on the plan for Day One, where certain groups are deleted and inserted elsewhere. Additions were also made in anticipation of the 1597 performance when Cysat was again in charge; on the original these can be seen to be in a paler ink.

For all the apparent wealth of detail, the fact remains that Cysat's drawings were made on the basis of past experience for his own benefit, and do not record every detail consistently for the benefit of present-day scholars. He drew in all the details which he knew from experience were likely to cause problems and left out everything which seemed to him self-evident and unproblematical. Thus, although the plans show where around the square the individual stalls are located by reference to the houses behind them, the plans provide no assistance to our attempts to understand the actual relationship between the rear of the stalls and the façades of the surrounding buildings.

The Bozen Palm Sunday Play was an innovation in 1514 and this is perhaps the reason why Raber made the sketch which is on page 1 of the manuscript [**F22**]. It is the subject of much controversy in its interpretation, since it is indeed only a 'sketch'. It is generally agreed that the play was staged in the Bozen parish church and whatever structure is here represented must fit into the church leaving sufficient room for services to continue and space enough for the audience. The plan's relevance to the following six performance days has not yet been examined by scholars.

F22   Vigil Raber's stage plan for the Palm Sunday Play, Bozen, 1514

Sterzing municipal archive manuscript: Ms Nro V, fol. 1 recto; dimensions 21.6 x 7.8 to 8 cms; published reproductions in *Sterzing*, vol. IV, p. 95; and in Harald Zielske's 'Die Bozener Passionsspielaufführung von 1514 und der Bühnenplan Vigil Rabers', *Daphnis* 23 (1994), pp. 287–307

This reproduction follows that of Professor Max Siller, 1996. The archway at the foot of the page is labelled '*porta magna*' [main door], with '*ingressus*' [entry] written above. Reading clockwise, the seven locations on the periphery of the central rectangle are assigned to 'Caiaphas', 'Annas', 'House of Simon the Leper', 'Hell', 'Angels with Choir', 'Synagogue', and 'Mount of Olives'. Within the rectangle the wording reads 'oben drauf' (on top) '*pinaculum*' (pinnacle); below comes '*Templum Salomonis*' (the Temple of Solomon). All the wording is in Latin except the item given a German gloss.

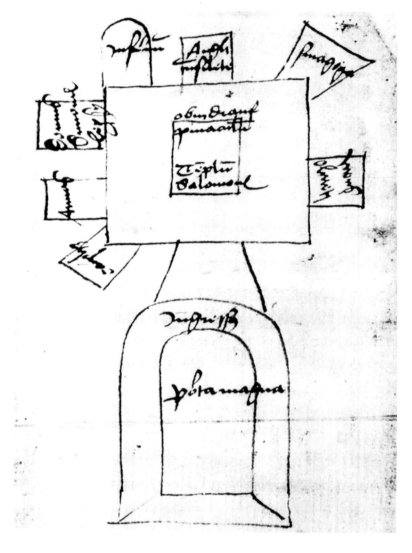

F23   (i) and (ii) Renwart Cysat's Lucerne stage plans for the first and second days of the Passion Play, 1583

Luzern, Zentralbibliothek, MSS L Sc 1:20 and 21, size A2; this translation is also published as endpapers to *Staging* © P. Meredith and J. E. Tailby

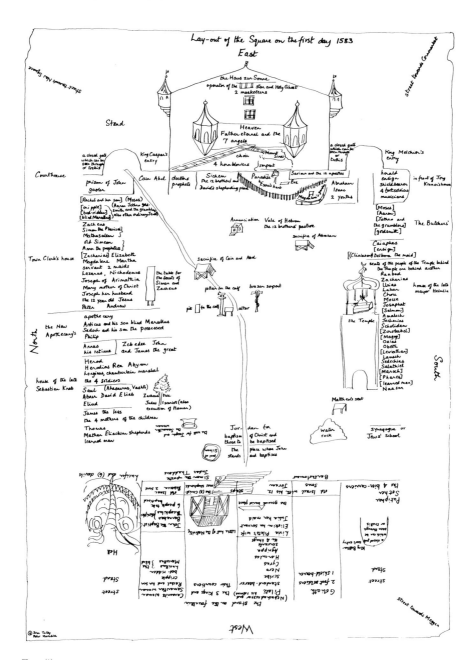

F23 (i)

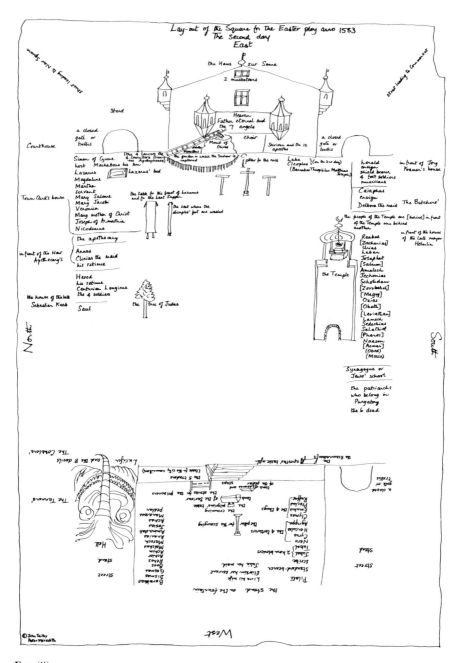

Lay-out of the Square for the Easter play anno 1583
The second day
East

the Haus zur Sonne

2 musketeers

Heaven Father eternal and the 7 angels

Stand

a closed gate or trellis

Courthouse

choir

Saviour and the 12 apostles

a closed gate or trellis

Mount of Olives

[the 4 Lancers the 4 Counsellors Dionis -ons Agathophonos]

the garden in which the Saviour is captured

pillar for the cock

Luke Cleophas (on the 2nd day)

(Barnabas Theophilus Matthias Joseph)

herald ensign shield bearer 4 foot soldiers musicians

in front of Jorg Kromer's house

Simon of Cyrene host Machabeus his son
Lazarus
Magdalene
Martha
servant
Mary Salome
Mary Jacobi
Veronica
Mary mother of Christ
Joseph of Arimathia
Nicodemus

Lazarus' bed

Caiaphas
Delbora the maid

The Butchers'

Town Clerk's house

the table for the front of Lazarus and for the Last Supper

the seat where the disciples' feet are washed

the people of the Temple are [behind] in front of the Temple one behind another

Reabod
[Zacharias]
Urias
Leban
Josaphat
[Salmon]
Amalech
Jechonias
Schobdam
[Zorobabel]
[Magg]
Ozias
[Obeth]
[Leviathan]
Lamech
Sedechias
Salathiel
[Phares]
Naasm
[Aaman]
(Obeth)
(Moise)

in front of the house of the late mayor Helmlin

the apothecary

in front of the New Apothecary's

Annas
Clinias the maid his retinue

the Temple

Herod
his retinue
Centurion Longinus
the 4 soldiers

the house of the late Sebastian Kaab

Saul

the Tree of Judas

North

South

Synagogue or Jews' school

the patriarchs who belong in Purgatory
the 6 dead

The Cobblers'

Lucifer

and the 8 devils

the apostles' table opp.

the Resurrection

a closed gate or trellis

The Tanner

[table for the city counsellors]

the 5 traitors

Hell

Stand
Street

Barabbas
Dismas
Gesmas
Roboas
Scribe
Pilate

Linus his wife
Electroin her servant
Standard-bearer
Pilate

the place for the pillar
the steps to the Saviour

Nacusson
Malchus
Actor
Rufus
Moses Esrom

Tubal
2 horn blowers

the steps in the prisoners

the pilgrims' table
Ara 4 thugs

the crowning table
the place for the scourging
the 4 torturers

Jubal
Lamech
Nero
Cyrus
Horculo
Naason
Agrippa
Ptolomeus
Emnibul
Climes

Stand
Street

the Stand on the fountain

West

© John Tailby
Peter Meredith

F23 (ii)

The most detailed information about costume [see also **F20**, **F21**] is to be found in Renward Cysat's writings concerning the Lucerne performances for which he was responsible. *Staging*, pp. 130–8 contains a translation of the greater part of the list for the first day of the 1583 performance in Lucerne. To complement it here is the complete list for the second day, which also contains considerable detail about properties for which actors were responsible [see **F24**]. In the opening paragraph several names are deleted and appear later with further detail added; these are omitted. See *Staging* p. 9 on the translation of terms describing parts of the square. [See also **F23**, the translation of the Lucerne stage plans.]

Lucerne Passion Play

F24   Costume list, Day Two, Lucerne, 1583

Luzern, Zentralbibliothek, MS 172, V, B, fos. 2 recto–33 verso: Denckrodel der Kleydung vnd andrer nottwendiger Sachen A° 1583; transcribed in German in M. Blakemore Evans, *The Passion Play of Lucerne*, New York and Oxford, 1943, pp. 208–14

The following roles and persons keep their costume the same as on the first day without alteration: Director, Lazarus, Martha, servant, Raabod, Naason, Jechonias, Sedechias, Joseph von Arimathia, Caiaphas, Annas, Ozias, Salmon, Aomar, Josaphat, Doctor Ambrose, Doctor Augustine, Doctor Chrysostomus, Doctor Gregory, Doctor Jerome, the Doctors' boys, Amalech, Josue, Johel, Sampson, Samuel, Lucifer, Astaroth, Beelzebub, Bürstlin, Brendlin, Fäderwüsch, Unkrut, Krüttlin, Glissglas, Herodes, Josias, Laban, Lamech, Uriel, First, Second and Third Angels, Raphael, Gabriel, Nicodemus, Pilate, his scribe, his banner-bearer, his wife, his [correctly 'her' ?] maid, Scholidam, Salathiel, Apothecary, Hornblowers, Phares, God the Father, Zorobabel, Synagogue or Jews' school, Semei their schoolteacher, Magog.

Magdalene
As on the first day, but in the manner she is dressed after her conversion. She is also to have Spica Nardi or Rosewater in a beautiful box, to pour over the Saviour's head at Lazarus' feast. This happens twice, at the said meal and previously at Simon the Pharisee's meal.

Herald, his cornet and squire [called *ensign* and *shield-bearer* on plans], four foot-soldiers
They are again equipped as the first day, except that the colour of costumes and banners are red this day, whereas they were white the first day.

Saviour
Is dressed as on the first day, but has his different hair and diadem.

Apostles

They are also dressed as on the first day subsequent to their conversion and calling. Peter and Andrew are each to have an old-fashioned dagger at the Last Supper. Peter is carrying his dagger in the garden [of Gethsemane – it is never given its full name].

Zacharias in the Temple

As on the first day after the baptism of John.

The three maids

Clinias in Annas'		stall	Jewish	proud, individualistic, not costly
Delbora in Caiaphas'			Jewish	
Julia in Pilate's			heathen, neat and tidy	

Achior, Ananias, Achas, Malchus, Manasses, Amon, Achim, Boos, Aminadab, Maroch, Barrabas, Rehos.

These are all bailiffs, rascally fellows. They are to be rough, arrogant, disreputable in behaviour, dressed in Jewish but warlike costume, tattered and strange in style, short and secular in dress, all different, no two alike.

Amon is the false witness against Christ.

Barrabas is the murderer who is captured and freed.

Barrabas and Boos are the two who lead out and crucify the two murderers or thieves, therefore they are to have their equipment for that: two ladders, cords, ropes, pincers; are also to have clubs made of leather, with blood-sponges at the front, to break the thieves' arms and legs. They loose the right-hand thief from the cross and the bier-carriers [four according to Plan for Day One] then take him to carry him away; the left-hand one the two devils loosen and take him into Hell.

Barrabas brings the four torturers a bottle containing wine, ropes and willow switches for the scourging. Otherwise as regards clothing, he is to be more differentiated and more like a robber than the others.

Malchus, Caiaphas' servant, is the one whose ear Peter cuts off. He is to have in one hand a lantern to carry in the garden and in the other a sponge with blood to hold up to his ear.

Achim is the companion of Malchus in the garden or at the Mount of Olives, he carries a resin pot (?) [*Hartz pfann*] or torch; he is also the one who brings the dice to the four under the cross to cast lots.

Ananias, Aminadab. These two carry torches in the garden to the Mount of Olives. Achior, Amon, Manasses, Maroch, Boos, Rehos. These all carry strange, old Frankish and differentiated arms and weapons, partisans, halberds, battle-axes and the like.

Barrabas does not process to the Mount of Olives since during that procession he commits the murder.

Manasses is to have at the Crucifixion a basket containing pincers, nails, hammers, ropes.

Maroch is to have at the Crucifixion a sponge on a long reed, a pot on which he wets the sponge.

Nero, Cyrus, Hercules, Agrippa
These four, who torture Christ, are to be dressed as stated previously for the first day, disreputable, warlike, tattered, but differentiated from the Jewish style, for they were heathens.
They are also to have their equipment: ropes, cords, a stool or block to sit Christ on; a pole when they want to suspend him by the feet; a stick, after that a reed, to put into the Saviour's hand in the mocking. Item: scourges and rods for the scourging; a crown of thorns and two soft green poles which can easily be bent for the crowning. Also a pot with blood colouring, to wet the scourges and rods.
Agrippa has a hammer and nailpunch like a cooper, with which he forces the crown into the Saviour's head.
Nero has at the Crucifixion a little bottle with wine on his belt.

The four torturers' assistants
Emulus belongs to Nero, Proclus to Cyrus, Clymax to Hercules, Ruffus to Agrippa. They are dressed as on the first day.
They fetch the equipment for their masters, the four torturers, in the sufferings of Christ; they also carry it in the entry and exit processions.
Emulus has ropes and cords; Proclus scourges; Clymax rods.
Ruffus the crown of thorns, poles. He also fetches the stool on which they sit the Saviour and the purple red robe in the crowning.
In the procession to the Mount of Olives they are to carry torches.

Herod
Is dressed as the first day. He is to have ready the long white robe to dress the Saviour in for the mocking.

Longinus, Centurio
Are also dressed as on the first day. But in the procession to the Mount of Olives they are in armour. Also in the leading out of the Saviour to Crucifixion likewise in armour; subsequently, when the Saviour dies on the cross, they both ride up to the cross on horseback and in armour.

Maria Salome and Jacobi
Are dressed as the first day. They are also to have their tins [*büchssen*] ready to buy ointment for the burial of the Saviour.

Veronica
Is to be dressed like these two Maries, but somewhat differentiated. Is to have the white cloth on which the face of Christ is copied, which she presses into the Saviour's face in the leading out [to Calvary].

Mary the Mother of Christ
Has her clothing with the white undergarment [*vnderkleid*] blue coat [*Mantel*], hose [*Hosen*], shoes, halo, the same as the first day. But on the second day a broad, white, clean cloth over her head, which is to hang down at both her sides to her knees and completely cover her hair.

Joseph of Arimathia and Nicodemus
Are dressed as on the first day.
Joseph is to have the long linen cloth in which to bury the Lord and the 'Aromata' or ointment box for the burial. He has pincers and the big nails in his pocket [the purpose of these is explained elsewhere: 'he drops them one by one as he is loosing the Saviour'] when the Lord is being loosed from the cross, likewise a long cloth, to lower the Lord with.

Simon of Cyrene
Helps the Saviour carry the cross, comes dressed as a old honourable friar/fellow (?) [*Brüederlein*], grey hair and beard, in the Jewish fashion, strange but not expensive.
He carries a jug of water and when the Jews push him under the cross, he drops the jug.

Judas Iscariot
Is dressed as the first day. He is to have his equipment and things ready for hanging himself and a live plucked cockerel in his bosom, as if it were his soul.

Dismas, Gesmas
Are dressed in a tattered, poor, strange fashion, as thieves and murderers.
Dismas is the one on the right, Gesmas the one on the left side.
The one on the left is to have red hair and beard, also a black squirrel around his neck or in his bosom, as if it were his soul.
The other black hair and beard, the beard short and well curled,[1] is also to have a clean white rag doll round his neck or in his bosom, as if it were his soul.

The traders in the Temple
Anticus   ]
Sem   ] each has a basket with doves
Cham a calf; Caleph two little lambs; Japhet two kids.
They are all to be dressed in the Jewish style, with short clothing, not costly, like Anticus, as is said about him for Day One, like traders.

Caiphas' ensign
Is dressed like the first day.
But in the procession to the Mount of Olives, in the leading out [to Calvary] and the Crucifixion he is in armour.

Pilate's standard-bearer
Is dressed like the first day.
But in the procession to the Mount of Olives, in the leading out [to Calvary] and the Crucifixion he is in armour.

Josaphat
Is dressed like the first day.
But in the procession to the Mount of Olives, in the leading out [to Calvary] and the Crucifixion he is the Jews' captain and in armour.

The Host of the Last Supper
Is dressed as a rich, honourable citizen in long clothing, though not as long as the Jews in the Temple, but also in Jewish fashion.
He is to have a little barrel of water, with which he greets the disciples.
He is to prepare the table for the Last Supper, including the Easter lamb, which is to be roasted, cut up and put back together again in advance.
After that wild plantain and lettuce (?) [*wilden lattich, salat darzuo*]
Item, wine, bread, small beakers or glasses and a pewter (?) [*zilgen*] beaker like a chalice, out of which the Saviour gives the disciples a drink. [A note elsewhere, MS 177, fo. 50 verso, ponders and decides: 'Should one have red wine for the Last Supper? It is to be white wine.']
Item, twelve of the big hosts [i.e. Communion wafers], one to give to each of the disciples. Item, a coal fire to burn the bones of the lamb. [MS 178, fo. 87 recto notes: 'The bones can be removed secretly and small pieces of wood put into the fire instead.']
A pitcher of water, bowl and towels, also the apron for the Saviour to put on for the foot-washing.

Young man, Machabeus' son [i.e. son of previous person in list]
Is also to be dressed in Jewish fashion, neat and tidy, brings the bowl to the Saviour for washing the feet. [MS 178, fo. 87 recto again: 'Machabeus' son, who is also called Marcellus [. . .] He is also to be in the garden at the Mount of Olives, when the Saviour is captured and the disciples flee. But he does not show himself until the disciples flee; over his body-stocking he is to wear a white coat/robe [*mantel*], which he drops when the servants want to hold him.']

Angel Michael
Is dressed as the first day, except that when he goes to the Mount of Olives he carries a chalice in his hand.

Lucas and Cleophas
Are to be dressed as two respectable pilgrims, with staves, hats and the like, also short black boots. [MS 178, fo. 88 recto: 'They are to equip their table on the stand at the foot of the square above the hole where the Saviour's tomb has been.' See 'the pilgrims' table' on the Plan for Day Two, **F23(ii)**.]

Urias
Is dressed as the first day. But on the second day he is to set up in the temple a moneychanger's table and have the silver coins to give to Judas, likewise four bags of money to give the four knights [i.e. tomb guards], and a seal and equipment to seal the tomb in the four places.

At a place in the temple he is to set up his moneychanger's table and sit at it when the traders have anything to do, likewise when Judas comes and when the knights come.

The Patriarchs in Purgatory
Adam, Eve in their costumes as on the first day.
David with hair and beard. A crown on his head and a harp in his hand.
John the Baptist also in his costume.
The remainder all the same, with grey hair and beards and all naked in body-stockings.

Marcellus the young man in the garden
Is to be naked in a body-stocking and be covered with a robe/coat [*mantel*] of soft white cloth or linen over it.

The dead for the Resurrection
Are dressed in body-stockings as though naked, but deathly pale in colour and as dead people with skeletons painted on, also on their heads artificial [literally 'made'] skulls. A bath wrap tucked under one arm [and] thrown over the shoulder, each carrying a skeleton in one hand.

They rise on the stand at the bottom of the square out of the grave into which the dead have been put when they are carried away [see 'the general burial place' on Plan for Day One and 'tomb of Lazarus and of the pedlar' on Plan for Day Two] and divide to go up both sides of the acting area [see *Staging*, p. 9] towards the Temple and the stalls, let the people see them as if they are appearing, without speaking, and immediately thereafter go back down through the grave that they came through.

[Cysat regularly reused the lists he made for himself, therefore this document ends with the following:]
A° 1597 Have been added:
Dionisius Areopatiga, Apollophanes – Philosophers. Are to be dressed in heathen style in long clothing.
Dionisius is to have a book, spectacles and a shaving-bowl with water.
Appollophanes [thus in Evans' transcription], a sphere or orb, as astrologers [or 'astronomers' ?] use.

---

[1] *kneblet*; according to Lexer, *Mittelhochdeutsches Taschenwörterbuch, knebel*, is a curler used in hair as punishment.

Corpus Christi Plays

The following details from Freiburg im Breisgau and Zerbst in Sachsen-Anhalt [see **F25**, **F26**, **F27**] show the only occasionally documented relationship between the Corpus Christi procession and play. [This material may be compared with **D10**, **I17**, etc.] In Freiburg the procession took place annually, the earliest surviving records dating from 1516, the play less frequently. In Zerbst the now lost early sixteenth-century text was only 399 lines long, some scenes having only a single line; the Freiburg text from the end of that century has 2,372 lines.

F25   The order of the Corpus Christi procession, Freiburg im Breisgau, 1516

Neumann, item 1568

The order of the procession on Corpus Christi Day in the fifteenth and sixteenth centuries:

First goes the schoolmaster with the procession and with cross and banner and the pupils with their decorated haloes

Painters: Adam and Eve with their group [*mit ir zuogehord*], Cain and Abel

Coopers' men: Abraham, Isaac, Josue and Caleph with their group

[Bread] Bakers: two prophets, the Annunciation, Emperor Augustus with their group

Priest[s]: Mary visits Elizabeth over the mountain [see Luke 1.39]; the shepherds, the angel, the crib [i.e. Nativity]

Tailors: Astronimus [= ???], the Magi

Priests: Simeon and Anna, Mary and Joseph at Candlemas

Shoemakers: Joseph and Mary in Egypt, Herod with his group

The society [fraternity ?] of the tailors' men: Palm Sunday with the twelve disciples; Mr Ludwig Oller with the Last Supper

Carpenters: Mount of Olives

Shoemakers' men's society: the scourging

Smiths' men's society: the crowning [i.e. mocking]

Coopers: Pilate leads Christ saying 'ecce, homo'; Annas and Caiaphas with their group

Butchers: the leading out [= Way to Calvary] with their group

Bernhart Gartner [possibly the name of the schoolmaster]: Mary and John following the cross

Goldsmiths and painters: erection of the cross with their group, the burial of the Lord and thereafter Mary lamenting

Clothmakers [*Tücher*]: the Resurrection and Apostles

Society [of]: St Sebastian [his scene]

Traders: St George with his group and St Christopherus

Citizens' sons: St Ursula with her group, St Appolonia and others

Paul Horgan's scene [No further explanation given!]

Tanners: Death, angels with instruments of torture

Smiths: Christ in the rainbow, Mary and John, the angel with the saved souls

Winegrowers [= ??]: the damned souls with the devil

Summary order of the guilds [zünpfkortzen ordnung] as they line up behind one another before the Holy Sepulchre and are to follow one another for Corpus Christi Day or for other such processions:

[In the manuscript each of the following words is on a separate line, without punctuation]

Butchers, coopers, painters, tailors, shoemakers, tanners, carpenters, bakers, winegrowers, traders, smiths, clothmakers, carters

F26   Preparations and finance, Freiburg im Breisgau, 1542–78

Neumann, items 1580–646; see also **F7**

(i) 5 May 1542. It is agreed to perform the procession with the play this year on Corpus Christi Day, as traditionally, without the living Lord on the cross, which is to be performed once in three years with the play [. . .]

(ii) 27 April 1545. Corpus Christi Day. It is agreed that since it is four years since the play on Corpus Christi Day with the scenes [figuren] and the Lord on the cross, it should be performed this year so that there shall be no loss of costumes and other things. But the expense of food and drink at the guilds in the morning is to be totally abolished. And it is to be negotiated with the butchers and landlords, that they will equip themselves so that visitors from elsewhere are provided with food and drink and are dealt with fairly as regards their money.

(iii) 7 May 1561. It is agreed according to old tradition to give those who are assigned to the foot of the cross [unders kreuz geordnet] on Corpus Christi Day the three pounds out of the common funds but the properties are to be saved and kept, so they they do not have to be made anew each year.

(iv) 26 May 1563. The painters here are to be commanded on oath to paint without delay everything for the Corpus Christi Play which still requires repairing and painting.

(v) 7 June 1563. It is agreed in order that Corpus Christi Day is well equipped [versehen], to instruct the scribes from the warehouse [kaufhaus] to organise and get the procession into good, advantageous order, according to the list they have, and Jacob Vifitz is to be ascribed to them [to supervise ?]. They are also to give the head of each guild a note [zedel] and with the order of procession, how they follow one another; and the priest is to be instructed to hold the office early in the morning before the procession. And after the completion of the procession the Crucifixion is to happen immediately before the refreshments, and a good space and room for it is to be made.

(vi) 4 June 1574. On Corpus Christi Day everything is to be organised and ordered according to old tradition, with the watch in armour, the carrying of the candles, everything else too in good order and with enthusiasm, so as not to become the object of mockery (?) [*damit man nicht zu spot komme*].

(vii) 23 May 1578. Corpus Christi Day is to be organised as two years ago and the Clerks of Works [*bauherren*] are to organise that barriers are made, which are wide enough, and benches in front of them, so that the leading members of the nobility and gentry [?] can sit round about, and nobody else is to be allowed inside such barriers, much less on the staging [*brugi*], apart from those who have speaking parts and are in this final play.

F27   *Grosses Regiebuch* for Zerbst Corpus Christi Play and procession, 1507

Neumann, item 3402

Organisation, ordering and description of the procession. A text on the significance and explanation of the scenes [*figuren*] which go in the procession on the Thursday in the Holy Pentecost week in the year fifteen hundred and seven.
[fo. 1:] ordering and organisation of the procession:
The oilmillers (?) [*Oelsleger*]: the creation of the world [*nach der (s)chepfer = ?*]
The bathkeepers [*bader*]: a tree with a serpent. Adam and Eve naked with twigs[1]
[. . .] When the lines are read, the angel is to expel Adam and Eve
Brewers' men: Cain with a club. Abel respectably dressed
Next scene: Abraham, a king, Melchisedek, wine and bread
Directors:[2] Abraham with a drawn sword, leading by the hand his son Isaac
The hatters: Jacob, already dressed as a patriarch
Directors: Moses with the tablets of the law
The sheet-makers [*lakenmecher*]: four of them carry the ark of the old covenant
szever and wood-turners: Jonas in the whale
The sheet-makers: David a king, with harp and servants
The master masons: four of them as ready to travel, carrying a vine. And a garden [*Engadi ?*] goes in front
The sheetmakers: Solomon a king, with his mother and their courtiers
The heads of Our Lady's [convent]; (Neumann footnote): The *Bruchstresser*[3] carry the enclosed garden [*ortus conclusus*] and its retinue. Mary's visit to Elizabeth over the mountain with two angels. As the text is read they are to embrace each other[4]
The Tailors [*wandsnyder*: cf. Mod Ger *Gewand 'garment'*]: the birth of Christ with the little house, with Mary and a child inside. To be carried by the barrel shifters [*ufc-zoger*][5]

The tailors: the three Magi, well equipped, the relics [*hilgetom*] in their hands; they point at the star on the little house

The heads of Our Lady's [Convent]: Joseph, an honourable man, well dressed with a flask and pouch. Mary on a donkey with a child. Joseph is to lead the donkey

The Bakers: Herod, a king, with a crown, on horseback, a sceptre in his hand. Well-armed servants with spears on which they harpoon children. Four women dressed in black, humble, wringing their hands, so that their coats [*mentell*] hang down from their shoulders. Are to pretend to weep

The Barbers: John the Baptist in a body-stocking, with a lamb on his arm, to which he points with two fingers 'behold the Lamb' ['*Ecce agnus*']

The barbers: Jesus with a devil. The devil has in his hands stones and a text 'If you are the son of God' ['*Si filius dei es*']. Likewise Jesus with a text: 'Not by bread alone' ['*Non in solo pane*'] Two angels with the text: 'And the angels' ['*Et angeli*']

The Ankuhn people [name of suburb]: Jesus with twelve Apostles, barefoot, Jesus in the middle, all with diadems

The carpenters: the scene of Herod with the beheading of John, dressed royally, together with his wife and daughter. four soldiers and four disciples of John in choir copes

The linenweavers (?) [*lynewefer*]: the raising of Lazarus from the grave. Jesus with two raised fingers, Lazarus in the grave with folded hands.

The coopers [*boddeker = Bötticher*]: Jesus with raised fingers on a donkey. Twelve Apostles. two young Jews in front throwing down cloths, two [more] who throw palms and sing 'This is' ['*Hic est*']

Pewterers [*Kannengiesser*]: Jesus and Judas. Jesus a text 'What you do, do more quickly' ['*Quid facis, fac citius*']. Judas a text 'Now, Lord I am' ['*Nuncquid ego sum domine*']

The farmers [*ackerleute*]: the Mount of Olives with Jesus and three Apostles when He is arrested

The tanners and shoemakers: Jesus with Judas, who is to kiss him. Here the previous twelve Apostles from Ankuhn shall come to this scene and stand in front of the sacrament until Jesus is taken prisoner. The Apostles are to run away, Judas is to have in his hand a big text: 'Greetings, master' ['*Ave rabi*']. At the same time they are to attack Jesus. Jesus attacked by four armed Jews, bound and dragged [off]

Annas with Jesus: here Jesus is to walk bound with Annas as a bishop on one side and on the other side a Jew who raises his hand to strike and carries in his hand a text 'That is how you reply to the bishop' ['*Sic respondes pontifici*']. On the market during the text Jesus is to fall down.

Brewers' men: St Peter with a long coat, a diadem. In one hand a text 'I do not know what you mean' ['*Nescio quid dicis*']. In his left hand a text: 'I do not know the man' ['*Non novi hominem*']. On each side a maid with texts. The one: 'You too were with Jesus of Nazareth' ['*Et tu cum Ihesu Naszareno eras*'], the other: 'And this man was with Jesus of Nazareth' ['*Et hic erat cum Iheso Naszareno*']

The honourable [town] council: Caiaphas with Jesus, bound, being led

Cobblers: Jesus with four Jews, a chain round his neck. Pilate on the right side, a white piece of wood in his hand and two banners before him

The honourable [town] council: Herod, beautifully dressed, a crown and sceptre before him. Jesus before him in a white garment and with a clasp (?) [*klatzer*]. Four Jews who lead Jesus bound

The shoemakers and tanners: Jesus at the pillar [i.e. scourging]. Two who hit him with rods

The shoemakers: Jesus on a stool [*stule*] Two who press the crown onto him with sticks. A Jew with a reed, a text; 'Hail, King of the Jews' ['*Ave, rex juedeorum*']

The aldermen/court assessors [*schepfen* = *Schöpfen*] Pilate, beautifully dressed. Jesus in a body-stocking with a red coat [*mantel*], a crown of thorns on his head. Two servants, one behind, one in front, with a bowl [of water] Pilate a text: 'Behold the man' ['*Ecce homo*']

The tailors: Jesus with a cross on his back. An old man who helps him carry it. Two thieves with crosses. Four Jews who lead him. Two Jews who lead the thieves. Two small Jews who throw him [to the ground ?] – Where the street is wide, the thieves are to go beside him, where narrow, behind

The traders [*cramer*]: a very well turned-out woman carrying the 'Veronica', modestly dressed. A cross set up

Darkness [Tenebre]

Mary modestly, well turned-out, John with Mary in a white coat, a naked sword turned towards Mary. After that Mary Madgalene with a box. Mary Cleophas dressed in black, with her [their ?] name[s] in her [their ?] hands. Centurion mounted on horseback, well turned-out; a servant at each side. In his hand the text 'Truly this man was the Son of God' ['*Vere filius dei erat iste*']. Longinus with a spear pointing upwards, well dressed. A boy who leads him.

Urbanus Richard: the Burial of our dear Lord

The smiths: the Resurrection of Jesus with a banner, a body stocking with five wounds, which is to be beside the grave. Two well equipped soldiers and two angels with white cloths. Also two graves, inside them two persons with white caps and folded hands

The farmers: St Stephen as an Evangelist [*Ewangelier*] two Jews who throw Stephen [to the ground]. Stephen is to have a reed in his hand

The coopers: twelve Apostles [again!] each with the sign of his torture, dressed in albs, wearing diadems on their heads with their names written on them; and each one with the text of one article of faith in front of his chest

The master sharpshooters: St Sebastian at a pillar, in body-stocking, pierced by arrows. Beside him one man with a bow, another with a crossbow

The heads of St Valentine's [church]: St George on horseback, as a knight in armour. A virgin with a crown, richly dressed, is to lead the dragon

The heads of St Bartholomew's [church]: St Ciriacus with a thick coat (?) [*diaken rocke*]. A diadem, the picture of a devil with him. St Lefin [?], a bishop's mitre and choir cope, a staff, pincers with a tongue. Lefinus and Nicholas together

The heads of St Nicholas' [church]: St Nicholas as a bishop, with a choir cope and mitre. A staff and three gold balls in his hands. His hand raised in benediction. St Lawrence as a Levite, a diadem, a grid and a reed in his hands

The furriers: St Gregory portrayed as a pope, with a mitre and cross. St Jerome as a cardinal, with mitre and cross, St Ambrose as a bishop, St Augustine as a bishop, a cross with three rays. They are all to have their names on their mitres

Die slechter koche [? = simple cooks[6]] St Michael as an angel, elegantly turned out, a cross in front of his head, a stole worn crosswise on his neck. Is to lead a devil on a chain

Die szeler [= counters? Of what?] St Christopher, barefoot, a child on the nape of his neck. He and the child diadem [and] cross on their heads. The child is to raise two fingers and a little old man is to carry a lantern

The heads of St Gertrude's [church]: Anna, dressed modestly. Together with Anna a young woman dressed in the style of Mary and a child in the style of Jesus, with a diadem. Elizabeth in courtly modesty with a minster [a model cathedral?] in her hand. All their names in their hands

The millers: St Maurice together with seven others, blacked up [*swartz beramit*] and in armour with a silken banner. Maurice a red shield with a yellow cross, good armour. All with crosses in front of their heads and loincloths

The heads of the Brotherhood of the Poor[7]: fourteen Holy Helpers [*Nothelfer*] with diadems and crosses on their heads. Jesus as a child in their midst. St Wendelin, a shepherd with a horn, sack and pouch

The heads of the Corpus Christi fraternity: St Katharine, beautiful, a crown and signs of martyrdom. St Margaret: a crown, most beautifully decorated, a dragon on her arm. St Barbara with a tower, chalice and host. St Dorothy leading a little boy by the hand with a basket of roses. After them follow as many virgins as possible, with their signs of martyrdom and their names in their hands

The sheetcutters [*lakenscherer*]: St Ursula, decked out royally, three rays in her hand. Before her a boy with a sceptre. One who carries her clothing behind her. Thereafter are to follow as many virgins as one can on the occasion assign to it, in white dresses, crosses before their heads, arrows, rays and other weapons in their hands. In groups of four

Joiners and painters: Death in a body-coloured garment, with a very effective death's head [*totenkappe*]; is to slink slowly, carry in his hand a scythe for cutting, is to remain from the start on the street [level?]

The bone breakers [*knochenhauer*]: Heaven. Jesus in front with a rainbow, so turned-out that one can see the five wounds. On one side Mary, a virgin, modestly dressed and with folded hands. On the other side St John with a diadem, also in a body-stocking and with a diadem. In the house of Heaven lutes, pipes, drums and all kinds of stringed instruments, as many as possible. In front of Heaven are to be children dressed in white, of all ranks: popes, bishops, cardinals, priests. One half of them an angel is to have on a rope leading to the right, in happy mood. The other half of the children of all ranks as stated above a devil leads on a chain; they raise their hands, weep and howl as the damned. A rainbow, a lily on the right side, a text: 'Come you blessed of my Father' ['*Venite, benedicti patris mei*']. On the left side a sword, a text: 'You cursed, go into eternal fire' ['*Ite, maledicti in ignem eternum*'] [. . .] At the judgement an angel shall carry a cross with all the arms of our Lord

The heads of the *hospital*: ten well decked-out virgins, five with burning lamps, happy. And five with dimmed lamps, sad and weeping

The shoemakers' men: Hell

[1]   The word is that applied to the twigs used in a sauna, hence the allocation of this scene to the *Bader*, who are also associated with nakedness.

[2]   According to a note by Sinteis in his edition, they were the owners of altars and the associated rents. See *Zeitschrift für deutsches Altertum*, vol. II, 1842, pp. 276–97.

[3]   According to Sinteis, a Zerbst street name.

[4]   As Bergmann points out, here follows the longest section of text, with prefigurations of the Virgin Mary.

[5]   According to a note by Sinteis.

[6]   No satisfactory translation for these two words has been found; *slechter* might also refer to butchers; other possible meanings of *koche* seem less likely.

[7]   According to a note by the editor Reupke transmitted by Neumann, p. 787, n. 14.

SHORT PLAYS ON RELIGIOUS SUBJECTS

Eschatological plays

Wise and Foolish Virgins

Though the surviving texts of and records[1] concerning such plays rarely match, the extant information from Thuringia provides an exception. Two versions of the Thuringian play survive, one from the third quarter of the fourteenth century, probably coming from Mühlhausen where it was found; the other dated 2 May 1428. Both are copies intended for reading, not associated with a performance; the older text is close to if not identical with that used in the 1321 Eisenach performance. The later text elaborates the speeches of the Foolish Virgins [see **F29**], giving them more individuality, but omits the dialogue between Jesus and the devils [*Teufelsszene*] besides the Latin stage directions and *incipits* for song [compare two versions in **F30**]. **F28(i)–(v)** reproduce in date order all the remaining references in Neumann to such separate performances, i.e. excluding such scenes as part of a Corpus Christi Play. With **F28(i)** compare **C21** which offers a different date and a slightly variant account of the incident.

1.   Neumann records two cases where he could not confirm the assertions of older scholars that *Zehnjungfrauenspiele* (literally Ten Virgins Plays) had been performed, from

Rattenberg am Inn where according to Dorrer there were several archival references to this play (Neumann, footnote to item 2353); and Köslin in Pomerania, now in Poland, where allegedly this play was especially popular in the fifteenth and sixteenth centuries (Neumann, item 1987).

F28   Performances of the Play of the Wise and Foolish Virgins

Neumann, items 1482, 1507, 2348, 1478, 2323

(i) Eisenach 4 May 1321 [. . .] there was a play at Eisenach[1] about the five foolish virgins, as the gospel describes. And when the five foolish virgins were damned, they behaved piteously and Our Lady and the saints all prayed for them, but that helped not at all. And this was played rather too harshly, for Mary and the saints do not pray for any of the damned, for they lack only God's will. So on Judgement Day God no longer wants to be gracious or merciful, but a strict judge. Until then in the present time He is gracious and merciful to us [. . .] Landgraf Friedrich der Freudige ['the Joyful'] also attended this performance and saw this and became very angry [. . .] It was scarcely possible to point out to him that this happened on Judgement Day and not before. And so he had a stroke and was lamed on one side and lost the power of speech, so it was hard to understand him, and thereafter he lived another three and a half years [. . .]

(ii) Frankfurt/Main 1492. In that winter they performed on the hill of Our Lady's Church a play about the seven [!] wise and seven [!] foolish virgins[2]

(iii) Pressburg [i.e. Bratislava] 1545. On the same day [27 May] paid also 14 d Viennese for sweeping the square after the performance of a holy play about the five foolish and wise virgins [title in Latin].

(iv) Eger [now Cheb in the Czech Republic], 1551: When they performed on the market the play of the five foolish virgins, to the actors 6fl [. . .]

(v) Munich 1552. 13fl 4s 6d paid to Master Jeronimus Ziegler, poet, as reward on account of a play [comedi] which he put on in honour of the honourable [town] council. It was about the ten virgins, five wise, five foolish, done in Latin and German. Payment made on 19 March, namely of the 12 talers, the ten belonging to him and the two [being] the reward of his followers.

---

[1] According to the Latin text of Neumann item 1481 [see C21], the performance was given by clerics and schoolboys [a clericis et scolaribus].

[2] If this is not simply an error, it would seem to be a case of making room for all who wanted to participate; compare the instruction to have as many virgins as possible in the scenes of St Dorothy and St Ursula in the Zerbst Corpus Christi play [see F27].

F29   Text of the Play of Wise and Foolish Virgins: the foolish rebuffed

Stadtarchiv Mühlhausen in Thüringen, Nr 20 'Ludus de decem virginibus', Hessische Landes- und Hochschulbibliothek, Darmstadt, Nr 3290 'Das Spiel von den zehen Junckfrauwen', *Das Eisenacher Zehnjungfrauenspiel*, ed. Karin Schneider, Texte des späten Mittelalters 17, Berlin 1964 [see **F28(i)**]

[The foolish attempt to join in the banquet attended by the wise virgins; s.d. after line 227] The foolish come singing to the wedding feast. [*Incipit* for their song] Second foolish one speaks:

'Lord Father, heavenly God, we implore you through your bitter death, which you suffered in the trial of the cross, spare us poor women, whose foolishness has delayed us. Now let us benefit from your great mercy and that of Mary your dear mother, and let us poor people enter your banquet.'

Jesus [*dominica persona* [as always]] [sings and speaks]:

'Anyone who has wasted the time of their youth and has not atoned for their sins, if they come and stand outside my kingdom, they will not be admitted.'

[The third is likewise rebuffed; the fourth suggests, after Latin *incipit*]:

'Since now God himself has refused us, let us implore Mary, the mild maiden and mother of all mercy, to have compassion on our great sorrow and implore her dear child on behalf of us poor women to have mercy on us.'

[Jesus is unmoved by her request and reminds her]: 'Mother, remember the words which they find written there: Heaven and earth should pass away before my word should be broken; according to that, all the heavenly host couldn't save one sinner.'

Lucifer to Jesus: 'Lord, believe me, you ought to be a just judge. Now let this cursed band go to Hell without a verdict.'

Jesus: 'There shall be just judgement. The cursed must go from me to the depths of Hell, for they are to become the companions of the devils.' [These four lines are repeated almost verbatim at the end of this scene. Mary's second attempt at intervention is ended abruptly by Jesus.]

F30   Text of the Play of Wise and Foolish Virgins: variant versions

[See **F29**, pp. 14–15]

(i) [Start of fourteenth century version: in Latin] Play about ten virgins. First the Christ figure [*Dominica persona*] enters with Mary and the angels singing the responsory '*Testimonium domini*' [extended by editor by reference to Psalm 18.8] Then the virgins singing the responsory '*Regnum mundi*' [extended by editor 'Hartkers Antiphonar S 208']

When this is finished the angels sing or rather [*sic*] the responsory [thus far all in Latin, now 6 short lines of German] Now be silent, dear people, and have things explained to you, be silent, let yourselves be informed about Jesus Christ, the dear Son of God, how sweet his name is to name.

[Latin] The choir sings the responsory '*Homo quidam fecit*' [extended by editor by reference to Luke 14.16.] Christ sings and stands up '*Dicite invitatis, ecce prandium meum paravi; venite at nuptias, dicit dominus*' [Continues in German] 'Messenger, I want to send you a long way into foreign parts to my dear friends; you are to make known to them and to all I hold dear [. . .]'

(ii) [Start of fifteenth-century version: all German, no Latin] The play of the ten virgins. Saint Augustine expounds for us the parable [*byspell*] of the ten virgins, five wise and five foolish, and it starts as follows here [switch to verse] Now pray to good Mary, the mother of God, that she intercedes with her son for us sinners.

God speaks to an angel: 'My friend, I want to send you a long way into foreign parts to my dear friends; you are to make known to them and to all I hold dear [. . .]'

The Rich Man and Lazarus

The *Erfurter Moralität* is a 1448 manuscript for reading, incorporating into the morality, some 18,000 lines long, dramatisations of three New Testament parables: the Wise and Foolish Virgins; the Prodigal Son; and the Rich Man and Lazarus. This is one of only two extant versions of the latter parable, of which the other is in a South Tyrolean text copied by Raber. His note dated 1539 on the outside of the manuscript states that he has had to copy this text again, since he has not recovered his copy lent out since 1520 [see **F13**]. This version takes 937 lines and thirty-three speaking parts, including all the members of the rich man's household, his five brothers and four peasants who constitute the final scene. It is clearly divided into scenes by the raising and lowering of a curtain. Towards the end, the relationship between play and reality blurs, immediately before and during the peasant scene.

F31   Text of the Play of the Rich Man and Lazarus, 1539

Sterzing, vol. v, pp. 237–66

[After 40 lines from Precursor:] When all is ready, then the curtain [*thüech*, literally 'cloth'] is to be taken away or down for the first scene [*figur*] [. . .]

The steward to Lazarus:

'Be quiet! My lord is now at table and cannot eat in peace because of you. So save your breath and find somewhere further away to sit.'

Then the curtain is closed.

Curtain away. Next scene.

[. . .]

Lazarus begins to die, speaks in sick fashion [*krancklich*]:

'Lord God, wretched man that I am, I cry up to you to your heavenly throne [. . .] and take me out of this wretched time [. . .] Jesus, I commend my soul to you at this hour.'

Then two angels come and the angel says:

'Be comforted, Lazarus, [. . .]'

The angels lead the soul before Abraham, the devils cry that they get nothing [. . .] Abraham says:

'Come here, my dear friend, receive your heavenly inheritance [. . .]'

Curtain closed. Exit Lazarus[1]

[. . .]

[. . . at end of next scene of Rich man in Hell, after speeches by two devils] then the devils jangle the chains and [there is] smoke and yells.

[. . .]

[The fourth brother: . . .] 'it belongs rightfully to me and my brothers, therefore I will fight you and go for your throats, you flatterers, spongers, devious gang!'

Then they draw their swords.

Curtain closes.

[the following scene shows the consequent injuries, in the text rather than any stage directions]

The steward laments:

[. . .] 'I laid claim to another's goods, it has cost me an arm. [. . .] Many a poor debtor I denied, and often wrongly did him out of his own.'

[. . .]

The entertainer [*spilman*]:

'And I am in great distress thanks to the hatred and fury of the five brothers, and have lost my right foot [. . .]' (lines 723–54)

The bailiff [*ambtman*]: 'What did I fight for? For possessions which are not mine [. . .] Note this, you people who are rich and generous, heed our example; be of generous hearts, so that the same does not happen to you as to my master and has now happened to us on his account; we give you that as a warning [*beyspiel* = *exemplum*?]'

Close curtain.   Open curtain. Scene 8 (*Precursor* then speaks, lines 806–21]

Curtain closes.

When everything is cleared away, the peasants enter looking in amazement

The second peasant: [. . .] 'He never let me off or made me a present of a single guilder. The poor got no mercy from him, therefore he is accused by me all the more readily, he always had in his service devious bailiffs.'

[. . .]

The fourth peasant [. . .]: 'The rich man was always after great possessions and has now died suddenly for it. I am not going to look round much for possessions, for the same could easily happen to me. I will get by as best I can, perhaps I shall still have bread to eat for the rest of my life, and leave the cares to someone who is more greedy [*gertiger*] than I am, I will just manage with my cattle.

Come on, you neighbours, let's not stand here any longer and after this unpleasantness [*unmut*] go to a good wine, where we will forget our sorrows, for at home we must eat only sour milk [= yoghurt!] We will get ourselves into a good mood, we are not likely to have it as good again! Come on! Come on! Let's go, for it is time.'
Precursor concludes [. . .]

---

1 Lazarus does not reappear, though this point is less than half way through the text.

Old Testament plays

Vigil Raber's 1515 copy of a play about David and Goliath [see **F32**] is a rare example of a short play, only 320 lines long, on a single Old Testament episode. It is intended explicitly as a warning against pride. Again here we see action implicit in the text as well as explicit stage directions. The start and especially the ending of this play is very like that of a Nuremberg *Fastnachtspiel* [see **F36**]; this ending is quoted in full.

F32   A Tyrol David and Goliath Play

Sterzing, vol. v, pp. 270–80

'[. . .] pride is a harmful ill and the beginning of all sin'
[David's putting on the armour has to be deduced from two successive speeches:
Saul:]
'. . . Put my armour on him, so that he will be all the safer.'
David to Saul:
'O king, the armour weighs me down. In it I cannot bend down.'
[After David's first confrontation with Goliath]
then the Israelites sing; then David again goes to Goliath, who says to him [. . .]
Goliath replies to David: 'Stand still, I advise you to do so. I am as strong as four of you – Yet he has got away from me and has taken my sword to boot [. . .]'
Then David strikes Goliath down with the [stone from the] sling saying: 'Take that! I send you that messenger, I hope it will be your final end [. . .]'
David shows the head of Goliath to the people.
[After this, surprisingly, King Saul has to ask his servant Abner who David is. David reminds King Saul of his promise and claims his daughter Mihol as his bride; she is very happy about it:] 'Him [David] I will have gladly and justly, for he has well deserved me.'
Then they can do a dance; after that the Herald [*Precursor*] concludes:
'You gentlemen, ladies, young and old, whatever you think of it, we have come to the end of the play. If anything in it displeased you, you are not to scold us for it,

for we go in for such entertainment only rarely, so we are not very well versed in it. Perhaps you prefer a dance. Strike up a tune for the ladies. Look at David dancing with his bride!'

Saints plays

These are far less numerous in German than in some other language areas. Very different kinds of information are available concerning performances of a play about the martyrdom of St Dorothy and one about St Alexius. The audience's behaviour at Bautzen [see **F33**] may be compared with that of the youths at Beverley [see **C65**].

F33   Fatalities at the Bautzen St Dorothy Play, 1413

Neumann, item 50; in Latin

On the Sunday before the feast of St Dorothy, which was February 5th, [. . .] the schoolmaster put on [*fecit*] a play about the suffering of the virgin St Dorothy with the authorisation of the town council; and when the performance was about half way through thanks to the disobedience and imprudence of those members of the public who climbed onto the roof in front of the *Kaufhaus* (where precious cloth is sold) [these words in German besides Latin] [. . .] a wall collapsed crushing many people of both sexes, so that 33 persons died that day and night [. . .]

F34   Cast list for the St Alexius fragment, *c.* 1460

Das rheinische Osterspiel der Berliner Handschrift ms. Germ fo. 1219, edited Hans Rueff, Berlin, 1925; includes the Alexius Fragment pp. 208–16. [Page 208 reproduces manuscript page 29 recto, a summary of the entry procession followed by a detailed list of the forty-three participants. All in Latin except names of devils.]

The persons concerned in the present play in terms of the procession

1st	The devils are to come out [*procedant*]
2nd	The pipers [*fistulatores*]
3rd	Two angels
4th	The Pope with the Lord [*Persona Dominica*]
5th	Two cardinals
6th	Caesar with his two soldiers
7th	The King of Spain with his two soldiers
8th	The King of Falfondia with his three soldiers, his wife and daughter follow him
9th	The King of Eufemia with his three soldiers, but without his wife (?) [*necne uxore*; she does not appear in the following detailed list]
10th	The cook's servant [*servus coquine*] with the poor man

11th   The blind man with his servant
12th   and finally there follows Death[1]

[1] The detailed list follows, one name per line, generally confirming the above summary with the following exceptions: besides the two devils at the beginning, items 14–24 are also the regular German names of devils, familiar from the religious plays (see note 1 to **F15** and **F24**). Further, the Lord and the angels appear only near the end of the list, in positions 37 to 39. Also the whole list of names are bracketed together and on the right is written: 'These persons are required of necessity for the present play' '[*Hec persone de necessitate requeruntur ad presens ludum*'].

II   Secular drama

SHROVETIDE OR CARNIVAL PLAYS

Like Latin *ludus*, English *play* and French *jeu*, the word *Fastnachtspiel*, here translated 'Shrovetide play' rather than 'carnival play', can be ambiguous, and not all
contemporary references make clear whether they refer to a dramatic performance. *Fastnachtspiel* can therefore mean any entertainment at Shrovetide, and
occasionally even the seasonal association is lost, see for example the 1510 entry
in **F35**.[1]

The genre first appears in the fifteenth century. The Nuremberg tradition has
been studied for over a century; the Lübeck tradition, from which only one play-
text survives, has recently been examined by Eckehard Simon.[2] South Tyrol is very
unusual in that there Shrovetide plays were fostered by the same people who
organised the religious drama performances, see **F16–F18**, **F31** and **F32**. We also
have occasional texts or information about performances from elsewhere: Bernd
Neumann's work on evidence from the Lower Rhine covers all genres, including
Shrovetide plays; and a few texts and references survive from, for example,
Switzerland.

It is generally asserted that the performers were the journeymen members of
craft guilds, *gesellen*. While the details of some of the Nuremberg entries below
make this highly likely, we must note that the same word is used for the performers elsewhere, about whom far less is known.

1. The same has happened in contemporary Britain, where the 'Notting Hill Carnival' in
    London takes place in August and the 'Bridgwater Guy Fawkes Carnival' in Somerset
    takes place in early November.
2. See 'Organizing and Staging Carnival Plays in Late Medieval Lübeck: a New Look at the
    Archival Record', *Journal of English and Germanic Philology* 92 (1993), pp. 57–72.

NUREMBERG

Both texts and council minutes[1] make clear that the Nuremberg plays were performed by groups who moved round the town in the days leading up to Ash

Wednesday, performing in several locations each day. Their plays are usually short, typically no longer than 400 lines, and in the most primitive *Reihenspiel* or 'revue play' each performer speaks only once, relating his speech to the central theme or telling an even taller story than his predecessor. If the speakers are given any title in the manuscript beyond 'First', 'Second', etc., then they are most frequently labelled 'fool' or 'peasant', and these designations are interchangeable.

Of the twenty-four entries relating potentially to drama belonging to the fifteenth century found by Theodor Hampe, only those which follow [see **F35**] relate at all clearly to Shrovetide plays. The usage is not sufficiently fixed to guarantee that only the allusions with rhymed text [*mit reimen*] were in fact plays. The sparseness and wording of these entries almost allow the interpretation that groups who intended only to perform within premises where they knew they were welcome did not need to obtain permission. (See especially the entry dated January 1495.) In several cases the syntax and wording of the minutes are awkward and unusual; the temptation to embellish beyond the actual wording has been resisted. The entries from after 1500 illustrate the way the meaning of *vasnachtspil* could be extended.

The surviving texts from Nuremberg are almost all in a small number of manuscript compendia. Keller's edition has long been criticised but never superseded. The extracts [see **F36(i)–(ix)**] are chosen to show typical features: opening and closing speeches which bind the play into the general Shrovetide revelries, including addresses to the host and guests and moving on to another venue; dances which include performers and audience; references to payment in kind especially drink; apologies for being too coarse, which account for the limitations imposed in several of the council minutes.

1.   In the Staatsarchiv Nürnberg since Nuremberg was incorporated into Bavaria in 1806. In these records the year runs from Easter to Easter.

F35   Shrovetide plays in Nuremberg council minutes, 1474–1522

Theodor Hampe, 'Die Entwicklung des Theaterwesens in Nürnberg von der zweiten Hälfte des 15. Jahrhunderts bis 1806: II. Teil', *Mitteilungen des Vereins für Geschichte der Stadt Nürnberg*, 13 (1899), pp. 98–237

5 February 1474. Item a Shrovetide [*sic*] is authorised to put on its play [*Item einer vasenacht vergonnt, ir spil zu haben*] in which the leaders are Michel Russ and Hans Rupprecht.

10 February 1476. The cloth workers' journeymen (?) [*tuchheftnergesellen*] are authorised to put on a Shrovetide play, but that they inform the magistrate [*pfentner*] who their leaders are and refrain from any impropriety.

10 December 1478. Pezensteiner is authorised [to put on?] a Shrovetide play on condition that the magistrate sees it and is informed.

Schiller the wire-maker is also authorised [to put on?] a Shrovetide play on condition that the magistrate, as above.

9 January 1479. Steinbruckner is authorised to run at Shrovetide dressed up as old women, but they [sic] must register with the magistrate.
Gutpier, coppersmith, is authorised [to put on ?] a morris dance [morischkotanz] and to have several dressed as peasants with it, but giving the magistrate description and names.

20 January 1483. Hans Preisensyn and Contz Wild are authorised to go around at Shrovetide decently dressed and without masks [one schempart] and to use seemly verse and to give their descriptions to the magistrate.

14 February 1484. Lienhart Coeler and his group [gesellschaft] are authorised to hold this year a Shrovetide play with a [female] chatterbox (?) [weschin].

19 January 1486. Master Hans, the barber,[1] and others of his relations are authorised to put on a seemly Shrovetide play with rhymed text, but that they do it with propriety and do not take any money for it.

4 February 1486. Several journeymen in Werd[2] are authorised to put on a Shrovetide play, but they are not to carry staves.
Several goldsmiths' journeymen are authorised to put on a Shrovetide play, but they are to behave with propriety and not carry staves.

3 February 1487. The honourable young journeymen are authorised to run about at Shrovetide in a group in Shrovetide costumes in the outfits of a moor (?) [des morn] and to use rhymed text, but the leader is to make himself known to the magistrate.

6 February 1487. The painters' apprentices are refused permission to put on a Shrovetide play.

12 January 1488. The honourable young journeymen, who intend to do a play with peasant action at Shrovetide, are authorised to perform it with propriety on the Monday[3] before Shrove Tuesday.
Likewise the armour-smiths are authorised to put on with propriety their planned play in peasant costume.

22 January 1495. Those from Werd [see note 2] and the other Shrovetide group, who wanted to run around during Shrovetide, are refused their requests, but if anyone wanted to go into houses with plays or rhymes, that is not to be forbidden.

5 February 1495. The journeymen who want to do a Shrovetide play with rhymed text about a court scene are authorised to do so, but that they are not to wear masks.

19 January 1496. The journeymen who want to put on a Shrovetide play with rhymed text are authorised to do so, but that they do not wear masks or run about in a crowd.

28 February 1497. The council has decreed that Wolf Keczel and Oswalt the servant of the company from Ravensburg shall each be punished with one month's imprisonment in a tower, half of which punishment they must undergo, for the other half each of them can pay a fine in lieu, because in a Shrovetide play they mocked Hans Zamasser as a fool.

23 February 1498. The court is to cease on the Monday before Shrove Tuesday and on Ash Wednesday.[4]

5 February 1500. Decreed that no Shrovetide [sic] shall be authorised to go with texts or other costumes or peasant costumes, except the *Schembart*.[5]

16 May 1510. The Poles, who are now here with their bears and trumpets, are allowed to do their Shrovetide play on the Whitsuntide holidays.

7 January 1513. The council has also decreed that [. . .] they refrain from all Shrovetide plays [*vassnachtischen spilen*] on Ash Wednesday and use instead the Monday before Shrove Tuesday, as happened some years ago.

14 February 1517. Those who are to perform a Shrovetide play in front of the town hall tomorrow are authorised to take some timbers from the [??] and to make a scaffold [*prucken*]on top.[6]

14 February 1522. The Shrovetide play in which a pope appears in a choir cope [*chormantel*] and a triple cross is carried before him, is totally banned and the sacristan in the Spital is to be roundly censured for having lent the cope for such a purpose, and he is to recover it.[7]

15 February 1522 [next day !] Those with the Shrovetide play in papal clothing are to be told again that they must refrain from such a play.

---

[1] I.e. Hans Folz, identified as author of at least eight extant plays; see **F36(iii)**.
[2] Wöhrd is today just east of the city walls.
[3] Now *Rosenmontag* in German, here *gailen montag* suggesting 'sexually uninhibited Monday'.
[4] Either this means that the court scenes [see e.g. the entry for 1495] could be played only on the Tuesday, or that it has no relevance to plays.
[5] This well-known non-dramatic Shrovetide event was performed regularly by the cutlers.
[6] This is the only evidence from Nuremberg for outdoor performance; in general outdoor performance in February seems implausible.
[7] Compare the unfortunate experience of Geoffrey of Gorham [see **C44**].

F36   Fifteenth-century Nuremberg play-texts

(i) Opening words of Keller 56; 483, 5–6

'Now listen and be quiet all, and take note, how you like the play.'

(ii) Start of Keller 38; 283, 5–13

The Herald [*Einschreier*] says: 'Strewth! I don't think we are right here. Come in here and look, dear friends, it isn't farmer Pilzan's house. Go out again in file. I can see that we went wrong. We were going to start something, but Old Nick has led us to a place which was not appropriate. But we may as well start it here after all.'

(iii) Start and finish of Keller 7; 66, 4–67, 6 and 74, 24–31

Gentlemen, we do not want to disturb you, but we have been directed this way especially, to see whether you could peaceably decide a matter. So, landlord, if you have a good wine, then let's be having it and pour it jolly quick! Let us drink a conciliatory cup and then drink until our heads are splitting [. . .]'

[The final speaker says] 'Landlord, if you want to be rid of these guests, then give [us] another drink all round and then let us say goodnight. Let's wait for another day to have further thoughts about the marriage and now turn our steps away from here. Who knows how it will work out in future? So says Hans Folz the barber.'[1]

(iv) Start and finish of Keller 47; 359, 3–16 and 364,15–24

[Title in one manuscript] *The deserving knights*

'Landlord, you should not take it amiss from us that we come to you so late tonight and you should also be happy with us. My lord the Emperor of Schnokenlant is arriving here with great honour. At home he was informed how much you desired [to meet] him. Now he has granted you this and is coming himself in his might and with all his knights. Thereby he will honour you here and will grant your requests, whatever you request this day and does not harm him' [. . .]

[At the end the Herald concludes] 'Landlord, now you have heard why the Emperor came to you. But don't take his entertainment amiss! He did it with good intention and has shown you his knights, so you have heard what each can do. Now give us leave, it is time. Tonight we must still go far and must sort out our affairs elsewhere. Landlord, good night and God be with you!'

(v) Conclusion of Keller 2; 39, 2–14

'[. . .] Wake up, peace! The dispute is over and let us feast and empty our beakers, cups and glasses and drink so that our cheeks are full to bursting, dance and leap and all be happy! Strike up, musician! A dance with a whoop! [presumably a dance ensues; then another speaker concludes:] Farewell, landlord, good night! If we have committed any impropriety in here, you should be nice and excuse us. If anyone comes in asking after us, tell him we have all left and are to be found in the next house.'

(vi) Conclusion of Keller 3; 45, 35–46, 16

'[. . .] But at the end I well perceived, when one told the other his deed, there was soon a solution to the dispute. Yet I am glad on their account and hope not to meet in any matters such quarrels and disputes. Strike up! Let us dance for joy!' [Presumably a dance ensues; then another speaker concludes:] 'Landlord, you must let us go. If we have done anything improper in your house, you should forgive us and throughout Shrovetide be of good cheer and not let sadness overcome you! If with our Shrovetide play [following the reading in Keller's footnote] we have been able to give you much pleasure, that will have been the delight and wish of all of us. But now we leave you peaceably, this will end in the next house.'

(vii) Conclusion of Keller 37; 281, 31–282, 9

'[. . .] Listen, friend! Don't beat the old whore! Don't let any procuress fool you! Landlord, say something to the matter too! Musician, you should make a dance for us, there's an end to it, and soon on our way, for we still have far to go. Landlord, now give us your blessing, not on account of eating or drinking, as one invites to hospitality. Only that we want to put you in a good mood, those of us who are here. God bless you all! We are off!'

(viii) Conclusion of Keller 55; 482, 24–9

'[. . .] Now we will put aside all that any one of us has ever done to another. Now, musician, strike up a dance to see whether I can delight my darling. If I don't find her here, perhaps I shall find her elsewhere.' [Presumably he then tries his luck in the dance with several women from the audience.]

(ix) Whole[2] of Keller 34; 269, 2–270, 10.

The Herald says: 'Dear friends, God be with you! A number of us are coming in and want to hold a court with you – one thing we cannot agree on. If we were not interrupting what is happening among you, we would like to settle it here very quickly.'
Accuser: 'Judge, I complain to you about this fool, who keeps slandering me in front of people, accuses me, throws burrs at me [i.e. casts aspersions], when I have never done him any harm. If I had only frightened his cockerel, then it would not enrage me. [sense unclear!]'
Respondent says: 'Judge, he is lying. I have a maid who he has told so many tales to and has unravelled so much yarn with, I found them all in a heap. I don't know what he persuaded her to do. It's enough to annoy a Jew.'
The judge says: 'As I regard the matter, it is not without cause that you are ill-disposed to one another. But in order that the dispute is ended, let each send for a quarter of wine and let the matter be completely settled.'
The Concluder [*Ausschreier*]: 'God bless you! You have things to do, and we have to look round further, where we are perhaps more esteemed than in here. I think we will go to the spinning room[3] and try our luck with the girls. My thanks to the person who gave us a drink.'

1 See **F35** under 19 January 1486.
2 The simplest *Reihenspiele* have a limited number of speeches of equal length, one per speaker; this is the shortest, consisting of 5 x 6 lines. Unlike the most 'primitive', however, these speeches do relate to one another coherently and form a simple 'action'.
3 The *Rockenstuben*, derived from the word for 'distaff', is notorious in these plays as a place for sexual dalliance.

LOWER RHINELAND

When considering archive material from this area, the problem again arises that not all entries referring to *spyl* or *spel* designate a dramatic performance. Serious plays as well as satirical and comic performances are recorded. References from Arnhem [see **H15**] and Deventer, geographically outside the scope of this section, are included for the interesting collateral information they provide.

F37   Performances at Shrovetide along the Lower Rhine

Bernd Neumann, 'Mittelalterliches Schauspiel am Niederrhein' in *Zeitschrift für deutsche Philologie* 94 (1975), *Sonderheft* [i.e. special number, with its own separate pagination] *Mittelalterliches deutsches Drama*, pp. 147–94, here pp. 167–75. Details are quoted according to town and date.

Arnhem   1395 [. . .] at Shrovetide the journeymen (?) [*gesellen*] performed Sir Neidhart's play.[1]

1396 the journeymen performed the play on the market square

1404 to the journeymen who performed [the play] about winter and summer

1411 a king and emperor play

Deventer   1436   [. . .] to the journeymen [?] who performed Theophilus' play

1470 [. . .] at Shrovetide [payment to performers] who performed the play about Lyske who wanted a husband who smelled of armour.

Wesel   1422 [payment for] Jerusalem, that was constructed of wood at Shrovetide on the market

Duisburg   1470 to the scholars who performed the play at Shrovetide [. . .]

1487 the journeymen who performed a play at Shrovetide

1499 a play performed on the market the mayor gave the performers [*speelluyden*] [. . .]

1505 a play performed at Shrovetide on the market, given to the performers [. . .]

Essen   1457 8s given to the journeymen who played the play of St Alexius[2]

1471 [. . .] when the young journeymen [*Jonge gesellen*, cf. Modern Germans *Junggeselle* = 'bachelor'] at Shrovetide performed the play [. . .]

1489 [. . .] to the Shrovetide kings who performed their play on the market [. . .]

1522 [. . .] given on Ash Wednesday to those who performed the play [this wording does not make clear which day the performance was]

Bocholt   1526 [allegedly on the square] the play of the Magi on the Wednesday
at Shrovetide

---

[1] See **F42–F44** on Neidhart plays.

[2] The dating at Shrovetide is deduced from the neighbouring items in the accounts; see **F34** regarding the only other known German Alexius play.

SOUTH TYROL

The archive material is in many cases not sufficiently explicit for us to be sure what kind of play, religious or secular, expenditure refers to. The texts collected by Raber state the date that they were copied but nothing about performance dates. These texts derive from widely differing sources, some clearly literary, some deriving from the quack-doctor scenes of the religious plays, some close to the Nuremberg tradition. No indication of Raber's immediate sources is given.

The items that follow are chosen to show the way in which the opening speech (*Einschreier*) partly resembles those from Nuremberg but also goes much further, for example in showing staging, and the use of the closing speech to return from the reality of the play to the reality of Shrovetide, including the use of a dance not involving the audience.

The play about Aesop is based closely on folios 29 recto to 45 verso of the text of Steinhöwel's translation of the fabulous life of Aesop, which appeared shortly after 1474. Unsurprisingly it has a clear plot, divided into scenes. Especially noteworthy is the appearance of stage directions such those quoted in **F38(iii)**.

F38   Shrovetide plays in Raber's manuscripts from South Tyrol

Sterzinger Spiele. Die weltlichen Spiele des Sterzinger Spielarchivs nach den Originalhandschriften, ed. Werner M. Bauer, Vienna, 1982

(i) Opening and end of 1/1; lines 1–43 and 536–78

The warriors play.
V. 1511. R [Raber's initials around the date; his usual way of marking the texts he copied; Eckehard Simon believes this is taken over from printed books]
A Shrovetide play about the warriors or giants
Precursor: 'Now pay attention, you gentlemen, all together, women and men, poor and rich, to what I am about to announce to you! A very entertaining Shrovetide play: how things happened long ago you will enjoy hearing and seeing. There on the Rhine lies a town called Worms, it was the seat of a lord known far afield called King Gibich; he had a daughter called Krimhild. By her pride she caused great wrong [. . .] Therefore you ought to remain quiet, you ladies ought not to be afraid, for you will see the swords flash; for it is all meant as entertainment, although each person takes it seriously. Therefore you gentlemen all together, we request you most decently that you take it aright that we have come in here to you today.

Therefore listen carefully and make quiet for us for a short time, move chairs and benches aside, Horny Seyfrid [= Siegfried] is very clumsy. So let us begin the entertainment. Here you see the noble queen standing.'

[. . .]

The Herald concludes the play: 'Sir Dietrich, you should desist from these matters, we ought to be going out into the street, where we have further business. Therefore all stand well back, since you have heard and seen what happened in former times and how each fought and how it turned out and how Sir Dietrich of Bern [i.e. Verona] departed from Worms with honour and won a garland from the noble queen Krimhild. And if we had offended anyone, we would like to request you now, that you take it in the right spirit, then everyone remains in a good mood, for we have come across mountains and high ridges, so that we are still mighty thirsty. Anyone who was intending to pour us out a drink should not hesitate long. With that we want to depart hence, the Dear Lord protect us all! And so we leave. God protect you, women and men!'

End of the play

200 43 couplets

Persons in the play 15:

Herald [*Precursor*]
King Gibich
Krimhild the daughter
Duke of Brabant the messenger
Dietrich von Bern [*perner*] ⎤
Hil[de]brant   ⎥
Wolfhart   ⎥
Wittich   ⎬ the heroes
Dietlieb   ⎥
Monk Ilsam   ⎦

Pusolt   ⎤
Asprian   ⎥
Staudenfues ⎬ the warriors
Walther   ⎥
Horny Siegfried ⎦

(ii) Opening and end of play iv/4; 270–294

The Father with Four Daughters [*Pater cum quatuor filias*] (*sic!*)
V. 1514. R.

Persons in this play 12:

Gummprecht

Priest [*plebanus*]
Girls' father
cliens
Merchant
Student
Musician [*Lutifigulus* = lutanist ?]

Hiltgart ⎤
Erntraut ⎟
       ⎬ [daughters]
Dorothea ⎟
Kun[i]gund ⎦

Beggar

The Shrovetide play starts [*Incipitur ludus carnis briui*]

Herald [= Gummprecht]: 'Step back and get out of my way, so that I can state my business properly! The mercy of the noble cool wine be with us always, since we are so thirsty after the salted *Bratwürste*. May God give us a good year so that all that may come our way. You dear sirs, now be quiet and note what I shall say to you! We want to start an entertainment, therefore clear the area [*plan*]. I am a messenger sent ahead, therefore note the argument in advance. A man of good standing is coming this way; he has a long honourable beard and brings with him four beautiful daughters, who all want husbands soon, this evening rather than tomorrow [. . .] Therefore be quiet and seemly, for it is going to be quite solemn.'
[. . .]
Father replies [to fourth daughter, aged twelve, who has just married a beggar]: 'Now off, I will forgive you everything, just don't oppose me in future, then we can be fresh and happy; therefore, N[ame], pluck your lute and let the strings sound happily so that the beggar can leap around.'
[Latin stage direction:] And thus they dance and after that the play is concluded by Gummprecht saying: 'Where has one heard in all one's born days such a wonder, for a girl is aged twelve and no longer wants to save her virginity but insists on having a husband, as this girl has done, who took this beggar? But you should all come to his wedding and give him an honourable [wedding] present so that he can support the youngest daughter.'
etc.
[Latin:] Written by me Vigil Raber, painter from Sterzing. 25th and 26th day of the month of April in Bolzano during the year 1514 etc.

> (iii) Stage directions in 'Esopus', play II/2, pp. 47–73; lines 178–80, 345–9, 398–400, 533–6, 631–6

Then Xantus leads Aesop away with him and Aesop goes with him as far as the house [. . .] Then Aesop puts a wooden bowl of washing-up water on the table and spreads out a dirty apron [. . .] Then for a while they are to eat some roast poultry or pigeon [. . .] There is to be a man offering birds, hens and cockerels, for sale; Aesop is to go to him and negotiate to buy them [. . .] Then the wife is to bend down with the jug in front of the peasant to wash his feet and the peasant is to put his feet out to be washed.

LÜBECK

Performances of Shrovetide plays in Lübeck are recorded from 1430 and were the exclusive preserve of two patrician societies who regarded it as part of their civic duty to put on these morally edifying plays. Only one text survives, but we have a list of the subject matter of seventy-three of the plays performed between 1430 and 1515 by the Confraternity of the Circle [*Zirkelbruderschaft*], whose emblem refers to their devotion to the Trinity. However, what survive are not titles but rather indications of the morals to be drawn from the performances.

Only in 1981 were scholars made aware of the survival of the records of a second group, the Merchants Company [*Kaufleutekompanie*], who modelled themselves on the *Zirkelbrüder* and also put on Shrovetide plays performed on a cart [*borch*] on the Sunday, Monday and Tuesday preceding Ash Wednesday. Their ordinances record in greater detail how performances were to be organised.

F39   Lübeck Merchants Company ordinances for Shrovetide plays, 1500

Antjekathrin Grassmann, 'Die Statuten der Kaufleutekompanie von 1500', *Zeitschrift des Vereins für Lübeckische Geschichte und Altertumskunde* 61 (1981), pp. 19–35. [Grassmann is transcribing from a nineteenth-century copy of the now lost 1500 document]

On Holy Innocents' Day [28 December] the stewards choose the Shrovetide play-makers [this is Eckehard Simon's translation of the word *dichtere*, which stresses that they were responsible for the organisation of the whole performance, not just composing the text], of whom there are to be four, the senior and junior brothers [*borgere*, i.e. full members] and the senior and junior candidate members [*gesellen*, the usual word for journeyman members of guilds]. And the senior members shall be calculated from the date of joining the company [. . .] and likewise the junior members. And when all the members have been playmakers, one is to start again with the most senior. And these Shrovetide playmakers receive from the stewards thirty marks towards the equipping of the cart.[1] After the Christmas holidays the Shrovetide playmakers are required to procure the Shrovetide play[-text] in good time. [How is not explained!] And thereafter the playmakers are to approach in turn those members of the Company whom they believe to be interested in acting and to invite those who are willing.

Then, three weeks before Shrovetide, these playmakers are to inform those who have agreed to participate how and in what way they are to dress and equip themselves and shortly thereafter they are to give each of them his text.

Then, a week after the texts have been distributed, the first rehearsal is to be held. And the fine is to be a quart of wine for any who does not appear in the company [house] by noon.

[. . .]

On the Saturday before Shrovetide one of the playmakers is to read the play to the senior members including those who are members of the city council [who are given the special title *heren*] to ask whether anything in the play needs altering[2]

[. . .]

And on the Sunday [preceding] Shrovetide each full member of the company, who is putting on the play, and also the playmakers if they are not themselves acting, are to be in the company [house] by twelve noon on pain of the aforesaid fine [a quart or gallon of wine] and the playmakers are to go up onto the cart, to check that everything is in order [literally 'that nothing is lacking']. Also all those who are due to follow the cart are required on pain of the same fine to return with the cart to the company [house]. Also each of them is to ensure that his servants keep away from the cart so as not to hinder the play [. . .]

[The document continues with details regarding the banquets which followed the performances each evening, Sunday and Monday in the company house, on Shrove Tuesday in the Lime Tree room in the *Ratskeller*, which still functions today as a restaurant beneath the town hall, as is common in German towns and cities. The text contains neither details about the performances nor any clues as where these took place.]

---

[1] The word is *borch*, which is used to denote both 'wagon, cart' and 'play'; *de borch halden* means 'to put on the play'. Lübeck here shows its close Hanseatic trading connections with Flanders where performances on carts are well attested [see **Section H**]; these are the only performances on carts in the German-speaking area.

[2] Since the first performance was next day, this left no real time for changes; as Eckehard Simon suggests, the very fact of this preliminary reading will have acted as the necessary curb.

HYBRIDS

Though the division between 'religious' and 'secular' plays is essentially valid [see introduction to this section] there remains a handful of awkward cases, especially where religious material has been given the externals of a Shrovetide play. Catholy noted several of these (Eckehard Catholy, *Das Fastnachtspiel des Spätmittelalters*, Tübingen, 1961, pp. 282ff.) including Keller play number 106, *Emperor Constantine*. The action of this play is based on a dramatisation of the Silvester legend from the *Passional*. It was authorised by the Nuremberg town council in August 1474, in a minute omitted by Hampe, as *The story of Constantine and Helen with the disputation of Silvester against the Jews*. As Catholy suggests, either the production encountered difficulties which delayed its performance, or it was so successful that a repeat performance at Shrovetide was decided on. The text recorded by Keller concludes with a whole series of features typical of Nuremberg Shrovetide plays and clearly they here serve to turn inherently alien material into a *Fastnachtspiel* [see **F40**].

In contrast Keller play number 1 by Hans Folz, known author of Shrovetide plays [see **F35** under 19 January 1486 and **F36(iii)**] but not of religious plays, is turned into a *Fastnachtspiel* by its opening, beginning with the title [see **F41**].

F40   Silvester as Shrovetide play, Nuremberg, 1474
Keller 106, 818, 21–819, 20

[That the final speaker in the basic action is a peasant we know from the fact that the next speaker is called 'another peasant'. The transition comes in the following speech with its local allusions] 'Now listen, be quiet, hear and pay attention! A plan is here announced to baptise all the Jews and Jewesses before sunrise on Sunday morning out there on the market square beside the *Schöner Brunnen*. [Still a feature of Nuremberg's market square.] And anyone wanting to buy an indulgence and having the intention to see it, should make his way there all the earlier.' [The second peasant's speech concludes] 'Strike up, musician, quickly, for they have waited for it a very long time, and let us then traipse on our way!'

[The third peasant's speech includes both local allusion and references to sword fighting and dancing] 'So I come traipsing along, lumbering through the muck and my name is Ott Eulenfist from Pirntan.[1] And I am a peasant who can do all kinds of things, fight, fence, run and wrestle, tease the ladies, dance and leap.'

[The final speech of all concludes with apology and promise] 'For the sake of joy and entertainment we came to you in good faith, whether [*sic*] we could entertain you all, and therefore gave you a religious piece; otherwise a lot of rascally stuff is produced, which we have omitted this year. But if God allows us to come back again next year, then we will deliver you a happy piece, which will perhaps give you more to laugh about.'

---

[1] = Otto Owl-fart from Birnthon, the place regularly symbolising the back of beyond in the *Fastnachtspiel* texts. It is about thirteen kilometers from the centre of Nuremberg, still undeveloped and remote.

F41   Religious dispute as Shrovetide play
Keller 1; 1, 1–2, 22

A Shrovetide play, The Old and New Covenants, the Synagogue, on converting the Jews in their Talmud.

The first peasant: 'Give way, turn around and tidy up before you are overrun and all this is shaken up, and besides don't spill the wine, pick up the cushions from the benches that they are spared your feet, carry children and cradles all out of the way, so that none of them are left exposed, move chairs and benches to one side and, in order that you can listen better, stand on them and prick up your ears and be quiet at the back, sides and in front; for anyone who was to open his mouth too much would have to be shown the way to the door! Let nobody move from their position, for where there is a lack of order, people go short on knowledge and reason, so employ wisdom and good order and let the Old and New Covenants come to you with great request!'

Another speaker: 'Sirs, one more thing is to be announced here. If any were standing here at this entertainment who had come uninvited and were to approach too close to us, these I would dismiss, so that they did not delay the entertainment. Therefore let nobody come too near who is not part of the play. And let nobody chatter at the back there when two people meet one another who have been roaming around for a while before they met. And let the dogs be chased out too, so that none is gnawing a bone or is so disruptive as to bark, so that anyone's words cannot be heard. When strangers and acquaintances are assembled, then lock up and let no one in. If anyone came in with amorous intentions, let him be a bit ashamed of himself and not too hasty in the matter, so that he does not make any particular disturbance. Keep quiet, those of you who are in the crowd, until we ourselves get to the end.'

NEIDHARTSPIELE

The central figure in these plays is derived from the thirteenth-century poet Neidhart von Reuental (*c.* 1180–post-1237), who added to the *Minnesang* tradition by introducing peasants as antagonists of the first person narrator, 'the knight of Reuental'. The sociological significance of this innovation beyond an artistic extension of the poetic genre is a matter for scholarly debate.

The central action of the *Neidhartspiele* is the finding of the first violet in May by Neidhart and its removal by the peasants before he can bring the duchess to see it. Its replacement by a pile of excrement deposited by one of the peasants, not always made explicit in the texts, brings down the duchess' wrath on Neidhart, who gains his revenge by defeating and mutilating the peasants.

We know of several performances of what appear to be *Neidhartspiele* [see **F42**]. Four texts survive, varying in length from the 66 lines of the St Paul Neidhart Play (mid- to later fourteenth century) [see **F43**], which some commentators consider incomplete, to the 2,624 lines of the Great Neidhart Play [*Das Grosse Neidhartspiel*] (early fifteenth century); the Lesser Neidhart Play [*Das kleine Neidhartspiel*] (late fifteenth century) has 236 lines and the Sterzing Neidhart Play [*Das Sterzinger Neidhartspiel*] 1,064 lines (this is a late fifteenth-century copy of a version from the middle of the century, i.e. not in Raber's hand). We also have the closely associated Sterzing Scenario [*Das Sterzinger Neidhartszenar*] [see **F44**] of similar date, giving *incipits* that match very closely the Sterzing play, combined with more elaborate instructions for staging which together add up to 926 short lines. The chosen selection of stage directions shows the organisation of movement between locations, dancing and fighting.

F42   Performances of Neidhart plays, 1479–1518

Eckehard Simon 'The Staging of Neidhart Plays with Notes on Six Documented Performances', *Germanic Review* 44 (1969), pp. 5–20

(i) Nuremberg town council minutes, 26 January 1479. Several young men are granted permission to perform a Neidhart dance [Simon argues in his article that it was in fact a play] on the Sunday 'Esto mihi' [= Quinquagesima, the Sunday before Lent] and the following Monday and Tuesday. Leaders: [five names follow].

(ii) Accounts of former Augustinian abbey of St Nicola, on River Inn just South of Passau, records for early February 1488. For the Neidhart dance 1 florin. [Simon notes that it is puzzling to find a stately monastery having anything to do with such a performance; he wants to regard this entry as a receipt, though it is presented as an expenditure.]

(iii) Town accounts of Pressburg, now Bratislava, on the Slovakian bank of the Danube, 1492. At Shrovetide the journeymen members of the guilds performed the Neidhart dance as entertainment; the council agreed to give them three shillings. [Dramatic performances in Pressburg are recorded between 1439 and 1545, see Neumann, items 2341–9.]

(iv) Town accounts of Eger, now Cheb, just in the Czech Republic, 1516. Given to the actors for the Neidhart play at Shrovetide, twenty-eight groschen.

(v) Town accounts of Laufen, on the German bank of the River Salzach north-west of Salzburg, February 1517. Given to Hans Steinmüller on account of the Neidhart play which he organised with the journeymen, the sum of two pounds from general funds. [The town council knew what to expect from such a performance and arranged for the attendance of the constable.] To the constable, for having been on duty at the council's instigation at the Neidhart play [. . .]

(vi) Town accounts of Burghausen, downstream from Laufen on the Austrian bank of the Salzach, 1518 or 1519. On the authorisation of the mayor and council, given to the weavers when they had performed the Neidhart play in front of the Town Hall, one Rhenish gulden. [This entry makes clear that the performance was outdoors, but the season is not stated.]

F43   The St Paul Neidhart Play

Neidhartspiele, ed. John Margetts, Wiener Neudrucke 7, Graz, Austria, 1982, pp. 11–13

[The opening speech by the *Proclamator* presupposes the duchess' invitation to find the first violet. After the duchess and Neidhart have each spoken once comes the

Latin stage direction:] Neidhart goes and places the flower under his hat [*sub pilleo*]. [He then has one more speech inviting her and her ladies to come see the flower; next stage direction] When the duchess has lifted up the hat: 'Alas! And again Alas! You shall be punished so that you never again lie and deceive a lady! You dreadful, worthless man! Your life is on the line!'

Neidhart replies somewhat shocked [*parum percussus*]: 'O noble lady of high birth, refrain from being angry with me and be well disposed to me! It has all happened without any fault of mine. A peasant has done it to harm me. It will cost him a leg.' Neidhart to the peasants: 'Tell me, you village lads, you boors, you milk-sop eaters [*dorf knappen/törpel muostrappen*], what vengeance have you taken on me that you broke off the violet and by your misbehaviour destroyed my enjoyment? That will cost you a leg each and leave you to walk home on crutches.'

[There is neither a clear indication that the flower has been replaced nor a statement that a fight or a dance actually ensues.]

F44   The Sterzing Neidhart Scenario

Neidhartspiele, pp. 123–58

When one first goes out to the acting area in procession [*in der Ordnung hynaus zun Schrannckn*[1]] then the wind musicians are to lead, and someone is to go with them to usher the crowd out of the way and make a space. Then the precursor shall go first and two knights of the duchess, and then the court chamberlain is to lead her. After that Neidhart with his knights lead the young ladies of the court. Following come Ennglmayr, Ellnschnprecht and their neighbours with their wives and servant girls. And when they all reach the acting area they are all to stop several paces short of it in processional order. And meanwhile the precursor alone is to go into the middle of the acting area and say as follows: [there follows the whole text of his speech]

After that another precursor says:
'Take note you men and also you women who want to see a delightful adventure [*hübsch Aubentewr*] here comes, etc.'

After that the play goes into the acting area in processional order; there chairs and benches are to be set up; the duchess and her ladies sit down in the top position; and a little lower on one side Neidhart and his knights and servants sit down; in the other position [*Ort*] opposite but lower, Ennglmayr and his fellows, together with their wives and servant girls, then the musicians play to the end of the tune [*Pfeyffent . . .aus*].

Then the duchess stands up with her young ladies and speaks in Neidhart's direction, who together with his knights is also to stand up.
[. . .]

Meanwhile Neidhart with his fellows walks around in a circle inside the barriers, looking for the violet and finally finds a violet in the middle of the acting area [*Plaan*], then he takes his hat off and addresses the flower thus:
'Be welcome, you noble little flower, how you delight my heart, all the honour, etc.,'
Meanwhile Neidhart with his knights and servants is standing around the violet, which pleases them, and they are talking to one another about it. Meanwhile the peasants get up secretly and Ennglmayr leads them aside to a position at the bottom of the acting area and they consult one another; after that Neidhart and his fellows return to their position and sit down, and then the peasants return to their position.

[. . .]

Then his wife goes back and sits down with the other neighbours and Ellsnchnprecht goes to the violet and with his equipment deposits a turd on it, covers it up again and as he is returning to his fellows meets his wife on the way, who says:
'Oh! Ellnschnprecht, my dear husband, now tell me what you have done,'
Then he says to her:
'Just look, dear Elsamuot, how my arse hurts, I have, etc.'

[. . .]

Now the duchess with her retinue stands up and puts the garland on Neidhart, saying: 'See, Neidhart my dear servant, I put the garland on you with great honour and, etc.' Now Neidhart orders the musicians to lead the way and says to them:
'Strike up, you musicians, it is time. We set no small store by this, we want etc.,'
Then the musicians lead the way playing and the whole play [i.e. cast] goes in a circle round the acting area in processional order and finally takes up positions. Then the musicians stand in their position and play for a dance, and Neidhart dances with the duchess, likewise the knights and young ladies, and the peasants with their wives and servant girls behind. And when they then take up positions in a circle around the violet, the peasants and their wives do not join the circle but go to their position and sit down.
Then the duchess speaks to Neidhart:
'See, Neidhart, you worthy man, here on this open space [*plaan*], uncover, etc.,'
Then Neidhart speaks to the duchess and points to the hat:
'O gracious lady of high esteem, here stands the noble delicate violet, it seems to me, etc.,'
Meanwhile Neidhart takes the duchess by the hand and the young ladies follow her; meanwhile the knights stand still, So he leads the lady to the violet, lifts up the hat and lets her see, then she turns away with a cry of revulsion [*pfuchytzt Sy darab*] And says to Neidhart: 'Neidhart, what is the meaning of this foul trick? Just look how like a violet that is, you have, etc.'

[. . .]

[The banished Neidhart sends his messenger Zyppryan with a letter challenging the peasants] So Ennglmayr receives the letter, meanwhile the messenger stands still. Then Ennglmayr shows it to his neighbours; they consult and decide to ask the messenger to read it out, so Ennglmayr says to Zyppryan:

'Dear messenger, we ourselves cannot read, for we never went to school, there, etc.' During this speech Zyppryan takes the letter from Ennglmayr and reads to all the peasants, very loudly. [On hearing the message] Then all the peasants shout and make fierce gestures and Zyppryan returns [and reports] to Neidhart. [The peasants come.] Then Neidhart and his knights step out into the acting area, and the peasants with their weapons also all step out to face them [. . .] Meanwhile the drummers beat to arms [*Das Veldgeschray*], and Neidhart and his fellows attack all the peasants and they strike one another; then Ellnschnprecht has one buttock cut off and Ennglmayr together with several other peasants are to pretend to be badly wounded; then Eberzannt is to shout very loudly to Neidhart and his knights [. . .] Then Neidhart and his fellows are to move away to a different position; and meanwhile Ellnschnprecht's wife is to come to her husband and sorrowfully say to him [. . .] Then Ellnschnprecht is to speak sadly with her somewhat apart and send her back home to her neighbours. And the peasants are to remain lying together in the open space. And a table and bench are to be set up elsewhere in the acting area, then a doctor comes with many tins and ointments to place on the table [. . .] Then the doctor sits down at the table; meanwhile the peasants bring Ellnschnprecht to him on a dung-barrow [. . .] Then the doctor and his servant set Ellnschnprecht up on the crutches; then the doctor and his servant are to move to another place in the acting area and remain there as though they had gone home. Meanwhile Clara, Ennglmayr's wife, comes to her husband who is to lie there and be very ill, with bandaged head and hands [. . .] Then their wives are to come to all their husbands, lament their injuries, and remain with them [. . .]

---

[1] The expression *zwüschen den schrancken* is regularly used by Cysat in the Lucerne material to designate the acting area 'inside the barriers'.

Section G
Italy

Edited by MICHAEL J. ANDERSON

Introduction

Although Dante and others may have dreamt of a strong ruler guiding the fortunes of a united Italy, the Italian peninsula was to remain divided throughout the Middle Ages and indeed until the second half of the nineteenth century. Its long coastline and relatively easy access by land and mountain passes from the north, coupled with its central position in the Mediterranean, enabled it to trade advantageously with Europe, Africa and the Levant. It also made it vulnerable to invasion, but the rugged mountainous interior, in particular the Appenine range which runs down the spine of Italy, made it difficult for any power, foreign or indigenous, to exert its rule over the peninsula as a whole.

Between the tenth and the fifteenth centuries there were few extended periods of peace and stability for Italy. The rivalry between Pope and Holy Roman Emperor for temporal power led to numerous and complex alliances, treaties and from time to time, outright conflict. But despite setbacks, the general pattern was one of rising prosperity as urban communities grew and experienced a standard of material and cultural development higher than almost anywhere else in Europe.

Although territorial boundaries were always being modified by war and treaty, Italy in the Middle Ages can best be described as falling into three parts. In the centre of the peninsula the Papal States extended in a broad band from Rome to the Adriatic coast. To the south lay the Kingdoms of Naples and Sicily, geographically the largest area of Italy to form (frequently with the inclusion of the island of Sardinia) a single political unit, falling successively under Arab, Norman, Angevin and Spanish rule. North of the Papal States Italy was divided into a host of dukedoms, principalities and republics, most of them owing allegiance to the Emperor. Whilst the economy of the Kingdoms of Naples and Sicily depended largely upon agriculture, the northern cities were home to the wealthy trading and banking enterprises which were to make Italy the richest and most sophisticated area of Europe during the Middle Ages. The states of Milan, Venice, Florence and Genoa could, individually, boast as much wealth as entire nations in northern Europe.

Most of the important cities of medieval Italy were already thriving communities in the Roman Empire, and it is hardly surprising that the combination of wealth, influence and tradition should have placed them at the centre of intellectual development. The first European University was founded at Bologna in 1088;

and the revival of interest in the art and literature of Greece and Rome which reached its climax in the fifteenth century had as its main centre Italy, and in particular the northern city-states.

Emphasis in most histories of Italy is naturally placed upon those aspects of art, literature and thought which were the forerunners of humanism and the Renaissance. But during the Middle Ages Italy shared with the rest of Christian Europe a thriving religious drama, albeit differing in a number of respects from the pattern established north of the Alps. Although an earlier generation of scholars took it for granted that the liturgical drama of the Middle Ages was introduced from France, more recent studies have argued for a more widespread and indigenous drama. The great cycles characteristic of England and France are not recorded for Italy, although elaborate Passion plays were performed in some cities as early as the tenth century, while 'new forces that allowed a more eloquent and human visualisation of Christ's anguish first appeared in the eleventh and twelfth centuries'.[1] In Cividale in north-west Italy a Passion play lasting two days seems to have been regularly performed in the late thirteenth century, and by the beginning of the fourteenth century its scope had been extended to include scenes of the Creation, Annunciation and Nativity [see **C7**]. *Sacre rappresentazioni*, religious plays dramatising episodes from the Bible or the lives of Christian saints and martyrs, mostly performed in churches by organised companies of *giovanetti* (youths), had by the late fifteenth century reached a highly developed form in Florence; they were skilfully written to exploit the dramatic potential of their subject matter and often contained spectacular staging devices. Even if their origins may not lie in the *laude*, religious songs recited by the *Disciplinati* or *Flagellanti*, companies of laymen under the powerful influence of the flagellant movement in thirteenth-century Umbria, it is noteworthy that the *laude* rapidly assumed a dramatic as well as a purely musical form.

The staging of drama in late medieval Italy, whether inside or outside the Church, relied on conventions broadly similar to those found elsewhere in Europe. 'Houses' or mansions, commonly referred to by modern scholars as *luoghi deputati*, were simultaneously present in the playing area to represent localities encompassed by the drama; a number of conventional units was used, one of the most important of which was the mountain which could open to reveal an interior setting, a Paradise or Inferno according to the needs of the drama [see **G26**]. For processional, open-air performances the *edifizio*, a construction built upon a wheeled float, was used, while for static drama the *ingegni* (devices) provided visual effects. The use of lighting and machinery, as well as of costumes and properties, was probably more advanced that anywhere in the rest of Europe by the fifteenth century, and the techniques used to stage divine descents, lighting and cloud effects, and spectacular transformation scenes in the Renaissance *intermedi* perhaps owe more than we commonly assume to the religious drama which preceded them. Renaissance artists contributed their skills to secular and religious drama alike, and it is hardly surprising that the new drama should also have influenced the old: by the sixteenth century the Florentine *sacre rappresentazioni* show the influence of the new staging principles by replacing the old multiple setting with a unified perspective scene.

Lack of adequate documentation makes it difficult for us to assess the contribution of the *giullari*, the itinerant mimes and *jongleurs* who offered lay entertainment at courts and festivities throughout the period.[2] In medieval Italy, as elsewhere in Europe, important events whether they were, like marriage, an important milestone in the life of the individual or, like Carnival or a local saint's day, part of a more communal experience, were marked by ceremonies, rites and festivities whose origins often lie in pre-Christian ritual [see **Section J**]. They included dance, procession and the exchange of dialogue, often developing into what could be defined as fully dramatic presentation.

The *maggio*, for instance, which survived as a part of popular culture in Tuscany and elsewhere until relatively recent times, has its origins in the pre-Christian *Calendimaggio* (May Day) celebrations which included rites to encourage the fertility of the crops and the well-being of the community. In its pre-dramatic phase it included processions of young men and maidens carrying a decorated branch or bush – the *maggio* – as well as an element of ritual combat, but developed into a simple folk-play whose stock characters included *il buffone* (the clown) and *il diavol* (the devil). The *bruscello*, which took its name from the bush decked out with flowers, bells and ribbons which was prepared for the open-air carnival celebration, in time turned into a dramatic treatment of a love affair and its obstacles, terminating in a marriage. The *mariazo* (or *mogliazzo*, *maridazo*) began its life as a short dialogue performed as part of a wedding ceremony, but became an independent entertainment in its own right. These folk-dramas are reminiscent of the mummers' plays and carnival plays from elsewhere in Europe [see **Section J**]. More sophisticated entertainments were also common: the *contrasto* was a literary composition in the form of a dialogue or argument between two opposing principles or characters, drawing on the medieval love of allegory; the extent to which they were composed for fully dramatic performance remains debatable.[3]

In general, these manifestations of popular culture were less carefully recorded than either the religious drama or the courtly festivities which formed the background to the revival of classical comedy, so that our knowledge of them for the most part relies on randomly preserved manuscripts or printed texts, usually without any form of stage directions, or upon more recent accounts of customs and practices which lingered on in Italy at least until the early years of this century. Modern scholarship, while less concerned to trace the evolutionary stages through which religious and secular drama passed, would argue for a continuum of performance practice between the many forms, religious and profane, of dramatic activity throughout the period covered in this section. Perhaps this is best symbolised by the word *festa*, which is the term for a public celebration or holiday, but also the word regularly used in the fifteenth and sixteenth centuries to describe a *sacra rappresentazione* or, on occasion, a secular folk-play.[4] Nor was this usage confined to popular culture: the courtly drama was simply one part of a festive celebration, often lasting for several days, to celebrate Carnival or some auspicious occasion, such as marriage or the visit of distinguished guests. Only when, in the middle of the sixteenth century, the first contracts were struck between groups of actors, to perform comedies before a paying audience, did the theatre move from what Taviani has called *un'economia di festa* to a market economy, *un economia di mercato.*[5]

NOTES

1. Sandro Sticca, 'Italy: Liturgy and Christocentric Spirituality', in Eckehard Simon (ed), *The Theatre of Medieval Europe: New Research in Early Drama*, Cambridge, 1991, p. 174.
2. See ibid.
3. Paolo Toschi, *Le origini del teatro italiano*, Turin, 1955; articles under the relevant headings in *Enciclopedia dello Spettacolo*, Rome, 1954–62.
4. As Cruciani has pointed out, the notion of the *festa* is key to the understanding of the development of theatre in Renaissance Italy: see Fabrizio Cruciani, 'Il teatro e la festa', in Fabrizio Cruciani and Daniele Seragnoli (eds.), *Il teatro italiano nel Rinascimento*, Bologna, 1987, pp. 31–52.
5. Ferdinando Taviani and Mirella Schino, *Il segreto della Commedia dell'Arte*, Florence, 1982, p. 359.

I   *Medieval traditions*

References to performance are widespread in Italy from the fourteenth century onwards, although somewhat random in their nature. Where narrative description is involved, features which attracted the narrator's interest may be given prominence, producing what may be a less than objective picture of the performance as a whole. However, it is evident that from an early date a delight in spectacle was often as important as the purely devotional features of the performance or ceremony. In Italy perhaps more than in any other part of Europe, by the middle of the fifteenth century, celebrated artists were devoting their skills to the construction of elaborate scenic devices, and this process was aided by the frequent use of spectacle and display as a means of asserting political supremacy, magnificence and generosity by the rulers of Italy: the artists, engineers, mechanics and artisans who constructed the floats and triumphal arches for public ceremonial readily turned their hand to the *edifizii* and *ingegni* of the religious drama, and we know more about the machinery and devices used than the acting style of the performers. Much of public ceremonial was based upon classical precedent (or supposed classical precedent),[1] and towards the end of the period we find revivals of classical drama competing for attention with religious drama.

While a corpus of technical knowledge accumulated around medieval performance, the rules governing the creation of drama were based more upon the nature of the event to be celebrated or commemorated rather than any concept of dramatic genre or aesthetic code of practice, and performances might accompany a sermon or an act of worship and be seen as an integral part of the whole event: it was not until the sixteenth century that drama was considered a form of art and treatises or theories of drama based upon the precepts of Horace and (later) Aristotle began to appear. They prescribed rules for the newly revived *commedia erudita* (comedies modelled on the works of the Roman dramatists Plautus and Terence) and the rarer examples of tragedy, almost entirely ignoring the medieval drama, which was regarded as rude and formless. But throughout the sixteenth century classical innovation and the medieval tradition existed side by side: while the theatrical celebrations in the Campidoglio in 1513 [see **G14**] were almost purely classical in their nature, the religious drama continued to develop throughout the century, indicating not only its popularity with the masses but also its artistic vitality.

1.   See Roy Strong, *Art and Power: Renaissance Festivals, 1450–1560*, London, 1984, a revised version of earlier publication *Splendour at Court: Renaissance Spectacle and Illusion*, London, 1973.

G1   A *festa* celebrated in Siena, 1273 (from an account of 1508)

A *Life* of St Ambrosio of Siena [Ambrogio Sansedoni (1220–87)] published in 1508, quoted in Alessandro d'Ancona, *Origini del teatro italiano*, Turin, 1891, vol. 1, pp. 101–3[1]

When the Messenger arrived in Siena with the letter announcing the removal of the decree of excommunication [*interdicto*] and the blessing of the city, the entire population responded with great joy and celebration: there were solemn celebrations of Mass and elaborate processions, with fireworks and the tolling of bells throughout the city. And it was determined that on the day of Ambrosio's entry into Siena the performance and spectacle [*Representatione et festa*] described below should be held in the main square [*piaza*] of Siena, showing how Ambrosio held an audience with the supreme Pontiff, and that on that day a fine horse race [*palio*][2] should be run, and that this festival should be celebrated each year, in memory of the blessing received in the miraculous way described above; and this festival was transferred to the day on which the blessed Ambrosio died. The dedication of the *Palio* took place at the church of St Domenico, where many candles were lit, with a procession of all the orders, accompanied by all the magistrates and high officials [*Presidenti*] of the city, each carrying a candle, and with all the guilds [*Arti*] with their contribution. Since he did not wish to participate in this ceremony, by reason of his humility, Ambrosio delayed his appearance, and proceeded straight to the performance and spectacle, building a large stage [*palco*], covered overhead in the manner of a vaulted roof supported by columns, with other decorations representing the sumptuous audience chambers of the Pope, and people within representing the person of the Pontiff and the Cardinals and other clerics [*secretari*] present in the splendour of the audience chamber, in addition to which there were present at the audience boys dressed in the form of Angels. And outside the Chambers were represented prelates, ambassadors and courtiers of different ranks. In the middle of the square were caves constructed out of wood painted to resemble large rocks surrounded by woods; and inside were men costumed in the form, some of devils, others of great dragons, and others in leather costumes made to look like serpents. These caves and the aforementioned chambers were closed, so that one could see nothing of the spectacle to be presented. The beginning of the performance [*festa*] was revealed in the following way: a white dove emerged from a place above the construction [*edifitio*] on a wire, with fire and flames issuing from his mouth, and concluded his swift flight in a large closed flower, placed at the top of the structure, from which there shortly emerged rockets and explosions, with an Angel announcing the *festa*, revealing the construction which had been prepared for the performance, where in devout language and strong voices there were recited all the words used by the blessed Ambrosio, which we have reported above. Then the Angels sang the most devout songs, thanking and praising God and the Virgin Mary, and playing many different instruments. Whereupon Angels moved out towards the people, singing devout songs declaring that they all thanked God and the Virgin Mary for the favour they had received, and that in future the people of this city would not oppose the sacred Church. Then another Angel appeared who sang verses in praise and honour of the blessed Ambrosio, and the person who represented Ambrosio came out of the audience chamber accompanied by the clerics and other courtiers, humbly begging that they might remain with him and accompany him; so that to prevent arguments among those who wished to accompany him, he withdrew to a private room. Then the Angels descended and mounted a carriage in which they moved around the square, singing and playing instruments. An Angel descended at speed, by a rope from the top of the aforementioned structure towards the caves containing the devils, and above those caves he sang verses against the devils. Then suddenly there was a great explosion of gunpowder [*spingarda*][3] and the devils, dragons and serpents emerged from their caves; the Angels chased after the devils, and two armed men on horseback appeared and battled against the dragons and serpents. Then the devils ran out of the square, and the dragons and serpents lay dead at the hands of the armed warriors, to signify that the souls of the persons from Siena who had been subjected to excommunication had escaped from the power of the demons. Then there was presented on the stage which had been erected [*nel edificio del palco*] the return of Ambrosio to the residence of the Pope Gregorio at his summons, representing the speech and the journey which Ambrosio wished to make across Europe to further the recapture of the Holy Land. Then the performance showed how, during that journey, the Devil appeared to Ambrosio in the form of a hermit, tempting him with much reasoning and subtlety of argument, that he should aspire to high office in the Church [. . .] And when the tempter had been killed, the Angel announced the conclusion of the spectacle [*festa*] with singing and music. All the Angels on the carriage together with the entire company for the performance withdrew to the convent of St Domenico, and thus the spectacle was concluded.

---

[1] The *Life* from which this passage is taken, although written in the sixteenth century, is based on contemporary accounts of the life of St Ambrosio, although it includes references to later events, including the transfer of the annual festival to the date of St Ambrosio's death (cf. d'Ancona, *Origini deltentro*, vol. I, p. 100, note); the description must also include accretions from later performances. The historical context of this event is the perennial strife between Guelf and Ghibelline: by espousing the Ghibelline cause Siena had earned the enmity of the papacy, and its prominent citizens had been excommunicated. Ambrosio successfully negotiated the lifting of the papal interdict.

[2] The *palio* or race, particularly the horse race celebrated annually in Siena, takes its name from the quantity of silk or other fine material originally offered as a prize.

[3] This is an anachronism, since gunpowder was not in use until the fourteenth century. Doubtless some other form of pyrotechnic was originally used.

G2   The collapse of a bridge during a *festa* in Florence, 1304

D'Ancona, *Origini del teatro*, vol. I, pp. 94–5; trans. Ferrari, *Staging*, p. 67

The inhabitants of Borgo San Friano, accustomed since the old days to produce the most original and varied spectacles [*guiochi*], published a proclamation that whoever wanted to get news of the other world should make sure of being on the Carraia bridge and along the banks of the Arno on the first day of May; and they constructed stages [*palchi*] on barges and boats on the Arno, on which they built a representation and likeness of Hell, with fires and other punishments and torments, with men disguised as demons of most horrible appearance and others who appeared like people in the form of naked souls, and they were put to various tortures with very great shouting and screaming and storming; and this appeared like a most terrible and frightening thing to hear and see. Many citizens went to see this new spectacle, and the Carraia bridge, which at that time was made of wood on piles, was so overburdened with people that it broke in several places and collapsed together with the people who were on it so that many people died and were drowned, and many were injured, so that the spectacle changed from jest to the truth, and, as the proclamation had said, through death many went to get news of the other world.

G3   The Siena Nativity Play, *c.* 1330

V. de Bartholomaeis (ed.), *Laude drammatiche e rappresentazioni sacre*, Florence, 1943, vol. II, pp. 208–9; trans. Ferrari, *Staging*, pp. 164–5

On the feast of the Nativity of Christ, the shepherds shall be first arranged with sheep and dogs and bagpipes and everything they need. First an angel shall come during Mass [*infra la messa*] over the hut [*capannucia*] with a light in his hand at the time of the *Gloria*, and he shall announce the *Gloria in Excelsis Deo*. The choir shall reply and the angels shall stand behind the canvas of the scaffold [*palco*]; they shall reply. After the *Ite Missa Est* has been said, an angel shall appear and announce the feast [*festa*]. When he has announced the feast, he shall go among the shepherds and remain in a hidden place until Jesus is born. After the birth of Jesus, he shall come out and announce to the shepherds that which he has to announce. And immediately there shall be amidst the shepherds thunder [?*uno scoppietto*] and lightning, at the proper time. After the annunciation of the angel, the Virgin Mary with Joseph and a handmaid shall go to be registered [*si vada a fare scrivere*]. And she shall come back and go on to the scaffold [*palchetto*]. When she has reached the scaffold and everything is ready, two angels shall come and lift the canvas, and Jesus shall be born; and the angel shall appear to the shepherds. And immediately the angels shall be at the hut. They shall come out and sing in chorus; and with great reverence they shall adore the Lord and, while the shepherds approach, they shall dance, and the angel who has announced to the shepherds shall depart from them and shall go to the hut with the others; and four stanzas of the *Verbum Caro* shall be sung while the child is swaddled. And when the child is swaddled the shepherds shall come to pray.

G4   The *Festa* of the Three Kings at Milan, 1336

G. Flamma, *De rebus gestis a Vicecomitibus*, quoted in d'Ancona. *Origini del teatro*, vol. I, pp. 97–8; reproduced in Emilio Faccioli (ed), *Il teatro italiano*, Turin, 1975, vol. I, pt ii, pp. 684–5

There were three crowned Kings on great horses accompanied by their attendants, each dressed differently and followed by pack-horses and a very large retinue. A golden star passed through the sky, moving ahead of the three kings, until they reached the columns of St Laurentino, where there was a figure in the likeness of King Herod, with his scribes and wise men. They were seen to ask King Herod where Christ was to be born, and after consulting many books his scribes replied that he should be born in Bethlehem, distant five miles from Jerusalem. On hearing this the three Kings set off wearing their golden crowns, carrying golden vessels containing gold, frankincense and myrrh, led by the star moving through the air, with a retinue of attendants and pack-horses, and preceded by the sound of horn and trumpet. Accompanied by monkeys, baboons and other animals of various kinds, they proceeded to the church of St Eustorgius. There beside the great altar was the stable with the ox and ass, and in the stall was the infant Christ in the arms of the Virgin Mother. The Kings offered Christ their gifts; then they were seen to fall asleep and a winged Angel told them that they should not return by the quarter of St Laurentin, but go by the Roman gate; and so it was done. Such a crowd of people, soldiers, clerics and nobles was present that scarcely anything similar had ever been seen. And it was decreed that this ceremony be repeated every year.

G5   Some expenses for fourteenth-century *laude*, Perugia, 1370–86

Extracts from two account books in the archives of the Confraternità dell'Annunziata of Perugia covering the period 1370–6, quoted in d'Ancona, *Origini del teatro*, Turin 1891, vol. I, pp. 207–8 (note)

11 Denari and 6 soldi[1] for the dove for the *festa*.
Purchase of thread [*refe*] to make the cord for the Dove.
And also there was given to Paulino when we made the Devotion[2] for Saint Paul, five soldi.
Also there was purchase of five pounds of oil for Christmas Eve [*la notte de natale*].
Also for a supply of straw for the said night. And there were the costs of the priests on the said night.
Also there was the purchase of wine when we presented the Devotion of the Magi.
For a porter who brought to the Fraternity a decorated cloth [? *panno indeco*] for the Devotion of the Limbo, 6 bolognini.[3]

For a porter who brought to the fraternity a likeness [*una faccia*] of St Peter martyr, 6 bolognini. To reward certain singers at the time of the Ascension, 3 bolognini.

[1] One soldo contained 12 denari.
[2] Devotion (*Devozione*) was a term used interchangeably with *Lauda*.
[3] The bolognino was a currency minted in Bologna.

G6   A spectacle at Pentecost, Vicenza, 1379

C. Pulce, *Annales*, quoted in d'Ancona, *Origini del teatro*, vol. I, pp. 98–100; reproduced in Faccioli (ed.), *Il teatro*, I.ii, 686–7

And on the day of Pentecost, 24 May, a priest from Vicenza [prepared] a prominent construction [*aedificio*] in front of the chapel of St Antony with two towers, on which were benches decorated with covers and beautiful tapestries. In the first of these towers were seated four persons wearing beautiful golden robes and bearing precious gems, in the likeness of four women representing our glorious Virgin and the other Maries. Round about, in great splendour, were seated twelve persons representing the twelve apostles, who rose one by one to hail the woman as the glorious Virgin. They chanted prophecies praising the Holy Spirit which they were about to receive; and then from different parts there arose diverse songs and melodies. Those who were seated in the other tower responded with songs of prophecy and made various gestures to show they were awaiting the Holy Spirit to enter into them. While they were performing thus someone appeared on the tower of the Bishop's palace: to the window of the tower a rope was attached which led down to the first clock-tower. There was a flash and a loud thunder-clap, and straight away there descended down this rope the image of a shining dove. Almost all fell to the ground in terror and amazement, beseeching God in hymns and chants that the promised Holy Spirit should descend upon them according to the prophecies. And on the clock-tower there appeared a person in the likeness of the great Prince of Judaea, mocking them and telling them that they were foolish and of little understanding.

While all of those who were present on the tower remained astonished, there were created fiery flashes accompanied by great claps of thunder, so that not only those who were on the building, but those who had come to attend the spectacle stood looking up in amazement towards Heaven, and then there descended by the rope three persons brilliantly lit in the likeness of doves, moving towards the first tower where there were those waiting for the Holy Spirit to enter them according to the prophecies which they sang. Overcome with astonishment almost all of them fell on their faces, and rising up after a little while, began speaking in various tongues. One became a Teutonic priest, who recited prophecies in the Gallic language, and likewise others recited the prophecies of the Holy Spirit in other tongues. The person representing the Prince of Judaea mocked them, and all those present, saying 'O foolish and deluded men! Now they are drunk, and this is clearly shown because, although they are Latin, they speak in Hebrew.' Finally those who were on the clock-tower, creating great flashes of lightning, chanted prophecies and named the Holy Spirit, so that the Prince of Judaea fell down on his knees and cried out, saying 'I see so many marvellous signs, which accord with the prophecies, that I can no longer disbelieve; but truly I believe that the Holy Spirit has descended upon these blessed men and those Holy Apostles.'

G7   Property list for the Play of St George, Turin (?), 1429

Giuseppe Boffito, 'Antica drammatica piemontese', *Giornale storico della letteratura italiana*, 30 (1897), pp. 344–6; trans. Ferrari, *Staging*, pp. 111–12

Here follow the things necessary to perform the play of St George, for the two days. First, for the banner of the Emperor Diocletian and the eagle above, in addition [*par dessus*[1]], 1 florin.

Item: for red standards: 6 ells of red cloth, 2 florins, 1 gros.
Item: for an idol made complete [*?toute entyere comisse*], three feet long: 5 yards of coarse cloth, 7 gross.
Item: for St Marcellin, St Cladien, St Cirin, St Anthony, and for the four martyrs whom Dacien first has beheaded, and for the wizard [? *magence*] Athainaise and St George: 11 ells of cloth, for each head one ell, for the said head, 22 gross.
Item: for a pot of aquavita.
Item: for the wood of the stakes [*rues*] which will be broken, not including the tin foil put over them so that they look like swords, 2 florins.
Item: for the said tin foil, 6 gross.
Item: another idol in which is hidden a person who speaks: 3 ells of cloth, 5 gross.
Item: four lbs of gold leaf to gild one of the idols, 16 gross.
Item: four lbs of silver [? *blanches*] foil for the other idol, 1 florin.
Item: two lbs of white paint [*blanc de puillie*] to do the flesh colour [*l'encarnacion*] of those who are or appear to be naked and also for the faces of the [false] heads, 5 gross.
Item: to dye yellow the aforesaid banner: 2 lbs of ochre [? *archiole/argile*] and 1 lb of rock alum [? *alon*], 6 gross.
Item: 1 lb of vermilion to cover [? *escouffar*] all the things necessary for the play, 10 gross.
Item: 6 lbs strong glue, 9 Genoese [? *gen*] gross.
Item: at most one lb of black earth, 1 gross.
Item: of rag [*destraxe*] paper to cover [*escouffer*] the heads of the idols, the haloes, the crowns, the pinnacles of a castle [? *d'un chastel*], one ream, 6 gross.
Item: for the said crowns of God, the Pope, the emperors, and the twelve souls [*armes*] and for the king and the queen a hundred and a half of gold leaf [? *or party*], 1 flor.
Item: for the wigs of the heads of the angels and the souls, eighteen cloth bases [*goiffes de toilles*], and for the eleven severed heads; for the wigs and beards, only for

the cloth on which all this shall be set and for the set bases, four ells of cloth, 8 gross.

Item: for 6 pairs of wigs for 6 angels both for the wood [*fust*] and everything else, 14 florins.

Item: for the herald of the emperors, for his emblazoned tabard, 2 ells of white cloth and 2 of red to make a tabard to match the banner and the standard, 2 gross and a half the ell and 4 gross an ell the red, in all 13 gross.

Item: for flax to make the hair of the angels and of the souls: 6 lbs, 6 gross.

Item: for four clean and large sheepskins to make the body of St George, full length, to seem naked, and for the making [*por la faczon*] of the said body, 1 flor.

Item: 2 cartloads of wood to heat [? *essuer*] the things necessary and to melt the glue. Total, without the wood and the making [*faczon*], 30 florins 4d gross. Given at Thonon on 8 April, the year of our Lord 1429.

[1] The account is written in French.

G8   Sermon and dramatic spectacle, Perugia, 1448

D'Ancona, *Origini del teatro*, vol. 1, p. 280; trans. Ferrari, *Staging*, pp. 248–9

On 29 March, which was Good Friday, the said Friar Ruberto started again his daily preaching in the square. On Holy Thursday he preached on Communion and invited the whole population to come on Good Friday; and at the end of the said sermon on the Passion he performed this play [*rappresentazione*]: that is, he preached at the top of the square outside the door of San Lorenzo where a platform was prepared [? *era ordinato un terrato*] from the door to the corner towards the house of Cherubino degli Armanne. And there, when it was time to show the Crucifix, out of San Lorenzo came Eliseo de Cristofano, barber at the gate of Sant'Agnolo, representing [*a guisa de*] the naked Christ with the cross on his shoulder and the crown of thorns on his head; and his flesh seemed beaten and scourged, as when Christ was scourged. And there several armed men [*armate*] took him to be crucified. And they went down towards the fountain, around the crowd, as far as the entrance to the Scudellare, and they turned [*argiero*] at the Exchange [*audienza del Cambio*] and returned [*argiero*] to the door of San Lorenzo and went on to the said platform [*terrato*]; and there, in the middle of the platform, someone [*una*] went towards him in the garb of the Virgin Mary dressed all in black, weeping and speaking sorrowfully, as was done in the similar play [*misterio*] of the Passion of Jesus Christ; and when they arrived at the scaffold [? *pergolo*] of Friar Ruberto, he stood there for a long time with the cross on his shoulder, and all the while the people wept and cried for mercy. Then they put down the said cross and took up a crucifix which was already there, and they erected the said cross; and then the wailing of the people grew louder. At the foot of the said cross, Our Lady started her lament together with St John and Mary Magdalene and Mary

Salome, and they said some stanzas from the lament of the Passion. Then came Nicodemus and Joseph of Arimathea, and they freed the body of Jesus Christ from the nails [*scavigliarono*], put it in the lap of Our Lady, and then laid it in the sepulchre; and throughout the people continued to weep loudly. And many said there had never been performed in Perugia a more beautiful and pious play [*devozione*] than this one. And on that morning six friars were professed [i.e. took their vows] [*? se fecero*] [. . .]

G9   Stage directions in a fifteenth-century Passion play text from Revello

La Passione di Revello, ed. A. Cornagliotti, Turin, 1976; trans. Ferrari, *Staging*, pp. 98–9, 108, 114, 125, 173

[*The Magi return home by boat*:] Here let there be a ship [*nave*] in which is a captain and his sailors among whom is one on the poop deck of the ship. [*The kings take passage on the ship and it sets sail.*] When [Balthasar] has spoken, the ship moves off and Freberic begins to sing the song written below [. . .]

While the ship is moving Freberic sings. The two war ships [*galeoti*] shall come to attack the ship. And the latter does not pay attention to them and goes on its way. And Freberic continues singing. And the warships shall come to the place where the ship was and remain there broken [*rotte*]. [*Later Herod passes that way and sees the war ships; believing them to be those of the kings, he orders them to be burnt.*] Then Herod's followers kindle and set fire to the war ships and burn them. Meanwhile, Herod goes on his way [. . .]

And when [Christ] is praying, the angel Uriel shall come and show him the Passion painted on a cloth. Then he shall stretch out on the stage [*zafaldo*] on his face, and underneath there shall be someone who shall paint his hands and face and hands with crimson paint as if he were sweating. And when he has been like this for a time he shall rise. And one of the angels shall come and without speaking wipe away the sweat [. . .]

When this has been said, Jesus shall go up on Mount Tabor, where shall be God the Father, the archangel Michael, Moses, Elijah. And a short distance away from the mountain shall be Lucifer, showing that he cannot look up at the mountain, but he shall be very eager to hear what is done and said. And when Jesus is on the mountain let there be a polished bowl [*bacillo*] which makes the brightness of the sun striking the bowl reflect on Jesus and towards his disciples. Then Jesus shall let fall his crimson garment and appear in white garments. And if the sun is not shining, let there be torches and other lights [. . .]

[*The Last Supper begins with a salad.*] And let Simon bring in first lettuces [*latuce*] with vinegar as a salad [*a modo d'insalata*] [. . .]

[*A shepherds' dance.*] Having said this Abiron [*a shepherd*] plays on his pipes. And the other shepherds dance in pairs. And Anania and his partner act as if [*finga*] they do not know how to dance like the others. [*Abiron rebukes them, seven lines.*] Then Abiron places himself at their head, dancing and playing and the other shepherds dancing [. . .]

G10   Religious and lay performances in Casteldurante, 1488

Part of a letter from B. Capilupi to Francesco Gonzaga, written in Urbino and dated 26 July 1488, quoted in A. Luzio and R. Renier, *Mantova e Urbino*, Turin, 1893, pp. 44–6; reproduced in Faccioli (ed.), *Il teatro*, I.ii, pp. 696–7

From the gate of the castle as far as the palace the street was strewn with lengths of fabric [*tela*], and in some places white wool; every angle was covered in greenery and twelve triumphal arches had been erected across the street, each one different from the other and decorated with the arms and devices of Your Lordship and figures of pagan spirits, vases in the ancient style and fountains, from two of which cascaded rose-tinted water. At the first arch by the gate there was a youth [*putto*] who recited poetry, and there were twelve knights dressed in silk who escorted Her Highness.

A triumphal chariot was driven from the palace to the square, in which on three sides were seated Caesar, S[c]ipio and Duke Frederick, wearing golden armour fashioned in the ancient style. A little below at the front of the chariot there sat a Sybil, and above on a raised platform there stood an Angel bearing the branch of a palm in his hand. First the Angel sang some verses, followed by all those who were taking part in the Triumph together with the Sybil. Two centaurs hauled the chariot and other beasts and birds were placed upon it: it would take too long to write a detailed description of these. Each one recited his verses: the carriage moved forward and accompanied the Lord and Lady to the Court.

Then on Sunday, the 27th [of July ?] was presented the play [*rappresentatione*] of the life of St John the Baptist. The stage which was prepared for this occasion extended the full length of Your Lordship's courtyard, with columns, mouldings and a roof [*coperto*] made of wood and painted in the ancient style. Between the two columns were devices, one of the Gonzagi and one of the Feltri, with branches of greenery and horns of plenty. On one side of the stage, to the right, there was the house of Zacharias, the father of St John; next to that was a house belonging to his neighbours, and then the house of Our Lady who went to visit St Elizabeth. Nearby was the temple where the birth of St John was foretold to Zacharias by the Angel, and where he was circumcised. A little way beyond that was the desert where he went to pay penance and where he and Christ were baptised. Then right in the middle of the stage was Herod seated on a high throne, surrounded below by his knights and councillors. Close by there was the treasure-chest [*credenza*] made in such a way that the coins could enter right inside. Close by was the Queen who was seated in the manner described above with her daughter [Salome] at her feet and her women around her. Nearby was the prison were St John was held and beheaded. Then there was a grotto from which the Sybil emerged. Beyond that, on the other side of the *loggia* [*baltresca*] three of the King's Barons were also seated on thrones, with their handmaidens in livery; each Baron was dressed distinctively and differently from the other two. All these were guests at the banquet at which St John was killed, and each one was dressed appropriately: in all there were about eighty persons, of whom thirty recited verses. This *festa* was presented in the square, near to the rock on top of which was Paradise, from which three times Angels descended in a cloud, by means of a rope. The first time an Angel remained in mid-air to announce the *festa*. The following two times the Angels descended to the stage to speak to Zacharias. On the ground, in a pit at the foot of the rock there was the Inferno, the mouth of which was formed from the head of a huge dragon whose open mouth appeared to lead down into the pit, with a machine [*edifficio*] which revolved with devils upon it, all holding different instruments which sent forth flames. After the death of St John the Queen was carried to this Inferno by a Devil suspended on a rope, with the greatest speed imaginable. The spectacle was greatly to be admired, especially the beheading of St John, which was made to seem truly genuine by means of a false head which was attached to the body of a real person.

This performance began at 19 hours and was concluded at 23 hours.

GII   Religious *feste* in Ferrara, 1489

G. M. Ferrarini, *Cronaca di Ferrara*, vol. I, pp. 293–5; reproduced in Faccioli (ed.), *Il teatro, italiano*, Turin, I.ii, pp. 697–9

The beginning of the Passion and the first act showed the Virgin Mary coming out with the three Maries, lamenting in the common tongue [*vulgarmente*] that the sinfulness of Eve had made it necessary for Christ to come to earth, to be made flesh and to suffer, and that her joy had been turned to grief, since her son Christ had been brought to trial before the Jews and condemned, and making other memorable speeches. At the conclusion of the first act Christ came out with his XII disciples, dressed in a worthy and appropriate manner, and held supper; and he washed the feet of all of them. The words of this act were in Latin, using those of the *Passio*; however, certain parts were omitted, and the whole was not recited word for word. The final act showed Christ taken by the Jews. After this final act a figure called Conchelle Domenico appeared, who represented the part of the blind man given sight by Christ. He made a speech in the common tongue, so that only twice was the common tongue used: all the rest was recited in Latin. The purpose of the blind man's speech was to describe how he went to find the Virgin Mary at her house to tell her that her son had been taken by the Jews. And after this speech the Passion was concluded; and that took place on the evening of the Thursday. Then everyone left the square, which had been full of spectators and the benches where they sat to listen, as had the wells [? *pozzoli*] of the Duke, the windows of the Ducal palace and other vantage-points in the square. And when it finished it was around two and a half hours after sunset.

On the morning of Good Friday, 17 April, at daybreak as is the custom, Master Baptista Paneto of the order of St Paul in Ferrara preached in the square, which was full of people who had come to see the Passion. The sermon was concluded by 12 o'clock, as the Duke wished, and with the Duke and his Lady standing on the wells [?] with their courtiers, the first Act to be presented on the Friday showed Annas and Caiaphas the high priest [*pontifice*], dressed in the costume of a high priest, Annas in the manner of a bishop when he stands at the altar in cope and mitre, with a host of Jews behind them, each dressed differently; and there were Herod and Pilate accompanied by a boy who carried their sword and headgear as is done for civil authorities, with others following behind. Herod had a Turkish cloak with brocaded gold, and was seated on a decorated throne. The other Jews who accompanied him formed a large number, some with artificial beards and some without, and some with elaborate headgear; they comprised more than fifty persons. They departed, and in the first act Judas appeared on the platform on the side facing the Jews, which was close to the benches on the other side of the platform facing towards the fountain. St John the Baptist came out walking towards him and when he saw Judas he began to reprimand him in the common tongue, saying many things against him, that he had sold his master, who had done so much good for him, and many similar things. Judas made no reply but paced up and down the platform in distress, frequently scratching his head and showing other signs of unhappiness. When St John had finished speaking he left. Judas went to return the coins he had been given to the Jews, and then pacing up and down he went through the motions of hanging himself; during which time, out of the mouth of a serpent constructed to face the platform on the side towards the fountain and representing the house of the Devil, there appeared a Devil – or rather someone disguised as a Devil – who went behind Judas and whispered in his ear *Hang yourself, Hang yourself!* And he threw a length of rope to him, to persuade him to hang himself. After having paced up and down for a long time, he went to the trunk of a tree which had been placed on the aforementioned platform, and he pretended to hang himself by the throat, but there was a device beneath the scene which was supporting him. Straight way the devil chopped down the trunk of the aforementioned tree, which was furnished with a green bough, and like a brigand he carried Judas off with his feet over his shoulder, still with the rope around his throat. Then Christ was brought before the Praetorium, and thus was performed the Passion. Shortly after Judas was hanged there came two Devils who took down his corpse and carried it into the serpent's mouth which represented the house of the Devil. After some further action Christ was taken down from the Cross by Nicodemus and two others and placed in the sepulchre: they sang hymns [*laude*] of praise before the Cross and while they were bringing Him to the sepulchre. And when He was brought to the sepulchre His mother the Virgin Mary held His dead body in her arms, and as she wept she recited words in the common tongue. So that in this Passion only four speeches were recited in the common tongue: the first was at the beginning of the Passion, in the words of Our Lady as mentioned above, the second scene was the blind man, the third scene, St John, the fourth and final speech the lament of Our Lady after the death of her son. All the others were in Latin, using the words of the *Passio*. All the dialogue [*tutti li parlamenti*] was recited in song, for all the Duke's singers [*cantori*] and others who could sing were the performers in this Passion. The final scene of this Passion was when Christ went to bring the holy fathers out of Limbo; they followed behind Him singing hymns, and all knelt at the foot of the Cross. Thus was this Passion concluded.

G12   Records of the Passion play performed in the Colosseum at Rome, 1498

Archives of the Confraternità del Gonfalone di S. Lucia, ed. M. Vatasso, *Per la storia del dramma sacro in Italia*, Rome, 1903, pp. 93–101; trans. Ferrari, *Staging*, pp. 46, 80, 92, 96, 123, 124, 139, 202–3

[*The Brotherhood of the Banner-Bearers of St Lucy*] deliberated and agreed that the producers [*of the play*] be allowed to spend every year twenty ducats or more for the said Passion, not including the meals [*for the musicians*], [. . .] and to have it performed on our site [*luogo*] at the Colosseum or on any other site the company may decide upon [. . .]

The tribunal [*tribunale*] of Pilate with four round columns in front and four square columns behind, with ceiling, frame [*cornice*], and all its other fittings [*fornimenti*].

Item. Another small tribunal on four small, round columns for Herod [. . .]

Item, two breadths of cloth with clouds [*anuvilate*] which were used for Heaven [*paradiso*] [. . .]

An iron girdle with little hinges [*a canchanetti*] for Our Lady.
A pair of big iron bars [*ferri*] with two clouds reinforced with wood [*armati de legno*] on which the angels come to the cross, with its beams.
Item: two iron strips to tie round the waist [*da cegnere*] with pieces divided at the back [*co li ferri dirietro spezzati*], which are hinged onto the aforesaid big iron bars for the angels.
Item: a construction of wood with nailed cross-members [*de legno carrato*] with an iron bar [*braccio*] and a cloud.
Item: for the said angel, an iron to tie round the waist of the angel, jointed, and to be hinged [*snodato da impernare*].
Item: a big iron rod with an iron cross-bar which ends in two hinges [*vanno in doi cancani*] used on [*in*] a column in Santa Maria Maggiore to make an angel appear.

Item: another, similar one, which was used for the appearance of Our Lady of the Snows [*a la Neve*].

Item: four iron bars [*ferri*] for angels which were used in the cloud or mandorla[1] [*amandola*] when they play the Assumption of Our Lady, with the cloud at her feet. Two big iron bars for angels, joined together in a cross, which were used [*se operavono*] at the feast of Santa Maria ad Martyres [? *Santa Maria Ritonna*].

Item: a long iron bar with the girdle and a cloud at its foot for Our Lady when she went up to Heaven [*salliva a cielo*].

Item: a hinged iron girdle [*a canchani*] for Our Lady inscribed twice [*scritta doi volte*]. A construction of wood with nailed cross-members with which Christ is taken to Heaven [*paradiso*] at the Resurrection [. . .]

The hanging with the painted angels, which is put behind the cross.
The other black hanging which is put at the front of the stage [*palco*].
A large white hanging, torn and sewn, with ropes.
Eleven breadths of light-blue cloth [*tela*] painted with stars, sewn in several places, each about two and a half rods [*canne*: 22 yards] in length [. . .]

The haloes [*diademe*] of pure gold [*oro fino*] for Christ and the Apostles, of which there are twelve in all, are kept by Antonio de Palitto, and two more, which makes it fourteen altogether.

Two crosses of gilded wood for the Resurrection and two banners of white silk with red crosses for the aforesaid Resurrection.

The veil with the painted Veronica.
A box with all iron nails [*ferri*] of the cross for the hands and feet etc.
Two copper lanterns [*lumiere*] on two poles [*aste*].
Items, there must be two more.
The iron lance for Longinus, joined and with a hollow shaft [*con l'asta busciata*][2].
A thick rope [*zaganella grossa*] in two long pieces.
Item: another piece of thick, shorter rope [*zaganella*]
Item: two rope halters.
A jar to hold water.
Five wooden crosses including the one which stands on Mount Calvary *infra annum* [. . .]

A cloak of light-blue cloth for Our Lady adorned with tinsel and little stars of batiste [? *battita*].

Item: another pinkish cloak [*de rosino*] with a ribbon of gold [*de ora*] for the Magdalene.

Item: another cloak of black mourning cloth for Our Lady.
A widow's skirt [*bonna (sic) vedovile*] of black cloth.
A Turkish dress [*turca*] of silk of different colours, worn, lined with yellow shot silk [*cagnante*].

Four little silk tunics in different colours for the Pharisees.

A rough tunic [*saltaimbarca*] of woollen mixture bordered with black, white and red.

A silk standard for Pilate, with the black scorpion on a yellow field.

Two banners for trumpets [*pendoni da tromette*] of red sendal [*zannato*] with S.P.Q.R. on them, and silk fringes of various colours and four buttons for each banner.

A skull-cap [*cacamauro*] of brocade for Caiaphas.

Two sheets [*traverse*] of red sendal [*zannato*].

Item: one of deep-blue sendal.

Item: two more of gold sendal.

Item: another of yellow sendal.

Item: another of yellow shot sendal [*zannato cangiante*]

Item: another large one of faded purple sendal.

Seven girdles of striped light-blue sendal.

Two pieces of girdle of deep-blue sendal [*zanzile*].

Four more girdles of faded old sendal.

Two cloths of buckram [*vocarame*] with red and light-blue roses for Christ at the Resurrection [. . .]

The officials and members of the company shall be obliged to meet in *S. Lucia* at the time of the service [*allo offitio*]: and there shall devoutly dress themselves in their tabards [*sacchi*] [. . .] and then they shall proceed with the Crucifix in procession to the Colosseum and go to the appointed by the said producers: and they shall observe silence throughout the said Passion: at the end of which they shall return in procession to *S. Lucia*.

[1] See **G13**.
[2] To contain a substance to represent Christ's blood.

G13   The operation of the *mandorla*

Designs from the *Zibaldone di disegni* of Bonaccorso Ghiberti (1451–1516), Biblioteca Nazionale, Florence, B.R.228, fols. 115 recto; 115 verso; reproduced in Mario Fabbri, Elvira Garbero Zorzi and Anna Maria Petrioli Tofani (eds.), *Il luogo teatrale a Firenze*, Milan, 1975, pp. 13–14

Sketches (i) and (ii) derive from a *zibaldone*, a notebook or common-place book in which writers and artists would enter material of interest to them, working designs, etc. (i) Section illustrating the means of operating the mandorla for an Annunciation device. (ii) Another arrangement for a mandorla. The *mandorla* (literally 'almond') was one of the most frequently used *ingegni* in medieval drama in Italy. The almond-shaped container would be lowered slowly from the roof or ceiling of the church, to open and reveal an angel within [See also **G17**, **G23iii**.]

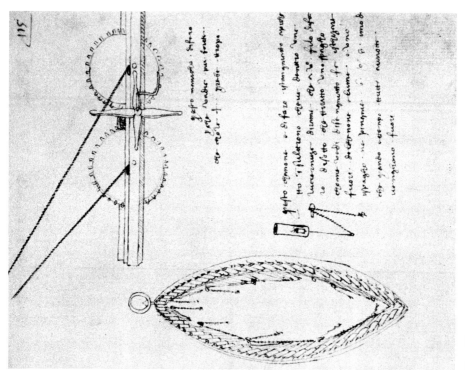

G13 (ii)

G13 (i)

G14 Performances in the Campidoglio, Rome, 1513

(a) The account given by Paulo Palliolo

Paulo Palliolo, *Narratione delli spectacoli celebrati in Campigdolio da Romani nel ricever lo Magnifico Juliano et Laurentio di Medici per suoi patriti*; reproduced in Fabrizio Cruciani, *Il Teatro del Campidoglio e le Feste Romane del 1513, con la ricostruzione architettonica del teatro di Arnaldo Bruschi*, Milan, 1968, pp. 21–67

[In September 1513 Roman citizenship was conferred upon Pope Leo X's brother and nephew, Giuliano and Lorenzo de' Medici; the performance of Plautus' comedy was only one of a series of celebrations held over two days to mark this important occasion. The specially constructed theatre in the Campidoglio (the Capitol) was used for a celebration of a Mass and a sumptuous banquet as well as the theatrical performance. For a fully documented account, and a hypothetical reconstruction of the building see Cruciani, *Il Teatro del Campidoglio*.]

Julio Arberino, a Roman gentleman of great and sagacious intellect and spirit, was placed in charge of the construction of the theatre. After the appointment of the best architects, builders and painters it was possible to find, he first of all knocked down some walls and buildings, and having levelled out some mounds [*tumuli*] in the ground to make the most prominent [*celebre*] road rising towards the Campidoglio wider and straighter: and there, in the square, he completed the construction of the theatre with great care and diligence. It is a temporary structure made of wood, square in shape [*in figura quadrata*]: lengthwise it extends towards the palace of the Senators 17 *canne*,[1] taking up much of the space of the steps ascending to the entrance; the width is 13 *canne*, with one side adjacent to the palace to the *Conservatori*, the other facing towards Araceli. The height is 8 *canne*. Inside it is surrounded on three sides by steps, or rather seats, 8 in number, rising in order one above the other: the highest is two and a half *canne* above the floor. At the foot of the lowest there is a wooden floor, or sloping stage [*spalto*] and this floor both covers the three sides of the theatre and adjoins the proscenium which is of equal height, three *canne* wide, and covers that side of the building which faces the steps, being the same width as the theatre. In the midst of this is the *cavea*, 11 *canne* long and 9 wide, surrounded on all sides from the floor to the afore-mentioned stage and proscenium with a great number and variety of paintings, which although they deserve to be described and commented upon at length, nevertheless (since each of the other paintings which we shall mention is equally or more worthy of praise), so as not to fill my pages with unnecessary laudations I shall not commend them at length, passing on to the description of the remainder.

Since I have used the word *canna* above, and perhaps you are not sure of its meaning, let me explain that the *canna* is the customary measurement in Rome, more than three *braccia*[2] in length in the usage of your country.

[There follows a description of the paintings and ornaments of the façade [*fronte*] of the theatre.]

The theatre from the inside

The fittings and ornaments of this theatre are not inferior in beauty or magnificence to the exterior; indeed in every quarter they equal them in excellence, as you will easily be able to judge for yourself.

Inside the aforementioned entrance to the theatre, on the right hand, is a tall and very ornate pillar in the form of a square column, on top of which is a life-size wolf suckling the two infant founders of Rome, a very ancient work and all made of metal. Likewise on the left-hand side is another pillar similar to the one already described, on which is placed the weighty hand of a colossus, so large that one of his fingers is as thick as a man's thigh, and in the hand there is held a large ball; this work too is of metal and formerly was gilded, but through the passage of time the gilding has become less visible.

The façade of the scena

Looking forward one sees the façade of the *scena* divided into five separate areas [*compassi*] by square columns, having bases and capitals covered with gold. In each area there is a doorway of the size found in a private house, all of them opening out on to the steps of the palace of the Senators. The lower part of this façade is decorated with four friezes. The first or lowest, two palms wide, is decorated with simple leaves; the second, two *braccie* wide, represent the sea full of marine gods and goddesses, sporting together on the flowing waves: Neptune is seen riding on his chariot drawn by dolphins, accompanied by Triton [. . .]

[There follows a fuller description of the scene.]

Above these cornices and the fourth frieze which we have described as surrounding the theatre, in each area there are figures and images which we shall describe in order, with their inscriptions.

In the first panel could be seen the armed vessel of Aeneas in the Tiber, and Aeneas himself landing, armed and with his Trojans, with eagles as their standard upon their flags. On the other side stood the Tuscans similarly armed, with lilies upon their flags. They received the Trojans in friendship, lending them assistance in founding the Empire, as the inscription accompanying it describes.

[There follow similar descriptions of the of the four panels.]

The comedy

After much playing of trumpets and pipes *Poenulus*, a comedy of Plautus, was presented, not translated into Italian but in Latin as it was originally presented.

[There follows a description of the plot.]

In the presentation of this comedy with its verses and the poetic fiction already described, no outsider [*forestiere*] took part, nor anyone from the lower orders, but only Romans, nearly all sons of the finest gentlemen of Rome, gracious and beautiful in appearance, educated in virtue and of tender years, so that in all their number only two were bearded: the others were still smooth-cheeked.

Their diction and pronunciation was wonderfully pleasing to all the audience and demonstrated clearly that they had been born and nurtured at the fount of Latium, and from there they had acquired that natural pronunciation of the words, which others could not acquire fully even after assiduous practice; for that is the birthplace of the Latin language.

Their costumes were all most elegant and assuredly most costly, from their head-gear down to their feet. They all wore flesh-coloured stockings [*calze*] to give the appearance of bare legs, in imitation of the custom of the ancients. Over these they wore a kind of short boot called a *soccus*, made of tanned leather dyed blue and decorated with silk ribbons. These *socci* were all covered with precious stones of various kinds, a wonderful sight inasmuch as the decorations on the footwear of a single performer were worth a huge sum. The other decorations which they wore were all different, so that I shall describe them separately one by one.

The first to appear on the proscenium was the Poet, whose costume was a very fine, full tunic and a shawl of gold cloth; on his head he wore the laurel crown, in his hand he held the book, and his *socci* were covered in jewels as we have described above. He recited the Argument of the play and retired into the scene [*dentro la scena*].

Then there came out the speaker of the Prologue, dressed in a similar tunic and *socci*, with a shawl of white damask lined with gold cloth and fastened over the shoulder according to the ancient custom, and folded around his head was a silk cloth of various colours, in the manner of a turban. And when he had recited the Prologue, he returned whence he had come out.

Then began a pleasant harmony, played upon the pipes, which lasted for a good length of time: and no other chorus or any other kind of music was heard throughout the comedy, apart from the trumpet sounded by the Herald when he made an announcement to the people. In this they were following the manner in which comedies were presented in the time of Plautus and Terence, in which there was no place for the chorus, but only the pipes, otherwise known as *tibie*, were employed, in even or odd numbers, on either the right- or left-hand side of the stage.

When the music was finished, the lover Agorastocles came forward, with a brilliant garland of gold on his head. He was wearing a very ornate silk shirt, shot with gold; the sleeves were of unusual width, and on the cuffs were bows of black silk. He wore a doublet [*saglio*] of gold cloth, covered with white damask slashed in various places so that the gold could be seen shining through. His cloak was of deep blue damask lined with gold brocade, which was fastened at his shoulder and thrown back, so that more of the lining than the exterior was visible, and the arms and most of his doublet was revealed. His *socci* were decorated with pearls and precious stones more richly than the rest. I should not omit to mention that none of the men's coats bore sleeves, to make a better showing of the magnificence of their shirts.

[The costumes of the other actors are all described in similar detail.]

The comedy concluded with applause, which was given with a good will and deservedly, when it was already around the hour of sunset: at which time all the actors, mimes and silent characters [*gl'histrioni, mimi et pantomimi*] presented themselves once more in formation upon the proscenium, in their costumes described above. To be sure it was a beautiful and magnificent thing to see them all together. Finally when they had all been sufficiently admired, they retired within the scene. Then the *Magnifico* Juliano and the others, with infinite charm, departed.

[1] The *canna* was a measurement of length which varied from under 3 metres in Florence to over 5 metres elsewhere.
[2] The *braccio* was a measure slightly more than half a metre in length.

(b)   A visual record

Book of sketches attributed to the German architect Andreas Coner, entitled *Architec[tura] civilis Andrea Coneri Antiqua monum[enta] Rome*, in Sir John Soane's Museum, London and reproduced in Cruciani, *Il Teatro*, Milan, tav. 2

This plan, of uncertain date, is considered to be a copy at one or two removes, of the original design: it was probably not drawn by Coner. It is discussed fully in Cruciani, *Il teatro*, pp. xliii–xliv and pp. 141ff. By courtesy of the Trustees of Sir John Soane's Museum.

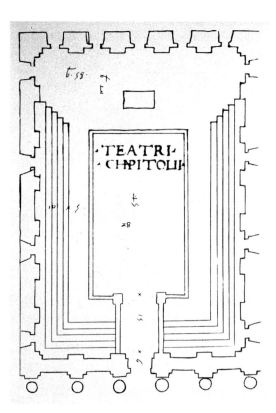

G15   An account of a Corpus Christi play at Modena, 1556

D'Ancona, *Origini del teatro*, vol. i, pp. 358–60; trans. Ferrari, *Staging*, pp. 268–70

At the Corpus Christi procession on 4 June of the year 1556, when Monsignor Gandolfo Sigone was bishop [*ordinario*], they performed the play [*si fece la Rappresentazione*] of how Nebuchadnezzar set up the gold statue forcing everybody to adore it; it was a thing [*la cosa*] no less beautiful and worthy than any other which had ever been performed and it proceeded in the following order. There was a most beautiful cart, surrounded by large canvas screens on which was painted with colours, flowers and figures the great history of the deeds of the aforesaid king: and these paintings were done by Messer Giovanni Tanasca, one of the Brothers of Charity [*fratelli amorevoli*]. The cart was framed all around by an alabaster frame and at the corners were some heads in relief, all gilded. On the cart there was a tall pillar [*pillo*], and on the pillar was a statue in relief three ells [*braccia*] high and all gilded which held a sceptre in its hand, and was made by Begarello. Behind the statue was a furnace ingeniously [*misteriosamente*] constructed and painted in which there were fireworks and people to make them burn at the appointed time. The rest of the play took place as follows. First came the King, richly attired and crowned, riding a most beautiful and finely caparisoned jennet [*gianetto*]; accompanying him there followed twenty noblemen from different nations, dressed in different ways according to the usage of their lands and all armed according to their custom. It was an admirable sight to behold the great variety of dress, all of silk richly adorned with gold and silver, and each wore on his head a helmet, a turban, or a hat following the fashion of his country; for some were Turks, others from northern Europe, or Tartars, Greeks, Moors, Arabs and from sundry other nations. These noblemen rode beautiful horses equipped according to their custom and each had his page at the stirrup, dressed in his livery, who carried on his left arm a shield made according to the custom of his land. The King was preceded by four horses more regally adorned than the others on which rode four pages in most beautiful and shining armour, one carrying the King's spear [*zagaglia*], another his rapier [*stocco*], another the shield, and another the sallet. One either side of the King there came on foot twenty grooms [*palafrenieri*] worthily clad in coats and sleeves of mail, and each one of them carried a halberd and the battle-axe with velvet and gold hangings. In this order they left [the house of] our Company and with royal magnificence set off to make their appearance in the cathedral. They were preceded, accompanied and followed by the people of the city in such numbers that it was barely possible and only with great effort to walk very slowly, so much so that there was much for the Brothers [*fratelli*] to do, who in great numbers and armed with staves [*aste*] kept the procession in good order. Having arrived at the cathedral, the King and the King's barons and pages dismounted and, leaving the horses with the footmen [*paggi pedoni*], in the same order accompanied the cart into the cathedral; they arrived before the Bishop and the other lords, and when the King gave the signal at the proper time, a proclamation [*bando*] was made by a trumpeter that everyone, of whatsoever condition or rank, should obey the King's command, namely that at the sound of the lute, harp, lyre, viol [*violina*], and violin each one should prostrate himself on the ground and adore the gold statue of the King his master. At the end of the proclamation the aforesaid instruments, which were accommodated on part of the cart, began to play in a most harmonious manner. As soon as they began to play the King and the whole Court fell to the ground and adored the golden statue. However three youths who were present – namely Sidrac, Midrac, and Edebnego – did not likewise prostrate themselves but remained standing, their eyes fixed on Heaven, inspired to adore the true God and scorn the statue of the King. When this was noticed they were immediately accused before the said King of scorning his commands, and he, having asked that they should be brought before him, told them that if they did not prostrate themselves with the others at the sound of the instruments to adore his statue he would have the furnace made three times hotter [*farrebe tre volte più accendere la fornace*] and have them thrown into the burning fire. They very promptly answered that they would adore no other than the God of Israel. The King was angry and commanded that they should be forthwith seized and bound and led to the furnace, which very appropriately sent forth flames in several places in such a way that they harmed the others but not the three youths, who right in the middle of the fire began to praise and bless their true God with beautiful and most learned verses inviting all creatures above and below the Heavens to share in these holy hymns of praise. On hearing such singing there were but few who did not shed tears of pity and emotion, moved by the well-sung verses. They finished their singing while the furnace continued to burn, but the flames were so carefully arranged that they harmed no one. After this beautiful and highly praised play [*Rappresentazione*] a motet was sung and the litanies were begun with a most harmonious music of voices and instruments, as beautiful as ever was heard in our city on such a day. Our Company received signal favour from the Bishop and the Governor who did not wish the singers of any other Company to stop and perform except ours. [Our Company] having started the litanies, everyone left the cathedral, together with the cart, and all took their places as before and in the same aforesaid order followed the procession, and the three youths remained in the furnace until the end of the procession. The matter [*la cosa*] had a beautiful beginning and a most beautiful ending, and was praised by the whole city. Camillo Panizzo devised and directed it. The author of the verses sung by the three youths was Messer Lodovico Castelvetro.[1]

---

[1] The author Lodovico Castelvetro (1505–71), a resident of Modena, wrote the influential commentary to Aristotle's *Poetics* (1570) which stressed the importance of the unities of place and time.

G16 Description of costumes and performance in a Sibyl play in Palermo, 1581

E. Di Marco, *Drammatiche rappresentazioni in Sicilia*, Palermo, 1876, pp. 17–37; trans. Ferrari, *Staging*, p. 140

And forthwith Human Nature shall appear, dressed in garments on which the four elements shall be painted, with a veil over her head which shall cover her to the waist.

When the queens have finished [their songs], eight prophets and eight sybils shall enter [*verranno*] in the following order: namely, from the right-hand side of the nave, which faces east, the Prophet Isaiah shall appear and recite his verse, and after him the Persian sibyl shall enter from that same side, and after she has spoken, another prophet and another sibyl shall speak on the opposite side, and so they shall continue every time, two on one side and two on the other.

When Isaiah has finished, the Persian sibyl shall come [*uscira*] from her cave, dressed in a golden dress with a white veil, singing the following verse [. . .]

Immediately the Phrygian sybil shall come forth in a purple garment, with naked arms, her hair flowing; and pointing her finger she shall sing [. . .]

Then the Hellespont sibyl shall come forth, old, wearing a peasant-like garment, with a veil arranged according to the ancient custom, and she shall sing [. . .]

Afterwards the Samian sibyl shall come forth with an unsheathed sword under her feet [*con una spada ignuda sotto i piedi*], with a delicate veil over her head, and richly dressed.

Afterwards the Delphic sibyl shall enter [*venirà*] dressed in a black garment, with her hair rolled up and plaited, with a horn in her hand.

Then the Tiburtine sibyl shall come forth, not very old, dressed in a pink-coloured garment, with a goatskin over her shoulders, her hair flowing, and a book in her hand.

Then the European sibyl shall come forth, young and beautiful, with a resplendent face, a very thin veil over her head, dressed in a garment sprinkled [? *toccata*] with gold.

II   *Theatre spectacles in Florence*

The mercantile wealth of Florence in the fifteenth century which made it a supreme artistic and intellectual centre, also created an ambience for the creation of some of the most elaborate and costly spectacles of the fifteenth century. The *sacra rappresentazione*, which came to displace the thirteenth-century Umbrian *lauda*, was widespread throughout central Italy but found its true home in Florence. Written in verse, usually *ottava rima*, and dealing with sacred subjects but increasingly infused with realistic detail, they were staged by companies mostly of young men, usually in churches but often in the open air. Many of the *sacre rappresentazioni* were written anonymously, but others were composed by named authors and appeared in manuscripts which were plainly intended to be read as popular literary compositions, and later in printed editions. Although published texts were printed in many Italian cities, the main centre for their production was undoubtedly Florence. The best-known author of *sacre rappresentazioni* was Feo Belcari (1410–84), whose *Rappresentazione di Abram ed Isac* (1449) was printed in numerous editions. Lorenzo de' Medici (1449–92) was the author of a number of sacred plays including *La Rappresentazione dei SS Giovanni e Paolo* (1449).

Many of the editions included woodcuts illustrating scenes from the action of the play. The relationship of these to the actual performance from which they ultimately derive is necessarily oblique, showing actions (for instance torture) which could not have taken place in performance in the manner illustrated unless dummies were employed (see **E22**, **E58**), or backgrounds which accord to the artistic conventions of the day rather than reproduce an image of the scenic representation of place. But the artist may be elaborating on the memory of an actual performance.

The admiring accounts of visiting foreign dignitaries [see **G18**, **G19**], and Vasari's determination to preserve for posterity an account of the machinery created by Filippo Brunelleschi [**G17**], are a clear indication that in Florence at least the medieval drama, even if it had not lost its devotional function, was considered as fully worthy of inclusion amongst the artistic achievements of the city.

G17   Giorgio Vasari's account of Brunelleschi's machinery for staging the Annunciation in Florence

Vita di Filippo Brunelleschi, in the edition of 1568 of Giorgio Vasari, *Le Vite de' più eccellenti Pittori Scultori e Architettori*, ed. Rosanna Bettarini and Paola Barocchi, Florence, 1971, vol. III, pp. 188–91. It is also translated in A. M. Nagler, *A Source Book in Theatrical History*, New York, 1952, pp. 41–3[1]

It is also claimed that the machines [*ingegni*] for the Paradise of St Felice in the *piazza* of the said city [Florence] were devised by Filippo to perform the spectacle, or *festa* [*rappresentazione, overa festa*] of the Annunciation, in the manner in which it had customarily been performed in that place in Florence. Indeed it was a wonderful thing and demonstrated the ingenuity and industry of its inventor: a Heaven [*cielo*] was displayed above full of living figures which moved, and an infinite number of lights flashing like lightning. But I shall describe in detail the nature of the devices for these machines, since everything is now in decline and those who had first-hand experience of them are no longer living and there is no hope that it will be repeated, since the monks of Camaldoli no longer live in that place, as at one time, but the nuns of St Peter the Martyr; and the building is in a terrible state of decay, since the struts which hold up the roof have fallen in. Now, between the two beams which supported the roof, Filippo, to produce this effect, had placed a domed structure [*una mezza palla tonda*] like a round bowl or a barber's basin placed upside down: this structure was made of light, pliant boards to which was attached a star made of iron which revolved in a circle around the said dome, being attached by a large iron ring to the centre, around which it revolved on its course. The whole of this device was supported by a strut of strong pinewood reinforced with iron, which lay across the roof-beams; and fixed on this strut was the ring which held the semicircular dome, which seen from the ground truly resembled a Heaven. At the foot of the circle, around the rim, there were wooden supports just large enough for someone to stand upon, and at the height of one *braccio* inside there was another iron support; and on each of these supports there was placed a youth of about twelve years, and with an iron harness around them at a height of one and a half *braccia* they were restrained so that they could not fall even if they had wished to. These youths, who were twelve in number, positioned as described on their stands, were dressed as angels with gilded wings and hair made of gold skeins; at the proper moment they took hold of each others' hands and through the movement of their arms seemed to be dancing, while the dome was continuously turning and moving. Inside it, above the heads of the Angels, there were three circles or garlands of lamps, fitted with certain little lights which could not spill, which from the ground appeared to be stars, while the planks, covered with cloth, resembled clouds. From the ring already mentioned there issued a large iron bar which had fixed to it another ring, to which was attached a soft hempen cord [*canapetto*] which, as shall be described, descended to the ground. The iron bar had eight branches [*rami*] which turned in an arc which filled the whole space of the dome, and at the end of each branch there was a platform the size of a trencher, and on each of these platforms was placed a young boy around nine years old, safely held there by an iron harness soldered at the height of the branch, but loosely so that they could turn to either side. These eight Angels, supported by the said iron structure, descended by means of a winch which was slowly unwound, lowering them eight *braccia* from the space in the dome to the platforms which supported the roof, so that they should be fully visible without obscuring the sight of the Angels who were situated inside the dome. The Angels were gathered together like a bunch of plucked flowers [*mazzo*], as it might be described, inside which there was a *mandorla*[2] of copper, empty inside, in which were placed some small lamps fixed to an iron structure resembling small cannons; and when a spring was held down they were all concealed within the copper *mandorla*, and when the spring was not depressed the light from all the lamps could be seen shining through the openings. When the gathering of Angels was in position, this *mandorla*, which was attached to the hempen cord, was lowered by the hempen rope by another winch, and moved slowly towards the stage [*palco*] where the *festa* was being performed. Upon the stage, just where the *mandorla* was to be positioned, there was a high platform with four steps which could be used as a mansion [*residenza*], in the centre of which there was an opening, just where the iron structure of the *mandorla* came to rest; under this mansion there was a man who, when the *mandorla* was in position, without being seen inserted a clamp so that it should stand firm and upright. Inside the *mandorla*, dressed as an angel, there was a youth of around fifteen years held by an iron harness to make sure he could not fall; in order that he should be able to kneel the harness was in three parts, so that when he knelt one part slid inside the other. And so when the gathering of angels had descended and the *mandorla* was in position, the man who had fixed the clamp now released the harness which was holding the Angel; he stepped out of it, walked on to the stage, and reaching the part where the Virgin was, he greeted her and proclaimed the Annunciation. He returned to the *mandorla* and the lights, which had been extinguished when he stepped out, were relit, and once more he was fastened into the harness which supported him, by the man concealed below. The *mandorla* was released from its clamp and borne aloft again, to the singing of the gathering of Angels and the movement of those above, which made it truly resemble a Paradise, all the more so because in addition to the Chorus of Angels and the gathering below, beside the outer surface [*a canto al guscio della palla*] there appeared a figure of God the Father surrounded by angels similar to those described above, all supported on an iron structure. So that the Heaven, the gathering of Angels, God the Father, the *mandorla* with innumerable lights and most sweet music, together truly resembled Paradise. Moreover, to enable the Heaven to be revealed and concealed, Filippo had constructed two large doors of five *braccia*, one on each side, with channels in which there were runners of iron or copper; the channels were greased so that when the doors were drawn on either side by a thin cord attached to a winch, they opened or closed as desired, drawing the two parts of the door together or opening them along the channels. The construction of the doors in this way served two purposes: first, when they were drawn they made a noise, because of their weight, which sounded like thunder: and second, when they were closed, they served as a platform where the Angels could prepare themselves, and provided space for the other things which had to be arranged inside. These inventions among others were created by Filippo, although others assert that they were invented much earlier. However that may be, it is worth recording them, because they are no longer in use.

¹ This account appears only in the second edition of Giorgio Vasari's *Life* of Brunelleschi (1568), when Vasari was himself engaged in the construction of stage machinery in Florence: see Patricia Lee Rubin, *Giorgio Vasari: Art and History*, New Haven and London, 1995, pp. 224–5.

² The *mandorla* (literally 'almond') was one of the most frequently used devices in the drama of medieval Italy [see also **G13**, **G23(iii)**].

G18   A *festa* of St John the Baptist in Florence, 1439

Description written in Greek in 1439: the original manuscript is no longer in the library at Turin and this translation is taken from the Italian version in d'Ancona, *Origini del teatro*, vol. I, pp. 230–1; trans. Ferrari, *Staging*, p. 240

On 23 June there is a big procession and a celebration in which the whole population takes part and during which they perform prodigies and almost miracles, or representations of miracles. For they resuscitate the dead; and the leader [*caporione*] routs the devils; they crucify a man, like Christ; and they perform the Resurrection of Christ; they dress up some men as Magi, and by means of men they represent the Nativity of Christ with the shepherds, the star, the animals and the crib. Moreover they have a procession with statues and relics of saints and effigies [*imagini*] and precious crosses, preceded always by trumpets and other musical instruments. How shall I describe how they represented St Augustine by means of one dressed as a friar, and they put him 25 ells [*braccia*] high, and he walked about and preached [?] But they also imitated hermits with beards, and they walked high on wooden stilts, and it was a most awesome [*orrendo*] sight. And we also saw some sacred images being carried around, some enormous, some impressive [*sublimi*], like sorrowful things [*come cosa dolorosa*]. What shall I say of St George who performs the miracle of the dragon? Having done all these things on 23 June, on the day of the 24th they showed all their riches and exhibited gold and silver in abundance and plenty of vestments, having on the day of the celebration consecrated in the Church of the Precursor first of all nearly one hundred banners and then thirty castles albeit of wood but splendidly made; and then candles and torches in great numbers and finally men who were kept in prison, carrying wreaths and olive branches. All these things were done with much pomp, with flutes and trumpets, and every other kind of ceremony [*onoranza*]; and one could see the whole of Florence revelling, both men and women, and the spectacle was great and splendid. Even the night was not dark, but bright and ablaze with lights. Not only on the lower part of the church, but also high up they had hung big lamps full of wax, a hundred pounds apiece, which lit up the night. As these things were being celebrated by the Florentines, we were made welcome by them to watch this festivity.

G19   The Annunciation and Ascension in Florence, 1439

Russian manuscript of the diary of Archbishop Abramo of Souzdal (now lost); this translation is taken from the German translation of A. Wesselovsky, 'Italienische Mysterien in einem russischen Reisebericht des XV. Jahrhunderts', *Russische Revue* 10 (1877), pp. 245–41, and compared with the Italian version of d'Ancona, *Origini del teatro*, vol. 1, pp. 246–53. It is translated in *Staging*, pp. 243–7. Where the meaning is difficult to determine, the translator has indicated the words used in both the German and Italian versions

A learned Italian has created in Italy a magnificent work. In a monastery in Florence there is a big church dedicated to the name of the Virgin [*SS Annunziata*] and over its entrance a scaffold [*Gerüst/tribuna*] ten and a half feet square was set up, with a small, skilfully constructed ladder [*Leiter/scala*] leading to it. Both scaffold and ladder were draped with curtains [*Vorhängen/tende*]. The scaffold was meant to represent the heavenly spheres from where the angel Gabriel is sent down to the Holy Virgin by God the Father; on top of the scaffold there is a throne on which a man of majestic appearance is seated, dressed in priestly robes with a crown on his head and the Gospel in his left hand, as God the father is represented. He is surrounded by many children artfully arranged around him and at his feet an image of the heavenly powers. Seven circles surrounded the throne and the children; the smallest of the circles had a diameter of about two ells [*ellen/braccia*], then there was another which was two spans larger, and so on, and there were a thousand lighted oil lamps on them. Four small children crowned and dressed as angels, holding cymbals, a cittern, or a tambourine in one hand, stood facing one another on the largest circle, amid the lamps. All this represented the seven heavens, the heavenly powers, and the inextinguishable angelic light, and everything was surrounded by the said curtain [*Vorhänge/cortine*]. In the middle of the church at a distance of 175 feet from the entrance there was, stretching from one wall to the other, a stone structure/bridge [*gerüst/ponte*] or partition [*tramezzo*], built on stone columns 21 feet high and 17½ deep, draped with red materials [*Stoffen/stoffe*]; on it, on the left, there was a wooden bed, also adorned with magnificent materials, and, beside it, close to the pillow, there was a richly covered seat. Seated on it there was a beautiful youth richly dressed in maiden's clothes with a crown on his head and holding a book which he was reading in silence, very much like the Virgin Mary to look at. On the same scaffold/platform [*Gerüst/palco*] there were four costumed men with long beards, long flowing hair, and narrow gold circlets on their heads. They were simply dressed in long, ample white surplices with girdles; a narrow scarlet band went from the right shoulder to the left side: their appearance and clothing were those of Prophets. All this, as well as that which was on the aforesaid higher scaffold [*Gerüst/tribuna*], was covered with precious Italian and French cloths [*Tüchern/panni*] and red curtains [*Umhängen/cortine*]. Five thin but strong ropes [*Stricke/canapi*] were stretched from the stone platform [*Estrade/palco*] in the middle of the church to the high scaffold facing it. Two of them were fastened not far from the young man dressed as the Virgin, and on them by means of a third, very thin rope [*Stricke/canapo*] the angel sent forth by God descends and then jubilantly returns up above after the Annunciation. The other three ropes lead precisely to the centre of the platform.

When the time comes to begin the great and marvellous spectacle, many people gather silently in the church, their eyes fixed on the scaffold in the middle of the church. After a short while the curtains and hangings are drawn back and one can see, seated on the magnificent seat by the small bed, the man who represented the Virgin. All this was full of beauty, wonder and grace. Then on the same platform appear the four Prophets, each of whom has a scroll [*Schrift/scritto*] in his hand, containing the ancient prophecies of the birth and incarnation of Christ. They move about on the platform, each looking at his own scroll, stretching out their right hands towards the upper scaffold [*tribuna*], which is still veiled, saying: 'Thence the salvation comes to mankind'; or one says to another, looking at his scroll: 'The Lord shall come from the South.' Then they dispute among themselves, after which each one tears up his scroll and throws it away as erroneous: then they take other scrolls and walk to the front of the scaffold and bow to each other, and each one examines his own scroll, striking it with his hand and arguing with his companions. One of them says: 'Thence shall God come to seek the lost sheep'; and another says other things. So they continue their dispute for about half an hour. Then the curtains of the upper scaffold open and from there comes a volley of shots imitating Heaven's thunder, and the Prophets with their scrolls are not seen again. Up on the scaffold is God the Father surrounded by more than five hundred burning lamps which revolve continually, going up and down. Children dressed in white, representing the angels, surround him, one striking the cymbals, others playing flutes or citterns in a scene of joyful and inexpressible beauty. After some time, the angel sent by God descends on the two ropes already mentioned to announce the conception of the Son. The angel is a beautiful, curly headed youth, dressed in a robe as white as snow, adorned with gold, exactly as celestial angels are to be seen in paintings. While he descends he sings in a low voice, holding a branch [*Zweig/ramoscello*] in his hand. The descent is effected in this way: behind him there are two small wheels secured, invisible from below because of the distance, into which the two ropes fit, while some people who cannot be seen stand up above and by means of the third very thin rope lower and lift up the angel. The angel, therefore, having descended and arrived before the Virgin Mary, who is resting, courteously addresses her, holding the aforementioned rod [*Ruthe*] in his hand. Then follows the Annunciation which is an abbreviation of the Ave Maria; to which the Virgin quickly stands up and answers in a sweet and modest voice: 'O young man, how dare you come to my threshold and enter my house? What foolish speech is this about God being with me and being incarnated in my womb? I do not trust your words, for I have no experience of marriage and I know no man. Go away, young man, lest Joseph should see you and cut off your head with an axe while you linger to address me in my house. I beg you, go away, or he will drive me out of the house too.' But, seeing her fear, the angel answers, 'Fear not, Mary; I am the archangel Gabriel, whom God has sent to you to announce the conception of his Son. Believe in what I say: you will conceive without seed; the Holy Spirit shall come upon you and the power of the highest shall overshadow you.' Having listened to these words, Mary lifts up her eyes and sees God in all his power and magnificence blessing her. She folds her hands in her lap and humbly says, 'Lo, I am God's handmaid: let what you have said befall me.' The angel hands over to her the beautiful branch [*Ruthe/verghetta*] and ascends. Mary remains standing, watching his ascent. In the meantime a fire comes from God and with a noise of uninterrupted thunder passes down the three ropes towards the middle of the scaffold, where the Prophets were, rising up again in flames and rebounding down once more, so that the whole church was filled with sparks. The angel sang jubilantly as he ascended, and moved his hands about and beat his wings as if he were really flying. The fire poured forth and spread with increasing intensity and noise from the high scaffold, lighting the lamps in the church but without burning the clothes of the spectators or causing any harm. When the angel arrives back at his point of departure the flames subside and the curtains close again.

I saw this marvellous and most skilfully contrived spectacle in the city of Florence, and I have described it to the best of my ability: but some of it was impossible to describe, for it was so inexpressibly beautiful.

In the famous city of Florence I saw something even more marvellous. According to an old custom, the Latin Church [*die Lateiner/i latini*] celebrates the memorial of the Ascension of Our Lord, who ascended to heaven to the Father on the fortieth day after the Resurrection. This celebration takes place on the Thursday of the sixth week after Easter in the Church of the Ascension of Our Lord [*Santa Maria del Carmine*]. This is what I saw. The church is 560 feet long from the front wall to the altar and is 140 feet wide. Like that of the church of SS Annunziata, of which I have already spoken, it has a stone platform [*Estrade/tramezzo*] 140 feet long standing on 28-foot-high columns. On this platform on the left-hand side can be seen a stone castle, magnificently adorned, with towers and bastions, representing the holy city of Jerusalem; opposite, against the wall, there is a hill, ten and a half feet high, to which leads a staircase, two spans from the floor. The hill is surrounded by red materials. Above it, at a height of about 56 feet, there is a wooden scaffold 28 feet wide and 28 deep with planking [*Brettverschlag/tavolato*] on all sides and beautifully painted beneath and all around. On the top of this scaffold there is a round opening of 14 feet in diameter, covered by a blue hanging, on which the sun, moon and surrounding stars are painted, representing the first heavenly sphere. When the time comes this hanging is lifted, which signifies that the gates of Heaven are opened; and inside a man can be seen with a crown on his head, representing God the Father: he stands in a miraculous way above the gates of Heaven, looking down on the Mount of Olives, where his divine Son, the holy Virgin, and the Apostles are standing together. He blesses them, apparently suspended in mid-air. Around him there are small children in great numbers with flutes, citterns and chime bells. Among these children, who represent the angels, and around God the Father there is a vast number of burning lamps. At the top of the opening which represents Heaven is fixed a paper disc, the bottom rim of which touches the upper rim of the opening and the top rim of which points upwards; on this, life-size angels are painted. Seven thin and strong ropes with skilfully constructed iron gear wheels go from the opening of Heaven to the Mount of Olives. A young man representing Jesus Christ in the act of ascending to the Father is beneath these ropes. Above the church altar, high up in the wall, there is a little stone room about 21 feet square; on the side of the church it is covered with a red curtain on which can be seen a crown in a circle, which ceaselessly revolves to the right and to the left. Everything is marvellously ordered and nothing similar has ever been seen.

Towards the ninth hour many people come to this church to watch the marvellous spectacle. When there is perfect silence in the crowded church, people turn their eyes to the platform and everything that has been prepared there. Then four young children dressed and attired as angels appear, each carrying a flowering rod [*Ruthe/ramo*], then another comes forth in the appearance of the Son of God and goes toward the city representing Jerusalem, and the angels precede him. He enters Jerusalem, and after a few minutes he comes out again accompanied by two young men dressed as women, who represent the holy Virgin and Mary Magdalene. Then he returns to Jerusalem and fetches Peter, prince of the Apostles, and after him all the other Apostles; and together with the holy Mother, the Apostles, and the four angels he proceeds towards the Mount of Olives. The Apostles walk barefoot and are dressed as they can be seen in holy paintings: some with beards and some without, just as they really were. When Jesus approaches the Mount of Olives he stops, turning his face towards Jerusalem, with the Mother and Magdalene standing on his right. The Apostle Peter, having knelt down before him and received his blessing, goes to his place. The others do the same, taking up their places, some to the right and some to the left of Our Lord. When they have done that, Jesus distributes gifts among them. He gives a net to the Apostle Andrew, saying: 'You will be a fisher of men.' Another receives a book, a third a sword, with the words, 'You will not suffer any harm from this, if you use it in my name.' Then Jesus proceeds to the Mount and climbs its ladder [*stiege/scala*]; the Mother and Magdalene stand on his right, the Apostles in their places at the foot of the Mount. Then Jesus says, 'Since everything concerning me is fulfilled, I return to my Father, who is also your Father, and to my God, who is also yours'; and he moves away to reach the summit of the Mount, where the machine with the ropes is prepared. The Apostles bow to one another, weep, and say sorrowfully, 'O Lord, do not forsake us, for we are orphans.' But Jesus answers, 'Do not weep, I will not leave you as orphans, I am going to my Father and I shall ask him to send you the Spirit of Consolation and Truth, who will teach you all things: for if I do not go, the Paraclete will not come to you.' After these and other words there is a clap of thunder, Christ appears on the top of the mountain, the heavens open, and God the Father can be seen miraculously suspended in the air, enveloped in a great light which pours forth from the innumerable lamps; the small children representing the angels move around him while harmonious music and sweet singing are heard. The taller angels which are painted on the disc also revolve around so that they seem to be alive. From the Heaven where God the Father is, a very beautiful and ingeniously devised cloud descends on the seven ropes: it is round and surrounded by revolving discs which move quickly; to right and left two children can be seen dressed as angels with golden wings. While the cloud is still on its way, Jesus takes two golden keys and says to Peter, 'You are Peter and upon this rock I will build my church, etc.', and blessing him, he gives him the keys. Then, with the help of the seven ropes he ascends towards Heaven, keeping himself upright, blessing Mary and the Apostles with his hand. It is a most marvellous and incomparable sight. The ropes are activated by invisible and most ingenious gear-wheels so that the person representing Jesus Christ seems indeed to be ascending by himself; and he reaches a great height without swaying. The holy Virgin and the Apostles, on seeing that the Lord is going away, shed tears. When he has reached the cloud, this envelops him from head to foot and the two angels who stand one on each side of him kneel down before him. At this moment many lamps which are also within the cloud are lit shedding splendid light. But Jesus continues to ascend, accompanied by the two angels, and as soon as he reaches the Father, the music stops and it grows dark. Then the Virgin and the Apostles turn their eyes towards the room above the altar: the curtain is pulled from the place which represents the upper heaven and the light comes back.[1]

---

[1] In 1439 representatives of the eastern and western Churches gathered in Florence in a vain attempt to reunite the two and settle their doctrinal differences through a Council of Reconciliation. Bishop Abramo was one of the Russian representatives attending, and wrote an account of the spectacle performed while the council was in progress. A hypothetical reconstruction of the staging arrange-

ments described by Abramo is found in Mario Fabbri, Elvira Garbero Zorzi and Anna Maria Petrioli Tofani (eds.), *Il luogo teatrale a Firenze*, Milan, 1975, pp. 55–6. For a further discussion of the text and its interpretation, see Ludovico Zorzi, 'La scenotecnica brunelleschiana. Problemi filologici e interpretativi', in Raimondo Guarino (ed.), *Teatro e Culture della Rappresentazione: Lo spettacolo in Italian nel Quattrocento*, Bologna, 1988, pp. 301–17.

G20   A change in the *Festa* of St John the Baptist, Florence, 1454

Manuscript written by Matteo di Marco Palmieri in 1454, quoted in d'Ancona, *Origini del teatro*, vol. I, pp. 228–9; trans. Ferrari, *Staging*, pp. 240–2

For St John the order of events was changed. It was customary to have the parade [*mostra*] on the 22nd, the procession with companies [*compagnie*], friars, priests, and floats [*edifizj*] on the morning of the 23rd, and the offerings [*offerte*] in the evening, and on the 24th the horse race [*palio*], and they were rearranged in this way: that is to say the parade should be on the 21st, and on the morning of the 22nd the procession with all the floats [*edifizj*]; what these were in the said year and how they processed I shall now proceed to tell. On the 22nd the cross from Santa Maria del Fiore led the way with all the choirboys and after them six cantors; next came the companies of Jacopo the tailor's cutter and Nofri the cobbler with about thirty boys dressed in white, and little angels; third, the float [*edifizio*] of the Angel St Michael, above which was God the Father in a cloud, and in the square before the Signoria [*al dirimpetto a' Signori*] they performed [*fecero Rappresentazione*] the battle of the angels when Lucifer was cast out of Heaven with his fallen angels [*maledetti*]; fourth, the company of ser Antonio and Piero di Mariano with about thirty boys dressed in white and little angels; fifth, the float of Adam which in the square performed the play [*fe' Rappresentazione*] of God creating Adam and Eve, and giving his commandment to them, and of their disobedience so that they were cast out of Paradise, with first the temptation by the serpent and other relevant events [*appartenenze*]; sixth, a Moses on horseback with a large group of mounted elders [*principali*] of the people of Israel and others; seventh, the float of Moses, which in the square performed the play [*fe' le Rappresentazione*] in which God gave him the law; eighth, several prophets and sibyls with Hermes Trismegistus and others who foretold the incarnation of Christ; ninth, the float of the Annunciation which performed its play [*fe' la sua Rappresentazione*]; tenth, the Emperor Octavian with many horsemen and the Sibyl, to perform the play in which the Sibyl foretold that Christ was to be born, and showed him the Virgin up in the sky [*in aria*] with Christ in her arms. And it happened that when the float was before the Signoria, and Octavian had dismounted and stepped on to the lower level of the float [*in sull'edifizio sotto*] – that is, into the temple – to start his performance, a German came upon them wearing only a loose shirt, and at the foot of the float he asked, 'Where is the King of Rome?' And there were some who answered, 'Look, he is there'; and showed him Octavian. He climbed on to the float: many believed that he was one of those who had to take part in the festival [*festa*] and therefore he was not hindered. First of all he seized the idol which was in the said temple and threw it in the square; then, turning to Octavian, who was dressed in purple velvet worked [*broccato*] in costly [*ricchissimo*] gold, he seized him, threw him headlong on to the people in the square, and then seized a pillar to climb up to some children who were standing above the said temple as little angels; and as he did this, some bystanders intervened having clubs [*mazze*] in their hands, and beating him fiercely they pulled him with difficulty to the ground. Having got up from the ground he again tried to climb up, but he was hit with clubs from below and from above and overpowered. Eleventh, the Temple of Peace [*Templum Pacis*] with the float of the Nativity to perform its play [*per fare la sua Rappresentazione*]; twelfth, a float in the shape of a magnificent and triumphal Temple, which octagonal temple was adorned all around with the seven Virtues and the Virgin Mary on the east side with the Christ Child, and around the temple Herod performed his play; thirteenth, the three Magi,with a troop of more than 200 horses most magnificently adorned, came to bring their offerings to the Christ Child; the Passion and Entombment were left out, as they were not felt to be appropriate to a festival [*non parve si convenisse a festa*]; fourteenth a mounted troop of Pilate's soldiers, detailed as guards to the sepulchre; fifteenth, the float of the Entombment, from which Christ arose; sixteenth, the float of Limbo, out of which he brought the Patriarchs; seventeenth, the float of Paradise, into which he led the said Patriarchs; eighteenth, the Apostles and the Maries, who were present at the Ascension [*Assunzione*]; nineteenth, the float of the Ascension of Christ, that is, the one from which he went to Heaven; twentieth, the mounted troop of three kings, queens, damsels, and nymphs with carts and other matters belonging to the Living [*appartenenze al vivo*]; twenty-first, the float of the Living and the Dead; twenty-second, the float of Judgement, with the stretcher for tombs [*barella de' sepolcri*], Paradise, and Hell, and its play [*Rappresentazione*] as in faith we believe it shall be at the end of time. All the above-mentioned floats performed their plays in the square before the Signoria, and these lasted until the sixteenth hour [after sunrise?: *in fino alle 16 ore*].

G21   Extracts from two *sacre rappresentazioni*, Florence c. 1463

Newbigin (ed.), *Nuovo Corpus*, vol. 139, pp. xii–xiv

(i) Dear brothers gathered in this place, we humbly appeal [to God], who through his grace in this present action will show us assembled here the outcome of his great ordering of events, and the times and degrees of his exalted virtue, which are deserving of our commendation in such a great performance [*tanta magna rappresentazione*] [. . .]

And the following matters which are set forth to us in the Bible, we shall contrive to represent them here; so may it please you to follow with your full attention the order of events which make such a fine and pious *festa*. And those of you who are come to watch, pray to God that he may help us to achieve this.[1]

[1] The manuscript of *La creazione del mondo* [The Creation of the World], from which this extract is taken, is ascribed to 1463 by Newbigin. These words form part of the opening speech from the Angel (vv. 9–16, 25–32).

(ii) The *festa* of the Prodigal Son is concluded. Then when the *festa* is over, an angel appears and recites this verse, thanking the public [*populo*]:

'I want to recite a verse to all of you here. If anything was lacking in this *festa*, I pray that you will excuse us, and we beg your forgiveness. For today you are dismissed: we pray that God will preserve you from troubles, and may you return here next year.'

After the angel has recited this everyone rises and performs a dance and sings a hymn of praise [*una lauda*][1]

[1] This speech (vv. 505–12) and the accompanying stage directions conclude *Il figliuol prodigo* [The Prodigal Son], also known as *Il vitello sagginato* [The Fattened Calf]. The *Sacra Rappresentazione* is attributed to Piero di Mariano Muzi of Florence, and dated around 1463.

G22   Extracts from a sixteenth-century *Sacra rappresentazione* (*La Storia di Santa Uliva*), Florence

De Bartholomaeis, (ed.), *Laude drammatiche*, vol. III, pp. 10–12 and 66–8. The text was first published in a modern edition by d'Ancona (*Sacre rappresentazioni dei secoli XIV, XV e XVI*, 3 vols., Florence, 1872)

(i) Now let four men come out dressed in white shirts, barefoot and wearing death-masks, with wigs upon their heads, and being all of the same kind, it would be better that each should carry in his hand two incense-burners which are long, and lit; and passing across the stage [*per la scena*] let them repeat twice, in a pious tone, the following verses:

> O false desires, O vain thoughts
> Which always form in the minds of men
> After some new anguish assails
> Our honest wishes and pure thoughts!
> Not only the common people, but famous emperors
> Are subject to this mutability.
> O thankless world, cruel and unhappy destiny,
> Which in a moment shows us life and death.

Having said this they leave.

Then Uliva and the others arrive at an Inn, and when they knock at the door the Innkeeper says:

GRUFFAGNA   It is we, who wish to stay the night.

INNKEEPER   You are a thousand times welcome.

GRUFFAGNA   We have travelled far on foot and are tired. And have need of your help, brother.

INNKEEPER   Please enter.

GRUFFAGNA   What have you to eat?

INNKEEPER   Ask as you wish.

GRUFFAGNA   I shall not refuse your offer.

INNKEEPER   Above all I have good bread and good wine.

GRUFFAGNA   Then bring us a jug of wine.

Then the Innkeeper prepares a meal. And while they are eating the Emperor on his throne [*in sedia*] says:

> Pride and fury have overcome me
> And made me act contrary to reason
> Against my daughter who has suffered so much.
> And I have condemned her to death unjustly
> Now I am alone, smitten and in despair
> By reason of my blind, insane decision.

(ii) Now the King descends from his throne and enters the Chamber with the Bishop.

While he is confessing, you should arrange for a woman wearing a cloak which is coloured and beautiful on top, with a garment underneath which is old and dark brown, with shoes of chamois leather upon her feet, and over them a pair of beautiful slippers. And let her have the faces of four different women, that is to say a mask which from one side is that of an elderly woman, from another side even more ancient, and from the third side of normal age, or not elderly at all, and finally there is her face without a mask; and on her head a diadem which covers all four of her faces, and is of various colours. Let her hold in her right hand a flaming torch, and in her left a knife bound with a rope. You should dress a youth in the same way wearing a cloak which is as ornate as possible, with a sword by his side. And let the youth have in his right hand a few cards, and under his left arm a gaming-table, and in his left hand a purse. Third, let a man appear with a long dark garment, poorly dressed and barefooted, with a large mask, a long white beard and hair, with his right hand held to his cheek. And let another man appear with him in a long garment of black skin, with the fur showing, and clad in stockings made of felt, wearing gloves of leather, with a finger held to his lips to indicate silence, and on his head a fur hat, with a dark mask and a long beard. Likewise you should dress a man in poor condition, his garments old and torn, his beard dishevelled and full of feathers, and his hair and clothes the same. Then let another appear, his clothes stained and dirty, his face swollen and coloured, without a hat on his head, holding chickens and wildfowl in his hand, and on his shoulders a roasting-spit. And after him let a man appear with two faces, one looking forward and one back, and let his costume from the front appear neat and clean, and from the back made of dirty and torn cloth, and let him also have some daggers and knives behind him, with a hat upon his head. And let the aforesaid persons station themselves as if they want to gaze upon the woman with four faces. And with these persons you should also costume seven women. Let the first be dressed in purple with rich and elaborate ornaments, and let her have for an emblem a serpent: let her display it in one hand, while the other adopts a threatening attitude; and note that over her costume she must wear a cloak, which should cover her down to her feet. The second shall wear a tan-coloured costume and have for her emblem a lion, without any decoration; and note that these two should have their hair braided into plaits, with nothing more upon their heads. The third dressed in yellow, her hair in disarray, with a hand upon the head of the animal which she has as her emblem, which is the wolf. The fourth dressed in red, with loose plaits, and for her emblem a pig. The fifth dressed in dark blue, with her hair parted, and her emblem a dog. The sixth dressed in black, with her hair loose, with an open book in her hand while with her other hand she shows her emblem, a he-goat. The seventh in a rose-pink costume, elegantly adorned, most of all upon her head: she should hold a mirror in one hand, with the other held aloft, and her emblem should be a peacock. Note that these women should appear to be riding upon their emblems, and since this will be difficult, depict them upon their breasts or wherever you find it convenient, in order that they shall be seen: and let all these persons enter in company with those described previously, and let them sing in two choruses the psalm mentioned below. When that is finished, let them return to the place from which they appeared. And this is the psalm: *Dixit stultum in corde etc.*, and the *Gloria* is not recited.[1]

---

[1] *La Storia di Santa Uliva* was one of the most popular of the Florentine *sacre rappresentazioni* throughout the sixteenth century, and is preserved in numerous manuscripts and printed texts (see Anna Maria Testaverde and Anna Maria Evangelista (eds.), *Sacre rappresentazioni manoscritte e a stampa conservate nelle Biblioteca Nazionale Centrale di Firenze*, Milan, Giunte regionale toscana and Editrice Bibliografica, 1988). It was elaborately staged, reached 1,480 lines in length and was presented over two days; the action included romantic as well as religious action and was interspersed with *intermedi* of a mythological and allegorical nature.

G23 Woodcuts from printed editions of fifteenth-century *sacre rappresentazioni*

(i) St Valentine, St Juliana and other martyrs

Woodcut from an anonymous play, *La Rapresentatione di Santo Valentino, & di Santa Giuliana, e altri Martiri*, Florence 1554; reproduced in Fabbri *et al.*, *Il luogo teatrale a Firenze*, p. 68

Although we cannot be certain that it represents an accurate reproduction of an actual peformance, this woodcut seems to indicate that by the middle of the sixteenth century the perspective scenery used in presentations of the classical *commedia erudita* was also seen in presentations of religious plays.

Detto quefto la fciolgano & bat/
tuta la menano dipanzi al Pre/
fetto.
Fatt'el comãdamẽto tuo fignor benigno
uedi come lhabbiam mal gouernata
& non ha luogo adoffo doue'l fegno
non fia,& ha la carne rileuata
& lei per quefto crede gir nel regno
di quel fuo Chrifto & effer poi beata
che mentre fuo corpo uergheggiato
habbian,ha fempre il fuo Iefu inuocato
Rifponde il Prefetto.
Per certo quefta gran cofa mi pare
ch'a farti tanto mal nulla non gioua
ma fe hor non ti ueggio rimutare
ti parra facci altri lamenti nuoui
& con cathene ti faro legare
e uo ch'aftare incarcerata pruoui
& s'io comincio forfe dadouero

ti muterai dal tuo uan penfiero
S. Giuliana al Prefetto.
Fãmi quel che tu uuoi chio nõ mi curo
di tua tormenti & te, non ftimo un fico
elqual ti ueggo come fetro duro
& non uuoi effer di Giefu amico
ma fempre fto con lanimo ficuro
inuer di te & intendi quel chio dico
che quanti ltratii mi fai & tormenti
mi fono allalma giubili & contenti
Il Prefetto irato dice a Ierui.
Prefto fu fate con forte cathene
fia'l corpo di coftei tutto legato
perche la uuol del male, e non del bene
& che al tutto le fia lacerato
ogni fuo neruo e offa,& ftar in pene
pel fuo penfier fciocco iniquo ingrato
& fate prefto uoi la incarcerate
ne pan,ne uino,& nulla non le date

Legonla con Cathene di ferro
& mettonla in prigione,& men
tre uanno, uno feruo dice a
lei.
Va pur auanti che forfe uedrai
quel che dir uillania a un Signore

perfida iniqua che del mal harai
po che ftar uuoi nel tuo iniquo errore
& in quefta prigione tanto ftarai
che forfe muterai tuo duro cuore
& nulla da mangiar t'arrecheremo
fe ben noi ti uedefsimo uenir meno
Mettonla

(ii) St Agatha, virgin and martyr

Frontispiece from *La rappresentatione di Santa vergine et Martire*, Florence 1558; reproduced in Anna Maria Testaverde and Anna Maria Evangelista (eds.), *Sacre rappresentazioni manoscritte e a stampa*, Milan, 1988, fig. 4

Although vivid representations of martyrdom were a regular feature of *sacre rappresentazioni*, it is unlikely that the degree of realism depicted in this woodcut was achieved in representation.

(iii) The Feast of the Annunciation

Woodcut from Feo Belcari, *La Festa della Annuntiatione di nostra Donna*, Florence, no date;
reproduced in Fabbri *et al.*, *Il luogo teatrale a Firenze*, p. 65

The woodcut is clearly an illustration of the operation of the *mandorla*, the
machine which descended from the roof of the church and opened to reveal an
angel, as described by Vasari [**G17**], and the design for whose mechanism is shown
in **G13(i)** and **(ii)**.

III   *Renaissance innovations*

The theatre of the Renaissance, based upon secular rather than religious texts, conforming to artistic rules and conventions set by classical precedent, and requiring a purpose-built theatrical space for its performance, came into being in late fifteenth- and sixteenth-century Italy, preceded by humanist comedies written, mostly for school or college performance, in Latin. The discovery of twelve hitherto unknown texts of comedies by Plautus in 1425 had led to a revival of interest in Roman comedy, and a growing understanding that it was essentially a theatrical and not a literary form. The publication of the first printed edition of Vitruvius' *De architectura* in 1468 [see **G24**] followed by an illustrated edition in 1511, led to a similar interest in the theatre building itself, the use of a purpose-built structure being a major departure from the medieval custom of transforming a church, street or *piazza* into a temporary playing space. (The third element of the modern theatre, the professional performers who earned their living from their acting skills, was to develop with the earliest companies performing what would later be termed *commedia dell'arte* from the middle of the sixteenth century onwards.)

Vitruvius, whose architectural treatise was the only one to survive from antiquity, had a profound effect upon Renaissance architecture: for the history of the theatre his significance lies not only in his prescriptive account of the architectural form of the theatre (difficult though it may have proved to interpret) but in his description of the three scenes for tragedy, comedy and satyr-play (v.vi). The concept of a unified setting appropriate to the dramatic *genre* which was being performed was in stark contrast to the unlocalised or multiple settings of most medieval drama. The classical sources, however, seemed ambiguous with regard to the extent to which the scene might change during the course of the play, and Renaissance practice, already familiar with the spectacular devices of medieval drama, seized upon every passage that seemed to offer a precedent for the changeable scenery which could accompany the *intermedi* which divided the acts of new, learned comedy (*commedia erudita*). The principles of perspective painting which transformed Renaissance painting were seen to reach their most complex form in a perspective scene for the theatre, where a three-dimensional town square, palace or rustic landscape was miraculously represented within the confines of the playing space, and significantly both Serlio's and Danti's descriptions of theatre scenes appear in the context of a discussion of perspective [see **G27**, **G28**].

It was not until the opening of the Teatro Olimpico (designed by Palladio, but not completed until after his death) in Vicenza in 1585 that Italy could boast a permanent theatre built upon Vitruvian principles: as Serlio indicates, the earlier structures were temporary, adapted as often as not to the needs of a rectangular banqueting hall or other similar space, and created as examples of princely magnificence. Classical precedent, indeed, was only one of the influences upon the new drama which eventually supplanted the medieval stage.

G24   Early performances of comedy and tragedy in Rome, 1486

From the dedication to Cardinal Raffaele Riario contained in the first printed edition of Vitruvius, *De architectura*, ed. Gaius Sulpicius (Giovanni Sulpizio), Rome, 1486; included, with a translation from the Latin into Italian, in Fabrizio Cruciani, *Teatro nel Rinascimento: Roma 1450–1550*, Rome, 1983, pp. 222–5

Indeed you were the first person to erect a beautifully decorated stage [*pulpitum*], five feet in height, in the centre of the square [*forum*] for a Tragedy, which we were the first in this age to teach youths to perform and recite [*cantare*] for the sake of arousing their emotions [*excitandi gratia*]; for the enaction of a Tragedy was something which Rome had not witnessed for many centuries.[1]

And after it had been performed in the great fortress of Hadrian [*in Hadriani mole*] in the presence of the blessed Innocenzo, then it was repeated at your home as if encircled by the seats of a circus [*tanquam in media circi cavea*], with all the spectators shaded by cloths; and you honoured the spectacle with your presence in the company of the people and many spectators of the same rank as yourself. You were also the first to present to our age the aspect of a painted scene [*picturatae scoenae faciem*], before which the followers of Pomponius performed a comedy.[2] For that reason the whole city looks to you with great eagerness for a new theatre [. . .]

[1] The tragedy whose performance is referred to was in all probability the *Hippolytus* of Seneca, in a production of 1486, presented first at Castel S. Angelo in the presence of Pope Innocenzo VIII and then at the home of Cardinal Raffaele Riario (1461–1521) near the Campo dei Fiori, Rome.

[2] The humanist Leto Pomponio (1428–98) was devoted to the revival of the customs and traditions of ancient Rome, including performances of comedy. This passage makes the earliest reference to painted scenery, but too briefly to give a clear account of the staging arrangements. See Fabrizio Cruciani, *Teatro nel Rinascimento: Roma 1450–1550*, Rome, 1983, pp. 219–22.

G25   Classical performances at Ferrara, 1499

Letter from Jano Pencaro to Isabella Gonzaga, written in Ferrara and dated 9 February 1499 (one of a series of four describing the nightly festivities), quoted in A. Luzio and R. Renier, 'Commedie classiche in Ferrara', *Giornale storico della letteratura italiana* XI (1895), pp. 182–9; reproduced in Faccioli (ed.), *Il teatro*, I.ii, pp. 700–2

My most illustrious lady and patron, having reached home today I consider it my duty to give an account to Your Highness of recent events and most of all of the

Comedies; all the more so having recently been in Mantua, making mention in the presence of certain gentlemen of the sums laid out by the most illustrious Duke, not only would they not believe me, but I was virtually accused of being a liar when I claimed that the amount spent was almost two thousand ducats. Having been in Ferrara and witnessed everything at first hand, I can vouch for the truth of what I have said. To portray to Your Ladyship how everything is set up I must beg you to have recourse to your imagination, and recall the great Hall as it was set up for the other Comedies. The scene for the actors [*la sena de comici*] runs, as is usual, the full length of the windows; at the head of the hall is the raised platform [for the audience]. The first row of seating is four feet above the floor not, as it used to be, one foot; and it rises up to nine rows in height. The platform which runs the length of the hall on scaffolds [*sopra modioni*], as Your Ladyship knows, is much larger than usual, insofar as where the scaffolds extended four clear feet from the wall they now extend eight, and now it rises to nine rows, almost to the height of the ceiling, with its cross-beams and columns all covered with bushes and greenery in the form of arms and devices of the Duke, which is a beautiful sight. All the platforms are spread with red, white and green cloths, and the rest of the Hall is decorated as formerly. At the other end of the Hall near the chest [*credenza*] a platform has been built with the same dimensions and decorations as the platform at the other end.

When the people had taken their place on these platforms, the comedy *The Eunuch*[1] was played before them last Thursday. About the play there is nothing further to say, since everyone can read it for himself, but the costumes and effects prepared for it are worthy of description. You should know that first of all there was a parade upon the stage of all those who played a part in each of the comedies, amounting to 133 persons, all attired in new costumes made for the occasion, some of satin, some of camlet [*zambelotto*], some of silk, some in cloth and some in other rich fabrics. Their costumes were adapted to their various characters, with some dressed as Greek slaves, some as servants, some as masters, merchants and women as required. After them those appearing in the *tramezi*[2] came on, 144 in number, also dressed in completely new costumes, some as peasants, others as pageboys, nymphs, clowns [*buffoni*] and parasites, and given that in some acts characters appeared for a second time, no costume was ever used more than once, so that in total there were 287 costumes, all of them new and for the most part dignified and solemn and very costly.

In the first *tramezo* a company of peasants appeared, who through their labour extracted the fruit of the well-tilled soil. At the beginning they leapt out suddenly, and performing a *moresca*[3] with hoes, they began to hoe the ground. With their every movement, action and rhythm they moved in perfect time with the music being played, so that it seemed that all these men were made to move by a single spirit, guided by the rhythm of the musician. So they came out and hoed the earth, planting golden seed with the measure and rhythm that I have described, so that every step, every gesture, every look was in time with the music. The corn which they had planted grew, and they began to reap it, and every swing of the scythe, every motion in collecting the wheat and tying it in bundles was carried out in time with the music; then with the same rhythm they threshed it, they winnowed it with shovels and stored it in sacks; and finally for relief after their labour they prepared a fine banquet with songs, music and dance: and with singing and merry-making they gave way to the second act.

In the second *tramezo* there came out twelve persons, led by a clown: they were dressed gracefully in silk with hose cut in a new fashion, with golden bells which were made to sound. After dancing a *chiaranza*[4] they performed a lively and very fine *moresca*.

In the third *tramezo* six nymphs appeared, led by a musician, light and free in their movements, and following them some unhappy youths, singing a song of lament in pleasant harmony, grieving over the perverse fate that had made them slaves of women who cared nothing for their misery, and held them captive like prisoners in chains.

In the fourth *tramezo* twelve persons appeared dressed in different costumes with new devices, each one of them carrying a wild fowl: one a pheasant, another a partridge, a hare [*lepore*], a peacock, etc. They moved across the scene to a new measure, and stopped in the middle to prepare the birds for a banquet, performing even the smallest action in perfect agreement with the music. And while they were at work plucking and skinning the birds a bear was seen to approach them, performing so naturally that many thought it was a real beast. The bear went for the group of revellers and they scattered everywhere in disorder, except for one who by mishap was unable to flee, and was killed by the bear and remained motionless on the floor. Turning to more pleasant prey, he ate the fowl and other meat which had been abandoned. Satisfied, the fierce beast began solemnly to gnaw at his nails; taking courage, the fugitives returned, cunningly surrounded the fearful animal and put him in chains, with even the smallest action being carried out in time to the music. Having bound the savage beast they went to the corpse and turning him over limb by limb they confirmed that he was dead. And only with much wit and intelligence could you determine whether this death was genuine or feigned. After removing the corpse they left the banquet with many lively actions. The fifth act followed, and at the conclusion every man and woman went to their home.[5]

[1] *The Eunuch* was Terence's most farcical comedy, and the most frequently revived of his plays in the Renaissance [see **A15**]. The parade of characters described by Pencaro indicates how the simplicity of Roman staging was elaborated during the Renaissance: the original cast list, including non-speaking parts, comprised less than twenty actors, and there would probably have been some doubling of roles.

[2] *Tramezo, intermedio, intermezzo* were all terms applied to the allegorical performances given in the interval between one act and another in performances of comedy. Originally musical, they developed into one of the chief vehicles for spectacular visual effects in Renaissance staging. Compare Nino Pirrotta and Elena Povoledo, *Music and Theatre from Poliziano to Monteverdi*, Cambridge, 1982.

[3] *moresca*: a semi-dramatic dance form (literally a 'moorish' dance, like the English Morris dance).

[4] *chiaranza*: a traditional dance form.

[5] The letter describes two further performances on successive nights: *The Eunuch* was followed by Plautus' *Trinummus* and its attendant *tramezi*, and there was a further performance of *The Eunuch*, apparently for female spectators, with new *tramezi*.

G26   A rotating mountain designed by Leonardo da Vinci, Milan, *c.* 1505

Sketches from Arundel MS 263, British Museum, London (fo. 224 and fo. 231); reproduced in Pirrotta and Povoledo, *Music and Theatre*, figs. 8 and 9

Sketches (i) and (ii) by Leonardo da Vinci show the design for a mountain which revolves and opens to reveal the interior of Hades with Pluto, God of the Underworld, enthroned. The performance for which these designs were prepared may have been a revival, or adaptation, of Poliziano's *Fabulo di Orfeo* (*c.* 1475), perhaps the first work in the Renaissance to represent classical mythology for performance within a dramatic structure. Povoledo argues that Leonardo's designs combine traditional staging conventions with the new 'demands of a unified set representing a specific location' (*Music and Theatre*, p. 297).

G26 (i)

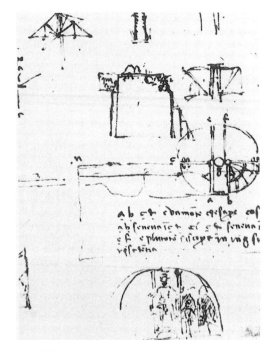

G26 (ii)

G27   Sebastiano Serlio's description of the theatre and its scenes, 1545

The Second Book of Sebastiano Serlio, *Regole generali di archittetura*, Paris, 1545, in the English version ('translated out of Italian into Dutch, and out of Dutch into English'), fols. 23–6, published by Robert Peake, London, 1611; reprinted with an introduction by A. E. Santaniello, New York, 1970

Sebastiano Serlio (1475–1554) worked as an architect and scene designer before setting himself the task, completed with difficulty at the end of his life, of writing a work on architecture which would serve his age in the way that Vitruvius' *De architectura* had served imperial Rome. For the first time in a treatise of this kind, the illustrations (reproduced below as (i), (ii), (iii), (iv) and (v)) were closely integrated with the text. For an account of Serlio's familiarity with scenic practice, see A. E. Santaniello (ed.), *The Book of Architecture by Sebastiano Serlio, London, 1611*, New York, 1980, pp. 3–15.

A TREATISE OF SCENES, OR PLACES TO PLAY IN

Among all the things that may bee [*sic*] made by mens hands, thereby to yield admiration, pleasure to sight, and to content the fantasies of men; I thinke it is placing of a Scene, as it is shewed to your sight, where a man in a small place may see built by Carpenters or Masons, skilfull in Perspective worke, great Palaces, large Temples, and divers Houses, both neere and farre off; broad places filled with Houses, long streets crost with other wayes: tryumphant Arches, high Pillars or Columnes, Piramides, Obeliscens, and a thousand fayre things and buildings, adorned with innumerable lights, great, middle sort and small, as you may see it placed in the Figure, which are so cunningly set out, that they shew foorth and represent a number of the brightest stones; as Diamonds, Rubins, Sapphirs, Smaragdes, Jacinthes, and such like. There you may see the bright shining Moone ascending only with her hornes, and already risen up, before the Spectators are ware of, or once saw it ascend. In some other Scenes you may see the rising of the Sunne with his course about the world: and at the ending of the Comedie, you may see it goe downe most artificially, where at many beholders have been abasht. And when occasion serveth, you shall by Arte see a God descending down from Heaven; you also see some Comets and Stars shoot in the skyes: then you see divers personages come upon the Stage, richly adorned with divers strange formes and manners of Apparell both to daunce Moriscoes and play Musicke. Sometimes you see strange beasts, wherein are men and children, leaping, running, & Tumbling, as those kind of beasts use to doe, not without admiration of the beholders: which things, as occasion serveth, are so pleasant to mens eyes, that a man could not see fairer made with mens hands. But for that we are entred into another maner of Perspective worke, therefore I will speake more at large thereof. This Perspective worke wherof I will speake, although it be contrary to those rules which are shewed before, because these aforesayd are imagined to be upon a flat wall: and this other rule because it is materiall and imbossed or raysed outward, therefore it is reason we observe another rule therein, according to common custome. First, you must make a Scaffold, which must bee as high as a mans eye will reach, looking directly forward; for the first part thereof which is marked C.[1] But the other part behind it, whereon the Houses stand, you must rayse by behind against the wall at least a ninth part thereof, that is, you must devide the playne Stage or Scaffold in nine parts; and then you must make the Scaffold higher by a ninth part behind: then before at B. which must be very even & strong, because of the Morisco dancers. This hanging downward of the Scaffold, I have found by experience to be very pleasing, for in *Vincente* [Vicenza] which is as sumptuous and riche a Towne as any in all *Italy*; there I made a Theater and a Stage of wood, then [than] the which, I thinke, there was never a greater made in our time, in regard of the wonderfull sights that there were seene, as of Wagons, Elephants and other Moriscoes. There I ordained, that before the hanging Scene there should be a Scaffold made by water compasse, which Scaffold was 12. foot broad, and 60. foot long, according to the place wherein it stood; which I found to be very pleasing and fit for shew. This first Scaffold, because it was right, therefore the pavement therof must not obey the Horizon, but the Quadrants, whereof on every side were foure square, from whence at the beginning of the rising Scaffold B. all the Quadrans went to the outtermost Horizon O.

which with their due distances do shorten very well. And for that some men have placed the Horizon of this Sciographies against the wall right above the Scaffold, whereby it seemeth the Houses runne all in one; therefore I determined to place the Horizon before the doore, which pleased me so well, that I used the same kind of order in all these kind of works: and so I counsell those that take pleasure in such Arts, to use and esteeme this way for the best, as I will shew in this Figure following, and also declared in the profill of the Theatre and Scene.

And because the preparation of Comedies are done in three sorts, that is, Comical, Tragical and Satiricall, I will first entreat of the Comicall, whereof the Houses must be made as if they were for common or ordninarie people, which for the most part must be made under roofes in a Hall, which at the end thereof hath a chamber for the pleasure or ease of the personages: and there it is that the ground of the Scaffold is made (as I said and shewed before) in the profil. Therefore C. is the first part being the flat Scaffold; and suppose that each Quadran containeth two foote on eyther side, so shal they upon the hanging Scaffold before on the Base be also two foot broad, which is marked B. And (as I sayd before) my meaning is not to place the Horizon hereof against the backe behind in the Scaffold, but as farre as it is from the beginning on the pavement B. to the wall, so farre I would also that men shall passe behinde through the wall, and so shall all the houses and other things show better in the shortening: and when by convenient distances you have drawne all the Quadrans towards the Horizon, & shortened them, then you must shorten the houses right with the foure square stones; which houses are the great lines marked upon the ground, aswell for those that stand upright, as those that shorten. All such houses I alwayes made of spars, or rafter or laths, covered with linnin cloth; making doores and windowes, both before and in the shortening, as occasion fell out. I have also made some things of halfe planks of wood, which were great helpe to the Paynters to set out things at life. All the spaces from the backe to the wall marked. A. shall be for the personages, to the which end the hindermost backe in the middle shall stand at the least two foot from the wall, that the personages may goe from the one side to the other, and not be seene. Then you must rayse a termination at the beginning of the pavement B. which shall be the poynt L. and from thence to the Horizon there shalbe a line drawne, as it is marked in the profil with prickes, which shall be of like height; and where that toucheth the hindermost backe of the Scene or Scaffold, there the Horizon of that backe shall stand: and that Horizon shall serve onely for that backe. But if you stretch a corde or any other thing to the termination L. then you may fasten a thread to it, to thrust backward or forward, ot use it out of the stedfast Horizon, & all the Ortographie of the houses before. But the Horizon which goeth through the wall, shall serve for all the shortening sides of the houses: and for that men should breake the wall, if they would use all this Horizon in grosse, which may not bee done, therefore I have alwayes made a small modell of wood and paper iust of the same bignes, and by the same modell set it downe in grosse, from piece to piece. But this way will fall out hard for some men to understand, neverthelesse, it will be necessary to worke by models and experiments, and by studie a man shall find the way: and for that a man can hardly finde any Halls how great soever, wherein he can place a Theater without imperfection and impediment; therefore to follow Antiquities, according to my power and abilitie, I have made all such parts of these Theaters, as may stand in a Hall. Therefore the part marked D. shall be the post scene, and the circular place marked E. shall bee the Orchestra: round about this Orchestra shall be the places for the noblest personages to sit, marked F. The first steps marked G. for the noblest women to sit upon. The place H. is a way, so is the part marked I. In the middle betweene these degrees are the steps the easier to goe up. The places marked K. must be made so great backward as the hall will afford, which is made somewhat slooping, that the people may see one over the others head.

Touching the disposition of Theaters and other Scenes, concerning the grounds thereof, I have spoken sufficiently; now I will speake of the Scene in Perspective worke: and for that Scenes are made of three sorts, that is, Comical, to play Comedies on, Tragicall, for Tragedies, and Satiricall for Satirs. This first shall be Comicall, whereas the houses must be slight for Citizens, but specially there must not want a brawthell or bawdy house, and a great Inne, and a Church; such are of necessitie to be therein. How to rayse these houses from the ground is sufficiently expressed, and how you shall place the Horizon: neverthelesse, that you may be the better instructed (touching the former of these houses, I have here set downe a Figure,[2] for satisfaction of those that take pleasure therein; but because this figure is so small, therein I could not observe all the measures, but refer them to invention, that thereby you may chuse or make houses which shew well as an Open Gallery, or lodge through the which you may see an other house. The hangings over or shooting out, show well in shortening works, and some Cornices cut out at the ends; accompanied with some others that are painted, show well in worke: so doe the houses which have great bearing out, like lodgings or Chambers for men, and especially above all things, you must set the smalest houses before, that you may see other houses over or above them, as you see it here above the bawdy house: for if you place the greatest before, and the rest behind still lesser, then the place of the Scene would not be so well filled, and although these things upon the one side be made all upon one floore: Neverthelesse, for that you place great part of the lights in the middle, hanging over the Scene or Scaffold, therefore it would stand better if the floore in the midst were taken away, and all the roundels and Quadrans which you see in the Buildings, they are artificiall light cutting through, or divers colors; which to make, I will shew the manner in the last of the Booke. The windowes which stand before, were good to be made of Glasse or Paper, with light behind them. But if I should here write all that I know to serve for this worke, it would be overlong to rehearse; therefore I referre that to the wit and discretion of those that exercise and practice themselves heerein.

Houses for tragedies, must bee made for great personages, for that actions of love, strange adventures, and cruell murthers (as you read in ancient and moderne Tragedies) happen always in the houses of great Lords, Dukes, Princes, and Kings. Therefore in such cases you must make none but stately houses, as you see it here in this Figure;[3] wherein (for that it is so smal) I could make no Princely Pallaces: but it is sufficient for the workeman to see the manner thereof, wherebye he may helpe himselfe as time and place serveth: and (as I sayde in the Comicall) hee must alwayes study to please the eyes of the beholders, and forget not himselfe so much as to set a small building in stead of a great, for the reasons aforesayd. And for that I have made all my Scenes of laths, covered with linnen, yet sometime it is necessary to make some things rising or bossing out; which are to bee made of wood, like the houses on the left side, whereof the Pillars, although they shorten, stand all upon one Base, with some Stayres, all covered over with cloth, the Cornices bearing out, which you must observe to the middle part: But to give place to the Galleries you must set the other shortening cloth somewhat backwards, and make a cornice above it, as you see: and that which I speake of these Buildings, you must understand of all the rest, but in the Buildings which stand far backward the Painting worke, must supplie the place by shadowes without any bearing out: touching the artificiall lights, I have spoken thereof in the Comicall worke. All that you make above the Roofe sticking out, as Chimneyes, Towers, Piramides, Oblisces, and other such things or Images; you must make them all of thin bords, cut out round, and well colloured: But if you make any flat Buildings, they must stand somewhat farre inward, that you may not see them on the sides. In these Scenes, though some have painted personages therein like supporters, as in a Gallery, or doore, as a Dog, Cat, or any other beasts: I am not of that opinion, for that standeth too long without stirring or mooving; but if you make such a thing to lie sleeping, that I hold withall. You may also make Images, Histories, or Fables of Marble, or other matter against a wall; but to represent the life, they ought to stirre. In the latter end of this Booke I will show you how to make them.

The Satiricall Scenes[4] are to represent Satirs, wherein you must place all those things that be rude and rusticall, as in ancient Satirs they were made plaine without any respect [concern], whereby men might understand, that such things were referred to Rusticall people, which set all things out rudely and plaineley: for which cause *Vitruvius* speaking of Scenes, saith, they should be made with Trees, Rootes, Herbs, Hils and Flowres, and with some countrey houses, as you see them here set downe. And for that in our dayes these things were made in Winter, when there were but fewe greene Trees, Herbs and Flowres to be found; then you must make these things of Silke, which shall be more commendable then the naturall things themselves: and as in other Scenes for Comedies or Tragedies, the houses or other artificiall things are painted, so you must make Trees, Hearbs, and other things in these; & the more such things cost, the more they are esteemed, for they are things which stately and great persons doe, which are enemies to nigardlinesse. This have I seene in some Scenes made by *Ieronimo Genga*, for the pleasure and delight of his lord and patron *Francisco Maria*, Duke of *Urbin*: wherein I saw so great liberalitie used by the Prince, and so good a conceit in the workeman, and so good Art and proportion to things therein represented, as ever I saw in all my life before. Oh good Lord, what magnificence was there to be seene, for the great number of Trees and Fruits, with sundry Herbes and Flowres, all made of fine Silke of divers collors. The water courses being adorned with Frogs, Snailes, Tortuses, Toads, Adders, Snakes and other beasts: Rootes of Corrale, mother of Pearle, and other shels layd and thrust through betweene the Stones, with so many severall and faire things, that if I should declare them all, I should not have time inough. I speake not of Satirs, Nimphes, Mer-maids, divers monsters, and other strange beastes, made so cunningly, that they seemed in shew as if they went and stirred, according to their manner. And if I were not desirous to be brief, I would speake of the costly apparel of some Shepheards made of cloth of gold, and of Silke, cunningly mingled with Imbrothery: I would also speake of some Fishermen, which were no lesse richly aparelled then the others, having Nets and Angling-rods, all gilt: I should speake of some Countrey mayds and Nimphes carelessly apparelled without pride, but I leave all these things to the discretion and consideration of the judicious workeman, which shall make all such things as their pattrons forme them, which they must worke after their owne devises, and never take care what it shall cost.

[1] The following passage is intended to be read in conjunction with illus. (i) and (ii) below.
[2] See illus. (iii) below. Since the number of performances of comedy far outweighed those of tragedy and satyr-play (which Renaissance dramaturgy interpreted as pastoral drama), Serlio devotes more space to a discussion of the practicalities of the comic scene.
[3] See illus. (iv) below.
[4] See illus. (v) below.

(i) Serlio's theatre: a cross-section

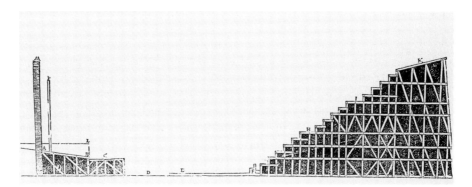

(ii) Serlio's theatre: ground plan

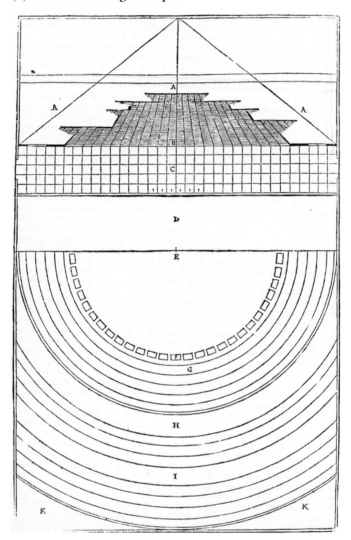

(iii) Serlio's comic scene

(iv) Serlio's tragic scene

(v) Serlio's 'satirical scene'

G28   Egnazio Danti explains the operation of changeable scenery, 1583

Iacomo Barozzi da Vignola, *Le due regole della prospettiva pratica, con i commentari del R.P.M. Egnatio Danti*, Rome, Zanetti, 1583

[Iacomo Barozzi da Vignola (1507–73) was a successful architect and author of treatises on architecture and perspective. Danti's commentary on his work contains what appears to be the first full account of changeable scenery on the Renaissance stage.]

Now, leaving aside the question of the differences between the tragic, comic and satiric scenes, since quite enough has been written about them by others and since they are outside the subject of our study, we shall explain here only how revolving scenes are made and how, in a moment, without the spectators realising it, the whole picture is changed, and from the semblance of a country place or a rustic village it is transformed into something else. In the figure [. . .] the way used to achieve this result may be seen. Let the line AB be the base of the upright face

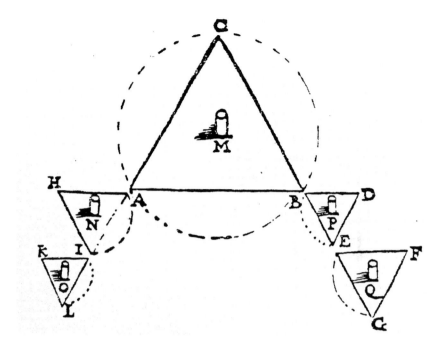

[*parete*], and let us assume it is desired to change this face, say, three times during the performance of the comedy: we should make three different faces, attaching them together so that they form a solid structure similar to a prism or a triangular column having at its extremities at the top and the bottom two equilateral triangles, whose base or ground plan will be the triangle ABC. These three faces must be built with wooden lasts strengthened by wooden beams running crosswise, and canvas must be stretched over this in order to be painted; in the centre M of the triangular base a pivot must be fixed, and similarly another one on the upper portion [of the structure] where it meets the point M. These must be secured with solid wooden bars so that the whole structure, which should touch the stage only around point M, can revolve on them. All the rest must stay free so that the rotation can take place with ease. Similarly the houses in relief should all be made in triangular form, so that the first surface of the scene LABG having served, for instance, for the first act, it can be turned in a moment and make another locality appear; for the position of the face AB will be taken by BC, and similarly with the houses in relief HA, KI, DE and FG will turn towards the front; and during two of the other *intermedi*, at the most suitable moment we can cause the other two surfaces of the upright face and the houses in relief to turn. And if we want to change the scene two times only, we shall decorate only two sides; if we want to change it four, five or six times, we shall decorate as many faces of our structures, just as we have done with three only in the above figure. It should be pointed out that while the scene is revolving and changing, it will be necessary to keep the spectators' eyes occupied with some *intermedio*, so that they do not notice the parts of the scene which are turning, and it is seen to have changed only when the *intermedio* is over.

I have heard that a scene was made in Castro for the Duke Pierluigi Farnese, by Aristotile da San Gallo, which changed twice, and I have seen a comedy recited in a similar setting [*in una simile scena*] in Florence, in the Ducal Palace, for the visit of the Archduke Karl of Austria in 1569, where the scene, designed by Baldassare Lanci da Urbino, changed twice. At the beginning of the comedy it showed the bridge at Santa Trinita and then, while the actors were represented as having gone to the villa of Arcetri, the second side was turned and the scene appeared full of gardens and country houses just as they actually are in Arcetri, with their vineyards and surrounding estates. When the scene changed a second time the suburb of Alberti was represented; and while the scene was being turned around [*mentre che la scena si girava*], it was concealed and filled by beautiful *intermedii* composed by M. Giovambatista Cini, a Florentine nobleman, who had also written the comedy. And I remember that the first time the scene turned the heavens opened [*s'aprì un cielo*], and a great number of men appeared in the air in the apparel of Gods, singing and playing music most pleasantly; and at the same time a cloud was lowered down under their feet and covered the scene while it was turning, so that when the cloud was lifted up again, there appeared on the scene the villa of Arcetri outside the gate of San Giorgio, near the walls of Florence, as already described; and in the meanwhile the Chariot of Fama passed over the stage, followed by many others who, singing another response, answered to the music being sung above. The other time the scene was being turned around it was likewise concealed by a cloud which came from the side, driven by winds, while the *intermedio* was being performed. On another occasion I saw a comedy represented in the same way in the presence of the Serenissimo Gran Duca Cosimo, by the company of the Vangelista, with a similar scene.

And indeed such scenes are well contrived, and they are a great source of pleasure and wonder to the eyes of those who do not know the means used to create them.

Section H
The Low Countries

Edited by ELSA STRIETMAN *and* LYNETTE R. MUIR

Abbreviations

Antwerp Rhetoricians	P. Visschers and J. F. Willems, 'Een woord over de oude Rhetorykkamers in het algemeen en over die van Antwerpen in het byzonder', *Belgisch Museum* 1 (1837), pp. 137–75
Antwerp, St Luke's guild	*De Liggeren en andere historische archieven der Antwerpse Sint-Lucasgilde*, ed. Philip Rombouts and Th. van Lerius, 2 vols., Antwerpen-Amsterdam, 1864–76; reprinted, Amsterdam, 1961
Archives de Lille	*Archives municipales de Lille (Affaires générales)*
Archives du Nord	*Archives départementales du Nord* B93–94, *Chambre des comptes* [of the Duchy of Burgundy]
Béthune	De la Fons de Mellicocq, *Mélanges historiques* in J. J. Champollion-Figeac, *Documents historiques inédits . . .*, vol. IV (1848), no. XIV, pp. 329–47; no. XXVIII, pp. 457–62
'Bishop of Fools'	Alan E. Knight, 'The Bishop of Fools and his Feast in Lille', in *Festive Drama*, ed. Meg Twycross, Cambridge, 1996, pp. 157–66
Bliscapen	*Die eerste bliscap van Maria en die sevenste bliscap van Onser Vrouwen*, ed. W. H. Beuken, Culemborg, 1978
Brabant *landjuweel*	E. van Autenboer, *Het Brabants Landjuweel der Rederijkers (1515–1561)*, Middelburg, 1981
Cornelis Everaert	J. F. Willems, 'Cornelis Everaert, toneeldichter van Brugge', *Belgisch Museum* 6 (1842), pp. 41–51
Dendermonde	Leo van Puyvelde, 'Het ontstaan van het moderne tooneel in de oude Nederlanden: De oudste vermeldingen in de rekeningen', *Verslagen en Mededeelingen der Koninklijke Vlaamsche Academie voor Taal-en Letterkunde*, 1922, pp. 909–52
Deventer	J. M. Hollaar and E. W. F. van den Elzen, 'Het vroegste tooneelleven in enkele Noordnederlandse plaatsen', *De Nieuwe Taalgids* 73 (1980), pp. 302–24
Diest	F. J. Raymaekers, 'Historische oogslag op de Rederijkkamers van Diest', *Vaderlandsch Museum* 3 (1859–60), pp. 90–129
Hummelen, *Stages*	Wim M. H. Hummelen, 'Typen van toneelinrichting bij de rederijkers', *Studia Neerlandica* 1 (1970), pp. 51–109

485

Lefèbvre *Lille*　　　　　　 Leon Lefèbvre, *Histoire du théâtre de Lille de ses origines à nos jours*, 5 vols., Lille, 1901–7

Mariken van Nieumeghen　 *Mariken van Nieumeghen*, ed. Dirk Coigneau, The Hague, 1982

Mons　　　　　　　　　　 *Le livre de conduite du régisseur et le compte des dépenses pour le Mystère de la Passion joué à Mons en 1501*, ed. Gustave Cohen, Strasbourg and Paris, 1925

Mystères　　　　　　　　 Louis Petit de Julleville, *Histoire du théâtre en France: Les Mystères*, 2 vols., Paris, 1880; reprinted Geneva, 1969

Oudenaarde　　　　　　　 B. A. M. Ramakers, *Spelen en figuren. Toneelkunst en processie in Oudenaarde tussen Middeleeuwen en Moderne Tijd*, Amsterdam, 1996

St Omer　　　　　　　　　 Justin De Pas, *Mystères et jeux scéniques à Saint-Omer aux XVe et XVIe siècles*, Mémoires de la Société des Antiquaires de la Morinie 31 (1912–13), pp. 343–77

Trou moet blijcken　　　　 *Trou moet blijcken* [facsimile edition of the books of the Haarlem Chamber of Rhetoric, 'De Pellicanisten'], ed. Wim Hüsken, B. A. M. Ramakers *et al.*, 8 vols., Assen, 1992–8

Veurne　　　　　　　　　 Ph. Blommaert, 'Rederijkkamers van Veurne en ommestreken', *Belgisch Museum* 2 (1838), pp. 357–74

Ypres　　　　　　　　　　 M. Vandecasteele, 'Een groots opgezet rederijkersfeest te Ieper in 1529', *Jaarboek 'De Fonteine'* 26 (1989), pp. 7–20

Introduction

The drama of the Low Countries cannot easily be defined as the product of a stable geographical area. Consisting of a number of independent regions, each with its own overlord and its own powerful and important towns, its boundaries do not coincide with the historical–political maps which, especially in the fifteenth and sixteenth centuries, demonstrate frequent changes which affected – and afflicted – the Low Countries [see map]. The title 'cockpit of Europe' is as appropriate for medieval Flanders and Brabant as for modern Belgium.

Ever since the break-up of the Carolingian empire and the treaty of Verdun (834), Lotharingia, the bilingual region from the Scheldt estuary down the eastern Rhineland to Burgundy, had been the subject of a tug of war between its two powerful neighbours, French-speaking West Francia (France) and German-speaking East Francia (the Holy Roman Empire).[1] In the late fourteenth century, the various independent states which had developed in this intermediate area became pawns in the power games of three warring powers – France, England and Burgundy, with the Emperor waiting his chance to intervene. Slowly but inexorably, these counties and duchies, with their fertile lands and rich cloth towns, found themselves transferred from one overlord to another as the Dukes of Burgundy constructed their great domain by a mixture of bribery, force, inheritance and marriage.[2] By the middle of the fifteenth century – the great age of medieval drama – the Burgundian Netherlands included not merely the principal regions of Flanders, Brabant, Hainault and Artois but also Picardy whose capital, Amiens, was a notable centre of French drama [see **C26**, **E9**].[3]

The death of the last Duke of Burgundy, Charles the Rash, in 1477, saw a revival of diplomatic activity as the powers struggled to gain control of the enormous inheritance of his sole child and heiress, Mary, whose marriage to Archduke Maximilian of Austria was to lead (through the marriage of their son, Philip the Fair, to Joanna, daughter of the Catholic Monarchs, Ferdinand and Isabella of Spain) to the integration of the Spanish Netherlands as part of the great Habsburg empire under the Emperor Charles V.[4]

This complex political situation was not made easier by the fact that three major languages, French, German and Dutch, existed side by side in a variety of dialects. The distinctions between the Germanic dialects were still fairly fluid and in many

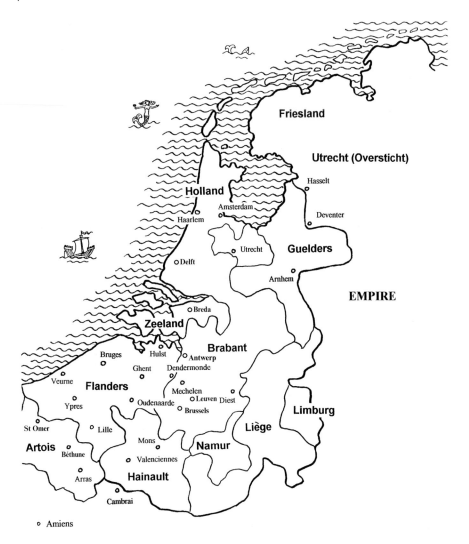

FRANCE

The Low Countries in the fifteenth century, showing principal provinces and cities.
(Drawing by Helen Taylor.)

cases only the political borders determined whether they would eventually be reckoned to be Dutch or German. Indeed the St Omer and Arnhem plays [see **H2**, **H15**] are closely linked to the German Shrovetide *Fastnachtspiele* [see **F35–F41**].[5] In bilingual Flanders and other southern provinces, further complications were added by the fact that a succession of rulers imposed French as the dominant language of court and administration.

Any treatment of the drama of the Low Countries must therefore take into account theatrical activities and plays in three languages. The French drama has always been treated as part of the theatrical heritage of France, but set side by side with its Dutch contemporaries, the similarities of performance and organisation are obvious, especially the use of wagon plays and processional drama and the widespread popularity of play competitions. Nor is there any real equivalent in France itself of the activities of the Rhetoricians, who were important in the culture of Dutch-speaking towns in the Low Countries [see **H11, H26**]. Of the four parts into which the material of this section has been divided, therefore, though Dutch records dominate the play contests (part II) and French Passions the non-processional religious plays (part IV), every division includes both Dutch and French material.

As is the case with all medieval and early modern literature, the surviving records and texts are a jumble of jigsaws with many pieces missing. As well as the normal deterioration of time, floods and wars, not to mention the religious destructiveness of Reformation and post-Reformation zeal, the armies of Louis XIV, Napoleon, Bismarck and Hitler have all done their part in obliterating the heritage of the Low Countries. However, some has survived, thanks to the industry of nineteenth-century scholars, in particular those Flemish speakers in the 1830s and 1840s without whose patient and painstaking work all knowledge of the drama of the Rhetoricians and their Chambers would have been lost from view entirely, because of the prevailing dominance of French language and French culture in the newly formed state of Belgium.

Only a small number of early editions are of plays, however, and hundreds still lie in archives and libraries, waiting to see the light of day and add their pieces to the jigsaw puzzle of the past. The French drama of the Low Countries has suffered a similar fate: two of the great Passion plays from Hainault, though described in 1880 by Petit de Julleville [see **H58**], still await an editor, while it is only the recent discovery of the (as yet unpublished) seventy-two plays of the Lille procession [see **H35**], the most important new addition to the corpus of French medieval drama since Gustave Cohen's great edition of the Mons director's copy in 1925,[6] that makes possible a genuinely bilingual approach to the drama of Flanders and Artois.

In Dutch, in addition to the liturgical and early vernacular religious plays from St Omer and Maastricht [see **B25(b), C16(iii)**], there are the so-called *Abele spelen* [see **H18**], a unique group of fourteenth-century plays on romance themes. The fifteenth century yields a much richer crop of texts, the majority of them religious plays, and this was also the period in which Chambers of Rhetoric came to be established in many towns.

In all regions, drama was now essentially 'community drama'. Archers' companies and craft guilds, Chambers of Rhetoric, neighbourhood groups, religious confraternities, all became involved in theatrical activities, especially from the 1440s onwards when the Burgundian dukes, chiefly Philip the Good, frequently paraded their splendour and their might in ducal entries and on other state occasions. Gradually a culture of theatrical display came into being which played an important and multifunctional part in the communications between prince and subjects. The performing and the visual arts, together with learning and poetry, became the carriers of the intricate social and political messages through which authority and authorities staked their claims and negotiated with each other.

A certain distinction can be made here between the reign of the Burgundians in the fifteenth century and that of the Habsburgs in the sixteenth. The involvement of the urban population does not differ in a practical sense but its emotional involvement and the citizens' own sense of power seem greater in the earlier period. Under Habsburg rule the distance between ruler and ruled seems to have widened, with grave implications for both. This was not a Burgundian triumph compared to a Habsburg failing; it was much more complicated, not the least of the contributing factors being the growing complexity of religious sects. The new Protestant creeds spread from Germany into, first, the southern Low Countries, where the printing presses of Antwerp became the major centre for the production and distribution of dissident literature.[7] The Chambers of Rhetoric quite rapidly became involved in the debates between the defenders of the Catholic Church and the supporters of the new religion in all its variety. The might of Church and State together attempted to root out dissident feeling and practice, with disastrous consequences for people, property, causes and the common weal.

Paradoxically, amidst the disturbances, armed conflicts and fearful reprisals against offenders of the status quo, drama flourished as never before. And, even more paradoxically, the Chambers of Rhetoric only and finally lost their creative and ideological impetus after the southern provinces came to be dominated by the forces of the Counter Reformation, and the northern provinces, as the Republic of the Seven United Netherlands, suffered a setback in this special form of creativity under the weight of the Calvinist Church [see **H64**].

It would be quite wrong, however, to give the impression that sixteenth-century drama concerned itself solely with religious issues. A certain secularisation developed both in the message and the medium of drama. This, however, was not so much a break with tradition as a shift of emphasis within the tradition. The sources from which drama gathered its material still consisted of the Bible and a variety of other religious writing, and plays using the traditional material from the medieval romances remain equally popular, although classical material was increasingly favoured.

But whereas in the French-speaking south, under Spanish, Catholic rule there was little change in the types of plays produced, elsewhere a certain difference in emphasis is noticeable, especially in the emergence of a new genre, the morality play or *spel van sinne*, which rapidly grew into a dramatic form that could not hide, but aimed to express, a multitude of sins. Using characters from scriptural, apocryphal, classical and contemporary writing, it concerned itself with the here and now of earthly, and daily, life and did so by deftly employing the ancient didactic tool of allegory. Influenced by a growing Protestantism, it also created a host of allegorical characters with pointedly moral and didactic names and for good measure invented some extra assistants to the forces of evil, the so-called *Sinnekens*. These characters, multifunctional in dramatic as well as in thematic respect, became a hallmark of the Dutch Rhetoricians' drama. Moreover, no other feature of sixteenth-century drama is so illuminating for the stagecraft of playwrights and performers alike, so revealing for contemporary attitudes and concerns, as the *Sinnekens*. The impetus for the morality play did not lie in a purely religious awareness but had to do with a different consciousness: that of the burgher in his natural environment, the town, where the term *burgher* implied the urban dwellers who had achieved a relatively sustainable or even comfortable level of existence and who were eager to distinguish themselves from the rabble, the poor, the illiterate, the peasant, the lower orders of servants and workers.

NOTES

1. The name Lotharingia survived in the dukedom of Lorraine which in the fifteenth century was technically part of the Empire but effectively under Burgundian rule. (Burgundy itself became part of France in the tenth century.)

2. For a useful outline of the formation of the Burgundian domain see Peter Spufford, 'The Burgundian Netherlands', in *Splendours of Flanders: Late Medieval Art in Cambridge Collections*, ed. A. Arnould and J. M. Massing, Cambridge, 1993, pp. 1–12.

3. For the purposes of this book, Picardy and Amiens have been treated as part of France since they were constantly changing hands, whereas from the end of the fourteenth century onwards, Artois, whose capital Arras had been so important in French drama in the thirteenth century [see **C85–C88**], became and remained part of the Low Countries (with bilingual forms of the names: Artois/Artesia and Arras/Atrecht) until the late seventeenth century [see **H3**].

4. The Duchy of Burgundy itself reverted to the French crown but *Franche Comté* (the County of Burgundy) was part of Mary's inheritance.

5. Other border areas include Maastricht and Limburg.

6. See Mons; for details of this and the other surviving French plays from this region see G. Cohen, *Le théâtre français en Belgique au moyen âge*. Brussels, 1953.

7. It is ironical that Béthune and Valenciennes, which staged major Corpus Christi tableaux and passion plays in the mid-sixteenth century [see **H34, H58–H62**] should have become hotbeds of Protestantism soon afterwards.

I   Organising and performing groups

Two principal kinds of groups performed plays in the Low Countries. Sometimes, especially in the French-speaking towns of Artois and southern Flanders, the players were grouped by neighbourhoods [*quartiers*], while in Mons (Hainault), there were also Confréries dedicated to a particular saint. Such groups or guilds are also recorded in a few Dutch-speaking towns such as Veurne and St Omer [see **H2**]. It is not known who originally presented the *abele spelen* (ingenious plays) composed in Dutch at the end of the fourteenth century [see **H18**].

At the beginning of the fifteenth century, the first *Rederijkerskamers* [Chambers of Rhetoric] were formed and the movement spread rapidly through the Dutch-speaking towns of both the northern and southern provinces. Often the Chamber of a major town[1] would act as a kind of legal overseer and patron to the Chambers in the surrounding area but the Rhetoricians always resisted attempts by the ruling dukes to get a firm grip on the Chambers [see **H5(ii)**]. The Chamber 'Jesus with the Balsamflower' in Antwerp, founded in 1493, was intended to serve as an overseeing institution, but the Chambers were not easily subdued. Many Chambers were still flourishing in the eighteenth century and a few, such as that at Veurne, still survive. There were also groups of Rhetoricians in French-speaking towns, though the term *Chambre de Rhetorique* is not used; the *Rhetoriciens*[2] gathered either in *Puys*, as at Lille, or by *quartier* [neighbourhood] as in Mons or Valenciennes [see **H11**, **H26**].

The neighbourhood plays seem generally to have been less learned and formal than those of the Lille Procession or the Chambers of Rhetoric and it is significant that no texts have survived. They were also on a more modest scale, to judge by the sums mentioned in accounts for both local performances and visits to the play-contests which were a feature of all parts of the Low Countries [see section II].

1. The Main Chamber in Flanders was 'De Fonteine', in Ghent. In Brabant, Antwerp was the centre of local government and therefore also of the Chambers of Rhetoric [see **H5**], though the political capital under both Burgundy and Spain was Brussels.
2. The *Compagnons de la Rhetorique* of Mons were awarded £6 for some *Jeux et Rhetorique* for the celebration of the coronation of *nostre sire* Charles V as Holy Roman Emperor in 1530 (Mons, p. xviii).

NEIGHBOURHOOD GROUPS AND CONFRERIES

H1 Some neighbourhood groups perform plays on wagons

(a) Neighbourhood plays on wagons banned in Lille 1382–1428

Lefèbvre *Lille*

[1382] Let no one be so bold [. . .] hereinafter to play any *jeu de personnaiges*, nor rimes, nor to have assemblies of one parish against another, or one street or square against another, or to have planted a tree or trees¹ [. . .] within the walls of this town. (p. 15)

[1398] It is forbidden] to perform on wagons [. . .] on the streets [*cauchies*] or squares of this town any plays in verse, on pain of a fine of 20s both for those who act against the ban as for any carter or wagoner who would transport the said players, or who owned the horses or horse – vehicles [*harnas*] on which these said plays were performed. (p. 15)

[1428] It is forbidden to play or have played *jeus de personnages* on wagons or otherwise, to unite in fine or large companies to award or receive prizes, whatever kind of play it may be [. . .] but let each remain in tranquillity [*a sacoyette*] without making noise or bustle on pain of a fine of £10.² (p. 15)

---

¹ It was apparently a May custom to plant trees outside the homes of young unmarried women.

² 'No prohibition of plays is found after the ban of 1428, though the ordinances forbidding assemblies, dances and other popular customs continued to be promulgated well into the sixteenth century.' Alan. E. Knight, 'Processional Theater as an Instrument of Municipal Authority in Lille', Société Internationale pour l'Etude du Théâtre Médiéval, Actes del VII colloqui . . . [Girona, 1992], Barcelona, 1996, pp. 99–103. The plays were controlled by making them part of the Procession de Lille [see **H35–H41**].

(b) Wagon plays rewarded by the St Omer authorities 1454, 1456

St Omer p. 350

[1454] To Jehan Descamps called Wastelet and his companions and to the son of the lady Leurant d'Antoing and his companions for the plays that they have done in the past. They have acted both before the *scelle* [the town hall] and before the dwellings [*hostels*] of my lord Bailiff and others in the town: to each of them 16s, making 32s and thereafter for each *carée* [carting], 4s.

[1456] For having made many entertainments and delights through plays on carts and wagons [*cars et carios*] [. . .] for each carting which in this period has amounted to 36 cartings [. . .] 4s. Making £7 4s.

(c)   Wagon plays also rewarded in Béthune, 1506

Béthune, p. 343

[1501] To some companions from [the *rue de*] Saint-Pry who performed plays and diversions [*esbatemens*] on wagons, [. . .] in celebration [. . .] of the joyful news of the betrothal [*alliance*] of the duc de Luxembourg to Madame Claude, daughter of the king of France: two measures of wine.

[1506] To some performers on wagons who performed diversions [*esbatemens*]: 6s.

(d)   The town contributes to parish wagon plays, Ypres, 1529

Ypres, p. 18

To] the companions who led [*beleedten*][1] the plays of the parishes of St Martin and St Nicholas and the Guild of Our Lady and for the expenses incurred in fitting out the wagons etc. £3

---

[1] Presumably this means they led the horses that pulled the wagons. For the 1529 procession see **H45**.

(e)   Wagon plays and the etymology of comedy?

Jacques Grévin, *Théâtre complet et poésies choisies*, ed. Lucien Pinvert, Paris, 1922, p. 8

As for me,[1] I am of the opinion that comedy took its name from the κώμη [entertainment][2] that is to say from the streets through which in these earliest times they were presented; and apparently this custom has persisted in Flanders and the Low Countries where the performers of comedies have themselves dragged from one crossroad to another [*trainer par les carrefours*] on wagons on which they perform their histories, comedies and farces.

---

[1] Jacques Grévin wrote a number of comedies in the sixteenth century, mostly for royal command or university performances. This quotation is from the *Bref discours pour l'intelligence de ce théâtre* which preceded the plays in *Le théâtre de Jacques Grévin*, Paris 1561. Cited here from the edition by L. Pinvert (Paris 1922).

[2] Liddell and Scott (*A Greek–English Lexicon*) define κώμης as 'a jovial festival with music and dancing [. . .] which usually ended in the party parading the streets.' Grévin's suggested etymology, however, lacks scholarly confirmation.

H2   Groups perform for local civic audiences

(a)   Carnival festivities in Deventer, 1364

Deventer, p. 306–7

Paid on the Monday before Shrove Tuesday for the echevins and the council and the good people whom they had invited and for Shrove Tuesday for the echevins and council for wine and for the food that they consumed together at the town hall: £65 11s 3 d.

Master Karstikine who made the galantines and baked the pies and flans: £3
Mosen who was their cook: 7s 6d
The servants who worked in the kitchen: 5s
For one hundred new plates: 5s
For the young ladies [*joncfrouwen*] for their play: 20s
For the young lords [*basseliers*][1] for their play: £2
For two minstrels: 15s

[1] Because of its location, Deventer gained early importance as a trading centre in the Lower Rhineland. It also became a centre of the *Devotio Moderna* and of the teaching order of the Brethren and Sisters of the Common Life. This may explain the unusual inclusion of groups of girls among the performers. The terms *joncfrouwen* and *basseliers* refer to young people of high class, as distinct from *iuvenes civitates* which occurs in other town accounts and indicates young burghers or burghesses [see **C60**].

(b)   Scholars perform a Passion play, Deventer, 1394

Deventer, p. 306

Item, for a quantity of wine brought on Low Sunday to some of the echevins [aldermen] and the council who had been instructed by our echevins to attend the play of Our Lord's Passion which the scholars performed in the marketplace, 8 groten.[1]

[1] For other early passion and resurrection plays in the Low Countries see Wim Hüsken, 'Civic patronage of Early Fifteenth-Century Religious Drama in the Low Countries', in *Civic Ritual and Drama*, ed. A. F. Johnston and W. Hüsken, Amsterdam, 1997, pp. 109–13.

(c)   Companions from St Omer perform entertaining plays, 1492, 1517

St Omer, p. 349

[1492] Item. Paid to Miquel Wincaire, landlord of St Margherite outside the Hault Pont gate, for the sum [*escot*] spent in his house by 7 or 8 companions from outside the said gate who had played a play of Peace on St John Baptist's day last. As a courtesy 18s.

[1517] To some companions from Hault Pont who on two separate days, viz. Holy Innocents Day [28 December] and New Year's Day [. . .] performed entertaining plays [*jeux e plaisance*] at the Scelle on the marketplace before most of the echevins [*messeigneurs*] [. . .] 8s.[1]

[1] In the last entry, 1529, the group were paid 6s for having performed a play before the abbot of St Bertin. For other plays in 1529 see **H46**.

(d)   Various groups in Mons perform saints' plays, 1459, 1491

Mons, p.xiv

[1459] Given by courtesy to several *compagnons* who on 2nd September performed a play of St Barbara [Barbe] on the marketplace, by order of the said echevins 12 measures [*lots*] of French wine, half white and half red, 53s.

[1491] To the *confrères*[1] of the Confrérie Madame Ste Barbe, was given by order of the ladies [the canonesses of St Waudrue][2] to help with their expenses in mounting a performance of the life of St Barbara on the marketplace over three days, 60s.

---

[1] The *compagnons* of 1459 would have been a neighbourhood group. The Confrérie of St Barbe was the guild of cannoneers. Performances of plays by Confréries of St George, St James, St John and St Quentin are also recorded between 1490 and 1521.

[2] The Canonesses of the principal church in Mons were generous patrons of the drama. The chapter accounts regularly record gifts to players between 1433 and 1535.

(e)   A variety of groups celebrate peace, Veurne, 1526

Veurne, p. 358

In Veurne[1] five guilds compete for the prizes put up by the town council on the occasion of the festivities for the peace of Madrid; prizes are for the play, and the farce. The society of the Weststraat won first prize for the play; the society of St Barbara first prize for the farce; the other competitors were those of the Market [*Heilig Kruis*], of the Zuidstraat and the Ooststraat.

---

[1] This reference is not from the original archive but from the editor's introduction.

H3   Groups meet for a joint celebration under their different leaders

(a)   The *Prince de jeunesse* meets the *Abbé de Liesse*, Béthune, 1462

Béthune, p. 344

1462 To Huart Naie, *prince de jeunesse*[1] for this year £6 in courtesy [*par courtoisie*] to help with the expenses which he and others of his followers sustained in going to Arras to attend on the *Abbé de Liesse* there, on *Gras Dimence*.[2]

---

[1] Each group in the town had its own leader. The Prince of Youth was chief of them all during his year of office.

[2] The Sunday before Lent.

(b)   Wine is given to many groups who attended the festival of the *Prince de jeunesse* in Béthune, 1500

Béthune, p. 345

1500 the 10th May, for the feast day of the Prince de Jeunesse [four cans of wine were given]

to the king of the *Sotz* from Lille [. . .],

to the prince de Saint-Jacques from Lille,

to the Cappitaine Pignon from Douay,

to the Carbonniers [charcoal-burners] from Douay,

to the Abbé de Liesse from Arras,

to the Bons-Enffans from Arras [. . .],

to the prince de Mal-Espargne [bad savings] from Arras,

to the prince des Lours from Arras,

to the prinche des Souldans from la ville d'Eure,

to the *gayant* [giant] de Saint-Pry,

to the prince de Saint-Jacques from Béthune.

(c)   The Valenciennes *Passion* is delayed because of the duties of the *Prince de plaisance*, 1547

Mystères, vol. II, p. 146

Quentin Coret, then the *Prince de plaisance* [pleasure] of the said town, undertook his tour to Lille and Tournai before our play which therefore had to be put off for two days.[1]

---

[1]   Coret was both a superintendant and an actor [see **H58**]

THE RHETORICIANS

H4   Naming and organising the Chambers of Rhetoric

(a)   The Guild of St Luke is now also called 'The Gillyflowers', Antwerp, 1480

Antwerp, St Luke's guild, p. 31

This year when Sir Jan de Buysenere, Knight, was Prince, it was decided that our Chamber would take the name 'The Gillyflowers' with the device 'United in affection'.[1]

---

[1]   In the sixteenth century, Antwerp also boasted two other independent Chambers of Rhetoric, 'The Olive Branch' and 'The Marigold'.

(b)   The coat-of-arms of the Gillyflowers of Antwerp, 1556

Brabant *landjuweel*, p. 137

The *wapenblazoen* was displayed on all ceremonial occasions including the processional entry of the Chambers into a city. In the centre is the winged bull of St Luke, patron of the painters' guild.

(c)   The two surviving guilds in Veurne unite in 1530

Veurne, pp. 358–9

It was proposed [. . .] that those same chambers[1] from now on would be one, that the old banners or standards would be abandoned and a new banner made, on which on one side the Holy Cross would be painted [. . .] and on the other side St Barbara. Furthermore the main altar of this guild should be the altar of the Holy Cross in St Walburg, where the main services and the annual Mass should be held, and now the blazons of the kings of the guild should be brought to the same chapel and left hanging there; only once a year there should be a solemn Mass in St Nicholas, on St Barbara's day, on her altar [. . .] This accord and union have been approved and confirmed by the magistrates of Veurne.

1 The Chambers of the Holy Cross with the device *Arm in de bors* (poor in the purse) and Holy Barbara with the device *Van zinnen jong* (young at heart).

(d)   The charter of a Chamber in Hasselt explains the choice of St Catherine as their patroness, 1482

J. F. Willems, 'Oorkonden van Rederijkkamers', *Belgisch Museum* 4 (1840), pp. 411–23

[17 August] We, Willem de Corte, lord of Hasselt, and Jan Huytenhove, lord in Hasselt, make known that [. . .] we have been asked [. . .] by divers good men and young men of our lordship, that they may institute, to maintain and enhance the noble art of Rhetoric, a Brotherhood, Guild, Confrérie and society, in order better to practise the art of Rhetoric [. . .] and [devotion] to the noble, pure virgin Saint Catherine who, more than all other male or female saints, may well be reckoned to be the patroness of all Rhetoricians, and that is well demonstrated by her legend: because in discussion [*disputando*] she convinced fifty learned men; and those learned men [*Rhetores*] were all doctors, masters [*magisters*] and great scholars, who had been commanded to convince her with their learning, and to make her move away from God, and she answered them with a great abundance of beautiful, flowery words, which she expressed, and taught them in such a way that they were all converted, and believed in God; which flowery language may well be counted as the foundation of Rhetoric, who says of herself: 'I am descended from both the root and the flower of eloquence.' (pp. 419–20)

(e)   Rhetoric is an art that cannot be learnt

Mariken van Nieumeghen, lines 505–13

I'm not very experienced in rhetoric. I'd love to practise it so as to be able to extol the seven liberal arts, but it's something that can't be learned, however much effort you put into it. Rhetoric's an art that has to come naturally. If you work hard enough at them, all the other arts can be learned by dint of study and instruction. But rhetoric is worth more than all of them: it's a gift from the Holy Spirit.[1]

1 The devil has undertaken to educate Mariken in the seven liberal arts [see **H17**] and she has already given proof of her skill in geometry. See Hans van Dijk, 'Mariken van Nieumeghen', *Dutch Crossing* 22 (1984), pp. 27–37.

H5   The Antwerp Chamber is very active

(a)   The city of Antwerp subsidises the Chambers

Antwerp Rhetoricians

In the year 1490 the players in Antwerp, where they are called 'The Gillyflowers' and 'The Marigolds', obtained from the town and will obtain every year from now on, 12 rhenish guilders for each society, to enjoy occupying themselves with Rhetoric. (p. 148)

(b)   Philip the Fair calls all the Chambers of Brabant to Mechelen, 1493

Antwerp, St Luke's guild

Item, these aforementioned Governors travelled to Mechelen because Archduke Philip[1] had commanded all the Chambers of Brabant to come there. In the Entry there we had a splendid borough of Antwerp [an image of the Antwerp city shield] on a waggon on which St Luke was painting Mary. (p. 47)

[1] The son of Mary of Burgundy and Archduke Maximilian of Austria, Philip nominally took over control of the former Burgundian Netherlands from his father after his mother's death in 1482, but was at the time less than four years old.

(c)   A successful performance in Antwerp, 1495

Antwerp, St Luke's guild

Item, they [the Governors of the Guild] caused to be performed the play of the King of Aragon,[1] which is 2,800 lines long and which was done so well and ingeniously that the Magistrates desired that it would once more be done on the Tuesday after it had been played on the Sunday which was the middle of Lent. And the same Governors commissioned in the same year a cloth that is hung before our Chamber, with an ox and the shield/arms of the painters on it. (p. 51)

[1] This was again performed by the Gillyflowers in 1529, probably in Antwerp itself.

(d)   One of Willem van Haecht's plays is performed, 1558

Antwerp, St Luke's guild

The Governors have had performed, in May of this year, the play of *Scipio*, a *spel van sinne*[1] composed by Master Willem van Haecht, *facteur*[2] of our Chamber, which play was very well acted before the lords of the town and the other Chambers. (p. 211)

[1] For the *spel van sinne*, see introduction, above.
[2] For the *facteur*'s duties, see **H6(ii)** and **(iii)**.

H6   The organisation of a Chamber of Rhetoric, Diest

Diest

(i) The chamber called 'The Eyes of Christ' is given a house in Diest

We, [seven names] echevins [*scepenen*] of Diest, testify [. . .] that they [two broth-ers] have instructed the *schoutaerd* [head of council] to keep gratis and for nothing, free of tax [? *voersom*] the house with grounds and all its appendages, situated on the land of the abbey [? *abbalie*] and with the grounds of Hendrik Missens and Machiel van Bontelen on either side, for the use of the company called 'the Eyes of Christ'[1] [. . .] until today for 7 schellingen, 7 old groet for expenses and a half engelschen[2] annually for ground rent and for the Lord's tax. (p. 123)

[1] The Chamber of 'De Christus-Oogen', founded 1502. Like so many names of Chambers, this too indi-cates a flower, i.e. *Lychnis coronaria*, or Rose Campion.
[2] For monetary terms see note following glossary.

(ii) 'The Lilies' of Diest reappoint their *facteur*, 1604

Anno 1604, the 14th of December our Leader, Prince, Deacons and other members, having come together in the Chamber of 'The Lilies',[1] have once more [. . .] bestowed on Master Lodewijck Vanden Berghe the post and office of *facteur*, since it is a time-honoured custom and tradition that all free[2] Chambers have a *facteur*. In which post Master Lodewijck will [. . .] oversee, show and teach the com-posers or amateurs of the aforementioned Chamber of the 'Lilies' how to write their refrains, acts [*ageringhe*][3] or any other poetry, in the best form or style etc. if they ask for help.

   Item, the aforesaid *facteur* shall be present in the Chamber, whenever the company is assembled, in order to reveal and to make known all matters, com-plaints, judgements and statements etc., whatever those might consist of, in the name of the Leader, the Prince, Deacons, Elders and the Company and to put down in writing all such judgements and complaints. (pp. 109–11)

[1] The company and the guild of 'The Lilies' of Diest, founded in honour of Our Lady and to honour and enhance the procession of the Assumption of Our Lady every year in the town of Diest, 1470.
[2] Free Chambers were officially recognised by the town government or its overlord and had an approved charter.
[3] The original term *ageringhe* means 'to act' but here seems to mean to recite or perhaps even to perform on stage.

(iii) The *facteur* has responsibility for the texts, casting and preparation of the plays

Item all *spelen van sinne*, farces, presentations or other performances, whether they will be played in the street, in front of the town hall or elsewhere, [the *facteur*] shall prepare for the occasion one month or six weeks or more in advance and request from the chest that which would be useful and proper; to which end he will have access to the chest, to the keys of the deacons and treasurers and having looked at the documents with plays, to bring the keys back, faithfully, according to his oath. [He] will prepare the roles of the plays and having done so will, with the advice of the deacons, give them to the most able people and command them to do their duty and learn them well.

Item every year, according to the praiseworthy and noble custom, the *facteur* shall bring a *spel van sinne*, a farce or another piece into the Chamber and honour it with the performance.

[He] shall also do everything in his power to enhance the honour and the well-being of 'The Lilies', for which the aforementioned company will reward our *facteur* with twelve Rhenish guilders annually, as well as, according to the old custom, free meals and free drink when he has guests for meetings. (p. 110)

(iv) The Chambers of Diest try to avoid friction over the choice of subjects for the plays, 1503

Item in order to avoid discord between 'The Lilies' and our fellow brothers of 'The Eyes of Christ' and create more affection and friendship between us, the aforementioned 'Lilies' desire that when one of the two Chambers wants to perform a *spel van sinne* or *esbattement*[1] that they will announce this to each other when the play has been copied into roles to be performed and that the play is then performed within the month and whoever first announces the play to the Leader, the Prince or the Deacons, shall perform it.

Item. For some specific reasons laid down by the Lord and the Town, they have further explained the last article of the aforementioned charter and declare hereby, that whenever one of the Chambers wants to perform, be it a *spel van sinne* or anything other, the *facteur* of the Chamber who wants to play should before he presents his script, take it upon himself to go to the Leader of the other Chamber and tell him under oath the subject and the play that they wish to perform. And if the other Chamber also wants to play and intended to perform the same play, the one who presented it first shall have first choice. And the other leader will command his *facteur* under oath, that he arranges to play another play and this the leaders and the *facteurs* and each of them will keep to under oath, without telling their members or anyone else in any way. Ordained by the Lord and the Town, 15 September 1503. (pp. 98–9)

[1] See glossary above for types of play.

H7   Duties and privileges of members of a Chamber
Diest

(i) Festivities for weddings of members

If one of our members is going to marry, he shall give his fellow members a dish of food and ten shillings and if he announces the marriage a fortnight before to the

Prince, Deacons or Treasurers, the companions have to perform an *esbattement*. If a bridegroom asks the companions, via the messenger, to go with him to his wedding, he who is not there at the appointed time, as he had been commanded by the messenger, with his gown with the device [of the Chamber] on it, will be fined half a shilling.

Item, the Chamber has to give the bridegroom a guild jug full of Rhenish wine; and whoever does not come when this is presented, will be fined a farthing apiece and the members who presented the jug can spend that on drinks. (p. 117)

(ii) Rules for rehearsals

When the companions rehearse an *esbattement* or *camerspel*[1] then they are allowed to drink a jug of beer at the expense of the Chamber; but if it is a *spel van sinne*, then they are allowed two jugs. When the companions are rehearsing a play, the main character of that play will determine the time of the rehearsal. And whoever is not there, if it is in his power, will have to pay half a shilling.[2] And that money the members can spend on drinks, unless he was unavoidably detained. (p. 119)

[1] For play types see glossary above.
[2] The terms of the Valenciennes contract [see **H60**] are very similar to the Rhetoricians' rules.

(iii) Casting by the *facteur* and deacons is final

If it were the case that the members wanted to perform a *spel van sinne, esbattement* or *tafelspel*[1] whoever is then sent a role by means of the messenger, by command of the *facteur*[2] and Deacons, will have to play that role or pay six shillings, of which the Chamber shall have three and whoever accepts the role will have the other three. And in the case that the members travel to a feast outside the town and perform there, whoever is sent a role for that will have to play it unless he pays six shillings, and will also get an official warning from the Chamber. And if someone has lost his role and cannot find it, he shall have to pay the fee for copying it; but if the Chamber incurred a loss or he did not keep his role secret, he shall have to submit to receiving a punishment from the Chamber. (p. 119)

[1] See glossary above.
[2] For the duties of the *facteur* see **H6(iii)**.

(iv) The treasurer keeps scripts and copies of roles

When a *spel van sinne*, an *esbattement* or a *tafelspel* has been performed then the members will have to give their roles back to the treasurer or forfeit half a shilling. (p. 119)

(v) Every member of the Chamber must help to build the scaffold

Item, when an extensive play is to be performed then every member will have to come and help to build the scaffold and no one will be able to absent himself or send apologies, except those who perform in the play; and if any one of the members fails to turn up, then he must send a similar man in his place and if he does not do so, then a man will be hired at his expense and in addition he will have to pay two shillings (p. 126).[1]

---

[1] Compare the situation in New Romney, Kent [see **D32**].

II   *Play contests and* landjuwelen

Play contests were a major feature of the cultural life of the Low Countries in the fifteenth and sixteenth centuries. Some were modest affairs, like that held in Arras in 1431, when the *Puy* organised a *concours* to which Cambrai, Douai and Valenciennes sent entries: 'They performed plays, and prizes were given for the best actors as well as the best poets.'[1] Others, like the great Brabant *landjuwelen*, involved numerous different Chambers of Rhetoric and were highly organised with elaborate performances and rich prizes [see **H13**].

1. Louis Petit de Julleville, *Le Répertoire du théâtre comique en France au moyen âge*, Paris, 1887, pp. 328–9.

H8   Different groups take part in contests
(a)   Lille wins a prize in Douai, 1418
Lefèbvre *Lille*; trans. *Staging*, p. 201

1418: To Girard Leborgne ['One-eye'] was given by courtesy to him and some companions, performers of entertainments with characters [*esbattements de personnaiges*], in honour of their having performed in an entertainment which was held at Douai where they gained a silver lion for the second prize and to help towards their expenses in taking part therein: £12.

(b)   The Bishop of Fools in Lille takes a group to Béthune, 1432
Lefèbvre *Lille*, p. 26

[1432] To Jehan Courtois, innkeeper, who, at the command of the echevins, paid to the Bishop of Fools and several companions of this town to support them for their expenses and costs when they went to Béthune to perform a *jeu de personnages*: £12.

(c)   A group from St Omer wins several prizes, 1462
St Omer, p. 362; trans. *Staging*, p. 201

1462: To Jehan Descamps, called Wastellet, Jacques de le Steghele, Bertelemieu Lartisien, Pierquin le Cordier, and others to the number of 24, who, for the honour of this town, have travelled to the town of Aire and maintained themselves there for five whole days, ending on the 28th day of this present month, in order to act there several plays, both moralities and *soties*, to win certain prizes which were being given by those of the said town of Aire to the best actors, in which those mentioned above have borne and acquitted themselves so well that they obtained the principal prize and two others, over one of which there was some discussion. For this and to help with their expenses in this matter, is [given] by order of their lordships [*messeigneurs*] on this last day of June 1462, £12.

(d) The Chambers of Courtrai and Nieuwpoort receive grants to participate in a competition, Ypres, 1529

Ypres, p. 19

Item paid by order of the magistrates of Courtrai to the Guild of St Anthony to help them [with the cost of] the voyage to Ypres, where they were bound in order to compete for a prize, £18.

[To] the Rhetoricians of this town [Nieuwpoort] to travel to Ypres to participate in the procession,[1] by order of the magistrates, paid £18.

---

[1] For the Ypres procession of 1529 see **H46**.

H9 'The Transfiguration' organises a competition, Hulst, 1483

Willems, 'Oorkonden van Rederijkkamers', pp. 411–23

(i) Directions for the length and matter of the plays

Item whoever shall at our drama festival and playing, show by means of a play or demonstrate the most beautiful and the best matter, in performing, of God, Mary, Our Lord's Transfiguration or about any other saint, male or female, spiritually or secularly, about the future of the world or the end of the world, of the joy of eternal life or about the sorrow or torments of hell, about the Old Testament or the New, with matter scriptural, natural or figurative,[1] with *exempla* or in verse, or any other material as each can and will comprehend, as you like, no less than five hundred nor more than six hundred lines, newly made, never heard or seen before, whether by moralisation or otherwise, beginning and ending with the same matter, and whoever shall do this best will receive from us and be presented with, as having performed best in the chief *spel van sinne*, as the highest prize, a beautiful costly silver cup, weighing a pound of silver, without the fashioning and the gold. (p. 413)

---

[1] 'Natural' and 'figurative' mean in words and in images, i.e. tableaux.

(ii) A special prize is promised for the best fool

Item, whoever will bring the most amusing fool, who will cause greatest amusement and tell the best jokes, and makes the people laugh most, he shall be rewarded by us with a costly statuette made of silver, worth, including the cost of making it, 3 shillings out of a Flemish pound.[1] (p. 415)

---

[1] See glossary above for money terms.

H10   The Ghent contest of 1539

(i) The elaborate stage used for the Ghent competition

Hummelen *Stages*, p. 52

At the top of the elaborate structure are shown the arms of Ghent [left] and the arms of The Fountain [right] and their motto: As you like it. At the bottom it says in Gothic script: Hereon the plays were performed. (All the plays were presented on the same stage during a competition.)

---

[1] Hummelen (p. 68) points to the similarity between the several '*huisjes*' [mansions] of the Ghent and other Rhetoricians' stages and the stage picture from Valenciennes [see **H60**].

(ii) 'The Gillyflowers' take part in the competition

Antwerp, St Luke's guild

This year we received tidings of a splendid feast organised by 'The Fountain' in Ghent,[1] where we triumphantly made our entry with many beautiful tableaux, characters and so forth and many lords, merchants and guildbrothers, beautifully dressed and for which we received a prize: three [silver] cups weighing four pounds; and for our badge that we displayed before the stage we received a beautiful silver fountain weighing three ounces. And we played a very good play there, for which we received the first and highest prize – four silver jugs together weighing nine pounds. And the *facteur* [received] for himself, a silver cup of four ounces and our fool had as his prize a silver monkey of four ounces.[2] (p. 136)

---

[1] This was the contest which led to trouble over doctrinal matters [see introduction above].
[2] Sometimes contests in Ghent seem to have been bilingual for in 1498 the *arbaletriers* [crossbowmen] of Mons won a prize there and 'some Rhetoriciens from Mons [. . .] gave several entertainments [*recreations*] and pleasures [*contentemens*] to the audience' (Mons, p. xv).

LANDJUWELEN IN BRABANT

The term *landjuweel* originated with the Archers' competitions of the fifteenth century and was adopted by the Brabant Chambers of Rhetoric which in the sixteenth century decided to organise a cycle of seven competitions meant to be held at three-yearly intervals in Brabant towns, organised by Brabant Chambers of Rhetoric and excluding any town or Chamber outside the Duchy. The *landjuweel* was sequential: the victor of the first contest had to organise the second and so on to the seventh. The first prize was not awarded for a *spel van sinne* but for an *esbattement*, a play with uncertain genre parameters, which had often been the entertainment, dramatic or other, performed at the contests of Archers' guilds. The prize awarded at these contests was a costly object made of silver, the *juweel* [jewel] given to the victor of the *land* [i.e the Duchy of Brabant] [see **H11**]. The term then came into use for the Archers' contests themselves, the earliest known instance of the use of the term being for the competition of the handbow archers in 1411 in Leuven. The towns hosting the *landjuweel* of the Brabant Chambers of Rhetoric were Mechelen, 1515; Leuven, 1518; Diest, 1521; Brussels, 1532; Mechelen, 1535; Diest, 1541; and Antwerp, 1561. The long gap between this last pair of contests was caused by the political and religious troubles that were besetting the Low Countries in those years. Other contests, such as the one in Ghent, the most important town in Flanders, in 1539 [see **H10**], well known because of the dissident religious ideas in some of the plays, were not *landjuwelen*: Ghent was not a Brabant town and its competition was not part of a series of seven. The last *landjuweel*, in Antwerp in 1561 [see **H12**], has always been the one in the limelight: it is very well documented and the fact that Antwerp was an internationally important port spread the fame of this competition. It was also the concluding contest and

Antwerp clearly wanted this to be a most memorable occasion that would fix the town's supremacy forever in men's minds. Yet it is important to be aware of the difference between this and the preceding *landjuwelen*. The Chambers of Rhetoric were heavily involved in religious and moral issues. After Ghent 1539 and in particular in the fifties and sixties, the Rhetoricians had acquired a bad name with the central government on account of their real and imagined heretical ideas and activities. Censorship of plays was widespread and thorough, and the Antwerp competition was hedged about with prohibitions. The plays and other activities were carefully screened and no whiff of religious or political ambivalence allowed. The theme of the competition finally chosen was 'That which inspires man most to create art.'

H11   Antwerp Chambers take part in many contests

(i) 'The Gillyflowers' win many prizes at Brussels, 1493

Antwerp, St Luke's guild, p. 47

Item, [the governors of 'The Gillyflowers'] travelled on behalf of Rhetoric to Brussels where the guild brothers won the highest prize, three silver bowls weighing nine ounces, for the *esbattement* [. . .]; another silver bowl for the most beautiful entry; a silver scale of two ounces for the Chamber which had come farthest; for the best prologue a silver statue of Mary of nine ounces. Laurens of Yperzele, our messenger at that time, won a personal prize for best character.

Item, they also got second prize for *Feast for a Bride.*

(ii) Antwerp organises a *landjuweel*, 1496

Antwerp Rhetoricians, p. 150

In May the lord magistrates ordained that a *landjuweel* should be proclaimed and the prizes for it were 36 silver Flemish marks and they sent messengers before Lent to the surrounding towns to invite them on St John's Day in the summer; and twenty-eight Chambers came, those from Leuven, Brussels, Nijvel, Lier, 's-Herenthals, Mechelen, Ghent, Zevenbergen, Aalst, Ostend, Roemerswaal, Amsterdam, Ypres, Oudenaarde, Dendermonde, Hulst, Axel, Courtrai, Sluis and others; and they had another 26 bowls made; and they cast lots [to determine] who would play first and it fell to those of 's-Herenthals; then those of Lier gained the top prize, i.e. two silver pots, one bowl and a hat with roses[1] and those of Roemerswaal got the second prize. The subject was: Which was the greatest mystery and most miraculous work that God had ever wrought for the salvation of mankind? And the answer which 'The Unlearned'[2] from Lier gave, by which they won the first prize, was: the gift of human nature.

---

[1] A frequent prize item, symbolising the rosary, as devotion to Our Lady was an important aspect of many Rhetoricians' Chambers.
[2] Also known as 'The Genista' or Broom.

H12   A splendid contest in Antwerp, 1561

(i) Invitations are sent to all the Chambers in Brabant

Antwerp, St Luke's guild

In this same year [1560] we were ordered by the magistrates of our town to send out four messengers to present the invitations concerning the *landjuweel* everywhere in the towns and freeholds of Brabant [. . .] The aforementioned messengers have announced everywhere that the gathering would begin on the third day in August 1561, as indeed happened; and it was such a magnificent feast, as had never been seen in Antwerp, where all the towns [gathered], each more splendid than the other, so much so that it is hard to describe, such triumphs as were celebrated, both of plays, illuminations, *facties*[1] and lavish banquets because the most important nobles of all the towns entered with the Chambers of Rhetoric and everything went very well considering that the town had never been as full as on that occasion [. . .] Those of 's-Hertogenbosch had the first prize for the *esbatement*, namely seven undeserved silver plates, earned because of prejudiced judging. The costs of these four messengers, their clothes, hiring of horses, living expenses and whatever else was needed, amounted to the sum of two hundred and seventy carolus guilders and eleven stivers. (pp. 222–3)

[1] See glossary for types of play.

(ii) Brussels wins first prize for the most beautiful entry

Brabant *landjuweel*

Asked which of the large towns would want to be considered for 'the most beautiful entry' prize, declarations are made by: those of Leuven that they will not compete for this; those of Brussels that they will want to be considered; those of Den Bosch say that they have come from afar and at their own expense without any financial assistance from anyone for which reason they submit themselves to the discretion of the jury; those of Mechelen commend themselves to the discretion of the jury. Following that it is decided that those of Brussels will be given the first prize for the most beautiful entry. (p. 95)

(iii) Lier receives first prize among the small towns

Brabant *landjuweel*

Asked which of the small towns want to be considered for this prize, those of Zoutleeuw commend themselves to the jury; those of Lier say that they have come with the greatest number; those of Herenthals commend themselves; those of Diest say that they came in with the most eloquent entry but commend themselves to the jury; those of Bergen think that they should get the first prize and that those of Lier should not carry it away since none of them were guildbrothers,[1] whereas those of Bergen are. Those of Lier claim that all those who set out with them from Lier are members from Lier; those of Herenthals do not dare to compete. Taking all this into account the judges have decided and declared that those of Lier will receive the prize for the most beautiful entry. (p. 96)

<hr>

[1] i.e. members of a Chamber of Rhetoric. Lier is a small town nine miles south-east of Antwerp.

H13 A number of procedural decisions have to be made

Brabant *landjuweel*

(a) Problems for the Mechelen Chamber of 'The Irisflower'

Those of 'The Irisflower' announce that one of their principal actors has had an accident so serious that the aforementioned person is in danger of dying, which has discommoded them greatly, so that they have to find someone in his place [and] they request that they will be allowed not to draw lots but wait as long as would be permitted. (p. 96)

(b) Precise instructions for the order of performances

When Leuven asks how many Chambers shall perform each day, it is decided according to the invitation charter that a Chamber shall perform every day, namely the first day in the afternoon the *punt*[1] and the *esbattement*, the following day before noon the *spel van sinne* and the *factie* in the afternoon after that. (p. 96)

<hr>

[1] The *poetelijck punt* was a tableau vivant, classical, mythological or biblical, shown on a stretcher or a wagon in processions or in front of the building where the members of the Chamber were lodged. It became an important part of the *landjuwelen* with its own separate prize. For the other play types see glossary above.

(c) A new Chamber is allowed to compete

[. . .] the Princes, leaders, deacons, elders and others of the Chambers of Rhetoric hereafter mentioned, in the town of Antwerp at the time of the *landjuweel* organised by the Guild of St Luke (also known as 'The Gillyflowers') having come together, since they have been presented with a request from the Princes, leaders, deacons and other common members of the guild named 'The Passionflower' of the town of 's-Hertogenbosch, after extensive deliberations have admitted and permitted, admit and permit hereby, that they [. . .] will be allowed with the other Chambers of Rhetoric in Brabant, to practise and use and may go everywhere [. . .] at *landjuwelen*, to towns, villages, freeholds and elsewhere to compete for prizes and to win, to enter, to play and to do all that can and must be done to enhance and to elevate Rhetoric. Thus decided [. . .] in the presence of those aforementioned the fourth day of the month of August 1561. In my presence being A. Grapheus.[1] (p. 97–8)

<hr>

[1] Grapheus was a secretary of the Antwerp town council.

H14   The 's-Hertogenbosch Chamber of St Catherine sends an invitation in verse to 'The Lilies' of Diest, 1615

Diest, p. 111

Cherish loyalty[1]

From 's-Hertogenbosch, this 4th of March, 1615

From the Catharinists: Honourable, discreet and noble Prince and competent officers as well, and to your members in general, we write this greeting with affection [. . .]

Rhetorica, who once was thrown down by grim Momo,[2] is now very pleasantly seated on Minerva's[3] triumphal chariot and elevated by the triumphant Catharinists, here in Sylvia[4] [. . .] You artistic spirits, open your mind and let art flow, then you will be praised. And we implore you: do remember all those who practise the noble, beautiful art of Rhetoric and bestow life unto her; that they may work with art to gain reward, is made clear by this invitation, for every person who best responds to our question will gain unstinted praise; thus, adherents of Minerva, apply yourselves diligently. This is our request that we present to you.

We pray you[5] for the sake of friendship, benevolent friends, that you do well and inspire all lovers of art and give them a copy of our invitation so that Rhetoric's praise may be broadcast and enlighten the ignorant who spurn all the glory of Rhetoric; then you will do us a great service. Equally, if you should require our services, we will do as much as we can. Nothing more remains to be said than to give you all cordial greetings and in particular to your *facteur* and Rhetoricians, our special friends.

Date as before.

This letter should be given to the honourable and very knowledgeable, sensible brothers of Rhetoric, that is of 'The Lilyflower', residing in Diest.(Pay the messenger.)

---

[1] The motto of the Chamber.
[2] Momus is the god of mockery and slander. The invitation is in a very characteristic rhetorical style full of classical allusions.
[3] Minerva is also the patroness of the arts.
[4] A wordplay on 's-Hertogenbosch which means 'the wood of the Duke'.
[5] This last part of the letter is in prose. The final words show that it was sent by special messenger.

III   Play-texts and tableaux

The plays performed by these community groups and Chambers varied enormously in subject matter and treatment. The only surviving French texts are those from the Lille procession [see **H35**] and the Passion plays from Mons and Valenciennes [see **H48–H62**]. In contrast, there are scores of Dutch plays, many of them, especially from the north, still unedited. The earliest surviving Dutch texts are the so-called *Abele Spelen* [Ingenious Plays] which survive in the Van Hulthem manuscript – a varied collection of medieval texts dating from circa 1410 – and add an early and special dimension to Dutch drama for *Gloriant, Esmoreit, Lanseloet van Denemerken* and *Van den Winter ende Vanden Somer* are serious secular courtly plays – virtually the only ones in Europe.[1] Each is followed by a farce (*sotternie*; compare the later French *sottie* [see **E88, E89** and **E90**]) and there are two separate *sotternien* as well. Nothing is known of the original performers, but there are records of performances in the fifteenth century.

From the fifteenth and sixteenth centuries, scores of Rhetoricians' plays have survived, especially the *spel van sinne*, a type of morality play peculiar to the Rhetoricians who also performed religious drama, farces and plays for royal occasions. Most of the material currently available is from the south but that is not to say that drama did not also occupy an important place in the cultural life of the northern provinces – it undoubtedly did. The archives of the Chamber of 'De Pellicanisten' in Haarlem, for example (better known by their device '*Trou moet blijcken*' [see **H18**]), contain many plays performed and/or originating in the Northern Low Countries and more material still awaits publication. The best-known Dutch drama, *Elckerlijc*, the original of the English *Everyman*, has no stage directions but the variety and range of Rhetoricians' plays can be seen in the stage directions from the play of the Wise and Foolish Virgins [*Spel van de V vroede ende van de V dwaeze Maegden*] which ends with the Judgement [see **H16**] and the list of plays by Cornelis Everaert [**H20**]. They also made great use of *togen* [tableaux; see **H21–H23**]. A number of plays introduced the motif of the play-within-a-play which was to become so popular in the Renaissance and later drama, the best-known example being that of Mariken van Nieumeghen [**H18**].

1.   The only other medieval play on a romance theme is the French *Estoire de Griseldis* (*c.* 1395), the story of patient Griselda, but romance plots are also found in a number of the Cangé Miracles of the Virgin [see **C30**].

H15   *Abele spelen* and Neidhart plays in Arnhem, 1395–1419

[Arnhem] *De Stadsrekeningen van Arnhem*, ed. W. Jappe Alberts, Groningen, 1967

1395: the performers who played Sir Nytert's play,[1] 12 quarts [of wine]: £3 4s. (II, p. 295)

1396: the performers who played the play in the marketplace: £6 12s. (II, p. 317)

1401: the same day [St Odulf's day, June 12th] when the performers did [the play] of the roses[2] in the marketplace: 27 quarts at 5 groats each, worth £9. (III, p. 13)

1404: the performers who played *Of the Winter and the Summer*:[3] 18 quarts worth £7 4s. (III, p. 61)

1411: the performers who played *The King and the Emperor* on the Old Market, £7 4s. (III, p. 177)

1419: the players who played Sir Nythert's play, 25 quarts at £3 and 5 gld. (III, p. 400)

---

[1] The Neidhart figure, found in many German *Fastnacht* plays [see **F42**, **F43**, **F44**], is based on the historical Minnesinger Neidhart von Reuental (*c.* 1180–post-1237) who was famed for his hatred of the peasantry.

[2] A play of the Rosary [**H11(ii)**, note 1].

[3] One of the *abele spelen*.

H16   Detailed stage directions for the Wise and Foolish Virgins, *c.* 1500

Het Spel van de V Vroede en de V Dwaeze Maeghden, ed. Marcel Hoebeke, The Hague, 1975; 2nd edn, 1979 [for similar plays see **C18**, **F28**, **F29**, **F30**]

Pausa. The foolish Virgins depart and the wise Virgins light their lamps during the interval. When the interval ends, then Fear-of-God, standing in her little house, speaks [. . .] (p. 121)

Then the foolish Virgins also sit down and fall asleep on the left side of the wise Virgins and their lamps go out. *Pausa.* Here a small interval occurs then some one makes a fearful sound and they all wake up, but they remain seated. Then someone calls out in a loud voice [the following] speech, but he cannot be seen [. . .] *Pausa.* Meanwhile the wise Virgins kneel down in front of Heaven and cause their lamps to burn brighter, and the foolish stand. (p. 126)

Pausa. Then [the foolish Virgins] go, in a leisurely way, towards the wise Virgins, not speaking until after Humility and Charity have spoken;[1] the wise Virgins stand and turn towards the crowd [Humility speaks]. Now the foolish Virgins turn towards the wise ones, imploring them [. . .] (p. 128)

Then they go away and the wise ones go towards the Bridegroom and Heaven is opened up again and the *Sanctus*[2] is sung. Meanwhile Our Lord and the Bride in front of Our Lord sit in joyous contemplation and two angels on either side swing smoking censers [. . .] (p. 130]

Then the Bridegroom goes towards them and they remain kneeling (p. 131). Saying this He raises Charity and remains standing there (p. 132). The Bridegroom raises Fear-of-God and takes each one in turn, after she has spoken [. . .] (p. 133)

Now He goes to Heaven and the wise Virgins bow towards him, and when He is in Heaven, the Bridegroom stands and the Bride and all the others kneel and the angels swing incense until the *Benedictus* has come to an end; then all the angels stand and the wise Virgins remain kneeling and sing: *Suscipe nos Domine* [Receive us Lord]. Then He crowns Charity and puts a ring on her finger, and then does the same with the others, one at a time, during the *pausa*. Once all of them have been crowned the Bridegroom seats Himself and the Bride next to Him. Then they sing *Te Deum laudamus, Sanctus*, and then they all kneel, but the Bridegroom alone remains seated. *Pausa*. When the *Te Deum* has been sung then the wise ones go and sit in front of the Bridegroom on a small bench and music is played during the *Pausa*; then Heaven is closed, and Hell opens (p. 135). *Pausa*. Then Hell is closed and the foolish ones come forward and speak [. . .] (p. 137). *Pausa*. Then they all kneel before Heaven in a row and [the Bridegroom] speaks again (p. 138). *Pausa*. Then the foolish Virgins stand up and turn towards the audience saying: [. . .] *Pausa*. Here the devils begin to clamour, speaking to the foolish Virgins [. . .] (p. 145). *Pausa*.

FINIS. Then they depart in joy: Our Lord first with the angels, and Mary after that with the Virgins, and they carry her cloak [. . .] (p. 154)[3]

---

[1] Both wise and foolish Virgins have names reflecting their virtues or follies.
[2] For liturgical pieces see glossary above.
[3] The play was probably written by Jan van den Vivere, priest of the church of Our Lady in Pamele, Oudenaarde. [See Oudenaarde pp. 48, 164–5 and **H35**.]

MARIKEN VAN NIEUMEGEN

The surviving version of the *Miraculous History of Mariken van Nieumeghen*, a printed text of the early sixteenth century, has no stage directions but the dialogue is interspersed with prose chapter headings which describe the action. The story is said to be based on a true story of a girl who became the devil's paramour but repented after watching a play of Our Lady and was saved.

H17   Mariken and her companion watch a play on a wagon

Mariken van Nieumeghen

Therefore Emmeken[1] and Moenen [the devil] travelled to Nieumeghen where they arrived on the day of the procession wherefore Emmeken was very glad [. . .]

Emmeken urged Moenen for so long to go and listen to the play that at last he consented, but he did it very reluctantly, as you have heard. (pp. 106–7)

Emmeken hearing this play[2] started to reflect on her sinful life, with a heavy heart [...] Therefore Moenen would have liked to prevent her from hearing the play, but she stayed and listened whether he wanted it or not [...] The longer Emmeken listened to the play, the more she thought about her sins. (pp. 114–17)

After these words Moenen the devil led Emmeken aloft higher than any house or church, so that her uncle and all the people saw it and they all wondered greatly not knowing what this might mean [...] When Moenen had carried Emmeken high up into the air he threw her down from above on to the street intending in that way to break her neck, which frightened everyone very much. And Sir Ghijsbrecht, her uncle, who also had been listening to the play, wondered what all this might mean and who it was who fell from such a great height. (p. 121)[3]

[1] Moenen, the devil with whom Mariken has lived for seven years, made her change her name because it was that of the Virgin.

[2] The wagon play shows Our Lady interceding for sinful mankind. She is opposed by the devil, Masscheroen.

[3] Through God's mercy Mariken is not killed. With the help of her uncle she seeks absolution for her sins and after long penance dies forgiven.

A CHAMBER'S PLAY-BOOK: THE 'TROU MOET BLIJCKEN' PLAYS

The plays of the *Trou moet blijcken* of Haarlem were collected in a large sixteenth-century manuscript which contains biblical plays, *spelen van sinne* and morality plays. The texts vary considerably in length and structure; some of them include detailed stage directions for performance [see **H18**]. The manuscript also contains some pages of accounts.[1]

[1] For the complete manuscript in facsimile with facing transcript see *Trou moet blijcken*.

H18 Directions for staging scenes interpolated in a morality play

Trou moet blijcken , vol. VIII

(i) Cast list for the play[1] with some costume details

Mankind: a finely dressed man.
Insatiable desire: a young woman seductively dressed
Avarice
A woman
One's own prophet[2]
Old and wretched/miserable: an old man soberly dressed

Many in need and distress: a soberly dressed woman with two or three children
Reason: a man [dressed] as a worthy [*statisch*] citizen
Scriptural instruction: a man [dressed] as a teacher
Fear of damnation: a man with a sword [27 recto].

[1] The play consists of extensive dialogue between the allegorical figures described in the list with two interpolated biblical scenes [*vertoninghen*] of Dives and Lazarus and the Last Judgement.
[2] i.e. a man who thinks he knows everything.

(ii) A scene of Dives and Lazarus

[The curtain has been closed on the dialogue then reopens] here they show Abraham with Lazarus in his bosom with four angels playing [music] which signifies Heavenly joy, and the Rich Man lying in Hell and two or three bellows-men blowing-up the fire as a sign of Hellish pain. And the Rich Man speaks [. . .] [38 recto]

(iii) Christ sits in judgement

[The curtain has been closed on the dialogue then reopens] here they shall show Christ sitting in judgement with seven or eight children and four angels, and the first angel blows his trumpet [then he speaks][1] [47 verso]

[1] Later souls on Christ's right and left speak as the saved and the damned.

H19   A multiple stage for a *spel van sinne*, 1696

Hummelen *Stages*, p. 73; trans. Wim Hüsken

The sketch shows a multiple stage with five banners – the one on the right named 'trouwe' [fidelity or loyalty] – above the five mansions, of which four are labelled: (left to right) prison [*gevangenissen*], audience chamber [*Houdensi Camer*] Statholder's room [*stathouwers Camer*] and inn [*herberge*]. At the far left and right (outside the line of banners) are two *sinnepoorten*: entrances, or gates for the *sinnekens*.[1]

[1] Hummelen discusses the similarities of this sketch (from the archive of the Rhetoricians of 's-Gravenpolder) to the stages used at Ghent [see **H10**] and Valenciennes [see **H61**]. Despite opposition by the authorities [see **H64**] and the rise of professional theatres in Amsterdam and The Hague, the Rhetoricians' drama continued in many towns until the late seventeenth century.

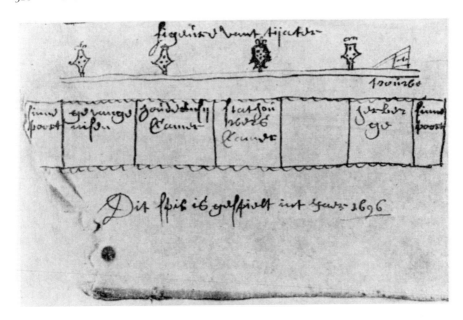

A RHETORICIAN PLAYWRIGHT

Although many of the authors of the scores of extant plays are known, it is unusual to find amongst the Rhetoricians a playwright who provides information about himself and his work. Cornelis Everaert of Bruges (1456–1556), however, dyer and fuller, clerk of the Archers, composed a list of his plays (which include political, commercial and medical subjects) with notes and details about the texts, their reception, success or failure, which allows us to form an idea of the variety of plays undertaken by one author. Performances might be on a wagon, a fixed stage or as part of a procession. Five of Everaert's plays are *toogspelen* in which the *togen* [tableaux] are the focus of language and action or the culmination of the play.

H20   Cornelis Everaert and his plays

Cornelis Everaert

(i) Prize-winning plays for special occasions

v.[1] The play of *The High Wind and the Sweet Rain*, made [. . .] in honour of Charles, our emperor, when the king of France was captured near Pavia [1525] [. . .] In 1528 this [play] won the first prize, a silver bowl, for the town [Bruges]. (p. 45)

II. *Esbattement Of the essence* written and made by me, Cornelis Everaert 1512, [. . .] won the first [prize] for the *esbatementen* in Nieuwpoort, a silver bowl. (p. 44)

x. The play of *Willing Labour and People who Trade* made and written by me, Cornelis Everaert, when the peace[2] was concluded between our emperor and Francis, [I] king of France [. . .] won a silver saltcellar in Bergen op Zoom. (p. 48)

[1] The numbers are those of Everaert's own list.

[2] This is the peace of Cambrai (1529), known as the *Paix des Dames* [the Ladies' Peace] because it was made by Margaret of Austria, regent of the Low Countries and Louise of Savoy, queen regent of France [see **H46(i)**].

(ii) A disastrous spelling mistake

vi. The play that was performed for the Aragonese[1] missed the first prize because the name on the *figuere* which symbolised the victory of our emperor was wrongly spelt, which name ought to have been written as Anon but was spelt as Naon. (p. 47)

[1] The 'Nation' of the Aragonese merchants in Bruges.

(iii) Some plays censored

xii. The play of war, [. . .] whose performance was forbidden because I hit upon the truth in it.

xiv. The play *Of unequal coinage*, [. . .] which I was forbidden to perform, and so I immediately wrote another, which follows hereafter and that was performed just as I had written it. (p. 49)

(iv) Several different kinds of plays are listed

i. The play of *Mary's little bonnet*,[1] an *exemplum* of a clerk who served the Virgin Mary, written and made by me C. E., 1509. (p. 44)

iii. The play of *Someone else's prosperity*, and this was my first wagon play, written and made by me C. E. in 1511 and copied by me in 1527. (p. 45)

xiii. *Esbattement Of farcical action and amusing proposal*, written for the archery feast in Ghistele, [1526]. (p. 49)

xxii. An interlude *Of the stream*, written by me C. E. 1512 for the Archers [of Bruges] and performed on January 20th. (p. 50)

xxxi. The [parable] play *Of the Vineyard*, made according to the Gospel of St Matthew chapter 20, and performed on the feast of the Annunciation to Our Lady, March 25th 1533. (p. 51)

[1] One of the prizes Rhetoricians could win was a hat decorated with roses, symbolising the Rosary [see **H11(ii)**].

(v) An elaborate tableau of Salvation

Pausa. Here they open the curtains and in the tableau should stand our Lord on the cross, which must resemble an olive tree, and before the cross must be written, on a banderole, in Latin: Come and see the works of the Lord who works wonders on the earth and makes wars cease even to the end of the earth (Psalm 45.9–10).[1] And outside [the curtains] in front of the tableau will be a banderole in Latin: From the mouth of children and babes is heard perfect praise (Psalm 8.3). Item. and down before the cross three young children must kneel, two boys and a girl and the one in the middle shall have a small banderole in his hand on which will be written: Grant us peace, Lord, in our time. The girl also will have a banderole on which will be written: Whoever is not against us will fight with us. The other boy [shall have] a banderole on which is written: Thou alone, Lord, our God. (pp. 48–9)

---

[1] References are given according to Vulgate numbering.

TABLEAUX VIVANTS AND RHETORICIANS' PLAYS

Image, speech and action were the three cornerstones of Dutch medieval drama, and it is clear that the variety of images was great: a painted text on a cloth or board; a group of silent characters in particular postures; a group of some silent, some speaking and/or gesturing characters; or a mixture of all these forms. By the time of the great contest in Ghent in 1539, it had become normal that the message of a play was expressed '*natuerlic*', by means of speaking, acting characters and '*figuerlic*', that is by iconographical means. Plays with one silent image or message (God the Father sitting on his throne) or with a group of silent characters and a painted message or image [see **H21**], or *toogspele* [demonstration plays] consisting of a whole series of images linked by text, were common. In processions the iconographic means of expression was of course most important, but plays on a fixed stage also made frequent and good use of images in a variety of ways

H21   'The Eyes of Christ' decide to fine members who do not take part in tableaux

Diest, pp. 119–20

When the members show *figueren*,[1] in particular silent characters, whoever does not want to take part, if the *Facteur* and Deacons have commanded it, will have to pay two shillings unless he can find someone as a substitute who is also a member of the Chamber and able to do it.

---

[1] *Figuere* [image, picture] is the technical term for a Rhetoricians' tableau.

H22   Tableaux may include speech and action

B. H. Erné and L. M. van Dis (eds.), *De Gentse Spelen van 1539*, 2 vols., The Hague, 1982, vol. II, pp. 426–431

lines 365ff. Tableau. Here Christ is shown hanging on the cross.

lines 387ff. Here Christ speaks, hanging on the cross.

lines 413ff. Tableau. Here Hell is destroyed.

lines 438ff. Tableau. Here is shown Christ rising and smiting death with his cross.

lines 449ff. 'Living Word' [a character] shows the shadow of death to 'Dying Man'.

lines 479 ff. Tableau. Here is shown Christ sitting on the right hand of his Father, having underneath him Sin, Death, Hell etc.[1]

---

[1]   The plays performed at the Ghent contest were the earliest collection of competition plays to be printed; see W. M. H. Hummelen. 'De eerste bundel met rederijkersspelen die bij een wedstrijd opgevoerd zijn, komt uit bij Joos Lambrecht Lettersteker te Gent', in Robert L. Erenstein *et al.* (eds.), *Een theatergeschiedenis der Nederlanden. Tien eeuwen drama en theater in Nederland en Vlaanderen*, Amsterdam, 1996, pp. 98– 105.

H23   A final tableau may underline the message of a *spel van sinne*

Man's Desire and Fleeting Beauty, trans. Robert Potter and Elsa Strietman, Leeds, 1994, pp. 88–9

Here the bower is opened and Man's Desire and Fleeting Beauty sit together embracing. And Death stands by them with a skull, or preparing to throw a spear but the lovers both turn away in horror and each holds up a hand as if trying to ward off Death. And on a tapestry in large letters are spelt out the words:

> ALL YOU LOVERS OF FAIR FLEETING BEAUTY
> PAY HEED TO THIS SHOW, WHILE YOU'VE BREATH:
> EMBRACE WHAT IS ETERNAL, LOVE RIGHTLY
> OR YOUR ONLY REWARD WILL BE DEATH.

The *Sinnekens*[1] keep quiet, frightened and fearful, long enough for the audience to read the above-mentioned message.

---

[1]   *Sinnekens* were the 'vices' in a *spel van sinne*.

IV   Plays for political and religious occasions

In addition to the regular local performances by groups and Chambers and the inter-city play contests, plays were also put on for special occasions, either political or religious. Many of the former involved royal or ducal births, marriages or visits to towns, while the latter included Corpus Christi and Passion plays. Often these were staged by special groups, and the variety of performance modes for both secular and religious drama was very considerable, ranging from single wagon plays to processions, from plays in churches to the great mansioned *hourd* of the French Passions.

PRINCELY CELEBRATIONS

French-speaking Béthune, on the border of Flanders, has a particularly rich record of drama to celebrate both Burgundian and French births, marriages and ceremonial entries and victories [see **H24**, **H25**]. Items under **H26** have been selected to show the very wide range of groups and plays involved on such occasions.

H24   Celebrations, Béthune, 1456, 1459

Béthune

(i) Awards for contributing to the festivities, 1456

Expenses on the occasion of the birth of the daughter of the Comte de Charolais[1] 102s [. . .] were distributed to the streets of the said town for various plays [*jus*], illuminations [*alumees*], and best-dressed [*plus belles*] companies,[2] prepared by them for this occasion. Viz:

To the rue Notre Dame for the best illumination 16s
To the rue St Vast for the finest company 16s
To the church for the best performance 12s
To the market for having done their duty well 12s
To the church clerks who were up on the stage singing songs while the companies [filed] past 4s. (pp. 337–8)

[1] Son and heir of the Duke of Burgundy.
[2] Groups dressed up for the occasion.

(ii) Special awards for those who acted plays

[. . .] To those of the church 20s, to those from the market 20s and to those from the shore [*rivage*] 20s, for having at the request of the authorities [*mesdits seigneurs*] sent for several plays from Cambrai, Arras and others which they performed over several days for the arrival of and in the presence of our most redoubted lord the Comte de Charolais in order to please and delight him in his town of Béthune. (p. 338)

(iii) Plays for the birth of a son to the Dauphin, 1459

To those of the market [. . .] for having played Rhetoricians plays [*jeus de retorique*] 12s
To those of the rue de Saint-Pry for playing the best *jeu de retorique* 16s
To those of the rue du Rivage [. . .] for having played [*jeu*] *de retorique* 12s
To those of the rue Notre Dame for having [. . .] performed plays *par personnaiges*.
For those of St Francis for having presented several *mystères* in mime [*par signes*] as the procession passed and repassed 12s. (p. 338–9)[1]

[1] The Dauphin in question is the future Louis XI, who reigned from 1461 to 1483.

H25   Many groups present tableaux for a royal visit, Béthune, 1483

Béthune

(i) Prizes promised to those who made the best tableaux and dumb-shows

To Jehan Gaumon, goldsmith, who [. . .] made several silver prizes [including] a dolphin, a daisy [*marguerite*][1] and a crown [. . .] to be given to those who would present the finest dumbshows [*remonstrances par seignes*] on the stages in the said town for the said visit. (p. 341)

[1] The Marguerite referred to is the three-year-old daughter of Marie of Burgundy. After her mother's death in 1482, she was betrothed to the Dauphin (the future Charles VIII) by the treaty of Arras.

(ii) Money given to all those who presented shows

Gifts [*courtoisies*] made by the said gentlemen [*sieurs*] to those who presented the said dumb-shows and entertainments [*joieusetez*] on stages for the said visit: the *charitables de St Eloy:*[1] 30s. The Companions of the church of Saint-Bertremieu; the Cordeliers; the crossbowmen; the Confrérie de Plaisance; the barbers, the butchers; the masons and stone-cutters; those of the *Sottie*: 12s [each group]. Two riders on hobby-horses [*chevaucheurs de bos*] 8s. (p. 341)

1 The *charitables de St Eloy* date back to a plague in the twelfth century when two farriers formed a *con-frérie* (under the name of their patron, St Eloy) for the purpose of burying the dead (one of the Seven Corporal Acts of Mercy). The *charitables* survive in Béthune to this day, providing free transport for coffins to the churchyard.

(iii) The stages are made of seasoned timber

To construct the stages in different parts of the town and also a high stage in front of the market hall it needed 37 pieces of wood from 20–24 feet long, 18–20 years old [. . .] All this cost 65s 5d.

[Another] 70 pieces of wood from 18–20 feet long for the stages: 52s 6d. (p. 341)

H26   Peace or victory: popular causes for performance, 1466–1520

Béthune

(a)   Plays to celebrate peace between Burgundy and Liège,[1] 1466

As a present made on Sunday 14 September [. . .] to those of St Bertremieu church and those of the *rues de Saint Pry* and *du Rivage* who on that day performed plays [*jus de personnaiges*] for this reason, to each of the streets and to those of the church were presented three measures of wine.

1 Charles le Téméraire of Burgundy was anxious to add the imperial bishopric of Liège to the Burgundian domain.

(b)   A play on New Year's Day, 1468

To Maitre Georges de Brelles, the Bishop of Fools,[1] 3 measures of wine for having performed and presented the destruction of Liège in front of the Halle [covered market]. (p. 340)

1 For the Bishop of Fools in Lille, see **H35**.

(c)   A celebration of peace, 1493

To the actors of the Confréries of Crossbowmen, of Archers de Plaisance, and to the clerks of St Bertremieu who, the day the said Peace was announced,[1] each acted a play *par personnaiges* on a stage in front of the market hall, for each play 8s which makes 24s. (p. 342)

1 By this peace the Habsburg Maximilian of Austria became Holy Roman Emperor, thus uniting the Low Countries to the Empire.

(d) Lille marks Charles V's visit to England, 1520

Archives de Lille 16255, fo. 155 recto

To Jan and Andrieu Pietdeaue, brothers, and Collart de Saint Legier, all Rhetoricians [*retorissiens*][1] for their salary for having, by order of the echevins, read and examined [*visité et examiné*] all the plays [to be performed] on this said day [5 June] both after dinner and after supper to entertain the people on account of this news,[2] to each of them 12s.

[1] There is a reference to Rhetoricians in Lille in 1499 (Knight suggests they were probably members of the Puy Nostre Dame established in the town in the late thirteenth century) and Rhetoricians from Arras visited Lille in 1532. For French Rhetoricians in Mons and Amiens, see **C26**, **H11**. The Valenciennes Rhetoricians took a play to Mons in 1527 (Mons, p. xix).

[2] That is, the news of the Emperor's arrival in England. Cardinal Wolsey was supporting the Empire against French claims in Italy.

H27 Royal entries in Antwerp

Antwerp, St Luke's guild

(i) Festivities for Maximilian and his son Philip, Antwerp, 1494

Item, in this year Maximilian, as King of the Romans [a title given to the Emperor; see **H26(c)**], entered into Antwerp with his son Philip, our prince, for whom great tableaux vivants with characters were organised amongst which was a splendid tableau ordered [to be made] by the Governors on the Marketplace with Venus, Juno and Pallas and so forth. And in the same year was held, on St Luke's Day, a poetry competition for [competitors] from outside and within [the town] in our Chamber, because on the same day a beautiful triumphal tournament with thirty helmets was held, because Blanche-Marie,[1] Maximilian's wife, came into Antwerp with a magnificent retinue. (p. 49)

[1] Better known as Mary of Burgundy. Her son was Philip the Fair (1478–1506), father of Emperor Charles V [see **H5(b)**].

(ii) Entry of King Philip II, Antwerp, 1555

[In 1555] When King Philip did enter here[1] incomparably triumphantly, then they and the elders have, with great enthusiasm, organised a magnificent representation of the Seventeen Netherlands, in front of the town hall in public, which Master Cornelis Grapheus had conceived. Another ingenious and poetic representation of the Chamber was that of Apollo and his nine Muses in triumph. Blessed is the country where the king comes in peace. For this service we were lavishly rewarded by the town with three sheep and wine [. . .]

Peter de Herpener had written a *factie*[2] how peace had re-established commerce, which much pleased our gracious king. It was played for him the first time in front of St Michael's abbey and was translated into Spanish for him by an interpreter.

We also performed, in front of the old house of the Archers, where there was a banquet for the lords of the Order [of the Golden Fleece] a play of the peace, called *Gooseman* composed neatly by Jan van den Berghe.[3] Peace creates Joy, but conflict hinders honour, virtue and prosperity. (pp. 189–91)

[1] The account is from a poem of forty-eight lines in alternating rhyme.
[2] See glossary above for play types.
[3] The *facteur* of the Chamber of the Gillyflowers [see **H4(a)**, **(b)**, **H10(ii)**, **H11(i)**].

PLAYS FOR RELIGIOUS FESTIVALS

H28   Dendermonde pays for a Resurrection play, 1391

Dendermonde, p. 110

Item, was given to the members of the company which played the play of Our Lord's Resurrection during Eastertide [. . .] 2s 9d gr.[1]

[1] For the 'great denier' see glossary above.

H29   A benefactress leaves money for a play, Leuven, 1474

Diest, pp. 35–6

[. . .] and before the altar of the Holy Sacrament or indeed elsewhere where the Mass of the Annunciation of the Blessed Virgin Mary will be held, which is celebrated on the fourth Ember day before the feast of the Nativity of Christ,[1] immediately after matins [. . .] before the altar of the benefactress. And in that Mass within the walls of the said church of Saint Jacob should always be played a history from the Old or the New Testament, according to the will of the aforesaid benefactress.

[1478] To Wensselyn for a scaffold to perform the play on, 6 gripen.[2]

Item on the Wednesday of the Emberdays before Christmas the Annunciation was performed, in the aforesaid church. Paid, by order of the churchwardens: for a pulley with which the Angel, who brought the message, was made to descend, to Jacop Meerman, carpenter, 15s.

[Item] for having made the scaffold, paid 6s. To Jan de Scrienmaker, for having made the chair in which the angel descended, 4s.

Item, to Claes the locksmith, for having put iron bands around the chair, 16s.
To the scribe, when the play was performed, 1s.

[1] For Ember days see glossary above.
[2] For money see glossary above.

H30   Horses in the Play of the Three Kings, Delft 1498

F. C. van Boheemen and Th. C. J. van der Heijden, *De Delfste Rederijkers 'Wij rapen gheneucht'*, Amsterdam, 1982, pp. 19–20

On the Sunday after Twelfth Night after vespers at 3 o'clock, a beautiful play was performed here in the church of the Three Kings who were [played by] priests. And they entered from several doors on horseback, each with his retinue, coming together in the middle of the church. And on the great organ there were angels singing *Gloria in excelsis* and down below shepherds were playing. And there was a fiery star shooting towards the high altar and remained standing there, showing there the Three Kings the new born King of the Jews in Bethlehem which was shown clearly with living people on the high altar, where these kings clearly and devoutly spoke [and partly sang] presenting their offerings. And after this play there was so much movement that the whole church was in motion. And the church was so full of people both upstairs and downstairs who came to watch as never before had been seen.

CORPUS CHRISTI

Corpus Christi was not a major occasion for plays in the Low Countries, though a few groups did 'adorn the passing procession' with plays in their neighbourhood, and in Oudenaarde plays and tableaux were included in the procession as early as 1409. Such plays were usually biblical but only in Béthune in 1549 is there anything like the craft-guild-sponsored, biblical cycles found in England and Germany.

The town of Nyeuwervaert, in the diocese of Breda, had a procession of Sacraments (with saints and biblical 'plays') on the Sunday before St John's Day to honour a miraculous Host found near the town in the 1460s. A *spel van sinne* survives which depicts the finding of the Host and the miracles. The only recorded performance is from 1500 but there may have been others.

H31   Corpus Christi plays in Oudenaarde, 1409–*c.* 1540

Oudenaarde

(i) The friars minor perform at Corpus Christi, Oudenaarde, 1409

[1409] Item [paid to] the friars as a courtesy and as a help with the cost and item [paid to] the friars for their expenses which they had incurred because of the play and *esbatement*[1] which they did in honour of the Holy Sacrament: £7 10sP. (p. 75)

---

[1]   This is the first mention of an *esbatement* in Oudenaarde and it is likely that this was therefore more than a tableau and involved speech and perhaps action.

(ii) Costly prizes for the most beautiful *figueren* in the Corpus Christi procession, Oudenaarde, 1413

[Then] the magistrates [bought] two golden brooches which weighed 10 old English [pounds] and a golden ring weighing three English [pounds]. These jewels were given to the companions[1] who made the best and most beautiful play in honour of the Holy Sacrament. (p. 83)

[1] These were presumably groups of townsfolk, but the procession was still organised by the friars at this date.

(iii) A clerk keeps the records of all the *figueren*, both moving and stationary, *c.* 1540

Figueren shown on scaffolds, beginning up the Hoochstraat and thus processing all around the town [. . .]: processing *figueren* first from the Old Testament [then] from the New Testament. (p. 78)

H32   The inhabitants of Pamele are rewarded with wine
Oudenaarde, p. 78

[1415] Item [given to] my lord the Deacon of Pamele,[1] who also, with the entire population of the village, celebrated in honour of the Sacrament [. . .] 12 jugs of wine.

[1417] [To] the good people of Pamele, who with their play and *esbatement* enhanced the procession [. . .] 10 jugs of wine.

[1] A village on the other side of the river from Oudenaarde. The whole region was under the feudal rule of the Lord of Pamele but by the late fifteenth century the village had become a mere suburb of the town.

H33   Haut Pont performs plays for Corpus Christi
St Omer

1413. To Pierre de Mussen for x cans [*kennes*] of wine at 2s 3d the measure, presented by order of the authorities to the companions from Haut Pont[1] who presented a *mystère* before the Holy Sacrament on Corpus Christi day [. . .] 40s. In addition to £4 cash [*monnaie courant*] [. . .] given to the said companions [. . .] to help pay for the costumes. (p. 347)

[1415–16] To Jehan Neudin and Willame Jaquemons for them and their companions living outside the Haut Pont gate [. . .] to present and set forth [*monstrer*] a *mystère* before the Holy Sacrament [. . .] 68s 7d. (p. 347)

1456. The echevins gave £6 for the costumes and making up the tree of Jesse and other things needful for preparing and carrying out the *mystères* they have promised to set forth and present to accompany and adorn the procession on Corpus Christi day as was done in former times by their predecessors living in the same neighbourhood. (p. 348)

[1] Haut Pont was a community of fishmongers and market gardeners near St Omer. The 1456 entry implies a revival of an old custom, with processional plays or tableaux.

H34   Corpus Christi pageants at Béthune from 1544
Béthune

(i) Pageants are presented by neighbourhood groups

[1544] The householders in the *rue de la croix* presented a display [*remonstrance*] of articles of the Passion. (p. 330)[1]

[1] Other tableaux staged include Christ's Robe and St Stephen but not the Passion.

(ii) A sequence of Passion scenes in 1548

The Last Supper, Jesus stretched [on the cross] on Mount Calvary; the Deposition, Pieta and the Burial. God being buffeted in the house of Annas, Judas hanging himself [. . .]. (p. 331)[1]

[1] The celebrations were not exclusively religious: 'To those Rhetoriciens [*de la Rhetorique*] who performed a morality and, thereafter, the farce: 6 measures of wine'. (p. 331 note 1)

(iii) A cycle presented mainly by the trade guilds, 1549

The linen-workers [*lingiers*]: the Annunciation with two characters [. . .]
The tanners and Cordwainers: the Nativity, with five characters and, on a third stage, the Three Kings with six characters [. . .]
The Barbers: the Garden of Olives, with 8 characters.
[. . .]
The Mercers and Jewellers: Jesus being nailed to the cross, with 18 characters; Ysaulde[1] forging God's nails [*les cloux Dieu*], 2 characters.
The dyers and sellers of satin [*satiniers de satin*]: the Crucifixion with several characters [. . .]
The glovers and woollen merchants: the Judgement, with several characters. (p. 332–3)

[1] This scene first appeared in 1546. The Smith's wife is also called Ysaude in the Valenciennes *Passion* performed in 1547 [see **H58**].

PROCESSIONS AND PLAYS FOR FEASTS OF OUR LADY

Many towns in the Low Countries, especially in the southern provinces of Flanders and Brabant, had *ommegangen* or processions for feasts of Our Lady, including Antwerp, Mechelen,[1] Diest [see **H6**] and Leuven.[2] Although all these processions included tableaux and decorated floats, the dramatically most important Marian festivals are the *Procession de Lille*,[3] the Brussels *Bliscapen* [Joys of Mary; see **H43**] and the Ypres *Thundaghe* [see **H46**].

[1] For details of the Mechelen procession and plays, see Hüsken, 'Civic Patronage', pp. 118–9.
[2] For details of the Leuven processions, see Meg Twycross 'The Flemish *ommegang* and its Pageant Cars', *Medieval English Theatre* 2 (1980), pp. 15–41, 80–98.
[3] The term *Grande Procession* used by some modern critics is never found in the Middle Ages.

THE LILLE PROCESSION

The *Procession de Lille*, founded in 1270 by Countess Margaret of Flanders, was originally an entirely religious occasion commemorating a miracle-working statue of Notre Dame de la Treille.[1] On the Sunday after Trinity[2] the Canons of St Peter's Church processed their most prized possession, a *fiertre* [feretory or portable reliquary] containing some of the milk and the hair of the Virgin Mary through the streets and around the city walls. The first reference to dramatic activity in the procession may be an ordinance of 1382, which forbids the playing of plays by neighbourhood groups but seems to make an exception for the procession. Another ordinance in 1402 gives instructions to the guilds that intend to perform '*aucuns jeux ou representations de vies de saints ou autrement*' [any plays or representations of saints' lives or other plays].[3] The organiser of the dramatic contest was for many years the Bishop of Fools [*evesque des fols*] elected annually from among the clergy of St Peter's Church [see **J15**]. The plays were performed by neighbourhood groups of young men from different streets [*rues*] or squares [*places*] whose traditional activities and violent rivalry between groups had been the subject of civic bans [see **H1(a)**]. Participation in the procession was encouraged by the award of prizes for the best play and best decorated wagon [see **H36**]. Barring a brief period between 1470 and 1475, the Bishop of Fools maintained control of the plays until 1527. However, the municipal authorities paid for the prizes and supported individual groups of players [see **H38**, **H39**].

1. The plays for the *Procession de Lille*, held annually on the Octave of Trinity Sunday, have only recently been discovered and are currently being edited. We are most grateful to Alan Knight for his help with this section, for transcripts of references from the unpublished records and for copies of his transcripts of the plays.
2. See 'Bishop of Fools'. Later a procession was also held on the feast of Corpus Christi.
3. See 'Bishop of Fools', p. 158.

H35 The Lille Bishop of Fools calls for plays for the procession, 1463

Archives du Nord, B93

To the honour of God and the glorious Virgin Mary, his blessed mother, and for the embellishment of the procession of this good city of Lille, we, Prelate [*prelat*] of Fools, stirred with willing heart by the deliberation of our council, intend to award, with God's help, the prizes listed below to groups formed in one neighbourhood with no outsiders, who come on the day of the procession on large or small wagons, wains, or portable scaffolds to present histories from the Bible, both Old and New Testaments, saints' lives approved by the Church, or Roman histories from ancient chronicles, each containing at least 300 lines and at most as you will. In the morning as the procession passes the plays are to be mimed in the squares designated by us or our deputies, and in the afternoon they are to be played before us, wherever we wish, in good and true Rhetoric. They must not have been played in this city within the last 16 years.[1]

---

[1] Much of this text is quoted (with translation) in 'Bishop of Fools', p. 159

H36 Examining and judging the plays, Lille, 1463, 1470

(i) Rules for those competing for prizes, 1463

'Bishop of Fools', p. 160

The company which, that day [of the Procession] after supper – or the next day, if it seems expedient – plays the funniest and most joyous farce, provided it has not been played in this city within the last 99 years [. . . will receive a prize].

Anyone wishing to compete for the said prizes must come to our palace of clerics [*palais des clers*] on the day of Corpus Christi between three and four o'clock in the afternoon, where lots will be drawn. He must bring the script of the history he wants to play and the banner of his leader or his neighbourhood. No one can win any of the above prizes who does not compete in both categories: farces and history plays.

(ii) The civic authorities appoint judges, 1470

Archives de Lille, 888

Paid to two Dominicans and two Franciscans] the day that they worked on the examination of the said histories and plays in order to award the prizes justly to those who have won them, which occupied them from morning to evening [cf. **H20**].

[To a group of men commissioned to] organise and award the prizes and to listen during the performance of the said histories and plays for any errors that might be made.[1]

---

[1] Knight suggests that the latter also probably judged the best decorated stage ('Bishop of Fools', p. 161).

H37   An informative prologue to one of the plays

'Bishop of Fools', p. 163

May the son of God omnipotent protect all who are here assembled, before, behind, and on all sides, and especially the Prelate of Fools, who, for the embellishment of the holy procession that is taking place today in Lille, issued his letters and proclamations to the city, requesting all to write new history plays containing meritorious works that are examples to people of doing good and avoiding evil. To that end we, of Saint Martin's Place, come before you, humbly requesting silence of all, that we may here show you a notable example of keeping justice in its course.[1]

---

[1] Prologue to *Le Juge d'Athenes*, one of the Roman plays of which there are four among the total of 72 in the Wolfenbüttel manuscript, comprising 43 Old Testament, 21 New Testament, 3 Christian legend and 1 morality.

H38   Tableaux of the Passion presented by a special group

(i) St Saviour's parish always presents the Passion

'Bishop of Fools', pp. 163–4

1470: [The Companions of St Saviour's Church played] several histories on the subject of the Passion of Our Lord Jesus Christ before the feretory of Our Lady as it moved from the said St Peter's Church to St Saviour's gate, as they are accustomed to do each year to adorn the said procession.[1]

---

[1] There is no Passion play in the Lille manuscript and Knight suggests the Passion was merely mimed: 'Because the same company always played the passion plays, it is probable that they had exclusive rights to the plays as did the Confraternity of the Passion in Paris. If that was the case they may not have [. . .] been part of the competition'.

(ii) The town council contributes for new costumes

Archives de Lille, 16219, fo. 117 recto

[1480] To the companions of the Gauguerie[1] by the council of echevins and the eight men[2] has been given in courtesy in support of the expenses sustained by them because of the several histories put on by them while going round the said procession, for its embellishment, viz. the Nativity, Passion and Resurrection of Our Saviour Jesus Christ, and especially as an advance for certain new costumes which they had to have because of some new histories shown by them [. . .] £12.

---

[1] The Place de la Gauguerie was in St Saviour's parish (Lefèbvre, *Lille*, vol. 1, p. 78).
[2] The 'Huit Hommes' were a part of the municipal government elected by the incumbents [*curés*] of the four oldest parishes in the city.

H39   Musicians and actors are rewarded by the town, 1480

Archives du Nord, B93

[1480] To Jehan Parent, Denisot of Longueville, [other names] and other gittern-ers[1] [*guistreniers*] and actors [*joueurs de personnages*] in this town of Lille, for having put on several plays and entertainments the day of the procession in the said town, and for its embellishment, has been paid 30s.

[1]   The gittern was a lute-like stringed instrument.

CRAFT GUILDS AND THE LILLE PROCESSION

In the sixteenth century, craft guilds presented tableaux as part of the procession, an innovation similar to that of the Béthune Corpus Christi procession [see **H34**]. In 1535 there were nineteen typological *figuren* [figures] each showing a New Testament 'type' and an Old Testament 'antetype', and these were followed by the Resurrection, the Harrowing of Hell and the Last Judgement. Like the St Saviour's Passion scenes, these floats were actually part of the procession rather than decorating the route as the plays did.

H40   'Figures' with antetypes presented by the craft guilds in the Lille procession, 1535

Archives de Lille, Affaires Générales 654, Item 3

Tanners: How Abraham made his son Isaac carry the wood on which he was to be sacrificed and he himself carried the fire and the knife, signifying [. . .]

Furriers: How Jesus was to be condemned by Pilate to carry his cross on which he would be crucified. [Note that the *pletiers* [furriers] say that it is more expedient to present Jesus carrying his cross] [. . .]

Bakers: How Jesus rose from the tomb, with his five wounds.

Chandlers and Candlemakers: How after his death Jesus went to Limbo to redeem the patriarchs.

Innkeepers: How Jesus will come to judge the quick and the dead.

H41   The council is willing to negotiate and remunerate

Archives de Lille, Affaires Générales 654, Item 3

The echevins and council of the town make it known that in honour of the forth-coming procession [. . .] they have ordered the craft guilds [*mestiers*] to present the histories they presented the previous year. Those who did them last year can do them again without anyone else being allowed to do them [on the same subject] and those who did not do them will have to do those agreed between them and the procurator of the town [. . .] And if there should be any guilds which want to postpone doing the said histories, they must declare it to the procurator of the town within eight days of this announcement[1] [. . .] And each guild which does a play will be given half a gold real in advance for expenses [. . .] And there will also be given to those who present the finest, most skilful and elaborate [*plus belle, industrieuse et riche*] history from the Old and New Testaments four gold carolus.

[1] A comparison of the list of 'figures' for the two years reveals that there was not one change of either guild or subject.

THE BRUSSELS PLAYS OF THE JOYS OF OUR LADY

The Brussels *ommegang* [procession] organised by the Guild of Archers on the Sunday before Pentecost, commemorated a legendary account of the flood which brought a miracle-working statue of Our Lady from Antwerp to Brussels. From 1448 onwards the morning procession was followed, in the afternoon, by a play representing one of the *Bliscapen* [Seven Joys of Mary] staged in turn in a seven-year cycle. Only the *Eerste* and *Sevenste Bliscapen* are extant. The play of the First Joy of Mary [the Annunciation] begins with the Fall of Man and includes Old Testament material and a Trial in Heaven. The Seventh Joy – The Assumption – is shorter and follows the traditional accounts closely. In the later sixteenth century the Chamber of the Cornflower took over the performances of the Seventh Joy and, according to a contemporary the stage was constructed 'in the form of the Colosseum'.

H42   *The Joys of Our Lady* are staged annually in Brussels in honour of the Virgin Mary

Bliscapen

(i) Time and place of the performance of the Joys of Our Lady are decided, 1448

Item it was decided that, as before, there shall be a performance of a play every year on the day of the procession, beginning at two hours after noon and on the Nedermarkt in Brussels. And these plays will be about the Seven Joys [*Bliscapen*] of Our Lady of which every year one shall be performed, a new one every year for seven years. And at the end of the seven years the series of seven about the same Joys will be started anew. And the town of Brussels will commission the making of a scaffold on which the play will be performed annually. (p. 12)

(ii) The Guild of Archers remains responsible for the performance of the plays up to the 1490s

1497 [. . .] the companions of the great guild who performed the play of Our Lady.

1498–9 [the same] who performed the play of Our Lady, in the market square. (p. 13)

H43 Lists of actors and props used in performances of *The Joys of Our Lady*

Bliscapen

(i) A cast list for the First Joy of Mary

Envy = Salome[1]
Lucifer[2]
The serpent = Will
Eve = Blinde
Adam = Van
God
Angel = Leers
Second child = Hans
Third child = Wuycke
First female neighbour = Draeyer[3]
Another

David
Job
Isaiah = Coninck
Bitter Misery = Draeyer
Passionate Prayer = Gillis
Mercy = Van
Justice = Blinde
Truth = Payge

The Son of God = Peeter
The Holy Spirit = Hans
Peace
Joachim=Tielman
First priest
Second priest = Coninck
Bishop = Cammin
Anna = Payge
Seth = Drayer

Second female neighbour,
third male neighbour,
fourth woman
Our Lady
First boy = Gillis
Second boy = Wil Davids
Third boy = Hans
Joseph
A girl = Heyle
A small boy = Lucas
Gabriel = Leers (p. 23)

---

[1] Salome who played Envy and Heyle [a girl] are clearly female.
[2] Not all the actors are named.
[3] Evidently some actors played more than one role (p. 23).

(ii) Costumes and props for the Seventh Joy, 1556 and 1566

God on the throne, a white alb and choir cope
God's hair [wig] and the crown
Four albs, three angels and hair
Crooks [for the Apostles]
Wings and a cope for St Michael, a sword, staff and armour

St John's white robe, the cloud, the pulpit
Jesus' robe; hair and beards for six or seven Apostles
Lucifer's Hell, costumes and heads [masks] for three or four devils
All three Heavens are made to open
Mary's clothes and girdle, the palm branch.
Grave, bier, shrine and shroud
The hands,[1] manna, and furthermore all the long robes, hoods and short coats
[*cleyn rocken*] available. (p. 25)

[1] For the legendary miracle of the Jew who touches the bier and whose hands remain fixed to it.

H44   Stage action in the Seventh Joy, the Assumption
Bliscapen

(i) St John travels on a cloud to Mary's house in Jerusalem

Here two angels shall arrive with a cloth and wrap it around St John and the cloth must shine like a cloud. And they shall take him, covered in this way to Mary's door, or in another way as seems best. (p. 164)

(ii) The funeral procession is disturbed

Here they [the Apostles] lift the bier and sing *Exit de Egypto, Alleluia*. And the angels in Heaven shall also sing and play the organ. Then the Jews arrive and start making a lot of noise. (p. 199)

THE YPRES PROCESSION OF OUR LADY

The *Thundach*, a feast-day peculiar to Ypres, commemorated the siege of the town by English and Ghent troops in 1383 from which the town was delivered by the intervention of Our Lady of the Ramparts [*Onse Lieve Vrouwe vanden Tuin*]. The feast was celebrated over several days [*Thundaghe*] in early August and included processions with *figueren*, prizes for the best poems in honour of the Virgin, an archers' competition and a large market [see **H45**, **H46**].

H45   Prizes for poems and *figueren* in the Ypres procession
Alphonse Vandenpeereboom, *Ypriana. Notices, Etudes, notes et documents sur Ypres*, 7 vols., Bruges, 1881, vol. v

(i) Costly prizes are prepared for the *Thundaghe* in 1409

To Melchior Broederlam for having made the design for the lily, the lion and the rose given [. . .] for the procession of the last *Thundach* and for determining the colours of the paint after they have been made of silver [. . .] £4

To master Jan de Koc, silversmith for making the aforesaid lily, lion, rose, bowl and cup by hand, providing the necessary gold to gild and enamel them according to the pattern and device designed by the aforementioned Melchior, in total paid by the treasurer [. . .] £25. (pp. 100–2)

(ii) Poems in honour of Our Lady also attract valuable prizes

[Paid] Master Jan van der Eechoute for having set to verse and written on a board the programme of prizes to be won for praising Our Lady

To Franz van der Loope, goldsmith, for two golden rings to give to those who will pronounce the best and most beautiful praise of the purity of the Virgin Mary, whether they are from inside or outside [the town] £4 16s. (p. 108)

(iii) The centenary of the first *Thundach* included *figueren* denoting deliverance, organised by five different groups, 1483

i. The guild of St Anne, motto: *Rosieren met melodie* [enhance with music]): Judith or the heroine who caused the siege of Bethulia to be lifted

ii. Guild of Our Lady of Alsembergh,[1] motto: *Door's Geest's weldaden, Zijn wij licht geladen* [through the benevolence of the Holy Spirit we are lighthearted]: King David's rage is appeased by wise Abigail [as Christ's anger against the inhabitants of Ypres was calmed by the intervention of Our Lady]

iii. Guild of St Maurice, motto: *Vreuchdenaers* [rejoicers]: The death of Christ or the deliverance of Mankind

iv. Guild of St Croix, also known as *de Mooren* [the Moors]: Sisera and Jael

v. Guild of the Guardian Angel, motto: *Getrouwe van Herten* [of loyal heart]: Esther or the deliverance of the Jews through prayers. (p. 183)

---

[1] This was a pilgrim confraternity. Four of the five plays treat of deliverance by women.

H46 Special preparations for the *Thundaghe*, Ypres, 1529

(i) The preparations for the August celebration are begun in January, 1529

Ypres, p. 14

[Paid to] Willem van Belle and seven other people for having been busy for five days at 12s, and 4 days at 6sP, with the making of the scaffolds for the celebration[1] in the marketplace [. . .] £4 4s

---

[1] The peace of Cambrai had recently been concluded; see **H20**.

(ii) The Fool is equipped with elaborate clothing

Ypres, p. 17

[Item paid] to Ghyselbrecht van den Kerckhove for supplying several pieces of woollen cloth to be made into a coat for the Fool in connection with the coming procession [. . .] £14 19s 6d.

[Item paid] to Jan Denys Parmentier[1] for having made the stockings and other articles of clothing to match the aforesaid coat [. . .] £12.

[Item paid] to Oliver Cortun shoemaker for supplying two pairs of shoes for the aforesaid Fool [. . .] 28s.

[Item paid] to Ghyselbrecht van den Hove because he has been entrusted with playing the Fool [. . .] £4.

[Item paid] to Loys the embroiderer for having embroidered the arms of the town on the aforementioned coat of the Fool [. . .] 12s.

[1] Parmentier, here used as a surname and an indication of a profession, means a tailor specialising in fine and costly materials.

(iii) The accounts reveal many details of the procession

Ypres, pp. 15–19

3. For the choir and parish priest of St Martin's, 2 jugs [of wine] [. . .] For the guild [staging] the play of Our Lady, and the carpenter and interpreters, 2 jugs

15. [To] Maerten van Pithem, painter, according to the conditions of the contract arranged with him for having decorated with paint the benches and the railings in front of the house of the justice of the peace [. . .] £6

22. As arranged by contract, to Daniel Homs for having lent red, white and yellow cloth and for having hung it up in the Dairy market [. . .] 10s

36. [To] various musicians; the young clerks who were in charge of the torches and the banners; and to those who carried the crosses of the four parishes; and to those who carried the canopy held above the Holy Sacrament[1] in the aforementioned procession on *Thundach* [. . .] £13 14s.

[1] The inclusion of the Sacrament in these processions is unusual.

(iv) Other towns compete for prizes during the *Thundaghe*

Cornelis Everaert, p. 50

[1529] This *esbattement* [of *Poor-in-the-Purse*] and the play hereafter following, of *Maria* [*compared with the throne of Solomon*],[1] was written by me Cornelis Everaert [see **H20**] for the guild of the town of Veurne, [. . .] both plays were performed in the town of Ypres after the Feast of Our Lady and won the third prize of honour.

[1] The throne of Solomon or of Wisdom is a well-known iconographical image of Our Lady. See G. Schiller, *Iconography of Christian Art*, 2 vols., London, 1971, vol. I, 46.

THE BRUGES PROCESSION OF THE HOLY BLOOD

It is not actually known when or how the celebrated relic of the Holy Blood came to Bruges. The traditional account of its being sent to Bruges from the Holy Land by Thierry of Alsace, count of Flanders in 1148 has now been discredited. The earliest definite reference to it is in 1256 and the first *ommegang*[1] is mentioned in 1291.

It is not until a century later that the term 'play' [*spel*] is mentioned in connection with the procession and it seems likely that the earliest 'plays' were in fact tableaux, though in 1457, the Dauphin (the future Louis XI) refers to the organisation of 'a very fine and excellent procession with plays [*spelen*]'. Other references suggest the use of large painted scenes and it is probable that over the years the variety and number of floats and presentations varied considerably. The procession is still held today on the feast of the Ascension, and still includes some short plays as well as the large tableaux on floats.

[1] For *ommegang* see glossary of terms above.

H47   Plays are included in the Bruges *ommegang*, 1396–1541

Wim Hüsken, 'The Bruges *Ommegang*', in Société Internationale pour l'Etude du Théâtre Médiéval, Actes del VII colloqui . . . [Gerona, 1992], Barcelona, 1996

(i) Payment for a play, town accounts, 1396

Presented to the companions of the play of the Twelve Apostles and Four Evangelists, who preceded the Holy Blood on the day of the procession, eighteen sixpences [xviiis, gro]. (p. 78)

(ii) A play of the Garden of Gethsemane, 1404–5

Idem, given to Janne van Marolus for the cost, the pain, and the trouble he had on the day of the *Ommegang* riding in front of the Holy Blood with Our Lady's Annunciation, with the Offering of the three Magi, with Our Lady's Childbed, King Herod, the City of Jerusalem, with the Table of the Twelve Apostles and with the Jesse Tree,[1] £36P. (p. 78)

[1] The title referred to in the Accounts shows little connection with the contents described. A Jan van Marolus was co-founder of the Chamber of the Holy Ghost (p. 78).

(iii) Some of the 'plays' could have been paintings, 1479

The Jesse Tree and the Supper and the Garden were shown there, the arrest, the flagellation and the Cross-bearing and many beautiful parts of Our Lord's Passion, such as Annas, Cai[a]phas, Herod and others very skilfully presented in paintings. (p. 78)

(iv) A specially elaborate *Ommegang* for Maximilian, 1478

And the plays of the Garden, of the Last Supper, and of other parts of Our Lord's Passion were performed, very richly decorated, and they had not been seen for many years. (p. 79)[1]

[1] The Emperor Maximilian of Austria (1459–1519) had married Mary of Burgundy in 1477.

(v) Later processions include legendary figures, 1541

[To repairing] Charlemagne and the four Sons of Aymon, the Jesse tree, the Giant[1] and the horse Bayard. (p. 79)

---

[1] Giants, and huge animals were well known in Spanish Corpus Christi processions and may have come to the Low Countries from Spain. In the sixteenth century many processions mingled religious and secular subjects [see **D10**].

PASSION PLAYS IN HAINAULT

Passion scenes connected with processions are recorded from Béthune, Bruges, and Lille, but there is no Dutch successor to the Maastricht *Passion* [see **C25**], and French-speaking Hainault is the only province in the Low Countries to have produced major Passion plays in the later Middle Ages. The principal town for drama was Mons, which has an extended tradition of performances, including Passions, from early in the fifteenth century, culminating in the great Passion play of 1501 for which we have the most important set of performance records of any French-speaking area. Among those present at the Mons play was a certain Jean Molinet (c. 1433–1507), a Rhetorician, who is probably the author of the original version of a twenty-day Passion play manuscript bearing the date 1549 and preserved in the library at Valenciennes, though it was not performed there. Indeed, in contrast to the regular theatrical tradition in Mons, although the Rhetoricians of Valenciennes held many meetings and took part in poetry and play contests elsewhere, only a single example of a major play performance is recorded from the town itself, that of 1547.

THE MONS PASSION PLAY

The records comprise the director's copy, with full stage directions and the first and last line of each speech,[1] the names of the actors, the town council minutes concerning the preparations of the play and the complete set of accounts. All the documents are quoted from the single volume [Mons] in which all the material was published by Gustave Cohen in 1925.

The stage [*hourt*] stretched across the marketplace and there was also extensive audience accommodation, the whole area (parq] being fenced round. The accounts give full details of the materials used and the cost of making things. References to costumes are rare because the players provided their own, with the exception of Jesus for whom several special costumes were made.[2]

---

1. The text of the play has been identified, line by line, by Cohen from the Passions of Gréban and Michel though some of the Old Testament material is original.
2. For details of God's costumes in this and other plays see Lynette R. Muir, 'Playing God in Medieval Europe' in *The Stage as Mirror. Civic Theatre in Late Medieval Europe*. Ed. Alan E. Knight. D.S. Brewer, 1997. pp. 25–50

H48   Some townsfolk want to perform the Passion, Mons, 1500

Mons, p. 588

[1500] There was a discussion of the request made by some of the townspeople to be granted permission to perform the Passion, also to be able to enclose the area of the said stage [*hourt*] and that the town should grant them help with the expenses, including the stage being built at the expense of the town. Agreed [. . .] that information should be sought on how things had been done in similar cases.

There was a discussion on the Mystery of the Passion to determine whether the town would have the stage [*hourt*] built at the town's expense. Agreed to assemble those who are taking part [*qui ont parchon*] next Sunday to learn if all will be ready for Whitsun and then ask the carpenters if they could complete the stage within the said time. Later in the month it was agreed in the matter of the Mystery of the Passion that they should send for Master Collart Ghossuin together with some of those who are organising the said Mystery to learn the cost of the stage [. . .] Agreed to perform the Mystery as soon as possible [*a toute diligence*] and the town to construct the stage.[1]

---

[1]   The town also paid for fetching the play from Amiens, having copies made and returning the original.

H49   Advertising the Mons performance

Mons, pp. 551, 588–9; trans. *Staging*, pp. 48–9

(i) A play competition planned

1 June. Notice was given at the said meeting that [. . .] the Lord Bailiff had advised that authorisation should be obtained to notify the good towns that whoever wanted should come and perform plays and entertainments [*jeux et esbattements*] in the evenings during the period of performance of the Passion and there should be some prizes and trophies. [. . .]

There was talk of having a prize for each day, to be played for in the evening after the end of the said *mystère*; the first of three ounces of silver, the second of two ounces of silver, and the third of one ounce. Agreed to award the said trophies and to have the performances near the fountain without touching the stage of the said *mystère*. (p. 588)

(ii) Safe conduct for visitors from neighbouring towns

Item: it seemed good to the said Lord Bailiff that safe conduct be given to the inhabitants of the good towns of this region who come to see the Passion against any debts that these said towns might have, and although the Lord Bailiff has indeed the power to grant such safe conduct, yet it seemed to him to be a good idea to obtain this authorisation from the Prince[1] who in this way would be informed of the performance of the said Passion. (p. 589)

[1] Philip the Fair, son of Mary of Burgundy and Maximilian of Austria [see **H5(b)**, **H27(i)**].

(iii) Notices posted on the city gates and letters sent to other towns

26 June. To Sire Jehan Bouchart, priest, for having made six notices to attach to the six gates of the town to advertise the date fixed for the performance of the said *mystère*, 12s. (p. 518)

[. . .] To Gerosme Fosset, for the fee for his journey to the towns of Valenciennes, Douai, Arras, Amiens, and Cambrai[1] to carry letters from the honorable echevins in connection with the said *mystère* and play festival [*Jeu de Rhetorique*] which took five days on horseback at 25s per day. (p. 551)

[1] Entries for 3 July list a total of eleven other towns to whom letters were sent.

H50   Regular rehearsals are held

Mons, pp. 557–8; trans. *Staging*, pp. 58–9

To Jehan Billet, for 48 days when he summoned the players to assemble for all the meetings for rehearsals made from the beginning of the said *mystère* in the Town Hall entered here by agreement with him £6. (p. 557)

To Jehan Barbet [. . .] who was reimbursed for what he had paid for a dinner [*desjeuner*] at the Stag, the day that they tried out God and the two thieves on the Cross, 19s. (p. 530)

H51   Admission charges and audience limitations

Mons, p. 591; trans. *Staging*, p. 64

There was a discussion about the commissioners [who were] to receive those who entered the stage enclosure [*le cloture du hourt*]: [four names] who for entry into the auditorium [*parq*] shall collect 12d from each person and as for those who are on the stands [*les hours*] near the houses [*marchissant as maisons*], they shall pay three sous each. And it was agreed that no one should enter the auditorium [*parq*] before nine o'clock in the morning and that children under ten, the old and infirm and pregnant women would not be admitted.

H52   Preparing and decorating the Hell

Mons, pp. 498–9, 511; trans. *Staging*, p. 91

To Jehan Helle called Vacquenot, for three and a half days employed in plastering Hell at 12s per day, he and his assistant, 42s, and for the hair put into the plaster [*mortier*] so that it can be painted on, 2s. Together 44s. (p. 498)

To Jaquemart du Bois, carter, for nine loads of clay brought by him to the said stage. (p. 499) [Several similar entries]

To Jehan Machon for a cartload of willow stumps [*teste de sauch*] which were used for the said Hell, with his fee for having uprooted them (he and his assistant) for two days: 24s. (p. 511)

H53   A boat on the Sea of Galilee

Mons; trans. *Staging*, p. 98

(i) Collecting the items needed

To Jehan de Gravelle called the shipwright [*bacqueteux*] for his salary for the wooden boat [*bacque* = a flat-bottomed ferry or canal boat] which he had agreed to make for the said *mystère* at the cost of £20 including delivery, has so far been paid £8. (p. 477) [Two further payments are listed]

To Jehan de le Fontaine, brewer, for the value [*interest*] of his beer-delivery cart [*chariot a mener cervoises par les rues*] lent by him during the said *mystère* to bring the wooden boat [*bacque*], inside which was made the great sea, from the quay to the said stage on the marketplace and which in the process was damaged, [. . .] 40s. (p. 584)

To Jehan Bracquet, boatman, for his salary for going by water to Jemappes to fetch a little wooden boat [*bacque*] [. . .] to be used on the sea of the said stage, 6s. (p. 533)

To Jehan Bouchart, carpenter, for a piece of wood 13 foot long and 6 inches square, which makes a supporting beam under the stage to support the *bacque* [this may be either the sea itself or the small *bacque* used on it]: 15s. (pp. 518–19)

Item for 5 sheepskins to make waves on the water, 29s. For another piece of leather for this purpose, 8s, and for the calfskin, 8s. (p. 531)

(ii) The stage directions show them in use

Here remind St Peter and St Andrew to approach the sea and go in and out of the boats [batelez] *several times, pretending to be fishing and moving their nets about.* (p. 147)

[Seven apostles, by the sea of Galilee] *enter the boat* [. . .] *St Peter steers the boat* [. . .] *then they prepare their trawls* [saines] *and their nets.* (p. 443)

Remind those who work the thunder effects to do their duty, following the contents of their cue sheet [billet de advertence] *and not to forget to stop when God* [i.e. Christ] *has said* 'Cease and be still'. (p. 169)

H54   The Valenciennes stage picture of the Sea of Galilee

Bibliothèque Nationale, Paris: Valenciennes MS 12536

The arrangement of the stage here seems to represent exactly the items mentioned in **H53**: the larger boat forming the sea has been sunk in the stage filled with water and presumably the sheepskin waves. The smaller boat is set on it and can be rocked by the pivot beam below the stage. For the whole picture, see **H61**.

H55   Costumes for Jesus

Mons

(i) A white robe and gold mask for the Transfiguration

[19 June] For 7 ells of white *treslis* [fine white cloth] to make a robe for God at the Transfiguration at 14s an ell: £4 18s. (p. 509)

[3 July] For 1¾ ells of white *trillis* [. . .] to make a pair of white hose [*chausses*] for God to wear at the Transfiguration.[1] (p. 527)

Note that here Jesus should go inside the mountain to dress himself in a white robe (and the whitest that can be found) with a mask [face] and hands of polished gold.[2] (p. 177)

---

[1] Jesus and the Apostles are normally barefoot.
[2] The accounts include a reference to 'gloves for God' (p. 552) which may be what are worn here. There would not be time to paint Jesus' face as is done for Raphael at the Resurrection: 'Note to warn the painter at this point to go to Paradise to paint Raphael's face red'. (p. 410)

(ii) How to fake Christs' nudity on the stage

Mons, pp. 364–5; trans. *Staging*, p. 146

Then [*the soldiers*] *pretend to strip him naked and lay him on the ground* (p. 364). [The Virgin Mary approaches] *Then Our Lady passes right through them and goes to Jesus and pretends to fasten her wimple round him, but there is one already there* (p. 365).

H56   Accounts and directions for the Last Supper

Mons; trans. *Staging*, pp. 125, 126, 143

(i) The accounts list the food needed

For a roast lamb on this day on the stage, for God keeping the Passover with his Apostles, etc.: 16s. For another lamb of paste, covered with roast fish, eaten on this day at the said Passover instead of the other [mentioned] above, because it was Saturday: 3s.[1] For lettuces on this day on the stage, eaten at the said Passover with the said lamb: 3d. For roast fish on this day on the stage, both to cover the said lamb made of paste and for the meal and supper taken on this day at the house of Simon the Leper: 30s [. . .] To Maistre Guillaume for eels on this day, used in one of the stage effects [*secrés*]: 2s.[2] (p. 571)

[1] Saturday was a fast day.
[2] Presumably the eels were used for the 'roast fish'.

(ii) Stage direction for the Eucharist

And there is no other food on the table except small white wafers [*fouaces*] *with the others[1] and the lamb, and Jesus takes a bread cake* [ung pain] *and breaks it in half and says:* [. . .] (p. 279)

[*After the washing of feet*] *Jesus should take a host* [hostie] *and hold it in his right hand and put the left over it.[2]* (p. 281)

[1] The reference in the second direction to a host suggests that the *fouaces* represent the hosts and the 'others' refers to the *pain* which he breaks.
[2] The gestures here are similar to the Eucharistic Manual Acts.

(iii) The Apostles wear special clothes

The Apostles should here be wearing white shoes [sorles] *on their feet and be girt with leather belts* [coroyes] *or sashes* [tarelles] *over their robes, their mantles taken off,[1] and with a white staff in their hands like a pilgrim's staff.* (p. 279)

[1] The Apostles' mantles were crimson (p. 292). Before they are called they wear their *habis mecaniques* [clothes of their craft] (p. 160) or *habit de pescheur* [fishermen's clothes] (p. 149).

H57   Day-by-day running costs for the Mons *Passion*

Mons; trans. *Staging*, pp. 126, 204

(i) Fresh food for the stage is bought each day

[Day One] For withered and fresh [*viezes et nouvelles*] apples, also cherries bought today for putting on the trees of Earthly Paradise: 5s. (p. 564)

[Day Two] For a piece of mutton on this day on the stage for the meal of the Three Kings' servants: 4s. For bread on this day on the stage, both for the said meal and for the children in Heaven: 5s. For three measures of wine on this day on the stage: 15s. For two barrels of beer on this day on the stage: 40s.[1] (p. 566)

[Day Four] For a shoulder of mutton, a breast of veal, and a chicken pie on this day on the stage for the Marriage at Cana: 16s. (p. 568)

---

[1] Entries for bread, wine and beer occur every day, also payments for meals for the actors and orga-nisers in the local inns.

(ii) A banquet on stage for all the actors

To Collart Doureau, cook in the same town [. . .] for his salary for preparing the supper for the actors in the Passion, given afterwards on the 13 July 1501 on the said stage, was paid, in addition to the £24 17s then given to the actors to celebrate together [*pour eulx recreer ensemble*], herewith, 50s. (p. 582)

THE VALENCIENNES PASSION

The text of the Valenciennes *Passion*, which was divided into twenty-five playing days, survives in two unpublished, illustrated manuscripts, copied about 1570 and now in the Bibliothèque Nationale.[1]

Manuscript 12536 also contains a document signed by the actors, from which it is easy to see that this was not a civic performance but an enlarged example of the kind of *ad hoc* group, bound together by legal contract, noted from Draguignan [see **E93**] and Toulon. The first part of the document (which was clearly written after the performance) gives detailed information about the organisation of the different aspects of the play including *secrets* and music. Then follow details of the financial arrangements including fines for failure to fulfil the contract, which are reminiscent of the rules of the Chambers of Rhetoric [see **H6**, **H7**] so it is not sur-prising to find that many of the actors listed at the beginning of the document were also *Rhetoriciens* [see **H58**]. Information about the actual staging can be deduced from the stage directions given in both the manuscripts and the lists of the *feintes* or *secrets* included at the beginning of each *journee* in the Rothschild manu-script.[2]

1 Both Valenciennes plays are based, like Mons, on the Gréban-Michel *Passions* but the twenty-day play shares the Flood play found in Mons, and both include extracts from the so-called Arras *Passion*, which survives in a manuscript of the 1460s (though it was probably written earlier). It is often attributed to Eustace Mercadé whose *Vengeance* play is found in the same manuscript. The *Passion* was certainly from the Low Countries, for extracts (including the Visitation and Magnificat) are used in the Lille plays as well as the two Valenciennes *Passions*.
2 An analysis of the play with full text of each day's list of *feintes* and reproductions of all the miniatures is given in Elie Konigson, *La Représentation d'un mystère de la Passion à Valenciennes en 1547*, Paris, 1969.

H58   The participants in the Valenciennes *Passion*, 1547

Mystères, vol. II, pp. 145–9

It is to be noted that to provide for the expenses and organisation of the said Passion, the said companions elected in Valenciennes [thirteen] supervisors both to be their masters and leaders and to ensure peace and unity if there should be any division or argument among them, and the said supervisors could punish and fine the said actor-companions [*compagnons jueurs*] for any misdemeanour without recourse to the magistrates. [Here is inserted the picture reproduced as **H59**.]

Item: it is also to be noted that the said thirteen and all the players who undertook the business, together agreed to pay any expenses incurred, if by chance there should be some disaster [*mortalité*] or war so that they could not act or carry out the said enterprise; in addition if anyone undertook to perform a role and then did not want to fulfil his undertaking, they could distrain on his person and his goods [. . .]

Here follow the names of the thirteen supervisors, some of whom were also actors: [they include]

Louys Wicart, supervisor and inventer of several *secrets*, which he himself directed and worked at the right time, and also he saw that the *silete* were performed without the *originateurs*[1] having to give any indication.

Jean Steclin, superintendent and inventer of several *secrets* and making them work, actor of several major roles like Herod Antipas, Jairus, Antipater and others [. . .]

Here follow the names of the three *originateurs*, Mesire Philippe Caraheu, priest [. . .] Roland Gerard, clerk of the *béguinage*,[2] Christoflin Hanelois, [. . .] *originateur*, [. . .] together with Louis Wicart organised and distributed the roles to the different actors as appropriate [*selon la faculté le queroit*] [. . .]

Here follow the names of the actors who did not share in the *obligation* [the financial agreement noted above].

Jehan Rasoir, actor [. . .] of the presence[3] of Our Redeemer Jesus Christ;

Gratien Guiot, actor of the presence of God the Father in Heaven [. . .]

Gilles Carlier, a young clerk [. . .] whom it pleased God to summon by accidental death during the said enterprise after having played the king of Iscariot, on whom may God have mercy.

[. . .]

Here follow the names of several young boys and young girls who played several roles [including]:

Josse de Ricque, player of several roles like the presence of Jesus Christ disputing in the Temple, Jairus' daughter and many others.

Guislain Rasoir played several roles as an angel and also the childhood of the Virgin Mary for the Presentation in the Temple.

[. . .]

The names of the young girls who took part [include] Jennette Caraheu, chosen to represent and play the person of the Virgin Mary and before that the role of Agar, St Anne's serving maid.[4]

---

[1] The term *originateurs* may suggest the prime movers in the organisation, the producers, or the compilers of the text which uses material from several earlier Passions especially Gréban and Michel.

[2] These lay communities of women were common in the Low Countries in the sixteenth century.

[3] The term '*presence de*' is used not only for the Persons of the Trinity but for several other roles including Judas.

[4] In Mons the Mary of the Presentation in the temple was played by a seven-year-old girl, and the Mary of the Annunciation and Nativity by a fourteen-year-old. *Notre Dame*, played by a man, took over at the scene of the Three Kings. It seems probable that Valenciennes followed a similar system though the name of the actor who played *Notre Dame* is not given in the list.

H59   Coloured painting of one of the Valenciennes superintendents

Bibliothèque Nationale, Paris: Valenciennes MS 12536, fo. 293 recto

The director wears late sixteenth-century costume: a violet doublet with red sleeves, yellow trunk-hose and stockings and black shoes. Like the character in the Fouquet miniature [see **E22**], he has a staff in his left hand, but his right holds a scroll rather than a book. Although there is no title given, the position of this picture in the midst of the document about the organisation [**H58**] makes the identity of this figure almost a certainty.

H60   The Valenciennes contract, signed by the actors.

Mystères, vol. II, pp. 149–52; trans. *Staging*, pp. 43–5

Here follows the detail of the obligation as it was drawn up and written on parchment.

Order for the play and *mystère* of the Passion and Resurrection [. . .] beginning on the Monday of Whitsuntide, in the year 1547.

Item. All the actors [*jueurs*] will be obliged to swear an oath and make a contract before a representative of the overlord and a notary to act on the days decreed by the supervisors unless they are excused by illness.

Item. The actors will be required to accept the roles offered to them by the supervisors and *originateurs*.

Item. The actors will be required to attend rehearsals [*records*] on the days and times appointed; if there is no reasonable excuse, each time they fail to appear they will be fined three farthings [*patarts*].

Item. Each actor will be required on playing days to attend and appear on the stage to rehearse, on pain of six farthings [. . .]

Item. All actors are forbidden to meddle with or be so bold as to murmur against the supervisors ordained and deputed to manage matters [. . .] on pain of such fine as the said supervisors shall exact.

Item. No actor shall leave the acting area until after the second session [*cambre*][1] without leave of the supervisors or reasonable excuse, on pain of ten farthings.

Item. No actor shall stand at the gate or meddle with taking the money but leave this to those deputed to do so by the said supervisors, on pain of 6 farthings.

Item. All the actor-companions given a role by the said supervisors shall be required to hand over each of them one gold ecu [= £6T] or equivalent when they accept the first role as contribution to the expenses if they wish to participate in the profits or losses [*au bon et au maulvais*], and also to pay any fines they may incur, and at the end each one will get back what he contributed unless there is a loss.

Item. That the actors who do not wish to contribute the aforementioned gold ecu shall agree to await whatever the supervisors shall give them for each day at the end of the performances.

Item. As for the gain and profit, if there is any, it shall be divided in two parts i.e. one half fairly and equally between all those who have contributed money: supervisors, actors, or administrators, and if one has paid out more than another he shall not therefore receive any larger amount; and the other half shall be divided among the actors and administrators only, by shares as ordained, according to their merits, by the said supervisors, and no actors or administrators shall [receive a share] without the agreement of at least seven of the said supervisors.

Item. That no man or woman should be admitted to the play without paying except the supervisors, actors, and administrators only, not including their wives, children, or family.[2]

[signing details]

[1] Each *journee* in this play is only about 2,000 lines, so it is possible that two were played on each day with a refreshment break in between (as at Mons).
[2] In Mons, wives of those taking the money were admitted free (p. 576).

H61   The drawing of the Valenciennes stage by Hubert Cailleau

Bibliothèque Nationale, Paris: Valenciennes MS 12536, fo. l verso–2

Each of the two manuscripts has such a drawing, but the two are not identical. The elaborate roofs are reminiscent of the contemporary Rhetoricians' stages [see **H10(i)**]. The pictures illustrating each day's action are said (in the manuscript) to be the work of one, Hubert Cailleau 'who also presented [*donna*] the portrait of the stage [*hourdement*] of the theatre, with Jacques des Moelles as it is shown in this book'. There is much difference of opinion among scholars as to the accuracy and reliability of the drawing, but it compares positively with the data from Mons. The locations shown are identified as Paradise, 'a hall', Nazareth, the Temple, Jerusalem, the Palace, the Bishop's house, the Golden Gate, the Sea [of Galilee], Limbo, and Hell.

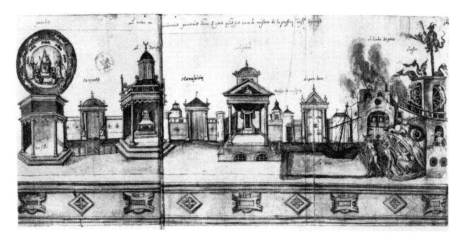

H62   The Valenciennes *Passion* makes a profit
Mystères, vol. II, pp. 151–2

Item that all those who who wanted to come and hear the said Passion, had to pay, great or small, the sum of six deniers on each occasion [*pour checune fois*] and those who wanted to go up onto a stage [*hordemont*] such as had been prepared there [...] would pay 12 deniers and the receipts for the 25 days added up to £4,680 14s 6d. [Sale of materials after the play brought in £728 12s 6d]

Item to set against the receipts, for the staging, the actors' costumes and all other properties [*ustensilles*] used for the *secrets* and other purposes, is the sum of £4,179 4s 9p. Balance [*benefice*] £1,230 2s 3d.[1]

[1] This is the only recorded play surplus – Mons, Châteaudun [**see E17**] and Romans [**see E19**] all made a loss.

CATHOLICS AND CALVINISTS BOTH OPPOSE PLAYS

It became increasingly difficult to put on plays in the Spanish Netherlands. The custom of a 'poor tax' was established early in the sixteenth century,[1] and in 1559 Philip II published an edict demanding that all plays of any kind, whether serious or comic, should be subject to strict censorship 'for the greater peace and tranquillity of our subjects and the public weal'.[2] In 1563 seven men who staged a play of the Golden Calf followed by a farce were imprisoned and made to do public penance, barefoot and carrying candles. There was also strong anti-theatrical pressure from the clergy recalling the trouble that had followed the Ghent contest of 1539: 'the men of Lille and the surrounding areas will kindle a fire which we shall have difficulty in quenching, with such assemblies of the people engendering great boldness and disputing over the Scriptures'.[3] At the same time, the Calvinists in the newly formed United Provinces also opposed plays as irreligious [see **H64**]. Regardless of these attacks, players still applied to do plays which were sometimes allowed [see **H63**]. Despite everything, then, the people of the Low Countries continued to enjoy their drama.

1.   Lefèbvre *Lille*, p. 28. The Low Countries had not, unlike France, previously had a law governing such payments [see **E6**].
2.   Ibid., p. 36.
3.   From a letter sent to Brussels in 1585 by the bishop of Tournai, Lefèbvre, *Lille*, p. 41

H63   Players apply for permission to stage the Passion, Lille, 1590

Lefèbvre *Lille*, p. 30

[1590] We, Jaspar Flameng [and others], all actors in plays and comedies [*comédies*] of this town of Lille, in order to attract the youth and the people of this town away from the taverns and wineshops on Sundays and holy days and to keep them in the town on these days without their leaving it, and also to avoid the rows and arguments [*noise et questions*] which often occur on these days as a result of drinking, these petitioners have the intention, with the help and assistance of their fellow actors and the permission of the most honoured lords, and indeed to provide an edifying example for the salvation of the said community, to present and perform at the next season of Easter in the town of Lille on the said Sundays and holy days at the accustomed hours, as has been done in times past, the Passion of Our Lord and Saviour Jesus Christ, as has been done in the past in the Court of Our Lord and King [the Palais du Rihours] and in other places; and the said petitioners promise to submit these [texts] beforehand and have them inspected and approved by the worthy Doctor Cupette and to submit them to you, my lords, at a time and place agreeable to you and to the satisfaction of your lordships. Having the intention also, in view of the cost and expenses that will be involved in this task, to charge 6d for each person on the understanding that they will pay to the poor[1] of the town the sum of £4 for each day that they perform, which the said petitioners would neither wish nor dare to do without your lordships' permission, which is the reason why these petitioners have addressed themselves to you, worthy and discreet gentlemen, beseeching you most humbly that you should grant them permission for this undertaking. And also they promise that in these plays they will conduct and comport themselves as they have done in the past in all honour and respectability without anything that can be criticised.[2]

[1] The permission was granted but the levy for the poor was raised to £5 per playing day.
[2] The play was repeated in 1593 and the same year the Rhetoricians performed 'Pyramus and Thisbe' to celebrate the Peace of Vervins.

H64   The Prince of Orange bans all performances of plays in Zeeland, 1583

C. P. Serrure, 'De Rhetorijkkamers van Zeeland', *Vaderlandsch Museum* 2 (1858), pp. 287–90

Item, as it has been found that because of public Rhetoricians' and similar plays and *Esbatementen* at this time many are irritated and scandalised – because it seems to originate in arrogance – and also because on such occasions ungodly and useless arguments and reasoning are set before the public, causing ungodliness, levity and disturbances,

THEREFORE, we have [decided] having taken advice as before, to forbid and prohibit explicitly those public Plays, and *Esbatementen* [from being performed] anywhere in this Province, until such time as will be decided otherwise [. . .] Given in the Court of Zeeland at Middelburgh, under the Seal of the aforementioned States herewith attached to this Edict, the eighth of February of the year 1583.

By his Excellency,[1]

On behalf of the Delegated Counsellors of the aforementioned States and at their behest.

By me Ch.Roels[2] (p. 290)

[1] 'William the Silent' (1533–84).
[2] Calvinist Holland continued to oppose the drama and in 1668 the consistory tried to prevent the Prince of Orange [later William III of England] from giving permission to the Queen of France's players to perform in The Hague. A final compromise was reached: the French would not present farces or scandalous plays; they would not perform on Sundays or holy days; and the prices of the seats would be doubled (thus serving both God and Mammon). See Paul Zunthor, *Daily Life in Rembrandt's Holland*, London, 1962, p. 84.

Section I
The Iberian Peninsula (including Majorca)

Edited by LOUISE M. HAYWOOD

Abbreviations

Álvarez Pellitero	Ana María Álvarez Pellitero, 'Aportaciones al estudio del teatro medieval en España', *El Crotalón: Anuario de Filología Española* 2 (1985), pp. 15–35
'Aragón'	Víctor García de la Concha, 'Teatro medieval en Aragón', in *La literatura en Aragón*, ed. Aurora Egido, Saragossa, Caja de Ahorros y Monte de Piedad de Zaragoza, Aragón y Rioja, 1984, pp. 33–49
Castilla	Miguel Ángel Pérez Priego, *Teatro medieval*, vol. II, *Castilla*, Páginas de Biblioteca Clásica, Barcelona, 1997
Cervera	Agustí Duran i Sanpere and Eulàlia Duran, *La Passió de Cervera: Misteri del segle XVI*, Biblioteca Torres Amat, n.s. 1, Barcelona, 1984
Chronicle of Muntaner	*The Chronicle of Muntaner*, trans. Lady Goodenough, Hakluyt Society, 2nd series, 47, 50, London, 1920, 1921 [Lady Goodenough's translation has been corrected and modernised against the *Crònica*, retaining Catalan theatrical terms.]
Crònica de Muntaner	Ramon Muntaner, *Crònica*, ed. E. B., Col. lectio Popular Barcino 19, 141–8, 9 vols., Barcelona, 1927, 1951–2
Cuéllar	*Religión y sociedad medieval: El catecismo de Pedro de Cuéllar (1325)*, ed. José-Luis Martin and Antonio Linage Conde, Salamanca, Junta de Castilla y León, 1987
Donovan	Richard B. Donovan, *The Liturgical Drama in Medieval Spain*, Toronto, Pontifical Institute of Mediaeval Studies, 1958
Festa d'Elx	*Festa d'Elx: edición inglesa de la Guía de la Festa d'Elx*, Alfons Lorens, Rafael Navarro Mallebrera, Joan Castaño García and trans. Pamela M. King and Asunción Salvador-Rabaza Ramos, Elche, Patronato Nacional del Misterio de Elche, 1990
Gillet	Joseph E. Gillet, '*Danza del Santissimo Nacimiento*, a Sixteenth-Century Play by Pedro Suárez de Robles', *PMLA* 43 (1928), pp. 614–34
Girona	Pep Vila and Montserrat Bruget, *Festes públiques i teatre a Girona: Segles XIV–XVIII (Notícies i documents)*, Gerona, Ajuntament de Girona, 1983

Gómez Moreno	Ángel Gómez Moreno, *El teatro medieval castellano en su marco románico*, Persiles 203, Madrid, 1991
Gracisla	*La coronación de la señora Gracisla*, in *Dos opúsculos isabelinos: 'La coronación de la señora Gracisla' (BN MS 22020) y Nicolás Núñez, 'Cárcel de Amor'*, ed. Keith Whinnom, Exeter Hispanic Texts 22, University of Exeter, 1979
Huerta Viñas	Ferran Huerta Viñas, *Teatre bíblic: Antic Testament*, Els Nostres Clàssics, Col. lectió A, 109–10, Barcelona, 1976
Lucas de Iranzo	*Hechos del Condestable Don Miguel Lucas de Iranzo (Crónica del siglo XV)*, ed. Juan de Mata Carriazo, Colección de Crónicas Españolas 3, Madrid, 1940
Massot i Muntaner	Josep Massot i Muntaner, 'Notes sobre la supervivència del teatre català antic', *Estudis Romànics* 11 (1962), pp. 49–101
Moll	Jaime Moll, 'Música y representaciones en las constituciones sinodales de los Reinos de Castilla del siglo XVI', *Anuario Musical* 30 (1977), pp. 209–43
Mota	Neil T. Miller, *Obras de Henrique da Mota: As origens do teatro ibérico*, Clássicos Sá da Costa, n.s., Lisbon, 1982
Romeu	Josep Romeu, *Teatre hagiogràfic*, Els Nostres Clàssics, Col. lectío A, 79–82, 3 vols., Barcelona, 1957
Shergold	N. D. Shergold, *A History of the Spanish Stage from Medieval Times until the End of the Seventeenth Century*, Oxford, 1967
Staging	see general bibliography [Wherever possible *Staging* translations have been compared with published transcripts and edited accordingly, using source language theatre terms.]
Stern	Charlotte Stern, *The Medieval Theater in Castile*, Medieval and Renaissance Texts and Studies 156, Binghamton, N.Y., 1996
Toledo	Carmen Torroja Menéndez and María Rivas Palá, *Teatro en Toledo en el siglo XV: 'Auto de la Pasión' de Alonso del Campo*, Anejos of the *Boletín de la Real Academia Española* 35, Madrid, 1977
Valencia	M. Sanchis Guarner, 'El Misteri assumpcionista de la Catedral de València', *Boletín de la Real Academia de Buenas Letras de Barcelona* 32 (1967–8), pp. 97–112
Vicente	Gil Vicente, *The Boat of Hell*, in *Three Discovery Plays: 'Auto da Barca do Inferno', 'Exortação da Guerra' and 'Auto da Índia'*, ed. and trans. Anthony Lappin, Warminster, 1996
Young	see general bibliography

Introduction

Perhaps the most frequently cited observation about dramatic activity in the Iberian Peninsula is Fernando Lázaro Carreter's observation that, 'The history of theatre in Spanish in the Middle Ages is the history of an absence.'[1] It is curious that this view still prevails despite the increasing number of studies and editions which are being published. This section brings together a selection of documents which certainly refutes the view that medieval drama has left no traces in the region, although these are not always in the form of performance texts or eyewitness accounts. The documents collected here represent three broad categories of drama: religious drama [also see **Section B**], processions associated with Corpus Christi [see **Section C**], and court pageantry. For reasons of brevity, documents concerned with the activities of *juglares* are excluded, although some of their activities may be appropriately regarded as performative or even paradramatic. Also omitted are other genres with performance potential, such as dramatic dialogues, disputations and sermons, with the exception of a Portuguese dialogue [see **I39**] which may have had links with the development of drama in that language.

It is unfortunate that the study of the drama of the Iberian Peninsula has yet to attract a collective project like the Records of Early English Drama, although the History of the Spanish Theatre project initiated by the late John Varey to print the records of early modern Spanish drama has done excellent work to further the accessibility of texts and records. Fortunately, since the pioneering work of Richard Donovan a number of important monographs, critical bibliographies, editions and articles have appeared and a selection of the main works is included in the general bibliography. Of particular interest to readers of what follows are Charlotte Stern's monograph *The Medieval Theater in Castile* (1996) and *Staging*, both of which provide further source documents in English translation.

In order to understand the development of medieval drama on the Iberian Peninsula and Majorca it is imperative to have a grasp of the historical and political background. The Iberian Peninsula was invaded by Muslims in 711 and throughout the late Middle Ages the Christian kingdoms struggled to gain control. The two communities lived together – along with a third religious group, the Jews – at war and in peace for nearly eight centuries. In the East there were strong links with the French and with Rome so that Aragon evolved more in step with the rest of Europe than the West. As the Christians gradually pushed forward their frontiers the kingdoms which comprised the Iberian Peninsula were in considerable flux [see **I1**]. Portugal became an independent kingdom in 1139. Castile first began its expansion as a country under Fernán González (931–70) and became a kingdom under Fernando I of León and Castile (1037–67). The thirteenth-century Christian expansionist push was successful; with Aragon under Jaime I (1213–85) taking Majorca (1229) and Valencia (1238), and Castile under Fernando III of Castile (1217–52) and of León (1230–52) and his son, Alfonso X 'the Wise' of Castile (1252–84), taking Córdoba (1236), Murcia (1243), Jaén (1246), Seville (1248) and Cádiz (1263) [see **I1**].

The process of the unification of Castile and Aragon began in 1410 when the death of Martin I of Aragon (reigned 1395–1410) led to a crisis in accession which resulted in the election of Fernando of Antequera, regent to Juan of Castile during his minority, as king of Aragon. This process culminated in 1469 with the marriage of Fernando of Aragon (reigned 1479–1516) and Isabel of Castile (reigned 1474–1504), known as the Catholic Monarchs, who united their crowns ten years later. Together they completed the reconquest with the seizure of Granada in December 1492.

The survival pattern of documents relating to the medieval theatre of the Iberian Peninsula and Majorca differs between the East and West. To the East the division corresponds to Aragon. From this area good documentary evidence survives for the historian of secular and religious theatre. To the West, Castile and Portugal provide a far scarcer source of documents [see **I2**]. Consequently the extracts presented in sections I and II below are grouped to reflect this pattern; however, in section III all materials are organised by topic. Documents are always grouped chronologically.

1.   'La historia del teatro en lengua española durante la Edad Media es la historia de una ausencia'; see Fernando Lázaro Carreter, *Teatro medieval*, Madrid, 1987, p. 9.

I1   Map showing the progress of the Reconquest

Angus Mackay, *Spain in the Middle Ages: From Frontier to Empire, 1000–1500*, London, 1977; reprinted 1983, p. xiv

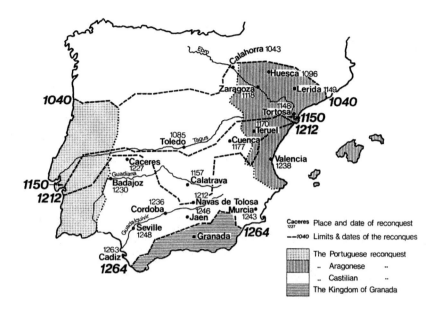

I2   Map of places from which documents are cited

© Peter Beaver, 1998

I   *Theatre and the Church*

THE EAST: ECCLESIASTICAL PROHIBITIONS

There is a strong tradition of Church and other religious theatre in the eastern portion of the Peninsula which has been fully documented. Nonetheless, just as elsewhere, ecclesiastical authorities expressed concern about what constituted appropriate performance inside church buildings [see **B26**, **B27**, **B28(c)**, **B30(a)**, **(b)**; **C32**; **J14**, **J17**]. Mossen Joan Martínez, *vicario general* to Francesc Ferrer Bishop of Majorca, in the fifteenth century, drew up a prohibition against the performance of *representacions* at Easter which was published in the cathedral and in parochial churches [see **I3**]. In 1517 Rodrigo del Mercado's *vicario general* repeated it and also forbade performances on 'the other days of Holy Lent' (Massot i Muntaner, p. 52). Further decrees in other areas followed which forbade performances which had not been granted express permission (Valencia, 1565, 1590; Gerona, 1691).

I3   Mossen Joan Martínez on *representacions*, Easter, 1470

Massot i Muntaner, p. 97

The Council of the honourable chapter of the said Cathedral of Majorca [. . .] prohibits [. . .] any secular person of whatever condition or estate [. . .] as much on Thursdays as on Good Fridays by day and at night from performing in the said churches, chapels or monasteries any *representacions*, and being in them or performing in them [*ni en aquelles sien ni entrevinguen*], except such *representacions* as are usually presented in the cathedral on Good Fridays during daytime, according to what is decreed in the *consueta* of the said cathedral.

THE WEST: CHURCH DOCUMENTS AND LEGAL INSTRUMENTS

Critics have repeatedly noted the paucity of early testimonies from the West to Church-sponsored theatre, from the most basic form of tropes to full-scale liturgical drama and religious theatre for performance in church. The few tropes surviving have been linked to practices in Catalan or French ecclesiastical centres. However, a careful collation of clerical documents and legal instruments suggests that religious drama in some form was performed in churches, and that this practice gave rise to more popular forms of entertainment which were then condemned by ecclesiastical authorities. The first such condemnation from the West of the Peninsula occurs in the *Primera partida*, section 34, of Alfonso X 'the Wise' of Castile's *Siete partidas* (1256–65) [see **C32**].[1]

1.   In some versions of the *Partidas* this *título* appears as number 35.

CLERICAL AND LEGAL CONDEMNATION

Imprecise condemnations, such as that expressed by Rodrigo Sánchez de Arévalo, bishop of Zamora (1404–70) in his *Speculum humanae vitae* [see **I5**], continued to be made as late as the fifteenth century. Indeed, some ecclesiastical pronouncements do no more than forbid clerics from associating with *juglares*, travelling minstrels and entertainers: for instance the Council of Valladolid (1228) or the *Statutes* promulgated by Tello, archbishop of Braga, in 1281, although in the latter the choice of vocabulary seems to suggest the existence of dumb shows, '*jograis, mimos e histriões*'.[1] Similarly general but nonetheless of interest is a confessional manual from León which gives advice on hearing the confessions of secular entertainers and which, in order to facilitate the confessor's task, defines the various types of *estriones* [see **I4**].[2] It may be compared with Thomas de Chabham's *Penitential* [see **A35**].

The value of these condemnations by ecclesiastics as proof of theatrical activity must be carefully weighed as they are often interdependent and/or rely heavily on edicts issuing from the Papacy. It has been argued, for example, that Alfonso's section 34 may derive from Pope Gregory's *Decretals*, which in turn gloss a decree of Pope Innocent III [see **B27(a)**, **(b)**]. Despite the textual dependence of much of Alfonso's section 34 on the *Decretals*, there may be independent corroboration of theatrical activity at Alfonso's court in the form of a Latin dramatic disputation. The king's secretary Juan Gil de Zamora's *Liber Mariae*, probably from the third quarter of the thirteenth century, contains a 'Four Daughters of God' disputation of a type which elsewhere was performed; however, its narrative setting and the lack of positive evidence make its presentation unlikely.[3]

1.   The original Latin text of Council of Valladolid, which translates Canon 16 of the Fourth Lateran Council (1215), is lost although a translation of 1266 is extant. I cite Tello from Gómez Moreno, p. 63.
2.   For observations about, and a partial edition of, Martín Pérez's *Libro de las confesiones* see Gómez Moreno, pp. 35–6, 139–43.
3.   Gil's version is of the same type as that in Caesarius of Heisterbach's *Libri VIII miraculorum* and Jacobus a Voragine's *Legenda aurea*, which are not associated with performance. The theme reappears in some sixteenth-century *autos* from the *Códice de los*

autos viejos: see Spurgeon W. Baldwin and James W. Marchand, 'A Dramatic Fragment of the *Four Daughters of God* from Medieval Spain', *Neophilologus* 72 (1988), pp. 376–9, n. 22.

I4   A Leonese confessional manual, 1312–17
Gómez Moreno, pp. 139, 141

Chapter 138. On *estriones* whose craft [*ofiçio*] is dangerous, and first on those who transform their bodies into other appearances.

Furthermore there is another dangerous craft which the Scriptures call *estriones*, of which there are four types: first are those who transform themselves to other likenesses, putting on masks [*vestiendo caras*] and other apparel in the semblances of devils and beasts, and they bare their bodies and blacken themselves [with ash] and make reprehensible movements and lewd faces and carry out very depraved and vile minstrelesque acts [*joglerías*] and alter their voices; and at times fights, deaths and other evils take place. And they do these things to give pleasure to the people, and some to earn something [. . .] All of these are in and live in great danger of their souls and they cannot do penance unless they stop these activities.

I5   A general condemnation of theatre, fifteenth century
Gómez Moreno, pp. 38–9[1]

It is decreed that the theatrical art is not in the least fit to be either performed or named [. . .] I do not know who comes out the more stupid, the *histrio* or someone who laughs at the *histrio*; perhaps the one who pays [for this], he is the most foolish.

[1] Dr Anthony Lappin of the University of Manchester very generously translated this extract for me.

ECCLESIASTICAL DISAPPROVAL

Synods and councils which refer to the performance of *juegos* and *representaciones* represent a broad geographical and chronological range, for example Toledo (1324), Cuellár (1325), Aranda del Duero (1473) [see **I13**], Oporto (1477), Alcalá (1480) [see **I6**], Ávila (1481) [see **I14**], Seville (1490, confirmed 1512), and Badajoz (1501) [see **I7**]. In an edict of 3 March 1515, Francisco de Herrera, *vicario general* to Cardinal Jiménez de Cisneros, prohibited religious *representaciones* on the grounds that they may be performed by the uneducated and therefore misrepresent scripture [see **I8**]; a similar concern is expressed by Fray Antonio de Guevara, bishop of Mondoñedo (Galicia), who further observes that such *representaciones* take place outside of churches and prevent the congregation from attending Mass [see **I9**].

The synods' and councils' acts deal with dramatic activity associated with a number of festivals ranging from the general to the specific, such as Christmas and

Easter, the Feast of Fools and vigils. The Synod of Oporto convoked and presided over by Dom Luìs Pires, bishop of Oporto on 11 December 1477 noted and condemned secular *jogos* [see **I10**]. It also prohibited *jogos* and *representações* in the Corpus Christi procession, and at Christmastide [*festa e noite de Natal*] banned all types of secular activity. The Synod of Don Pedro of Cuéllar, bishop of Segovia, on 8 March 1325, is typical in its condemnation of performances which distract the congregation from the solemnity of the festival; however, it also makes specific reference to the play of the Maries, most probably a *Visitatio sepulchri* [see **I11**]. This is not the only document which preserves details of particular celebrations. A *Consuetudinario y Martirologio* from the Cathedral of Palencia (first half of the fifteenth century) contains a full description of a *Depositio et Elevatio*.[1]

Indeed, the secular nature of celebrations associated with the Feast of Fools came in for particular and repeated condemnation [for examples see **B24**, **B27(a)**, **B28**, **B30**, **C32(a)**, **J14**, **J17**, etc.]. The Synod of Segovia celebrated in Aguilafuerte by Don Juan Arias Dávila, bishop of Segovia, in June 1472 describes the types of secular celebrations associated with the Feast of Fools and condemns them by indicating that they are improper and slight God [see **I12**]. Canon 19 of the Council of Aranda (1473) legislated against indecent performances and, in particular, the use of disguises during the Feast of Fools and on some other high days and on the occasion of First Masses, but permits the institution of the Boy Bishop [*episcopellus*] provided it is carried out with due reverence [see **I13**; see also **B24**, **B28**, **J16**, **J18**, **J19**]. Later prohibitions concerning the celebration of the *episcopellus* and related ceremonies were also ratified by the synods of Ávila (1481) [see **I14**], Jaén (1511) and Calahorra and la Calzada (León, 1553). Finally, the Synod of Oporto (1477) [see **I15**] and chapter 9 of the constitution (1490) of Cardinal Diego Hurtado de Mendoza, archbishop of Seville, confirmed by provincial council presided by Don Diego Deza, 1512, are two of a number expressly concerned with secular theatrical activities and entertainments associated with vigils.[2]

1. See Álvarez Pellitero, pp. 29–30 and also **B5**.
2. Where consecutive items dealing with the same issues are quoted, I cite the first in full and only give the points of significant difference for subsequent documents.

GENERAL CLERICAL PROHIBITIONS

I6   A decree of the Synod of Toledo, Alcalá, 1480

Jesús Menéndez Peláez, *Teatro en Asturias de la Edad Media al siglo XVIII*, Gijón, 1981, p. 25

Amongst the other things which with all our heart and soul we desire is the honour and decency of the Holy Churches . . . in which often during some of the year's *fiestas* and other days under the cover of commemorating holy and contemplative things, ugly, reprehensible *juegos* are performed and impious and extremely dissolute words are spoken which distract from contemplation and move [the congregation] more to derision than inspire devotion to the *fiesta* or solemnity. And therefore we prohibit and reprove such profanation and defilement, and we order by statute when such festivals [require] for the sake of their sacred ceremony [*por solemnidad*] the performance of *representaciones* to bring the past to memory, that such words should not be said nor should reprehensible things be said or done which bring near to the faithful scandal or the cooling of devotion. We order that the two oldest Dignitaries and the president who are to be present [*que residieren*] each day on which the *representaciones* are to be held preside over what is said and done, over which we give them accountability [*conciencia*] and we grant them the power and authority to prevent all impiety and immodesty in deed and word.

I7   The Synod of Badajoz, 1501

Álvarez Pellitero, p. 33

(i) Reports of immodest *representaciones*

[. . .] under the guise of commemorating holy and contemplative things, *representaciones* of the *misterios* of the Birth and of the Passion and Resurrection of Our Lord, Redeemer and Saviour Jesus Christ take place which are carried out in such a manner as widely to provoke the public to derision and distract them from contemplation and proper devotion to the feast and solemnity and, what is worse, impious and very dissolute things are said and done.

(ii) Penalties for involvement

[. . .] we ban and prohibit the custom, which would be better called profanation and defilement, of doing and saying the impieties in churches which are said and done on Christmas Night under the cover of the joy which all faithful Christians ought to feel on that holy night, uttering, in the place of the blessings of the lessons of Matins, cacophonies and singing ugly and reprehensible songs, and getting up to other impious things.

I8   The edict of Francisco de Herrera, Toledo, 1515

Trans. Stern, p. 88

[. . .] acts of *representación*[1] such as of the Birth of Our Redeemer and Saviour Jesus Christ and of His sacred Passion and other *representaciones* of other *abtos de devociones* because they are performed by untutored and ignorant people who make and compose many diverse poems and stories in which they inject many and diverse errors concerning our holy Catholic faith [shall be prohibited.]

---

[1] I correct Stern's translation against the original as she quotes it. Note that she renders 'abtos de rrepresentación' as plays.

I9   A synodal decree of Fray Antonio de Guevara, 3 May 1541

Álvarez Pellitero, p. 34

Further it has come to our attention through the aforementioned pastoral tour [of the diocese] that at the sacred time of Lent and Holy Week many idle people become involved in performing *representaziones* [*sic*], in the style of worldly plays [*farsas*], which give rise to many improprieties; namely, that much is said in them that is not in the Gospels and, likewise, that they provoke much laughter and pleasure in those who listen to them, and, similarly, people fail to attend High Mass [*misa maior*] on Sundays and *fiestas* on account of gathering together where these *representaziones* [*sic*] are performed which are entirely not in praise but rather in vituperation of Christ.

CONDEMNATION OF CHRISTMAS AND EASTER PERFORMANCES

I10   The Synod of Oporto on appropriate Christmas performances, 1477

Luiz Francisco Rebello, *O primitivo teatro português*, Biblioteca Breve 5, Lisbon, 1977, p. 35; translation adapted here from Vicente, p. 10 [cf. **B27(b)**]

Neither *chanceletas* nor any other songs may be sung, nor may *jogos* be performed in the choir of the church, unless it be a good and devout *representação* such as that of the Manger [*Presépio*] or of the Wise Kings, or others like these, which should be done with all piety [*honestidade*] and devotion and without laughter or other disturbance.

EASTER

I11   The Synod of Cuéllar, 1325

Cuéllar, p. 242

Further, clerics ought not consort in [*non deven usar de*] minstrelesque acts or with jesters [. . .] Furthermore *juegos* must not take place in churches unless they are *juegos* or *fiestas* such as those about the Maries and about the *monumento*,[1] but clerics should take care not vitiate the holy liturgy on account of such *juegos*.

---

[1] Álvarez Pellitero (pp. 25–7) argues that the Spanish term *monumento* refers to a *Depositio Christi* [see **B5(d)**, **B9(a)**] rather than to the *sepulchrum* visited by the Maries.

FEAST OF FOOLS

I12   The Synod of Segovia, June 1472

Castilla, p. 210

On St Stephen's, St John the Evangelist's and the Innocents' days and certain other feast-days [*días festivales*] whilst Mass and other Divine Offices are being said, it is customary to tell jokes, to perform tricks, scandalous acts [*escarnio*] and to say and do reprehensible, ugly and immodest things by which Our Lord is slighted, which ought to be very alien in a house of prayer and Divine Office.

I13   The Council of Aranda, December 1473

Gómez Moreno, p. 64

(i) Description of the practice

On the feast-days of the Birth of Our Lord Jesus Christ and of Saints Stephen and John and of the Holy Innocents, as well as on other feast-days and even on the solemn occasion of First Masses, whilst the Holy Mass is being celebrated *ludi theatrales*, masques, *monstra*, spectacles and many other equally indecent things are done in church – raucous acts and lewd songs and burlesque sermons are said to such an extent that they vitiate the Divine Office and lead the people to be irreverent.

(ii) Prohibition

Throughout the cathedrals, metropolitan and other churches in our province we therefore, with the approval of the Council, prohibit all such corrupt practices [. . .] during the celebration of the Divine Office.

(iii) Permission for certain diversions

We do not intend to prohibit [by this] devout *repraesentationes* which move the people to devotion on high days or on any other day.

I14   The Synod of Ávila, 1481

Moll, pp. 227

(i) Feast of Fools' customs described

[. . .] during the recitation of Mass and the other Divine Offices, [men] appear as a matter of custom in disguise [*acostumbran fazer çaharrones*], wearing clothing contrary to their estate such as the apparel of women or friars and other different costumes, putting on other faces [*poniéndose otras caras*] than those our Lord desired to give them, dressing absurdly [*faciéndose homarraches*], uttering many jokes, scandalous comments [*escarnios*], and doing and saying lewd, ugly and indecent things.

(ii) Consent to *Episcopellus* [the Boy Bishop]

[...] but by this we do not ban or prohibit the pious and devout performance of the *obispillo* and the things and acts pertaining to it.

VIGILS

I15   The Synod of Oporto, 1477
Álvarez Pellitero, p. 32

During vigils [...] we order and strictly prohibit, under pain of excommunication, men as well as women, religious and secular, who to fulfil their devotion should wish to hold vigil in any church or monastery, chapel or hermitage, from carrying out or allowing or giving rise to *jogos*, *momos*, songs and dancing; nor should men dress in women's clothing nor women in men's, nor should they ring handbells nor church bells [*sinos nem canpãas*] nor [play] organs, lutes, guitars, viols, drums or any other instrument nor carry out other improprieties which very often provoke and cause the wrath of God to be visited on them and on the earth.

THE EAST: CHURCH-SANCTIONED RELIGIOUS DRAMA

Catalan liturgical manuscripts such as tropers and *consuetas* prove invaluable sources for liturgical and extra-liturgical theatre. The twelfth-century Ripoll Troper contains a *Visitatio sepulchri* which includes the oldest documented European *mercator* dialogue between the Maries and a seller of spices [see **C1**], whilst the Gerona *Consueta* of 1360 in its provision for eight Latin liturgical plays describes the use of a special *sepulchrum* in the *Visitatio sepulchri* [see **B11(a)**, **(b)**] Thriving traditions were centred around Gandía, Valencia, Gerona, and Majorca.

Extra-liturgical religious theatre is also in evidence. The celebration of Corpus Christi processions in the eastern portion of the Peninsula is well documented: from Barcelona, for example, come proclamations concerning the procession from 1320 onwards [see **C79**, **80**] with a first extant list of pageants dating from 1415, and a very extensive list for 1424 [see **I17**]. The city council commissioned Johan Çalom to build several new pageants, including floats of the Creation and Bethlehem with a complex use of canopies and wagons, for which an agreement was signed on 20 April 1453 (*Staging*, pp. 71–2). At Gerona such a procession began around the same date with inventories dating from 1470 [see **I20**]. In 1391 Barcelona's records describe costumed angels walking in the parade, while at Valencia between 1400 and 1408 a variety of costumed figures accompanied the floats, which were wheeled or carried *rocas* or *rochas* [see **C80**]. A dedicated storage building for the floats was probably begun in 1435, extended in 1441 and finished in 1447.[1] By 1571 *representacions* were performed on most of the floats, of which there were eleven.[2] From Saragossa proclamations concerning Corpus Christ have been documented from 1423 to 1502. The celebration of Corpus Christi on the

Iberian Peninsula shows a development from a simple procession with musicians and costumed walkers through the use of floats with tableaux to spoken or sung plays [see **C78**, **C79**, **C80**, and **I16**, **I17**, **I18**].

In 1355 a play commemorating the Passion of Christ was performed in the market square at Pollença (Majorca) before the townsfolk, although no text survives [see **I16**].[3] In the same year the municipal council's account books included those for a play of the three Maries [*joch de III Meries*], first mentioned in 1349.[4] From Cervera documentary evidence shows that a Passion play was performed at the church of Santa Maria from 1481 and a *Misteri de la Passió* by Pere Ponç and Baltasar Sança from 1534 is extant [see **I18**]. Very important medieval and early Renaissance Assumption plays survive from Tarragona (probably the earliest vernacular example of the form), Valencia [see **I21**] and Elche [see **I19**, **I53**], the last of which is still performed today. The earliest record to refer to the *Festa d'Elx* [the Elche Assumption] is a 1370 letter from Doña María of Aragon whilst the earliest extant reference to the performance is in a petition of September 1530 from the Cofraría de la Humil Verge María to the municipal council requesting that it pay the cost of gilding the Virgin's chair. *Consuetas* survive from 1625 but a no longer extant version may have been in existence by the end of the fifteenth century.

The important Llabrés manuscript, also referred to as the Palma codex, compiled by Miguel Pasqual in the late 1590s contains forty-nine biblical and hagiographic plays, including a very small number in Castilian. It includes texts with complex staging, including a Resurrection scene in the *Consueta de Juy* (see *Staging*, pp. 88–9) and the appearance of St Francis bearing stigmata in the *Consueta de Sant Francesc* (*Staging*, p. 110) [also see **I67**].

The thriving tradition of liturgical drama in Gerona, well documented from the 1470s onwards, illustrates the extent to which theatre was incorporated into worship in the eastern portion of the Peninsula in the later Middle Ages. An inventory of the treasury of the cathedral at Gerona contains details about the plays performed during Lent whilst the *Llibre d'Obra* documents a payment for the construction of *cadafals*. Finally an ordinance adopted at Gerona in 1539 gives a full description of a *Visitatio sepulchri*, including references to the three Maries' costumes and to the other characters involved in the play [**see I20(iii)**].

1.   See Henri Mérimée, *L'Art Dramatique à Valencia depuis les origines jusqu'au commencement du XVIIe siècle*, Toulouse, 1913, p. 20.

2.   See H. Corbató, *Los misterios del Corpus de Valencia*, Berkeley, 1932, pp. 82–3 and 150–2.

3.   As the document is from May 1355 it is quite likely that the Passion play formed part of Corpus Christi celebrations.

4.   These documents have not been included for reasons of space. They can be consulted in Gabriel Llompart, 'La fiesta del "Corpus Christi" y representaciones religiosas en Barcelona y Mallorca (siglos XIV–XVIII)', *Analecta Sacra Tarraconesia: Revista de Ciencias Historicoeclesiásticas* 39 (1966), pp. 43–45.

116   A Passion play in the market square, Pollença, May 1355

Massot i Muntaner, p. 71

It was announced by the venerable Guilelmo Niell, at the little bay of Pollença before Our King, that on the day before a certain Sunday with nearly all of the commonalty and people of Pollença being in the market square of the aforementioned place, a *representatio* and remembrance [*memoria*] of the Passion of Our Lord Jesus Christ was performed [*fiebat*].

BARCELONA

117   Some *representacions* in the Corpus Christi procession, Barcelona, 1424[1]

A. Duran i Sanpere and Josep Sanabre, *Llibre de les solemnitats de Barcelona*, vol. 1, *1424–1546*, Barcelona, Institució Patxot, 1930, pp. 18–9

The *representacions* administered by the Cathedral:

First, Moises and Aaron; Ezekias and Jeremiah; Elijah and Elisha [Heliseu]; Ezekiel and Jonah; Abacuch [?] and Zachariah; Daniel and Isaiah; St John the Baptist, alone; the judges of St Susannah; St Susannah with the angel and Daniel; Judith with a handmaiden; St Raphael and Tobiah; the Annunciation of the Virgin Mary with the angels singing, 'A Deu magnifich' [the Magnificat].

The *entremés* of Bethlehem or the Nativity of Jesus Christ: the first King of the Orient mounted, alone; the second King, mounted and alone; the third King, mounted and alone; six Jews with capes and caps [*gramalles*].

The *entramés* [*sic*] of the Innocents with Rachel underneath; armed men [*l'homens d'armes*]; King Herod and his two wise men [*doctors*]; the *Alamanys*;[2] the twelve angels who sing, 'Loem la ostia sagrada'.

[*Representacions* administered] by the Monastery of St Anne:

Joachim and the shepherd; Sts Anne and Elizabeth; St Helen with the Emperor Constantine, with his wise men [*doctors*] and knights; St Mary the Egyptian with Zosimas and the lion; Sts Paula and Perpetua; St Elmo; St Heutriz (?).[3]

---

[1] *Staging* (pp. 127–8) lists properties stored at other sites and gives the full list for St Anne's.
[2] Probably the painters referred to as 'Alemany' and who have charge of other *entreméses*.
[3] St Heutriz is a female saint: I have been unable to identify her.

I18   A Passion cycle, Cervera, 1481–8

(i) First extant references to the play, 1481

Cervera, p. 17

Further, payment made by the bursar [*clavari*] to Bernardí Cardona and Pere Poujades to make the *cadafal* in the principal church where the *representació* of the *Passion of Jesus Christ* is being performed [*hon se féu*] this year, eleven sous.

(ii) Payment to Rochamora for a cadafal, 1486

Cervera, p. 17

Given to Jaume Rochamora, *verguer*, twenty sous which the town advanced for the erection of a *cadafal* in the principal church of the said town, which was used to perform the *representació* of the *Passion* which was ordered by the ordinary council celebrated on 5 March just passed.

(iii) Council order of 5 March for Good Friday, 1488

Cervera, p. 17

And further, the said honourable council wish, order and command that in praise and reverence of the most Holy Passion of Our Lord God Jesus Christ, a *representació* of it be performed on the next Easter Sunday, committing the town elders [*senyors de pahers*] to request of the priests of the venerable clergy [*preveres del venerable clero*] and other persons who will be suitable and necessary in this, that they should take responsibility for the said *representatió*. And that the expenditure for the said *representació* be made from the subvention of twenty sous.

I19   The Elche Assumption Play recorded, 26 September 1530

Festa d'Elx, p. 26, note 28

[. . .] the Assumption of the said very glorious Virgin Mary takes place in the month of August every year [. . .]

I20   Dramatic activities, Gerona, 1470–1546

(i) Inventory of the cathedral treasury, 1470, 1473, 1474, 1538, 1546

Girona, pp. 135–6

1470, item two *moniments*, one for the *representació* of the Resurrection
1473, two commissioned to assist the *representacions* of the Passion of the Lord

which was carried out on Sundays in Lent so that they be carried out with greatest reverence.

15 March 1474, the canons [*canonges*] took turns at overseeing the *representacions* [*per torn de las representacions*] and *jochs* on Easter Day

9 March 1538, the *representació* on Lenten *dominicas* according to the narrative [*hystorial*] of the Gospels is the responsibility of a canon

22 March 1546, the curate [*vicari*], because of his great expertise, was charged with the *representació* of the Passion of the Lord and the Seven Deadly Sins.

(ii) The construction of cadafals, Easter 1487

Girona, p. 136

I paid mestre Julià, the principle master of the said work, for the *cadafals* of the Easter *entremesos*.

(iii) Ordinance adopted by the cathedral chapter, 1539

Young, vol. II, p. 504

[. . .] therefore according to the order of ancient times let the *representationem*, popularly known as *The Three Maries* [*Les tres Maries*], be performed on the Easter festival of the resurrection of Our Redeemer Jesus Christ, for the present in the church of Gerona every year at Matins [. . .] namely, once the trope of the last responsory [*verbetta*] is said, the three Maries dressed in black as is the custom shall begin the accustomed verse after the invitatory psalm has been sung, and singing they go to the high altar where a *cadafale* will have been set up with many lights [*multa luminaria*] and there will be the Apothecary, his wife and small son and also the Merchant and his wife who shall not enter until the third lesson is finished and there they will perform [*fiat*] the *representatio* of the request for the unguent to anoint the most holy Body of Christ, as is the custom. When these same people doing the *representationem* come to the church there must be no small drums or drums [*tympana sive tabals*] nor trumpets nor any other types of music nor black men nor women [*niger neque nigra*] as servants nor are cakes and wine-flagons [??? *crustula, sive flaons*] to be thrown in any way. These, we observe, tend more to mockery than to knowing God, to the laughter and irreverence of the people and disturbance of the divine office.

VALENCIA

121 The Valencia Assumption first dated, 1569

Valencia, p. 97

In the year fourteen hundred and sixteen on the fifteenth of August the triumphant Assumption of Our Lady began to be celebrated [*se començó de hazer fiesta*] at the Cathedral of Valencia. And on account of it being on a Saturday the first year, it was decreed that it be celebrated for three days without interruption.

Church-sanctioned processions took place in connection with ecclesiastical celebrations at the Cathedral of Zamora. In 1273 the *monaziellos* [acolytes, choirboys]
received permission to process from the Hermitage of St Mark to the cathedral itself
on Palm Sunday and later to use the castle door for a *representación*. Account books
from León document expenditure on various plays [*juegos, representación, remembranza*] in the fifteenth century for the seasons of Christmas, Epiphany and Easter
[see **I23**].

The visit of the Catholic Monarchs, Isabel and Fernando, to Saragossa in 1487
gave rise to extraordinary expenditure on a Nativity play [see **I65**]. Nativity and
Passion plays survive from Toledo where the celebration of Corpus Christi was the
main dramatic activity: there are records of some thirty-three plays and far
greater expenditure seems to have been made in their preparation and maintenance than for other religious festivals.[1] The Toledo Corpus procession, first defi-
nitely documented in 1418, predates the Seville one in 1454 and brings forward the
earliest date by which Corpus celebrations were found in the Crown of Castile. The
surviving accounts for the Seville procession include payments for musicians in
costume as angels, several actors and a *roca* (Shergold, p. 97). As part of the 1501
Corpus celebrations in Salamanca Lucas, possibly Lucas Fernández, organised
juegos which seem to have included a Shepherds' play (Shergold, p. 84).

Non-liturgical records, such as account books, also refer to the production of
other *representaciones* in the cathedral and its chapels; however, it is difficult to tell
whether such plays were liturgical and the extent to which they were mimetic. The
city of Murcia's municipal archives include a list of Corpus Christi *juegos* from May
1471 [see **I26**]. Alonso del Campo was in charge of the accounts of the chapel of
San Blas at the Cathedral of Toledo and was responsible for the Corpus Christi
plays and a Passion play, which was most probably presented in the cathedral on
Good Friday [see **I25**]. It seems likely that he reworked earlier material, including
a performable Passion play from the fourteenth century or earlier.[2] The first sixth
of the Passion play has full stage directions [see **I25(iii)**]. An inventory of del
Campo's goods taken after his death includes a number of masks and two moulds,
one for a woman's face and the other for an angel (*Toledo*, pp. 196–7 and *Staging*,
p. 188). Accounts documents from León have records from 1452 for a Sibyl piece
[see **I64**], from 1458 for Magi [see **I23(i)**] and Passion plays [see **I23(ii)**] and from
1507 for a shepherds' play [see **I23(iii)**]. Finally, Don Miguel Lucas de Iranzo, constable of Jaén, numbered Christmas amongst the festivals celebrated by his court
[see **I24** and **I37, I51, I58**].

1. *Staging*, pp. 252–8 reprints accounts of the Corpus Christi expenses (including those
    for costumes and floats) for 1493.
2. See Alberto Blecua, 'Sobre la autoría del *Auto de la Pasión*', in *Homenaje a Eugenio
    Asensio*, Madrid, 1988, pp. 79–112.

ZAMORA

I22   Palm Sunday celebrations, Zamora, 1273–9

(i) A procession, 1273

Facsimile in *Las edades del hombre: libros y documentos en la Iglesia de Castilla y León*, Burgos:
Caja de Ahorros de Salamanca, Junta de Castilla y León, Caja de Ahorros del Círculo
Católico de Burgos, 1990, p. 304; Gómez Moreno, p. 66

The house [. . .] into which the *monaziellos* go on Palm Sunday when they come
from the procession from [the hermitage of] San Marco.

(ii) Clerics present a *representación* at the castle gate, 1279

Gómez Moreno, p. 66

[. . .] to sing the lines [*viessos*] and carry out the *representaçión* of Our Lord on Palm
Sunday.

LEÓN

I23   Dramatic presentations, León, 1458–1507

(i) Epiphany and Magi plays

Gómez Moreno, pp. 72–3

8 January 1458, payment to the choir boys for the *juegos* which they performed at
Epiphany.[1]
1459, payment to Banuncia to make the Three Magi [*para facer los reyes magos*], 100
mrs.
1460, payment to Banuncia for the Magi, 100 mrs.

[1] Gómez Moreno copies no fee. I have been unable to check the original documents.

(ii) A Passion play, 1458

Gómez Moreno, p. 73

1458, to those who performed the *representación* of the Passion on Good Friday [*el
viernes de la cruz*], 107 mrs.

(iii) A Shepherds' play, 1507

Gómez Moreno, pp. 72 and 73

1507 As a gift to the shepherds who performed the *Remembranza* of Our Lord on
Christmas Night, a ducado.

124   The Constable of Jaén prepares for Christmas, 1464

Lucas de Iranzo, p. 154

For the evening [of Christmas day] he ordered that the *Estoria* of the Birth of Our Lord and Saviour Jesus Christ and of the shepherds be performed in the said principal church at Matins, as was and is required on the feast and birthday of Our Lord God.

125   Dramatic presentations, Toledo, 1470–99

(i) A Christmas Shepherds' play, 1470

Toledo, p. 36

Item, I gave by another order signed by Don García de Ayala and by the head chaplain [*capellán mayor*], 200 mrs, which were ordered to be given to the shepherds who performed the Christmas night *rrepresentaçión*: this command was made on 17 January.

(ii) A Passion play, 1474

Toledo, pp. 36, note 74, 138, note 178

Item, another order for the said Pero Díaz, *refitolero*, to give 300 mrs to George de Bryuega[1] to perform the Passion *rrepresentaciones*, done on 6 April [14]74 signed by the head chaplain and Bachelor Alonso García.

[1] This document is also transcribed on p. 138, where this surname is rendered 'Bryuesa'.

(iii) Alonso del Campo's *Auto de la Pasión*, 1486–99

Toledo, pp. 159–63

To the oratory in the garden
First prayer in the garden
 My friends, wait here whilst I go to the garden to pray. How my soul is sad unto death, how I must suffer greatly and my body is groaning and my heart faltering. Keep vigil with me, my friends, do not abandon me [*no me seas desconosçidos*].
Here he will go away [from the others] and kneel down and say to the Father:
 My compassionate Father, hear my prayer [. . .]
Here he will get up and go to the disciples and say:
 Could you not watch with me for one single hour, friends? [. . .]
 He will go back and pray [torna aora] for the second time and he will say:
 Father, I know not what to do [. . .]

Here he will return to the disciples and look at how they are sleeping and he will stay silent [callará] and go back to pray [bolverse a a orar] for the third time, and say:
Father, if it is Your will that above all I should die [. . .]
Here the angel shall next appear bearing the Instruments [ensinias] of the Passion and he will show each one individually at the appropriate time

Lord, your Father heard you from your first prayer and did not reply to you because He found no way to give you succour as you must know well that your coming, Lord, was to suffer death and in so doing to save [guaresçer] all the lost people. You will suffer much grief and very grave insult. Oh divine beauty! From this chalice of bitterness you must drink [en ti s'a d'esequtar]. You, oh Lord, will be accused with false accusations, whipped, crowned and afterwards crucified between two robbers. First you will be seized by those whom you have taught, and you must be spat upon by them, and mocked and cruelly slighted by the Jews [judaycos varones].[1] You will suffer unjustly countless thousands of injustices [a sin rrazón mill cuentos de sinrazones] because your Passion consists of infinite passions.

---

[1] The word *varón* in the phrase *judaycos varones* probably reflects the tradition that the *principes iudorum*, and not all the Jews, were responsible for Christ's death.

I26   Corpus Christi processions, Murcia, May 1471
Gómez Moreno, p. 75

Further it was ordained and commanded that Juan Tallante and the bachelor Antón Martínez de Cascales, aldermen [regidores], with the members of the Chapel discuss imposing an eight-day tax [ynpusiçión] on meat to help with the Corpus Christi juegos, which are written below, because otherwise the Council [Consejo] could not meet the expenditure which must be made as it has other financial commitments which it cannot fail to meet:
Paradise
The Holy Fathers
St Jerome [Gerónimo]
Bethlehem
Judgement
St Michael
St George
St Francis

II   Court theatre and pageantry

Disguisings played an important role in court ritual from the thirteenth century onwards, particularly on state occasions [see **C86–C90** and **I27–I31, I33, I36, I37(i), I38**]. They also took the form of *entremeses* or entertainments performed between dishes at banquets or as preludes to dancing after dinner [see **I29, I30(ii)**]. The chronological presentation of material in this chapter reveals increasing sophistication and technical artifice. Disguisings include realistic-looking boats [see **I42–I44**] and the elaborate use of wagons [see **I31, I33**] and machines [see **I49, I51–I52, I54, I58**]. Successful properties were reused on different occasions; for example, some of the pageants used in 1269 by Jaume I 'the Conqueror' to welcome his son-in-law Alfonso 'the Wise' of Castile [see **C32**] to Valencia [see **I28**] were adopted for the 1286 coronation of Alfonso III at Saragossa, whilst the play performed for the coronation of Fernando of Antequera borrowed properties used in the Valencia Corpus Christi processions [see **I32**].[1]

1. Secondary sources are divided as to whether the date of Jaume's reception of Alfonso was 1269 or 1272–4.

THE EAST

Court theatre and pageantry are documented from the first third of the thirteenth century in the eastern portion of the Peninsula. The *Chronicle* of Ramon Muntaner describes a series of pageants that used quite elaborate machinery, and which included the civic receptions enjoyed by King Jaume I of Aragon after the conquest of Valencia [see **I27**], and the reception King Jaume extended to Alfonso 'the Wise' when the latter visited Valencia [see **I28**]. *Entremeses* are associated early on with the presentation of dishes at banquets, as seen at the coronation of Queen Sibila in 1381 [see **I29**]. More elaborate disguisings and *entremeses* were held to celebrate later coronations such as those of Martín I of Aragon and Fernando of Antequera, both in Saragossa [see **I31, I33**]. Fernando of Antequera's coronation entertainment is particularly interesting for a variety of reasons: it may have been composed by Enrique de Villena (1384–1434); it used Valencian Corpus Christi properties [see **I32**], and it includes spectacular aerial machinery, including a terrifying portrayal of Death [see **I33, I49**]. Finally, a late example of court pageantry is found in the celebrations at Gerona of the conquest of Granada from the Moors [see **I34**].

RECEPTIONS

I27   A civic reception for King Jaume I of Aragon, 1238

Crònica de Muntaner, vol. I, p. 31; trans. *Chronicle* of Muntaner, p. 25

And so he went likewise to visit Montpellier, which he had greatly wished to visit. And in every place he went, great processions were made and thanks given to Our Lord, the true God who had saved them; and there were dances and *jocs* and diverse amusements.

I28   A royal reception for Alfonso of Castile, Valencia, 1269

Crònica de Muntaner, vol. I, p. 57; trans. *Chronicle* of Muntaner, pp. 58–9

In every place the people of the King of Aragon arranged great processions and *jocs* for them [. . .] They came to the city of Valencia and when they were in that city, no one could describe the *jocs*, diversions, the round tables, the platforms for jousts and 'wild knights' [*cavallers salvatges*], lists, tournaments and exercises of arms, the galleys and armed ships which seamen dragged along the main street [*Rambla*] in carts [*carretes*], the battles of oranges and the tapestries.

AN *ENTREMÉS*

I29   An *entremés* at the coronation of Queen Sibila, 1381

'Aragón', p. 46

Further, a splendid *entremés* was brought at the end of the course, which is a lovely peacock displaying its tail and on a magnificent structure [*bastiment*] around which were many other types of fowl covered in cloth of gold and silver and this peacock was served very high [*fou servit fort altament*][1] and presented at the table of the said lady to the accompaniment of instruments, stringed as well as of other types, with the *mayordomo*, knights and maidens advancing ahead of it and the said *entremés* had on its front [*en sos pits*] a *cobla* which said this, 'To you my gift, Lady of Worth [. . .]'

---

[1] The meaning of 'fort altament' is unclear here. It may mean that the dish was served with great ado or may refer to the way it was prepared.

CORONATIONS AT SARAGOSSA

130   The coronation of Alfonso IV of Aragon, Easter Day 1328

Crònica de Muntaner, vol. IX, pp. 19, 26; trans. *Chronicle* of Muntaner, pp. 724, 730

(i) Wild men in the procession

And so, by the grace of God, amidst a great noise of trumpets and drums and dulcimers and cymbals and other instruments, and with *cavallers salvatges* who all shouted 'Aragon! Aragon!' and the names of all the families to which the higher nobility [*richs homens*] belonged, they [King and his retinue] came to the church of San Salvador [. . .]

(ii) An *entremés*

And the Infante En Pedro, with two nobles – all three hand-in-hand and he in the middle – came first singing a new dance he had composed; and all those who were bringing in the dishes responded. And when he came to the King's table he took the bowl and tasted the contents and set it before the King, and then set down the carving board. And when he had thus placed the first dish before the said King, and finished the dance, he took off the robes he was wearing, namely a cloak and tunic of cloth of gold dressed with ermine and many pearls, and gave them to his *juglar*, and at once, other very rich garments were ready for him, which he put on. And he maintained the same sequence with all the other dishes served; at each dish which he carried he sang a new dance which he had composed [. . .]

131   The coronation of Martin I, king of Aragon, 1399

'Aragón', pp. 47–8

Before dinner at the Aljafería [. . .] they performed an *invención* of a great spectacle in the manner of a starry sky which had several steps, and on these there were various Saints' images [*bultos*] with palm leaves in their hands and on high God the Father was painted in the midst of a great crowd of seraphim and their lovely voices were heard, accompanied by various musical instruments singing many *villancicos* and songs in honour and praise of the festival. From the sky a large *bulto* descended like a cloud which came to rest on top of the King's seating area [*apartador*]. From inside of this cloud there descended someone dressed as an angel singing wonderfully; and going up and down several times he scattered all around many with short poems written out [*muchas letrillas y coplas*], some on red paper, others on yellow and others on blue paper, written in different inks [. . .] a great snake came out, made very lifelike, of very unusual inventiveness which blew flames of fire from its mouth and around which swarmed many men armed with weapons, shouting and bellowing as if they wanted to kill it but it defended itself [. . . later] a large realistic-looking rock or crag and on the top of it there was a figure of a very large tawny lioness, which had a large opening like a wound on her left side. From this rock on the patio many rabbits, hares, partridges, turtle doves and many other birds started up from it and began to fly around the patio and also some wild boar appeared [. . .] the armed men who had stayed on the patio after the death of the snake approached the rock and surrounded it showing that they wished to climb it to kill the lioness. But many men issued from the same rock, dressed as Wild Men, who, preventing the others from climbing it [. . .] and from the lioness's wound a very handsome boy came out dressed in the royal arms with a crown on his head, and a drawn sword in his right hand as a sign of victory and began to sing very sweetly

I32   A request for the use of Valencia Corpus Christi properties, 1413

Trans. *Staging*, p. 188

Then the honoured Micer Johan Mercader, Governor of the Kingdom of Valencia, came before the Council and showed a letter of credence from the King [Fernando of Antequera] and informed the Council that the King begged and asked the said Council to lend for his coronation festivities the masks, wings, and albs [*testes, ales e camjs*] of the angels, which the said city had for the feast of Corpus Christi. And he said that he would offer to give all necessary assurances that he would have them returned to the city as soon as the above-mentioned celebrations were over. Concerning this request, the council, after a vote, decided that the said masks, wings, albs, and other ornaments of the angels of the Corpus Christi procession should be lent to the King, and to the said Governor on his behalf. It was agreed, however, that the said Governor should give assurances and should appoint a person of Valencia who would be able to guarantee the return to the city of the said items immediately after the coronation in the condition they were in when lent, without damage or hurt. And on the same subject the said Council asked the honoured representatives chosen to attend the said celebrations that while they were in Saragossa they should immediately afterwards recover the said items and have them sent back quickly and securely.[1]

[1] This appears to have been done; see **165**.

I33   *Entremeses* for the coronation of Fernando of Antequera, 1414

Castilla, pp. 242–6

As the said dish was eaten, first God the Father moved all the heavens and from there a great cloud came and descended in front of the table at the level of the French cloths [*paños*] which were hung in the hall about a lance's height from the floor and an angel came out of the cloud singing, carrying in his hand a drawn sword and saying two verses thus in Catalan [*limosín*]: [Two octaves follow in which the angel bids Fernando to be a robust ruler and to heal the schism in the Church]

This said, the cloud lifted the angel to the heavens and those in Paradise played their instruments making a very joyous melody [. . .] And Pride rose and spoke two verses which told who he was and all about his evil deeds. He was dressed in cloth of gold [. . .]

Avarice then rose and told of all the avaricious things he does, and he uttered two verses which spoke of his faults, and he was dressed in old clothes patched in many colours.

Lust rose, dressed in red [*colorado*] cloth beautifully shot with gold. She had a mirror in her hand, and making lewd and immodest faces she recited two stanzas about all her unbridled stains.

Envy rose, dressed in light tawn cloth with a yellow face, stopping all the time and acting sad and sorrowful, suffering greatly at the good fortune of others. He pronounced two verses about his ill grace and deficiency [*mengua do morían*], despairing of the good luck of others.

Gluttony rose, dressed in dark green, with much food before him, and he proclaimed two verses about how he was still famished.

Anger rose, dressed in white with her clothes covered in flames of fire and holding a dagger in her hand. She had a great and angry bearing, making as if to stab herself in the breast, and she said two verses, without stopping her actions and as if tearing her clothes.

Laziness rose and he was dressed in black. He had a book in his hand which he seemed to drop and could not pick up out of laziness, and he delivered two verses about his laziness and wretchedness.

And once the Seven Deadly Sins had finished, on the second step above their demons were the Seven Virtues who opposed the said sins and they stood up. First Humility was dressed in light grey cloth with a very modest head dress [*tocado*] and his modest eyes showing very great humility. He praised patience in two verses and forgave those who trespassed against him. And the angel who was behind him said two more verses praising Humility, putting a crown on his head.

[The other Virtues speak in turn, each has a symbolic feature, and is crowned by an angel who sings: Largesse, in modest green, throws down a skirt full of coin; Chastity, in white with gold brocade, looks modestly at no one; Love-One's-Neighbour, in purple [*cárdena*]; Temperance, in red and gold eats with restraint from a plate of food; Patience, dressed in green, is slapped and begs God to forgive her aggressor; Diligence, dressed in white, reads devoutly from a book and sings that Man should love God.]

Once Diligence's angel had spoken the Heavens revolved and, in the middle of the room, out came a cloud on which rode Death, who was very ugly and covered in skulls, snakes and tortoises. He came in this way: a man dressed in close-fitting yellow leather which resembled his own skin, his head was a fleshless skull and leather [hood] without nostrils or eyes which looked very ugly and very frightening, and he beckoned to all sides, calling now to some, now to others in the hall.[1]

Once this was done, the cloud returned to the Heavens and the *mayordomo* came in with the second dish [preceded by the fire-breathing griffin after which came] a large *roca* like a painted wooden *castillo* on wheels and in the middle of the said *castillo* there was a vase of Saint Mary with its very large, polished silver, white lilies.

In the said *castillo* there were six maidens singing songs very sweet to hear and on a crag on the *castillo* there was a very large, crowned gold eagle. Around its neck was a necklet of the device of the vases of the King of Aragon [the same as the vase of Saint Mary], and the vase in the middle of the *castillo* revolved when the *roca* was moved, and thus the second dish was brought into the hall through the door.

Then God the Father moved the heavens and all the angels and archangels played their instruments, and the patriarchs and prophets sung their songs very marvellously, and the first cloud which first came out before the table of the King came out into the air and on it rode an angel who carried a very beautiful gold vase with its lilies. And in a song he told that he was the ambassador of the resplendent Virgin who sent the King that vase so that he might always carry it in his conquests. He spoke two verses praising Pope Benedict as the true Pope, saying that the King should enforce this as he had the imperial device.[2]

Once the angel had pronounced its embassy he returned to Paradise and in this way the dishes were brought to the table and the pies [*pasteles*] were opened and birds flew out round the room.

[The griffin, with men dressed as Moors, fought the eagle which nonetheless came down from the *castillo* to the ground and did reverence to the King. During the struggle the gold vase was broken open and a boy wearing the royal arms of Aragon emerged, sword in hand and killed the griffins and Moors, and the eagle mounted the crag again.]

---

[1] This paragraph is partially translated in *Staging* (pp. 138–9). Stern (p. 99) cites an edition which gives '*llevaba a unos e a otros por la sala*', 'he carried this group and that one through the hall'.

[2] These were the years of the Great Schism in the Roman Catholic Church; at the Council of Constance [see **C15**] (1414–18) Pope Benedict XIII was deposed, and Martin V elected in his place (and that of several other claimants). Antequera supported Benedict.

THE CONQUEST OF GRANADA CELEBRATED

134   Celebrating the conquest of Granada, Gerona, 30 and 31 December 1492

Girona, pp. 64–5 (source: *Manuale Negociorum Iuratorem Gerunde*, 1492, fo. 20 recto [Arxiu Municipal de Girona])

After lunch the canons and clergy of the cathedral held a very beautiful *representatió* in the cathedral square, in which a Cardinal, an apostolic legate, pretended to have come from Rome to crown our King as Emperor and Queen as Empress and the aforementioned Cardinal was dressed in a purple cape and scarlet cap [*capell*] and accompanied by bishops and prelates [. . .] There was a splendid and very honourable *cadafal* and here this Cardinal dismounted, and the man who was the King and the woman, the Queen, did likewise. They ascended the said *cadafal* and everyone followed and there was much solemnity made at the said coronation [. . .]

On Tuesday after lunch the honourable judges went to see the *representació* and *entramesos* which were performed in the square of les Cols in the said city. They pretended it was the city of Granada with the Moors inside it, and that outside there were pavilions and tents and the King and Queen were there with the Cardinal of Spain, the Dukes of Seville and Cádiz, the Count of Cabra and the Chief Knight Commander [*Comenador maior* . . .] and they performed [*representaren*] the capture of the city of Granada here very magnificently.

THE WEST

Documents detailing court pageantry from the West are extant from the fifteenth century. As in the East, court disguisings were associated with state occasions. Two of the documents included here describe disguisings at marriage celebrations [see **136, 137(i)**]. The first details the celebrations in 1451 at Lisbon of the marriage of Leonor, sister to Afonso V of Portugal, to Frederick III, Holy Roman Emperor, which was solemnised in Rome the following March. The second is from the chronicle which the Constable of Jaén, Don Miguel Lucas de Iranzo (fl. 1459–71), commissioned. This is an especially valuable source which describes the yearly cycle of dramatic activities as well as occasional events [see **137(ii), (iii)**]. Don Miguel rose high under Enrique IV and set himself up as an image of nobility.

Just as the constable used disguisings as occasional entertainments, Princess Isabel, later Isabel 'the Catholic' of Castile, commissioned a disguising from Gómez Manrique to celebrate the majority of Prince Alfonso in 1467 in which she performed along with members of her court [see **138**]. The ladies were disguised as the nine Muses, one acted as expositor [*reportadora*] and spoke the dedicatory epistle which explained the idea of the *momos* whilst each of the others held a symbolic icon [*pintura*] explained in verse. Fernando of Aragón, her husband, enjoyed a sumptuous civic reception from Valladolid in 1509[see **141**].

Gomes Eanes de Zurara's *Crónica da Tomada de Ceuta* (c. 1450) conveys the planning involved in the preparation of a court disguising [see **135**]. Whilst amongst early Portuguese court activities the work of Anrique de Mota (1470–80 to post-1545) is of note. He wrote five dramatised dialogues which were collected in Garcia de Resende's *Cancioneiro geral* (1516). His *A Lamentação da Mula* [see **139**], probably written between 1499 and 1503, is included here because, although Mota's dialogues may not have been performed, they may have influenced later dramatists. Finally, Ochoa de Ysásaga, the ambassador of the Portuguese court, in a letter of 1500 to the Catholic Monarchs reported some elaborate secular celebrations at Christmastide which formed part of the Christmas celebrations which he had witnessed at Lisbon [see **140, 144**].

I35   *Momos* at the Portuguese court, Lisbon, *c.* 1414

Mota, p. 47

To increase his amusements Prince Dom Anrique ordered right away that noble celebrations [*festas*] be held in Viseu, like those which his brother, the Count of Barcellos, had ordered to be celebrated with all the lords, bishops, the lesser [*fidalgos*] and other nobles who were in the region [. . .] The Prince sent to Lisbon and Oporto for cloth of silk and of wool and embroiderers [*brolladores*] and tailors to make liveries and *momos* according to what is truly appropriate to this *festa* [. . .] and when on the Christmas Eve [*vespera de natall*] he saw that all these things were ready and many adornments placed on the lists [*corregimientos de justas*] and other trappings of various sorts and from the city and the villages around about streams of people [*cheas de gemte*] came so that it seemed to some foreigners who were passing through there that the town was none other than a regal court.

I36   Royal wedding celebrations, Lisbon, 1451

Mota, p. 48

And afterwards every day that the Empress [Leonor] was in the city before her departure, there were always sumptuous banquets, to which the King and Queen were often invited, and also the Ambassadors and Princes, like the splendid *momos* which the Prince Dom Fernando organized himself. And others of even greater splendour and singular imagination [*envençam*] which the Prince Dom Anrique ordered to be done along with others of many Lords and lesser nobility [*fidalgos*], and above all those of the King, in which he challenged the knights to Royal Jousts, which took place in the Rua Nova . . . The Prince Dom Fernando saw how his knights-errant [*ventureiros*] dressed in long-haired wigs [*guedelhas*] of fine silk like Wild Men [*salvajens*], mounted on good horses dressed and covered with the figures and colours of animals, some recognisable and others deformed . . . And after the jousts there were bullfights, tourneys and more *momos*, banquets and many *entremeses* with great *envenções*[1] at high cost.

---

[1] For *envenções*, see glossary above.

JAÉN

I37   Disguisings at the court of the Constable of Jaén, 1461–4

(i) Marriage celebrations, 1461

Lucas de Iranzo, pp. 47–8

At the sound of them [*duçaynas*] after the said Constable and Countess, and his sister, Juana, and brother, and others had danced for a while, a troop of gentlemen of the house came in disguised as foreigners [*personas estrangeras*], masked [*con falsos visajes*] and dressed in a very novel and elegant way, that is to say in a fine, very pale green cloth, pretending that they had escaped from a cruel captivity and that freedom had been granted to them on condition that they came to do service and honour at the said *fiesta* of the said Constable and Countess. They danced for more than three hours.

(ii) Processional celebrations for Epiphany, 1462

Lucas de Iranzo, pp. 70–1

When the Countess and the ladies Doña Guiomar Carrillo, her mother, and his sister Doña Juana, with many other ladies and maidens were in the highest tower of their dwelling watching, and many other people mounted and on foot [were] in the streets and at windows, on walls and roofs with many torches and lanterns so that it seemed like midday on account of the great brightness of the light, the said Constable left the house of Fernando de Berrio, alderman [*regidor*] of the said city, whence the departure was ordered, which is to the church of the Magdalene, and he crossed nearly the whole city in this way.

He came [. . .] in a doublet lined in gold with a short jacket on top with his coat of arms worked in very fine yellow cloth, very well shod in black embroidered shoes, on his head a very well-made royal crown and wearing a mask, a drawn rapier in his hand and well seated on his horse like a noble knight.

In front were two pages [. . .] twelve mounted gentlemen [. . .] and another knight on a very large horse, who carried a flag. They were all dressed in this livery, with masks and crowns on their heads, in memory of the Three Kings, whose *fiesta* was being celebrated [. . .]

When they arrived [at the lists] then they all removed the masks. A prize of two brocade doublets was offered to the first two knights to enter the lists [. . .]

(iii) Epiphany, 1464

Lucas de Iranzo, p. 162

After dinner the *mastresalas* cleared the tables. Then it was commanded that the *Estoria* of when the Kings came to worship and to give their gifts to Our Lord Jesus Christ be performed. When this was done, and viewed with great devotion, it was ordered that the collation be served; this done, his worship withdrew to his chamber.

138   *Momos* for the birthday of Prince Alfonso of Castile, November 1467

Gómez Manrique, *Momos*, in *Teatro castellano de la Edad Media*, ed. Ronald E. Surtz, Madrid, 1992, pp. 95–101

A brief treatise which Gómez Manrique made at the command of the very illustrious Lady, Princess Doña Isabel, for *momos* which her excellency performed with the following *fados*[1]

Most illustrious and fortunate prince, and most powerful King and sovereign Lord,

[The epistle begins by telling Prince Alfonso that the Muses have heard of his fourteenth birthday, the age of majority, and know all that his past and future holds[2].] And because travelling such a great distance of [many] lands was dangerous to our female estate and youthful age with great sacrifices and prayers we asked the high gods [. . .] to transform our persons into other forms so that without danger to our reputations we should be able to come before your royal highness. These gods, having heard our fair request, suddenly covered eight of us in these beautiful feathers and the ninth, the bearer of this short letter, with these pelts of white fur [*d'estas vedijas de blanchete*] which your excellency sees. And thus we are brought before your Majesty, not with rich gifts of gold nor of precious stones because we have none and do not desire them, nor do you, very powerful King and Lord, have need of them, as it is enough for you to be Lord of the lords of these things; but with the increased love which your noble sight has caused us, we present the following *fados* to your highness, which, putting aside the other gods, we beg that He alone who created you plainly grant to you.

Mencía de la Torre carried the following fado:

To your royal excellency we, these *fados*, come led and guided by divine essence. Each of us with our figure in turn will give you a *fado*; I order by my painting that luck and fortune obey your desire.

[The other court ladies who speak are Doña Elvira de Castro, Doña Beatriz de Sosa, Isabel Castaña, Doña Juana de Valencia, Doña Leonor de Luxán, Beatriz de Bobadilla, and Isabel herself – they wish for him the virtues necessary for a King.]

---

[1] *Fado* literally means 'fate'; here it alludes to the *devisas* and *letras* which the ladies offer Alfonso as gifts and prophecies.

[2] Alfonso died in the year he obtained his majority.

I39   Anrique de Mota's *A Lamentação da Mula*, c. 1499–1503

Mota, pp. 420–2

The owner speaks with the Mule when they are just about to go:

Everyone is leaving already; let's get out whilst the going's good.

MULE   But the departure is in an evil hour for whoever travels with me.

MASTER   Get a move on [?*Andrai rijo*] – these people will see you.

MULE   God forbid that anyone should do me such ill as would please [my owner] [. . .]

Farewell of the Mule on his departure:

MULE   Lords of Bombarral, with your permission I go – you would do me a great kindness if you remember my suffering [. . .].

It was several days from there to Alcoentre where Dom Henrique was; he found the Mule

who recounted to him everything which had befallen him on his day's pilgrimage from which he was now returned:

MULE   I am very pleased to find you, my Lord, in this land and am compelled [? *a guerra*] to tell you that I was given nothing to eat. If you want to hear, I will tell you of my inherent suffering, the great pain and grief which I endured.

I40   Christmastide celebrations at the Portuguese court, 1500

Gómez Moreno, pp. 147–8

And then the minstrels began to play very loudly and then many *momos* with *ynvençiones*, each with trumpets in front, came out as will be described.

At the end of the room was made a large curtained retreat [*retraymento con paños*] from which an enchanted garden came out with a large quince tree inside [which was] very well made with many thick branches full of burning candles. On top of the tree [there was] a very frightening dragon with three ferocious heads and six long limbs [*largos manos*] and its tail wound around the tree trunk and the garden was enclosed [*estava cubierto al derredor*] with fine linen hangings. And six ladies were inside, dressed in the French style [. . .] and in their hands burned painted torches [. . .] The garden arrived before the Queen [. . .] and as the ladies came out, Doña Angela, in name of them all, gave a letter [*escripto*] to the Queen which said the following:

[The letter explains that the ladies, from their Ethiopian garden of Love, are empowered by the gods to give remedy to lovers and tells the Queen of a knight who begs them to intervene on his behalf, and that of his men, to invoke her aid.]

After this, the *carro* was removed from there and the King came in to a great fanfare of trumpets with twenty of the principal knights of his court all disguised [*echos momos*] with masks and crests [*çimeras*[1]] and they danced twice around the hall. After this the King began to make his way to the dais and the Queen, when she realised it was he, got up and went out to meet him. [They danced and then each of the other knights in turn approached his lady, removed his mask, handed his lady a letter and the couple danced.]

[1]   The *çimera*, or crest, often comprised the *divisa* or visual part of an *invención*: see Ian Macpherson, 'Text, Context and Subtext: Five *invenciones* of the *Cancionero genera* and the Ponferrada Affair of 1485' in *The Medieval Mind: Hispanic Studies in Honour of Alan Deyermond*, ed. Ian Macpherson and Ralph Penny, London, 1997, pp. 259–74.

I41   A civic reception for Fernando the Catholic, Valladolid, 1509

Gómez Moreno, pp. 153–8

The entrance was through the Puerta del Campo, at which was built a great *cadahalso*, where the first triumph was, which was of Fortune, arranged in the following way:

It was decorated with very opulent hangings. Fortune was dressed [*cubierta*] in brocade, pearls and gold and a precious crown. Around her she had a gilded wheel as high as two men [*estados*], on which our fortunate king had put his feet. Its sign said, 'Don Fernando, Catholic King of Spain.' Below this wheel there were many fallen kings as is customary. Right above the arch was a *mote* in large letters which could be read from a great distance, which said, 'If Fortune had more, she would give you more.' When his Highness arrived, Fortune took a gilded club and affixed a great nail and stilled the wheel, saying in a loud voice which could be heard very clearly, the verse which follows [. . .]

When the wheel was fixed and this verse pronounced, she turned to the King and removed her crown and kneeling began to speak thus, 'High King of great power [. . .]'. When Fortune had finished speaking, six singers [*cantors*] of excellent voice and skill began to sing this *villancico*; and if its sound could be printed then it would seem much better, 'Bound by the hand of God [. . .]'

On His Majesty's entering the city, there were many *castillos* with pleasing *inuenciones*, many *cadahalsos* and pavilions with things of great joy [. . .] The second Triumph was in the square, which was of the Seven Virtues arranged on a great throne according to their nature in dress as in the insignias which belonged to them, each with their garlands of laurel. As his Highness arrived, they all stood up. On the top of the arch was a *mote* which said, 'More accomplished than anyone, God desired that you possess all seven.' The first to speak was Faith, and they each spoke in turn until Strength spoke, who was the last [the Virtues were Faith, Charity, Hope, Justice, Temperance, Prudence and Strength. After Strength's speach, a *villancico* was sung, 'Let, oh let, such a couple come in a fortunate hour' ['*Vengan, vengan, en buen ora tales dos*'].

The third Triumph was on the east *costanilla*. It was as great thing to see in costume [*atauío*] as in *inuençion*. In it was *Fama*, placed at its highest point and dressed according to her nature, who on top of the brocade and metallic-plate [? *chapado*] which she wore had on wings, sword in hand. Under her were placed in good order all those famous forbears deserving of her company with their crowns and signs, who were:

> The emperors. Julius Caesar. Octavius. Alexander the Great. Trajan. King David. Constantine. King Solomon. Don Alfonso.[1] Hannibal. Judas Maccabeus. Scipio. Count Fernán González, armed and white.[2] Hector. The Cid.

On top of the arch was a *mote* which said, 'You, the trunk of *Fama* and all of these the branch.'

Above of all this was a great lion which frightened everyone (it was so ferocious!) and it had the arms of our city between its claws. And when his Majesty arrived, he tore them to shreds and was left with the royal arms. *Fama* stood up as did the aforementioned and she began to speak, 'You did as I desired [. . .]' At this triumph were many singers [*cantors*] and when *Fama* had finished speaking, they began to sing this *villancico*, 'How unequalled is the news [. . .]'

The fourth Triumph was Time, which triumphs over all things. He had under him *Fama* and Fortune and was armed in white with a clock in his hand. He pointed with his hand to a *mote* which said, "'What I do is end *Fama*, Fortune and their glory [. . .]'

---

[1] Most probably Alfonso X 'the Wise'

[2] Count Fernán González was the first Count of Castile and as such is viewed as the founding father of Castile and, consequently, of Spain.

III Theatre and performance

Many of the documents cited in the two previous chapters contain information concerning aspects of performance and staging in the Peninsula and in them many similarities with staging conventions elsewhere in Europe can be seen, such as the use of pageant wagons [see **I17, C80**], processional performance [see **I22, I26, I28, I30(i), I37(ii)**] and 'place-and-scaffold' staging [see **B17, I20(iii)**], for which playing spaces included the interiors of churches, secular buildings and public places such as market and town squares [see **I16, I34**]. The documents presented here illustrate a series of Hispanic staging practices and indicate the financial implications of building the necessary properties and, in at least one case, rehearsing the cast. Three aspects of drama in the Iberian Peninsula remain to be treated: first, the presentation of Death and the later development of a dramatic tradition focusing on the Dance of Death; second, the frequent use of dance in shepherds' plays; and, finally, the beginning of the rise of the actor-manager.

STAGES AND STAGING: SHIPS

Mobile presentation and court pageant made notable use of ships. In an early appearance at the coronation of Alfonso III of Aragon they served as no more than stations which could be used in a 'battle of oranges' [see **I42**]; however, at the wedding of Prince Afonso of Portugal and Princess Isabel of Spain in 1490 realistic-looking vessels were used in a disguising of the Knight of the Swan [see **I43**] and in 1500 again at the Portuguese court realistic brigs were employed in a disguising [see **I44**]. Gil Vicente's *Play of the Ship of Hell* [*Auto da Barca do Inferno*] (published late 1517 or 1518) is an allegorical discovery play which uses the Ship of Fools motif [see **I45**].

I42 The coronation of Alfonso III of Aragon, Saragossa, 1286

Crònica de Muntaner, vol. v, pp. 15–16; trans. *Chronicle* of Muntaner, p. 384

[. . .] the seamen had two armed ships constructed, of those flat ones used on the river; on them you might have seen battles of oranges, of which they had over fifty loads brought from Valencia.

143   A royal wedding between Portugal and Spain, 1490

Garcia de Resende, *Vida e Grandíssimas Virtudes e Bondades do Rey dõ João o Segundo*, Evora, 1545, pp. lxxiiii–lxxvi; trans. Shergold, pp. 129–30

The King [John II] appeared in the character of the Knight of the Swan, and he and his eight companions made their entry, each one set on canvas painted to resemble water. The King's boat was preceded by a white swan and, as the vessels advanced they discharged their artillery, and minstrels played upon trumpets and drums. In the prow of the King's ship stood an knight in full armour, who in the name of the King addressed a *breve* to the Princess, saying that it was his wish to serve her at her wedding feast, and to champion her by challenging all comers to joust. The king-at-arms then proclaimed the joust and its conditions, the trumpets blew [. . .][1]

[1]   I have been unable to consult a primary source for this extract and therefore give Shergold's text.

144   Christmastide celebrations at the Portuguese court, 1500

Gómez Moreno, p. 149 [see **140**]

After this there came eight pilgrims who, going to Santiago with their pilgrim's staffs and conch shells in a brig made with artifice and arriving at the door of the hall, disembarked and one in the name of all gave a letter [*escripto*] to the King, which said this 'The news is growing, holy King [. . .]'

145   Gil Vicente's *Auto da Barca*, 1517–18

Vicente, pp. 46–53[1]

USERER   O alas! Who made me blind?
DEVIL   Shut up; here's where you'll cry.
When the userer boards the boat, he finds the nobleman embarked, and says, taking off his cap:
    Saint Joanna de Valdes! It's not your lordship!
NOBLE   Give your manners to the devil [. . .]
Simple Simon [Joane o Parvo] enters and says to the pilot of Hell:
    Ho, thingummyjig!
DEVIL   Who is it?
SIMON   It be me! Be this hulkin' tub ours?
DEVIL   Whose?
SIMON   The fools'.
DEVIL   It's yours; come on board.
SIMON   Should I jump or should I fly? Oh, ma grand-daddy's grief, at th' end I fell right sick, an' I died damn quick, it were ma' number that come up.
DEVIL   What did you die of?

SIMON   O' what? 'Appen, o' t' trots.

DEVIL   Of what?

SIMON   O' t' pooey shits, tha' mangy git!

DEVIL   Come on board, put your foot down there.

SIMON   Oh, oh, tha' sambook's[2] tippin' over!

DEVIL   Board, you great ball-less fool, for the tide's slipping away.

SIMON   Wait a mo', wait a mo', oh! And where are we goin' ta go?

DEVIL   To the port of Lucifer.

SIMON   Ah, ha, ha!

DEVIL   Oh, Hell, get on board!

SIMON   Hell, hellfire and damnation! Phew, phew, cuckold's boat! [Simon insults the Devil at length, clearly disbelieving him.]

   The fool [i.e. Simon] goes to the Angel's boat and says:

SIMON   Ho, boat there!

ANGEL   What do you want me to do?

SIMON   Will tha take me over there?

ANGEL   Who are you?

SIMON   'Appen, someone.

ANGEL   You shall cross if you wish. [The Angel explains that Simon's sins are not borne of malice, therefore he is to be saved, adding that they will wait to see if anyone else deserves to be saved.]

A cobbler enters wearing his apron and loaded with lasts and comes up to the hellish boat. He says:

   Ho, boat there!

DEVIL   Who goes there? Oh, Saint Cobbler the honourable, how come you've come so laden?

COBBLER   I was ordered to come like this. And to where's the journey?

DEVIL   To the lake of the damned.

---

[1]   Lappin's is a lively translation in which he attempts to capture the rustic tone of the language used by the fool Simon. I have made minor adaptations.

[2]   Lappin gives 'sampan' (p. 49) in his translation but explains that a 'sambook', although little known in English, was a 'small sailing-boat used in the Indian Ocean, sewn together with ropes' (p. 99).

PLACE-AND-SCAFFOLD STAGING

As in the drama of medieval Britain and France [see **Sections D** and **E**], much use of scaffold-and-place staging was made, particularly in vernacular religious plays for performance in church. Indeed there was a thriving tradition of scaffold-and-place staging at the Cathedral of Palma (Majorca). An Easter Tuesday Mary Magdalene ceremony is first documented in a manuscript of the fourteenth to fifteenth century and fully described in a *consueta* of 1511 [see **B17**] whilst the famous Llabrés manuscript [see **I47, I60–I61, I67**] contains scripts which include detailed staging directions. Also from the East, is the Prades Assumption (1420) which used various structures (*barracha, loch, casa, hortatori, sepulchre*) [see **146**]. Of particular note is Llabrés *Consueta del Rey Asuero* which begins with complicated staging in the interior of a church, most likely the Cathedral of Palma [see **147**]. The Catalan play of St Eudalt is extant in a manuscript copied in 1549 but is thought, on linguistic grounds, to date from the fifteenth century [see **148**]: it is also preceded by full staging directions, including a cast list.[1]

---

[1] See Romeu, vol. I, p. 56.

146   The Prades Assumption, Tarragona, 1420

Joan Pié, 'Autos sagramentales del sigle XIV', *Revista de la Asociación Artístico-Arqueológica Barcelonesa* I (1896–8), pp. 674–5; trans. *Staging*, pp. 79–80

The place where this *representació* is to be presented is to be arranged as follows:
   Firstly, the Jews are to make a splendid house [*una bella barracha*] for themselves. Further, Lucifer and the other devils [are to] make a place which is to be a large Hell [*un loch quey sía infern gran*]. And they are to take there an anvil [*anclusa*] and hammers [*mayls*] to make a loud noise when the time comes. Further, Paradise [*parays*] is to be fitted out with fine purple cloth, rich curtains, and ties [*benes ó clòs*] where Jesus is to be with angels and archangels. Also St John the Baptist, patriarchs, prophets, virgins, and other blessed souls. Further, there is to be constructed a house [*casa*] for the Virgin Mary in which there is to be a fine bed, furnished with fine curtains, and in front of the house there is to be a fine oratory [*un bell hortatori*] where the Virgin may say her prayers. Further, there is to be made in another place a fine tomb [*un bell sepulcre*] where the Virgin Mary is to be placed when she departs this life, and here some fine white garments are to be made for her to wear when Jesus brings her back to life. She is to be led to Paradise. Further, it is to be arranged that when the angel who brings the palm to the Virgin Mary returns to Paradise, there is to be a noise with explosions [. . .]

147   *Consueta del Rey Asuero*, fifteenth century (?)

Huerta Viñas, pp. 237–8

In order to perform the present *consueta* four *cadefals* are necessary; thus, two on each side of the church. The first is to be beside the mayor's bench [*banche del balle*], on it will be King Ahasuerus, very richly attired, with crown, cape and sceptre in his hand, with two door-keepers [*porters*], one on each side of the *cadefal*; further seven eunuchs [. . .] Thus there are ten characters for this *cadefal*: that is, two door-keepers, seven eunuchs, the King.
   The second *cadefal* will be a little lower down, on which [is] Queen Vashti, first wife of King Ahasuerus, richly attired, with her royal crown and two maids; further, two eunuchs and Hegai and Hatach dressed in their long robes. Further Esther, after she has been chosen as Queen, with her two maids. Before, however,

her election she will be with Mordecai in some other place in the church [*en algun loch apartat de la església*]. The characters add up to the following: the Queen Vashti, two maids, two eunuchs, Hegai, Hatach, Ster [*? Zeresh*], Mordecai.

On the other side there will be two other *cadefals* to the right of these two. On the first, opposite Ahasuerus', there will be four wise men with their long robes and beards, and these are to be Ahasuerus' councillors. Four wise men.

On the fourth *cadefal* there will be Haman with two servants and two messengers, a bailiff, three sergeants, a trumpeter, an executioner. Finally, they will have wood to make a gallows on the same *cadefal*, when it becomes necessary. Haman, two servants, one bailiff, three sergeants, two messengers, one trumpeter, one executioner.

148   *Consueta de Sant Eudalt*, fifteenth century (?)

Romeu, vol. II, pp. 67–9

[Cast list]

Sent Tou [Eudalt]	Tomàs Fabra
First Knight	Sabastià Bosch
Second Knight	Jaume Pau
Door-keeper	Mossèn Quera[1]
Prancassi	Alamany Bosch
Angel	Miquel Baxador
St Ramon	Mossèn Brocons
St Vicent	Mossèn Albert
St John Prevere	Sabastià Bosch
Layman [Profano]	Mossèn Carbonell
Alexandrina	Alguer
Kings William and Valentin	Mossèn Fexes
Bailiff	Jaume Cabana
Executioner	Ribes
Executioner	[No name given]
Devil	Planes
Bailiff	Jaume Cabana
Devil	Planes

Here follows the *Misteri* or *Representatió* of the glorious St Eudalt, as is told in Latin in his legend, written [*conpost*] in the town of Sent Joan les Abbadesses [near Ripoll] in the month of April in the year of Our Lord 1549.

First let there be made a beautiful *catafal* with a very well curtained canopy,[2] on which is St Eudalt together with two knights of his company, to whom St Eudalt begins, and speaks.

After this let there be made on one side of the woods a hermitage where St Prancaci [*sic*] will be; on another side let there be a splendid *catafal* for the Layman and Alexandrina, where they are to be with some servants; on another side let there be made [*gornida*] a fountain which, as St Eudalt is there and is to pray begging for water, at that same time is to begin to flow. Let there be, further, another *catafal* for King William, on which he is to be with his knights, near which is to be made a prison for St Eudalt as will be necessary. On another side let there be a *catafal* for King Valentin, on which he is to be with his knights and all his company.

This is what must be provided and obtained to play [*jugar*] and perform [*representar*] the present *misteri* of the glorious St Eudalt.

The characters who are to act in the present *representatió* are:

St Eudalt; two Knights; the door-keeper; St Prancaci; the Angel; St Ramon; St John Prevere; St Vicent the Minor; a Layman; Alexandrina; King William, a bailiff; two executioners; King Valentin, a bailiff; two executioners. As for any others, this is at the discretion of the actors [*representadós*].

[1] The names preceded by the honorific 'Mossèn' are probably those of priests (Romeu, vol. ii, p. 67).
[2] Romeu (vol. ii, p. 67) argues that there should be a canopied throne.

AERIAL MACHINERY

Many medieval Hispanic dramatic performances make use of aerial machinery. These include systems of winches and ropes to move characters and properties horizontally through space as well as the devices for vertical movement such as those associated with Assumption plays. Aerial machinery was a central feature at the celebrations of the coronation of Leonor of Albuquerque (died 1436), Fernando of Antequera's queen, in Saragossa, 1414, where the Duke of Gandía had the actor playing Death play a prank on Borra, the court jester [see **149**; also see **133**]. From Valencia [see **150**] there is an inventory of equipment used in the construction and decorating of an *araceli*. At the court of Don Miguel Lucas de Iranzo, the Magi are guided by a star hoisted on a cord [see **151**]. The fictional *Gracisla* offers an interesting description of a Triumph of the Wheel of Fortune and House of Fame which includes some aerial business [see **152**]. *Gracisla* is a late fifteenth-century anonymous prose and verse account of a fictional court of love at which the eponymous Lady Gracisla is judged to be the winner. Her victory is celebrated with court disguisings described in some detail [see also **159**].

The outstanding example of the use of aerial machinery is the Festa or Misteri d'Elx [Elche], a spectacular Assumption of the Virgin which is still staged every August and is currently performed in the Church of St Mary (founded in 1672). The Festa can be confidently dated to the fifteenth century, although it may be earlier. The music includes some medieval plainchant and courtly lyric but it is mostly Renaissance polyphony. The Festa uses two aerial machines, the pomegranate or cloud and the *araceli* or *recélica*, both capable of carrying musicians, which descend through a trapdoor in a canvas sky to a platform positioned at the juncture of the transepts and intruding slightly into the choir. Ground-level access to the platform is along a gangway [*andador*] running from the main door of the church [see **153**].

149 Death visits a banquet for Leonor of Albuquerque, Saragossa, 1414

Shergold, p. 121; trans. *Staging*, p. 95 [also see **133**]

The jester was in the hall where the Queen was eating, and when Death came on the cloud [*la nube*] as he had done for the King as we have said. [The jester] showed great fear on seeing Death and shouted loudly at it not to come near him. Then the Duke of Gandía sent word to the King, who was at the window watching the Queen dine, that when Death descended and the jester began to shout, he [the Duke] would take him underneath and tell Death to throw him a rope and pull the jester up to him. And this was done. When Death came out on his cloud before the table, Mossen Borra started to shout, and the Duke carried him underneath Death who threw down a rope which they tied to the body of the said Borra, and Death wound him up. Here you would have marvelled at the things Mossen Borra did and at his wailing and at the great fear which seized him, and, whilst being pulled up, he wet himself into his underclothes, and the urine ran on to the heads of those who were below. He was quite convinced he was being carried off to Hell. The King and those who watched were greatly amused. Mossen Borra went in Death's power to Heaven.

150 A Valencian Assumption play, early fifteenth century

Valencia, pp. 100–1; trans. *Staging*, p. 231

When she [the Virgin Mary] has finished her speech she shall stand up, and if she is able to reach the representations [*forma*[1]] of Christ's feet she is to touch them with her lips or hands. And then she is to return devoutly to her house [*casa*], and when she reaches the door she is to turn towards the altar, then go and sit down on her seat.

Very shortly afterwards, because of not having time, she is to stand up then kneel and, looking up towards heaven with folded hands, is to say the following *cobla* to the melody of 'Ab cant d'auzells':

[Mary prays to Christ that she may join him]

And immediately she is to sit on her seat. Claps of thunder [*trons*] are to be made and the angel is to descend [*devall*]. And when the angel is before the Mary, she is to look at him very humbly, and the angel is to sing [. . .]

---

[1] I have used the more recent edition by Sanchis Guarner against *Staging*'s use of Alcahalí's transcription. Note that Sanchis Guarner gives *dorma* for *forma*.

151   A moving star at the court of the Constable of Jaén, 1462

Lucas de Iranzo, pp. 71–2; trans. *Staging*, p. 250

After they had dined and the tables had been cleared away a lady entered the hall, mounted on a little donkey [*un asnito sardesco*] with a child in her arms. She was acting the part of [*representaba ser*] Our Lady the Virgin Mary with her blessed and glorious Son, and Joseph accompanied her. And with great devotion the said Constable received her and handed her up to his seat [*asiento*], placing her amongst the said Countess [his wife], the Doña Guiomar Carrillo, her mother, Doña Juana, his sister, and the other ladies and maidens present.

The said Constable withdrew to a room [*una camara*] at the other end of the hall. Shortly afterwards, he came out of the said room with two pages, both very well dressed, with masks [*visajes*] and crowns on their heads like the Three Wise Kings, each with a goblet in his hands, with their gifts. And thus they advanced through the hall very slowly in a most dignified manner [*muy mucho paso con muy gentil con-tenençia*], looking at the star which guided them, which was attached to a cord [*un cordel*] there in the said hall. And thus they arrived at the far end where the Virgin was with her Son and offered the presents amidst a great fanfare of trumpets, drums and other instruments.

152   A Triumph of Fame and Fortune from *Gracisla*, c. 1500

Gracisla, p. 27

So as all the knights and ladies who had come together in Paris finished praising this Lady Gracisla, Fortune arrived along some golden cords which were high up in the hall, and she came through the air above them with a wheel in her hand, and some ladies were rising up it [*subían por ella*] and others fell and others were below it and on top of her wheel there was a splendid chair [*silla*], on which Fortune had to seat Gracisla. And this was all very skilfully made from models [*maçonería*] and so well made that everyone looked at it in amazement. And with great restraint Fortune arrived before the triumph [*trihunfo*] where *Fama* was seated crowning Gracisla, who, after being crowned and praised by all to the highest degree which my wearied pen reveals to you, was seated by Fortune on the highest part of her wheel, just as if she were alive, and in this way Fortune then began to speak the following verse [. . .]

153   The Elche Assumption, 1709

Trans. *Festa d'Elx*, pp. 37–9[1]

(i) The *núvol* or *granada*

When Mary has finished singing this plea, the doors of Heaven, which are represented in *La Festa* in the dome of the church, are opened. Heaven is made up of a
canvas painted with clouds which completely covers the main drum of the dome.
Only a square aperture, coinciding with the centre of the *cadafal*, can be opened
and closed by means of sliding doors [*les ports del cel*]. Through the gap left by these
doors a machine known as the cloud [*núvol*] or pomegranate [*granada*] begins to
descend, first appearing in the form of a sphere, suspended by a stout rope. It is
crimson, and its exterior is adorned with geometrical patterns and gilt decoration.
From the lower end hangs a beautiful golden tail.

Once it has gone through the door of the Heaven, and by means of guy ropes,
the pomegranate starts opening into eight wings or segments. Its interior, which
is completely covered in golden tinsel paper, reveals a boy dressed in a sky blue robe
with wings on his shoulders, who represents an angel. In his hands he holds a
golden palm. The opening of Heaven and the emergence of the aerial machine are
accompanied by organ music, pealing of bells and a fireworks display. When the
cloud has descended a few metres, this show of jubilation ends, and the angel, after
dropping a handkerchief full of pieces of golden paper representing very fine
golden rain, begins his singing. He greets Mary with this song, announcing to her
that Christ has listened to her pleas and accedes to her wishes.

---

[1]   The English text, based on a *Consueta* of 1709, is from the guide to the modern performance.

(ii) The *araceli* or *recélica*

Trans. *Festa d'Elx*, p. 46

When this deeply moving chant of the apostles is over, the doors of Heaven open
again and the descent of an aerial machine called the *araceli* or *recélica* begins. This
is a machine with the configuration of the reredos of an altar, built of iron,
wrapped in golden foil. It is made up of four ledges symmetrically placed around a
central niche. On the upper ledges there are two kneeling men-angels who play the
guitar and the harp respectively. On the lower edges there are two boy-angels, each
with a small guitar. The central niche is assigned to the so-called *Angel Mayor*, who
appears standing up and wearing a priestly alb and stole. This character has to be
played by a priest. As soon as the *recélica* has come through the doors of Heaven,
a rain of golden tinsel paper falls on the stage. The angelic choir starts its singing,
telling Mary of her coming Assumption [. . .]

HEAVEN

The *entremeses* performed at the coronation of Fernando of Antequera in 1414 [see **154**; also see **133**, **149**] were especially elaborate and the actions of God the Father in Heaven served a unitary function in the allegory of the Vices and Virtues, probably by Enrique de Villena. The *entremeses* constituted an extremely ambitious project and consequently used elaborate staging techniques; however, some of the machinery and properties was borrowed from the Valencian Corpus Christi processions [see **132**].

154   The staging of Heaven in the allegory of the Vices and Virtues, 1414

Castilla, pp. 240–1

Before the first dish came a very handsome golden griffin, as big as a horse [*rocín*], wearing a golden crown as a necklet. It came breathing fire all the way to make room for the dishes to be brought through the people which could not otherwise be brought so easily through the mob.

And in this great hall above the door where they entered a great, tall *cadalso* had been built to resemble the heavens which were made thus: there was a high scaffold [*andamio*] above the door and in the middle were three wheels, one on top of the other, and the middle one was larger than the others. On each side of the wheels were eight steps which were filled in [? *avía ocho gradas de cada parte todas las ruedas, e en llenadas e enbutidas*]. The wheels, all the scaffold and the steps were the colour of the sky and above the wheels on the last one was a sky which was higher than the others on which were two boys who were very well dressed in cloth of gold and one was crowning the other in remembrance of when God crowned Saint Mary. These three wheels were full of men dressed in white with large gilded wings and white masks [*rostros sobrepuestos*] who resembled angels and [they were] so splendid that they really seemed like angels. And these three wheels moved one against the other like the heavens which move whenever they desire [*quando se mueven cada que querían*]. And these angels and archangels played instruments and sang [. . .] and whenever the wheels of the heavens moved, the heaven above with the boys stayed in the same place, and did not move, and on the four highest steps were seated princes, prophets and apostles, each with the symbol in his hand by which he was recognised.

On the first step of the other wheels one above the other [? *otra contra ayuso*] were seven men dressed as the Seven Deadly Sins and below them on the boards [*tablas*] at their feet were painted seven devils' heads resembling the Seven Deadly Sins. On the second step were seven boys masked and disguised [*con rostros e sobrepuestos*], who resembled devils who tormented the Seven Deadly Sins. On the third step were the Virtues, on the fourth, seven angels.

On the arrival of the aforementioned King at his table [. . .] the heavens of the angels and archangels began to move and they played their instruments, and the patriarchs, prophets and apostles sang '*Te Deum laudamus*' and other hymns and songs praising and thanking our Lord for the solemn coronation and anointing which the said King had received very devoutly [. . .]

STAGING THE PASSION

The direct portrayal of the Crucifixion is a particularly challenging piece of stage business. Three Castilian texts are notable for affective but indirect presentation: Alonso del Campo's *Auto de la Pasión*[1] [see **I25(iii)**], Gómez Manrique's *Representación del Nacimiento de Nuestro Señor* [see **I55**] and the Burgos *Ecce homo* [see **I56**]. Ronald E. Surtz has argued that plays associated with Franciscan convents, such as Gómez Manrique's *Nacimiento*, portray difficult stage business whilst those associated with the University of Salamanca tradition, such as those by Juan del Encina and Lucas Fernández, narrate such events.[2] The *Auto* and *Representación* each depicts the presentation of the Instruments of the Passion to Christ, the *Nacimiento* to the Infant Christ and the *Auto* to Christ in the Garden of Gethsemene.

1. Note that Alonso del Campo may have reworked older, probably fourteenth-century material.
2. See his 'The "Franciscan Connection" in Early Spanish Theater', *Bulletin of the Comediantes*, 35 (1983–4), pp. 141–52.

I55   Gómez Manrique, *Representación*, 1458–68

> *Representación del Nacimiento de Nuestro Señor*, in *Teatro castellano de la Edad Media*, ed. Surtz, pp. 75–86

Instruments of the Passion [martirios] which they present to the Child
> *The Chalice*

O Holy Child born for our redemption! It is necessary that your holy Majesty drink this pain-filled [*dolorido*] chalice of your cruel Passion to save humanity which was lost through Eve.

The Pillar and Rope

And to this pillar your blessed body, oh powerful King of Heaven, will be tied with these ropes.

The Scourges

With these cruel scourges very enraged executioners [*sayones*] will break your ribs to wash away our sins.

The Crown [of Thorns]

And after your body [*tu persona*] [has been] wounded with whips they will put on you this crown of sorrowful [*dolorosa*] thorns.

The Cross

On this holy cross your body will be put. At that time there will be no light and the temple will fall.

The Nails

With these nails, Lord, your feet and hands will be nailed. You will suffer great pain for wretched human beings.

The Lance

With this very cruel lance your side will be pierced and that which was prophesied will be clear beyond doubt.

Song to quieten the Child

Be quiet, my son, little boy. Pray be quiet, Lord, our Saviour, your suffering will not last long. Angels in heaven, come to console this little boy, beautiful Jesus. This was the reparation, although it cost dear, of that bitter people captive in Egypt. This worthy saint, Child so gracious, came to redeem the afflicted lineage. Let us sing joyfully, gentle sisters, as we are the wives of blessed Jesus. (pp. 83–6)

I56   The Burgos Passion *paso, Ecce homo*, 1520

Joseph E. Gillet, 'Tres pasos de la Pasión y una égloga de la Resurrección (Burgos, 1520)', *PMLA* 47 (1932), pp. 958–9; trans. *Staging*, p. 164

In this short scene [*contemplacion*] of the *Ecce homo*, an honourable man leads Christ round a hall by a rope around his neck and with his crowns of thorns very much suffering from his torture. When Our Lady sees this man, so disfigured, she asks St John, 'Who is he?', and St John answers that her it is her son. Then Our Lady makes a certain lament [*es/clamacion*] to the people:

MARY   My laments [*el suspirar*] prevent me from asking [. . .]

PUPPETS, DOLLS AND MODELS

Dolls and models were frequently used to facilitate the presentation of difficult stage business, such as torture and violence [see **I60–I6I**; cf. **E22**, **E58**, **E59**], or were used in conjunction with actors and elaborate machinery as, for example, to represent the soul of the Virgin in Assumption plays [see **I57**, **I62**]. A model dragon which breathed fire and spat out burning captives appeared at Jaén [see **I58**]. The fictional *Gracisla* (*c.* 1500) contains an elaborate description of a Triumph which includes a model Wheel of Fortune [see **I52**], and House of Fame peopled by models, and a puppet show [see **I59(i), (ii)**].

I57   A Valencian Assumption play, early fifteenth century

Valencia, p. 105; trans. *Staging*, p. 236

When Christ has finished, the Mary shall fall into the arms of the handmaidens [*donzelles*] as if dead [*faent com es morta*] to loud thunder, and they are to place Mary beneath the *cadafal*. And they are to carry up the image [*ymage*] and say all the rest of the Office.

On the second day [*iornada*] when St Michael has returned the soul to the body, those who are beneath the *cadafal* are to take the image quickly, making loud thunder and smoke. The living person [*la viva*] is to emerge suddenly.

I58   A fire-breathing dragon at the court of Don Miguel de Iranzo, Jaén, 1461

Lucas de Iranzo, p. 51; trans. *Staging*, p. 121

At the door of a room at the other end of the hall, opposite the Countess, there appeared the head, very large and made of painted wood, of the said serpent and by artifice it propelled the said boys from its mouth [*lançó por la boca*] one by one, breathing fiery flames. And at the same time the pages, as they wore tunics, sleeves and hoods soaked in spirits [*agua ardiente*] came out burning so that it seemed that they were really aflame.

I59   *Gracisla*: a disguising, *c.* 1500

(i) House of Fame

Gracisla, p. 20

Fame was in the other corner, in the form of a very beautiful lady, with a linen blindfold tied over her eyes, as she is usually depicted; and she was seated on top of gold *carros* with the dead nobles who were worthy of perpetual remembrance, and other virtuous ladies from Antiquity of whom books [*escripturas*] narrate infinite praises, and all these were models [*maçonería*], so wonderfully made that they seemed alive. And above everything else there was a seat [*silla*] on the right hand side of Fame, where the lady was to be put who was lucky enough to win that crown on account of her worth and merit.

(ii) Puppet show

Gracisla, pp. 42–3

Gracisla had, in the air on golden cords [*cordeles dorados*] which were attached from some of the hall's walls and from some small gilded *castillos* which were on the hall's ceiling [? *por el cielo*], Hector and Achilles come out with all the other knights, Trojans and Greeks wielding their weapons [. . . Troy] was so well fashioned from wood [. . .] it was a marvel to see that is was the handiwork of such skilful men that the people [*personas*] actually seemed alive except that they were small.

I60   Majorcan *Representació de Judith*, sixteenth century

Huerta Viñas, pp. 230–1; trans. *Staging*, p. 110

Having said this, she enters the chamber. And Holofernes is to be sleeping in the bed; and there is to be made a head like his, so that it can be held and cut from a dummy body [*una stàtua*]. And kneeling, she says:

[prays to God]

Now she shall get up, take his knife, which is to be on the bolster, and taking the head by its hair, Judith says:

[prays to God].

This said, she is to cut off Holofernes' head and take it to the handmaiden.

161   The Majorcan *Consueta de Sant Crespí y Sant Crespinià, germans, fills de un rey Sarraý*, sixteenth century

Romeu, vol. III, p. 200; trans. *Staging*, p. 110

They are to be beheaded. Where they are standing, there are to be two dead bodies which are to be dummies [*de bulto*] filled with straw, and the heads of two masks with noble expressions [*màscaras molt gentils*].

162   Festa d'Elx, 1709

Trans. *Festa d'Elx*, p. 46

When the *Araceli* arrives at the *cadafal*, without stopping the singing it goes through the stage by a great central trapdoor which has been opened secretly by the hands inside the stage. Its stay within the stage, however, will be very brief: the time necessary for the *Ángel Mayor* to collect a small image of the Virgin dressed in white veiling. This tiny carved model represents the soul of Mary.

INVENTORIES AND ACCOUNTS FOR PROPERTIES AND MACHINES

Three fifteenth-century inventories of the equipment needed for the construction of properties and machinery appear next: the Valencian document lists materials for the construction of aerial machines [the *araceli* for the Virgin and the *peanya*, 'pedestal', for the Angel] [see **163**]; an account book from the León inventory refers to a Sibyl play [see **164**]; and the third records the extraordinary expenses incurred at the Cathedral of Saragossa for a Christmas Nativity to be presented before the Catholic Monarchs [see **165**].

163   The Valencia Assumption: construction of properties, 1440

Valencia, pp. 111–12; partial trans. *Staging*, p. 94

I bought the following things for the building [*per obs*] of the said *representació*:
one thin sheet of wood used by sieve-makers [*fulla prima de fust des cedaçers*] to
    make the rays [*raigs*] of the *Araceli* [. . .];
a dozen sheets of gold foil to cover the said rays;
14 quires [*mans*] of paper for the clouds for the *Araceli* and the angel's *peanya* [. . .];

two pounds of tinplate [? *lata*] for the *Araceli* and the angel's *peanya* and for the
angels' wigs [*xapellets*] and the dove's wings [*per a la palometa ales . . .*];

8 alnes [= 1 metre] of canvas to provide the bodies [? *cossos*] for the *Araceli* Mary
[*la Maria del Araceli*] and the pedestal angel [*àngel de la peanya . . .*];

tin [?] and 2 tinsel sheets to make the wings of the angel which descends from the
dome [*cimbori . . .*];

9 pounds of paste [*aygua-cuyta*] to glue the clouds and wings and the Mary's [*la
Maria*] and the angels' bodies and other trimmings [. . .];

a pound of white wax to make the angel's bunch of lilies [*lo ram de flor de llir . . .*];
verdigris to colour the leaves of the said flower, putty and turpentine [. . .];

7 ounces of fine copper-zinc thread [*fil de lautó*] for the angels' chaplets and for the
lilies and many other things.

164 Accounts for a Sibyl play, León Cathedral, 1452–1520
Gómez Moreno, p. 72

1452 25 December The *provisor* ordered on this day that the Sibyl [*Sevilda*] and
the *juglares* who went with her be given 20 mrs.

1487 Spent by the *admor* for the lunch of the Sibyl of bread, meat, wine and two
pairs of chickens and candles, 170 mrs.
Further, one pair of gloves and 100 pins for the Sibyl, 18 mrs.
Given to the Sibyl as is customary, 50 mrs.
Given to the two trumpeters and to a rattle-shaker [? *sonajero*], 12 reales.

1488 To the Sibyl, 50 mrs.
Further to the drum players [*tamborines*] and the rattle-shakers and a
blind man who played a fanfare [*Ravé*], 9 reales.

1520 The cost of leading [*adiestrar*[1]] the Sibyl with the work of the person who
dresses her, and the lunch for her and the women who went with her and
the pins [*las que con ella fueron y alfileres*], total sum of 147 and a half mrs.
I gave the Sibyl's drum-player [*tamborín*], 3 reales.
To the Count's trumpeters who accompanied the Sibyl, 204 mrs.
To the Sibyl, 2 reales, and some gloves, half a real.
The lunch for the officials who went with the Sibyl cost, 4 reales.
The horse for the Sibyl, half load at a cost of four and a half *reales*, 153
reales.

[1] *Adiestrar* may mean 'to train'.

165 Accounts for a mystery presented before the Catholic Monarchs, Saragossa, 1487
Gómez Moreno, p. 73; partial trans. *Staging*, pp. 55, 56, 92, 145, 187, 190

Extraordinary expenses for the building of the *cadahalsos* ordered by the
Archbishop and the Chapter for the *representación* of the birth of Our Saviour on

the night of Christmas Day of 1487, which was done for the service and contemplation of their Majesties the Catholic Monarchs, the Prince Don Juan and the Princess Doña Isabel.

For the heads of the ox and the ass, for the stable and the pieces of tinsel, 7 sueldos. A pound of combed cotton [*cotón cardado*], 3s. Three of red combed wool, 5s. Some bristle wigs for the prophets, 4s 6d. Seven pairs of gloves for the angels, 6d. For the hire of seven women's wigs for the angels, 6d. A pair of clubs to move the winch [*pujar el torno*] where Mary was seated, 4d. 22 polished, round nails [*clavos palmeras, limados, redondos*], for the angels to turn around on the wheels, 1s 6d. A pair of gloves for the man who is acting God the Father.

I also made a payment on the second day of Christmas for dismantling the platform [*tablado*] on which their Majesties sat on Christmas Night, for the Queen's retinue wished to take it saying that they were royal insignia [*que eran insignias reales*] [see **I32**]; to dismantle and store the wood safely, 2s. On the third day of Christmas to dismantle the *cadahalsos* of the Shepherds' *entremés* to make way for the Feast of the Innocents, 5s. For half a pound of gold [*oro de bacín*] for the heavens and angels' wheels, 6s. For a sheet of tinsel for the stars, 2s. Three pounds of paste for sticking on the clouds and stars, 1s 6d.

The Chapter ordered that Maese Just be given as a gift for the supervision of the whole Nativity *representación*, 5 gold florins or 80s. To their Majesties' minstrels for the music which they made, 2 gold florins or 32s. Further to Maese Paphan for so many parts which he composed (?) [songs in five voices or gatherings] [*quinternos que fizo notados*] to be sung by the prophets, to the Mary and Jesus, half a gold florin or 8s. To the woman who was the Mary, to Jesus and to Joseph who were husband, wife and child, so that the *misterio* and *representación* should be more devout, the Chapter ordered the payment of 2 gold florins or 32s.

DEATH

Shergold (p. 119) has commented on the early appearance of the beckoning figure of Death at the coronation celebrations of Fernando of Antequera [see **I33, I49**; cf. **D64**] a decade before the paintings at the Cemetery of the Holy Innocents in Paris. In the light of this, the controversy surrounding the performative nature of the Castilian *Danza general de la Muerte* [see **I66**] and the existence of a Catalan dramatic version, extracts are included here [see **I67**].

I66   *Danza general de la muerte*, mid-fifteenth century (?)

Ana Maria Álvarez Pellitero, *Dança de la muerte* in her *Teatro medieval*, Colección Austral 157, Madrid, 1990, p. 293

Prologue to the translation
Here begins the *Danza general* which deals with the way Death tells and warns all living beings [*criaturas*] to remember the brevity of their lives and not value life more than it deserves. And similarly Death tells and requires them to see and listen

attentively every day to what wise preachers, giving them good and beneficial advice, say and advise: that they strive to do good works to obtain a broad pardon for their sins. And, next, showing in practice [*mostrando por espiriença*] what has been said, calling and requiring all the estates of the world to come willingly or otherwise. Beginning thus:

Death

I am Death guaranteed to all living beings who are and who will be in this temporal world [*el mundo durante*].

167   *Representatió de la Mort*, possibly by Francesc d'Olesa, *c.* 1540

José Romeu Figueras, 'La *Representatió de la Mort*, obra dramática del siglo XVI, y la *Danza de la Muerte*', *Boletín de la Real Academia de Buenas Letras de Barcelona* 27 (1957–8), pp. 209–11

The rich man falls dead and the devils carry him away. And Death hides. Enter a poor man; the poor man speaks:

The Poor Man: All my life is toil; I have not even one hour of rest and my spirit falters [. . .]

Death appears and says:

Death: Come to me, friend [*compañó*], leave [? *aflagit de*] poverty behind. Do not fear, I am Death, to whom you have given your devotion [*a qui teniu devosió*], your desire is granted [. . .]

The Poor Man falls dead and Death hides. And a gambler enters with playing cards [*cartas*] *in his hands* [. . .]

DANCE

Despite the repeated prohibition of dancing during the celebration of First Masses [see **169**], religious dance was performed by clerics as part of the celebrations of certain feasts [see **168, 171**]. In Toledo, dance formed part of the ceremony of the elevation of Don Juan Martínez Silíceo in 1546 to cardinal.[1] The celebrations included a *Danza de Salvajes*, or Dance of Wild Men, and the dance of the *seises*, a solemn dance performed by choirboys, which is thought to have originated in the Mozarabic rite and a version of which is still performed in the Cathedral of Seville.[2]

The presence of dance in what appears to be an extra-liturgical performance of a vernacular antiphon from Toledo is also of note in this connection. As early as 1785 Felipe Fernández Vallejo wrote a description of dramatic performances at the Cathedral of Toledo in which he described a ceremony for Lauds on Christmas Eve which was in existence by the late sixteenth century and which continued to be performed when he wrote, with minor modification but without the dance. Vallejo drew his information from a late fifteenth-century manuscript by Juan Chaves de Arcayos [see **170(i)**]; this was considered lost, but Donovan located it along with a further Toledo ceremonial from the end of the fifteenth century containing a version of a Christmas Lauds ceremony, important for its combination of Latin tropes and the vernacular '*Bien vengades, pastores*', a version of the antiphon *Pastores dicite* [see **I70(ii)**]. References to dance in Shepherds' plays occur throughout the sixteenth century, one example of which is Suárez de Robles' *Danza del Santo Nacimiento*, printed in 1561 [see **I72**], whilst others may be found in the *Códice de autos viejos*.

1. See Joseph E. Gillet, 'The "Memorias" of Felipe Fernández Vallejo and the History of Early Spanish Drama', in *Essays and Studies in Honor of Carleton Brown*, New York and London, 1940, pp. 270–2.
2. On the *seises* see ibid., pp. 620–1, and Shergold, p. 45.

I68   Shepherds dance at the Portuguese Court, Christmastide 1500

I. S. Révah, 'Manifestationes théâtrales pré-vicentines: les *momos* de 1500', *Bulletin d'Histoire du Théâtre Portugais* 3 (1952), p. 94, and Gómez Moreno, p. 145 [see **I40, I44**]

The King, leaving the Queen in gallery, went down below to where his curtained seat [*sitial*] was, and they listened solemnly to matins, with organs, singing [*chançonetas*] and shepherds, who entered the chapel presently dancing and singing *Gloria in excelsis Deo*.

I69   The Synod of Badajoz, 1501

Moll, p. 214

[. . .] at that solemnity [First Masses] clerics ought not sing profane songs nor dance[1] nor undress [*se pongan en cuerpo*] putting on secular clothes nor performing other *representaciones* and *juegos*, except that which may accompany the First Mass with all the clerics decently dressed [i.e. in religious habit].

1 The Spanish phrase is '*ni baylen, ni dancen*'.

I70   Toledo Shepherds' dance, *c.* 1500

(I) 'Bien vengades'

Arcayos MS, Toledo Cathedral Library, MS 42.29; pr. Donovan, pp. 185–6

There the *cantors* ask the following questions in plain chant and the choir directors [*scoapsicoles*] hold two of those little shepherds by the hand and ask them together with the *cantors* the following:

QUESTION Welcome, shepherds, be welcome. Shepherds, where did you go? Tell us what you saw?

RESPONSE   Be welcome, Shepherds of the flock, tell us the good news [*mandado*].
   Be welcome. [Response. And to this the *cantors* always reply:]
SHEPHERDS   We saw the flower of flowers was born in Bethlehem, my lords.
RESPONSE   Be welcome.
SHEPHERDS   This flower which has been born today will give us the fruit of life.
RESPONSE   Be welcome.
SHEPHERDS   A boy-child and King of the Heavens that has been born today as
   consolation.
RESPONSE   Be welcome.
[SHEPHERDS]   He is between two animals, wrapped in poor swaddling clothes.
RESPONSE   Be welcome.
[SHEPHERDS]   The mother who bore him remained virginal and pure.
RESPONSE   Be welcome.
[SHEPHERDS]   We pray Son and Mother that it may please them to save us.
RESPONSE   Be welcome.

On finishing the singing of these verses, the shepherds will say a *villancico*, dancing
and singing between the Gospel lectern [? *aguila*] and the pew of choristers who
were wearing vestments [*caperos*].

(ii) Late fifteenth-century Toledo ceremonial

University of Madrid Library, Sección de Derecho, MS 149, *Ordinarium Toletanum*; pr.
Donovan, p. 48

The two caped *cantors* are to sing the *Laudes absolute, Natus est nobis*. They go on in
the usual way until the line of *Laudate Dominum de celis* where they say '*ut faciat in
eis judicium conscriptum*'. When this line is finished the *cantors* shall say the antiphon which begins, *Pastores dicite*.

And, once finished, the shepherds from the highest step of the high alter shall
say, '*Infantem vidimus* [. . .]'

Once this is finished, the directors of the caped choir say, *Laudate Dominum in
sanctis eius*. And then they should repeat the antiphon, *Pastores dicite*. When the
antiphon is finished, the shepherds say at the door of the archbishop's choir,
Infantem vidimus. Then the robed *cantors* say, *Laudate eum in virtutibus eius*. And
when this verse is finished the *cantors* repeat, *Pastores dicite*.

When this is finished, the shepherds say from inside the choir, *Infantem vidimus*.
This done the two robed *cantors* say, *Bien vengades pastores, etc*. And the boy shepherds [*pastorçicos*] respond, telling the things they saw. And they dance and sing a
little. And they go to change.

I71   Contract between Gonzalo Guerra and the Tanners' Guild, Seville, 1540

C, López Martínez, *Teatros y comediantes sevillanos del siglo XVI*, Seville, 1940, p. 99; trans. *Staging*, p. 173

I undertake to provide at Corpus Christi this year a dance composed of seven dancers: the Magi, a lady, and three pages. The seven dancers will come out of a pavilion, and the Magi will go up to Mary and the Child Jesus, who will be effigies [*que han de ir de bulto*] at a crib [*portalico*] together with St Joseph, a mule and an ox and a drummer, and will offer gifts and worship. I shall present myself, with the dancers, at the time when the procession and banner of the said guild comes out of the cathedral, and we shall accompany the procession dancing for as long as it lasts, for a fee of 8 gold ducats. Further I will undertake to give you a preview [*el ensayo*] of the dance at Whitsun.

I72   Suárez de Robles, *Natividad*, 1561 (?)

Gillet, pp. 624–33; trans. *Staging*, pp. 174–5

The shepherds are to enter in two lines preceded by a psaltery [*psalterio*] or a kettle drum [*tamborino*] player to whose rhythm [*son*] they are to dance up to the middle of the church, and there they will make a few figures [*laços*]. After the shepherds are to come the angels with candles and, if it can be arranged, eight angels carrying the canopy of the Most Holy Sacrament under which will be Our Lady and St Joseph, and they shall go up to the steps of the high altar, where there is to be a cradle like a manger, and in it they shall place the Child Jesus. Our Lady and St Joseph kneel, their hands positioned as if in prayer [*contemplación*], the angels [are] to be distributed on each side facing one another and looking at the Child. Whilst they are in this position, the shepherds shall have finished dancing, and then an angel shall go into the pulpit and say the following and as the shepherds listen, they are to seem afraid and look up here and there.

ANGEL   Do not be afraid [. . .]

Here the angel disappears and those at the Nativity sing this *villancico*:

Glory to God in the highest [. . .]

Here the angels stop singing and the shepherds speak, beginning with Anton, the first, without moving from their positions:

ANTON   There near the city [. . .]

Here they dance a figure and dance towards the Nativity, and before they stop they dance the same figure there before it, and when they have finished the angels sing this *villancico*, and the shepherds reply:

ANGELS   Sweet shepherds [. . .]

When the singing is finished, being in the same order as hitherto, the first shepherd, who is Anton, says:

ANTON   Illustrious company [. . .]

Now Anton comes out dancing and, after having made some steps [*alguna mudança*], he remains kneeling and says:

ANTON   I adore you [. . .]

Here he can offer a rattle or something else. Then the instrument is played at the rhythm at which Anton is to get up dancing, and at the same time Rebanado will come forward, and both will dance to the same rhythm, one dancing back to his place, and the other to the place where Anton knelt, and they shall stop at the same time. The others are to do the same.

[Business of presenting and receiving the gifts takes place – Anton and Rebanado introduce a song to be sung as the shepherds return to their flocks.]

Now the shepherds sing this *villancico*, beginning first with Anton and Rebanado, and then the others. After singing the verse, the angels must sing, saying, 'Here in Bethlehem'. When the shepherds have made a figure, stopping they sing a verse, the angels respond, and they are to dance again, and they will do this until they have finished all the verses, which are to be sung to the tune of others which go, 'At the gates of the King a flower &c', 'There in Bethlehem, Our God is born'.

EARLY ACTOR-MANAGERS

From the early sixteenth century named individuals took responsibility for the production of dramatic pieces for presentation during the Corpus Christi procession at Seville. In 1538 Mutio the Italian 'de la comedia' requested payment for his group for the *carros* they provided [see I73]; in 1540 Gonzalo Guerra signed a contract with the Tanners' Guild for a Magi dance [see I71]; and in 1543 Lope de Rueda produced an Assumption play for the guild of wine merchants and makers of wine skins [see I74].

I73   Mutio, 'Italiano de la comedia', petitions for expenses, Seville, 1538

José Sánchez Arjona, *El teatro en Sevilla en los siglos XVI y XVII: estudios históricos*, Madrid, 1887, p. 43

The Italians who produced the two *carros* at the *fiesta* of Corpus Christi, request from your honour that – as it is customary to distribute gifts [*joyas*] to those who show the best will and work on such a day – they having done everything that they could, that your honours [*sic*] be so good (although there be little of merit in them [the Italians] which may be enjoyed), that everything be as they request with that brevity which your honour's pleasure and their necessity require, so that they may go on their way and free themselves from such debts as they have run up to maintain such a notable pleasure.

174   Lope de Rueda's Assumption Play, Seville, 1543

Shergold, p. 100

To bring out on Corpus Christi day on two *carros* the *Auto* of the Assumption of Our Lady, how and as it was performed last year, in the year of our Lord 1542, or better if possible, all at my expense, providing the cast [*gente*], costumes, angels, singers [*cantores*], the wax [for the torches] which the Apostles will carry burning, and a curtained bed for the sum of 24 gold ducats.

Section J
Traditions of the people: customs and folk drama

Edited by THOMAS PETTITT *and* LEIF SØNDERGAARD

Introduction and abbreviations*

The inclusion in this volume of a separate section on customs and folk drama is more a reflection of modern scholarly convention than of medieval reality. The notion of folk drama as a distinct form of theatrical activity, the province of folklorists rather than theatre historians, emerged at the end of the nineteenth century within a residualist concept of folklore as the survival, in more civilised (medieval or modern) times, of cultural activities characteristic of earlier (savage or barbaric) phases of cultural evolution. In these terms folk drama preserves, albeit in degenerate form, ancient cultic rituals designed to preserve or enhance the reproductive capacities of crops, herds, or men, and hence the survival of the community. It ill becomes a theatre historian to express an opinion whether this is right or wrong, but it may be legitimate to note that the evolutionary anthropology underpinning this view, most forcefully and comprehensively represented by Sir James Frazer's *The Golden Bough,* was dismissed by anthropologists in the early part of the last century; that this view of folklore in general and folk drama in particular, having been adhered to long enough to bring their discipline into academic disfavour, has been emphatically rejected by folklorists themselves over the last couple of decades. More practically, whatever the origins of a given observance, they can be of significance for the student of medieval drama only if they retained some living significance in the Middle Ages, and this must be a matter of historical documentation rather than speculation. In the present context, however, the theory of ritual origins is most significant in the history of scholarship as the effective *definition* of folk drama, distinguishing it from other varieties of theatrical activity (for many of which ritual origins have nonetheless also been claimed): once it is questioned, the matter of demarcation becomes a pressing and virtually insuperable problem.

The 'folk' in folklore and folk drama (and the 'people' in 'traditions of the people') is theoretically susceptible to sociological specification, 'peasants and craftsmen' (roughly corresponding to one of the three 'estates' in medieval theory) being an attractive option available from studies of early popular culture. But con-

*The editors of this section gratefully acknowledge assistance from Kurt Villads Jensen and Reinhold Schröder with the work of translation.

ventional wisdom in the latter field suggests that their culture was unlikely to have been exclusive to them. There was, rather, a 'little tradition' of popular culture in the broad sense, common to both folk and élite (and the two other 'estates'), with the latter, however, also participating in a 'great tradition' of literate and literary culture in which they alone were qualified by leisure, education and refinement to indulge. Liturgical drama and school plays evidently belong to the great tradition, but most of what we call medieval theatre, from mummings and May games to mystery cycles and masques, belonged to the little tradition of common culture. Within this field, differences are of degree rather than kind, and demarcations consequently arbitrary. A late medieval 'mumming' of the London establishment to a royal palace (as at Kennington in 1377 [see **D65**] will have been bigger and better than, but essentially the same custom as, the humbler house-visits of French peasants or German urban craftsmen [see e.g. **F35–F44**]. There are no definitive criteria which would warrant distinguishing between the perambulation of a decorated plough or a riding of St George and the dragon as 'folklore', and a royal entry or a lord mayor's parade as 'pageantry'.

Distinctions are much easier following the post-Renaissance withdrawal of the élite from the popular, common culture and the effective shift of theatre into the great tradition, leaving the less privileged classes to persist in their traditional practices, which are then rediscovered (and renamed 'folklore') by the élite in the nineteenth century. 'Folk drama' *is* a legitimate term for the more dramatic of these rediscovered traditions as they were when rediscovered, but applying it retrospectively would simply make most medieval drama folk drama (which is why German scholarship calls mystery and miracle plays *Volksschauspiele*).

The most effective available term is undoubtedly 'custom', and it is feasible to distinguish a 'customary drama', an integral feature of traditional activities associated with recurrent festivals or festive occasions, as opposed to dramatic activities largely independent of any customary context, say performances by itinerant entertainers (and later the professional actors), or monologues, songs and narratives whose performance might have a dramatic aspect. But by this criterion too most medieval drama is 'customary'; a mystery cycle at Corpus Christi is no less a seasonal custom than a Robin Hood Play at Whitsun or a *Fastnachtspiel* at Shrovetide.

There remains only the arbitrary, but effective, criterion of dramatic elaboration. The degree of mimesis in customary performance varies between customs, or within a given custom over time or between local traditions. At some point, when the action is more representational than presentational, when the guise is more costume than disguise, when comportment is more impersonation than display, when the words are dialogue rather than speeches, when the progress of the performance is more a plot than a sequence of items, then it is possible to claim we are in the presence of drama as well as custom, of a play rather than a show or a ceremony. Customary performances with a fully-fledged dramatic element (such as farces, *sotties*, *Fastnachtspiele*) thus qualify as 'theatre', and figure elsewhere in this volume. What follows therefore largely comprises records of customs in forms which do not fully qualify, in conventional terms, as drama, or in which the play is emphatically subservient to the customary context.

The essentially oral nature of traditional culture means that written records are always in some way exceptional, and essentially secondary to the activity itself. Medieval documentation, with the execption of normative sources such as regulations and occasional outbursts by church councils or reforming bishops, is largely restricted to relatively uninformative entries recording payments to, or receipts from, performers 'with the star', 'with the plough', 'who performed the sword dance', or the like. Since specifying the source often requires more words than the record itself, we have largely avoided these in favour of the more voluble accounts of sixteenth-century sources which reflect a time when the customs were seen as problematic and in need of reform or abolition (while nonetheless indicating that they are traditional and derive from pre-Reformation times). The notion of a 'long' Middle Ages extending, in some aspects of culture, to the late eighteenth century, may also be invoked in deploying later evidence. We have occasionally had recourse to dramatic texts, to the extent that they reveal performance aspects, and to later antiquarian or folkloristic accounts, but only for traditions with a satisfactory medieval documentation (hence the otherwise surprising omission of the English mummers' plays), but with the appreciation that while these may record 'survivals' of medieval customs, a survival is by definition still alive, and changes are likely to have occurred.

The following abbreviations are used throughout this section.

Kirchmair/Googe	Thomas Kirchmair/Kirchmeyer ('Naogeorgus'), *Regnum Papisticum* (1553); translated as *The Popish Kingdome, or reigne of Antichrist, written in Latine verse by Thomas Naogeorgus, and englyshed by Barnabe Googe*, London, 1570; facsimile reprint ed. Robert Charles Hope, London, Chiswick Press, 1880. [Googe's translation is not in itself evidence that all these observances were practised in England.]
Mueller *Caesarius*	*Saint Caesarius of Arles. Sermons*, trans. Mary M. Mueller, 3 vols., New York and Washington, 1956–73.
Vaultier	Roger Vaultier, *Le folklore pendant la guerre de cent ans d'après les lettres de rémission du trésor des chartes*, Paris, 1965.

I. Pre-Christian origins?

The collapse of the anthropological framework for the ritual origins of custom and folk drama does not in itself rule out such origins; it merely means they have to be demonstrated by conventional historical means, in exploring the pre-Christian practices of European cultures (effectively Celto-Germanic and Graeco-Roman), rather than by appeal to exotic tribal practices elsewhere in the world. We accordingly include a selection of early records which might be invoked in such a project. Given the emphasis on fertility in the ritual origins theory, and the hints in the records that some customs were indeed seen as promoting the growth of crops, the cult of Freyr, the Norse god of fertility, is a natural focus of interest. The first of the following items [J1] suggests a distinctly dramatic element in cult practices, while the second [J2] indicates a luck-bringing perambulation anticipating many later traditions. We also include two documents relative to the question of continuity between pagan and Christian religious sites and practices: the celebrated instruction from Pope Gregory addressing the church mission to the Anglo-Saxons urging them to rededicate pagan sites and practices to the new religion [J3], complemented by an outburst from Caesarius of Arles [J4], chronologically earlier but later relative to the local conversion to Christianity, condemning precisely the continued practices at heathen shrines (and another document below [J5] records his attack on pagan practices in churchyards).

THE CULT OF FREYR

J1   **Saxo Grammaticus on the Freyr cult at Uppsala**

Saxo Grammaticus, *Gesta Danorum* (a history of Danish kings from prehistoric times onwards, *c.* 1200), book VI; pr. Saxo Grammaticus, *The History of the Danes, Books I–IX*, trans. Peter Fisher, ed. Hilda Ellis Davidson, 2 vols., Cambridge, 1979, vol. I, p. 172

[On the adventures of the legendary warrior, Starkather, who quits Sweden after a seven-year sojourn.]

[. . .] for, living at Uppsala in the period of the sacrifices, he had been disgusted with the womanish bodily movements, the clatter of actors on the stage, and the soft tinkling of bells.

J2   The perambulations of Freyr and his 'wife'

The Tale of Ogmund Dytt (probably of the thirteenth century, an episode in *The Great Saga of Olaf Tryggvason*), pr. *Two Tales of Icelanders. Ögmundar tháttr dytts og Gunnar Helmings. Olkofra thattr*, ed. Ian Wyatt and Jessie Cook, Durham, 1993, pp. 1–16; trans. John McKinnell, *Viga-Glums Saga. With the Tales of Ögmund Bash and Thorvald Chatterbox*, Edinburgh, 1987, pp. 132–44 (this episode, pp. 141–3)

[A Norwegian, Gunnar Helming, is falsely suspected of a murder, and flees to Sweden.]

Great heathen sacrifices were held there at that time, and for a long while Frey had been the god who was worshipped most there – and so much power had been gained by Frey's statue that the devil used to speak out of the mouth of the idol, and a young and beautiful woman had been obtained to serve Frey. It was the faith of the local people that Frey was alive, as seemed to some extent to be the case, and they thought he would need to have a sexual relationship with his wife; along with Frey she was to have complete control over the temple settlement and all that belonged to it [. . .] Gunnar got on with people better the longer he stayed there, because of his entertaining conversation and other excellent qualities. Once more he came to speak with Frey's wife and asked about his position. She answered: 'People have taken a liking to you, and I think it would be a good idea for you to stay here over the winter and go to the feasts with the Frey and me when he goes to ensure good crops for the people – yet he dislikes you.'

[Their journey takes them over mountain passes, and when they are struck by a blizzard all the retainers except Gunnar abandon them. Gunnar himself eventually tires, and decides to sit in the cart, provoking a fight with the idol which Gunnar, with God's aid, wins:]

Then the devil which had been hidden in the idol went rushing out of it, and only a hollow log of wood was left – and he broke that to pieces. Afterwards he gave the woman two choices – either he would abandon her and look out for himself, or else she was to say when they came to settled country that he was Frey. She said she would much rather say that. Then he put on the clothes of the idol, and the weather began to clear.

At last they came to the feast which had been prepared for them [. . .] Now it seemed to the people an omen of great importance that Frey had shown his power by bringing himself into settled lands with his wife in such weather that everyone had fled from them, and what was more, that he could now walk with other men, and ate and drank like other people. They went round to feasts throughout the winter. Frey was always very silent with other people. But it did happen that he wouldn't allow living beasts to be slaughtered before him as before, and would accept no sacrifice and no oblations except gold and silver, good clothing or other precious things. But when some time had passed, it became clear that Frey's wife was pregnant. That was taken to be excellent, and the Swedes were now delighted with this god of theirs; the weather too was mild and all the crops so promising that nobody could remember the like.

J3 The Gregorian compromise, 601

The Venerable Bede, *Historia ecclesiastica gentis Anglorum, c.* 731 (transcribing a letter sent by Pope Gregory, 601, to Abbot Mellitus, with instructions for the mission converting England to Christianity); pr. *A History of the English Church and People*, trans. Leo Sherley-Price, revised R. E. Latham, Penguin Classics, Harmondsworth, 1955; reprinted 1968, pp. 86–7

[. . .] when by God's help you reach our most reverend brother, Bishop Augustine, we wish you to inform him that we have been giving careful thought to the affairs of the English, and have come to the conclusion that the temples of the idols among that people should on no account be destroyed. The idols are to be destroyed, but the temples themselves are to be aspersed with holy water, altars set up in them, and relics deposited there. For if these temples are well built, they must be purified from the worship of demons and dedicated to the service of the true God. In this way, we hope that the people, seeing that their temples are not destroyed, may abandon their error and, flocking more readily to their accustomed resorts, may come to know and adore the true God. And since they have a custom of sacrificing many oxen to demons, let some other solemnity be substituted in its place, such as a day of Dedication or the Festivals of the holy martyrs whose relics are enshrined there. On such occasions they might well construct shelters of boughs for themselves around the churches that were once temples, and celebrate with devout feasting. They are no longer to sacrifice beasts to the Devil, but they may kill them for food to the praise of God, and give thanks to the Giver of all gifts for the plenty they enjoy.

J4 Condemned by Caesarius of Arles, early sixth century

Caesarius of Arles, *Sermon* 54 (Gaul, early sixth century); trans. Mueller *Caesarius*, vol. 1, 269–70

5. [. . .] Christians should not fulfill vows to trees or adore fountains [. . .] So, if a man has any kind of shrines on his land or in his country house, trees or altars near his estate where miserable men are wont to fulfill such vows, if he does not destroy them and cut them down, he will doubtless be a participant in those impious practices which are carried on there [. . .] See the misery and foolishness of men: they pay honour to a dead tree, but despise the living God [. . .]

6. It further occurs to me that some people, through either simplicity or ignorance or, what is certainly more likely, gluttony, do not fear or blush to eat of that impious food and those wicked sacrifices which are still offered according to the custom of the pagans. For this reason I exhort you, and before God and his angels I proclaim, that you should not come to those devilish banquets which are held at a shrine or fountains or trees.

II   *Seasonal customs*

Customary activities are amenable to categorisation from several perspectives, for example in terms of their social auspices: there are customs or variants of customs specific to households (from the royal court to the peasant cottage), institutions (colleges, monasteries, cathedrals), communities (cities, parishes), and associations (craft and religious guilds), and even more customs involving a structured encounter between two such groups (e.g. a house visit). Function similarly provides a system of categories: some customs are merely celebratory, others seem more demonstrative, asserting rights or expressing attitudes (benevolent or malevolent). Yet others are performed for their effect: to enhance fertility; to bring good luck and good health; to cause inconvenience or harm; many are designed mainly to collect money or achieve a share of festive refreshment. There are pastimes (engaged in by all present); entertainments (distinguishing clearly between performers and spectators), and ceremonies; the activities can be physical (dancing, fighting), visual (the exhibition of costumes or objects), aural (music, song, speech), and more or less dramatic. In presenting the material, we have opted for categorisation by incidence, distinguishing customs whose incidence is tied to a seasonal or calendrical pattern, and those with some other rhythm (or none). The only major awkwardness in this approach results from geographical discrepancies: it does seem to be the case (and not an illusion reflecting documentation patterns) that while in England the centre of gravity of the winter season was Christmas – New Year – Twelfth Night, in continental Europe the major focus was rather on Shrovetide/Carnival (sometimes seen as the culmination of an extended Christmas period). In consequence several customs which in England (at least in recent centuries) are associated with Christmas (plough-trailing; sword dancing; mumming) are documented on the continent in connection with Shrovetide. There is a similar tendency for customs (explicitly) symbolising the beginning of summer to occur at different calendrical dates in different parts of Europe and at different periods.

J5   Condemned by Caesarius of Arles, early sixth century

Caesarius of Arles, *Sermon* 55; trans. Mueller *Caesarius*, vol. I, 271

There are some people who come to the birthday festivals of the martyrs for this sole purpose, that they may destroy themselves and ruin others by intoxication, dancing, singing shameful songs, leading the choral dance, and pantomiming in a devilish fashion.

J6   Prohibited by Edmund Grindal, archbishop of York, 1570–6

Archbishop Grindal's Register, York, Borthwick Institute of Historical Research, Reg. 30 Grindal, fo. 130 verso; pr. REED, *York*, vol. I, p. 358

Item that the minister and churchwardens shall not suffer any lords of misrule or summer lords or ladies or any disguised persons or others at Christmas or at May games, or any minstrels, morris dancers or others at rushbearings, to come unreverently into any church or chapel or churchyard and there dance or play any unseemly parts with scoffs, jests, wanton gestures or ribald talk, namely in the time of divine service or of any sermon.

CHRISTMAS AND NEW YEAR

[*New Year beast-guise*]

J7   Condemned by Caesarius of Arles, early sixth century

Caesarius of Arles, *Sermon* 192, 'On the Calends of January'; trans. Mueller *Caesarius*, vol. III, pp. 26–30. By permission of Catholic University of America Press

[. . .] in these days miserable men, and what is worse, even some who are baptised, assume false forms and unnatural appearances, and certain features in them are especially worthy of laughter or rather of sorrow. For what wise man can believe that men are found to be of sound mind, if they are willing to make themselves a small stag or to be changed into the condition of wild beasts? Some are clothed in the skins of sheep, and others take the heads of wild beasts, rejoicing and exulting if they have transformed themselves into the appearance of animals in such a way that they do not seem to be men.

J8   Condemned by Burchard of Worms, *c.* 1010

Burchard of Worms, *Decretal*, book XIX, *Corrector et medicus*, ch. V, no. 99; pr. *Patrologia Latina*, CXL, 537–1058; trans. John T. McNeill and Helena M. Gamer, *Medieval Handbooks of Penance. A Translation of the Principal 'libri poenitentiales' and Selections from Related Documents*, New York, 1938, reprinted 1965, pp. 334–5

Hast thou done anything like what the pagans did, and still do, on the first of January in [the guise of] a stag or a calf? If thou hast, thou shalt do penance for thirty days on bread and water.

J9   The Byzantine Dance of the Goths, tenth century

Constantine VII Porphyrogenitus, *De Caeremoniis Aulae Byzantinae* (*c.* 953, a systematic description of court ceremonial, compiled for the benefit of his successors), book I, ch. 83; pr. Karl Kraus, 'Das Gotische Weihnachtsspiel', *Beiträge zur Geschichte der deutschen Sprache und Literatur* 20 (1985), pp. 224–7, trans. Minna Skafte Jensen

[It is not suggested that this is the same custom as that documented in the two preceding entries.]

On the ninth day of the Twelve Days, when the rulers are sitting at dinner, the one which is also called the Harvest Dinner, those who are to perform the *gothicon* assemble by the two entrances to the great dining hall with the nineteen sofas, in the following manner: On the left side, where the *Drungarius* of the Fleet also stands, the Master of the Venetan section takes up his position together with a few ordinary members and the pandura-players with their instruments, and behind him the two Goths, wearing hides turned inside out[1] and masks of different forms, holding shields in their left hands and sticks in the right. Correspondingly on the right side, where the *Drungarius* of the Night Watch also stands, the Master of the Prasinan section takes up his position together with a few ordinary members and the pandura-players with their instruments and behind him the two Goths, wearing hides turned inside out and masks of different forms, holding shields in their left hands and sticks in the right.[2]

And after the conclusion of the ball-game, when the Ruler orders the Master of the Table to lead them in, then the Master of the Table at once gives a signal to the Master of the Theatre, and as he goes out himself, he orders them to go in. And as they run and strike the shields with the sticks they are holding, and carry out the striking, they say, 'tul, tul'. And continuing to say this they approach the neighbourhood of the royal table until they are only a little distance from it, and from there the two groups join together and assume a ring formation, with one group enclosed in the ring, and the other group surrounding them on the outside. And they do this three times, after which they separate, and take up positions in their usual places, the Venetans' group on the left, the Prasinans' group on the right, together with the ordinary members of both parties, and both groups sing the *gothicon*, i.e. the following, while of course the pandura-players also perform their native melody:

'gauzas. bonas. bekedias. hagia. gaudentes. elkebonides. enkertys. hagia. bona. hora. tutu. bantes. bona amore. episkyantes. idesalbatus. nana. deus. deus. sebakiba. nana. deumonogyngybele. gybilus. gybelares. nana. gybilus. gybelares. nana. tu gegdema. de tulbele. nikato tuldo. nana. As Ezekias armed himself against the Assyrian enemies. anana. as he put all his trust in God the lover of man. nana. he has conquered all nations and the tyranny of the ungodly. hagia. the Saviour, the good rulers. nana. everything which is inimical to you will be enslaved at your feet. iber. iberiem. tu ingerua. gergerethro. nana. sikadiase peretures.'[3]

And next the masters together with the ordinary members say the *alphabetarion*:[4]

'Anana. You will be wreathed by the hand of the Almighty God, ruler, from heaven. You will be seen as the prize of victory, lords of the world, benefactors. You will be seen as noble by your opponents, in that you give the Romans life-giving benefits.'

And next the masters say again thus:

'hagias ta. anate anetane. Your commands are stronger than weapons against all enemies. The life and wealth of the Romans are truly the fall of other tribes. You have been found like the wall of the state. God has given you boughs of the same throne, benefactor.'

And when the masters then say to the Goths, '*ampaato*', the Goths form a circle at the nod of the same masters, and as they beat the shields with the sticks and say 'tul, tul', they surround from within the masters of the two groups, and as they again draw apart and resume their usual places, and again the masters begin to say,

'I***, K***, L***, M***'

and again is done as was previously described, and as the Goths separate and take up their own positions the masters say:

'N***, X***, O***, P***',

and again is done as was previously described, and as the Goths separate and take up their own positions the masters say:

'R***, S***, T***, Y***'.

And again is done as was previously described, and as the Goths separate and take up their own positions the masters say:

'The light, your virtues, has let justice ascend into the power of the sun. May Christ be with each one, as he wreathes your temples, you who rule through your own votes, as lords and rulers over the frontiers of the Empire.'

And after the completion of the *alphabetarion* they say:

'God will give many years to your holy kingdom.'

And the Goths beat the sticks on the shields still saying 'tul, tul', and run out, the group of the Venetans to the left, the group of the Prasinans to the right.

¹ This is generally taken to mean that the rough (furry ?) side is worn outwards (giving an animal-like impression), in contrast to inwards (as would be normal when the hide was used as a coat).
² There may be reference here to two of the four stables whose horses competed in the Roman circus: the 'Blues' (Venetans) and the 'Greens' (Prasinans).
³ The meaning of these lines is much discussed: they seem to contain Greek, Latin, and (possibly) Germanic words, and the text may well have suffered corruption in scribal transmission. One attempt at a translation is that of C. Müller, 'Ein altgermanisches Weihnachtspiel, genant das gotische', *Zeitschrift für deutsche Philologie* 14 (1882), pp. 442–60, whose German translation is here rendered in English:

> Rejoice, the noble company: *Hagia*!
> Enjoy the day of the festival with combat: *Hagia*!
> Raising the trumpet at this gracious time.
> Watching with delight.
> Nana, the God, the God, is saved;
> On days of festival, Nana,
> Divine celebration.
> Joy; rejoicers;
> Joy; rejoicers.
> You, who on the final day arise, beautiful Tul;
> Victory, O Tul, O Nana!   (p. 453)

Scholarship is divided between a Germanic tendency, which would like to see the observance as a survival of something genuinely Gothic, and those who see it as essentially Byzantine. For a recent discussion in English of the account see Terry Gunnell, *The Origins of Drama in Scandinavia*, Woodbridge, 1995, pp. 72–6.
⁴ Evidently a euology in which each line began with a letter of the Greek alphabet, for parts of which the account supplies only the letter concerned.

The parade of Christmas and his wife

J10   Yule's suppression ordered by the Ecclesiastical Commission, York, 1572

Letter to York City Council. Act Book 1572–4, fos. 41–1 verso. Borthwick Institute of Historical Research, York; pr. REED, *York*, vol. i, p. 369

[. . .] whereas there hath been heretofore a very rude and barbarous custom maintained in this city, and in no other city or town of this realm to our knowledge, that yearly upon St Thomas' Day before Christmas, two disguised persons called Yule and Yule's wife should ride through the city very undecently and uncomely drawing great concourses of people after them to gaze, often times committing other enormities. Forasmuch as the said disguised riding and concourse aforesaid besides other inconveniencies tendeth also to the prophaning of that day appointed to holy uses, and also withdraweth great multitudes of people from divine service and sermons. We have thought good by these presents to will and require you, and nevertheless in the Queen's Majesty's name by virtue of her Highness' commission for causes ecclesiastical within the Province of York, to us and others directed straightly to charge and command you, that ye take order that no such riding of Yule and Yule's wife be from henceforth attempted or used [. . .]

The Christmas Lord

J11   The Twelfth-Day King described by Thomas Kirchmair, 1553

Thomas Kirchmair/Kirchmayer ('Naogeorgus'), *Regnum papisticum* (a Reformist attack on Catholic observances, 1553 [see **B8**, **B34**, **J33**, **J47**, **J61**]; pr. Kirchmair/Googe, pp. 45b–46a

Here sundry friends together come, and meet in company,
And make a king amongst themselves by voice or destiny:
Who after princely guise appoints, his officers alway,
Then unto feasting do they go, and long time after play:
Upon their boards in order thick the dainty dishes stand,
Till that their purses empty be, and creditors at hand.
Their children herein follow them, and choosing princes here,
With pomp and great solemnity, they meet and make good cheer:
With money either got by stealth, or of their parents left [eft],
That so they may be trained to know both riot here and theft.

J12   Thomas More compares William Tyndale to a Christmas Lord

Sir Thomas More, *A Confutacyon of Tyndales Answer*, 1532 (a contribution to Reformation polemics); pr. *The Complete Works of Sir Thomas More*, vol. VIII, *A Confutacyon of Tyndales Answer*, ed. Louise A Schuster *et al.*, part 1, New Haven and London, 1973, p. 42

[Anyone considering Tyndale and his followers] would he not believe that these men were some sort of friars following an abbot of misrule in a Christmas game that were clothed [pricked] in blankets, and who then should stand up and preach upon a stool and make a mocking [mowing] sermon? And as debased [lewd] sermons as they make in such wicked [naughty] games, would God that these men's earnest sermons were not yet much worse. But surely as evil as the other is, yet is there more harm and more deadly poison too in this one sermon of Tyndale's [. . .] than in a hundred sermons of Friar Frappe, that first gapes and then blesses, and looks holily and preaches ribaldry to the people that stand about. For there is not the worst thing that Friar Frappe preaches in a base [lewd] sport, but father Tyndale writes much worse in very great earnest, and much worse than the other abuses the scripture relating to it. The other [Friar Frappe] when he preaches that men may lawfully indulge themselves sexually [go to lechery] he commonly makes up some foolish [fond] texts out of his own head [. . .] The other rogue [ribald] [Frappe] in his stupid [fond] sermon meddles only with fleshly vices and worldly wantonness [. . .] Never was there any scoffing Friar Frappe preaching upon a stool that dare play the knavish fool on such a fashion as you shall see Tyndale do here.

J13   The Christmas Lord invades the church, Bampton, 1615/16

PRO State Papers Domestic SP14/86, no. 34 (a complaint against William Howard by his Protestant neighbours); pr. REED, *Cumberland/Westmorland/Gloucestershire*, p. 218

[. . .] at Christmas last, at Bampton in Westmorland, [. . .] the tenants and servants of the lord William [Howard], assisted with others of the parish, did erect [*sic*] a Christmas Lord, and resorting to the church, did most grossly disturb the minister in time of prayer, the minister himself granting a kind of toleration for that, he for the most part liveth with the Lord William at his table, but never pray together. The Christmas misrule men drank to the minister reading a homily in the pulpit, others stepped into the pulpit, and exhorted the parishioners to an offering for maintenance of their sport, the minister continuing still his service, others of the Lord William's own servants came in savage manner disguised into the church, in the time of prayer, others with shooting of guns, others with flags and banners borne entered the church, others sported themselves in the church with pies and puddings, using them as bowls in the church aisles, others took dogs counterfeiting the shepherd's part when he feeds his sheep, and all there in the time of divine service.

Feast of Fools and Boy Bishop

See **B24**, **B28** for other items relating to the Boy Bishop and the Feast of Fools. It has been thought useful to reproduce Bishop John Grandisson's condemnation [**J14**] in the current context, although it appears in a slightly different version as **B28(a)**. For the rather specialised function exercised by the Bishop of Fools at Lille, see **H8(b)**, **H35**.

J14   The Feast of Fools condemned by the Bishop of Exeter, 1333

Letter from Bishop John Grandisson to Subdean and Canons of Exeter Cathedral. Register of Bishop John de Grandisson, Devon Record Office, Chanter 4, fo. 174 verso; pr. REED, *Devon*, ed. John Wasson, Toronto, 1986, pp. 6–7, trans., p. 319

[. . .] We have learned, not without serious displeasure, from the account of trustworthy persons that some vicars and other ministers of the said church, having put on masks, do not even fear to practise in a manner worthy of condemnation dissolute behaviour, laughter, jeering, and other excesses irreverently as an offence to God and a marked impediment to divine worship and a scandal to our very church during the solemnities of the church service and especially in this famous feast of the Holy Innocents: thus, through their mimings' obscene ravings, they cheapen the honour of clerics in the sight of the people [. . .]

J15   The Bishop of Fools in Lille, 1366

Royal Pardon. Trésor des Chartes, Archives Nationales, Paris, JJ 97; pr. Vaultier, p. 88

[. . .] the clerks of the church of St Peter of this town commonly have a game and disport every year between New Year and Candlemas in which they choose a bishop called the Bishop of Fools, and this disport lasts a certain time, and at the end of this game they are accustomed to eat and drink together, and thus it happened that between the New Year and Candlemas last past, about the day of [the Conversion of] St Paul [25 January], after the said clerks had finished and completed their said game and disport, they went to dine together at the house which is called the clerks' house.

J16   The Swabian Boy Bishop's Play, *c.* 1420

Houghton Library, Harvard University, MS Ger 74; pr. Eckehard Simon, 'Das Schwäbische Weihnachtsspiel. Ein neu entdecktes Weihnachtsspiel aus der Zeit 1417–1431', *Zeitschrift für deutsch Philologie* 94 (1975), *Sonderheft*, 30–50 [Simon, 'The Home Town of the "Schwäbische Weihnachtsspiel" (*c.* 1420) and its Original Setting', *Euphorion* 73 (1979), pp. 304–320 argues that the play was performed in Constance, around 1420, probably by the Boy Bishop and his company from the Cathedral School.]

Herald
Listen, and be quite quiet everywhere.
Mark what I shall say to you!
What I tell you is true,
that many years ago
here on earth was born
the true Lord Jesus Christ,
of a pure virgin.
Now note what is my message.

[There follows a summary of the Nativity story: the Bethlehem stable, the star, the circumcision, the three kings, Herod's threats and the flight into Egypt.]

Now will we in a little while
in a play present
the matters which have been mentioned here
concerning Mary, Joseph, and their child.

Bishop/Chaplain
The peace and forgiveness of the Holy Ghost
be with you, noble lord and lady, and most of all with us.
Honourable Lord, hither come Joseph, Mary, and their child
and others of their young servants
with papal and proper licence
to require your contribution with a good heart.
To this end our holy Father the Pope,
Who took the name Martin in the Cathedral,

Who has dominion here as in Rome,
proclaims to your graces and all those in the streets,
great mercy and great indulgence.
To all people who show them their aid;
through me, his very willing chaplain,
Mary and the glorious God,
to them I promise indulgence for all faults.

[Simon places here a scene, not heralded in the Prologue, in which an angel announces the Nativity to the shepherds, who visit the stable at Bethlehem; it comes after the end of the play in the manuscript. As it stands, the play, which now follows, mainly comprises a Latin hymn of rejoicing [*Resonet in laudibus*], sung by the angels and echoed, in German, by Joseph. A Latin instruction indicates differences between the play as performed in the church [*in alteri*] and in houses [*in domibus*], presumably during the visits signalled later in the text. The Magi and Herod do not appear, but warning of the latter's plans prompts the Holy Family to flee, Joseph carrying the cradle on his back, and motivates the players' request for the audience's largesse:]

Third Angel
Now pay attention all together
Both poor and rich!
Here are Joseph and Mary and their child
And also others of their servants.
They wish to go from hence
And flee into the land of Egypt.
Therefore Joseph the loyal man asks you
that you will freely aid him,
with a contribution to the glorious God;
For that he thanks you in all seriousness.
Whoever has not hotcakes or cookies,
Let him give us money, and God will still reward him.

Joseph's Servant
Joseph, now listen carefully,
I have always been your faithful servant.
We should not be diverted,
We should set out.
The way leads to the house of N:[1]
that we should not leave.
There is a parlour, which is very warm,
that is where we should rather go.
He himself will well receive us,
and enjoy all gladness with us,
for the honour of Mary and her child
And also other of your servants.

Maidservant
Jesus, my dearly beloved lord,
See here you have some porridge.
It is made for you with care,
And is very good food for you.

Fourth Angel
We will no longer stay here,
We shall now return home;
[. . .]
God give us all a good new year.

Something should be briefly sung

Bishop/Chaplain again
Noble lord, Mr N, and you other men!
Pay attention to me the Pope's chaplain;
[. . .]
Be advised, both young and old,
If anyone because of guilt needs the Pope's powers[2]
Let him come to me in the house of Mr. N,
there tonight my own power expires.
I a poor chaplain complain of this,
then I will again often be a poor man,
Had it lasted longer
I would surely have done better for myself.

play pipes[3]

---

[1] The name is evidently to be specified according to circumstances.
[2] i.e. to take advantage of the Pope's powers to grant indulgence.
[3] Literally 'pipe up [or off]': *Pfeiff uffa*.

J17   A condemnation by the Faculty of Theology, University of Paris, 1445

Letter to bishops and chapters of France, 1445; pr. and trans. E. K. Chambers, *The Mediaeval Stage*, 2 vols., Oxford, 1903; various reprints; vol. I, p. 294, note 2. By permission of Oxford University Press

Priests and clerks may be seen wearing masks and monstrous visages at the hours of office. They dance in the choir dressed as women, panders or minstrels. They sing wanton songs. They eat black puddings at the horn of the altar while the celebrant is saying Mass. They play at dice there. They cense with stinking smoke from the soles of old shoes. They run and leap through the church, without a blush at their own shame. Finally they drive about the town and its theatres in shabby traps and carts; and rouse the laughter of their fellows and the bystanders in infamous performances, with indecent gestures and verses scurrilous and unchaste.

J18   The Feast described by Sebastian Franck, 1534

Sebastian Franck, *Weltbuch*, 1534, 'The Strange Customs of the Franks'; pr. *Bräuche und Feste im fränkischen Jahreslauf*, ed. Josef Dünninger and Horst Schopf, Kulmbach, 1971, p. 11

On St Nicholas's Day [6 December] the schoolboys elect from among themselves a Bishop and two Deacons; they sit in their vestments led in a procession into the church until the service is over [*für ist*], then the Nicholas Bishop with all his train goes and sings before people's houses: and this is not begging but the Bishop collecting a tax.

J19   Boy Bishop perambulations banned in England, 1541

Proclamation of Henry VIII, Altering Feast Days and Fast Days, 1541; pr. *Tudor Royal Proclamations*, ed. Paul L. Hughes and James F. Larkin, vol. i, *The Early Tudors (1485–1553)*, New Haven, 1964, no. 203 (pp. 301–2). By permission of Yale University Press

[. . .] And whereas heretofore divers and many superstitious and childish observations have been used, and yet to this day are observed and kept in many and sundry parts of this realm, as upon St Nicholas, St Catherine, St Clement, the Holy Innocents, and such like, children be strangely decked and appareled to counterfeit priests, bishops, and women, and so be led with songs and dances from house to house, blessing the people and gathering of money, and boys do sing mass and preach in the pulpit, with such other unfitting and inconvenient usages, rather to the derision than to any true glory of God, or honour of his saints: the king's majesty therefore, minding nothing so much as to advance the true glory of God without vain superstition, willeth and commandeth that from henceforth all such superstitious observations be left and clearly extinguished throughout all this his realm and dominions [. . .]

Perambulations and house visits

J20   Edict of the Duke of Savoy prohibiting pre-Christmas *quêtes*, 1430

Decreta Sabaudorum, Turin, 1586, fo. 7 recto; trans. Sam Kinser, 'Wildmen in Festival', *Oral Traditions in the Middle Ages*, ed. W. F. H. Nicolaisen, Binghamton, 1995, pp. 145–60

In some years on holy days and above all on Saint Catherine's Day [25 November] or close to these dates, some despicable folk change themselves into the appearance of devils by donning deformed costumes. Carrying arms in and out of households, they run and roam through the streets and public places of our cities, villages and rural areas, bringing ruin. And they violently accost peasants and various other simple, quiet people, and sometimes strike them, and force them to give them money, while heaping upon them other injuries which are offensive to God and man. (p. 153)

J21   Description of *Perchtenlauf* in the Salzburg region, nineteenth century

Ignaz von Kürsinger, *Ober-Pinzgau oder der Bezirk Mittersill*, Salzburg, 1841, p. 166; pr.
Hans Moser, 'Kritisches zu Tradition und Dokumentation des Perchtenlaufens', in
*Volksbräuche in geschichtlichen Wandel. Ergebnisse aus fünfzig Jahren volkskundlicher
Quellenforschung*, Munich, 1985, pp. 41–57

Young vigorous lads, to the number of eight to ten, form an association, two of
whom represent ugly old figures, armed with old brooms; these are the *Berchten*
[. . .] They are usually accompanied by a grotesque crowd [*Karricatur*] composed
of clowns, vagabonds and other rabble, and this assemblage is followed by the
dancers, in festive clothes, with bright sashes tied around them, and on their heads
a crown with high waving cock feathers, from which numberless brightly
coloured ribbons cascade down over shoulder and back. Their faces hidden in
masks, they have hanging at the end of the back a cowbell [. . .] They announce
their approach with quick and well-coordinated footsteps, then form a circle, in
which they perform the most impressive evolutions with incredible speed and precision, a sustaining rhythm provided by the tramp of their feet on the wooden
floor. From time to time in the course of the dance they suddenly let their bells
sound, then again silence them [. . .] They go from parish to parish, visiting the
houses of the better sort, where their exertions in the dance are rewarded with
spirits and bread, after which they return peacefully to their work. (p. 41)

J22   Payments to *Perchtenlauf* participants, Markt Diessen, Bavaria, late sixteenth century

Local Archives, Town Hall, Markt Diessen am Ammersee, Upper Bavaria. Chamberlain's
Accounts; pr. Moser, 'Kritisches zu Tradition und Dokumentation des Perchtenlaufens',
pp. 41–57

1582: Item additionally dispensed on the 6 of January this year to those, who
hunted the *Percht*, 8kr.

1586: In addition given to those who hunted the *Percht* at Christmas 1585, 1ss 5dn.

1600: Item given as drinking money to those who hunted the *Percht*, 1ss 22dn, 1h.

J23   New Year perambulations with a masked boy, Rome, 1140–3

Canon Benedict of St Peter's, *Liber Polypticus* (an account of Roman customs, 1140–3); pr.
Georgio Brugnoli, 'Architipi e no del Carnevale', in *Il Carnevale dalla tradizione Arcaica alla
tradizione colta del Rinascimento*, ed. M. Chiabo and F. Doglio, Rome, 1989, pp. 41–61

These are the Roman plays that are common at the Kalends of January.

On the eve of the Kalends late at night the youths get up and carry around a shield,
and one of them is masked, with a drum hanging from his neck. Whistling and

sounding the drum they go around to the houses, and swing around [*circumdant*] the shield; the drum sounds, the [one with the] mask [*larva*] whistles. This game over, they receive a reward from the master of the house according to what pleases him. Thus they do in each and every house. On that day, they eat all kinds of vegetables. And in the morning two boys of their number get up. They are given olive branches and salt and enter into the houses. They salute the household: 'joy and gladness be in this house'; they throw a handful of leaves and salt into the fire and say, 'so many children, so many piglets, so many lambs', and wish for all good things, and before the sun rises they eat either honeycomb or something else sweet, so that the whole year will go well for them, without disputes and without great labour. (pp. 59–60)

J24   Prohibition of disguised perambulations, London, 1418

Corporation of London Records Office. City of London Letter-Book I, fo. ccxxiii; pr. *Memorials of London Life in the XIIIth, XIVth and XVth Centuries*, ed. H. T. Riley, London, 1868, p. 669

The Mayor and Aldermen charge on the King's behalf, and this City, that no manner of person, of what estate, degree, or condition that ever he be, during this holy time of Christmas be so hardy in any wise to walk by night in any manner of mumming, plays, interludes, or any other disguisings with any feigned beards, painted visors, deformed and coloured visages in any wise, upon pain of imprisonment of their bodies, and making fine after the discretion of the Mayor and Aldermen; with the exception that [outake] it be lawful to each person for to be honestly merry as he can, within his own house dwelling.

J25   Convivial visit, Arras, 1450

Royal Pardon. Trésor des Chartes, Archives Nationales, Paris, JJ 184; pr. Vaultier, pp. 97–8

The young companions, children of citizens, of the said city and others are accustomed to gather together and go around on the eve of the Festival of the Kings to the houses of their neighbours the said citizens and other people of this town, and bring by way of disport and gladness at the solemnity of the said festival some small trinket [*joyaulx*], gift or present, accompanied by the sound of minstrels or other joyous instruments and to play in the house of the citizen or other where they entered a game called *montine*. And if these companions lose in the said game in the given household where they have entered, they are chased out for fun without being offered drink, and if they win they are given a drink and honoured. It happened that on the eve of the said Festival of the Kings last past, certain young companions gathered and dressed up in various clothes in order to go to the houses of their neighbours, citizens and other people of the said town of Arras where it seemed good to them, to bring in their gifts and to play the said game of *montine* or to indulge in other pastimes [. . .] And to this end they went to or sent for the said supplicant who customarily plays the fife and drum in the said town of Arras, and who went [with them] to earn money to feed his said wife and children, the which young companions and the said supplicant who played the said fife and drum entered the house of a certain Jehan Lesueur [. . .]

The Three Kings and the star

J26   Attacks on performers, Tölz (Baden-Württemberg), 1496–7

County Court Records of Fines, 1496–7; City Archives, Landshut; pr. Hans Moser, 'Neue Materialen zur Sternsinger-Forschung', in *Volksbräuche im geschichtlichen Wandel: Ergebnisse aus fünfzig Jahren volkskundlicher Quellenforschung*, Munich, 1985, pp. 74–97

Walthasser Örrtl beat Hewsl, the clerk, at night time, and chased him, when he was going round with the star; he gives 7ss dn.

Hennsl Schöttl from Lenggries helped to beat and chase the clerks who were going round with the star; he gives 9ss dn.

Jorg Denngk is accused on account of the crime he committed against the school-master with the star, since he beat them and took their weapons; he gives 10 sch. Item Hanns Dennk's son helped the aforementioned Jorg Denngk to chase the schoolmaster; he gives 50dn. (p. 77)

J27   Payments to performers at St Peter's Monastery, Salzburg, sixteenth century

Abbot's Accounts, Stiftsarchiv St Peter; pr. Moser, 'Neue Materialen zur Sternsinger-Forschung', pp. 74–97

1541. Item to the singers with the star on [the day of the] Three Kings, 1t 2ss dn. 1551. Item given for the play from Reichenhall about the gifts of the three kings, 2ss 20dn. (pp. 78–9)

J28   A Danish cleric observes performers, 1661

Bishop J. Bircherod, *Diary*, entry for 6 January 1661 (in Odense); pr. Hilding Celander, *Stärngossarna, deras Visor och Julespel*, Stockholm: Nordiska Museet, 1950, p. 34

In the evening, when I saw the players who went around with the star, and among them the figures dressed in white who were supposed to represent the three holy kings, in my simplicity I allowed myself to imagine that they really had come from the East.

The hobby horse

J29   Divine punishment of a hobby-horse dancer, France, c. 1260

Étienne de Bourbon, *Tractatus de diversis materiis praedicabilibus* (a collection of *exempla*); pr. A. Lecoy de la Marche, *Anecdotes historiques, legendes et apologues, tirés du recueil inédit d'Étienne de Bourbon*, Paris, 1877, no. 194, pp. 168–9

It happened in the diocese of Elne, after a preacher in that country had preached against and prohibited the many dances which were conducted in churches and on the eves of saints, and after certain young people of a particular village who customarily came and mounted on a wooden horse, and masked and armed, led dances on the eves of the feasts of the church, in the church and in the cemetery, had given up the dances in accordance with the words of the preacher and their prohibition of of their priest, and when the people were observing the vigil and praying in the church, a certain youth came to his companion, inviting him to join the customary game. But when the latter rejected the game, saying it had been prohibited by the words of the preacher and the priest, the other armed himself, cursing anyone who gave up the customary game because of the prohibition. But when the said youth entered the church, where men were observing the vigil in peace and prayer, on his wooden horse, as he entered the church, fire broke out around his feet and totally consumed him and his horse.

J30   Abbots Bromley Hobby Horse and Horn Dance Gathering, 1686

Robert Plot, *Natural History of Staffordshire* (1686), p. 434; pr. E. C. Cawte, *Ritual Animal Disguise*, Cambridge, 1978, p. 65

At Abbots, or now rather Pagets Bromley, they had also within memory, a sort of sport, which they celebrated at Christmas (on New-year, and Twelfth-day) called the Hobby-horse dance, from a person that carryed the image of a horse between his legs, made of thin boards, and in his hand a bow and arrow, which passing through a hole in the bow, and stopping upon a shoulder it had in it, he made a snapping noise as he drew it to and fro, keeping time with the Music. With this Man danced 6 others, carrying on their shoulders as many Rain deers heads, 3 of them painted white, and 3 red, with the Arms of the chief families (viz. of Paget, Bagot, and Wells) to whom the revenues of the Town chiefly belonged, depicted on the palms of them, with which they danced the Hays, and other Country dances. To this Hobby-horse dance there also belonged a pot, which was kept by turns, by 4 or 5 of the chief of the Town, whom they call'd Reeves, who provided Cakes and Ale to put in this pot; all people who had any kindness for the good intent of the Institution of the sport, giving pence a piece for themselves and families; and so strangers [foreigners] too, that came to see it: with which Money (the charge of the

Cakes and Ale being defrayed) they not only repaired their Church but kept their poor too: which charges are not now perhaps so cheerfully borne.

Plough-trailing

J31   Plough-trailing banned by royal authority, England, 1548

Injunctions for the Deanery of Doncaster issued by commissioners conducting the royal visitation of 1548; pr. *Visitation Articles and Injunctions of the Period of the Reformation*, ed. W. H. Frere and W. McC. Kennedy, 3 vols., London, 1910, vol. II, *1536–1558*, pp. 171–5

8. Item. Forasmuch as drunkenness, idleness, brawls, dissension and many other inconveniences do chance between neighbour and neighbour by the assembly of people together at wakes, and on the Plough-Monday; it is therefore ordered and enjoined that hereafter the people shall use, make, or observe no more such wakes, Plough-Mondays, or drawing of the same, with any such assembly or rout of people, or otherwise, as hath been accustomed, upon pain of forfeiting to the King's Highness 40s. for every default, to be paid by the owner of the plough and householder whereunto the said plough is drawn or wakes kept. (p. 175)

J32   Antiquarian description, Derbyshire, mid-nineteenth century

Frederick W. Ll. Jewitt, 'On Ancient Customs and Sports of the County of Derby', *Journal of the British Archaeological Society* 7 (1851), pp. 201–2

On Plough Monday, the 'Plough-bullocks' are still occasionally seen; they consist of a number of young men from various farmhouses, who are dressed up in ribbands, their shirts (for they wear no coats or undercoats) literally covered with rosettes of various colours, and their hats bound round with ribbands, and decorated with every kind of ornament that comes in their way; these young men yoke themselves to a plough, which they draw about, preceded by a band of music, from house to house collecting money; they are accompanied by the fool and Bessy; the fool being dressed in the skin of a calf, with the tail hanging down behind, and Bessy, generally a young man in female attire, covered with a profusion of ribbands and other meretricious finery. The fool carries an inflated bladder tied to the end of a long stick, by way of a whip, and which he does not fail to apply pretty soundly to the heads and shoulders of his team; to these personages are usually added two or three more drivers, armed with similar bladders, and a ploughman and attendants. When anything is given, a cry of largess is raised, and a dance performed around the plough; but if a refusal to their application for money is made, they not infrequently plough up the pathway, door stone, or any other portion of the premises that happen to be near.

SHROVETIDE AND CARNIVAL

Maskings and perambulations

J33 Carnival condemned by Thomas Kirchmair, Germany, 1553

Thomas Kirchmair/Kirchmayer ('Naogeorgus'), *Regnum papisticum* (1553) [see **B8, B34,** **J11, J47, J61**]; pr. Kirchmair/Googe, pp. 48a–b

But some again the dreadful shape of devils on them take,
And chase such as they meet, and make poor boys for fear to quake.
Some naked run about the streets, their faces hid alone,
With visars close, that so disguised, they might be knowne of none.
Both men and women change their weed, the men in maid's array,
And wanton wenches dressed like men, do travel by the way,
And to their neighbours' houses go, or where it like them best,
Perhaps unto some ancient friend or old acquainted guest,
Unknown, and speaking but few words, the meat devour they up,
That is before them set, and clean they gulp down [swinge of] every cup.
Some run about the streets attired like monks, and some like kings,
Accompanied with pomp and guard, and other stately things.
[. . .]
Some like wild beasts do run abroad in skins that diverse be
Arrayed, and eke with loathsome shapes, that dreadful are to see:
They counterfeit both Bears and Wolves, and Lions fierce in fight,
And raging Bulls. Some play the Cranes with wings and stilts upright.
Some like the filthy form of Apes, and some like fools are dressed,
Which best beseem these Papists all, that thus keep Bacchus' feast.
But others bear a turd, that on a Cushion soft they lay,
And one there is that with a flap doth keep the flies away.

J34 Carnival regulations at Überlingen, South Germany, c. 1496

Überlingen City Archives, Council Minutes 1496–1518, pp. 158–9; pr. Dieter H. Stolz, 'Die Fasnacht in Überlingen', in *Masken Zwischen Spiel und Ernst*, no ed., *Beiträge des Tübinger Arbeitskreises für Fasnachtforschung*, Tübingen, 1967, pp. 65–107

Carnival Ordinance
No one should make any one else dirty, or besmirch them, or wear a devil's costume in any way other than that they can be recognised, and no one should throw anyone into the spring. Item whoever has borrowed the devil's costume from the Warden of St Nicholas [. . .] must be answerable to him for it. But whoever has made a devil's costume at his own expense he may keep it, provided that he is willing to lend it out for the procession in God's honour. (pp. 84–5)

J35   Maskers debarred from the Sacrament, Regensburg, Germany 1459–60

State Library of Bavaria (Bayerische Staatsbibliothek), Munich, MS Clm. 2611 (document from Monastery of Regensburg, specifying those who are unqualified to receive the sacrament); pr. Hans Moser, 'Zur Geschichte der Maske in Bayern', in *Masken in Mitteleuropa*, ed. Leopold Schmidt, Vienna, 1955, pp. 93–141

All those who have transformed themselves into devils, horses, calves and thus danced on Ash Wednesday [. . .] and all men who have dressed in women's, monks' or priests' clothes, or women who have disguised themselves in men's clothing, [. . .] performing plays, japes or rhymes in scorn and despite of priests, confessors, or any holy Christian thing [. . .] (p. 110)

J36   Danish prohibition of masked perambulations, 1520

Draft of Royal Ordinance for Schools; pr. *De tre ældste danske Skuespil*, ed. Birket Smith, Copenhagen, 1874, p. 13

Hereafter shall no priest, clerk or scholar disguise himself at Shrovetide as a Herald, Monk, or in the appearance of a mummer in order to perambulate and to beg and commit other follies, as they have done hitherto. Whoever offends against this will lose his skin [i.e. be whipped].

J37   Carnival regulations for Nuremburg, 1469

Civic ordinances issued by the Mayor and Corporation; pr. *Nürnberger Polizeiordnungen aus dem XIII bis XV Jahrhundert*, ed. Joseph Baader, Stuttgart, 1861; reprinted Amsterdam, 1966, pp. 92–4

[marginal note:] Proclamation of the Sunday after Epiphany, 1469

We, the Mayor and council of the City of Nuremburg, on account of extraordinary circumstances, wish most earnestly to enjoin, that henceforth no one, man or woman, at any time of the year, by day or by night, shall reverse any clothing or garment or alter it, and especially that they shall not change or distort their face with anything, but that they behave and show themselves in such a way that they are quite recognisable. Exempted from this, however, are the youths who have our permission for the protection of the butchers in their customary Shrovetide dance, and others who specifically receive our permission [. . .]
[. . .]
We furthermore hereby earnestly request, that neither the wild men nor anyone else, for any reason chase or run after Christians or Jews yelling at them [. . .] Similarly neither the wild men nor anyone else shall bully, push, strike, scratch or in any other way harm or inconvenience others [. . .]

Since during the Shrovetide last past certain persons in the manner of plays and rhymes performed frivolous, improper, indecent and unseemly words and actions, not only in the houses but also elsewhere by day and by night, being a sinful, annoying and shameful and unseemly thing to undertake and perform before honest people and above all before maidens and women, to prevent this our lords of the Council earnestly and emphatically request that henceforth at any time, and particularly at the time of Shrovetide, no one, either man or woman, young or old, whosoever they be, in any way exercise or use such indecent and unseemly words or actions in rhymes or in other form, and not only in visiting houses but anywhere else behave honestly, decently and in seemly fashion [. . .][1]

[1] For Shrovetide plays in Nuremberg, see **F35**, **F36**, **F40**.

Beast and wild-man-customs

J38   Roman beast-slaying tournament, twelfth century

Canon Benedict of St Peter's, *Liber Polypticus* (1140–3); pr. Georgio Brugnoli, 'Architipi e no del Carnevale', in *Il Carnevale dalla tradizione Arcaica alla tradizione colta del Rinascimento*, ed. M. Chiabo and F. Doglio, Rome, 1989, pp. 41–61

Concerning carnival games

On the Sunday before Lent, after dinner the cavalry and footsoldiers rise and drink together. After the footsoldiers have put aside their shields they go to Mount Testaccio; the Prefect goes with the knights to the Lateran. The Lord Pope leaves the palace and rides with the Prefect and the cavalry to Mount Testaccio, and just as there the city had its beginning, so there on that day the pleasures of our bodies have their end. They perform the game before the Pope, so that no contention arises among them. In killing a bear, the Devil is slain, that is the tempter of our flesh. When bullocks are killed, the pride of our pleasure is slain. In the killing of a cock, the lechery of our loins is slain, so that we thereafter may live chastely and soberly in the struggle of the soul, so that at Easter we shall be worthy to receive the body of Christ. (p. 60)

J39   Venetian pig hunt with wild men and bears

Giovanni Boccaccio, *Il Decamerone* (1348–53), Day IV, story 2; trans. Richard Aldington, *The Decameron of Giovanni Boccaccio*, 2nd edn, London, 1969, vol. I, p. 286. © The Estate of Richard Aldington.

[A lecherous friar, Alberto, pursued by the family of a woman he has seduced, seeks refuge in the house of a Venetian. The latter, intending ultimately to betray him, suggests he escape by adopting a festive disguise.] 'There is only one way of doing this. There is a festival today[1] where one man leads another dressed like a bear or a wild man of the woods or one thing or another, and then there is a hunt in the Piazza di San Marco, and when that is over the festival ends. Then everyone goes off where he pleases with the person he has brought in disguise' [. . .]

Friar Alberto did not at all like the idea, but he was so much afraid of the lady's relatives that he agreed to it, and told the man where he wanted to go, and how he should be led along. The goodman smeared him all over with honey and then covered him with feathers, put a chain round his neck and a mask on his face. In one hand he gave him a large stick and in the other two great dogs which he had brought from the butcher [. . .] He then led his wild man of the woods to a column in a con-spicuous and elevated place [in the Piazza di San Marco], pretending that he was waiting for the hunt [. . .] And when the goodman saw that the Piazza was full of people, he pretended that he was going to unchain his wild man; but instead he took off Friar Alberto's mask and shouted, 'Gentlemen, since the pig has not come to the hunt and since the hunt is off, I don't want you to have gathered for nothing [. . .]

[1] While the custom is known to have been performed on the Thursday before Shrovetide (*Giovedi Grasso*), it is evident from the narrative that this is not the day on which the story takes place: no pigs appear, and the disguised friar attracts more attention than would otherwise have been the case. For discussion of the custom's wider scenario in which pigs and a bull are condemned to death, hunted and killed, see Edward Muir, *Civic Ritual in Renaissance Venice*, Princeton, 1981, pp. 161–4 and 180, note 133.

J40   Folk-play of the capture of a wild man, 1566

Pieter Bruegel the Elder, *The Masquerade of Ourson and Valentine* (1566), woodcut, Bibliothèque Albert I, Brussels; pr. Jacques Lavalleye, *Pieter Bruegel the Elder and Lucas van Leyden: the Complete Engravings, Etchings and Woodcuts*, London, 1967, p. 146

Based on an earlier drawing by Bruegel, this woodcut depicts a scene which reap-pears as a detail in Bruegel's celebrated *Combat between Carnival and Lent*, although its customary associations may be with Candlemas rather than Carnival, strictly speaking. Evidently a dramatisation of some version of the popular romance, *Valentine and Orson*, the folk-play includes the scene where the wild man, Ourson, is hunted by his brother, while a king, a female character (probably a princess) and a ring also have significant roles. Behind the performers, gatherers can be seen col-lecting money from spectators.

Sword-dance and sword-dance play

J41   Payment to sword-dancers in Flanders, 1389

Bruges City accounts; pr. Louis Gilliodts-van Severen, *Inventaire des archives*, 3 vols., Bruges, 1871–5, vol. III, p. 119; trans. Stephen D. Corrsin, *Sword Dancing in Europe: a History*, Enfield Lock, 1997, p. 17. By permission of the Folklore Society and Stephen D. Corrsin.

Item: Given on command of the mayor to the sailors performing at Shrovetide about the city with swords 4 shillings 3 pence.

J42   Swedish sword-dancing described by Olaus Magnus, 1555

Olaus Magnus, *Historia de gentibus septentrionalibus* (Rome, 1555); facsimile reprint introduced by John Granlund, Copenhagen, 1972, book XV, chapter XXIII; trans. Peter Fisher and Humphrey Higgens, *Olaus Magnus, A Description of the Northern People, 1555*, ed. P. G. Foote, vol. III, Hakluyt Society, 2nd series, 187, London, 1998, p. 748. (With the kind permission of the Hakluyt Society, and through the good offices of Peter Foote)

On the Sword Dance or Soldiers' Morris

For training their young men the Götar and Swedes of the North have another game, too, in which they drill themselves by leaping about among naked swords and unprotected thrusting blades. As they grow up they learn this through a certain athletic routine under instruction from experts and a dance leader, while accompanying themselves with singing. They demonstrate this sport chiefly during Shrovetide, the time of masquerade, to use the Italian term. Before this particular season young men practise in large numbers for eight days in continual dancing, with their swords raised, but sheathed in their scabbards, circling round three times. Next they draw their swords, raise them in the same way, and presently hold them stretched out. They then revolve at a gentler rate, each taking the point or hilt of another's weapon; next they change their formation and range themselves in a hexagonal figure, which they call a rose, and almost immediately undo it by withdrawing and lifting their swords, so that in consequence a square rose appears over all their heads. Finally, by violently clashing their swords together sideways and with a swift leap backwards, they bring the game to an end. The rhythm is given by pipes or old songs, or by both together, so that the dancing is slow at first, then more energetic, and lastly quite furious. But unless you see the thing with your own eyes, this presentation of mine scarcely allows you to grasp what a handsome, noble sight it is when, at the briefest bidding of one person, a whole mass of armed men briskly arrange themselves for this sport. Clerics are permitted to practise and take part in this entertainment, since it is all conducted in a most honourable fashion.

J43   Swedish sword and bow dances illustrated

Olaus Magnus, *Historia de gentibus septentrionalibus* (Rome, 1555); facsimile reprint
introduced by John Granlund, Copenhagen, 1972, book xv, woodcut illustrating chapter
23, p. 517

For Olaus Magnus' account of the sword-dances, see **J42**; he describes bow
dancing in chapter 24 (p. 518): they 'follow much the same routine' as the sword
dances, except that the leader is called the 'King', and 'in order to perform this with
more merriment and noise, they tie little, tinkling, copper bells below their knee'
[trans. Fisher and Higgens, as Olaus Magnus].

Carnival interludes

J44   The Danish Interlude of the Unfaithful Wife

[Probably performed, as a fund-raising venture, by the pupils of Our Lady's School,
Odense, at the Shrovetide revels of local craft guilds.]
Royal Library, Copenhagen, MS Thott 780; pr. *Fastelavnsspillet i Danmarks senmiddelalder*,
ed. Leif Søndergaard, Odense, 1989

[*Herald*]
Wassail! Good day, dear friends,
All you who are in here,
To you all be respect and honour,
Both men and women.
I am come here for your pleasure;
I spent a day in a crowd
And I travelled here on a broken sledge,
And I was in great danger.
If you will give room and be still as well
And do not chatter too loudly,
I shall tell you a little of God's word,

So you will thank me.
For the company that is in here,
if it wishes to hear them,
[The actors] will contrive a little play;
That they will do soon.
Then you will see a fair rose,
Who will be approached by many wooers,
For she is a good one to lie with,
I've known that well for a long time.
First comes a peasant with great desire
That he might gain her consent,
But then comes his wife and drags him off
And so tries to separate them.
Thereafter a monk will court her,
And dance a morris in his cowl,
Until there comes a haughty courtier,
Who gives his back a good thrashing,
And drives him back into his monastery,
Where he's in no position to woo;
So he gets little honour,
And nor does he get his will.
The courtier with his clever wiles
Tries to tempt the woman,
Until he is certain
That he will win her love.
He who now will not keep quiet
And will not watch the play,
I shall give him a blow on the backside
So his rump will ache [. . .]

[The action of the play follows closely the Herald's summary, but with additional episodes – which may indeed be later additions – in which the Peasant, told he is too filthy and hairy for a wooer, visits a bathhouse, only to have his beard singed and smeared in ordure by an unsympathetic attendant, and the Courtier appeals to an old witch for help, the latter (in vain) conjuring up a devil to whisper lascivious thoughts into the lady's ear, and then (successfully) frightening her into submission by convincing her that a weeping dog is the witch's daughter, bespelled by a courtier whose advances she had refused [see **A36** for a similar plot-motif in *Dame Sirith*].]

> *Herald*
> In this play you have now heard
> How the Old Woman brought them together.
> If any of you wish to try out this trick,
> You must get the advice of the Old Woman;
> Like a little devil she knows many tricks,

As you have now seen, that's for sure.
Now wassail to you all,
If you are happy, things are fine.
And with that will I now go out the door,
    But first give me a drink.

The end of Christmas/Carnival

J45   A Swedish 'dispute' of Christmas and Lent, fifteenth century

Stockholm, Royal Library MS D 4a (Codex Verelianus) from 1457; pr. Gustaf Ljunggren, *Svenska dramat intill slutet af sjuttende århundrate*, Lund, 1864, pp. 133–4; trans. Leif Søndergaard and Thomas Pettitt, 'The Flyting of Yule and Lent: a Medieval Swedish Shrovetide Interlude', *Early Drama, Art and Music Review* 16.1 (autumn 1993), pp. 1–11

Next follows how Yule and Lent dispute.

> *Lent*
> It is my duty first to wish
> Health and happiness to King and Bishop!
> I am the one who is called Lent,
> I am accustomed to keep watch over sin and vice;
> Anyone who knows he has been sinful,
> He is afraid to come to me.
>
> *Yule*
> My lords King and Bishop both,
> I crave of you help and mercy.
> I am she who is called Yule
> I do not hide myself from Lent.
> Lent will be against me,
> My lord King be my servant
> I hope that I shall live well
> My lord King you must give me my rights,
> For both poor and rich know
> That Lent will never be like that.
>
> *Lent*
> I shall teach you a better attitude:
> Drink and eat a good deal less,
> Do not sit long at your table,
> But also go and listen to God's word sometimes.
>
> *Yule*
> I'll tell you, Lent, what you must do:
> Go to the sermon now as always;
> Let me sit here with my food,
> And fill my horn, we'll not be parted.

Lent
That won't do you much good,
Scoffing so many sweet things:
You fill your habituated belly with rubbish,
So the soul is diseased with your sin.

Yule
I think you are too haggard, Lent,
You're pale and thin, weedy and brownish;
God will fully know how to judge
Which of us will first come to heaven.

Lent
I'm trying to give you a lesson:
Let us all scourge our backs
Ready to meet our father confessor
And humbly do penance for all our sins.

Yule
It's your occupation to hear confessions,
To sit in church and do nothing else;
If I come to you Good Friday night
I reckon that should be good enough.

Lent
So comes he who is called Mortification,
He will scourge your back
So you won't be able to get away,
And you'll be punished for old and new sins.

Yule
I shall surely see to it
That he doesn't scourge my bare back
[text breaks off]

J46   The Norwich procession of Christmas and Lent, 1443

Petition of citizens of Norwich, 1448, Norfolk Record Office; pr. *The Records of the City of Norwich*, ed. W. Hudson and J. C. Tingey, Norwich and London, 1906, vol. I, pp. 345–6

And where that it was so that one John Gladman of Norwich which was ever and at this hour is a man of sober [sad] disposition and true and faithful to God and to the King, of disport as is and ever hath been accustomed in any City or Borough through all this realm on Shrove [fastyngong] Tuesday made a disport with his neighbours having his horse trapped with tinsel and otherwise disguising things crowned as King of Christmas in token that all mirth should end[,] with the twelve months of the year before him each month disguised after the season thereof, and Lent clad in white with red herrings' skins and his horse decked [trapped] with oyster shells after him in token that sadnes and abstinence of mirth should follow and an holy time; and so rode in diverse streets of the City with other people with him disguised making mirth and disport and plays [. . .]

J47   Ash Wednesday observances criticised by Thomas Kirchmair, 1553

Thomas Kirchmair/Kirchmayer ('Naogeorgus'), *Regnum papisticum* (1553) [see **B8**, **B34**, **J11**, **J33**, **J61**]; pr. Kirchmair/Googe, p. 49a

Some bear about a herring on a staff, and loude do roar,
Herrings, herrings, stinking herrings, puddings now no more.
And hereto join they foolish plays, and doltish doggerel rhymes,
And what beside they can invent, belonging to the times.
Some other bear upon a staff their fellows horsed high,
And carry them unto some pond, or running river nigh,
That what so of their foolish feast, doth in them yet remain,
May underneath the flood be plunged and washed away again.

EASTER AND ASSOCIATED FESTIVALS

J48   The Death of Jack of Lent: a London procession of 1553

The Diary of Henry Machyn, ed. J. G. Nichols, London, 1848; reprinted New York, 1968, p. 33

The 17th day of March[1] there came through London, from Aldgate, Master Maynard, the Sheriff of London, with a standard and drums, and after giants both great and small, and then hobby-horses [. . .] and after great horses and men in coats of velvet, with chains of gold about their necks, and men in harness, and then the morris dance, and then many minstrels; and after came the sergeants and yeomen on horseback with ribbons of green and white about their necks, and then my Lord Justice late being lord of misrule rode gorgeously in cloth of gold, and with chains of gold about his neck, with hands full of rings of great value; the [. . .] sergeants rode in coats of velvet with chains of gold; and then came the dullo and a soldan, and then a priest shriving Jack of Lent on horseback, and a doctor his physician, and then Jack of Lent's wife brought him his physician and bade him save his life, and he should give him a thousand pounds for his labour; and then came the cart with the wyrth[2] hanged with cloth of gold, and full of banners and minstrels playing and singing and afore rode master Coke, in a coat of velvet with a chain of gold, and with flowers.

[1] E. K. Chambers, *The English Folk-play*, Oxford, 1933; reprinted 1969, pp. 157–8, notes that from its place in the sequence of entries this one is more likely to refer to 27 March, which was Palm Monday in 1553.
[2] Uncertain meaning: 'wreath'? 'Worthies'?

J49 A Scottish Priapic dance at Easter, 1285

Chronicon de Lanercost; pr. *Chronicles of Lanercost, 1272–1346*, trans. H. Maxwell, Glasgow, 1913, pp. 29–30

About this time [1285], in Easter week, the parish priest of Inverkeithing, named John, revived the profane rites of Priapus, collecting young girls from the villages, and compelling them to dance in circles to the honour of Father Bacchus. When he had these females in a troop, out of sheer wantonness, he led the dance, carrying in front on a pole a representation of the human organs of reproduction, and singing and dancing himself like a mime, he viewed them all and stirred them to lust by filthy language. Those who held respectable matrimony in honour were scandalised by such a shameless performance, although they respected the parson because of the dignity of his rank.

J50 The Bishop of Worcester condemns hocking, 1450

Bishop John Carpenter of Worcester, letter to diocesan clergy, 1450; Oxford, Bodleian Library, MS Bodley 692 (Notebook of John Lawern); pr. REED, *Herefordshire/Worcestershire*, pp. 349–50, trans., pp. 553–4.

An unmistakable rumour of grief has filled the inner reaches of our spirit with bitterness about a noxious corruption tending to reduce persons of either sex to a state of [spiritual] illness which, we are sorry to say, we should think has escaped the notice of none of you, how on one set day usually, alas, when the solemn feast of Easter has ended women feign to bind men, and on another day men feign to bind women, and to do other things – would that they were not dishonourable or worse! – in full view of passers-by, even pretending to increase church profit but earning a loss for the soul under false pretences.

J51 The Coventry Hocktide show performed at Kenilworth, 1575

Robert Laneham, *A Letter: whearin, part of the entertainment vntoo the Queenz Maiesty, at Killingworth Castl, in Warwik Sheer in this Soomerz Progress 1575 iz signified: from a freend officer attendant in the Coourt, vnto hiz freend a Citizen, and Merchaunt of London* (London, 1575); pr. REED, *Coventry*, pp. 272–5

And hereto followed as good a sport (methought) presented in a historical manner, by certain good hearted men of Coventry, my Lord's neighbours, there, who [. . .] made petition that they might renew their old historical show: whose argument was how the Danes formerly here in a troublous season were for quietness' sake borne withall and suffered in peace, that anon by outrage and intolerable insolence, abusing both Ethelred the then king and all estates everywhere besides: at the grievous complaint and counsel of Huna, the king's chieftain in wars, on St Brice's night, AD 1012 (as the book says) that falls yearly on the thirteenth of November were all dispatched and the realm rid [of them]. And for because the matter mentions how valiantly our English women for love of their country behaved themselves, expressed in actions and rhymes after their manner, they thought it might move some mirth to her Majesty the rather [. . .]

Captain Cox came marching on valiantly before, clean trussed and gartered above the knee, all fresh in a velvet cap (master Goldingam lent it him) flourishing with his sword, and another fence-master with him: thus in the vanward making room for the rest. After them proudly pricked on foremost, the Danish lance-knights on horseback, each with the alder-pole martially in their hand. Even at the first entry the meeting waxed somewhat warm, that by and by kindled with courage on both sides, grew from a hot skirmish unto a blazing battle; first by spear and shield, outrageous in their races as rams at their rut, with furious encounters that together they tumble to the dust, sometime horse and man, and after fall to it with sword and target, good bangs on both sides, the fight so ceasing but the battle not so ended, followed the footmen, both the hosts the one after the other; first marching in ranks, then warlike turning, then from ranks into squadrons, then into triangles, from that into rings, and so winding out again. A valiant captain of great prowess, as fierce as a fox assaulting a goose, was so hardy to give the first stroke, then get they grimly together, that great was the activity that day to be seen there on both sides, the one very eager in pursuit of prey, the other utterly stout for redemption of liberty; thus quarrel enflamed fury on both sides. Twice the Danes got the better [of the others], but at the last conflict, beaten down, overcome, and many led captive by our English women.

SPRING AND SUMMER

The expulsion of Winter/Death

J52   The expulsion of winter described by Sebastian Franck, sixteenth century

Sebastian Franck, *Weltbuch* (Tübingen, 1534), fo. 51 recto; pr. *Bräuche und Feste*, ed. Dünninger and Schopf, p. 47

In some places at mid-Lent they make a man or scarecrow of straw, constructed and laid out like a corpse, and the assembled youths carry it around the neighbouring villages. In some places they are well received and refreshed and served with dried fruits, milk and peas. Others, who take it as a sign of an impending death, receive them badly, and drive them from their farms with curses and sometimes blows.

The conflict of winter and summer

J53 The Aalborg (Denmark) Corpus Christi Guild, 1441

Constitutions of the Corpus Christi Guild (the Parrot Guild), Aalborg, 1441; pr. *Danmarks Gilde- og Lavsskraaer fra Middelalderen*, ed. C. Nyrop, vol. I, Copenhagen, 1889; reprinted 1977, pp. 621–2

Item whoever is appointed to cast lots for [performing] winter and summer on behalf of the guild and does not do so, or who does cast lots but does not go through with it, according to custom, whether his lot fall to be winter or summer, must pay a fine of one barrel of strong ale; and any brother who is appointed to accompany and assist winter or summer, either indoors or outside, and does not do so, must pay a fine of one mark of wax.

J54 A Swedish performance described by Olaus Magnus, 1555

Olaus Magnus, *Historia de gentibus septentrionalibus* (Rome, 1555); facsimile reprint introduced by John Granlund, Copenhagen, 1972, book XV, chapter VIII, 'De ritu fugandae hyemnis, & receptione aestatis', and chapter IX, 'Ad idem', trans. Fisher and Higgens, *Olaus Magnus*, vol. II, pp. 733–4. With the kind permission of the Hakluyt Society, and through the good offices of Peter Foote

[Chapter VIII]

But the Southern Swedes and the Götar [. . .] hold a different ceremony. On the first of May, when the sun is passing through Taurus, the magistrates of the cities commission two squadrons, or cohorts, of riders, consisting of tough young men who make a show as if they are about to advance to some hard battle. Of these the one is commanded by a leader appointed by lot; he bears the name and costume of Winter and, clad in various pelts and armed with pokers, scattering snowballs and chunks of ice to prolong the cold, he rides about as if he has won a victory. He pretends and acts as if he is all the less yielding, because icicles can still be seen hanging outside the heated cabins. The leader of the troop of riders on the other side, representing summer, is called Count Floral. He is garbed in the green boughs of trees, together with leaves and flowers, which have been found with difficulty, and wears summery clothes that afford little protection. Like Duke Winter, he comes into the city from the countryside, though each from a different place and with different arrangements. Contesting with their lances, they give a public entertainment to demonstrate that summer overcomes winter.

[Chapter IX]

Since, then, each side eagerly desires to conquer, the one which seems to borrow strength from the mildness or harshness of the weather on that day presses upon the other with greater force. If after they have ended their jousting a bitter winter wind is still blowing chill, the person who represents winter takes hot ashes mingled with burning sparks of fire from pots or other containers and rides round flinging them at those who are watching. Similarly, those who follow him in his troop and have the same kind of clothing and equipment gallop about hurling fire-balls at the spectators. Now in case the man who personifies summer, along with his cohort of riders, should be deprived of his desired embellishment because of green branches or flowers are not to be had, he wears birch leaves or lime twigs which have long before been ingeniously made to grow green by watering them inside warm buildings. These, borne out secretly but carried back openly, he now displays, as though they were brought from the forest. When this happens, the champions of winter attack the more violently, because Nature has been cheated and they will not let victory be gained by fraud or a peaceful procession end the affair. However, the favourable opinion of the bystanders, who refuse to tolerate any longer the harsh reign of Winter, confirms the result by a just and proper deci-sion, and to everyone's joy the victory is awarded to Summer. The latter completes his conquest by providing a splendid banquet for his companions, and validates with liquor what he could hardly have gained with lances.

St George's Day, May Day and Maying

J55   Pieter Bruegel depicts St George's Day customs, 1559

Pieter Bruegel the Elder, engraving, *The Fair of St George's Day* (1559), Bibliothèque Albert
I, Brussels; Lavalleye, *Pieter Bruegel the Elder*, pl. 57.

Amidst miscellaneous revelry and entertainment the engraving depicts an elab-orate sword-dance (see **J42** for a documentary source) and, immediately behind, an enactment of St George's combat with the dragon, anxiously watched by the princess, her father and a lamb, probably similar to the St George 'ridings' recorded for late medieval English towns. In the background on the right spectators watch a performance mounted on a traditional booth stage.

J56   Philip Stubbes attacks Maying, 1583

Philip Stubbes, *The Anatomie of Abuses*, London, 1583; facsimile reprint, New York and London, 1973, fos. M3b–4a

Against May, Whitsunday or other time, all the young men and maids, old men and wives run gadding over night to the woods, groves, hills and mountains, where they spend all the night in pleasant pastimes, and in the morning they return bringing with them birch and branches of trees, to deck their assemblies withall, and no marvel, for there is a great Lord present amongst them, as super-intendant and lord over their pastimes and sports, namely, Satan prince of Hell. But the chiefest jewel they bring from thence is their May-pole, which they bring home with great veneration, as thus. They have twenty or forty yoke of oxen, every ox having a sweet nosegay of flowers placed on the tip of his horns, and these oxen draw home this May-pole (this stinking idol rather) which is covered all over with flowers, and herbs bound round about with strings from the top to the bottom, and sometimes painted with variable colours, with two or three hundred men, women and children following it with great devotion. And thus being reared up, with handkerchieves and flags hovering on the top, they strew the ground round about, bind green boughs about it, set up summer halls, bowers and arbours hard by it. And then fall they to dance about it like as the heathen people did at the dedication of the idols, whereof this is a perfect pattern, or rather the thing itself. I have heard it credibly reported (and that *viva voce*) by men of great gravity and reputation, that of forty, three-score, or a hundred maids going to the wood over night, there have scarcely the third part of them returned home again undefiled.

Whitsun

J57   A Robin and Marion play in Angers, 1392

Royal Pardon. Trésor des Chartes, Archives Nationales, Paris, JJ 142, 173; pr. Vaultier, p. 72
[see **C84(ii)** for further details concerning *Robin et Marion*]

Jehan le Begue and five or six other scholars his companions went to play in dis-guise in the town of Angiers [*sic*] a game which is called Robin and Marion, as it is customary to do each year at the Whitsun fairs in the said town of Angiers by the people of the region, scholars and sons of the citizens and others. In the company of this Jehan le Begue and his associates there was a young girl in disguise, and as they went dancing through the said town they met four or five sons of citizens of the town, dancing and playing the said game of Robin and Marion, who, when they noticed that in the company of the said scholars there was a young girl, they accosted them and attempted to take away from them the said young girl.

Robin Hood plays

J58   A Paston serving-man as Robin Hood, 1473

Letter from John Paston II to John Paston III, 16 April 1473; pr. *Paston Letters and Papers of the Fifteenth Century*, ed. Norman Davis, 2 vols., Oxford, 1971, vol. 1, no. 275, pp. 460–1

[. . .] I have been and am troubled by my over generous and courteous dealing with my servants, and now by their ingratitude. Plattyng, your man, chooses today to bid me farewell tomorrow at Dover, notwithstanding the fact that Thryston, your other man, is away from me, and John Myryell and W. Woode, who promised you and Dawbeney,[1] God have his soul, at Caister that if you would take him in to be with me again, then he would never depart from me; and on that basis I have kept him these three years to play [in?] Saint George, and Robin Hood and the Sheriff of Nottingham,[2] and now when I am in need of good horsemen, he is gone into Barnesdale, and I am without a keeper.[3]

[1]   Paston's right-hand man, killed at the siege of Caister Castle, September 1469.
[2]   Norman Davis suggests that Paston kept too modest a household for Woode to have been retained to perform, and is here waxing ironic: Woode has been more active participating in traditional entertainments than in his domestic duties.
[3]   W. W. Greg, *Collections Part II*, Malone Society 1908, prints what he believes to be the surviving fragment of the text (once owned by the Pastons) which Woode performed.

J59   Sir Richard Morison disapproves, *c.* 1536–9

Sir Richard Morison, 'A Discourse Touching the Reformation of the Lawes of England' (*c.* 1536–9); British Library, MS Cotton Faustina C. ii; pr. Sydney Anglo, 'An Early Tudor Programme for Plays and Other Demonstrations Against the Pope', *Journal of the Warburg and Courtauld Institutes* 20 (1957), pp. 176–9

In summer generally [commonly] upon the holy days in most places of your realm, there are plays of Robin Hood, Maid Marian, Friar Tuck, wherein besides the lewdness and ribaldry that there is opened to the people, disobedience also to your officers is taught, whilst these lusty lads [good bloods] go about to take from the sheriff of Nottingham [some]one who for offending the laws should have suffered execution. (p. 179)

J60   Hugh Latimer disapproves, 1549

Hugh Latimer, sermon preached before Edward VI, April 1549; pr. Hugh Latimer, *Sermons Preached Before Edward VI*, ed. E. Arber, Birmingham, 1869, pp. 173–4

I came once myself to a place, riding on a journey homeward from London, and I sent word over night into the town that I would preach there in the morning because it was [a] holy day; and methought it was a holy day's work. The church stood in my way, and I took my horse, and my company, and went thither. I thought I should have found a great company in the church, and when I came there, the church door was fast locked. I tarried there half an hour and more, at last the key was found, and one of the parish comes to me and says, 'Sir this is a busy day with us, we cannot hear you, it is Robin Hood's day. The Parish are gone abroad to collect [gather] for Robin Hood, I pray you prevent [let] them not.' I was fain there to give place to Robin Hood, I thought my surplice [rocket] should have been regarded, though I were not, but it would not serve, it was fain to give place to Robin Hood's men. It is no laughing matter, my friends, it is a weeping matter, a heavy matter, under the pretence of gathering for Robin Hood, a traitor, and a thief, to put out a preacher, to have his office less esteemed, to prefer Robin Hood before the ministration of God's word.

Midsummer

J61   Bonfires, dances and the burning wheel in sixteenth-century Germany

Thomas Kirchmair/Kirchmayer ('Naogeorgus'), *Regnum papisticum* (1553) [see **B8**, **B34**, **J11**, **J33**, **J47**]; pr. Kirchmair/Googe, p. 54b

Then doth the joyful feast of John the Baptist take his turn,
When bonfires great with lofty flame, in every town do burn:
And young men round about with maids, do dance in every street,
With garlands wrought of Motherwort, or else with Vervain sweet,
And many other flowers fair, with Violets in their hands,
[. . .]
When thus till night they danced have, they through the fire amain
With striving minds do run, and all their herbs they cast therein,
And then with words devout and prayers, they solemnly begin,
Desiring God that all their ills may there consumed be,
Whereby they think through all that year, from Agues to be free.
Some others get a rotten wheel, all worn and cast aside,
Which covered round about with straw, and tow, they closely hide
And carried to some mountain's top, being all with fire light,
They hurl it down with violence, when dark appears the night:
Resembling much the Sun, that from the heavens down should fall,
A strange and monstrous sight it seems, and fearful to them all:
But they suppose their mischiefs all are likewise thrown to hell,
And that from harms and dangers now, in safety here they dwell.

J62   Perambulation of stick-dancers in sixteenth-century Switzerland

Gilg Tschudi, *Die urallt warhafftig Alpisch Rhetia* (Basel, 1538 [written 1528]), Hiv.; pr. Hans Moser, 'Zur Geschichte des Winter- und Sommer-Kampfspiels', *Bayerischer Heimatschutz*, 29 (1983), pp. 33–45

[. . .] there is a custom derived from heathen times, in which some years[1] they assemble together, mask themselves and put on armour and weapons, each one taking a big strong stick or cudgel, and in this manner go in a company from one village to another, making high leaps and doing other strange things, and as they truly say, after they have taken off their armour and have terminated their business, they can never make such jumps so high and so far. They run at full tilt into each other, knocking and punching with great force, from which they are known as 'stickers' in the region, doing it – they maintain this superstition – so that their grain will do better. (p. 41)

[1] A clearly related account by a near-contemporary Swiss historian, Johannes Stumpf, adds here, 'mostly at the time of midsummer'; quoted in full in Sir James Frazer, *The Golden Bough*, 3rd edn, part VI, *The Scapegoat*, London, 1913; reprinted 1980, p. 239, note 2.

Harvest

J63   A hay-making feast in Nottinghamshire, early fifteenth century

Memorandum on customs of Norwell Manor, reign of Henry IV (1399–1413). Southwell Cathedral Library, *Liber Albus*; trans. William Dickinson, *Antiquities, Historical, Architectural, Chorographical, and Itinerary, in Nottinghamshire, and other Adjacent Counties*, I. 2, Newark, 1803, p. 151; reproduced Ian Lancashire, 'Records of Drama and Minstrelsy in Nottinghamshire to 1642', REED *Newsletter*, 2.2 (1977), pp. 15–28

[In return for mowing the lord's meadows in Northing the 24 tenants are to eat in the Prebendal-house] and, after dinner, they are to sit and drink, and then go in and out of the hall three times, drinking each time they return, which being done, they shall have a bucket of beer, containing eight flagons and an half, which bucket ought to be carried on the shoulders of two men through the midst of the town, from the Prebendal-house unto the aforesaid meadow, where they are to divert themselves with plays [sports?] the remainder of the day, at which plays the Lord shall give two pairs of white gloves. (p. 16)

J64   A French Harvest Queen, 1451

Royal Pardon. Trésor des Chartes, Archives Nationales, Paris, JJ 185; pr. Vaultier, pp. 106–7

On the fourth day of August last past Jaques Gallet, his wife Jehannette, their daughter Galoise, and other reapers and harvesters of our trusty and well-beloved Guillaume de Soyecourt, Lord of Torchy, they being in the fields of the said Guillaume for disport, did raise and parade a banner and then carried the said Jehannette as Queen of their field, as harvesters are accustomed to do for disport to the community at that season. And this being made known to Jaques Boussart the elder, miller of the said place of Torchy and father of the present supplicant, who is a jovial man, as also to this supplicant and other reapers of the said village of Torchy, they assembled in great numbers with the intention of going in jollity and disport to the field of the said Guillaume de Soyecourt in order to seize the Queen and the banner of the said harvesters. And to this end they went to drink together, as it is customary to do in these circumstances. And with this friendly and festive intention without malice or hatred the said Jaques Boussart dressed and disguised himself in the manner of a messenger or herald, and fixed to his chest a shield of wood in the manner of a blazon and took a piece of parchment without writing on it on which he hung a platter of wood which he pretended was a seal. And he also took a pistol without gunpowder and without intent to fire it. In this condition he mounted on a horse or a mare. Someone else took a clay trumpet and some other instruments to blow and play merrily. And in this manner they went together merrily and trumpeting to the field of the said Guillaume, where the said Jaques pretended to read from the said piece of parchment without writing, speaking several japes and merriments, and the other blew the said trumpet. And thus the harvesters of the said Guillaume were assailed, and they defended themselves merrily. And there were those taken and struck to the ground on the one side and the other. Likewise the said Jaques was pulled from the aforementioned beast and then remounted. And finally the said banner and Queen were captured and taken to the public square of the said town. And the belt and dagger of this Jaques were removed, and the said Queen was tied with his sash for disport, and the said Jaques Gallet, who was inclined to be choleric, was not pleased.

III *Occasional customs*

Many customs have an incidence other than the seasonal or calendrical, and in several ways. There are for example distinctly traditional practices (illustrated below by the case of festive dance-songs **J65, J66, J67, J68, J69, J70**) which, while invariably performed under the auspices of seasonal festivals or occasional celebrations, are not strictly tied to any particular one: a household's Christmas revels, a summer festival in the churchyard, or a lying-in feast would all provide a suitable context. A more predictable rhythm is provided by observances (not all actual rites of passage) triggered by significant transitions in the life of an individual: birth (observances in connection with the lying-in, the christening, and the mother's 'churching'), coming of age, marriage (handfasting; wedding), and death (the wake and the funeral) [see **J71, J72**]. Other customs mark important moments in the official rather than the personal biography, for example the assumption of office (e.g. mayor; monarch). There are, finally, customs whose incidence is basically sporadic, prompted by an exterior incident to which a reaction (positive or more usually negative) is felt requisite: a price or rent rise, an unpopular wedding, an incident of husband beating or cuckoldry, a rumour of sexual deviance. The response in these cases generally takes the form of a mocking parade (*charivari*) [see **J73, J74, J75**] or a satirical game [see **J76, J77, J78**].

FESTIVE DANCE-SONGS

J65 Dance-songs condemned by the Council of Rome, 826

Council of Rome (826), canon 35; pr. L. Gougaud, 'La danse dans les églises', *Revue d'histoire ecclesiastique* 15 (1914), pp. 5–22; 229–45

There are some, mostly women, who take pleasure in coming to church on festivals and holy days and on the nativities of saints not for the sake of these, as they should, but for dancing, singing wicked words, performing and leading dance-songs, in the manner of pagans [. . .].(p. 12)

J66   The dancers of Kölbigk, eleventh century

Oxford, Bodleian Library, MS Rawlinson C938 (thirteenth century), fos. 22b–25a,
appendix to Goscelin's *Life of St Edith* (1080); pr. Ernst Erick Metzner, *Zur frühesten
Geschichte der europäischen Balladendichtumg: Der Tanz in Kölbigk*, Frankfurt, 1972, pp. 43–4

[This belongs to the 'Theoderic' tradition of the Kölbigk legend, the account of one
of the sinners, whose involuntary dancing was purportedly cured by the miraculous intervention of St Edith at Wilton in England: it is probably the ultimate
source for the more familiar account in Robert Mannyng's fourteenth-century
Handlynge Synne [see **C33**].

On the night of the Nativity of our Lord [. . .] we twelve companions, in our folly
and madness, came to the place called Kölbigk, to the church which is dedicated
to the holy martyr Magnus and to his sister St Buccestra. Our leader was named
Gerlevus, and the other twelve [*sic*] are added here for completeness' sake. We were
as follows: Theodericus, Meinoldus, Odbertus, Bovo, Gerardus, Wetzelo, Azelius,
Folpoldus, Hildebrandus, Alvuardus, Benna, Odricus. Why hesitate to recount our
unhappy fate? The whole cause of our accursed gathering was that we comrades
together intended, in our pride and to no good end, to seize a girl, the daughter of
Rodbert, the parish priest. The girl was called Ava. Neither the Lord's vigil, nor the
thought of Christianity, nor the piety of the faithful, congregated at the church,
nor the sound of the divine liturgy, could discipline our indecency into desisting
from such a shameful act.

We sent the two girls, Merswind and Wibecyna, who [. . .] inveighled away from
the church her whom we had sought as our prey, to participate in our ring-dance
of sin [. . .] Ava was brought to us like a little bird in a net, and Bovo, who was senior
in both years and depravity, welcomed them as they came.

We took each other by the hand, and started our ring-dance of confusion in the
churchyard. Gerlevus was chosen as the leader of our madness, and began the following song:

> Bovo rode through the leafy wood;
> And led the beautiful Merswind.
>   Why do we stand still?
>   Why do we not go?

When the holy service of the night was concluded, and the first Mass due to the
honour of this night begun, we danced with even greater noise as if to drown out
God's servants and the praise of God with our polluted ring-dance. When the priest
heard it, he went from the altar to the church door and in a loud voice urged us to
respect sacred things and to come to the church service in a Christian manner. But
when no one would be quiet or listen to him on account of their corrupt hearts,
the priest, with divine zeal, imposed on us, through the holy martyr Magnus, God's
vengeance, and, he said, we should never cease this 'service' without God's leave.
When he had said this, he bound us with the judgement he had spoken in such a

way that none of us could stop doing what had been started, and no one could be separated from another [. . .] We could not for one moment stop going round in our ring-dance, stamping the ground with our feet, making jumps or ridiculously clapping our hands or continuing to sing the same song. Again and again the refrain of our song of punishment returned to taunt us:

> Why do we stand still?
> Why do we not go?

– we could neither resist nor alter our dancing circle.

J67   Festive dance with work-mimes, Wales, late twelfth century

Giraldus Cambrensis, *Itinerarium Cambriae* (*c.* 1188), book I, ch. II; pr. Chambers, *The Mediaeval Stage*, vol. II, p. 189, note I; trans. Lewis Thorpe, Gerald of Wales, *The Journey through Wales and the Description of Wales*, Harmondsworth, 1978, pp. 92–3

[Speaking of the church of St Eluned, on the top of a hill near Brecon Castle, Brecknockshire.] Each year on the first day of August her feast-day is celebrated with great solemnity [. . .] On that day great crowds of ordinary folk assemble there from far and wide [. . .] You can see young men and maidens, some in the church itself, some in the churchyard and others in the dance which threads its way round the graves. They sing traditional songs, all of a sudden they collapse on the ground, and then those who, until now, have followed their leader peacefully as if in a trance, leap in the air as if seized by frenzy. In full view of the crowds they mime with their hands and feet whatever work they have done contrary to the commandment on sabbath days. You can see one man putting his hand to a plough, another goading his oxen with a stick, and as they go singing country airs, to lighten the tedium of their labour. This man is imitating a cobbler at his bench, that man over there is miming a tanner at his work. Here you see a girl pretending that she has a distaff in her hand, drawing out the thread with her hands, stretching it at arm's length, and then winding it back on to the spindle; another, as she trips along, fits the woof to the warp; a third tosses her shuttle, now this way, now that, from one hand to the other, and, with jerky gestures of her tiny tool, seems for all the world to be weaving cloth from the thread which she has prepared. When all is over, they enter the church. They are led up to the altar and there, as they make their oblation, you will be surprised to see them awaken from their trance and recover their normal composure.[1]

---

[1] For singing-games involving work-mimes in recent folk tradition see A. B. Gomme, *The Traditional Games of England, Scotland and Ireland*, 2 vols., London, 1894–8; reprinted New York, 1964, vol. II, pp. 362–74.

J68   A dance-game at a thirteenth-century Danish lying-in feast

Durham Cathedral Chapter Library MS. B.IV.19. (A collection of Latin *exempla* compiled by an anonymous English Franciscan in the second half of the thirteenth century, including material copied from contemporary published collections and original material from oral tradition [as evidently in this instance]); pr. Jørgen and Axel Olrik, 'Kvindegilde i Middelalderen', *Danske Studier* (1907), pp. 175–6

If we are speaking of uninhibited games I shall not omit to repeat something I had from Brother Peder, who was once in the train of Concedus, the inspector of the order, and who subsequently succeeded him in that post after the latter's death. He told me and several other brothers in Dublin that in his homeland, Denmark, it is the custom that when women are lying-in the neighbouring wives come and help them to keep cheerful with dancing and uninhibited songs. So it happened that one time when a group of women had assembled for a lying-in and were intent on making a row in accordance with the country's evil custom, they assembled a bundle of straw and formed it into the likeness of a man, with arms of straw, put a belt and hat on him, and called him 'Bovi'.[1] Then they performed their ring-dance, and two women jumped up and sang with him between them, and between the verses, as the custom is, they turned to him with unseemly gestures and said to him: 'Sing with us, Bovi, sing with us; why are you silent?' And at once the devil, who had these wretched women in his power, replied: 'Oh yes, I shall sing!' and he (not the bundle itself of course, but the devil sitting in it) screamed out and gave such a powerful yell that some of them fell down dead, while others were struck with such horror and fear that they were ill for a long time afterwards and barely escaped with their lives. (p. 175, note 1)

---

[1] It has not escaped notice that the name is very similar to the 'Bovo' of the analogous dance-game reported from Kölbigk [see **J66**].

J69   Song and dance condemned by Thomas of Chobham, *c.* 1220

Thomas of Chobham, *Summa confessorum* (instructions for priests conducting confession, *c.* 1220); pr. Thomas of Chobham, *Summa confessorum*, ed. F. Broomfield, Paris, 1968, p. 292; trans. Sandra Billington, *A Social History of the Fool*, Brighton, 1984, p. 2. [See also **A35**]

It is known that until now there has been the perverse custom in many places, where on any holy feast day wanton women and youthful fools gather together and sing wanton and diabolical songs the whole night through in the churchyards and in the church to which they lead their ring-dances and practice many other shameful games. All such activity is to be prohibited with the greatest diligence, if it is possible.

J70   The dance-game of King Valdemar, Gotland, seventeenth century

Hans Nielssøn Strelow, *Guthilandiske Cronica* (Copenhagen, 1633), pp. 168–70, under the year 1361; reprinted *Danmarks gamle Folkeviser*, vol. IV, ed. Svend Grundtvig, 1869–83; reprinted Copenhagen, 1966, p. 480

When the people of Gotland heard of King Valdemar [of Denmark's] arrival and expedition, they were by no means concerned, in view of the large forces they could deploy, but made great scorn and pastime of it (although none should scorn their enemies) in their assemblies, revels and feasts, in that they made a game of his military preparations which was to be played by groups at all their assemblies, particularly at Shrovetide, as it is still played in our Christmas revels: they take each other by the hands, make a circle or ring, and Valdemar is to go outside [it] and try to sneak in; the one he gets past must be punished.

WAKE GAMES

J71   Wake games condemned by Regino of Prüm, tenth century

Regino, Abbot of Prüm [Lorraine], *Libri duo de synodalibus causis et disciplinis ecclesiasticis* (tenth-century compilation of regulations); trans. McNeill and Gamer, *Medieval Handbooks of Penance*, pp. 318–19. Reprinted by permission of the publisher

canon cccxcviii. That diabolical songs be not sung at night hours over the bodies of the dead. – Laymen who keep watch at funerals shall do so with fear and trembling, and with reverence. Let no one there presume to sing diabolical songs nor make jests and perform dances which pagans have invented by the devil's teaching. For who does not know that it is diabolical, and not only alien from the Christian religion, but even contrary to human nature, that there should be singing, rejoicing, drunkenness, and that the mouth be loosed with laughter, and that all piety and feeling of charity be set aside, as if to exult in a brother's death, in the place where mourning and sobbing with doleful voices for the loss of a dear brother ought to resound? [. . .] And therefore such unsuitable rejoicing and pestiferous songs are on God's authority to be wholly forbidden.

J72   Wake games in late seventeenth-century England

John Aubrey, *Remaines of Gentilisme and Judaisme* (late seventeenth century); pr. *Three Prose Works*, ed. John Buchanan-Brown, Carbondale, 1972, p. 173

At the funerals in Yorkshire, to this day, they continue the custom of watching and sitting-up all night till the body is interred. In the interim some kneel down and pray (by the corpse), some play at cards, some drink and take tobacco: they have also mimical plays and sports, e.g. they choose a simple young fellow to be a Judge, then the suppliants (having first blacked their hands by rubbing it under the bottom of the pot), beseech his Lordship: and smut all his face. They play likewise at Hot Cockles.[1]

[1] A game in which a blindfolded figure has to guess who has hit him; it may have inspired one of the torments inflicted on Christ in the Chester Cycle (Play 16).

CHARIVARI

J73   The *charivari* in *Le Roman de Fauvel* (early fourteenth century)

These are additional lines in Paris, BN MS fr. 146, fos. 1–45 by Raoul Chaillou du Pesstain (see *Le Roman de Fauvel*, ed. Arthur Långfors, SATF, 64 (Paris, 1914–19; reprinted New York, 1968), pp. 135–8), pr. ibid., appendix, 'Notice et Extraits de l'Interpolation du Manuscrit E', lines 679–770ff.

Fauvel reckons that the time has come
To go to bed: so without delay
He jumps into bed to lie with her
But never was such a *charivari*
Made by homeless tramps
As they do at the crossroads
Of the town and along the streets.
[. . .]
Those who participate push forward everywhere
[. . .]
Some have all back to front
Dressed and put on their clothes;
Others have made their disguise
Out of large sacks and monks' cowls
One could scarcely recognise them,
They were so painted and deformed.
They were bent on nothing but mischief.
One of them carried a big frying-pan,
Another a roasting spit, a gridiron, and a
Pestle, yet another a copper pot
And all pretended to be drunk;
Another a bowl, and they all beat
So loud that all were astounded.
Another one had cowbells
Sown to his thighs and his buttocks
And above them large bells
Which rang clear as he moved;
Others had drums and cymbals
And large instruments, ugly and dirty,
And rattles and harrows
With which they made such a great row and loud noise

It can't be described.
One pushes forwards and another pulls,
For they drew with them a cart
And in the cart there was
A mechanism with cartwheels,
Strong, stiff and excellently made
So that when they turned
Six iron rods clashed together
Which were nailed in the hub
And well attached; Oh listen!
Such a loud and unexpected noise
So awful and so horrible
They produced when they struck together
That you could not have heard God's thunder.
Then they raised up a shouting
The like was never heard before;
One of them exposed his arse to the winds,
Another smashed shutters;
One broke windows and doors;
Another threw salt in the wells;
And a third threw turds in people's faces.
They were so ugly and savage.
On their heads they wore bearded masks,
And with them they brought two coffins
In which there were people too skilled
At singing the devil's songs.
One cried of panniers and winnowing fans;
Another of the part whence comes the wind.
There was a huge giant
Who went ahead howling,
Wearing a fine cloak;
I think it was Herlechin
And all the rest his rout
Who followed him in a mad rage.
He was mounted on a tall hack
So fat that, by St Quinault,
You could have counted its ribs
And climb them one by one like laths
Ready to be covered with tiles or shingles.

J74   A 'skimmington' in Quemerford, Wiltshire, 1618

Depositions before Wiltshire Quarter Sessions, 1 June 1618. Wiltshire and Swindon Record Office, Trowbridge, Quarter Sessions Great Rolls, W.S.R.O.A1/110/Trinity 1618, no. 168; pr. B. H. Cunnington, 'A "Skimmington" in 1618', *Folklore* 41 (1930), pp. 288–90

The information of Thomas Wills of Quemerford in the parish of Calne, County of Wilts, cutler, and Agnes his wife taken the first day of June anno domini 1618.

And about noon came [. . .] from Calne to Quemerford [a] drummer named William Watt, and with him three or four hundred men, some like soldiers, armed with pieces [guns] and other weapons, and a man riding upon a horse, having a white night cap upon his head, two shining horns hanging by his ears, and a counterfeit beard upon his chin made of a dear's tail, a smock upon the top of his garments, and he rode upon a red horse with a pair of pots under him and in them some quantity of brewing grains, which he used to cast upon the press of people, rushing over thick upon him in the way as he passed.

And he and all his company made a stand when they came just against these examinates' house, and then the gunners shot off their pieces, pipes and horns were sounded, together with cowbells and other small bells which the company had amongst them, and rams' horns and bucks' horns carried upon forks were then and there lifted up and shown. [The crowd dragged Agnes Wills out of the house, beat her, and trod her in a muddy hole.]

J75   A skimmington ride illustrated by William Hogarth, 1726

William Hogarth, engraving (one of twelve) to illustrate 1726 edition of Samuel Butler's *Hudibras* (orig. 1664), part II, canto II, lines 585ff; pr. Joseph Burke and Colin Caldwell, *Hogarth. The Complete Engravings*, London, 1968, illus. 103.

[Hudibras is the portly man riding from right to left, the other figures belong to the custom, which is also described at some length in Butler's text. Note left of centre the female figure beating with a large spoon (the 'skimmington') the 'husband' who both rides backwards on the horse and spins from a distaff.]

SATIRICAL GAMES AND PLAYS

J76   A play against the shoemakers, Exeter, 1352.

Letter from Bishop John de Grandisson to the Archdeacon of Exeter, Register of Bishop John de Grandisson, entered 9 August 1352. Devon Record Office: Chanter 3, fo. 172 verso; pr. REED, *Devon*, pp. 9–10, trans. pp. 323–4

[...] we learned some time ago that some impudent sons of our city of Exeter, inordinately given over to wanton behaviour [and] foolishly contemptuous of things usefully devised for their needs and those of all the populace, are proposing, as they had agreed and are planning among themselves, to practise openly on this very Sunday in a public place of our aforesaid city an objectionable diversion [...] as invective and a reproach against the shoemakers and also against their craft, wherefore, as we have learned, serious disputes, rancours, and brawls are sprouting forth vigorously and growing, [...] among the aforesaid craftsmen and those taking part in the said sport, both leaders and supporters. [They are to be instructed to desist.] Moreover, because the aforementioned craftsmen, who, as we have heard from the clamorous report of the people, so excessively receive and extort in selling their wares more than the just price in modern times from those contracting with the same [they are not to charge more than the authorised price].

J77   A play against abbey servants, France, 1460

Royal Pardon. Trésor des Chartes, Archives Nationales, Paris, JJ 189; pr. Vaultier, p. 89

[On the Feast of the Holy Innocents (28 December) a group of young men] went to play a farce after supper in the hall of the Abbess of Béthencourt where there were several nuns and other young people. Those mentioned above said in their play that Toussain and Gauvain du Four [...] had drunk the wine of the said nuns and eaten their capons, and this was because it was said that the said Toussain and du Four had as paramours certain of the nursemaids of the said nuns.

J78   A mock groaning at Westonbirt, Gloucestershire, 1716

Holford Papers, Gloucestershire Record Office, D. 1956, Holford and Westonbirt papers (letter of 28 November 1716 from Francis Goodenough to Sir Richard Holford); pr. David Rolinson, 'Property, Ideology and Popular Culture in a Gloucestershire Village 1660–1740', *Past and Present* 93 (November 1981), pp. 70–97

[Rumour claimed that a local man, George Andrews, had committed sodomy with a young man from Gloucester, Walter Lingsey. As no criminal proceedings were instituted, members of the community arranged a public feast, at which a satirical 'mock groaning' (labour and birth) would be performed, with Lingsey playing himself.]

Walter Watts' wife furnished Lingsey with a mantua petticoat, white apron and head-clothes that he might look something like a woman. One Rolfe of Luckington was the midwife. After the invited company, which was numerous, had pleased themselves with the ale and good things, Lingsey by their assistance was delivered of a child, viz. a wad of straw made up and dressed with clothes in that form, which they said was a male child, whereupon the company drank plentifully and rejoiced up [sic] exceedingly at the birth. After a little while they resolved to have the child christened, and picked upon one of their company, Samuel Wallis by name (a scandalous fellow) to be parson, who some say raised the child to the churchyard and there (for he could not get into the church) after he had pronounced so much of the form of Baptism as he could remember christened the child, whom the godfathers, whose names I do not know (for there was no godmother) named George. The said parson threw water upon it and said I baptise thee in the name of the Father the Son and the Holy Ghost. After this was done the company fell to their rejoicings and continued their mirth until the barrel was empty and then sent and invited some of the women of the place to wait with the lying-in woman as they termed Lingsey. (p. 73)

Bibliography

GENERAL

Axton, Richard, *European Drama of the Early Middle Ages*, London, Hutchinson, 1974; University of
  Pittsburgh Press, 1975
Barber, Richard and Juliet Barker, *Tournaments: Jousts, Chivalry and Pageants in the Middle Ages*,
  Woodbridge, Boydell and Brewer, 1989
Bevington, David (ed. and trans.), *Medieval Drama*, Boston, Houghton Mifflin Co., 1975
The Book of Saints: a Dictionary of Servants of God Canonized by the Catholic Church, compiled by the
  Benedictine monks of St Augustine's Abbey, Ramsgate, 6th edn, London, A. & C. Black, 1989
The Cambridge History of the Bible, vol. II, *The West from the Fathers to the Reformation*, ed. G. W. H.
  Lampe, Cambridge University Press, 1969
Chambers, E. K., *The Mediaeval Stage*, 2 vols., Oxford, Clarendon Press, 1903; various reprints
Colish, Marcia L., *Medieval Foundations of the Western Intellectual Tradition, 400–1400*, Yale Intellectual
  History of the West, New Haven and London, Yale University Press, 1997
Davidson, Clifford (ed.) *The Saint Play in Medieval Europe*, Early Drama, Art and Music Monograph Series
  8, Kalamazoo, Western Michigan University, Medieval Institute Publications, 1986
Davidson, Clifford, *The Iconography of Heaven*, Early Drama, Art and Music Monograph Series 21,
  Kalamazoo, Western Michigan University, Medieval Institute Publications, 1994
Davidson, Clifford, C. J. Gianakaris *et al.* (eds.), *Drama in the Middle Ages: Comparative and Critical Essays*,
  AMS Studies in the Middle Ages 4, New York, AMS Press, 1982
Davidson, Clifford and T. H. Seiler (eds.), *The Iconography of Hell*, Early Drama, Art and Music
  Monograph Series 17, Kalamazoo, Western Michigan University, Medieval Institute Publications,
  1992
Davidson, Clifford and John H. Stroupe (eds.), *Drama in the Middle Ages: Comparative and Critical Essays
  Second Series*, AMS Studies in the Middle Ages 18, New York, AMS Press, 1990
Davidson, Clifford and John H. Stroupe (eds.), *Medieval Drama on the Continent of Europe*, Kalamazoo,
  Western Michigan University, Medieval Institute Publications, 1993
Doglio, Federico, *Teatro in Europa: storia e documenti*, vol. I, Milan, Garzanti, 1982
Farmer, David Hugh, *The Oxford Dictionary of Saints*, Oxford, Clarendon Press, 1978
Hardison, O. B., Jr., *Christian Rite and Christian Drama in the Middle Ages. Essays in the Origin and Early
  History of Modern Drama*, Baltimore, Johns Hopkins University Press, 1965
Hindley, Alan (ed.), *Drama and the Community: People and Plays in Medieval Europe*, Medieval Texts and
  Cultures of Northern Europe 1, Turnhout, Brepols, 1999
Holmes, George (ed.), *The Oxford Illustrated History of Medieval Europe*, Oxford University Press, 1988
Johnston, Alexandra F. and Wim Hüsken (eds.), *Civic Ritual and Drama*, Ludus II, Amsterdam, Rodopi,
  1997
Kelly, J. N. D. *The Oxford Dictionary of Popes*, Oxford University Press, 1986

Kipling, Gordon, *Enter the King: Theatre, Liturgy, and Ritual in the Medieval Civic Triumph*, Oxford, Clarendon Press, 1998
Knight, Alan E. (ed.), *The Stage as Mirror: Civic Theatre in Late Medieval Europe*, Woodbridge, Boydell and Brewer, 1997
Konigson, Elie, *L'Espace théâtral médiéval*, Paris, Centre National de la Recherche Scientifique, 1975
Lexikon der christlichen Ikonographie, ed. Engelbert Kirschbaum *et al.* 8 vols., Rome etc., Herder, 1968–74; reprinted 1994
Markus, R. A., *The End of Ancient Christianity*, Cambridge University Press, 1990
Meredith, Peter and John E. Tailby (eds. and trans.), *The Staging of Religious Drama in Europe in the Later Middle Ages: Texts and Documents in English Translation*, Early Drama, Art and Music Monograph Series 4, Kalamazoo, Western Michigan University, Medieval Institute Publications, 1983
Migne, Jacques Paul (ed.), *Patrologiae cursus completus: series Latina*, 221 vols., Paris, 1841–64
Muir, Lynette R., *The Biblical Drama of Medieval Europe*, Cambridge University Press, 1995
 'Playing God in Medieval Europe', in Knight (ed.), *Stage as Mirror*, pp. 25–50
Nagler, A. M., *The Medieval Religious Stage: Shapes and Phantoms*, New Haven and London, Yale University Press, 1976
The New Cambridge Medieval History, vol. II, *c. 700–c. 900*, ed. Rosamond McKitterick, Cambridge University Press, 1995
Records of Early English Drama, ed. Alexandra F. Johnston, University of Toronto Press, 1979
 Chester, ed. Laurence M. Clopper, 1979
 York, ed. Alexandra F. Johnston and Margaret Rogerson, 1979
 Coventry, ed. R. W. Ingram, 1981
 Norwich 1540–1642, ed. David Galloway, 1984
 Cumberland/Westmorland/Gloucestershire, ed. Audrey Douglas and Peter Greenfield, 1986
 Devon, ed. John Wasson, 1987
 Cambridge, ed. Alan H. Nelson, 1987
 Bristol, ed. Mark Pilkington, 1997
 Dorset, ed. Rosalind Conklin Hays and C. E. McGee, 1999
 Cornwall, ed. Sally Joyce and Evelyn S. Newlyn, 1999
Rey-Flaud, Henri, *Le cercle magique: Essai sur le théâtre en rond à la fin du Moyen Age*, Paris, Gallimard, 1973
Rubin, Miri, *Corpus Christi: the Eucharist in Late Medieval Culture*, Cambridge University Press, 1991
Simon, Eckehard (ed.), *The Theatre of Medieval Europe: New Research in Early Drama*, Cambridge Studies in Medieval Literature 9, Cambridge University Press, 1991
Smalley, Beryl, *The Study of the Bible in the Middle Ages*, Oxford, Clarendon Press, 1941; 3rd revised edn, Oxford, Blackwell, 1983
Smoldon, William, *The Music of the Medieval Church Dramas*, ed. Cynthia Bourgeault, Oxford University Press, 1980
Société Internationale pour l'Etude du Théâtre Médiéval: Proceedings of Triennial Colloquia
 The Drama of Medieval Europe, proceedings of the colloquium [held at the University of Leeds 10–13 September 1974], ed. Richard Rastall, Leeds Medieval Studies 1, Graduate Centre for Medieval Studies, University of Leeds, 1975
 Le Théâtre au Moyen Age, Actes du deuxième colloque [held at Alençon, 11–14 July 1977], ed. Gari R. Muller, Montreal, L'Aurore/Univers, 1981
 Between Folk and Liturgy, proceedings of the third colloquium [held at Dublin, 8–12 July 1980], ed. Alan J. Fletcher and Wim Hüsken, Ludus III, Amsterdam, Rodopi, 1997
 Atti del IVᵒ Colloquio . . . [held at Viterbo 10–15 July 1983], ed. Federico Doglio, Viterbo, Centro Studi sul Teatro Medioevale et Rinascimentale, 1984
 Le théâtre et la cité dans l'Europe médiévale, Actes du Vème colloque . . . [held at Perpignan 7–13 July 1986], ed. Edelgard E. DuBruck and William C. Macdonald, *Fifteenth-century Studies* 13 (1988) [Special issue]
 Evil on the Medieval Stage, papers from the sixth triennial colloquium [held at Lancaster 13–19 July 1989], ed. Meg Twycross, *Medieval English Theatre* 11 (1989), [published 1992]

Formes Teatrals de la Tradició Medieval, Actes del VII colloqui [held at Gerona, 29 June–4 July 1992], ed. Jésus-Francesc Massip, Barcelona, Institut del Theatro, 1996

Southern, Richard, *The Seven Ages of the Theatre*, London, Faber, 1962

Spufford, Peter, *Handbook of Medieval Exchange*, London, Royal Historical Society, 1986

Sticca, Sandro (ed.), *The Latin Passion Play: its Origins and Development*, Albany, State University of New York Press, 1972

The Medieval Drama, Albany, State University of New York Press, 1972

Stratman, Carl J. (ed.), *Bibliography of Medieval Drama*, Berkeley, 1954; 2nd revised edn, 2 vols., New York, Frederick Ungar, 1972

Tydeman, William, *The Theatre in the Middle Ages. Western European Stage Conditions c. 800–1576*, Cambridge University Press, 1978

Veltrusky, Jamilla P., 'Medieval Drama in Bohemia', *Early Drama, Art and Music Review* 15 (1993), pp. 51–63

Vince, Ronald M., *A Companion to the Medieval Theatre*, New York and Westport, Greenwood Press, 1989

Wickham, Glynne, *The Medieval Theatre*, London, Weidenfeld and Nicolson, 1974; 3rd edn, Cambridge University Press, 1987

Wright, Stephen K., *The Vengeance of Our Lord. Medieval Dramatizations of the Destruction of Jerusalem*, Studies and Texts 89, Toronto, Pontifical Institute of Mediaeval Studies, 1989

Young, Karl, *The Drama of the Medieval Church*, 2 vols., Oxford, Clarendon Press, 1933

SECTION A   THE INHERITANCE

Albertus Magnus, *Opera omnia*, ed. Augustus Borgnet, 38 vols., Paris, 1890–9

Aquinas, St Thomas, *Summa theologiae*, ed. and trans. Thomas Gilby, 60 vols., London, Eyre and Spottiswoode, 1964–6

Bennett, J. A. W. and G. V. Smithers (eds.), *Early Middle English Verse and Prose*, Oxford, Clarendon Press, 1968

Birch, Walter de Gray (ed.), *Cartularum Saxonicum: a Collection of Charters Relating to Anglo-Saxon History*, 3 vols., London, Whiting & Co., 1885–99

Bollandus, Johannes, *Acta sanctorum*, ed. Jean Carnandet, 61 vols., Paris, etc., V. Palmé, 1863–83

Bonfante, Larissa (trans.), *The Plays of Hrotswitha of Gandersheim*, New York University Press, 1979

Buecheler, F. and A. Riese (ed.), *Anthologia Latina*, Leipzig, Teubner, 1894; revised Riese, 2 vols., Leipzig, Teubner, 1906

Butler, Sister Mary Marguerite, *Hrotswita: the Theatricality of her Plays*, New York, 1960

Campbell, Jackson J. (ed. and trans.), *The Advent Lyrics of the Exeter Book*, Princeton University Press, 1959

[Cassiodorus, Magnus Aurelius], *Variarum Libri XII [Variae]*, ed. Å. J. Fridh, in *Magni Avrelii Cassiodori Senatoris Opera*, vol. 1 (Corpus Christianorum, Series Latina XCIV), Turnholt, Brepols, 1973

Variae, ed. and trans. S. J. B. Barnish, Liverpool University Press, 1992

Chambers, E. K.   *see general bibliography*

Davis, Nicholas, '*Spectacula Christiana*: a Roman Christian Template for Medieval Drama', *Medieval English Theatre* 9 (1987), pp. 125–52

Dümmler, E. (ed.), *Epistolae Karolini aevi*, vol. II, *Monumentae Germaniae Historica*, Berlin, Weidmann, 1895

Dumville, David N., 'Liturgical Drama and Panegyric Responsory from the Eighth Century? A Re-examination the Origin and Contents of the Ninth-century Section of the Book of Cerne', *Journal of Theological Studies* n.s. 23 (1972), pp. 374–406

Elliott, Alison Goddard (trans.), *Seven Medieval Latin Comedies*, New York, Garland, 1984

Fowler, Roger (ed.) *Wulfstan's Canons of Edgar*, EETS (OS 266), Oxford University Press, 1972

Fulgheri, Andrea Dessà (ed.), *Babio*, in Ferrucio Bertini (ed.), *Commedie latine del XII e XIII secolo*, vol. II, Sassari, Gallizi, 1980

Galleé, Johan Hendrik (ed.), *Altsächsische Sprachdenkmäler*, 2 vols., Leyden, 1894

Giraldus Cambrensis, *De rebus a se gestis, Invectionum libellus, Symbolum electorum*, ed. J. S. Brewer, J. F. Dimock and G. F. Warner (Rolls Series, 21, vol. 1), 8 vols., London, 1861–91

Haddan, Arthur West and William Stubbs (eds.), *Councils and Ecclesiastical Documents Relating to Great Britain and Ireland*, 3 vols., Oxford, 1869–78; reprinted Oxford, Clarendon Press, 1964

Holmes, Urban T., Jr., 'Ludos scenicos in Giraldus', *MLN* 57 (1942), pp. 188–9

[Isidore of Seville] *Isidori Hispalensis Episcopi etymologiarum sive originum, Libri XX*, ed. W. M. Lindsay, 2 vols., Oxford, Clarendon Press, 1911

Jones, Joseph R., 'Isidore and the Theater', *Comparative Drama* 16 (1982–3), pp. 26–48

Jürgens, Heiko, *Pompa diaboli. Die lateinischen Kirchenväter und das antike Theater*, Tübingener Beiträge zur Altertumswissenschaft 46, Stuttgart, Kohlhammer, 1972

Kelly, Henry Ansgar, *Ideas and Forms of Tragedy from Aristotle to the Middle Ages*, Cambridge Studies in Medieval Literature 18, Cambridge University Press, 1993

Loomis, R. S., 'Some evidence for secular Theatres in the Twelfth and Thirteenth Centuries', *Theatre Annual* (1945), pp. 33–43

Mansi, J. D. (ed.), *Sacrorum Conciliorum et decretorum nova et amplissima collectio*, 31 vols., Florence/Venice, 1759–98, reproduced in 53 vols., Paris, Welter, 1901–27; reprinted Graz, Akademische Durch- und Verlaganstalt, 1960–1

Marshall, Mary H., 'Boethius' definition of *persona* and medieval understanding of the Roman theater', *Speculum* 25 (1950), pp. 471–82

'Theatre in the Middle Ages: Evidence from Dictionaries and Glosses', *Symposium* 4 (1950), pp. 1–39, 366–89

Migne, Jacques Paul (ed.)   *see* general bibliography

Nicoll, Allardyce, *Masks, Mimes and Miracles: Studies in Popular Theatre*, London and New York, Harrap, 1931

Ogilvy, J. D. A., 'Mimi, scurrae, histriones: Entertainers of the Early Middle Ages', *Speculum* 38 (1963), pp. 603–19

Olson, Glending, 'The Medieval Fortunes of *Theatrica*', *Traditio* 42 (1986), pp. 265–86

Pike, Joseph B. (trans.), *Frivolities of Courtiers and Footprints of Philosophers* [selections from John of Salisbury's *Policraticus*], Minneapolis, University of Minnesota Press, 1938; reprinted New York, Octagon Books, 1972

Richard of Devizes, *Chronicle of the Time of King Richard the First*, ed. John T. Appleby, London, Thomas Nelson, 1963

Robertson, James Craigie and J. B. Sheppard (eds.), *Materials for the History of Thomas Becket*, (Rolls Series 67), 7 vols., London, 1875–85

Rubel, Helen F., 'Chabham's *Penitential* and its Influence in the Thirteenth Century', *PMLA* 40 (1925), pp. 225–39

St John, Christopher (trans.), *The Plays of Roswitha*, London, Medieval Library, 1923

Societas Aperiendis Fontibus, *Epistolae Karolini aevi*, vol. IV, *Monumentae Germaniae Historica*, Berlin, Weidmann, 1925

Taylor, Jerome (ed. and trans.), *The Didascalicon of Hugh of St Victor*, New York, Columbia University Press, 1961

Thorpe, B. (ed.), *Ancient Laws and Institutes of England*, Commissioners of the Public Records of the Kingdom, 2 vols., London, Record Commission, 1840

Traube, Ludowick (ed.), *Poetae Latini aevi Carolini*, 4 vols., Berlin, Weidmann, 1881–1923, vol. III, *Monumentae Germaniae Historica*

Tunison, Joseph S., *Dramatic Traditions of the Dark Ages*, University of Chicago Press; London, Fisher Unwin, 1907

Weissman, Werner, *Kirche und Schauspiele. Die Schauspiele im Urteil der lateinischen Kirchenväter unter besonderer Berücksichtigung von Augustin*, Coll. Cassiciacum 27, Würzburg, Augustinus-Verlag, 1972

Young, Karl   *see* general bibliography

SECTION B   LATIN LITURGICAL DRAMA

Amalarius of Metz, *De Ecclesiasticis officiis*, in Migne (ed.), *Patrologiae cursus completus series Latina*, vol. cv, cols. 985–1242

Bailey, Terence, *The Fleury Play of Herod*, Toronto, Pontifical Institute of Mediaeval Studies, 1965
The Processions of Sarum and the Western Church, Studies and Texts 24, Toronto, Pontifical Institute of Mediaeval Studies, 1971

Baxandall, Michael, *South German Sculpture 1480–1530*, London, Her Majesty's Stationery Office, 1974

Bevington, David (ed. and trans.)   *see* general bibliography

Bischoff, Bernhard (ed.), *Carmina Burana*, vol. I, part 3 of *Die Trink- und Spielerlieder, die geistlichen Dramen. Nachträge*, ed. Otto Schumann and Bernhard Bischoff, Heidelberg, winter, 1970

Boutell, Charles, *The Monumental Brasses of England*, London, George Bell, 1849

Brooks, Neil C., *The Sepulchre of Christ in Art and Liturgy*, University of Illinois Studies in Art and Literature 7, no. 2, Urbana, 1921

Campbell, Thomas P., and Clifford Davidson (eds.), *The Fleury Playbook: Essays and Studies*, Early Drama, Art, and Music Monograph Series 7, Kalamazoo, Western Michigan University, Medieval Institute Publications, 1985

Chambers, E. K.   *see* general bibliography

Clayton, H. J., *The Ornaments of the Ministers as Shown on English Monumental Brasses*, Alcuin Club Collections 22, London, Mowbray, 1919

Coleman, William E. (ed.), *Philippe de Mézières' Campaign for the Feast of Mary's Presentation*, Toronto Medieval Latin Texts, Toronto, Pontifical Institute of Medieval Studies, 1981

Collins, Fletcher, Jr., *The Production of Medieval Church Music-Drama*, Charlottesville, University Press of Virginia, 1972
Medieval Church Music-Dramas: a Repertory of Complete Plays, Charlottesville, University Press of Virginia, 1976

Davidson, Clifford *et al.* (eds.), *Studies in Medieval Drama in Honor of William L. Smoldon on His 82nd Birthday*, Kalamazoo, Western Michigan University, 1974

Davison, Nigel, 'So Which Way Round Did They Go? The Palm Sunday Procession at Salisbury', *Music and Letters* 61.1 (January 1980), pp. 1–14

De Boor, Helmut, *Die Textgeschichte der lateinischen Osterfeiern*, Hermaea, Germanistische Forschungen n.s. 22, Tübingen, Niemeyer, 1967

Dickinson, Francis Henry (ed.), *Missale ad usum insignis et praeclarae ecclesiae Sarum*, Burntisland, Pitsligo; Oxford and London, Parker, 1861–83; reprinted Farnborough, Gregg, 1969

Donovan, Richard B., C.S.B., *The Liturgical Drama in Mediaeval Spain*, Studies and Texts 4, Toronto, Pontifical Institute of Mediaeval Studies, 1958

Drumbl, Johann, *Quem quaeritis? Teatro sacro dell'alto medioevo*, Rome, Bulzoni Editoro, 1981

Dunn, E. Catherine, 'Voice Structure in the Liturgical Drama: Sepet Reconsidered', in Taylor and Nelson (eds.), *Medieval English Drama*, pp. 44–61

Egan-Buffet, Máire and Alan J. Fletcher, 'The Dublin *Visitatio Sepulchri* Play', *Proceedings of the Royal Irish Academy* 90, C, no. 7 (1990), pp. 159–241

Flanigan, C. Clifford, 'The Liturgical Context of the *Quem queritis* Trope', in Davidson *et al.* (eds.), *Studies In Honor of William Smoldon*, pp. 45–62
'The Liturgical Drama and its Tradition: a Review of Scholarship 1965–1975', *Research Opportunities in Renaissance Drama* 18 (1975), pp. 81–102; 19 (1976), pp. 109–36
'Karl Young and the Drama of the Medieval Church: an Anniversary Appraisal', *Research Opportunities in Renaissance Drama* 27 (1984), pp. 157–66
'The Fleury *Playbook*, the Traditions of Medieval Latin Drama and Modern Scholarship', in Campbell and Davidson (eds.), *The Fleury* Playbook, pp. 1–25
'Medieval Latin Music-Drama' in Simon (ed.), *Theatre of Medieval Europe*, pp. 21–41

Fowler, J. T. (ed.), *Rites of Durham being a Description or Brief Declaration of all the Ancient Monuments, Rites & Customs Belonging or being within the Monastical Church of Durham before the Suppression written 1593*, Surtees Society 107, Durham, 1902

Hardison, O. B. Jr.   *see* general bibliography

Hartzell, K. D., 'Diagrams for Liturgical Ceremonies, late 14th Century', in R. A. Skelton, and P. D. A. Harvey (eds.), *Local Maps and Plans from Medieval England*, Oxford, Clarendon Press, 1986, pp. 339–41

The Holy Bible Translated from the Latin Vulgate, Diligently Compared with the Hebrew, Greek, and Other Editions in Divers Languages, London, Herder, 1955

Hope, W. St John, and E. G. Cuthbert F. Atchley, *English Liturgical Colours*, London, SPCK, 1918

Hughes, Andrew, *Medieval Manuscripts for Mass and Office: a Guide to their Organization and Terminology*, University of Toronto Press, 1982

Hunt, E. D., *Holy Land Pilgrimage in the Later Roman Empire*, AD 312–460, Oxford University Press, 1984

King, Archdale A., *Eucharistic Reservation in the Western Church*, London, Mowbray, 1965

Legg, J. Wickham, *The Sarum Missal, Edited from Three Early Manuscripts*, Oxford, Clarendon Press, 1916

Lexikon der christlichen Ikonographie   *see* general bibliography

Lipphardt, Walter (ed.), *Lateinische Osterfeiern und Osterspiele*, Ausgaben deutscher Literatur des 15.–18. Jahrhunderts 5, 6 vols., Berlin and New York, de Gruyter, 1975–81

Littlehales, Henry (ed.), *The Medieval Records of a London City Church (St Mary at Hill)* AD 1420–1559, EETS (OS 125, 128), London, 1904, 1905

Marshall, Mary H., 'Aesthetic Values of the Liturgical Drama', *English Institute Essays, 1950*, New York, Columbia University Press, 1951, pp. 89–115; reprinted in Taylor and Nelson (eds.), *Medieval English Drama*, pp. 28–43

Maskell, William, *Monumenta ritualia Ecclesiae Anglicanae*, 3 vols., London, 1846; 2nd edn, Oxford, Clarendon Press, 1882; reprinted Farnborough, Gregg, 1970

McGee, Edward, 'The Role of the *Quem Queritis* Dialogue in the History of Western Drama', *Renaissance Drama* n.s. 7 (1977 for 1976), pp. 177–91

Ogden, Dunbar H., 'The Use of Architectural Space in Medieval Music-Drama', in Davidson *et al.* (eds.), *Studies in Honor of William Smoldon*, pp. 63–76

'Set Pieces and Special Effects in the Liturgical Drama', *Early Drama, Art and Music Review* 18 (spring 1996), pp. 76–88; 19 (fall 1996), pp. 22–40

Proctor, Francis and Christopher Wordsworth, *Brevarium ad usum insignis ecclesiae Sarum*, 3 vols., Cambridge University Press, 1886

Pynson, Richard, *Processionale ad usum Sarum, 1502*, facsimile reprint, Musical Sources 16: The Use of Sarum 1, Clifden, Boethius Press, 1980

Schwarzweber, Annemarie, *Das heilige Grab in der deutschen Bildnerei des Mittelalters*, Freiburg im Breisgau, Eberhard Albert, 1940

Sekules, Veronica, 'The Tomb of Christ at Lincoln and the Development of the Sacrament Shrine: Easter Sepulchres Reconsidered' in *Medieval Art and Architecture at Lincoln Cathedral*, British Archaeological Association Conference Transactions, 1982, VIII, Leeds, 1986

Sheingorn, Pamela, *The Easter Sepulchre in England*, Early Drama, Art and Music Reference Series 5, Kalamazoo, Western Michigan University, Medieval Institute Publications, 1987

Simon, Eckehard   *see* general bibliography

Smoldon, William L., *The Music of the Medieval Church Dramas*, ed. Cynthia Bourgeault, Oxford University Press, 1980

Smoldon, William L. (ed.), *The Play of Daniel: a Medieval Liturgical Drama*, revised David Wulstan, Plainsong and Mediaeval Music Society, Sutton, 1976

Swayne, Henry James Fowle (ed.), *Churchwardens' Accounts of S. Edmund & S. Thomas, Sarum, 1443–1702*, Salisbury, Wilts Record Society, 1896

Symons, Dom Thomas (ed.), *Regularis Concordia*, London, Nelson, 1953

Tanner, Norman P., S. J. (ed.), *Decrees of the Ecumenical Councils*, 2 vols., London, Sheed and Ward; Washington DC, Georgetown University Press, 1990

Taylor, Jerome and Alan H. Nelson (eds.), *Medieval English Drama: Essays Critical and Contextual*, University of Chicago Press, 1972

Tyrer, John Walton, *Historical Survey of Holy Week, its Services and Ceremonials*, Alcuin Club Collections 29, Oxford University Press, 1932

Warren, Frederick E. (trans.), *The Sarum Missal in English*, 2 vols., Library of Liturgiology and
  Ecclesiology for English Readers, London, Alexander Moring, De La More Press, 1911
Woolf, Rosemary, *The English Mystery Plays*, London, Routledge and Kegan Paul, 1972
Wordsworth, C., 'Inventories of Plate, Vestments etc. belonging to the Cathedral Church of the Blessed
  Mary of Lincoln', *Archaeologia* 53 (1892–3), pp. 1–82
Wright, John, *The Play of Antichrist. Translated with an Introduction*, Medieval Sources and Translations
  7, Toronto, Pontifical Institute of Mediaeval Studies, 1967
Young, Karl   *see* general bibliography

SECTION C   EXTRA-LITURGICAL LATIN AND EARLY VERNACULAR DRAMA

Le jeu d'Adam (Ordo representacionis Ade), ed. Willem Noomen, Paris, Champion, 1971
  Adam A twelfth-century play, trans. Lynette R. Muir, Leeds Philosophical and Literary Society, 1968
Adam le Bossu, *Le jeu de la feuillée*, ed. Ernest Langlois, Paris, Champion, 1911; reprinted 1965
  Adam de la Halle: Le Jeu de la feuillée, ed. Jean Dufornet, Ghent, Editions Scientifiques, 1977
  Le jeu de Robin et Marion, suivi du *Jeu du pèlerin*, ed. Ernest Langlois, Paris, Champion, 1924; reprinted
  1958
[Alfonso X el Sabio] *Primera partida*, ed. Juan Antonio Arias Bonet, University of Valladolid, 1975
Altteutsche Schauspiele, ed. Franz Josef Mone, Quedlinburg and Leipzig, G. Basse, 1841
Axton, Richard and John Stevens (trans.), *Medieval French Plays*, Oxford, Blackwell, 1971
Baud-Bovey, Samuel, 'Sur un "sacrifice d'Abraham de Romanos"', *Byzantion* 13 (1938), pp. 321–34
[Bertrandon de la Brocquière] *Le voyage d'Outremar de Bertrandon de la Brocquiere*, ed. Charles H. A.
  Schefer, Paris, 1892
Bevington, David (ed. and trans.)   *see* general bibliography
Jean Bodel, *Le jeu de Saint Nicolas*, ed. F. J. Warne, Oxford, Blackwell, 1951; reprinted 1968
Bullarum diplomaticum et privilegiorum sanctorum Romanorum pontificum . . . , Taurinensis editio . . . , 25
  vols., vol. III (1181–1268), A. Tomassetti, 1858
Chambers, E. K.   *see* general bibliography
[Geoffrey Chaucer] *The Riverside Chaucer*, ed. Larry D. Benson, Oxford University Press, 1988
Clark, Robert A., 'The "Miracles de Nostre Dame par personnages" of the Cangé Manuscript and the
  Sociocultural Function of Confraternity Drama', UMI Dissertation services, 1994
Cline, R. H., 'The Influence of Romance on Tournaments of the Middle Ages', *Speculum* 20 (1945), pp.
  204–11
Cohen, Gustave, *Etudes d'histoire du théâtre en France au moyen âge et à la Renaissance*, Paris, Nizet, 1950
Courtois d'Arras. Jeu du XIIIe siècle, ed. Edmond Faral, Paris, Champion, 1911; reprinted 1961
Le Cycle de mystères des premiers martyrs, ed. Graham A. Runnalls, Geneva, Droz, 1976
The Cyprus Passion Cycle, ed. August C. Mahr, Notre Dame, University of Indiana Press, 1947
[St John of Damascus] *St John Damascene on Holy Images, followed by three sermons on the Assumption*,
  trans. M. H. Allies, London, T. Baker, 1898
D'Ancona, Alessandro, *Origini del theatro in Italia*, 2 vols., Florence, Le Monnier, 1877; 2nd edn. [as
  Origini del teatro italiano], 2 vols., Turin, Ermanno Loescher, 1891; reprinted Rome, 1981
Davidson, Audrey E. (ed.), *The 'Ordo Virtutum' of Hildegard of Bingen*, Early Drama, Art and Music
  Monograph Series 18, Kalamazoo, Western Michigan University, Medieval Institute Publications,
  1992
De Bartholomaeis, Vincenzo, *Origini della poesia drammatica italiana*, Turin, Società Editrice
  Internazionale, 1924; 2nd edn, 1952
De Bartholomaeis, Vincenzo (ed.), *Laude drammatiche e rappresentazioni sacre*, 3 vols., Florence, Le
  Monnier, 1943
Dronke, Peter (trans. and ed.), *Nine Medieval Latin Plays*, Cambridge Medieval Classics 1, Cambridge
  University Press, 1994
Du Cange, Charles Du Fresne, Sieur, *Glossarium mediae et infimae Latinitatis cum supplementis integris D.
  P. Carpenterii, et additamentis Adelungii et aliorum digessit G. A. L. Henschel*, 7 vols., Paris, Firmin
  Didot, 1840–50

Dufournet, Jean, *Adam de la Halle à la recherche de lui-même*, Paris, Société d'Edition d'Enseignement Supérieur, 1974

Duran i Sanpere, Agustí, *La fiesta del Corpus*, Barcelona Histórica y Monumental 2, Barcelona Aymá, 1943

Eustathius, *Proemium* [Preface] to *Interpretatio hymni Pentecostalis Damasceni*, in Migne (ed.), *Patrologiae cursus completus*, vol. cxxxvi, cols. 507–8

Die Frankfurter Dirigierrolle, in *Das Drama des Mittelalters*, ed. Richard Froning, Deutsche National-Litteratur 14, 3 vols., Stuttgart, 1891–3, reprinted 1964

[Geffroy de Paris] *La Chronique métrique attribuée à Geffroy de Paris*, ed. Armel Diverrès, University of Strasbourg, 1956

St Germanus, *In Annunciationem SS Deiparae*, in Migne (ed.), *Patrologiae cursus completus*, vol. xcviii, cols. 319–40

Hassall, W. O. 'Plays at Clerkenwell', *MLR* 33 (1938), pp. 564–7

Jeanroy, Alfred (ed.), *Le jeu de Sainte Agnes, drame provençal du XIVe siècle*, Paris, Champion, 1931

[*Le Jour du jugement*] *Etudes sur le théâtre français au XIVe siècle. Le Jour du jugement, mystère français sur le grand schisme . . . et les Mystères de sainte Geneviève*, ed. Emile Roy, Paris, E. Bouillon, 1902

La Piana, Giorgio, *Le Rappresentazioni sacre nella letturatura Bizantina dalle origini al secolo IX*, Grottaferrata, Tip.Italo-Orientale 'S. Nilo', 1912

'The Byzantine Theater', *Speculum* 11 (1936), pp. 171–211

Loomis, Roger Sherman, 'Chivalric and Dramatic Imitations of Arthurian Romance', in *Medieval Studies in Memory of A. Kingsley Porter*, ed. Wilhelm R. W. Koehler, Cambridge, Mass., Harvard University Press, 1939, pp. 79–97

'Edward I, Arthurian Enthusiast', *Speculum* 28 (1953), pp. 14–27

[Mannyng, Robert] *Robert of Brunne's 'Handlyng Synne'*, ed. Frederick J. Furnivall, EETS (OS 119, 123), 1901, 1903

Meredith, Peter, 'The York Cycle and the Beginning of Vernacular Religious Drama in England', in *Le laudi drammatiche umbre delle origini*, Atti del v Convegno di Studio (Viterbo, 22–25 Maggio 1980), Centro di Studi sul Teatro Medioevale E Rinascimente, 1981, pp. 311–33

Milá y Fontanals, Manuel, *Orígenes del teatro catalán*, in *Obras completas*, 8 vols., Barcelona, 1888–96

Mittelniederländisches Osterspiel, ed. J. Sacher, *Zeitschrift für deutsches Altertum* 2 (1842), pp. 303–50

Miracle de l'enfant ressuscité, ed. Graham A. Runnalls, Paris, Minard; Geneva, Droz, 1972

Miracles de Nostre Dame par personnages, ed. Gaston Paris and Ulysse Robert, Société des Anciens Textes Français, 8 vols., Paris, Didot, 1876–83

Muir, Lynette R. *see* general bibliography

Mystères inédits du quinzième siècle, ed. Achille Jubinal, 2 vols., Paris, Téchener, 1837; reprinted Geneva, Slatkine, 1977

Neumann, Bernd, *Geistliches Schauspiel im Zeugnis der Zeit. Zur Ausführung mittelalterlicher Dramen im deutschen Sprachgebiet*, Münchener Texte und Untersuchungen zur deutschen Literatur des Mittelalters 84, 85, 2 vols., Munich and Zurich, Artemis, 1987

Non-Cycle Plays and Fragments, ed. Norman Davis, EETS (SS 1), Oxford University Press, 1970

[*Paschon Christos*] *Grégoire de Nazianse La Passion du Christ Tragédie*, ed. André Tuilier, Sources chrétiennes 149, Paris, Editions du Cerf, 1969

[Pope Pius II (Aeneas Sylvius Piccolomini)] *Commentarii rerum memorabilium . . .* (Rome, 1584), trans. F. A. Gragg and L. C. Gabel, Smith College Studies in History 22, 25, 30, 35, 43, Northampton, Mass., Smith College, 1936–57

Roy, Emile, *Etudes sur le théâtre français du XIVe et du XVe siècle La Comédie sans titre . . . et les Miracles de Notre-Dame par personnages*, Dijon, Damidot; Paris, E. Bouillon, 1902; reprinted Geneva, Slatkine, 1900

Rubin, Miri *see* general bibliography

Runnalls, Graham A., 'Medieval Trade Guilds and the *Miracles de Nostre Dame par personnages*', *Medium Aevum* 39 (1970), pp. 257–87

[Rutebeuf] *Le miracle de Théophile*, ed. Grace Frank, Paris, Champion, 1975

[Sarrasin] *Le Roman de Hem [1278]*, ed. Albert Henry, Les belles lettres, Paris, 1938

La Seinte Resurreccion, ed. T. Atkinson Jenkins and J. M. Manly [completed by Mildred K. Pope and Jean G. Wright], Anglo-Norman Text Society 4, Oxford, Blackwell, 1943

Shergold, N. D., *A History of the Spanish Stage from Medieval Times until the End of the Seventeenth Century*, Oxford, Clarendon Press, 1967

[*Spiegel Historiael*] Lodowijk van Velthem, *Continuation of the Spiegel Historiael 1248–1316*, ed. Hermann Vander Linden, Willem de Vreese *et al.*, 3 vols., Brussels, Commission Royale d'histoire, 1906

Le 'Sponsus', Mystère des Vierges sages et des Vierges folles, ed. Lucien-Paul Thomas, Paris, Presses Universitaires de France, 1951

Sticca, Sandro, *The Latin Passion Play*   *see* general bibliography

[John Stow] *A Survey of London . . .* , ed. Charles Lethbridge Kingsford, 2 vols., Oxford, Clarendon Press, 1908; reprinted 1971

Symeon of Thessalonica, *Dialogue against the Heretics*, in Migne (ed.), *Patrologiae cursus completus*, vol. CLV, cols. 33–176

[Toulon cast list] *Revue des Sociétés savantes*, series 5, vol. VIII (1874), p. 259

Trabalza, Ciro, 'Una lauda umbra e un libro di prestanze', in *Scritti vari di Filologia (A Ernesto Monaci gli scolari 1876–1891)*, Rome, 1901

Tunison, Joseph S.,*Dramatic Traditions of the Dark Ages*, University of Chicago Press; London, Fisher Unwin, 1907

Varey, John E., 'Minor Dramatic Forms in Spain with Special Reference to Puppets', Doctoral thesis, Cambridge University, 2 vols., 1950

Das Wiener Passionsspiel, in *Das Drama des Mittelalters*, ed. Richard Froning, in Deutsche National-Litteratur 14, 3 vols., Stuttgart, 1891–3, reprinted 1964

Das Wiener Passionsspiel (ed. Ursula Hennig), Osterreichischen Nationalbibliothek zu Wien 92, Göppingen, Kümmerle, 1986

Wenzel, Siegfried, 'An Early Reference to a Corpus Christi Play', *Modern Philology* 74 (1977), pp. 390–4

Wyatt, Diana, 'Performance and Ceremonial in Beverley Before 1642: An Annotated Edition of Local Archive Materials', D. Phil. thesis, University of York, 1983

Young, Karl   *see* general bibliography

SECTION D   ENGLAND, IRELAND, SCOTLAND AND WALES

Alford, John A. (ed.), *From Page to Performance Essays in Early English Drama*, East Lansing, Michigan State University Press, 1995

Beadle, Richard (ed.), *The Cambridge Companion to Medieval English Theatre*, Cambridge University Press, 1994

Belsey, Catherine, 'The Stage Plan of *The Castle of Perseverance*', *Theatre Notebook* 28 (1974), pp. 124–32

Berger, Sidney E., *Medieval English Drama. An Annotated Bibliography of Recent Criticism*, New York and London, Garland Publishing, 1990

Bevington, David, '*Castles* in the Air: the Morality Plays', in Simon (ed.), *Theatre of Medieval Europe*, pp. 97–116

Briscoe, Marianne G. and John C. Coldewey (eds.), *Contexts for Early English Drama*, Bloomington and Indianapolis, Indiana University Press, 1989

Butterworth, Philip, *Theatre of Fire. Special Effects in Early English and Scottish Theatre*, London, Society for Theatre Research, 1998

Cawley, A. C. *et al.* (eds.), *The Revels History of Drama in English*, vol. I, Medieval Drama, London, Methuen, 1983

Clopper, Lawrence M., 'The History and Development of the Chester Cycle', *Modern Philology* 75 (1977–8), pp. 219–46

Davenport, W. A. (ed.), *Fifteenth-Century English Drama. The Early Moral Plays and their Literary Relations*, Cambridge, D. S. Brewer, 1982

Davis, Norman (ed.), *Non-Cycle Plays and Fragments*, EETS (SS 1), Oxford University Press, 1970

Dawson, Giles (ed.), *Records of Plays and Players in Kent, 1450–1642*, Malone Society Collections 7, London, Malone Society, 1974

Denny, Neville (ed.), *Medieval Drama*, Stratford-upon-Avon Studies 16, London, Arnold, 1973

Duffy, Eamon, *The Stripping of the Altars. Traditional Religion in England 1400–1580*, New Haven, Yale University Press, 1992

Dutka, JoAnna, *Music in the English Mystery Plays*, Early Drama, Art and Music Monograph Series 2, Kalamazoo, Western Michigan University, Medieval Institute Publications, 1980

'The Lost Dramatic Cycle of Norwich and the Grocers Play of the Fall of Man', *Review of English Studies* 35 (1984), pp. 1–13

Galloway, David and John Wasson (eds.), *Records of Plays and Players in Norfolk and Suffolk 1330–1642*, Malone Society Collections 11, London, Malone Society, 1980

Gardiner, Harold C., *Mysteries End*, New Haven, Yale University Press, 1946

Gibson, Gail McMurray, *The Theater of Devotion. East Anglian Drama and Society in the Late Middle Ages*, University of Chicago Press, 1989

Happé, Peter, *English Drama Before Shakespeare*, London, Longman, 1999

Hutton, Ronald, *The Rise and Fall of Merry England The Ritual Year 1400–1700* Oxford University Press, 1994

Johnston, Alexandra F. (ed.), *Editing Early English Drama: Special Problems and New Directions*, New York, AMS Press, 1987

'What if No Texts Survived? External Evidence for Early English Drama' in Briscoe and Coldewey (eds.), *Contexts for Early English Drama*, pp. 1–9

'"All the World was a Stage"; Records of Early English Drama' in Simon (ed.), *Theatre of Medieval Europe*, pp. 117–29

Johnston, Alexandra, F. and Wim Hüsken (eds.), *English Parish Drama*, Ludus I, Amsterdam, Rodopi, 1996

Kahrl, Stanley J., *Traditions of Medieval English Drama*, London, Hutchinson, 1974; University of Pittsburgh Press, 1975

'The Staging of Medieval English Plays' in Simon (ed.), *Theatre of Medieval Europe*, pp. 130–48

Kahrl, Stanley J. (ed.), *Records of Plays and Players in Lincolnshire 1300–1585*, Malone Society Collections 8, London, Malone Society, 1974

King, Pamela, M., 'Spatial Semantics and the Medieval Theatre', in *Themes in Drama*, vol. IX, *The Theatrical Space*, ed. James Redmond, Cambridge, 1987

Kolve, V. A., *The Play Called Corpus Christi*, Stanford University Press, 1966

Lancashire, Ian, *Dramatic Texts and Records of Britain. A Chronological Topography*, University of Toronto Press, 1984

Longsworth, Robert, *The Cornish Ordinalia, Religion and Dramaturgy*, Cambridge, Mass., Harvard University Press, 1967

Lumiansky, R. M. and David Mills, *The Chester Mystery Cycle: Essays and Documents*, Chapel Hill, University of North Carolina Press, 1983

Meredith, Peter, '"Make the Asse to Speake" or Staging the Chester Plays', in *Staging the Chester Cycle*, ed. David Mills, Leeds Texts and Monographs 9, University of Leeds, School of English, 1985, pp. 49–76

'Scribes, Texts and Performance', in Neuss (ed.), *Aspects of Early English Drama*, pp. 13–29

'The Professional Travelling Players of the Fifteenth Century: Myth or Reality?', in *European Medieval Drama 1997*, papers from the Second International Conference on 'Aspects of European Medieval Drama', Camerino, 4–6 July 1997, ed. Sydney Higgins, Tempo di Spettacoli, 2 vols., University of Camerino, 1997, pp. 25–40

Mill, Anna J., *Medieval Plays in Scotland*, St Andrews University Publications 24, University of St Andrews, 1927; reprinted New York, Blom, 1969

Mills, David, 'Approaches to Medieval Drama', *Leeds Studies in English* 3 (1969), pp. 47–61

Mills, David (ed.), *Staging the Chester Cycle*, Leeds Texts and Monographs 9, University of Leeds, School of English, 1985

Nelson, Alan H. *The Medieval English Stage: Corpus Christi Pageants and Plays*, University of Chicago Press, 1974

Neuss, Paula (ed.), *Aspects of Early English Drama*, Cambridge, D. S. Brewer, and Totowa, Barnes and Noble, 1983

Pettitt, Thomas, 'Early English Traditional Drama: Approaches and Perspectives', *Research Opportunities in Renaissance Drama* 25 (1982), pp. 1–30

Phythian-Adams, Charles, 'Ceremony and the Citizen: the Communal Year at Coventry', in *Crisis and Order in English Towns 1500–1700: Essays in Urban History*, ed. Peter Clark and Paul Slack, University of Toronto Press, 1972, pp. 57–85

Potter, Robert, *The English Morality Play. Origins, History and Influence of a Dramatic Tradition*, London, Routledge and Kegan Paul, 1975

Rastall, Richard, 'Music in the Cycle Plays', in Briscoe and Coldewey (eds.), *Context for Early English Drama*, pp. 192–218

   The Heaven Singing: Music in Early English Religious Drama 1, Cambridge, Brewer, 1996

Salter, F. M., *Medieval Drama in Chester*, University of Toronto Press, 1955; reprinted New York, Russell and Russell, 1968

Schmitt, Natalie Crohn, 'Was There a Medieval Theatre in the Round? A Re-examination of the Evidence', *Theatre Notebook* 23 (1968–9), pp. 130–42; 24 (1969–70), pp. 18–25; reprinted in Taylor and Nelson (eds.), *Medieval English Drama*

Sharp, Thomas, *A Dissertation on the Pageants or Dramatic Mysteries Anciently Performed at Coventry*, Coventry, 1825; reprinted Wakefield, 1973

Simon, Eckehard (ed.)   *see* general bibliography

Southern, Richard, *The Medieval Theatre in the Round*, London, Faber and Faber, 1957; 2nd revised edn, 1975

Stevens, Martin, *Four Middle English Mystery Cycles. Textual, Contextual, and Critical Interpretations*, Princeton University Press, 1987

Taylor, Jerome and Alan H. Nelson (eds.), *Medieval English Drama: Essays Critical and Contextual*, University of Chicago Press, 1972

Tydeman, William, *English Medieval Theatre, 1400–1500*, Theatre Production Studies, London, Routledge and Kegan Paul, 1986

Wickham, Glynne, *Early English Stages, 1300–1660*, 3 vols., London, Routledge and Kegan Paul, 1959–81 (vol. I: *1300–1576* (1959))

Withington, Robert, *English Pageantry. An Historical Outline*, 2 vols., Cambridge, Mass., Harvard University Press, 1918–20

Woolf, Rosemary, *The English Mystery Plays*, London, Routledge and Kegan Paul, 1972

Wyatt, Diana *see* bibliography to Section C

Reference should also be made to the volumes of dramatic documents in the Records of Early English Drama series (general editor Alexandra F. Johnston), and to the periodicals *Medieval English Theatre* and *Medieval and Renaissance Drama in England*, edited from Lancaster and New York respectively.

SECTION E   FRANCE

Advis et Devis des Lengues, composé par Bonivard 1563, *Bibliothèque de l'Ecole des Chartes*, series B, vol. V, Paris, 1849

Axton, Richard and John Stevens (trans.), *Medieval French Plays*, Oxford, Blackwell, 1971

[Bar-sur-Aube] ed. Vallet de Vireville, *Bibliothèque de l'Ecole des Chartes*, series A, vol. III, Paris, 1841, pp. 450–1

Bibolet, Jean-Claude (ed.), *Le Mystère de la Passion de Troyes*, 2 vols., Geneva, Droz, 1987

Bordier, Jean-Pierre, *Le jeu de la passion: le message chrétien et le théâtre français (XIIIe–XVe siècles)*, Paris, Champion, 1998

Bouchet, Jean, *Annales d'Aquitaines*, Paris and Poitiers, E. de Marnef, 1524 [subsequent edns expanded and corrected]

   Epistres morales et familieres du traverseur, Poitiers, 1545; reprinted New York, Johnson Reprint Co., 1969

[Bourges] *Extraicts des fainctes qu'il conviendra faire pour le mistère des Actes des Apostres*, ed. Auguste-Théodore de Girardot, *Annales Archéologiques*, Paris, 1854, pp. 8–24

Thiboust, Jacques, *Relation de l'ordre de la triomphante et magnifique monstre du mystère des Saints Actes des Apostres . . .*, Bourges, Manceron, 1838

Britnell, Jennifer, *Jean Bouchet*, Edinburgh University Press, 1986

Butterworth, Philip, '"The Martyrdom of St Apollonia" and "The Rape of the Sabine Women" as Iconographical Evidence of Medieval Theatre Practice', in *Essays in Honour of Peter Meredith*, ed. Catherine Batt, Leeds Studies in English 29, University of Leeds, 1998, pp. 55–68

Chevalier, Ulysse and Paul-Emile Giraud (eds.), *Mystère des Trois Doms représenté à Romans en 1509 publié avec . . . des documents relatifs aux représentations en Dauphiné du XIVe au XVIe siècle*, Lyons, Brun, 1887

Chocheyras, Jacques, *Le Théâtre religieux en Savoie au XVIe siècle*, Geneva, Droz, 1971

Le Théâtre religieux en Dauphiné du Moyen Age au XVIIIe siècle, Geneva, Droz, 1975

Clark, Robert L. A., 'The "Miracles de Nostre Dame par personnages" of the Cangé Manuscript and the Sociocultural Function of Confraternity Drama', UMI Dissertation services, 1994

Cline, R. H., 'The Influence of Romances on Tournaments of the Middle Ages', *Speculum* 20 (1945), pp. 204–11

Cohen, Gustave, *Histoire de la mise en scène dans le théâtre religieux français du Moyen Age*, Brussels, Académie Royale, and Paris, Hayes, 1906; 2nd edn, Paris, Champion, 1926; revised 3rd edn, Paris, Champion, 1951

Le Théâtre en France au Moyen Age, 2 vols., Paris, Rieder, 1928–31

Etudes d'histoire du théâtre en France au moyen âge et à la Renaissance, Paris, A-G. Nizet, 1956

[see also *Mélanges . . . offerts à Gustave Cohen*]

Couturier, Maurice and Graham A. Runnalls (eds.), *Compte du mystère de la Passion: Châteaudun 1510*, Société Archéologique d'Eure-et-Loir, 1991

Craig, Barbara (ed.), *'La Creacion', 'La Transgression', and 'L'Expulsion' of the 'Mistere du Viel Testament'*, University of Kansas Humanistic Studies 37, Lawrence, Kansas, 1968

Deierskauf-Holsboer, Wilma S., ' Les Représentations â Athis-sur-Orge en 1542', in *Mélanges . . . offerts à Gustave Cohen*, pp. 199–203

De la Chesnaye, Nicolas, *La Condemnation de Banquet*, ed. Jelle Koopmans and Paul Verhuyck, Geneva, Droz, 1991

[Draguignan] 'Régistre des ordonnances . . . de Draguignan', *Revue des sociétes savantes*, 6th series, vol. III (1876)

Duplat, André (ed.), *Andrieu de La Vigne: Le Mystère de saint Martin*, Textes littéraires français, Geneva, Droz, 1979

Durbin, P. T. and Lynette R. Muir (eds.), *La Passion de Semur*, Leeds Medieval Studies 3, University of Leeds Press, 1981

Frank, Grace, *The Medieval French Drama*, Oxford and London, Clarendon Press, 1954; 2nd edn., 1960

Gosselin, Edouard H., *Recherches sur les origines et l'histoire du théâtre à Rouen*, Rouen, 1868

Gouvenain, Louis de, *Le théâtre à Dijon (1422–1790)*, in *Mémoires communales de la Côte d'Or*, vol. XI, Dijon, Commission des Antiquités du Département de la Côte d'Or, 1885–8, pp. 239–407

Gringore, Pierre, *Oeuvres complètes*, ed. Charles d'Héricault and A. de Montaiglon, 3 vols., Paris, P. Jannet, 1858–77

Gros, Gérard, *Le poète, la Vierge et le prince du puy. Etude sur les puys marials de la France du Nord du 14e siècle à la Renaissance*, Paris, Klincksieck, 1992

Gros, Louis, *Etude sur le mystère de l'Antéchrist et du jugement de Dieu, joué à Modane en 1580 et 1606*, Chambéry, Editions réunies, 1962

Harvey, Howard G., *The Theatre of the Basoche. The Contribution of the Law Societies to French Medieval Comedy*, Harvard Studies in Romance Languages 17, Cambridge, Mass., Harvard University Press, 1941

Henrard, Nadine, *Le théâtre religieux médiéval en langue d'oc*, Bibliothèque de la Faculté de Philosophie et de Lettres de l'Université de Liège CCLXXIII, Geneva, Droz, 1998

Hindley, Alan, 'Histoire locale du théâtre français: Moyen Age et Renaissance', *Le moyen français* 35/36 (double volume) (1994/5), Montreal, Ceres, pp. 129–59

Howarth, William D. (ed.), *French Theatre in the Neo-Classical Era, 1550–1789*, Theatre in Europe: a Documentary History, Cambridge University Press, 1997

Husson, Jacomin, *Chroniques de Metz de Jacomin Husson 1200–1525*, ed. H. Michelant, Metz, 1870
Journal d'un bourgeois de Paris sous Charles VI et Charles VII, ed. André Mary, Paris, Jonquières, 1929
Kipling, Gordon, 'Theatre as Subject and Object in Fouquet's "Martyrdom of St Apollonia"', *Medieval English Theatre* 19 (1997), pp. 26–80 [for a opposing view see Graham A. Runnalls, 'Jean Fouquet's "Martyrdom of St Apollonia" and the Medieval French Stage', *ibid.*, pp. 81–100; see also Kipling's 'Fouquet, St Apollonia, and the Motives of the Miniaturist's Art; a Reply to Graham Runnalls', *ibid.*, pp. 101–20]
Knight, Alan E., *Aspects of Genre in Late Medieval French Drama*, Manchester University Press, 1983
Konigson, Elie, *La Représentation d'un mystère de la Passion à Valenciennes en 1547*, Paris, Editions du Centre Nationale de la Recherche Scientifique, 1969
Lazar, Moshé (ed.), *Le Jugement Dernier (Lo Jutgamen General), Drame provençal du XVe siècle*, Paris, Klincksieck, 1971
Lebègue, Raymond, *Le Mystère des Actes des apôtres: contribution à l'étude de l'humanisme et du protestantisme français au XVIe siècle*, Paris, Champion, 1929
     Etudes sur le théâtre français, 2 vols., Paris, A-G. Nizet, 1977–8, esp. vol. I, pp. 11–126
Lecoy de la Marche, [Richard] A. (ed.), *Extraits des comptes et mémoriaulx du roi René*, Paris, Ecole des Chartes, 1873
[Le Doyen, Guillaume] *Annales et Chroniques du pais de Laval . . .*, ed. M. H. Godbert and Louis La Beaulière, Laval, 1839
Le Moigne, F.-Y. (ed.), *Histoire de Metz*, Toulouse, Privat, 1986
Le Verdier, Pierre (ed.), *Mystère de l'Incarnation et de la Nativité représenté à Rouen en 1474 . . .* , Société des bibliophiles normands, 3 vols., Rouen, Cagniard, 1884–6
Louandre, F.-C., *Histoire d'Abbeville et du Comté de Ponthieu jusqu'en 1789*, 2 vols., Paris and Abbeville, 1844–5
Mazouer, Charles, *Le théâtre français du Moyen Age*, Paris, Sedes, 1998
Mélanges d'histoire du théâtre du Moyen-Âge et de la Renaissance offerts à Gustave Cohen . . ., Paris, Librairie Nizet, 1950
Michel, Francisque (ed.), *Le mystère de Saint Louis, Roi de France*, Westminster, Roxburghe Club, 1871
[Michel, Jean] *Le 'Mystère de la Passion' de Jean Michel* [Angers 1486], ed. Omer Jodogne, Gembloux, Duculot, 1959
Muir, Lynette R., 'Women on the Medieval Stage: the Evidence from France', *Medieval English Theatre* 7.2 (1985), pp. 107–19
     'Audiences in the French Medieval Theatre', *Medieval English Theatre* 9.1 (1987), pp. 8–22
Oulmont, Charles, *La Poésie morale, politique et dramatique à la veille de la Renaissance. Pierre Gringore*, Paris, Champion, 1911
     'Pierre Gringore et l'entrée de la reine Anne de Bretagne en 1504', in *Mélanges offerts à M. Emile Picot*, 2 vols., Paris, E, Rahir, 1913
Petit de Julleville, Louis, *Histoire du théâtre en France. Les Mystères*, 2 vols., Paris, Hachette, 1880; reprinted Geneva, Slatkine, 1969
     Les comédiens en France au Moyen Âge, Paris, L. Cerf, 1885
     Répertoire du théâtre comique en France au Moyen Age, Paris, L. Cerf, 1886
Port, Célestin, *Documents sur l'histoire du théâtre à Angers*, Bibliothèque de l'Ecole des Chartes 22, Paris, 1861, pp. 69–80
Raimbault, Maurice, 'Une représentation théâtrale à Aix en 1444', *Revue des Langues Romanes* 7 (1933–6), pp. 263–74
Rey-Flaud, Henri *Le cercle magique   see* general bibliography
Roy, Emile, *Le Mystère de la Passion en France du XIVe au XVIe siècle . . .* , 2 vols., Dijon, Damidot, 1904; reprinted Geneva, Slatkine, 1974
Runnalls, Graham A., 'Medieval Trade Guilds and the *Miracles de Nostre Dame par personnages*', *Medium Aevum* 39 (1970), pp. 257–87
     'Le Mystère de la Passion à Amboise au Moyen Age: représentations théâtrales et texte', *Le moyen français* 26, (1990), pp. 7–86
     Etudes sur les mystères, Paris, Champion, 1998
     Les mystères français imprimés (Bibliothèque du XVe siècle), Paris, Champion, 1999

Samaran, Charles (ed.), 'Le Miracle de St Nicolas: prologues', *Romania* 51 (1925), pp. 191–7

Serrigny, Ernest (ed.), *La Représentation d'un mystère de saint Martin à Seurre, en 1496 . . .*, Dijon, Lamarche, 1888

Servet, P. (ed.), *Le Mystère de la résurrection [Angers (1456)]*, Textes littéraires français 435, 2 vols., Geneva, Droz, 1993

Söderhjelm, W. and and A. Wallens Köld (eds.), *Le Mystère de saint Laurent*, Acta Societatis scientiarum fennicae XVIII, Helsinki, 1891, pp. 111–287

Thomas, Antoine, 'Note d'histoire littéraire: Le Théâtre à Paris à la fin du XIVe siècle', *Romania* XXI (1893), pp. 606–11

Trois jeux des rois, ed. Yves Giraud, Norbert King, and Simone de Reyff, Freiburg, Universitätsverlag, 1985

[Vigneulles, Philippe Gérard de] *La Chronique de Philippe de Vigneulles*, ed. Charles Bruneau, 4 vols., Metz, Société d'histoire et d'archéologie de la Lorraine, 1927–33

Gedenkbuch des Metzer Bürgers Philippe von Vigneulles, aus den Jahren 1471–1522, ed. Heinrich Michelant, Bibliothek des litterarischen Vereins in Stuttgart XXIV, 1852

Vitale-Brovarone, Alessandro, *Il quaderno di segreti d'un regista provenzale del Medioevo: Note per la Messa in scena d'una Passione*, Alessandria, Edizioni dell'Orso, 1984

Zimmerische Chronik, ed. Karl A. Barack, Bibliothek des Literarischen Vereins 91–4, [vol. III, pp. 226 -8] Tübingen, 1869

SECTION F   THE GERMAN-SPEAKING AREA

Bauer, Werner M. (ed.), *Sterzinger Spiele. Die weltlichen Spiele des Sterzinger Spielarchivs nach den Originalhandschriften (1510–1535) von Vigil Raber und nach der Ausgabe Oswald Zingerles (1886)*, Wiener Neudrucke 6, Vienna, Österreichischer Bundesverlag, 1982

Bergmann, Rolf, 'Spiele, Mittelalterliche geistliche', in *Reallexikon der deutschen Literaturgeschichte*, vol. IV, Berlin, de Gruyter, 1979

Katalog der deutschsprachigen geistlichen Spiele und Marienklagen des Mittelalters, Munich and Zurich, Artemis, 1986

Brett-Evans, David, *Von Hrotsvit bis Folz und Gengenbach. Eine Geschichte des mittelalterlichen deutschen Dramas*, 2 vols., Berlin, Erich Schmidt, 1975 [Withdrawn by the publisher in the face of universal critical condemnation of its unreliability.]

Catholy, Eckehard, *Das Fastnachtspiel des Spätmittelalters. Gestalt und Funktion*, Hermaea 8, Tübingen, Niemeyer, 1961

Fastnachtspiel, Sammlung Metzler M 56, Stuttgart, Metzler, 1966

Evans, M[arshall] Blakemore, *The Passion Play of Lucerne: an Historical and Critical Introduction*, New York, MLA, and Oxford University Press,1943

Grassmann, Antjekathrin, ' Die Statuten der Kaufleutekompanie von 1500', *Zeitschrift des Vereins für Lübeckische Geschichte und Altertumskunde* 61 (1981) pp. 19–35 [Transcribes from a nineteenth-century copy of the now lost 1500 document.]

Hampe, Theodor, 'Die Entwicklung des Theaterwesens in Nürnberg von der zweiten Hälfte des 15. Jahrhunderts bis 1806: II. Teil', *Mitteilungen des Vereins für Geschichte der Stadt Nürnberg* 13 (1899), pp. 98–237

Keller, Adalbert von (ed.), *Fastnachtspiele aus dem fünfzehnten Jahrhundert*, Bibliothek des Literarischen Vereins in Stuttgart, vols. 28–30 (1853) and *Nachlese*, vol. 46 (1858); reprinted Darmstadt, 1965–6

Liebenow, Peter K. (ed.), *Das Künzelsauer Fronleichnamspiel*, Ausgaben deutscher Literatur des 15. bis 18. Jahrhunderts, Reihe Drama II, Berlin, de Gruyter, 1969

Linke, Hansjürgen, 'Drama und Theater', [chapter 4] in *Die deutsche Literatur im späten Mittelalter*, part 2: *1250–1370*, ed. Ingeborg Glier (Geschichte der deutschen Literatur von den Anfängen bis zur Gegenwart, ed. Helmut de Boor and Richard Newald), Munich, Beck, 1987, pp. 153–233, 471–85

'Germany and German-Speaking Central Europe' in Simon (ed.), *Theatre of Medieval Europe*, pp. 207–24

Lipphardt, Walther and Hans-Gert Roloff (eds.), *Die geistlichen Spiele des Sterzinger Spielarchivs*, Berne and Frankfurt-on-Main, Peter Lang, 1980 – vol. I [revised edition 1986] contains the plays in the

'Debs Codex' [see **F16**]; vol. II (1988) contains 'Lienhard Pfarrkirchers Passion' of 1486, and the 1496 and 1503 versions of the Sterzing Passion Play; vol. III (1997) contains the Passion Play copied by Raber in 1514 after that year's performance; the 'Passion von Hall' obtained for 1514; the fragment of a further version of a Passion Play; plus three shorter plays: *Ludus paschalis* (1520), *de nativitate domini*, and a *planctus* with prophets; vol. IV (1990) contains two Palm Sunday plays; a Last Supper play; an Ascension Day play and a Pentecost play; vol. V (1980) contains in much smaller font five previously unpublished plays: two related versions of a dramatisation of St John's Gospel, both incomplete; a court scene entitled *Ain recht das Christus stirbt*; a dramatisation of the parable of the Rich Man and Lazarus; a short David and Goliath play; vol. VI.2 contains the commentary on the music; vol. VI.1 is intended to present all relevant directorial [*Regie*] material.]

Margetts, John (ed.), *Neidhartspiele*, Wiener Neudrucke 7, Graz, Akademische Druck- und Verlaganstalt, 1982

Meier, Rudolf (ed. and trans.), *Das Innsbrucker Osterspiel: Das Osterspiel von Muri. Mittelhochdeutsch und Neuhochdeutsch*, Universal-Bibliothek 8660/61, Stuttgart, Reclam, 1962

Michael, Wolfgang F., *Das deutsche Drama des Mittelalters*, Grundriss der germanischen Philologie 20, Berlin and New York, de Gruyter, 1971

Mone, Franz Josef (ed.), *Schauspiele des Mittelalters*, 2 vols., Karlsruhe, C. Macklot, 1846; reprinted Aalen, Scientia, 1970

Neumann, Bernd, 'Mittelalterliches Schauspiel am Niederrhein', *Zeitschrift für deutsche Philologie* 94 (1975), *Sonderheft* [i.e. special number, with its own separate pagination] *Mittelalterliches deutsches Drama*, pp. 147–94

Geistliches Schauspiel im Zeugnis der Zeit. Zur Aufführung mittelalterlicher Dramen im deutschen Sprachgebiet, Münchener Texte und Untersuchungen zur deutschen Literatur des Mittelalters 84, 85, 2 vols., Munich and Zurich, Artemis, 1987

Rueff, Hans (ed.), *Das rheinische Osterspiel der Berliner Handschrift ms. Germ fo. 1219*, Berlin, Weidmann, 1925 [includes at pp. 208–15 the Alexius fragment [see **F34**]]

Rueff, Jacob, *Adam und Heva*, ed. Hermann Marcus Kottinger, Bibliothek der gesammten deutschen National-Literatur 26, Quedlinburg and Leipzig, G. Basse, 1848

Das Züricher Passionsspiel [Jacob Rueff, Das lyden vnsers Heren Jesu Christi das man nempt den Passion, 1545], ed. Barbara Thoran, Bochum, Dr N. Brockmeier, 1984

Schneider, Karin (ed.), *Das Eisenacher Zehnjungfrauenspiel*, Texte des späten Mittelalters und der frühen Neuzeit 17, Berlin, Erich Schmidt, 1964

Schottmann, Brigitta (ed. and trans.), *Das Redentiner Osterspiel. Mittelniederdeutsch und Neuhochdeutsch*, Stuttgart, Reclam, 1975 [the play is translated into modern German with commentary]

Siller, Max, 'Zu den Editionen der geistlichen Tiroler Spiele', in *Literatur und Sprache in Tirol*, ed. Michael Gebhart and Max Siller, Innsbruck, Universitätsverlag Wagner, 1996

Simon, Eckehard, 'The Origin of Neidhart Plays. A Reappraisal', *Journal of English and Germanic Philology* 67 (1968), pp. 458–74

'The Staging of Neidhart Plays. With Notes on Six Documented Performances', *Germanic Review* 44 (1969), pp. 5–20

'Neidhart Plays as Shrovetide Plays. Twelve Additional Documented Performances', *Germanic Review* 52 (1977), pp. 87–98

'Organizing and Staging Carnival Plays in Late Medieval Lübeck: a New Look at the Archival Record', *Journal of English and Germanic Philology* 92 (1993), pp. 57–72

Steinbach, Rolf, *Die deutschen Oster- und Passionsspiele des Mittelalters*, Kölner germanistische Studien 4, Cologne and Vienna, Böhlau, 1970

Tailby, John E., 'Die Luzerner Passionsspielaufführung des Jahres 1583: Zur Deutung der Bühnenpläne Renward Cysats', in *The Theatre in the Middle Ages*, ed. Hermann Braet *et al.*, Louvain University Press, 1985, pp. 352–61

'The Role of the Director in the Lucerne Passion Play', *Medieval English Theatre* 9 (1987), pp. 80–92

'Lucerne Revisited: Facts and Questions', in *Essays in Honour of Peter Meredith*, ed. Catherine Batt, Leeds Studies in English 29, University of Leeds, 1998, pp. 347–58 [contains details of earlier articles in German]

'Drama and Community in South Tyrol', in *Drama and the Community: People and Plays in Medieval Europe*, ed. Alan Hindley, Medieval Texts and Cultures of Northern Europe 1, Turnhout, Brepols, 1999, pp. 148–60

'Mystery Plays', in *Encyclopedia of German Literature* ed. Matthias Konzett, Chicago, Fitzroy Dearborn, 1999

Touber, Anthonius H. (ed.), *Das Donaueschinger Passionsspiel*, Universal-Bibliothek 8046, Stuttgart, Reclam, 1985

Ukena, Elke (ed.), *Die deutschen Mirakelspiele des Spätmittelalters. Studien und Texte.*, Europäische Hochschulschriften Series 1, 115, 2 vols., Berne and Frankfurt-on-Main, Peter Lang, 1975

Wackernell, Joseph E. (ed.), *Altdeutsche Passionsspiele aus Tirol*, Graz, K. K. Universitätbuchdruckerei und Verlags-Buchhandlung 'Styria', 1897; reprinted Walluf, Sändig, 1972

Wuttke, Dieter (ed.), *Fastnachtspiele des 15. und 16. Jahrhunderts*, Universal-Bibliothek 9415, Stuttgart, Reclam, 1973; 2nd edn, 1978

Wyss, Heinz (ed.), *Das Luzerner Passionsspiel*, Schriften herausgegeben unter dem Patronat der Schweizerischen geisteswissenschaftlichen Gesellschaft 7, 3 vols., Berne, Francke, 1967

Zucker, Adolf E. (trans.), *The Redentin Easter Play. Translated from the Low German of the Fifteenth Century with Introduction and Notes*, Records of Civilisation, Sources and Studies 32, New York, Octagon Books, 1941; reprinted 1961 [Not consulted for *Theatre in Europe* purposes.]

SECTION G   ITALY

Allegri, Luigi, *Teatro e spettacolo nel medioevo*, Bari, Editore Laterza, 1988

Apollonio, Mario, *Storia del teatro italiano*, 2 vols., Florence, Sansoni, 1943–6; reprinted 1981

Banfi, Luigi (ed.), *Sacre rappresentazioni del Quattrocento*, Turin, UTET, 1963

Barr, M. Cyrilla, *The Monophonic Lauda and the Lay Religious Confraternities of Tuscany and Umbria in the Late Middle Ages*, Early Drama, Art and Music Monograph Series 10, Kalamazoo, Western Michigan University, Medieval Institute Publications, 1989

'Music and Spectacle in the Confraternity Drama of Fifteenth-Century Florence: the Reconstruction of a Theatrical Event', in *Christianity and the Renaissance. Image and Religious Imagination in the Quattrocento*, ed. Timothy Verdon and John Henderson, New York, Syracuse University Press, 1990, pp. 376–404

Bonfantini, Mario (ed.), *Le sacre rappresentazioni italiane; raccòlta di testi dal secolo XIII al secolo XVI*, Milan, Bompiani, 1942

Coppola, Domenico (ed.), *Sacre Rappresentazioni Aversane del secolo XVIe*, Biblioteca dell' 'Archivum Romanicum' series 1. 56, Florence, Leo S. Olschki, 1959

Cornagliotti, Anna (ed.), *La Passione di Revello*, Turin, Centro Studi Piemontesi, 1976

Cruciani, Fabrizio, *Il Teatro del Campidoglio e le Feste Romane del 1513*, Milan, Edizioni Il Polifilo, 1968

Teatro nel Rinascimento: Roma 1450–1550, Rome, Bulzoni, 1983

'Il teatro e la festa', in Fabrizio Cruciani and Daniele Seragnoli (eds.), *Il teatro italiano nel Rinascimento*, Bologna, Il Mulino, 1987, pp. 31–52

D'Amico, Silvio (ed.), *Enciclopedia dello Spettacolo*, 9 vols. (3 supplements), Rome, Le Maschere, 1954–62

D'Ancona, Alessandro (ed.), *Sacre rappresentazioni dei secoli XIV, XV e XVI*, 3 vols., Florence, Le Monnier, 1872

Origini del teatro in Italia, 2 vols., Florence, Le Monnier, 1877; 2nd edn [as *Origini del teatro italiano*] 2 vols., Turin, Ermanno Loescher, 1891; reprinted Rome, 1981

De Bartholomaeis, Vincenzo, *Origini della poesia drammatica italiana*, Turin, Società editrice internazionale, 1924; 2nd edn, Nuovo biblioteca italiana 7, 1952

Il teatro abruzzese nel medio evo, Bologna, Zanichelli, 1924; reprinted 1979

De Bartholomaeis, Vincenzo (ed.), *Laude drammatiche e rappresentazioni sacre*, 3 vols., Florence, Le Monnier, 1943

Eisenbichler, Konrad (ed.), *Crossing the Boundaries: Christian Piety and the Arts in Italian Medieval and Renaissance Confraternities*, Early Drama, Art and Music Monograph Series 15, Kalamazoo, Western Michigan University, Medieval Institute Publications, 1991

'Confraternities and Carnival: the Context of Lorenzo de' Medici's *Rappresentazione di SS Giovanni e Paolo*', in *Medieval Drama on the Continent of Europe*, ed. Clifford Davidson and John H. Stroupe,

Kalamazoo, Western Michigan University. Medieval Institute Publications, 1993, pp. 128–39
Fabbri, Mario, Elvira Garbero Zorzi and Anna Maria Petrioli Tofani (eds.), *Il luogo teatrale a Firenze*, Milan, Electa Editrice, 1975
Faccioli, Emilio (ed.), *Il teatro italiano*, vol. I, *Dalle origini al Quattrocento*, part I, Turin, Einaudi, 1975
Fagiolo, Maurizio, *La scenografia. Dalle sacre rappresentazioni al futurismo*, Florence, Sansoni, 1973
Falvey, Kathleen, 'Italian Vernacular Religious Drama of the Fourteenth to Sixteenth Centuries: a Selected Bibliography on the *Lauda drammatica* and the *Sacra rappresentazione*', *Research Opportunities in Renaissance Drama* 26 (1983), pp. 125–44
Fortini, Arnaldo, *La lauda in Assisi e le origini del teatro italiano*, Assisi, Edizioni Assisi, 1961
Galante Garrone, Virginia, *L'apparato scenico del dramma sacra in Italia*, Turin, Rosenberg and Sellier, 1935
Guarino, Raimondo (ed.), *Teatro e Culture della Rappresentazione: Lo spettacolo in Italiano nel Quattrocento*, Bologna, il Mulino, 1988
Larson, Orville K., 'Bishop Abraham of Souzdal's Description of *Sacre Rappresentazioni*', *Education Theatre Journal* 9 (1957), pp. 208–13
Molinari, Cesare, *Spettacoli fiorentini del Quattrocento*, Raccolta Pisana di saggi a studi 5, Venice, Neri Pozza, 1961
Teatro, Milan, Arnaldo Monadori, 1972
Musumarra, Carmelo, *La sacra rappresentazione della Natività nella tradizione italiana*, Florence, Leo S. Olschki, 1957
Newbigin, Nerida (ed.), *Nuovo corpus di sacre rappresentazioni fiorentini del Quattrocento*, Bologna, Commissione per i Testi di Lingua, 1983
Feste d'Oltrarno: Plays in Churches in Fifteenth-Century Florence, 2 vols., Florence, Leo S. Olschki, 1996
Pallen, Thomas, *Vasari on Theatre*, Carbondale, Southern Illinois University Press, 1999
Pirrotta, Nino and Elena Povoledo, *Music and Theatre from Poliziano to Monteverdi*, Cambridge University Press, 1982 [first published as *Le due Orfei*, Turin, Eri, 1969]
Ponte, Giovanni (ed.), *Sacre rappresentazioni fiorentine del Quattrocento*, Milan, Marzorati, 1974
Ricci, Giuliana, *Teatri d'Italia*, Milan, Bramante, 1971
Simon, Eckehard (ed.)   *see* general bibliography
Sticca, Sandro, 'Italy: Liturgy and Christocentric Spirituality', in Simon (ed.), *Theatre of Medieval Europe*, pp. 169–88
Tortoreto, Walter, *Genesi di una sacra rappresentazione abruzzese*, L'Aquila, DASP, 1983
Toschi, Paolo, *L'antico dramma sacro italiano*, 2 vols., Florence, Libreria Editrice Fiorentina, 1925–6
Dal dramma liturgico alla rappresentazione sacra, Florence, Sansoni, 1940; reprinted with additions as *L'antico teatro religioso italiano*, Matera, Montemurro, 1960
Origini del teatro italiano, Turin, Einaudi, 1955
Trexler, Richard C., 'Florentine Theater, 1280–1500. A Checklist of Performances and Institutions', in *Medieval and Renaissance Theater and Spectacle* ed. Robert J. Rodini, *Forum Italicum* 14 (1980), pp. 454–75
[Vitruvius] *The Ten Books of Architecture*, trans. M. H. Morgan, Cambridge, Mass., Harvard University Press, 1926

SECTION H   THE LOW COUNTRIES

Archives départementales du Nord B93–94, *Chambre des comptes* [of the Duchy of Burgundy]
[Arnhem] *De Stadsrekeningen van Arnhem*, ed. W. Jappe Alberts, Teksten en Documenten uitgegeven door het Instituut voor Middeleeuwse Geschiedenis, (eds. W. Jappe Alberts and F. W. N. Hugenholtz), vol. XV, Groningen, J. B. Wolters, 1967
Beuken, W. H. (ed.), *Die eerste bliscap van Maria en die sevenste bliscap van Onser Vrouwen*, Culemborg, Tjeenk Willink, 1978
Brandt, George W. (ed.), *German and Dutch theatre, 1600–1848*, Theatre in Europe: a Documentary History, Cambridge University Press, 1993
Champollion-Figeac, J. J., *Documents historiques inédits tiré des collections manuscrites de la Bibliothèque Nationale et des archives ou des bibliothèques des départements*, vol. IV (1848), no. XIV, pp. 329–47; no. XXVIII, pp. 457–62

[Chastellain, Georges], *Oeuvres de Georges Chastellain*, ed. Kervyn de Lettenhove, 8 vols., Académie royale de Belgique, Brussels, Heussner, 1863–6

Cohen, Gustave (ed.), *Le livre de conduite du régisseur et le compte des dépenses pour le Mystère de la Passion joué à Mons en 1501*, University of Strasbourg; Paris, Champion, 1925

Le théâtre français en Belgique au moyen âge, Nôtre passé 7, Brussels, La renaissance du livre, 1953

Coigneau, Dirk (ed.), *Mariken van Nieumeghen*, The Hague, Nijhoff, 1982

De Pas, Justin, *Mystères et jeux scéniques à Saint-Omer aux XVe et XVIe siècles*, Lille, Mémoires de la Société des Antiquaires de Morinie 31 (1912–13), pp. 343–77

Dufournet, Jean (ed.), *Le Garçon et l'Aveugle*, Paris, Champion, 1982

Erenstein, R. L. *et al.* (eds.), *En theatergeschiedenis der Nederlanden. Tien eeunen drama en theater in Nederland en Vlaanderen*, Amsterdam, Amsterdam University Press, 1996

Erné, B. H. and L. M. van Dis (eds.), *De Gentse Spelen van 1539*, 2 vols., The Hague, Nijhoff, 1982

Grévin, Jacques, *Théâtre complet et poésies choisies*, ed. Lucien Pinvert, Paris, Garnier, 1922; reissue 1961

Hoebeke, Marcel (ed.), *Het Spel van de V Vroede en de V Dwaeze Maeghden*, The Hague, Nijhoff, 1975; 2nd edn, 1979

Hollaar J. M. and E. W. F. van den Elzen, 'Het vroegste toneelleven in enkele Noordnederlandse plaatsen', *De Nieuwe Taalgids* 73 (1980), pp. 302–24

Hummelen, Wim M. H., *Repertorium van het Rederijkersdrama, 1500–c. 1620*, Assen, Van Gorcum, 1968

[Addenda in *Dutch Crossing* 22 (1984), pp. 105–28]

'Typen van toneelinrichting bij de rederijkers', *Studia Neerlandica* 1 (1970), pp. 51–109

'Types and Methods of the Dutch Rhetoricians' Theatre', in *The Third Globe. Symposium for the Reconstruction of the Globe Playhouse. Wayne State University 1979*, ed. C. Walter Hodges, S. Schoenbaum and Leonard Leone, Detroit, Wayne State University Press, 1981, pp. 164–254

'The Biblical Plays of the Rhetoricians and the Pageants of Oudenaarde and Lille', trans. Susan Mellor, in *Modern Dutch Studies: Essays in Honour of Peter King*, ed. Michael Wintle and Paul Vincent, London, Athlone, 1988, pp. 88–104

Hüsken, Wim, 'The Bruges *Ommegang*', in *Formes teatrals . . .*, ed. Jésus-Francesc Massip [*see* Société Internationale pour l'Etude du Théâtre Médiéval in general bibliography], pp. 77–85

'Civic patronage of Early Fifteenth-Century Religious Drama in the Low Countries', in *Civic Ritual and Drama*, ed. Alexandra F. Johnston and Wim Hüsken, Ludus II, Amsterdam, Rodopi, 1997, pp. 107–23

Hüsken, Wim, B. A. M. Ramakers, *et al.* (eds.), *Trou moet blijcken*, 8 vols., Assen, Uitgeverij Quarto, 1992–8

Kipling, Gordon, 'The Idea of the Civic Triumph: Drama, Liturgy and the Royal Entry in the Low Countries', *Dutch Crossing* 22 (1984), pp. 60–83

Knight, Alan E., ' The Sponsorship of Drama in Lille', in *Studies in Honor of Hans-Erich Keller*, ed. Rupert T. Pickens, Kalamazoo, Western Michigan University, Medieval Institute Publications, 1993, pp. 275–85

'Processional Theater as an Instrument of Municipal Authority in Lille', in *Formes teatrals . . .*, ed. Jésus-Francesc Massip [*see* Société Internationale pour l'Etude du Théâtre Médiéval in general bibliography], pp. 99–103

'The Bishop of Fools and his Feast in Lille', in *Festive Drama*, ed. Meg Twycross, Cambridge, D. S. Brewer, 1996, pp. 157–66

'Beyond Misrule: Theater and the Socialization of Youth in Lille', *Research Opportunities in Renaissance Drama* 35 (1996), pp. 73–84

'Faded Pageant: the End of the Mystery Plays in Lille', *Journal of the Midwest Modern Language Association* 29 (1996), pp. 3–14

'Processional Theatre and the Rituals of Social Unity in Lille', in *Drama and the Community: People and Plays in Medieval Europe*, ed. Alan Hindley, Medieval Texts and Cultures of Northern Europe 1, Turnhout, Brepols, 1999, pp. 99–109

see also France

Konigson, Elie, *La Représentation d'un mystère de la Passion à Valenciennes en 1547*, Paris, Centre National de la Recherche Scientifique, 1969

Lebègue, Raymond   *see* France

Lefèbvre, Leon, *Histoire du théâtre de Lille de ses origines à nos jours*, 5 vols., Lille, Lefèbvre-Ducrocq, 1901–7

[Lille] *Archives municipales de Lille (Affaires générales)* [*see also* Knight, Alan E., above]

Muir, Lynette R. 'Le théâtre hennuyer à la fin du moyen âge', in *De la représentation du mystère de Valenciennes de 1547 à la Post-modernité. Etudes rassemblées et présentées par Amos Fergombe*, Presses universitaires de Valenciennes 24 (1998), pp. 29–40

Petit de Julleville, Louis   *see* France

Potter, Robert and Elsa Strietman (trans.), 'Man's Desire and Fleeting Beauty. A Sixteenth-Century Comedy', *Dutch Crossing* 25 (1985), pp. 29–84; reprinted Leeds, 1994

Ramakers, B. A. M. *Spelen en figuren. Toneelkunst en processie in Oudenaarde tussen Middeleeuwen en Moderne Tijd*, Amsterdam, University Press, 1996

Raymaekers, F. J., 'Historische oogslag op de Rederijkkamers van Diest', *Vaderlandsch Museum* 3 (1859–60), pp. 90–129

Rombouts, Philip and Th. van Lerius (eds.), *De Liggeren en andere historische archieven der Antwerpse Sint-Lucasgilde*, 2 vols., Antwerpen-Amsterdam, 1864–76; reprinted Amsterdam, N. Israel, 1961

Small, George, *Georges Chastelain and the Shaping of Valois Burgundy*, Woodbridge, Boydell and Brewer, 1977

Strietman, Elsa, ' The Low Countries', in Simon (ed.), *Theatre of Medieval Europe*, pp. 225–52

Twycross, Meg, 'The Flemish *ommegang* and its Pageant Cars', *Medieval English Theatre* 2 (1980), pp. 15–41; 80–98

Van Autenboer, E., *Het Brabants Landjuweel der Rederijkers (1515–1561)*, Middelburg, Merlijn, 1981

Van Dijk, Hans, 'Mariken van Nieumeghen', *Dutch Crossing* 22 (1984), pp. 27–37

Van Dijk, Hans, Wim Hummelen, Wim Hüsken, and Elsa Strietman, 'A Survey of Dutch Drama before the Renaissance', *Dutch Crossing* 22 (1984), pp. 97–131

Van Puyvelde, Leo, 'Het ontstaan van het moderne tooneel in de oude Nederlanden: De oudste vermeldingen in de rekeningen', *Verslagen en Mededeelingen der Koninklijke Vlaamsche Academie voor Taal-en Letterkunde*, 1922, pp. 909–52

Vaughan, Richard, *Philip the Bold. The formation of the Burgundian State*, London, Longman, 1962

Valois Burgundy, London, Allen Lane, 1975

[Veurne] Blommaert, Ph., 'Rederijkkamers van Veurne en ommestreken', *Belgisch Museum* 2 (1838), pp. 357–74

Visschers, P. and J. F. Willems, 'Een woord over de oude Rhetorykkamers in het algemeen en over die van Antwerpen in het byzonder', *Belgisch Museum* 1 (1837), pp. 137–75

Willems, J. F., 'Oorkonden van Rederijkkamers', *Belgisch Museum* 4 (1840), pp. 411–23

'Cornelis Everaert, toneeldichter van Brugge', *Belgisch Museum* 6 (1842), pp. 41–51

Worp, Jacob A., *Geschiedenis van het drama en van het tooneel in Nederland*, 2 vols., Groningen, J. B. Wolters, 1904, 1908

[Ypres/Yperen] Vandecasteele, M., 'Een groots opgezet rederijkersfeest te Ieper in 1529', *Jaarboek 'De Fonteine'* 26 (1989), pp. 7–20

Vandenpeereboom, Alphonse, *Ypriana, Notices, études, notes et documents sur Ypres*, 7 vols., Bruges, A. de Zuttere, 1881

[Zeeland] Serrure, C. P., 'De Rhetorijkkamers van Zeeland', *Vaderlandsch Museum* 2 (1858), pp. 287–90

Zumthor, Paul, *Daily Life in Rembrandt's Holland*, trans. Simon Watson Taylor, London, Weidenfeld and Nicolson, 1962

SECTION I   THE IBERIAN PENINSULA (INCLUDING MAJORCA)

Blecua, Alberto, ' Sobre la autoría del *Auto de la Pasión*', in *Homenaje a Eugenio Asensio*, Madrid, Gredos, 1988, pp. 79–112

Cátedra García, Pedro M., 'Escolios teatrales de Enrique de Villena', in *Serta philologica F. Lázaro Carreter*, Madrid, Cátedra, 1983, vol. II, pp. 127–36

Corbató, Hermengildo, *Los misterios del Corpus de Valencia*, University of California Publications in Modern Philology 16, Berkeley, University of California Press, 1932

Delgado, Feliciano, 'Las profecías de Sibilas en el ms 80 de la catedral de Córdoba y los origenes del teatro nacional', *Revista de Filogía Española* 67 (1987), pp. 77–87

Deyermond, Alan, 'El teatro medieval', in his *Historia y crítica de la literatura española*, vol. I, *Edad Media*, Barcelona, Crítica, 1980, pp. 451–60

'El teatro medieval', in his *Historia y crítica de la literatura española*, vol. I.I, *Edad Media; primer suplemento*, Barcelona, Crítica, 1991, pp. 359–65

Diago Moncholi, Manuel V. (ed.), *Teatro y práctias*, vol. I, *El Quinientos valenciano*, Valencia, Institución Alfonso el Magnánimo, 1984

Díez Borque, José María (ed.), *História del teatro en España*, vol. I, *Edad Media; siglo XVI; siglo XVII*, Persiles, vol. 152, Madrid, Taurus, 1983

Donovan, Richard B., *The Liturgical Drama in Mediaeval Spain*, Toronto, Pontifical Institute of Mediaeval Studies, 1958

'Two Celebrated Centers of Medieval Liturgical Drama: Fleury and Ripoll', in *The Medieval Drama and its Claudelian Revival*, ed. E. Catherine Dunn *et al.*, Washington DC, Catholic University of America Press, 1970, pp. 41–51

Duran i Sanpere, Agustí, *La fiesta del Corpus*, Barcelona Histórica y Monumental 2, Barcelona, Aymá, 1943

García Soriano, Justo, *El teatro universitario y humanístico en España: estudios sobre el origen de nuestro arte dramático; con documentos, textos inéditos y un catálogo de antiguas comedias escolares*, Toledo, Rafael Gómez-Manos, 1945

Gillet, Joseph E., ' Tres pasos de la Pasión y una égloga de la Resurrección (Burgos, 1520)', *PMLA* 47 (1932), pp. 949–80

'The "Memorias" of Felipe Fernández Vallejo and the History of the Early Spanish Drama', in *Essays and Studies in Honor of Carleton Brown*, New York University Press, 1940, pp. 264–80

Hook, David and Alan Deyermond, 'El problema de la terminación del *Auto de los reyes magos*', *Anuario de Estudios Medievales* 13 (1983), pp. 269–78

Lázaro Carreter, Fernando, *Teatro medieval*, Odres Nuevos, 4th edn., Madrid, Castalia, 1987

[León] *Las edades del hombre: libros y documentos en la Iglesia de Castilla y León*, Burgos, Caja de Ahorros de Salamanca, Junta de Castilla y León, Caja de Ahorros del Círculo Católico de Burgos, 1990

Llabrés, Gabriel, 'Repertorio de "Consuetas" representadas en las iglesias de Mallorca (siglos XV y XVI)', *Revista de Archivos, Bibliotecas y Museos* 5 (1901), pp. 920–7

Llompart, Gabriel, 'La fiesta del "Corpus Christi" y representaciones religiosas en Barcelona y Mallorca (siglos XIV–XVIII)', *Analecta Sacra Tarraconensia: Revista de Ciencias Historicoeclesiásticas* 39 (1966), pp. 25–45

'La fiesta del Corpus y representaciones religiosas en Zaragoza y Mallorca (siglos XIV–XVI)', *Analecta Sacra Tarraconensia: Revista de Ciencias Historicoeclesiásticas* 42 (1969), pp. 181–209

López Morales, Humberto, *Tradición y creación de los orígenes del teatro castellano*, Colección Romania, Series Literaria, Madrid, Alcalá, 1968

López-Ríos, Santiago, 'Los "desafíos" del cabellero salvaje: notas para el estudio de un juglar en la literatura peninsular de la Edad Media', *Nueva Revista de Filología Hispánica* 43 (1995), pp. 145–59

'La parodia del caballero salvaje en el episodio de Camilote de la *Tragicomedia de Don Duardos*', in *Comentarios de textos literarios hispánicos: Homenaje a Miguel Ángel Garrido*, ed. Esteban Torre and José Luis García Barrientos, Madrid, Síntesis, 1997, pp. 259–72

Mackay, Angus, *Spain in the Middle Ages: from Frontier to Empire, 1000–1500*, London, Macmillan, 1977; reprinted 1983

McKendrick, Melveena, *Theatre in Spain, 1490–1700*, Cambridge University Press, 1989; reprinted 1992

Macpherson, Ian, 'Text, Context and Subtext: Five *invenciones* of the *Cancionero general* and the Ponferrada Affair of 1485', in *The Medieval Mind: Hispanic Studies in Honour of Alan Deyermond*, ed. Ian Macpherson and Ralph Penny, Tamesis Monografías A 170, London, Tamesis, 1997, pp. 259–74

Massip, Jesús Francesc, *Teatre religiós medieval als països catalans*, Monografies de Teatre 17, Barcelona, Edicions 62, 1984

Massot i Mutaner, Josep (ed.), *Teatre medieval i del Renaixement*, Barcelona, Edicions 62, 1983

Mérimée, Henri, *L'Art Dramatique à Valencia depuis les origines jusqu'au commencement du XVIIe siècle*, Bibliothèque Méridionale, 2nd series 16, Toulouse, Edouard Privat, 1913

Oleza Simó, Joan (ed.), *Teatro y práctias escénicas*, vol. II, *La comedia*, Tamesis Monografías A 123, London, Tamesis and Institución Alfonso el Magnánimo, 1986

Pié, Joan, 'Autos sagramentales dels sigle XIV', *Revista de la Asociación Artístico-Arqueológica Barcelonesa* I (1896–8), pp. 673–86; pp. 726–44

Quirante Santacruz, Luis (ed.), *Teatro y espectáculo en la Edad Media: Actas, Festival d'Elx 1990*, Elche, Instituto de Cultura 'Juan Gil Albert'; Diputación de Alicante y Ajuntamente d'Elx, 1992

Révah, I. S., 'Manifestationes théâtrales pré-vicentines: les *momos* de 1500', *Bulletin d'histoire du théâtre Portugais* 3 (1952), pp. 91–105

Romeu i Figueras, José, 'La *Representatió de la Mort*, obra dramática del siglo XVI, y la Danza de la Muerte', *Boletín de la Real Academia de Buenas Letras de Barcelona* 27 (1957–8), pp. 181–225
  'El teatre assumpcionista de tècnica medieval als països catalans', in *Estudis de llengua i literatura catalanes oferts a R. Aramon i Serra*, 4 vols., Barcelona, Curial, 1984, vol. IV, pp. 239–78

Romeu i Figueras, José (ed.) *Teatre hagiogràfic*, 3 vols., Barcelona, Barcino, 1957

Rouanet, Léo (ed.), *Colección de autos, farsas y coloquios del siglo XVI*, Bibliotheca Hispánica, 4 vols., Barcelona, L'Avenç, 1901; reprinted Hildesheim, Georg Olms, 1979

Rubio García, Luis, *La procesión de Corpus en el siglo XV en Murcia y religiosidad medieval*, Murcia, Academia Alfonso X el Sabio, 1983

Sanchis Guarner, M., 'El Misteri assumpcionista de la catedral de València', *Boletín de la Real Academia de Buenas Letras de Barcelona* 32 (1967–8), pp. 97–112

Shergold, N. D., *A History of the Spanish Stage from Medieval Times until the End of the Seventeenth Century*, Oxford, Clarendon Press, 1967

Shoemaker, W. H., *The Multiple Stage in Spain during the Fifteenth and Sixteenth Centuries*, Princeton Univerity Press, 1935

Stebbins, Charles (ed. and trans.), 'The *Auto de los Reyes Magos*: An Old Spanish Mystery Play of the Twelfth Century', *Allegorica* 2 (1977), pp. 118–43

Stern, Charlotte, *The Medieval Theater in Castile*, Medieval and Renaissance Texts and Studies 156, Binghamton, New York, Renaissance Society of America, 1996

Sturdevant, Winifred, *The 'Misterio de los reyes magos': its Position in the Development of the Mediaeval Legend of the Three Kings*, Johns Hopkins Studies in Romance Languages and Literatures 10, Baltimore, Johns Hopkins University Press, 1927; reprinted New York, Johnston Reprints, 1973

Surtz, Ronald E., 'El teatro en la Edad Media', in José María Diéz Borque (ed.), *História del teatro*, vol. I, pp. 61–154
  'The "Franciscan Connection" in Early Castilian Theater', *Bulletin of the* Comediantes 35 (1983–4), pp. 141–52
  'Spain: Catalan and Castilian Drama', in Simon (ed.), *Theatre of Medieval Europe*, pp. 189–206

Surtz, Ronald E. (ed.), *Teatro medieval castellano*, Madrid, Taurus, 1983
  Teatro castellano de la Edad Media, Madrid, Taurus, 1992

Walsh, John K. and Alan Deyermond, 'Enrique de Villena como poeta y dramaturgo: bosquejo de una polémica frustrada', *Nueva Revista de Filología Hispánica* 28 (1979), pp. 57–85

SECTION J   TRADITIONS OF THE PEOPLE: CUSTOMS AND FOLK DRAMA

Alford,Violet, *The Hobby Horse and Other Animal Masks*, London, Merlin Press, 1978

Axton Richard, 'Origins and Traditions' (part I), in *European Drama of the Middle Ages*, London, Hutchinson, 1974; University of Pittsburgh Press, 1975, pp. 17–74

Berce, Yves-Marie, *Fête et révolte. Des mentalités populaires du xvie au xviiie siècle*, Paris, Hachette, 1976

Bernheimer, Richard, *Wild Men in the Middle Ages: a Study in Art, Sentiment, and Demonology*, Cambridge, Mass., Harvard University Press, 1952

Billington, Sandra, *A Social History of the Fool*, Brighton, Harvester Press, 1984

Cawte, E. C., *Ritual Animal Disguise. A Historical and Geographical Study of Animal Disguise in the British Isles*, Cambridge, Brewer, for the Folklore Society, 1978

Chambers, E. K., 'Folk Drama' (book II) in *The Mediaeval Stage*, pp. 89–419
  The English Folk-Play, Oxford, Clarendon Press, 1933; reprinted 1969

Corrsin, Stephen D., *Sword Dancing in Europe: a History*, Enfield Lock, Hisarlik Press, 1997

Feste und Feiern im Mittelalter. Paderborner Symposion des Mediävistenverbandes, ed. Detlef Alterburg *et al.*, Sigmaringen, Jan Thorbecke, 1991

Forrest, John, *The History of Morris Dancing, 1458–1750*, University of Toronto Press, 1998

Gaignebet, Claude and Marie-Claude Florentin, *Le Carneval: essais de mythologie populaire*, Paris, Payot, 1974; 2nd edn, 1979

Gunnell, Terry, *The Origins of Drama in Scandinavia*, Woodbridge, Brewer, 1995

Halpert, Herbert and George Morley Storey (eds.), *Christian Mumming in Newfoundland. Essays in Anthropology, Folklore and History*, University of Toronto Press, 1969

Heers, Jacques, *Fêtes, jeux et joutes dans les sociétés médiévales d'occident à la fin du moyen âge*, Montreal, Institute d'études médiévales, 1971

Helm, Alex, *The English Mummers' Play*, Folklore Society, Mistletoe Series 14, Woodbridge, Brewer, for the Folklore Society, 1981

Hutton, Ronald, *The Pagan Religions of the Ancient British Isles*, Oxford University Press, 1991

The Rise and Fall of Merry England: the Ritual Year, 1400–1700, Oxford University Press, 1994

The Stations of the Sun: a History of the Ritual Year in Britain, Oxford University Press, 1996

Ladurie, Emmanuel le Roy, *Carnival: a People's Uprising at Romans, 1579–1580*, London, Scolar Press, 1979; reprinted as *Carnival in Romans: a People's Uprising at Romans*, Harmondsworth, Penguin, 1981

Laroque, François, part 1 of *Shakespeare's Festive World: Elizabethan Seasonal Entertainment and the Professional Stage*, Cambridge University Press, 1991, pp. 3–175

Le Goff, Jacques and Jean-Claude Schmitt (eds.), *Le Charivari: Actes de la table ronde organisée à Paris (25–27 avril 1977) par l'École des Hautes Études en Sciences, Sociales et le Centre National de la Recherche Scientifique*, Paris, The Hague and New York, Mouton and l'Ecole des Hautes Etudes en Sciences Sociales, 1981

Marcus, Leah S., *The Politics of Mirth. Jonson, Herrick, Milton, and the Defense of Old Holiday Pastimes*, Chicago University Press, 1986

Masken in Mitteleuropa. Volkskundliche Beiträge zur europäischen Maskenforschung, ed. Leopold Schmidt, Vienna, Selbstverlag des Vereines für Volkskunde, 1955

Meschke, Karl, *Schwerttanz und Schwerttanzspiel im germanischen Kulturkreis*, Leipzig and Berlin, Teubner, 1931

Mezger, Werner, *Narrenidee und Fastnachtsbrauch. Studien zum Forleben des Mittelalters in der europäischen Festkultur*, Konstanz, Universitätsverlag Konstanz, 1991

Moser, Dietz-Rüdiger, *Fastnacht-Fasching-Carnival. Das Fest der 'Verkehrten Welt'*, Graz, Kaleidoskop, 1986

Moser, Hans, *Volksbräuche in geschichtlichen Wandel. Ergebnisse aus fünfzig Jahren volkskundlicher Quellenforschung*, Munich, Deutsche Kunstverlag, 1985

Narrenfreiheit. Beiträge zur Fastnachtsforschung, ed. Hermann Bausinger *et al.*, Tübingen, Tübingen Vereinigung für Volkskunde, 1980

O Suilleabhain, Sean, *Irish Wake Amusements*, Cork, Mercier Press, 1967

Rey-Flaud, Henri, *Le charivari: les rituels fondamentaux de la sexualité*, Paris, Payot, 1985

Schutt-Kehm, Elke M., *Pieter Bruegels d. A. 'Kampf des Karnavals gegen die Fasten' als Quelle volkskundlicher Forschung*, Frankfurt-on-Main, Peter Lang, 1983

Thompson, Edward P., 'Rough Music', chapter 8 of *Customs in Common*, London, Merlin Press, 1991

Tiroler Volksschauspiele. Beiträge zur Theatergeschichte des Alpenraumes, ed. Egon Kühebacher, Bozen, Athesia, 1976

Underdown, David, *Revel, Riot and Rebellion. Popular Politics and Culture in England, 1603–1660*, Oxford, Clarendon Press, 1985

Vaultier, Roger, *Le folklore pendant le guerre de cent ans d'après les lettres de rémission du trésor des chartes*, Paris, Librairie Guénégaud, 1965

Wagner, Siegfried, *Der Kampf der Fasten Gegen die Fastnacht. Studien zu Form, Funktion und Entwicklung des Systems von Fastnacht und Fasten im Spätmittelalter und der Frühen Neuzeit*, Diss. Albert-Ludwigs-Universität zu Freiburg im Breisgau, Munich, tuduv, 1986

Warner, E. A., *The Russian Folk Theatre*, The Hague and Paris, Mouton, 1977

Welsford, Enid, *The Court Masque. A Study in the Relationship Between Poetry and the Revels*, Cambridge University Press, 1927

Wiles, David, *The Early Plays of Robin Hood*, Cambridge, Brewer, 1981

Index

In a work of this scope it is clearly impracticable to list supplementary details for every entry. Priority has therefore been given to highlighting items of particular theatrical significance. Geographical locations adopt their present-day affiliation; dates are AD unless otherwise stated.